M000247557

LAWS AND SOCIETIES IN GLOBAL CONTEXTS

This book seeks to situate sociolegal studies in global contexts. Law and society scholarship in the United States and elsewhere typically assumes one legal system and one society and explores the relationship between them. Such a narrow endeavor perpetuates a European-based international relations model that too often conflates law, culture, and the nation-state. A more global sociolegal perspective engages with multiple laws and societies within and across national borders and recognizes diverse sociolegal systems based on very different historical and cultural traditions, interacting on multiple local, national, regional, and global levels. This more global perspective also reveals an array of transnational issues including regional conflicts, genocide, mass immigration, environmental degradation, and climate change that have consistently defied resolution via the traditional international system of governance. The approach to global legal pluralism outlined here seeks to provide a framework for envisioning new global governance regimes that move beyond state-based solutions to deal with trenchant transnational challenges.

Eve Darian-Smith is a professor in the Global & International Studies Program at the University of California, Santa Barbara. She holds degrees in history and law from the University of Melbourne and sociocultural anthropology from Harvard and the University of Chicago. Her research engages with issues of legal pluralism and explores the changing role of law and legal institutions in the context of globalization. Her first book, *Bridging Divides: The Channel Tunnel and English Legal Identity in the New Europe*, was the winner of the USA Law and Society Association Herbert Jacob Book Prize. Subsequent books include *Laws of the Postcolonial*; *New Capitalists: Law, Politics and Identity Surrounding Casino Gaming on Native American Land*; and, most recently, *Religion, Race, Rights: Landmarks in the History of Anglo-American Law*. She has also published another five edited volumes/special issues. She is on numerous editorial boards and is a former associate editor of the *Law & Society Review* and *American Ethnologist*.

Laws and Societies in Global Contexts

Contemporary Approaches

EVE DARIAN-SMITH

University of California, Santa Barbara

CAMBRIDGE
UNIVERSITY PRESS

CAMBRIDGE
UNIVERSITY PRESS

32 Avenue of the Americas, New York NY 10013-2473, USA

Cambridge University Press is part of the University of Cambridge.

It furthers the University's mission by disseminating knowledge in the pursuit of education, learning, and research at the highest international levels of excellence.

www.cambridge.org
Information on this title: www.cambridge.org/9780521130714

© Cambridge University Press 2013

First published 2013
Reprinted 2013

A catalog record for this publication is available from the British Library.

Library of Congress Cataloging in Publication data
Darian-Smith, Eve, 1963–
  Laws and societies in global contexts : contemporary approaches /
  Eve Darian-Smith.
    p. cm.
  Includes bibliographical references and index.
  ISBN 978-0-521-11378-6 (hardback) – ISBN 978-0-521-13071-4 (pbk.)
  1. Sociological jurisprudence. 2. Law – Philosophy. I. Title.
  K370.D37 2013
  340´.115–dc23   2012036703

ISBN 978-0-521-11378-6 Hardback
ISBN 978-0-521-13071-4 Paperback

To Phil with love

Contents

List of Figures

Acknowledgments

The people I would like to thank are too numerous to mention. Over the years, and in many different contexts, friends, mentors, colleagues, students, and family members, as well as a range of people that I have talked to in places such as legal aid offices, courtrooms, shops, bars, bus stops, and on the street have helped challenge my ideas about law and reflect on what law means to people of different cultures, classes, races, religions, and belief systems. I am indebted to all of them and am enormously grateful for the time each person shared with me. As always, I thank my wonderful mentors who have played such an inspirational role over the years – Donna Merwick and Greg Dening, Sally Falk Moore, John Comaroff, and Peter Fitzpatrick. I also thank my colleagues in the Global & International Studies Program at the University of California, Santa Barbara, who have provided me with such a welcoming and exciting institutional home, and John Soboslai for advising and helping me with technical issues in the preparation of the manuscript. Finally, I am very thankful to my husband Phil McCarty for all his love, support, patience, and conversations, and my twins Ellie and Sam who gave me many kisses and cuddles along the way to encourage my writing.

1 Introduction: Sociolegal Scholarship in the Twenty-First Century

BRIEF DESCRIPTION OF LAW AND SOCIETY SCHOLARSHIP

Law and society scholarship, or sociolegal scholarship as it is typically called outside the United States, has contributed enormously to understanding how law works in complex social, cultural, economic, and political contexts. As an interdisciplinary field of inquiry, sociolegal scholarship ranges from deeply theoretical explorations to more empirically based examinations of how law operates in meaningful and dynamic ways among and between peoples, communities, societies, institutions, states, regions, spaces, times, properties, corporations, environments, texts, and material objects. Drawing on theoretical and methodological perspectives from both the social sciences and the humanities, sociolegal scholarship has expanded in recent decades to embrace an extensive array of substantive topics and fields of inquiry.[1]

Within the United States, the Law and Society Association was established in 1964 and the *Law & Society Review* was first published in 1966. The law and society movement emerged within the civil rights activism and cause-lawyering efforts of the 1960s, but its intellectual roots were in the American New Deal and the school of thought called legal realism that was concerned with exposing law as a mechanism of power (Levine 1990; Trubek 1990; Garth and Sterling 1998; Tomlins 2000; Feeley 2001; Sarat 2004:2–4, 2008; Friedman 2005). Today

---

[1] Law and society scholarship and sociolegal scholarship (sometimes referred to as the sociology of law) have distinct intellectual legacies. For instance, sociolegal scholarship as it developed in Britain drew more explicitly from European political and social theory, particularly within the field of sociology and to a lesser degree anthropology. In the United States, the law and society movement emerged in the 1960s and drew explicitly from the legal realism school of the 1920s and 1930s and its concern with law as a mechanism of power. Notwithstanding these differences, throughout this book the terms "law and society scholarship" and "sociolegal scholarship" are used interchangeably as umbrella terminology for a wide range of legal analysis that has expanded in recent decades to include perspectives, substantive concerns, and methodologies from across the social sciences and humanities (see Sarat 2004; Ewick 2008).

the U.S. law and society movement has a presence in social science and humanities departments of higher education institutions across the nation, and is also embraced to varying degrees within major law schools. The USA Law and Society Association has a robust national and international membership and promotes cross-discipline and cross-national research through its Collaborative Research Networks and International Research Collaboratives. The Association's journal, the *Law & Society Review,* is considered the leading publication in the field (Scheingold 2008). Smaller but arguably more cutting-edge sociolegal associations exist, or are emerging, within a number of countries such as Germany, Canada, Britain, Australia, India, Israel, China, Chile, Spain, and Mexico. Notably, the Japanese Association of the Sociology of Law was established in 1947 and is the oldest sociolegal association in existence. In addition to these formal professional organizations, there is a range of interdisciplinary scholarly communities engaged in humanistically oriented critical sociolegal scholarship, such as the Association for the Study of Law, Culture and the Humanities, whose members may identify with LatCrit theory, feminist legal theory, legal history, and critical race theory as well as a range of other theoretical orientations involving literature, narrative, or semiotics. There is also a strong social-science-oriented community of legal scholars centered around places such as the International Institute for the Sociology of Law in Onati, Spain.

The primary mission of sociolegal scholarship broadly construed is to better understand the social, cultural, political, and economic contexts in which law operates in practice, be it in the past or the present. The hope is that such knowledge will make law more widely accessible, equitable, and just. To achieve this goal, sociolegal scholars are interested in the gap between law in the books (known as doctrinal law, black letter law, or positivist law) and law in action as it plays out among and between peoples, places, histories, and institutions. Law and society scholars are critical of doctrinal law as it is typically taught in law schools because it presents a one-size-fits-all set of abstract legal principles that supposedly apply to a variety of situations and legal actors. Against this legal abstractionism, law and society scholars argue that studying doctrinal law alone does not tell the full story about how and under what conditions law is imagined, produced, formalized, enforced, reformed, or made meaningful for different political constituencies and individuals in any given community.

An example where studying doctrinal law fails to tell the full story is the field of criminal law. Law students typically study criminal law as a set of rules that establish acceptable conduct and punishments if those rules are broken. But the study of criminal law does not usually take into account or explain how people interpret those rules, under what conditions rules may be broken, whether and by whom rules are enforced, manipulated, subverted, or resisted, and how social and political action may feed back into the legal system to define new crimes or determine that certain behaviors should no longer be considered criminal. The issue of battered woman's syndrome is a case in point. This is an example where placing the criminal act of murder in wider contexts that take into account long-term spousal abuse, conditions of gender oppression, and psychological desperation whereby some women feel they have no alternative to committing violence can provide mitigating evidence that lessens the first-degree murder charge (see Tolmie 1997, 2002). Without understanding the significance of these wider contexts, and taking account of them in determining what may be an appropriate punishment, sociolegal scholars suggest that certain women may be unjustly held accountable for acts of violence that they were not entirely responsible for because of the structural inequities built into our social systems.

As the preceding example illustrates, sociolegal scholars argue that law has a life beyond law texts. Hence, law must be analyzed in the wider spheres where it is interpreted by people, in turn shaping their social relations and ways of operating in the world. These arenas of legal interaction, or what is often referred to as law in action, may be within obvious settings such as parliaments, law courts, and police stations, as well as in less obvious and non-intuitive places such as schoolrooms, entertainment venues, and sports arenas (Macaulay 1987). Law and society scholars also argue that people are not passive recipients of the law, but in their everyday practices influence and shape law and legal processes. In other words, people are not static objects upon which law causally operates. People can imagine new forms of legal engagement and may resist or reframe prevailing legal norms, regulations, and categorizations. Often cited in support of this approach to law is Clifford Geertz's famous line that law is a way of "imagining the real" (Geertz 1983:184). This dynamic, reflexive, constitutive engagement between law as laid down in the books and the individuals and societies that law is meant to govern helps explain how and why law changes over time, and underscores that at any one moment in time law both reflects the status quo and is responding to accommodate shifting cultural values, norms, societal demands, and ways of being. This mutually constitutive relationship between law and society is a hallmark of contemporary sociolegal scholarship.

The idea of studying the difference between how law is presented in law books and the ways law is constituted and practiced in real life has had an enduring legacy over the past four decades. While some law and society scholars have been critical of "gap studies" from their early inception (Abel 1973;

Nelken 1981), they nonetheless remain a defining characteristic of sociolegal scholarship (Seron and Silbey 2004; Calavita 2010). Despite the enormous expansion of substantive topics in law and society scholarship over the decades, the law and society movement continues its original mission to contextualize legal processes and embrace critical perspectives that expose law's explicit and implicit relationship with political and economic power (see Abel 2010). As Mark Suchman and Elizabeth Mertz have noted, "this counter-hegemonic tendency has, if anything, strengthened in recent years, as the movement has worked to preserve or enhance its inclusiveness toward historically disadvantaged groups, critical and postmodern perspectives, and nonpositivistic agendas" (Suchman and Mertz 2010:568).

This book seeks to broaden the counter-hegemonic trend in law and society scholarship. My hope is that such a broadening will also deepen the relevance of sociolegal scholarship in multiple fields of inquiry (beyond law schools) as we advance further into the twenty-first century. What I propose is the adoption of a more expansive global perspective in law and society research so as to move beyond a state-centrist or state-framed interpretation of law. This is necessary, I suggest, to better analyze how law operates both within and beyond national jurisdictions and so opens up opportunities to discuss new forms of legality that may not neatly correlate to conventional state-based legal institutions or notions of citizenship. More pragmatically, a global sociolegal approach is essential in order to think through legal strategies that may help address the world's contemporary challenges, risks, and demands that are not bound within or contained by national jurisdictions. These challenges include such things as human trafficking, drug cartels, terrorist networks, poverty, labor exploitation, mass human migrations, climate change, declining public health, threats to food and water security, and natural resource depletion that today exist on a global scale and directly and indirectly affect every one of us, whatever local community we may live in.

In arguing for the need to embrace a global perspective with respect to sociolegal inquiry, this book differs from conventional introductory texts on law and society scholarship available in the United States. Some of these texts deal specifically with sociolegal theory as it has developed in Western thought since the nineteenth century (see Travers 2009): some are edited volumes that showcase classic and contemporary articles by leading figures in law and society scholarship (see Abel 1995; Sarat 2004; Bonsignore et al. 2005; Macaulay et al. 2007); others present discussion by one author and are explicitly designed as teaching texts for undergraduate students (Barkan 2008; Walsh and Hemmens 2010; Friedrichs 2011; Vago 2011). Whatever the precise emphasis, format, and relative quality of these texts, they revolve almost exclusively around law and legal process in the United States and cover a range of predictable topics such as social control, lawmaking, legal administration, courts and juries, dispute resolution, capital punishment, crime, the legal profession, and so on.

My concern with these texts as a whole is that they are overwhelmingly parochial. They typically present U.S. law as if it is the only legal system operating in the world and, moreover, one that does so in a geopolitical silo unaffected by international affairs or events external to its national borders such as war, immigration, or climate change. One consequence of this parochialism is that these introductory law and society texts rarely – if at all – mention the comparative, international, and global dimensions of sociolegal scholarship. If they do, it is usually tagged on as a final section or chapter (i.e., Sarat 2004; Travers 2009). Against this parochial trend, one recent law and society textbook explicitly seeks a global approach (Friedman et al. 2011). Unfortunately, this book presents this approach rather simplistically by expanding the "geographical area" to include comparisons between the United States and other countries dealing with conventional sociolegal topics such as the legal profession or dispute resolution. Here, too, research exploring the forces of globalization on national legal systems is relegated to a final section of the volume rather than being foregrounded as a central theme informing subsequent chapters.

In contrast to the provincialism of much sociolegal research in the United States (especially as reflected in introductory law and society texts), there is a growing body of legal research that appreciates that all law, even at local community levels, should be read through a lens that takes into account the increasing forces of globalizing cultural, political, and economic interactions. Notable among these scholars are legal anthropologists who for many years have been actively involved in exploring the concept of legal pluralism and showing the global dimensions of legal interaction within colonial and postcolonial regimes (see Moore 1992; Benda-Beckmann et al. 2009a; Griffiths 2002; Merry 2006, 2007). Beyond this small group of ethnographically oriented scholars, however, the turn toward a global sociolegal perspective has been slow to materialize. Mainstream U.S. law and society scholarship is primarily fixed on a state-centered approach, reflecting perhaps the disciplinary constraints of sociology and political science representing the intellectual training of the majority of USA Law and Society Association members. Whatever the reason, much sociolegal research in the United States lags behind other fields of inquiry in its dogged resistance to think beyond the nation. Revealingly, Lawrence Friedman, a figure long associated with the U.S. law and society movement, wrote as late as 2002 that "the globalization of law is a topic that has entered the consciousness of legal scholars only recently. This is not mere fashion – it is a response to real processes and events" (Friedman 2002:23).

This book is a modest attempt to present recent sociolegal scholarship that approaches law from a global perspective, even when explicitly examining national or subnational legal processes. It is not intended – as some of the aforementioned introductory texts do – to present the major approaches in law and society research and include a canon of "classic" articles that everyone should read. Nor is it intended to dismiss any existing sociolegal texts that are all valuable in various ways and on which this book necessarily builds. Rather, I seek to highlight some emerging ideas about law that bring into question the taken-for-granted assumptions that endure in much sociolegal research. My hope is to (1) problematize the dominance of Euro-American legalism;[2] (2) highlight the need to embrace (rather than resist) legal pluralism and alternative conceptualizations of what constitutes law, justice, and rights; and (3) at the same time encourage emerging conversations among scholars and legal practitioners in the global North and global South about law that may be applicable to dealing with the complex, ambiguous, and pressing global challenges of our contemporary moment.[3] In short, this book is not intended as a summary of new directions within sociolegal scholarship, but rather as an urging for a rethinking of some of the basic assumptions about what constitutes law in a global world, in an effort to ensure that law and society research remains significant and relevant in the coming decades.

THE BOOK'S THREE OBJECTIVES

The first objective of this book is to move sociolegal conversations beyond the taken-for-granted frame of the nation-state and push the reader to think more

[2] I use the term "Euro-American" as shorthand to refer to European, Anglo, and American legal systems, or what is commonly thought of as Western law. There are, of course, substantive differences between these jurisdictions, and it is important to appreciate that the "West" is no more homogenous than the "East" as an identifying category. That being said, Euro-American legal systems share common cultural values that emerged in the Enlightenment and substantiate an understanding of law based on individualism and an individual's capacity to possess property, express identity, and claim rights (see Collier et al. 1996).

[3] I use the terms "global North" and "global South" to designate the vast disparities of resources and relative international power between the wealthy developed countries (the north) and poorer and less-developed countries (the south). This is an artificial distinction and does not correlate geographically to northern and southern hemispheres. Nor should the global south be thought of as exclusively consisting of poor, undemocratic, and undeveloped nations, given that within any one country there may be vast disparities of relative wealth and opportunity. Hence the global south perspective more accurately represents poor and marginalized people living within first- and third-world countries. That being said, the north-south divide loosely correlates to countries described as high-income and advanced economies and low-income and developing economies by the World Bank and International Monetary Fund, and corresponds to levels of wealth and poverty as monitored by the UN Human Development Index.

flexibly and critically with respect to the enormous legal issues and scales of risk confronting all communities and societies irrespective of whether they are legally contained within national jurisdictions or not. These are issues such as environmental degradation and threats to global health, abuse and defense of human rights, as well as the impact resulting from the movement of peoples attributable to wars, poverty, epidemics, and natural disasters. These pressing contemporary issues require new approaches to legality that transcend nation-states and their bounded geographical territories. According to Rafael Domingo, a Spanish jurist and legal theorist, in his book titled *A New Global Law*:

> The indispensable pluralism of a global society clashes with the nation-state's pretense of exclusivity. Numerous declarations of the universality of human rights and various historical milestones such as the birth of the EU or the establishment of international tribunals call into question the reach and future of the concept of sovereignty, in spite of certain cosmopolitan efforts to reconceptualize it. Rather, an open society requires new mechanisms for articulating and meeting the needs of civil societies, needs that cannot always be met via the bureaucratic structures of sovereign power, which are ultimately based on obsolete doctrine. (Domingo 2010:66; see also Onuma 2010)

Unfortunately, to date, much of the small but growing body of scholarship on law and globalization continues to adopt a state-centered approach. This approach supports a traditional comparative methodology that explores and contrasts how law operates in different countries around the world (e.g., Nelken 2002; Halliday et al. 2007). In other words, almost all of the existing sociolegal literature frames discussion about law and globalization through sites of national and international law and organizations (see Halliday and Osinky 2006; for a notable exception, see Berman 2005). For instance, some scholars explore the impact of international legal institutions on national legal professions and judiciary (Sarat and Scheingold 2001; Dezalay and Garth 2002, 2010, 2011; Bierman and Hitt 2007). Other scholars examine how international legal institutions such as the International Monetary Fund (IMF), World Bank, and the United Nations impact national legal systems (Halliday and Carruthers 2009). Still other scholars are interested in the rising legal and economic power of countries such as Brazil, Russia, India, China, and South Africa (BRICS). A substantial amount of this research is concerned with global trade, commercial integration and arbitration, private informal networks amongst legal practitioners and corporate entities, and the regulatory basis of what is known as *lex mercatoria* or mercantile law (see Dezalay and Garth 1998; Braithwaite and Drahos 2000; Appelbaum et al. 2001; Flood

2002; Wolf 2004). A prevailing assumption in this kind of sociolegal research (at least research emanating within the United States) is that nation-states still operate primarily as sovereign legal units that negotiate and collaborate with, and possibly adapt and make concessions to, other nations.

In 1996, Susan Silbey, then president of the US Law and Society Association, gave a presidential address titled "'Let Them Eat Cake': Globalization, Postmodern Colonialism, and the Possibilities of Justice" (Silbey 1997). This address ushered in, at least in my mind, a new era of critical sociolegal scholarship that bravely exposed the decentering of the regulatory state and its complicity in the emerging power of global corporate capitalism with respect to the rest of the world. Unfortunately, this remarkable speech, which was published the following year in the *Law & Society Review,* did not launch a broad wave of critical new thinking. As a result, to this day, relatively few sociolegal scholars problematize the concept of state sovereignty; explore the intermediary role played by NGOs and corporate actors in shaping global, international, national, and local legal instruments; examine the impact of regional forms of collective legal authority such as the African Union, European Union, or Association of Southeast Asian Nations (ASEAN); engage with emerging legal concepts such as universal jurisdiction; examine the transnational legal challenges presented by environmental degradation, climate change, and mass movements of people across borders and regions; or discuss how non-state legal institutions as promulgated through global justice movements such as the World Social Forum may be destabilizing conventional international/national legal terrains. Let me be clear – I am not saying that academic work is not being done with respect to these topics of legal globalization, only that it is has a limited presence within mainstream law and society scholarship as presented at professional meetings and published in leading sociolegal journals in the field.[4]

In contrast to a state-centered approach, this book stresses the legal relations between and within local, regional, national, international, transnational, and global legal arenas, and emphasizes that the lines of demarcation between these sites and scales are dynamic and porous. What is argued is that there is an urgent need to decenter the nation-state in an effort to reveal global legal interconnections between peoples, places, cultures, ideologies, religions, economies, and political systems. Importantly, decentering the nation-state

---

[4] There are, of course, notable exceptions such as Santos (1995); Boyle and Preves (2000); Klug (2002); Slaughter (2002); Maurer (2004); Merry (2006); Coutin (2007); Walby (2007); Barbour and Pavlich (2010); Benda-Beckmann et al. (2009a, 2009b); Halliday (2009); and Yngvesson (2010).

should not be interpreted as disempowering or marginalizing the nation-state. Rather, as noted by Franz von Benda-Beckmann and his colleagues, "states and their varying populations are enmeshed in horizontal and vertical legal relationships that crosscut one another both within and beyond territorial borders.... Such processes allow for new forms of governance that challenge the law's hegemony (as pronounced by states) through establishing alternative legalities of power" (Benda-Beckmann et al. 2009b:23). In light of such observations, a fundamental assumption underscoring this book is that it is not possible to take the geopolitical boundaries of the nation-state as given, nor view states as discrete and autonomous legal units operating within international, transnational, and global domains.

The second objective of this book is to push readers to think more flexibly and critically with respect to the production and meaning of legal knowledge and legal norms at the substate level. Hence related to the first goal to engage with legal processes *beyond* the nation-state is the renewed need to critically engage with legal processes *below* the federal level. I emphatically stress that embracing a global legal perspective does not mean that states and their domestic legalities are less important in the twenty-first century. On the contrary, the state remains a central feature of contemporary sociolegal research. The difference is that today the modernist myth of states being sovereign and self-contained within a Westphalian international system is no longer credible (Falk 1998). Similarly, the myth that a state represents one legal system and contains within it a singular cultural interpretation of law is no longer tenable.

In re-examining the production of domestic national legalities in a heightened era of globalization, it is essential to acknowledge that monocultural societies no longer exist (if in fact they ever did). There is not a pre-given "society" through which law operates, because societies are always in the process of becoming (Pavlich 2011). Today we are witnessing a rising presence of multicultural communities around the world, particularly in Europe and North America. These culturally rich subnational and transnational communities with distinctly different norms and values – and often with considerable social networks and economic links to peoples and places in Latin America, Africa, Asia, and the Middle East – present possibilities of new legal knowledge emerging within Western national boundaries. We can already see this in some legal settings such as UK family courts paying greater attention to Shari'a law (see Chapter 2), or the use of the culture defense within U.S. and other national law courts, which makes concessions to people from different cultural, religious, and legal systems. That the culture defense can be used in biased ways, favoring the values of certain cultural groups such as, for example, Asian Americans over African Americans, is beyond the scope of this discussion (see Roberts 1999:6–7; Renteln 2004; Cotterrell 2006:99–108; Foblets and Renteln 2009; Connolly 2010). My point is that whether the accommodation of alternative, perhaps non-Western, legal norms and cultural values is embraced or resisted, the taken-for-granted assumption in much sociolegal research that a national legal system maps onto a homogenous "society" is no longer acceptable.

This brings me to the third objective of this book, which is reflected in its title *Laws and Societies*.[5] In urging sociolegal scholars to engage with complex legal processes *beyond nations* and in problematizing how legal knowledge is constituted *within nations*, my third goal is to demonstrate the necessity to see these multiple arenas of legal activity as intrinsically related, mutually constituted, and always in dynamic interaction. Laws at the global/transnational level, laws at the federal/state level, and laws at the domestic/local level should all be viewed as elements of an interconnected and unfolding global legal system. In this interconnected realm, William Twining notes, "it is illuminating to conceive of law as a species of *institutionalised social practice* that is *oriented to ordering relations* between *subjects* at one or more *levels* of relations and of ordering" (Twining 2009:116).

In calling for a pluralizing of laws and societies, most sociolegal scholars would say "of course" and have no problem conceptually with this idea. That being said, much law and society scholarship remains bogged down in an anachronistic world view that is increasingly out of step with contemporary global geopolitical realities. Much law and society scholarship continues to take as pre-given entities "law" and "society" and seeks to illuminate what kind of law and what kind of society is present at any one moment in time. Much law and society scholarship ignores a legal "thickening" or what is often referred to as legal pluralism within and between and across countries, institutions, cultures, religions, actors, and various sites, scales, and spheres of legal engagement (for notable exceptions see Merry 2006, 2007; Barzilai 2008). These complex and interconnected geopolitical realities cannot be adequately analyzed through a conventional law and society approach that takes law and society as preexisting analytical frames. As George Pavlich has asked, "If neither law nor society is cast as fixed objects, whose essence can be determined, the character of early forms of study in the law and

---

[5] Here, and in many other ways besides, I am indebted to Peter Fitzpatrick. The title of my book plays off and builds upon Fitzpatrick's essay "Law and Societies" (1984) and his subsequent groundbreaking work; see Fitzpatrick 1992, 2001.

society field appears ripe for significant modification" (Pavlich 2011:9; see also Cotterrell 2009). And, I would add, reassessment of conventional law and society scholarship becomes most urgent in the context of globalization. This is because any acknowledgment of a pluralizing of laws and societies profoundly problematizes the immutability of the nation-state and relatively simplistic studies that compare and contrast how law operates in different countries around the world (i.e., Friedman et al. 2011; for a notable exception, see Menski 2006).

In thinking about global legal interactions in the twenty-first century we can learn from the work of legal historians and anthropologists who have long recognized the direct and indirect legal exchange between colonizers and colonized and the legal pluralism that developed as a consequence of that exchange (see Comaroff and Comaroff 1991; Lazarus-Black 1994; Cohn 1996; Moore 2004; Chanock 2007; Mawani 2009). From the sixteenth through to the nineteenth centuries, European countries that set up colonial outposts in the Old and New Worlds imposed their legal systems on the people they oppressed, and in turn, they were influenced by their involvement with the cultures and laws of the people they colonized. As a result, disparate elements of "foreign" law were inadvertently incorporated back into the European homelands of colonial powers (Anghie 2005; Benton 2010; Darian-Smith 2010a:138–146). In short, the legal systems of imperial nations were inevitably altered as a result of long-term legal engagement with their colonial subjects, whether or not it was recognized by the dominant European powers at the time.

Today, as in the past, Western legal systems in the global North are subject to unpredictable influences from their interaction with non-Western legal systems in the global South. Even if the country is a global superpower, such as the United States, its legal interaction with the wider world changes that country's legal system even though this may not be considered desirable or be immediately self-evident. Because law is a dynamic field and, as discussed earlier, is constituted by and through the people it governs, there are always some forms of legal reception, accommodation, and adaptation on all sides that may open up new spaces of legality that embody different legal concepts, logics, symbols, aesthetics, metaphors, and meanings. Importantly, and often not recognized in scholarly conversations about law and globalization, interactive exchanges between states and global processes happen both within and beyond the framing parameters of national jurisdictions (for a notable exception, see Sassen 2002, 2008). These decentered interactive legal processes through various levels, scales, territories, and spaces are what this book urges us to explore more carefully.

WHAT IS A GLOBAL SOCIOLEGAL PERSPECTIVE?

In arguing for what I call a global sociolegal perspective, I turn to more general theories of globalization. These theories typically focus on the mechanisms and technologies that have speeded up communications and enabled ever-faster movements of things, peoples, and knowledge systems around the world (Held et al. 1999). Sociolegal discussions of law and globalization tend to follow this general theoretical lead. As discussed earlier, these legal discussions typically take the nation-state as the starting point and then focus on the increasing proliferation of international business law, international trade regulations, international commercial arbitration, and international courts as evidence of global interconnectivity. Further evidence of legal globalization often cited by scholars is the existence of a shared global legal culture "of lawyers and business people who travel on the same jets, who have the same habits, use the same laptops and cell phones, dress the same and speak a common language" (Friedman 2002:31–32; Friedman et al. 2011).

In calling for a global sociolegal perspective, I mean something rather different. I believe that counting the proliferation of international lawyers and speed of international economic transactions, and noting the predominance of self-important, English-speaking, black-suited men lugging heavy briefcases in and out of the business section of airplanes does not adequately account for what is actually happening in a globalizing legal world. I urge us to move away from the obvious global legal exchanges and material trappings and learn to appreciate that all classes and races of people – many of whom may never have flown in an airplane and may not be explicitly linked with a wider world – nonetheless still feature in a global sociolegal perspective. One does not have to hold an investment portfolio, drink Coca-Cola, or access the Internet to be analytically and ethically relevant (see Santos and Rodriguez-Gavarito 2005). Thus, a rice farmer in rural China who no longer can send her child to school, an indigenous person from the Amazon Basin who walks 300 miles to file a formal complaint against forest deforestation, a Texan shopkeeper who feels increasingly insecure and buys three sub-automatic shotguns, or a young unmarried woman from Niger who no longer can get access to HIV medicine or contraception have all been affected in various ways that can be linked to changes in how law, politics, and economics are playing out in a globalizing world. Notes the global governance scholar, Mary Kaldor, globalization is a complex process in which "people's lives are profoundly shaped by events taking place far away from where they live over which they have no control" (Kaldor 2007:74). All of these people are pertinent to a global legal perspective, because as David Held reminds us, we live in a world of "overlapping communities" in which "the fate and fortune of each of us are thoroughly intertwined" (Held 2004:x).[6]

As sociolegal scholars, we should not and cannot ignore the "contribution of the masses" (Rajagopal 2003a:402). We need to be concerned with how globalization affects peoples in different ways that include a relatively small, cosmopolitan, plane-hopping legal elite and the millions of peoples from various classes, cultures, ethnicities, and religions whose understanding of law may appear "traditional" or "backward." We also need to move past fetishizing globalization's obvious material manifestations. As the sociologist Philip McCarty cautions, we need to stop trying to quantify the speed and frequency of point-to-point interactions and instead adopt a global perspective that:

> has the power to show us connections we could not have otherwise seen or imagined. A global perspective suggests that important connections exist between events and processes even when events appear to be disconnected and separated by time, space, or even our own categories of thought. When we look we find that the local is connected to the global, past to the present, north to south, rational to irrational, legal to illegal, function to dysfunction, and intended consequences to unintended consequences. By changing the way we see connections, a global perspective has the power to destabilize our modern and linear understandings of cause and effect in the social world (McCarty 2012:3).

Building upon more nuanced understandings of the general phenomenon of globalization, a global sociolegal perspective means adopting a "global imaginary" that destabilizes our modern and linear understandings of what law is, where law appears, and how law works (on the global imaginary, see Steger 2009). Writes Patricia Ewick in her urging sociolegal scholars to embrace methodological and theoretical eclecticism, this entails a willingness "to see our plots unravel" (Ewick 2008:15). This opening up of the logics of understanding means "seeing" new constructions of persons, goods and practices deemed legally legitimate or illegitimate in the global arena (Coutin et al. 2002). Moreover, it means that analyzing law within nation-states cannot be disconnected from law's global historical formation – often through colonialism and imperialism – as well as a range of global challenges that influence and frame every country's contemporary legal system. In short, a global

---

[6] This argument runs counter to the views expressed by prominent legal academics such as A. Vaughan Lowe who writes in the foreword to the book *Transnational Legal Processes*, "Does globalization reflect the state of the world? It is undeniable that there is a part of society that is internationalized. But how typical is that part? Or to put what is essentially the same question in a different way, how much of the reality of life on this planet is accommodated within the perspective of globalization? Not, I suspect, very much" (Lowe 2002:vi).

sociolegal perspective means recognizing that domestic law as it plays out within states is, and always has been, constitutively linked to issues of global economic, political, and cultural power as manifested both within and beyond national jurisdictions.

In the United States, two examples of the constitutive links between global, international, regional, state, and local legal issues are the following. In the run-up to the 2012 presidential elections there were considerable efforts made by the Republican Party to disenfranchise minority voters in states such as Mississippi, Texas, and South Carolina (*New York Times* Nov. 18, 2011). A global sociolegal perspective suggests that these Republican political efforts and the appeal of the Tea Party cannot be disconnected from such things as (1) Islamophobia associated with events of 9/11 and the wars on terror, (2) high unemployment rates as a result of pressures of a global economic recession, and (3) xenophobic and racist fears of rising rates of immigration and non-white birth rates. However, to date in U.S. academic or media circles, there is very little conversation that contextualizes the current wave of American right-wing nativism within larger unfolding global events, even though, curiously, discussion in the United States about the rise of right-wing political parties in Europe tends to be framed by a more encompassing global/international perspective.

Similarly, the moratorium on the death penalty by Oregon Governor John Kitzhaber in 2011 should be read, at least in part, through a global sociolegal perspective. The United States is the only major Western democracy that sanctions capital punishment.[7] Moreover, the United States has resisted pressure by the United Nations to suspend the use of the death penalty and to follow a global trend that has resulted in twenty-five countries abolishing the death penalty since 2000, and a total of fifty-nine countries abolishing it since 1990. The United States represents a democratic anomaly and joins countries such as China, Pakistan, North Korea, Cuba, and Iran, which all allow the death penalty and are regularly criticized for their lack of due process and abuse of human rights. As a result of aligning with these countries on the death penalty, the United States has come under increasing pressure from other Western nations to end what is often called a "barbaric practice."[8] In 2011, German

---

[7] The death penalty is banned under the European Convention on Human Rights and abolished in fifty of fifty-one European countries. The only country where it is permitted is Belarus, which gained its independence from Russia in 1991. For a country to join the European Union it has to eliminate capital punishment within its domestic legal system.

[8] "In the long run, the reason why international opposition to the death penalty may finally be having a significant impact on the US is that this opposition is more cohesive than ever before. The United States' closest allies in Europe and North America are unanimous in rejecting the death penalty and they do not hesitate to let their views be known. New countries can only be admitted to the growing European Union, a body whose size and economy may soon equal

pharmaceutical companies refused to sell a drug used in lethal injections to the United States and cited its decision in purely ethical terms (Stafford 2011). Other countries such as Mexico, Canada, and France have refused to extradite criminals to the United States on the grounds that they may face the death penalty (Clarke and Whitt 2007). While very rarely mentioned in law and society scholarship on capital punishment, international and global contexts inform – directly and indirectly – a shifting attitude toward abolishing the death penalty within the United States (Clarke et al. 2004; Bohm 2007; LaChappelle 2012). In other words, Governor Kitzhaber's moratorium on the death penalty did not happen within a geopolitical vacuum and should be understood against a backdrop of changes in international law and the United States' growing global legal consciousness.

In this book, I urge law and society scholars to take a more holistic approach to legal phenomena and to be open to seeing links between seemingly unrelated realms that may raise non-intuitive relationships and interconnections. This kind of eclectic and creative legal thinking is necessary to imagine adequate structural solutions to pressing national and global issues such as health, poverty, war, racism, labor exploitation, water and mineral resource depletion, and climate change – all of which disproportionately affect women and minority communities. These issues are further complicated by the historical colonial injustices and contemporary economic inequities that exist between the global North and the global South. Such disparities contextualize and inform all law and society scholarship, even that of the most local and micro and personal. As sociolegal scholars, it is important to acknowledge and explore how these historically interconnected geopolitical actualities play out within any given legal system, including those of Western industrialized nations.

OBSTACLES TO EMBRACING A GLOBAL SOCIOLEGAL PERSPECTIVE

As mentioned earlier, this book seeks to broaden and deepen a counter-hegemonic trend in sociolegal scholarship. This is not an easy task for a variety of reasons. A primary problem is a looming crisis in the legitimacy

---

or surpass the US, if they renounce the death penalty. Courts in countries such as Canada and Mexico, and throughout Europe, have begun to consistently refuse extradition as long as the death penalty is a possibility in the U.S. And, on the issue of the execution of juvenile offenders, every country of the world, with the possible exception of Somalia, has ratified the Convention on the Rights of the Child forbidding such executions. In the face of such consistent and adamant challenges to the death penalty, the US risks becoming isolated at a time when it can least afford it" (Dieter 2003).

Figure 1. Occupy London. Tents in front of St. Paul's Cathedral, London, October 16, 2011. Photograph by Neil Cummings, Wikimedia Commons.

of Western legality (see Falk et al. 2012). In the United States, for instance, popular disillusionment in law as a vehicle for democracy has been recently expressed across the conservative and progressive political spectrum in Tea Party and Occupy Wall Street activist movements. Today, unlike moments in the past such as in the civil rights era of the 1960s, law is not typically embraced for its emancipatory potential or seen as a strategy by which to resist or change the status quo.

In other Western countries there is similar disillusionment in law that is widely viewed as a mechanism of power rather than as a resource for a common good (see Figure 1). The days-long street riots in England and the horrific massacre of seventy-seven Norwegians in Oslo by a lone desperate gunman – both of which occurred in July 2011 – are flashpoints emblematic of peoples' disenchantment with the prevailing system. As Richard Falk has noted with respect to the worldwide 2011 Occupy Movement, "The movement was indistinct in its contours and goals, seemingly dedicated to the realization of democratic values on a global scale, particularly with respect to the global economy, but without any confidence that desirable ends could be reached by way of conventional politics: elections, political parties, institutional lawmaking, and governmental policies" (Falk 2012). In short, there is a growing gap between the concepts of legality and legitimacy and a general demoralization in the democratic promise of Western law within Western nations. Ironically, the same level of despondency was not evident among Middle East populations involved, at least initially, in the Arab Spring of 2011.

This crisis in the legitimacy of Western legality is not surprising. Under the weight of neoliberal market logics and conservative social values, law has become, Brian Tamanaha reminds us in his groundbreaking book *Law as Means to an End* (2006), explicitly instrumental. Today, particularly in the United States, law is seen not as an objective authority composed of fundamental principles of justice, customary rights, and public welfare, but rather a technical apparatus for making plans that conform to individual or group interests (Shapiro 2011). Law has become a commodity to be bought and sold by both state and private corporate interests. Law is now considered by legal practitioners and the wider society as an "empty vessel that can be applied to achieve any end" (Tamanaha 2006:219). As witnessed in the United States, law can be massaged and manipulated to justify torture, deny workers a living wage, and protect oil companies whose shoddy practices have caused billions of dollars in damages but whose liability is legally capped at only a fraction of the actual injury (see Scarry 2010). What we are now facing, Tamanaha argues, is "the rule of some groups over others *by* and through the law, more so than a community united under a rule of law that furthers the common good" (Tamanaha 2006:225). In this context of Western law's declining legitimacy, it is hard to promote a counter-hegemonic sociolegal perspective that both critiques legal instrumentality and proffers law as a site of hope for righting global injustices (see, however, Bartholomew 2012).

A second related problem follows from the first. This is the general lack of funding for critical sociolegal scholarship. The increasing corporatism of universities and for-profit research translate into less funding for critical scholarship of any sort, let alone critical sociolegal scholarship (Shaker and Heilman 2008; Brown 2010a). Over the past two decades, research funding has been severely cut back in the United States, the UK, and Australia, and it is now almost impossible to attract support for research that does not have an obvious policy orientation, reform recommendation, or prescriptive basis (Bonnor 2007; Paraskeva 2010; Ravitch 2010). In short, sociolegal scholarship that is not instrumental, defined as empirical, or speaks to interest group agendas is typically marginalized, undervalued, and under-resourced. Not surprisingly, sociolegal scholarship that has little value in measurable economic terms and points to the legal and social inequalities built into "anti-democratic" neoliberal state policies is increasingly vulnerable (Harvey 2006:27). As Rosemary Hunter and others have noted, critical sociolegal scholars are left fighting for their "own institutional survival" (Hunter 2008:125). This is particularly the case if scholars are not interested in serving the predominantly conservative agendas of law schools and legal practice.[9]

Today, within law and society scholarship an emphasis on legal instrumentality is championed by the Empirical Legal Studies (ELS) movement and the New Legal Realism Movement (NLR), both of which are largely associated with U.S. law school scholars, quantitative methods, and conceptually narrow and formulaic projects that seek to inform policy decision making (Macaulay 2005; Chambliss 2008; Nourse and Shaffer 2009; Suchman and Mertz 2010). "Empirical" in the context of the ELS movement is used in a narrow way and so is rather different from how the term is used elsewhere, such as in the UK's 2006 Nuffield Report on legal research (Genn and Wheeler 2006). Within the United States, there are distinct differences between the approaches of ELS and NLR to sociolegal inquiry, with ELS tending to "highlight the top-down institutions of the state" and NLR highlighting "the bottom-up normative contexts of civil society" (Suchman and Mertz 2010:564). That being said, both ELS and NLR are "creatures of the legal academy, and take their problematics and their tone largely from that setting." Both address doctrinal legal issues and seek prescriptive solutions as well as "share an aspiration to reach legal audiences from whom doctrine and policy are paramount" (Suchman and Mertz 2010:565). In short, what unites these two self-identifying groups of scholars is "the pull of the policy audience" and a shared assumption that law can be reformed (Sarat and Silbey 1988; see also Tomlins 2000).

Why is this trend toward explicit legal instrumentalism and a policy-driven research orientation significant, and why should we care? According to Mark Suchman, one of the problems with legal scholarship becoming more and more empiricist is that "it might leave less and less room for theoretical analyses that critique the social foundations of the legal enterprise itself" (Suchman 2006:3). In other words, the trouble with the agenda of ELS and NLR is that if the intellectual project is to make the current legal system better – irrespective of whose interests inform what "better" means – then ELS and NLR scholars are necessarily limited in an ability to imagine other forms of legal interaction. If scholars cannot interrogate the meaning of law from outside the practice

---

[9] The economic recession beginning in 2008 did not herald an abrupt or decisive change in funding for critical sociolegal scholarship in the United States. Rather, current fiscal uncertainties have accelerated trends in state policies that over the past decades have deliberately targeted and undermined public education and curtailed intellectual critique (see Cuban 2004; Newfield 2008; Krugman 2012).

of law itself, or even recognize that this is essential, then they are also precluded from imagining legal processes and the production of legal knowledge in wider global contexts that are culturally plural and spatially fluid and may be politically and economically distanced from state institutions.

Paul Kahn in his book *The Cultural Study of Law* articulates these concerns in another way. His central argument is that we need to study the culture of law in the same way that we study other cultures since "[e]ach has its founding myths, its necessary beliefs, and its reasons that are internal to its own norms" (Kahn 1999:1; see also Fitzpatrick 1992, 2001; Rosen 2008). Only by stepping outside the paradigm that believes in law as an object of power and so is focused on reforming it for a particular purpose, can, Kahn argues, we achieve some conceptual distance and begin to explore how law is understood as meaningful practice. Writes Kahn:

> We have to remember that the rule of law is neither a matter of revealed truth nor of natural order. It is a way of organizing society under a set of beliefs that are constitutive of the identity of the community and of its individual members ... It is both a product of history and constitutive of a certain kind of historical existence. To study the rule of law outside the practice of law is to elaborate this history and to expose the structure of these beliefs. This project is substantively and methodologically independent of any practical judgments about alternative forms of political order. The issue is not whether law makes us better off, but rather what is it that law makes us (Kahn 1999:6).

The ELS and NLR movements, which favor an instrumental understanding of law, do not bring the legal system itself into question, only its functional mechanisms. The questions that ELS and NLR scholars ask are not what is law and how does it shape our social organization, consciousness, and imagination. Rather, they ask how to make law better according to the values of particular interest groups, political parties, and state interests, be these progressive or conservative in nature. The problem with this narrow intellectual inquiry is that, writes Kahn, by "Standing within law, we are always in danger of allowing law to fill our entire vision. A cultural study of law reminds us not only that people have lives of meaning outside of law's rule, but also that many of our richest and deepest experiences must be protected from the imperialism of law's rule" (Kahn 1999:138–139).

I take Kahn's insights very seriously. We are facing a future where democracy – as we imagine it should be – is gravely threatened on a number of fronts that includes the dismantling of public education and concurrently a growing disbelief in the possibility of transparent and accountable government and judiciary. The legitimacy of law and its relevance to ordinary people is at stake.

A consequence of this threat to democracy is that we may also be facing a future where there no longer exists the intellectual capacity to imagine alternative understandings of law, justice, or common good beyond that articulated by a political and economic elite.

CHAPTER OUTLINE AND FORMAT

The chapters that follow are interconnected, and hence, their presentation as distinct intellectual conversations is in many ways artificial and contrived. That being said, the chapters have been organized around scholarly inquiries that overlap theoretically and substantively, and foreground certain issues that I regard as overlooked in much sociolegal scholarship but which can no longer be ignored as we march forward into the twenty-first century. These include a more nuanced approach to the production of legal knowledge and, hence, to the meaning and constitution of law itself (Chapter 3), the shifting spatial and temporal legal relations between states and other legal actors and institutions (Chapter 4), the limits of human rights discourse and humanitarian intervention and the growing threat to peace and security particularly in certain parts of the world (Chapter 5), and the enduring global injustices of racial discrimination that play out in battles over religion, environment, and health (Chapter 6).

What links all the chapters are thematic themes and contemporary challenges as discussed in Chapter 2. At the heart of this chapter is a conversation about the politics of deciding whose understanding of law dominates the global arena, which in turn forces us to acknowledge the socio-cultural biases that are built into Western legal jurisprudence and the assumed values and subject positions embodied in Euro-American law. At the end of each chapter are excerpted readings that are intended to build upon the general discussion and upon each other, presenting specific examples of sociolegal engagements with the chapter focus. Unfortunately, copyright fees were prohibitively expensive for articles that I would have liked to include such as Susan Silbey's article "Let Them Eat Cake": Globalization, Postmodern Colonialism, and the Possibilities of Justice" (1997); Sally Engle Merry, "International Law and Sociolegal Scholarship: Toward a Spatial Global Legal Pluralism" (2007); Boaventura de Sousa Santos, "Law: A Map of Misreading. Toward a Postmodern Conception of Law (1987); Mariana Valverde "Authorizing the Production of an Urban Moral Order: Appellate Courts and their Knowledge Games" (2005), and David Engel "Globalization and the Decline of Legal Consciousness: Torts, Ghosts, and Karma in Thailand" (2005). In my view, these articles are all important and should be read by anyone who is interested in current directions in sociolegal scholarship.

With respect to the readings that are included in this volume, the idea is to let the reader engage with a variety of theoretical and methodological approaches in the hope of provoking further thoughts and imaginings about what law is and what it means to whom. My chapter discussions and the accompanying articles are not intended to be conclusive or definitive in any way. On the contrary, I have deliberately framed my writing and selected the readings on the basis of accessibility and in the hope of nurturing new conversations, questions, investigations, and research.

LIST OF SUGGESTED READINGS

1. Abel, R.L. (2010) Law and Society: Project and Practice. *Annual Review of Law and Social Science* 6:1–23.
2. Benda-Beckmann, Franz von, Keebet von Benda-Beckmann and Anne Griffiths (eds.) (2009) *The Power of Law in a Transnational World: Anthropological Enquiries.* New York and Oxford: Berghahn Books.
3. Boyle, Elizabeth H. and Sharon E. Preves (2000) National Politics as International Process: The Case of Anti-Female-Genital-Cutting Laws. *Law & Society Review* 34(3):703–737.
4. Domingo, Rafael (2010) *The New Global Law.* Cambridge: Cambridge University Press.
5. Falk, Richard, Mark Juergensmeyer and Vesselin Popovski (eds.) (2012) *Legality and Legitimacy in Global Affairs.* Oxford: Oxford University Press.
6. Fraser, Nancy (2005) Reframing Justice in a Global World. *New Left Review* 36(Nov–Dec).
7. Kahn, Paul W. (1999) *The Cultural Study of Law: Reconstructing Legal Scholarship.* Chicago: University of Chicago Press.
8. Pavlich, George (2011) *Law and Society Redefined.* Oxford: Oxford University Press.
9. Sarat, Austin (ed.) (2008) Special Issue: Law and Society Reconsidered. *Studies in Law, Politics, and Society* 41.
10. Silbey, Susan S. (1997) 1996 Presidential Address: Let Them Eat Cake": Globalization, Postmodern Colonialism, and the Possibilities of Justice. *Law & Society Review* 31(2):207–236.
11. Steger, Manfred (2009) *The Rise of the Global Imaginary: Political Ideologies from the French Revolution to the Global War on Terror.* Oxford: Oxford University Press.

12. Suchman, Mark C. and Elizabeth Mertz (2010) Toward a New Legal Empiricism: Empirical Studies and New Legal Realism. *Annual Review of Law and Social Science* **6**:555–579.
13. Twining, William (2009) *General Jurisprudence: Understanding Law from a Global Perspective*. Cambridge: Cambridge University Press.

Excerpts From:

Sassen, Saskia (2008) Neither Global nor National: Novel Assemblages of Territory, Authority and Rights.[10] *Ethics & Global Politics* 1(1–2):61–79.

Published under the Creative Commons Attribution-NonCommerical 3.0 Unported license.

NEITHER GLOBAL NOR NATIONAL: NOVEL ASSEMBLAGES OF TERRITORY, AUTHORITY AND RIGHTS

Saskia Sassen (2008)

Introduction: Mapping An Analytic Terrain

A key yet much overlooked feature of the current period is the multiplication of a broad range of partial, often highly specialized, global assemblages of bits of territory, authority, and rights (TAR) that begin to escape the grip of national institutional frames.[11] These assemblages cut across the binary of national versus global. They continue to inhabit national institutional and territorial settings but are no longer part of the national as historically constructed. They exit the national through a process of denationalization that may or may not lead to the formation of global arrangements.

These assemblages are enormously diverse. At one end we find private, often very narrow, frameworks such as the lex constructionis, a private 'law' developed by the major engineering companies in the world to establish a common mode of dealing with the strengthening of environmental standards in a growing number of countries, in most of which these firms are building.[12] At the other end of the range they include far more complex (and experimental) entities, such as the first ever global public court, the International Criminal Court; this court is not part of the established supranational system and has universal jurisdiction among signatory countries.[13]

Beyond the fact of the diversity of these assemblages, there is the increasingly weighty fact of their numbers-over 125 according to the best recent

---

[10] This is based on a larger project published as *Territory, Authority, Rights: From Medieval to Global Assemblages* (Princeton University Press 2006; New Updated Edition 2008), henceforth referred to as Territory. There readers can find full bibliographic elaboration of the issues raised here.

[11] This is clearly an analysis that emerges from European history, with all the limitations that entails. Critical here is Gayatri Spivak's thinking about the diverse positions that can structure an 'author's' stance. Donna Landry & Gerald MacLean (Eds) (1996) The Spivak reader. New York and London, Routledge.

[12] See generally Teubner, Gunther (Ed.) (1997) Global law without a state. Aldershot, UK: Dartmouth Publishing.

[13] See Sadat, Leila Nadya, & Richard Carden, S. (2000) The new international criminal court, Georgetown Law Journal, 88(3), 381–474.

count.[14] Their proliferation does not represent the end of national states, but it does begin to disassemble the national.

Central to the argument in this paper is that although for now these are mostly incipient formations, they are potentially profoundly unsettling of what are still the prevalent institutional arrangements (nation-states and the supranational system) for handling questions of order and justice. One of the consequences of the sharpening differentiation among domains once suffused with the national, or the supranational, is that this can enable a proliferation of temporal and spatial framings and a proliferation of normative orders where once the dominant logic was toward producing unitary spatial, temporal, and normative framings. A synthesizing image we might use to capture these dynamics is that we see a movement from centripetal nation-state articulation to a centrifugal multiplication of specialized assemblages. This multiplication in turn can lead to a sort of simplification of normative structures: these assemblages are partial and often highly specialized formations centered in particular utilities and purposes. The valence of these particular utilities and purposes can range from the search for justice (the ICC) to narrow self-interest (Lex constructionis).

What distinguishes these novel assemblages is that they can de-border, and even exit, what are today still ruling normative orders. Further, and equally important if not more so, they can constitute particularized 'normative' orders internal to each assemblage which easily amount to mere utility logics. These assemblages are not only highly specialized or particular, they are also without much internal differentiation, thereby further reducing normative orders to somewhat elementary utilities. This is still a minor process in the larger scale of our geopolity. But it may well be the beginning of a multi-sited disruption of its existing formal architecture. It is a process that lifts a variety of segments (involving dimensions of TAR) out of their nation-state normative framing, thereby reshuffling their constitutional alignments. Not even well-functioning states with their powerful raison d'etat can quite counteract the particularized normativities of each of these assemblages, and their easy slide into narrower utilitarian logics.

This slide into utilitarian logics is not always bad. In the case of a single-minded pursuit of human rights, we can see many positive outcomes. But a similarly single-minded pursuit of profits and disregard of state welfare functions is troubling. There is, then, multivalence in this process of multiplying lower-order normative framings. But whether good or bad, the de-bordering of national normative frames is a change, and it carries implications for how we are to handle the often complex interactions of larger normative issues.

My argument is then that these developments signal the emergence of new types of orderings that can coexist with older orderings, such as the nation-state

---

[14] See http://www.pict.org

and the interstate system, but nonetheless bring consequences that may well be strategic for larger normative questions. These developments are both strategic and particular, and hence often illegible, requiring diverse modes of decoding.

Emphasizing this multiplication of partial assemblages contrasts with much of the globalization literature. That literature has tended to assume the binary of the global versus the national, and hence to focus on the powerful global institutions that have played a critical role in implementing the global corporate economy and have reduced the power of 'the state'. I rather emphasize that the global can also be constituted inside the national, i.e. the global city, and that particular components of the state have actually gained power because they have to do the work of implementing policies necessary for a global corporate economy. Thus my focus in the larger project (2006) and in this particular paper opens up the analysis of what is described as 'globalization' to a far broader range of actors, and it repositions the powerful global regulators, such as the (reinvented) IMF or the WTO as bridging events for an epochal transformation, rather than as the transformation itself. The actual dynamics getting shaped are far deeper and more radical than such entities as the WTO or the IMF, no matter how powerful they are as foot soldiers. These institutions should rather be conceived of as powerful capabilities for the making of a new order-they are instruments, not the new order itself. The multiplication of partial assemblages examined in this paper signals a new ordering that begins to unsettle older frameworks that have held together complex interdependencies between rights and obligations, power and the law, wealth and poverty, allegiance and exit-albeit always imperfectly.

In what follows I first discuss the features of some of these assemblages, then examine questions of method and interpretation that shape this particular conceptualization of current transformations, and conclude with a discussion of their normative and political implications. Both self-evidently global and denationalizing dynamics destabilize existing meanings and systems.

Specialized Assemblages as New Types of Territoriality

If you see through the eye of the national state, these assemblages look like inchoate geographies. But they are actually the bits of a new type of ordering, a reality in the making. Perhaps starting with some actual elementary spatial instances might help illuminate some of the issues for politics and normative questions to which I return in the second half of this essay. These are instances where we can detect a process of at least partial denationalizing of TAR. Here, then, follow some of these instances.

I will use the concept of territoriality, usually used to designate the particular articulation of TAR marking the modern state, in a slightly different way so as to capture a far broader range of such articulations. But the national state does function as the standard against which I identify the following four types of territoriality assembled out of 'national' and 'global' elements, with each individual or aggregate instance evincing distinct spatio-temporal features. (In the larger project, 2006, I examine yet other emergent assemblages.) These four types of instances unsettle national state territoriality, that is to say, the institutional framing of territory that gives the national state exclusive authority in a very broad range of domains. The territory of the national is a critical dimension in play in all four instances: diverse actors can exit the national institutionalization of territory yet act within national territory, and do so in ways that go well beyond existing extraterritorial arrangements. What gives weight to these four types of instances is not simply a question of novelty but their depth, spread, and proliferation. At some point all of this leads to a qualitatively different condition. We can conceive of it as emergent institutionalizations of territory that unsettle the national encasement of territory.

A first type of territoriality is being constituted through the development of new jurisdictional geographies. Legal frameworks for rights and guarantees, and more generally the rule of law, were largely developed in the context of the formation of national states. But now some of these instruments are strengthening a non-national organizing logic. As they become part of new types of transnational systems they alter the valence of older national state capabilities. Further, in so doing, they are often pushing these national states to go against the interests of national capital. A second type of instance is the formation of triangular cross-border jurisdictions for political action, which once would have been confined to the national. Electronic activists often use global campaigns and international organizations to secure rights and guarantees from their national states. Furthermore, a variety of national legal actions involving multiple geographic sites across the globe can today be launched from national courts, producing a transnational geography for national lawsuits.

The critical articulation is between the national (as in national court, national law) and a global geography outside the terms of traditional international law or treaty law. A good example is the lawsuit launched by the Washington-based Center for Constitutional Rights in a national court against nine multinational corporations, both American and foreign, for abuses of workers' rights in their offshore industrial operations, using as the national legal instrument the Alien Torts Claims Act. In other words, this is a global three-sited jurisdiction, with several locations in at least two of those sites-the locations of the headquarters (both the US and other countries), the locations of the offshore factories (several countries), and the court in Washington. Even if these lawsuits do not quite achieve their full goal, they signal it is possible to use the national judiciary for suing US and foreign firms for questionable practices in their operations outside their home countries. Thus, besides the much noted new courts and instruments (e.g. the new International Criminal Court, the European Court of Human Rights), what this example shows is that components of the national rule of law that once served to build the strength of the national state, are today contributing to the formation of transnational jurisdictions. Another instance is the US practice of 'exporting' prisoners to third countries (rendition), de facto to facilitate their torture. This is yet another instance of a territoriality that is both national and transnational. Finally, diverse jurisdictional geographies can also be used to manipulate temporal dimensions. Reinserting a conflict in the national legal system may ensure a slower progression than in the private jurisdiction of international commercial arbitration.[15] Diverse jurisdictional geographies can also be used to manipulate temporal dimensions. Reinserting a conflict in the national legal system may ensure a slower progression than in the private jurisdiction of international commercial arbitration.

A second type of specialized assemblage that is contributing to a novel type of territoriality is the work of national states across the globe to construct a standardized global space for the operations of firms and markets. What this means is that components of legal frameworks for rights and guarantees, and more generally the rule of law, largely developed in the process of national state formation, can now strengthen non-national organizing logics. As these components become part of new types of transnational systems they alter the valence of (rather than destroy, as is often argued) older national state capabilities. Where the rule of law once built the strength of the national state and national corporations, key components of that rule of law are now contributing to the partial, often highly specialized, denationalizing of particular national state orders. For instance, corporate actors operating globally have pushed hard for the development of new types of formal instruments, notably intellectual property rights and standardized accounting principles. But they need not only the support, but also the actual work of each individual state where they operate to develop and implement such instruments in the specific context of each country. In their aggregate this and other emergent orderings contribute to produce an operational space partly embedded in particular components of national legal systems which have been subjected to specialized denationalizations;[16] thereby these orderings become capabilities

---

[15] Territory, Chapter 5.
[16] Territory, Chapters 4 and 5.

of an organizing logic that is not quite part of the national state even as that logic installs itself in that state. Further, in so doing, they often go against the interests of national capital. This is a very different way of representing economic globalization than the common notion of the withdrawal of the state at the hands of the global system. Indeed, to a large extent it is the executive branch of government that is getting aligned with global corporate capital and ensuring this work gets done.

A third type of specialized assemblage can be detected in the formation of a global network of financial centers. We can conceive of financial centers that are part of global financial markets as constituting a distinct kind of territoriality, simultaneously pulled in by the larger electronic networks and functioning as localized micro- infrastructures for those networks. These financial centers inhabit national territories, but they cannot be seen as simply national in the historical sense of the term, nor can they be reduced to the administrative unit encompassing the actual terrain (e.g. a city), one that is part of a nation-state. In their aggregate they house significant components of the global, partly electronic market for capital. As localities they are denationalized in specific and partial ways. In this sense they can be seen as constituting the elements of a novel type of multi-sited territoriality, one that diverges sharply from the territoriality of the historic nation-state.

A fourth type of assemblage can be found in the global networks of local activists and, more generally, in the concrete and often place-specific social infrastructure of 'global civil society'.[17] Global civil society is enabled by global digital networks and the associated imaginaries. But this does not preclude that localized actors, organizations, and causes are key building blocks of global civil society as it is shaping up today. The localized involvements of activists are critical no matter how universal and planetary the aims of the various struggles-in their aggregate these localized involvements are constitutive. Global electronic networks actually push the possibility of this local-global dynamic further. Elsewhere I have examined[18] the possibility for even resource-poor and immobile individuals or organizations to become part of a type of horizontal globality centered on diverse localities. When supplied with the key capabilities of the new technologies-decentralized access, interconnectivity, and simultaneity of transactions-localized, immobilized individuals and organizations can be part of a global public space, one that is partly a subjective condition, but only partly because it is rooted in the concrete struggles of localities.

[17]   This term remains underspecified in the view of many. But there is now a vast scholarship that has documented various features, measures and interpretations. See for instance, the Annual Global Civil Society volumes published by Oxford University Press.

[18]   *Territory*, Chapter 7.

In principle, we can posit that those who are immobile might be more likely to experience their globality through this (abstract) space than individuals and organizations that have the resources and the options to travel across the globe. These globalities can assume complex forms, as is the case with first-nation people demanding direct representation in international fora, bypassing national state authority, a longstanding cause that has been significantly enabled by global electronic networking. They can also be more indirect, as is the case with the Forest Watch network which uses indigenous residents in rain forests around the world who can detect forest abuse long before it becomes visible to the average observer. They then pass on this information to what are often long chains of activists eventually ending in the central office; the early links in the chain, where the deep knowledge resides, are typically not via digital media nor are they in English.

We can see here at work a particular type of interaction between placeless digital networks and deeply localized actors/users. One common pattern is the formation of triangular cross-border jurisdictions for political action which once would have been confined to the national. Local activists often use global campaigns and international organizations to secure rights and guarantees from their national states; they now have the option to incorporate a non-national or global site in their national struggles. These instances point to the emergence of a particular type of territoriality in the context of the imbrications of digital and non-digital conditions. This territoriality partly inhabits specific subnational spaces and partly gets constituted as a variety of somewhat specialized or partial global publics.

While the third and fourth types of territoriality might seem similar, they are actually not. The subnational spaces of these localized actors have not been denationalized as have the financial centers discussed earlier. The global publics that get constituted are barely institutionalized and mostly informal, unlike the global capital market, which is a highly institutionalized space both through national and international law, and through private governance systems. In their informality, however, these global publics can be seen as spaces for empowerment of the resource- poor or of not very powerful actors. In this sense the subjectivities that are emerging through these global publics constitute capabilities for new organizing logics.

These emergent assemblages begin to unbundle the traditional territoriality of the national, albeit in partial, often highly specialized ways. In cases where the global is rich in content or subject to multiple conditionalities, its insertion in an institutional world that has been historically constructed overwhelmingly as a national unitary spatio-temporal domain is eventful. It is the combination of this embeddedness of the global along with its specificity.

Although these four types of emergent territorialities are diverse, each containing multiple, often highly specialized and partial instances, all three evince specific features. First, they are not exclusively national or global but are assemblages of elements of each. Second, in this assembling they bring together what are often different spatio-temporal orders, that is, different velocities and different scopes. Third, this can produce an eventful engagement, including contestations and the frontier zone effect, a space that makes possible kinds of engagements for which there are no clear rules. The resolution of these encounters can become the occasion for playing out conflicts that cannot easily be engaged in other spaces. Fourth, novel types of actors can emerge in this assembling, often with the option to access domains once exclusive to older established actors, notably national states. Finally, in the juxtaposition of the different temporal orders that come together in these novel territorialities, existing capabilities can get redeployed to domains with novel organizing logics.

These emergent assemblages begin to unbundle the traditional territoriality of the national historically constructed overwhelmingly as a national unitary spatio- temporal domain.

Normative and Political Implications

The centrifugal multiplication of specialized and/or particular assemblages of TAR is a partial rather than all-encompassing development. Yet its character is strategic in that it unsettles existing normative arrangements and produces a new type of segmentation. One way of formulating the consequences is in terms of novel types of systemic inequality and novel locations for the normative.

We can begin with the novel types of systemic inequality that are being produced. These are kinds of inequality that can cut across every scale, nation-state, major city, and state apparatus. It is not the kind of intra-systemic inequality that emerges from inside a unitary, albeit highly differentiated system, such as a nation-state. Nor is it the kind of inequality that exists between developed and less developed regions of the world. These are two types of recognized and named inequalities, and we have developed massive institutional and discursive domains to address them; although all this effort has only partly reduced those inequalities, they are a recognized target for existing efforts and resources.

In contrast, the proliferation of specialized assemblages that exit the grip of existing normative frames and cut across countries produces a kind of inequality we might conceive of as multiplying particular types of intersystemic segmentations, where the systems are these particularized assemblages.

It is, then, also a kind of inequality that can coexist with older and recognized forms of differentiation inside countries and among countries. But it is to be distinguished from these.

Secondly, on the locations for the normative, these assemblages tend to have rules for governance wired into the structures of their system in a way reminiscent of how free markets function. That is to say, these are not explicated rules and norms. The new forms of unaccountable power within the executive branch of government and in global markets illustrate this; but so does the world of NGOs, perhaps especially when they function internationally. This wiring of rules and norms in the structure itself of the system can be distinguished from formalized systems for governance where rules and norms are meant to be explicated and are located both inside and outside the system itself in that they are accountable to external authorities.[19]

We can see here a disaggregating of the glue that for a long time held possibly different normative orders together under the somewhat unitary dynamics of nation-states. The multiplication of partial systems, each with a small set of sharply distinctive constitutive rules produces a proliferation of simple systems. This also brings with it a reshuffling of constitutive rules. Not all of these new specialized assemblages contain such constitutive rules, but it is evident in a number of those that constitute themselves precisely as disembedded from state authority and normativity and as systems of justice and authority (for instance, the ICC), including private systems of justice (for instance, international commercial arbitration).[20]

Perhaps it is tempting to see in these trends arrangements akin to European feudalism, a period marked by the absence of centralized national states. Some of the globalization literature positing the weakening, and even 'disappearance' of the nation-state has made this type of argument. I see this as a mistake (2006: Part One). In identifying a multiplication of partial orders I find a foundational difference with the medieval European period, one when there were strong broadly encompassing normative orders (the church, the empire) and the disaggregations (the feuds, the cities) each contained within them a fairly complete structure involving many if not most aspects of life (different classes,

---

[19] I intend this to capture a considerable diversity of formations. For instance, Hezbollah in Lebanon can be seen as having shaped a very specific assemblage of TAR that cannot be easily reduced to any of the familiar containers-nation-state, internal minority-controlled region, such as the Kurdish region in Iraq, or a separatist area such as the Basque region in Spain. It intensifies the difference with the 'home country' and in fact extends beyond the latter through specific translocal networks and more diffuse subjectivities. This type of development strengthens types of territorial and authority fractures that the project of building a nation-state sought to eliminate or dilute.

[20] I develop these issues at length in Territory, Chapters 5, 6, and 8.

norms, systems of justice, and so forth). Today these assemblages are highly specialized, partial, and without much internal differentiation. In contrast, the localized and limited world of the manor or the fief of the medieval lord was a complex world encompassing constitutive rules that addressed the full range of spheres of social life.

The multiplication of partial, specialized, and applied normative orders is unsettling and produces distinct normative challenges in the context of a still prevalent world of nation-states. Just to mention one instance, we can deduce from these trends that normative orders such as religion reassume great importance where they had been confined to distinct specialized spheres by the secular normative orders of states. Thus I posit the rise of religion in the last two decades is part of a new modernity rather than a fallback on older cultures, no matter how 'traditional' its contents. It is a systemic outcome of cutting-edge developments. In brief, this can then be shown to be not pre-modern but a new type of modernity, arising out of the partial unbundling of what had been dominant and centripetal (secular) normative orders into multiple particularized segmentations.[21]

This incipient formation of specialized or particularized orders extends even inside the state apparatus. I argue that we can no longer speak of 'the' state, and hence of 'the' national state versus 'the' global order. There is a novel type of segmentation inside the state apparatus, with a growing and increasingly privatized executive branch of government aligned with specific global actors, notwithstanding nationalist speeches, and a hollowing out of the legislature whose effectiveness is at risk of becoming confined to fewer and more domestic matters.[22] A weak and domesticated legislature weakens

[21] We also see these incipient novel mixes of TAR in far less visible or noticed settings. For instance, when Mexico's (former) President Fox met with undocumented Mexican immigrants during his visit to the US in May 2006, his actions amounted to the making of a new informal jurisdiction. His actions did not fit into existing legal forms that give sovereign states specific types of extraterritorial authority. Nonetheless, his actions were not seen as particularly objectionable; indeed, they were hardly noticed. Yet these were, after all, unauthorized immigrants subject to deportation if detected, in a country that is now spending almost two billion dollars a year to secure border control. No INS or other police came to arrest the undocumented thus exposed, and the media barely reacted, even though it was taking place at a time when Congress was debating whether to criminalize illegal immigrants. Or when Chavez, seen as an 'enemy' of sorts by the US government, is somehow enabled (through the state-owned oil enterprise) to bring oil to the poor in a few major cities in the US. All of these are minor acts, but they were not somehow acceptable or customary even a short time ago. I see these practices as producing novel types of mostly informal jurisdictions, and these are, in the last analysis, assemblages of TAR.

[22] Territory, Chapter 4. In fact, nationality itself is a legal format undergoing change (see, for instance, Karen Knop (2002) Diversity and Self-Determination in International Law. Cambridge: Cambridge University Press; Kim Rubenstein and Daniel Adler (2000) 'International

the political capacity of citizens to demand accountability from an increasingly powerful and private executive, since the legislature gives citizens stronger standing in these matters than the executive. Further, the privatizing of the executive partly has brought with it an eroding of the privacy rights of citizens-a historic shift of the private-public division at the heart of the liberal state, even if always an imperfect division.[23]

A second critical divergence is between the increasing alignment of the executive with global logics and the confinement of the legislature to domestic matters.[24] This results from three major trends. One is the growing importance of particular components of the administration, such as ministries of finance and central banks (respectively, Treasury and Federal Reserve in the US), for the implementing of a global corporate economy; these components actually gain power because of globalization. Secondly, the global regulators (IMF, WTO, and others) only deal with the executive branch; they do not deal with the legislature. This can strengthen the adoption of global logics by the executive. A third becomes evident in such cases as the Bush-Cheney Administration's support for the Dubai Ports' proposed management of several major port operations in the US. In contrast to these trends, the legislature has long been a domestic part of the state, something which begins to weaken its effectiveness as globalization expands. This then also weakens the political capacity of citizens in an increasingly globalized world.

The participation of the state in the implementation of a corporate global economy engenders a particular type of international authority for the state vis a vis global firms and it engenders a kind of internationalism in state practice. But for now the deployment of this authority and new internationalism

Citizenship: The Future of Nationality in a Globalized World', Indiana Journal of Global Legal Studies 7(2): 519–48). Nationality can no longer be easily deployed as a singular condition. Some of the main dynamics at work today are destabilizing its singular meaning, for example, the granting of dual nationality. Peter J. Spiro (2008) Citizenship Beyond Borders and the incorporation of international human rights norms in national law (Harold Hongju Koh (1997) 'How is International Human Rights Law Enforced?', Indiana Law Journal 74(4): 1397–1417). In this regard nationality may well evolve into an instance of Benhabib's "constitutive tensions in liberal democracies." For a more detailed discussion of these issues see the special issue on Benhabib's work and my response in the European Journal of Political Theory, Vol. 6, No. 4, 431–444 (2007).

[23] This is a complicated issue that I do not address here, but see (Territory, Chapter 6). One question is whether there is a necessary relationship between an increasingly privatized executive branch and the erosion of citizens' privacy rights.

[24] An issue here is the relationship between this executive branch alignment with global logics, on the one hand, and, on the other, the proliferation of various nationalisms. I address this in Territory, Chapters 6 and 9. Helpful here is Calhoun's (1997) proposition that nationalism is a process articulated with modernity; this makes room for the coexistence of globalization and nationalization. Craig Calhoun 1997. Nationalism, University of Minnesota Press.

have largely been confined to supporting private corporate interests. Such a conceptualization introduces a twist in the analysis of the state and corporate economic globalization because it seeks to detect the actual presence of private agendas inside the state, rather than the more common focus in the globalization literature on the shift of state functions to the private sector and the growth of private authority.[25] Further, it differs from an older scholarly tradition on the captured state, which focused on cooptation of states by private actors.[26] In my own research I emphasize the privatization of norm-making capacities and the enactment inside the state of corporate private logics dressed as public norms.[27] An important question is whether these new properties of state practice could be reoriented to questions concerning the global common good. For this to become an aim, a number of issues need to be addressed. What type of state authority is this mix of public and private components: most importantly, could it accommodate interests other than private corporate ones? Does the weight of private, often foreign, interests in this specific work of the state become constitutive of that authority and indeed produce a hybrid that is neither fully private nor fully public? My argument is that we are seeing the incipient formation of a type of authority and state practice that entail a partial denationalizing of what had been constructed historically as national. This denationalizing consists of several specific processes, including importantly, the re-orienting of national agendas towards global ones, and the circulation inside the state of private agendas dressed as public policy. But this denationalizing also can open up space for non-corporate international agendas.

For the purposes of this essay it matters whether this participation by the state in global processes and the consequent partial denationalization, can also take place in domains other than that of economic globalization. Among these are recent developments in the human rights regime which make it possible to sue foreign firms and foreign dictators in national (rather than international) courts. Can denationalization be extended to aims other than those of global corporate actors, including an attempt to develop a global economy with broader social justice aims, and aims other than economic ones.[28]

---

[25] For example, Cutler, C. (2000) 'Globalization, law, and transnational corporations: a deepening of market discipline', in: T.H. Cohn, S. McBride & Wiseman, J. (Eds) Power in the global era: grounding globalization, 53–66. London, Macmillan.

[26] Panitch, 'Rethinking the Role of the State.' op.cit. Cox.

[27] Territory, Chapters 4 and 5; Sassen (1996) Losing control? Sovereignty in an age of globalization. New York, Columbia University Press, Chapter 2.

[28] For example, Lourdes Beneria (2003) Global tensions: challenges and opportunities in the world economy. New York, Routledge; Max Kirsch (Ed.) (2006) Inclusion and exclusion in

Elsewhere I have argued that yes, like globalization, denationalization can be multivalent: it can include the endogenizing into the national of the global agendas of diverse actors, not only corporate firms and financial markets, but also human rights and environmental agendas.[29] The existence of a dynamic and growing transnational sphere[30] becomes critical at this juncture as it can sustain this entry by national actors into global struggles using national instruments.[31] Sometimes these processes of denationalization allow, enable, or push the construction of new types of global scalings; other times they continue to inhabit the realm of what is still largely national.

An issue in all of this is the considerable illegibility, ultimately, of this shift from a centripetal to a centrifugal logic. We cannot quite see that this centrifugal logic has replaced important segments of the centripetal logic of the nation-state. This is partly because the national state continues to be the dominant ordering institution and because war and militarized border controls mark the geopolitical landscape and have mostly been sharpened rather than diluted in much of the world. It leads many observers to overlook the fact that wars and borders can coexist with centrifugal logics. Even more difficult to apprehend is the fact that through processes of denationalization some of the components of the nation-state and the state apparatus are themselves part of the new centrifugality. Elsewhere I have shown how this trend holds even for particular segments of the executive branch of government,[32] in spite of varied nationalisms. The ongoing prevalence of strong state politics and policies may well increasingly be a matter more of raw power than the more complex category that is authority. The new types of wars, whether 'civil' or international, suggest this rise of raw power over authority. Even as

the global arena. New York, Routledge; Kate E. Tunstall (Ed.) (2006) Displacement, asylum, migration: the 2004 amnesty lectures. Oxford, Oxford University Press; Linda Lucas (Ed.) (2005) Unpacking globalisation: markets, gender and work. Kampala, Uganda, Makerere University Press; Natalia Ribas-Mateos (2005) The Mediterranean in the age of globalization: migration, welfare, and borders. Somerset, NJ, Transaction; Rami Nashashibi (2007) 'Ghetto cosmopolitanism: making theory at the margins', in: Sassen, S. (Eds) Deciphering the global: its spaces, scales and subjects, 241–262. New York and London, Routledge.

29 Territory, Chapters 8 and 9.

30 For example, Khagram, S., Riker, J.V. & Sikkink, K. (Eds) (2002) Restructuring world politics: transnational social movements, networks, and norms. Minneapolis, MN, University of Minnesota Press; Valentine M. Moghadam (2005) Globalizing women: transnational feminist networks. Baltimore, Johns Hopkins University Press; Nancy A. Naples & Manisha Desai (2002) Women's activism and globalization: linking local struggles and transnational politics. New York, Routledge.

31 Territory, Chapter 6.

32 Territory, Chapter 4.

the raw power of national states in many cases has increased, this may not necessarily mean that sovereign territorial authority has become more significant. This distinction is critical to the analysis in the larger project on which this essay is based.[33]

Important to my argument is that some of the most complex meanings of the global are being constituted inside the national, whether national territories and institutions or national states. A good part of globalization consists of an enormous variety of subnational micro-processes that begin to denationalize what had been constructed as national-whether policies, laws, capital, political subjectivities, urban spaces, temporal frames, or any other of a variety of dynamics and domains.[34] This argument can perhaps be developed most persuasively at this time through an examination of the critical role of national states in setting up the basic conditions, including governance structures, for the implementation of a global economy.[35] Ministries of finance, central banks, legislatures, and many other government sectors have done the state work necessary to secure a global capital market, a global trading system, the needed competition policies, and so on.

Conclusion

Both self-evidently global and denationalizing dynamics destabilize existing meanings and systems. As the unitary character of the nation-state becomes disaggregated, even if only partially, sovereign authority is itself subject to partial

---

[33] Territory, Chapter 4.

[34] A focus on such subnationally based processes and dynamics of globalization requires methodologies and theorizations that engage not only global scalings but also subnational scalings as components of global processes, thereby destabilizing older hierarchies of scale and nested scalings. Studying global processes and conditions that get constituted subnationally has some advantages over studies of globally scaled dynamics, but it also poses specific challenges. It does make possible the use of longstanding research techniques, from quantitative to qualitative, in the study of globalization. It also gives us a bridge for using the wealth of national and subnational data sets as well as specialized scholarships such as area studies. Both types of studies, however, need to be situated in conceptual architectures that are not quite those held by the researchers who generated these research techniques and data sets, as their efforts mostly had little to do with globalization. I develop this in Saskia Sassen (2007) A sociology of globalization. New York, W. W. Norton.

[35] For example, Alfred C. Aman (1998) 'The globalizing state: a future-oriented perspective on the public/private distinction, federalism, and democracy,' Vanderbilt Journal of Transnational Law, 31, 769–870. Giselle Datz (2007) 'Global-national interactions and sovereign debt- restructuring outcomes', in: Sassen, S. (Eds) Deciphering the global: its spaces, scales and subjects, 321–350. New York and London, Routledge; Rachel Harvey (2007) 'The subnational constitution of global markets', in: Sassen, S. (Eds) Deciphering the global: its spaces, scales and subjects, 199–216. New York and London, Routledge; Territory, Chapters 1 and 2; Balakrishnan Rajagopal (2003) International law from below. Cambridge, Cambridge University Press.

disaggregations. The weakening of the centripetal dynamic of the nation-state also can generate exit options for the disadvantaged. Denationalization is the category through which I attempt to capture these transformations because they are not necessarily global in the narrow sense of that term. This is a historicizing categorization with the double intent of de-essentializing the national by confining it to a historically specific configuration and making it a reference point by positing that its enormous complexity and large capture of society and the geopolity make it a strategic site for the transformation-the latter cannot simply come from the outside. What this categorization does not entail is the notion that the nation-state as a major form will disappear. Rather that, in addition to being the site for key transformations, the state will itself be a profoundly changed entity.

Except for the most superficial and self-evident instances (e.g. globalized consumer markets), this constituting and shaping of global dynamics inside the national generally gets coded, represented, formulated or experienced through the vocabularies and institutional instruments of the national as historically constructed. This is to be expected insofar as nation-states and national states are enormously complex organizations, with often very long histories of developing the needed capabilities. In contrast, the current phase of global institutions and processes is young and is an as yet thin reality. Part of the research task is, then, decode, and, more generally, discover and detect the global inside the national.

These and other denationalizing dynamics (e.g. the insertion of human rights in national judiciary decisions) have additional consequences. They begin to disassemble bits and pieces of the nation-state and the state apparatus itself as containers. This disassembling is one dynamic feeding the multiplication of partial, often highly specialized, cross-border assemblages of bits of TAR once lodged inside the national. Many of these are beginning to function as formal or informal entities for both operational and governance tasks in a growing range of global processes stretching across nation-states. The clearest normative implication is a proliferation of particularized normative orders, including their downgrading to utility logics. Whether this is the beginning of a phase that might still see the formation of larger and more encompassing normative orders remains an open question in my reading.

All of this points to at least three distinct subjects for further research and theorization. One concerns the degree of specificity of these emergent assemblages that result from the partial disassembling of unitary nation-state framings. That is to say, what is the extent of their normative and analytic legibility? The second concerns the level of complexity and power these assemblages can evince given their as yet elementary character compared to the internal diversity, organizational complexity, and social thickness of the national. A third subject concerns the move away from unitary normative and spatio-temporal alignments inside nation-states as a result of this proliferation of multiple assemblages. In brief, what are the normative and political implications of these moves toward centrifugal dynamics and away from the centripetal dynamics that have marked the development of nation-states.

2   Interconnected Themes and Challenges

This chapter outlines themes that run throughout the book. These themes are twofold, build upon each other, and together provide the ultimate challenge for long-term peace and human security in the twenty-first century. The first theme is that law is a dynamic artifact of cultural engagement. This means that all law – however defined – is constituted through its cultural and social environments and imparted with meaning by the people who experience and engage with it. This leads to the second theme. In situating law within international and global settings, it is argued that law has been (and continues to be) constituted through its interaction with other legal systems that are similarly culturally constituted. The world is made up of assemblages or "constellations" of overlapping legal systems that embody a diverse range of cultural values, norms, and meanings (Benda-Beckman et al. 2009b:4). These legal systems are in constant tension with, and concurrently defined through, interactions with each other. Compounding the complexity is that some legal systems are seen to hold greater authority and legitimacy. The result is a complex of legal interconnectivity in which some countries' laws (i.e., U.S. law, German law) are presented as more legitimate and valuable than others that may not be obviously territorially defined or centrally state-based (i.e., Shari'a law, Bedouin law).

I urge readers to hold these two persistent and interlocking themes (law as culture and assemblages of legal systems) in mind while reading the chapters that follow this one. These themes underscore the complexity of a global sociolegal perspective and should foreground legal analysis. Perhaps the most challenging issue confronting law in the twenty-first century, and possibly the only one offering a tangible means to overcome disparities and differences in legal and cultural systems, is to pursue the idea of global governance. Global governance, at least in principle, aspires to transcend state boundaries and national self-interests. As an idea, global governance provides an inclusive platform for pluralistic systems of legal meaning and cultural perspective. Yet how is it possible to achieve a form of global governance that truly respects legal pluralism and does not advocate that one legal system and one cultural position is superior to another? Related to this first question, how can we establish a global governance regime that is consensually endorsed yet sufficiently authoritative that it would be capable of dealing with pressing world problems such as global climate change, global poverty, and global depletion of natural resources? These two interrelated questions represent the ultimate legal challenge confronting all of us.

LAW AS (MULTI)CULTURAL ARTIFACT

It is often forgotten in Western legal arenas – especially among law students and legal practitioners – that law is a product of cultural processes and always involves political, economic, and socio-cultural dimensions. Law cannot be thought of as existing outside specific cultural contexts because it only has meaning and significance amidst people with shared understandings of how a particular society is organized and functions. Law, in short, is a cultural artifact. It is both the product of social, cultural, economic, and political interactions and at the same time constitutes the epistemological foundations that shape the very modes of engagement creating it. It is not something distinct from society, but part of society itself. As Carroll Seron and Susan Silbey note, "Law is *in* society, or laced through, between and in society's culture" (Seron and Silbey 2004:31; see also Cotterrell 2004, 2006).

This approach to law, commonly known as the constitutive theory of law (see Hunt 1993; Ewick and Silbey 1998), does not distinguish between law and culture, but interprets law as culture. Naomi Mezy, in her essay titled "Law as Culture," notes that in this circuitous system of meaning:

> law's power is discursive and productive as well as coercive. Law participates in the production of meanings within the shared semiotic system of a culture, but it is also a product of that culture and the practices that reproduce it. A constitutive theory of law rejects law's claim to autonomy and its tendency toward self-referentiality.... Whether called constitutive theory or legal consciousness, this understanding of the mutual constructedness of local cultural practices and larger legal institutions provides a way of thinking about law as culture and culture as law. At their most radical, these theories question the common conviction that law is "still recognizably, and usefully, distinguishable from that which it is not" (Mezey 2001:47; see also Roberts 1999).

Building upon the idea that law is a cultural artifact, it follows that because culture is not a static concept and is constantly evolving and adapting to shifting social values and relations, then law too is intrinsically dynamic. Despite law often appearing as an objective, apolitical, and fixed set of rules, law is constantly responding to cultural, social, and political changes in any society, just as social changes are in part a response to prevailing legal norms. In other words, law is a dynamic field of institutional, conceptual, and behavioral processes. Thinking about law as part of a cultural field of interaction is widely embraced by sociolegal scholars (i.e., Sarat and Kearns 1999; Sarat and Kearns 2000; Goldberg, Musheno, and Bower 2001; Sarat and Simons 2003; Bracey 2006).

However, outside sociolegal academia, thinking about law as a dynamic cultural process is not typically understood or acknowledged by legislators, legal practitioners, law school instructors, or the wider public. People living in Euro-American legal systems have historically tended to think of law not in terms of its constitutive construction, but in terms of its instrumental efficacy in regulating and controlling society for the general benefit of all (see Introduction). Law is seen as functionally necessary to determine a predictable and foreseeable future – a world where contractual obligations are enforced, property rights protected, harms compensated, and violence managed. Without law, it is generally conceded there would be chaos and mayhem. The legal writings of Hobbes, Locke, Rousseau, and other English and French Enlightenment thinkers remind us that law was put in place to defend a collective morality and common good, as well as to defend ordinary people from the oppressive power of kings and political elites. It is important to remember that this functionalist understanding of law developed in the context of capitalism and colonialism and is particular to the nationalist impulses and emergent democratic aspirations of European nations that began to develop in the seventeenth and eighteenth centuries (Darian-Smith 2010a).

In other cultural contexts around the world very different understandings of law exist to that which developed in the West, as discussed further below. At this point, I want to stress that as a cultural artifact, law reflects deeply held cultural assumptions. A modernist and prevailing Euro-American assumption is that law neatly maps onto a state-based "imagined community" that is culturally homogenous, religiously uniform, politically contained, and nationally identifiable (Anderson 1983). This assumption can be presented as an equation: law = culture = nation. As Roger Cotterrell argues, "These assumptions seemed, until recently, unproblematic because the unity of culture was an object of faith in classical common law thought. The rise of legal positivism shifted attention from cultural bases of law to its political sources in legislation and obscured the issue of the consequences of cultural change" (Cotterrell

2006:101). However, Cotterrell goes on, "in contemporary conditions of considerable (and perhaps only partly mapped) cultural diversity such a position may no longer be tenable" (Cotterrell 2006:100).

Acknowledging and learning to cope with (if not embrace) the problematic relationship posed by cultural and legal diversity is perhaps more important today than ever before given the enormous movement of peoples around the world. Millions of people seek to gain access into Europe, North America, the Middle East, and to a lesser degree, into Africa and Australia. Not all the international movement of peoples is from poorer to wealthier countries, but the majority of the movement follows this pattern as people pursue labor opportunities, seek security from political and religious conflict and war, search for healthier living environments that can offer clean water and food, are displaced by climate change manifested in such things as coastal flooding and perpetual droughts, and desire to be with family members who may have already established themselves in new homelands. According to the 2010 *World Migration Report*, ten years ago there were 150 million migrants. Today the number of migrants has grown to 214 million, "and the figure could rise to 405 million by 2050 as a result of growing demographic disparities, the effects of environmental change, new global political and economic dynamics, technological revolutions and social networks" (World Migration Report 2010:xix).

Held amongst the millions of people on the move are diverse ethnic and religious value systems that in turn inform very different cultural interpretations of law. Within any one country there now exists a wide range of values and perceptions of what constitutes law and what law means (see Figure 2). Is law a symbol, a ritual, a rule, a cosmology, a divine scripture, an ideology, or concurrently all of these? The consequence, as noted earlier by Cotterrell, is that no longer tenable is the idea that law neatly correlates to a singular cultural identity (see Dudziak and Volpp 2006). In short, cultural and legal pluralism are interrelated and are an unavoidable feature of the twenty-first century. And this plurality of legal understandings within any one country undermines the simplistic modernist presumption that law = culture = nation.

Unfortunately, the reality of legal pluralism can create enormous social, cultural, and political tensions. One example of this is the increasing acknowledgment of Shari'a law, or Islamic law, in industrialized countries such as the United States and Britain (Moore 2010; Bowen 2011a). Typically, Shari'a law is evident in these countries, if at all, in specialized forums of religious arbitration. These forums involve private issues such as marriage, child custody, or the division of familial assets. Unfortunately, in the United States the idea of Shari'a law being recognized in arbitration before religious tribunals has set off a frenzy of hatred and bigotry, particularly among evangelicals and political

Figure 2. Mall cultural in Jakarta, Indonesia. Photograph taken by Jonathan McIntosh. 2004.

conservatives (CBS, October 13, 2010).¹ Despite efforts to quell a bigoted backlash against anything associated with Muslim peoples, Shari'a law became an issue in the 2012 political platforms of Republican presidential candidates Herman Cain and Newt Gingrich. Cain declared he would be "uncomfortable" including a Muslim in his cabinet because "there is a creeping attempt to gradually ease Shari'a Law and the Muslim faith into our government" (Cain, 2011). For Gingrich, Shari'a law is a concern akin to terrorism, and he often declared in his campaign speeches that "Shariah is a mortal threat to the survival of freedom in the United States and in the world as we know it."²

---

¹ In this context, it may not be surprising that some states in the United States are calling to ban Shari'a law even when there is no evidence of it being used or referred to in practice. For example, in the state of Oklahoma 70% of voters approved an amendment in 2010 that read, "The courts shall not look to the legal precepts of other nations or cultures. Specifically, the courts shall not consider international law or Sharia law." Tellingly, this amendment was subsequently ruled unconstitutional.

² "Shariah (literally, 'the path to the watering place') is a central concept in Islam. It is God's law, as derived from the Koran and the example of the Prophet Muhammad, and has far wider application than secular law. It is popularly associated with its most extreme application in

In Australia, Britain, and other European countries, reaction to the accommodation of Shari'a law within certain legal proceedings is perhaps less publicly hostile but no less controversial and politicized (Moore 2007, 2010). For instance, the archbishop of Canterbury, Dr. Rowan Williams, will never be forgiven by many British people for his saying in 2008 that some accommodation between British law and Shari'a law was "inevitable," and the then Lord Chief Justice of England, Lord Philips, will always be remembered for agreeing with him (see Ahdar and Aroney 2010). According to Mehdi Hasan, "the hysteria around sharia has become the modern-day equivalent of the 1950s Red Scare, with Islamists replacing communists 'under the bed' – on both sides of the Atlantic.... The very word [sharia] sends chills down the spine of not just conservatives but liberals, too. It conjures up horrific associations of hand-chopping, flogging and stoning" (Hasan 2011).

A second, perhaps less controversial, example of legal pluralism is that of the laws of indigenous peoples that are slowly being acknowledged within Western societies (see for example Anker 2007; Cunneen 2010; Woo 2011; Miller 2012). Historically, native peoples have been the most oppressed and marginalized of all minorities. Their legal norms were completely ignored by colonizing Europeans who typically thought that indigenous peoples lived without any legal structure and denigrated them as "lawless." Today, the marginalization of native peoples is changing as some indigenous communities begin to exercise political and economic pressure, most notably within Latin American countries (Brysk 2000; Sieder 2002; Cleary and Steigenga 2004). Even in the United States, Native Americans can no longer be entirely ignored and relegated to far away reservations,

societies like Afghanistan under the Taliban, including chopping off a hand as punishment for thievery. But it has always been subject to interpretation by religious authorities, so its application has varied over time and geography, said Bernard G. Weiss, professor emeritus at the University of Utah and an authority on Islamic law. 'In the hands of terrorists, Shariah can be developed into a highly threatening, militant notion,' Professor Weiss said. 'In the hands of a contemporary Muslim thinker writing in the journal Religion and Law, Shariah becomes an essentially pacifist notion.' The Arab Spring has set off a lively political and scholarly debate over the growing power of Islamists in Egypt, Tunisia and Libya. But those are all overwhelmingly Muslim countries. The idea that Shariah poses a danger in the United States, where the census pegs Muslims as less than 1 percent of the population, strikes many scholars as quixotic. Even within that 1 percent, most American Muslims have no enthusiasm for replacing federal and state law with Shariah, as some conservatives fear, let alone adopting such ancient prescriptions as stoning for adulterers, said Akbar Ahmed, chairman of Islamic studies at American University in Washington, who spent a year traveling the United States and interviewing Muslims for his 2010 book 'Journey into America: The Challenge of Islam.' The notion of a threat from Shariah to the United States 'takes your breath away, it's so absurd,' Dr. Ahmed said. He sees political demagoguery in the anti-Shariah campaign, which fueled rallies against mosques in the last two years from Manhattan to Tennessee." (*New York Times* Dec 21, 2011, article by Scott Shane).

dismissed from mainstream society (Darian-Smith 2004, 2010b; Cattelino 2006, 2007). Against long-standing forms of cultural, economic, and political discrimination, indigenous laws – which include collective and non-possessory rights to land and cultural property – are being acknowledged by some national governments for the first time. This is a positive step, even if these indigenous legal rights are a long way from being fully protected and raise a variety of complicated challenges to liberal legal categories and concepts (see Engle 2010).

The trend toward recognizing indigenous legal systems and native peoples' complex relationship to land, water, and other natural resources has been emerging in international law since the 1970s, supported by forums such as the International Indian Treaty Council (1974), World Council of Indigenous Peoples (1975), UN Working Group on Indigenous Populations (1985), and the UN Permanent Forum on Indigenous Issues (2002). Many of these groups played a role in the International Labour Organization (ILO) Convention Concerning Indigenous and Tribal Peoples of 1989. The ILO treaty has now been ratified by almost all Latin American countries and ensures that the rights of native groups over legal status, lands, and environment are at the center of many states' political concerns (Warren and Jackson 2002; Rodríguez-Piñero 2006). Importantly, writes the international law theorist Jorge Esquirol:

> legal pluralism need not undermine state law. Indeed in Bolivia and Ecuador for example, it may turn out to actually reinforce it with an agenda of internal legal pluralism. The new constitutions there promote plurinational legal institutions and legal culture. These would require a new fusion of the traditional state apparatus to accommodate the different world views and organizational preferences of the multiple and distinct ethnic and racial communities in countries of the region (Esquirol 2011).

Building on similar observations, the anthropologist Michael Brown notes that "Despite the region's [Latin America] history of military rule and indifference to human rights, indigenous groups have fundamentally reshaped national politics in Ecuador, Peru, and Bolivia. Less sweeping but still significant impacts have been felt in Mexico, Brazil, Venezuela, Colombia, Nicaragua, and Panama" (Brown 2004:245–246; see Goodale 2006).

In 2007 the ratification of the UN Declaration on the Rights of Indigenous Peoples focused additional world attention on indigenous sovereignty, self-determination, and individual and collective native rights (Xanthaki 2007; Wiessner 2008; Allen and Xanthaki 2011; Charters and Stavenhagen 2010). In the words of UN Special Rapporteur S. James Anaya, the Declaration represents an important contribution to international customary law by presenting "an authoritative common understanding, at the global level, of the minimum content of the rights of indigenous peoples" (cited in Wiessner 2008:1162). Despite the United States' initial failure (along with Canada, Australia, and New Zealand) to endorse the UN treaty, the twenty years of work culminating in the 2007 Declaration have invigorated new thoughts about indigenous/state relations and new political theories that take into account competing and overlapping legal jurisdictions at international, national, and subnational levels (Ivison et al. 2000; Barker 2005; Wiessner 2008). Of significance in moving conversations about human rights in new directions, the UN Declaration on the Rights of Indigenous Peoples derived from a long process of input and consensus building among representatives of tribes, indigenous organizations as well as member-states. In doing so, those involved in producing the 2007 UN Declaration actively sought participation from representatives of non-state members in an effort to make the document more inclusive and more legitimate.[3] It is also unique in that it is the first UN Declaration to specifically include the recognition of collective indigenous rights alongside the rights of individuals.

The extent to which Western countries recognize and accommodate indigenous jurisprudential traditions within dominant Euro-American legal systems is hard to determine. Within the context of intellectual property law, for instance, there have been minor adjustments made by some countries to incorporate native interpretations of the rules governing traditional knowledge. This has involved both state law becoming more receptive to indigenous ways of knowing and being, and native law adapting to become more translatable into Western legal concepts and categorizations (Anderson 2009; Antons 2009). Cynically, one could argue that this process is driven more by economic self-interests – on the part of both native and non-native communities – than any real desire to engage with multiple and alternative legal systems of meaning. Be that as it may, there is a growing, albeit reluctant, effort by some industrialized nations to recognize very different epistemological and jurisprudential frameworks (see Black 2010; Sieder 2010; Darian-Smith 2010b; Gover 2011). This does not mean, of course, that the majority of indigenous peoples around the world are no longer subject to extreme violation and abuse. Nor does it mean that the commodification and exploitation of indigenous

---

[3]   In a similar way, the Yogyakarta Principles were established through the efforts of non-state UN members. The Yogyakarta Principles are a set of principles related to sexual orientation and gender identity that was first discussed by a group of international human rights jurists and experts in 2006 at Gadjah Mada University in Yogyakarta, Indonesia. These principles do not form part of international law as they were endorsed by a group of legal experts but not officially adopted by UN member-states. Nonetheless, the Principles are meant to help in the interpretation and application of all human rights treaties.

knowledge by the West is not a serious and ongoing issue (see Mgbeoji 2005; Whitt 2009; Marrie 2010). However, what it does mean is that acknowledging and learning to deal with competing legal systems is becoming more common and hopefully more familiar. This is a move in a direction that takes seriously the presence of legal pluralism and the opportunities for legal collaboration that may emerge in these processes (see Ivison 2002).

To date – as mentioned in the Introduction – legal pluralism remains a site of inquiry and theoretical discussion among a relatively small number of sociolegal scholars (see Santos 1995; Twining 2000:194–244; Tamanaha 2001:171–205; Benda-Beckman 2002; Griffiths 2002; Merry 2007; Barzilai 2008). This seems rather shortsighted and naïve. No doubt Euro-American law will continue for many decades to be the dominant legal system around the world. But beneath the veneer of national and international legal stability there is already an emergent insistence among non-Western societies to acknowledge alternative legal conceptualizations and norms that may not easily correlate to what we in the West recognize as the rule of law and related notions of rights and justice. This has become glaringly apparent in transitional justice efforts in post-conflict societies where local community notions of justice may differ dramatically from how it is conceived by international courts and legal agencies (see Chapter 5). Presumably, as the global balance shifts to accommodate new economies, and new political and cultural pressures are brought to bear on the global scene, discussions among sociolegal scholars about legal pluralism will by necessity become increasingly mainstream.

Importantly, any move by Western nations toward embracing legal plurality must amount to more than cursory recognition of alternative non-Western jurisprudential traditions such as Shari'a law or indigenous law. Boaventura de Sousa Santos has argued for the concept of "interlegality" in an effort to move legal scholars to think about different legal orders not "as separate entities coexisting in the same political space, but rather, the conception of different legal spaces superimposed, interpenetrated, and mixed in our minds, as much as in our actions" (Santos 1995:472–473). In other words, accommodation of legal pluralism requires acknowledgment and also a sincere willingness to lay ourselves open to new experiences in "which codes and norms are mixed in reality and in the contents of our minds" (Santos 1987:297–298, 1995; Darian-Smith 1998; Manderson 2000:177).[4] This suggests that Western legal scholars must overcome their Eurocentrism and be prepared to empathize

---

[4]   As discussed in Chapter 3, within sociolegal scholarship the turn to legal aesthetics, and the focus on new models of connectivity, subjectivity, and cultural logics across time and space as suggested by actor-network theory and affect theory, offer ways to think about a more radical legal pluralism that alters "the law within ourselves" (Manderson 2000:176).

and communicate openly with others (Berman 2010). More fundamentally, it means that Western scholars should acknowledge processes of interlegality and also be prepared to adjust their ways of knowing, thinking, and behaving with respect to law such that they engage with others' legal traditions in a manner on par with how they engage with their own. Unfortunately, given the rise in right-wing xenophobic nationalism across all industrialized Western nations in the early decades of the twenty-first century, navigating toward this form of inclusive and transformative radical legal pluralism will be – at the very least – an intensely political project.

OVERCOMING LEGAL ORIENTALISM

One move toward an inclusive legal pluralism, as discussed earlier, is to recognize how legal Orientialism has historically shaped the development of modern Euro-American law from the sixteenth century to the present (Ruskola 2002; Anghie 2006; Falk 2009:39–54; Nader 2009:62–65; Darian-Smith 2010a). Such a recognition forces us to think about how racial and cultural biases continue to inform globally dominant legal concepts and assumptions of Western legal superiority and may open up ways in which to challenge or resist these dominant legal understandings of the world.

What is legal Orientalism? The concept of legal Orientialism draws expressly upon the work of Edward Said, a leading figure in postcolonial theory. Said coined the word "Orientalism" to refer to the ways Western societies throughout the nineteenth century constructed their identity and self-understanding through imagining their difference to the Arab and Muslim world (Said 1978; 1993; for critiques of Said, see Mackenzie 1995; Halliday 1996). Essential in this process was the West's stereotyping of the Orient, which included a range of Eastern cultures that included the Middle East as well as China, Japan, and South Asia. Orientalist discourses emanating from Europe were not exactly the same as those emanating from the United States because they were usually directed toward the Middle East and China, while in the United States Orientalist rhetoric was usually directed to the Philippines and targets closer to home (Little 2008; Brody 2010; Francavigilia 2011). These differences typically correlated to a country's imperial and colonial interests and often changed over time accordingly. However, what united these various forms of Orientalist rhetoric and material practice was the (assumed oppositional) relations between an exoticized and irrational Other and a civilized and rational Occident.

Typically, Western Orientalist discourses about the East were negative and reinforced a presumed hierarchy of Western superiority and Eastern inferiority. However, this was not always the case, particularly in the earlier seventeenth and eighteenth centuries when Enlightenment philosophers and missionary Jesuits often praised Chinese people for their ingenuity and skill (see Gregory 2003; Mungello 2009). However, by the nineteenth century Western attitudes had crystallized into derogatory stereotypes (Ruskola 2002:fn175). Europeans promoted themselves as modern, rational, moral, and lawful in contrast to a projection of Eastern societies as premodern, irrational, immoral, and lawless. But as insisted upon by Said, this did not mean that the "Orient was *essentially* an idea, or a creation with no corresponding reality" (Said 1978:5). Rather, "The Orient is an integral part of European *material* civilization and culture ... with supporting institutions, vocabulary, scholarship, imagery, doctrines, even colonial bureaucracies and colonial styles" (Said 1978:2).

Law was an important material means by which the West constructed the East, providing an ideological and conceptual frame through which Euro-American Orientalist discourses about the Other's inferiority became manifest. Europeans, it was argued, had law and were lawfully minded people, whereas the Chinese and other Oriental peoples were not. Hence, at the same time that commentators such as Alexis de Toqueville were remarking upon the emphasis given to law in the United States (de Toqueville 1835), Western lawyers, historians, and social theorists were pointing to the lack of law in countries such as China, which was essentially viewed as a backward "stagnant" society in which lawlessness reigned (Ruskola 2002:181–187, 213–215).

Legal Orientalism served a variety of purposes. The most obvious of these was that it helped confirm the marginality of the East in contrast to the centrality of the imperial West on the world stage. European and American scholars argued that Eastern jurisprudential traditions were based in custom, ritual, and religion in contrast to the so-called rational and scientific legal systems of modern Western nations. Declaring non-Western legal systems inferior helped to justify European law and culture as a superior civilization, worthy of world leadership and dominance. Orientalist rhetoric also provided the rationale for Western nations to marginalize Asian peoples within their domestic jurisdictions. For instance, in the United States Orientalist rhetoric provided the basis for the Chinese Exclusion Act (1882). This act suspended Chinese immigration into the country and prevented those Chinese people already living in the United States from ever being granted citizenship. Under the act, it was argued that Chinese people were nonlegal subjects because they were incapable of understanding American law and so deserved to be excluded from the new republic (Ruskola 2002:215–217; Park 2004).

Postcolonial legal scholars argue that the oppositional rhetoric between Eastern and Western legal traditions was essential for the development of modern Euro-American law. In other words, European law emerged historically through a perceived difference with non-Western legal concepts. According to the critical legal scholar Duncan Kennedy, international law must be understood in relation to "a distinction between the West and the rest of the world, and the role of that distinction in the generation of doctrines, institutions and state practices" (Kennedy 1997:748). This perceived difference helped shape the international legal system, which required the "invention of legal primitivism" to legitimate the West's universal aspirations (Gathii 1998; Bowden 2005; Anghie 2006; Wilf 2009). If one accepts this argument, then it follows that Western law has Orientalist assumptions historically built into its language, structure, and procedures. This suggests that contemporary Euro-American law, and the international legal system on which it is built, remains to this day intrinsically and pervasively cultural and racially biased (see Pahuja 2011; Westra 2011).

A few, but increasingly outspoken, critical legal scholars argue that legal Orientalism endures in twenty-first century international law and global legal relations (see Otto 1996; Rajagopal 2003b; Haldar 2007; Falk et al. 2008). Legal Orientalism continues to fuel assumptions about Western legal superiority over third world nations and has been deployed in a range of national and international legal forums such as asylum and refugee claims (Akram 2000). Moreover, legal Orientalism is evident in the ways the global North interprets law in the Middle East, particularly in the wake of the events of 9/11, as well as how the global North views law in China, Africa, and Latin America. According to Jorge Esquirol:

> The writing in English on Latin American Law follows mostly in either the "law and society" or the "law and development" type perspectives. While much of this scholarship is quite useful and sheds significant light on development in Latin America, it also leaves out a significant part of the picture. Indeed, this omission often leads to a disappointingly predictable "Orientalizing" structure that results in negative diagnoses of the problem of "law" in Latin America from a neocolonial and hegemonic perspective (Esquirol 2011).

I argue, as have others, that recognizing what Esquirol calls "Orientalizing structures" is vital in facing the problems of the future. This does not mean, as the international legal scholar Teemu Ruskola remarks, that we can ever entirely overcome our cultural biases and present a non-Orientalist perspective (Ruskola 2002:222). Rather, argues Ruskola, we can move toward what he calls an "ethics of Orientalism" that centers attention on the political, economic, and cultural conditions in which essentialized notions of Others and hierarchies of legal superiority emerged (Ruskola 2002:225). I take from Ruskola's argument that there is little point in chastising Western countries for their arrogance and ignorance, as tempting as that may be. A more productive strategy is to ask why certain Orientalist images of law developed and were accepted, why they continue to resonate in the contemporary world, and what could be done to dilute these negative stereotypes that undermine international law and are preventing sincere global dialogue and creative legal collaboration.

One thing that is certain is the need to move past the rhetoric of legal Orientalism and a modernist hierarchy of legal authority based on simplistic binaries of scientific v. nonscientific, rational v. nonrational, secular v. religious, and civilized v. uncivilized legal systems. De-Orientalizing the twenty-first century's normative global order and stereotyped legal divides is seen – by some scholars and analysts at least – as ultimately necessary for the stability and peace of global, international, national, regional, and local relations (Santos 2007; Falk 2009:52; Onuma 2010). As the Nigerian legal scholar Ikechi Mgbeoji eloquently stated, "the North and South are mutually vulnerable, sharing a common destiny, which cannot be realized unless notions of a civilized self and barbaric other are abandoned" (Mgbeoji 2008:152; see also Nederveen Pieterse 2006).

ASPIRATIONS OF GLOBAL GOVERNANCE

Another approach toward an inclusive legal pluralism, and one related to the preceding discussion on legal Orientalism, is to take seriously the aspirations of global governance. The idea of some sort of world governance system that transcends national borders and self-serving state interests has a long history, but it was the euphoria of the post-World War II period that cemented in the minds of an international community the idea of global governance as the key to establishing peace in the modern era. Its early institutional manifestation was in the establishment of the United Nations and the Bretton Woods monetary system in the immediate postwar years. Since the mid twentieth-century, global governance institutions, networks, and legal forums have become steadily more complicated and extensive than this earlier state-based format of international control, yet the same basic idea of political, economic, and legal collaboration endures.

The precise meaning and feasibility of global governance mechanisms is much theorized and debated (see Nayyar 2002; Held and Koenig-Archibugi

2003; Whitman 2005; Wilkinson 2005; Benda-Beckmann et al. 2009; Camilleri and Falk 2009; Held 2009; Bjola and Kornprobst 2011). Very simply, global governance refers to the political networks, institutions, mechanisms, and agencies required to solve problems that confront multiple states or regions, and it is needed when there are limited alternative enforcement mechanisms available. Global governance is different from the concept of a world government, although the two ideas are related (see Yunker 2011). The central difference is that global governance mechanisms – unlike a federally based world government – are decentralized and diffuse and not so easily co-opted by oppressive or authoritarian powers (Falk 2009:14). Moreover, global governance seeks to include national governments, international organizations, as well as a wide range of non-state actors, NGOs, and various community agencies in formulating global directives, policies, regulation, and accountability. The primary aspirations of all global governance networks are to provide transparency and accountability in efforts that ensure peace and security for all people. In recent decades these aspirations have necessarily expanded to include the management and security of the natural environment and the protection of the world's biosphere.

Particularly since the end of the Cold War, the idea of some form of global governance has again captured the imaginations of political and legal practitioners, corporate organizations, and commercial operators, academics, and activists. This interest reflects the obvious limitations of the concept of autonomous state sovereignty in an increasingly interconnected world and also reflects the proliferation of legal actors, agencies, and non-state rule-making institutions that have emerged to deal with the new legal networks and demands presented by global market expansion (Slaughter 2002). In the words of David Held, a leading scholar of globalization:

> Global governance today is a *multilayered, multidimensional* and *multi-actor* system. It is multilayered in so far as the development and implementation of global policies involve a process of political coordination between suprastate, transnational, national and often substate agencies. Attempts to combat AIDS/HIV, for instance, require the coordinated efforts of global, regional, national and local agencies. It is multidimensional in so far as the engagement and configuration of agencies often differs from sector to sector and issue to issue, giving rise to significantly differentiated political patterns. The politics of, for example, global financial regulation is different in interesting ways from the politics of global trade regulation. Further, many of the agencies of, and participants in, the global governance complex are no longer purely intergovernmental bodies. There is involvement by representatives of transnational civil society – from Greenpeace to Jubilee

2000 and an array of NGOs.... Accordingly, global governance is a multi-actor complex in which diverse agencies participate in the development of global public policy. Of course, this essentially pluralistic conception of global governance does not presume that all states or interests have an equal voice in, let alone an equal influence over, its agenda or programmes – not at all (Held 2004:79–84).

Held's last point in the preceding paragraph requires emphasizing. Contemporary forms of global governance do not necessarily imply equal participation in and access to new institutions and organizations of political and legal power. According to John Ruggie, as rules favoring global market expansion have grown and arbitration of economic disputes have become more enforceable, there is a concurrent diminishing of laws that seek to protect ordinary people and non-corporate interests. Notes Ruggie, "rules intended to promote equally valid social objectives, be they labor standards, human rights, environmental quality or poverty reduction, lag behind and in some instances actually have become weaker" (Ruggie 2003:96–97). The horrifically disquieting result is that "patent rights have trumped fundamental human rights and even pandemic threats to human life." (Ruggie 2003:96–97). In the contemporary context of uneven legal applications and protections, the need to reconfigure existing global governance mechanisms becomes paramount. Writes Jan Aart Scholte, "Without adequate transplanetary regimes, positive potentials of contemporary globalization can go unrealized and negative prospects can go unchecked" (Scholte 2011:110).

Unfortunately, it is impossible to deny that today's global governance complex is unequivocally facilitating world inequalities and inequities. The sociologist Howie Winant sees these global inequities as falling along racial lines and has called this twenty-first century process a "re-racialization of the world" (Winant 2004). People living in the global north may object to the characterization of global inequities being racially and ethnically configured. Certainly all people, wherever they live, are potentially subject to exploitation, poverty, environmental disaster, and disease. As underscored by the 2011 Occupy movements, people living in the wealthiest countries are not buffered from the impact of global economic recession, high unemployment, labor exploitation, or environmental disasters caused by oil spills and tsunamis. That being said, the vast percentage of the world's populations – the hundreds of millions of people who live at or below poverty living in the global South – bear the brunt of power inequities in the international and global arena. As will be discussed in Chapter 6, these global power asymmetries and the global governance mechanisms that, up to this point, have sustained them have already caused untold injury to non-Western communities subject to the "slow violence" of such things as mineral and fossil fuel extraction, seeping toxic waste, genetic deformity, and irreversible biosphere degradation (Nixon 2011; Bond 2012).

In the context of increasing trends of global disparity, Richard Falk offers a chilling warning. Writes Falk, without "drastic normative adjustments in the interaction of states and regions as well as an accompanying social regulation of the world economy, global governance is almost certain to adopt highly coercive methods of stifling resistance from disadvantaged societies and social forces" (Falk 2009:13). This gloomy forecast, however, is countered by Falk's determined optimism in the possibility of a "humane" form of global governance that could take the shape of a global parliament and enable opportunities for global democracy (Falk 2009:14). This call for a humane form of global governance is what Falk calls a "necessary utopianism," and is, he argues, worth pursuing as a process valuable in and of itself rather than measured only in terms of its pragmatic feasibility. Balakrishnan Rajagopal, along with other third world critics, adds that to move beyond the inequities built into international law, global governance mechanisms need to incorporate the perspectives of social movements and require "a theory of resistance ... to ensure that the voices of ordinary people, who are increasingly marginalized by the current global world order, are properly heard" (Rajagopal 2003a:420; Baxi 2006b; Chimni 2006). Considering the limited options that are currently available and capable of deflecting trends in global economic and political disparity, I want to believe in Falk's optimism and at the same time agree with Rajagopal's demand that future advances can only be achieved if ordinary people are allowed to participate in shaping appropriate global responses.

In the twenty-first century, aspirations of global governance have to take seriously the evolving complexity of legal plurality and its multicultural dimensions, as well as the enduring historical legacy of legal Orientalism. The denigration by the West of non-Western laws and cultures is no longer tenable or justifiable. There is an emerging perception, even amongst the wealthiest and most powerful industrial nations, of the limits to Euro-American imperialism and its current exploitation of the world. As China's reemergence as a global superpower solidifies, and countries such as Brazil, Russia, India, and South Africa emerge as economic global players, the arrogance of the global North is being slowly chipped away. As a result, difficult questions are now being asked, and scenarios impossible to imagine twenty years ago are being raised that position the West, and specifically the United States, as no longer the dominant or leading force in the global arena (i.e., Guardiola-Rivera 2010; see also Chakrabarty 2000). These questions include the following: What would be necessary to provide security for all human beings, irrespective of race, class, gender, age, or religion? How will states, regions, and cities govern diminishing natural and mineral resources without resorting to further escalations of violence and terror? Is it possible to move beyond the gross economic and political inequities between a global South and global North and the accompanying cultural biases and Orientalist assumptions these inequities engender? How realistic is the aspiration to establish a new global legal order? How would such a global legal order be structured, managed, and enforced? All of these questions turn on creating a humane system of global governance that recognizes the complexity of legal plurality and comes to terms with the cultural and ethnic biases built into existing international and national laws. Accommodating legal pluralism and overcoming legal Orientalism together define the ultimate challenge in pursuing a global sociolegal perspective and will, one hopes, become more central to all law and society scholarship in the coming years.

LIST OF SUGGESTED READINGS

1. Anghie, Anthony (2005) *Imperialism, Sovereignty, and the Making of International Law.* Cambridge: Cambridge University Press.
2. Bracey, Dorothy H. (2006) *Exploring Law and Culture.* Long Grove, IL: Waveland Press.
3. Camilleri, Joseph A. and Jim Falk (2009) *Worlds in Transition: Evolving Governance Across a Stressed Planet.* Surrey: Edward Elgar.
4. Coutin, Susan Bibler, Bill Maurer, and Barbara Yngvesson (2002) In the Mirror: The Legitimation Work of Globalization. *Law & Social Inquiry* **27**(4):801–843.
5. Falk, Richard, Balakrishnan Rajagopal, and Jacqueline Stevens (eds.) (2008) *International Law and the Third World: Reshaping Justice.* London and New York: Routledge-Cavendish.
6. Held, David (2009) Restructuring Global Governance: Cosmopolitanism, Democracy and the Global Order. *Millennium. Journal of International Studies* **37**(3):535–547.
7. Mezey, Naomi (2001) Law as Culture. *Yale Journal of Law & the Humanities.* **13**:35–67.
8. Rajagopal, Balakrishnan (2003) *International Law From Below: Development, Social Movements and Third World Resistance.* Cambridge: Cambridge University Press.
9. Razack, Sherene (2008) *Casting Out: The Eviction of Muslims from Western Law and Politics.* Toronto: University of Toronto Press.

10. Sen, Amartya (2011) *The Idea of Justice.* Cambridge, MA: Belknap Press of Harvard University Press.
11. Thomas, Caroline (2001) Global Governance, Development and Human Security: Exploring the Links. *Third World Quarterly* **22**(2):159–175.
12. Westra, Laura (2011) *Globalization, Violence and World Governance.* Leiden and Boston: Brill.

Excerpts From:

Mezey, Naomi (2001) Law as Culture. *Yale Journal of Law & the Humanities.* 13:35–67.

Reproduced with permission from the *Yale Journal of Law and the Humanities.*

LAW AS CULTURE

Naomi Mezey[5]

Introduction

The notion of culture is everywhere invoked and virtually nowhere explained. Culture can mean so many things: collective identity, nation, race, corporate policy, civilization, arts and letters, lifestyle, mass-produced popular artifacts, ritual. Law, at first glance, appears easier to grasp if considered in opposition to culture – as the articulated rules and rights set forth in constitutions, statutes, judicial opinions, the formality of dispute resolution, and the foundation of social order. In most conceptions of culture, law is occasionally a component, but it is most often peripheral or irrelevant. Most visions of law include culture, if they include it at all, as the unavoidable social context of an otherwise legal question – the element of irrationality or the basis of policy conflicts. When law and culture are thought of together, they are conceptualized as distinct realms of action and only marginally related to one another. For example, we tend to think of playing baseball or going to a baseball game as cultural acts with no significant legal implications. We also assume that a lawsuit challenging baseball's exemption from antitrust laws is a legal act with few cultural implications.[6] I think both of these assumptions are profoundly wrong, and that our understandings of the game and the lawsuit are impoverished when we fail to account for the ways in which the game is a product of

[5] Associate Professor of Law, Georgetown University Law Center. My thanks to Heidi Li Feldman, Mark Kelman, David Luban, Leti Volpp, and Robin West for their comments on earlier drafts of this essay and to Rachel Taylor and Philip Ferrera for superb research assistance. The many comments I received from my colleagues at the Georgetown Faculty Workshops and from the participants of the Legal Studies as Cultural Studies Conference have improved this paper in ways large and small; I am particularly grateful to the insights of Lama Abu-Odeh, Sam Dash, Katherine Franke, Michael Gottesman, Angela Harris, Gillian Lester, Michael Musheno, Gary Peller, Milton Regan, Mike Seidman, Girardeau Spann, and Mark Tushnet. Thanks finally to Austin Sarat, Jonathan Simon, and the *Yale Journal of Law & the Humanities* for the opportunity to write and present this essay, and to Clifford Rosky and John Pellettieri for their very fine editing suggestions.

[6] *See, e.g.,* Flood v. Kuhn, 407 U.S. 258 (1972); Toolson v. N.Y. Yankees, 346 U.S. 356 (1953); Federal Baseball Club v. Nat'l League, 259 U.S. 200 (1922).

law and the lawsuit a product of culture – how the meaning of each is bound up in the other, and in the complex entanglement of law and culture.

If we are to make headway in understanding legal studies as cultural studies and legal practice as cultural practice, then a contingent clarification of the vague concept of culture is an important threshold question. The goal of this interdisciplinary project is to understand law not in relationship to culture, as if they were two discrete realms of action and discourse, but to make sense of law as culture and culture as law, and to begin to think about how to talk about and interpret law in cultural terms.

This Essay participates in an increasingly lively discussion within law and sociolegal studies about what we ought to mean by culture and what culture can mean for law. These questions have gained urgency of late thanks to recent efforts to investigate the relationship of culture to law, and vice versa, and to make a place in legal studies for a cultural analysis of law.[7] The engine of this investigation has been the popularity and usefulness of the interdisciplinary methods of cultural studies, which have been particularly keen to invade those disciplines, like law, which have traditionally insisted on their own formal integrity. Yet cultural studies suffers from the same definitional distress as culture itself: No one is exactly sure what it means to others and everyone is loath to offer their own working definitions.

Another motivation for the academic pairing of law and culture emerges from the fact that political "culture wars" are being waged ever more explicitly on legal terrain. Congress, for instance, is increasingly confident that it can change culture through legislative initiative. Take, for example, Congress's reaction to the shootings at Columbine High School and youth violence more generally. The rhetoric of the mostly partisan debate, as well as the substance of the proposed legislation,[8] focused more on regulating youth culture (in the

---

[7] Austin Sarat and Thomas Kearns have been indefatigable champions of this cause with their series of books in law, jurisprudence, and social thought. *E.g.*, Cultural Pluralism, Identity Politics, and the Law (Austin Sarat & Thomas R. Kearns eds., 1999); Law in the Domains of Culture (Austin Sarat & Thomas R. Kearns eds., 1998); Law In Everyday Life (Austin Sarat & Thomas R. Kearns eds., 1993); *see also* Guyora Binder & Robert Weisberg, Literary Criticisms of Law (2000); Rosemary J. Coombe, The Cultural Life of Intellectual Properties: Authorship, Appropriation and the Law (1999); Robert M. Cover, Narrative, Violence, and the Law: The Essays of Robert M. Cover (Martha Minow, Michael Ryan & Austin Sarat eds., 1993); Patricia Ewick & Susan S. Silbey, The Common Place of Law: Stories from Everyday Life (1998); Paul W. Kahn, The Cultural Study of Law: Reconstructing Legal Scholarship (1999); Legal Studies as Cultural Studies: A Reader in (Post)Modern Critical Theory (Jerry Leonard ed., 1995). However, many of the important predecessors in this area have worked primarily in anthropology and American studies. *E.g.*, James Clifford, The Predicament of Culture: Twentieth-Century Ethnography, Literature, and Art (1988); Jane M. Gaines, Contested Culture: The Image, the Voice, and the Law (1991); Clifford Geertz, Local Knowledge: Further Essays in Interpretive Anthropology (1983).

[8] Juvenile Justice Reform Act, H.R. 1501, 106th Cong. (1999).

form of movies, video games, and overly secularized public schools) than on regulating guns.[9] Like Congress, the Supreme Court is increasingly divided over whether the issues before them are issues of law or culture.[10] Congress is right that legislation can change culture, but it is right for all the wrong reasons. It is more likely that culture will be influenced by law in ways never intended or anticipated by Congress. This common slippage between the purposes and meanings that appear to animate a particular legal rule (or even the absence of a rule), and the actual effects of a rule as it circulates through cultural practice, is the object of inquiry in a cultural interpretation of law. Slippage, a concept on which I will elaborate later, identifies the dislocation between the production of legal meaning and its reception and re-articulation, all of which are mutually informed and always cultural. This dislocation in turn locates the inevitable intersection of law and culture.

Law as Culture

[L]aw, rather than a mere technical add-on to a morally (or immorally) finished society, is, along of course with a whole range of other cultural realities from the symbolics of faith to the means of production, an active part of it.

-Clifford Geertz[11]

As Geertz has said, law is one way in which we make sense of the world, one way of organizing meaning, one "distinctive manner of imagining the real."[12]

---

[9] I do not want to suggest that regulating guns is not an act with cultural implications, merely that legislators are increasingly overt in their attempts to use law to reform culture, however cynical those attempts might be. The House did not entertain measures to make parents pay more attention to their children, or to expand mental health coverage, or to encourage jocks to treat Goths with more respect, but it discussed just about every other Columbine explanation. The widespread sense among members was that the era of big government may be over, but when tragedy strikes, Americans still expect at least the appearance of action from their politicians. In a typical swipe, Rep. Louise M. Slaughter (D-NY) described the debate as "full of solutions in search of problems." Michael Grunwald, *Culture Wars Erupt in Debate on Hill,* Wash. Post, June 18, 1999, at A1.

[10] *See also* Romer v. Evans, 517 U.S. 620 (1996). In *Romer,* the majority found that a Colorado referendum targeting homosexuals violated the Equal Protection Clause because it could not be explained by anything other than animus toward the class it affected. 517 U.S. at 632. Justice Scalia, writing in dissent, claimed that the majority had "mistaken a Kulturkampf for a fit of spite" by a group of tolerant Coloradans who were merely trying to express their cultural preference for heterosexuality. *Id.* at 636. Because Scalia found that nothing in the law prevented Coloradans from doing so, he argued that the Court should not resolve the issue based on its own preferences in an otherwise purely cultural debate. *Id.*

[11] Geertz, *supra* note 2, at 218.

[12] Geertz, *supra* note 2, at 184.

Law is simply one of the signifying practices that constitute culture and, despite its best efforts, it cannot be divorced from culture. Nor, for that matter, can culture be divorced from law. "To recognize that law has meaning-making power, then, is to see that social practices are not logically separable from the laws that shape them and that social practices are unintelligible apart from the legal norms that give rise to them."[13] Therefore, if one were to talk about the relationship between culture and law, it would certainly be right to say that it is always dynamic, interactive, and dialectical – law is both a producer of culture and an object of culture. Put generally, law shapes individual and group identity, social practices as well as the meaning of cultural symbols, but all of these things (culture in its myriad manifestations) also shape law by changing what is socially desirable, politically feasible, legally legitimate. As Pierre Bourdieu puts it, "law is the quintessential form of 'active' discourse, able by its own operation to produce effects. It would not be excessive to say that it creates the social world, but only if we remember that it is this world which first creates the law."[14]

But perhaps we should not speak of the "relationship" between law and culture at all, as this tends to reinforce the distinction between the concepts that my description here seeks to deny. What I am after is not to make sense of law *and* culture, but law *as* culture. This dynamic understanding of law as culture is influenced directly by Patricia Ewick and Susan Silbey's important book *The Common Place of Law*, in which they "conceiv[e] of law not so much operating to shape social action but *as* social action."[15] This conceptualization is related more generally to what many in sociolegal studies call a constitutive theory of law,[16] in which law is recognized as both constituting and being constituted by social relations and cultural practices.[17] In other words, law's power is discursive and productive as well as coercive. Law participates in the production of meanings within the shared semiotic system of a culture, but it is also a product of that culture and the practices that reproduce it. A constitutive theory of law rejects law's claim to autonomy and its tendency toward

---

[13] Sarat & Kearns, *supra* note 7, at 10.

[14] Pierre Bourdieu, *The Force of Law: Toward a Sociology of the Juridical Field*, 38 Hastings L.J. 814, 839 (1987); *see also* Ewick & Silbey, *supra* note 2, at 39 (1998) (describing "a reciprocal process in which the meanings given by individuals to their world become patterned, stabilized, and objectified. These meanings, once institutionalized, become part of the material and discursive systems that limit and constrain future meaning-making.").

[15] Id. at 34–35.

[16] *See, e.g.,* Alan Hunt, Explorations in Law and Society: Toward a Constitutive Theory of Law (1993); Law in Everyday Life, *supra* note 2, at 27–32; Susan S. Silbey & Austin Sarat, *Critical Traditions in Law and Society Research*, 21 Law & Soc'y Rev. 165 (1987).

[17] Naomi Mezey, Out of the Ordinary: Law, Power, Culture and the Commonplace, 26 Law & Soc. Inquiry 145 (2001).

self-referentiality.[18] As Alan Hunt explains, "It serves to focus attention on the way in which law is implicated in social practices, as an always potentially present dimension of social relations, while at the same time reminding us that law is itself the product of the play and struggle of social relations."[19] Whether called constitutive theory or legal consciousness,[20] this understanding of the mutual constructedness of local cultural practices and larger legal institutions provides a way of thinking about law as culture and culture as law. At their most radical, these theories question the common conviction that law "is still recognizably, and usefully, distinguishable from that which is not law."[21]

While I agree that law and culture do not exist independently of each other, I disagree that their necessary interconnections make them indistinguishable from one another. Even acknowledging that the negotiation of legal meaning is always a cultural act, I believe that we still can, and should, distinguish between the kinds of power assigned to the law and legal actors, and the way power and resistance are exercised among the least powerful. To talk about the making and contestation of meaning is necessarily to talk about power. "Power is seen in the effort to negotiate shared understandings, and in the evasions, resistances, and inventions that inevitably accompany such negotiations."[22] It is partly in the different forms that power takes that law and culture are still recognizably distinct. Their differences are greatest when legal power manifests itself as state-sanctioned physical force or ideological influence. Indeed, most critical theorists of law think that law's hegemonic, ideological character is more effective than its violence.[23] While the differences between legal and cultural exercises of power are significant,[24] I think they are also too often exaggerated.[25] For example, law's hegemonic power depends deeply on

---

[18]   *See* Hunt, *supra* note 50, at 304–05.

[19]   *Id.* at 3.

[20]   Ewick and Silbey use the term legal consciousness "to name participation in the process of constructing legality... [E]ach person's participation sustains legality as an organizing structure of social relations." Ewick & Silbey, *supra* note 2, at 45.

[21]   *Id.* at 19.

[22]   Austin Sarat & William L.F. Felstiner, Divorce Lawyers and Their Clients: Power and Meaning in the Legal Process II (1995).

[23]   Robert Gordon gives one of the classic statements of the hegemonic power of law: "[T]he power exerted by a legal regime consists less in the force that it can bring to bear against violators of its rules than in its capacity to persuade people that the world described in its images and categories is the only attainable world in which a sane person would want to live."Robert Gordon, *Critical Legal Histories*, 36 Stan. L. Rev. 57, 108 (1984). For the original source on "hegemony," see Antonio Gramsci, Selections from the Prison Notebooks of Antonio Gramsci 242, 245–246 (Quintin Hoare & Geoffrey Newell Smith eds. & trans., 1971).

[24]   Robert M. Cover, *Violence and the Word, reprinted in* Cover, *supra* note 2, at 203.

[25]   Sarat and Felstiner offer a valuable corrective when they describe the power in the lawyer-client interactions they observed as "not possessed at all. It is mobile and volatile, and it circulates

culture to be effective, and much of the violence evident in culture likewise depends on inequalities directly and indirectly attributable to law.

Law as culture might be understood in a number of different ways. I want to suggest three possibilities. First, one might analyze the relationship between law and culture by articulating the unspoken power of law in the realm of culture. Second, one might think about the relationship by emphasizing the enduring power of culture over legal institutions and decision-making. Lastly, one might reject the distinctions suggested by a "relationship" between the two and seek to synthesize law and culture, by pointing to the ways in which they are one and the same. None of these understandings is wrong, and many of the examples that I give of each one could be recharacterized as belonging to the other two. Yet even though the distinctions are fragile, they enable us to appreciate what law as culture can mean.

A. The Power of Law

First, law as culture might mean emphasizing the pervasive power of law and excluding the possibility that there is an autonomous cultural realm that could be articulated without recourse to law. Here, culture is a colony in law's empire. "We live," as Ronald Dworkin puts it, "in and by the law. It makes us what we are: citizens and employees and doctors and spouses and people who own things."[26] This version of law as culture is best exemplified by the realist insight, elaborated by critical legal scholars, that law operates even when it appears not to, that legal permissions and prohibitions are in force in the most intimate and nonlegal relationships – indeed, that legal rules structure the very baseline from which we negotiate our lives and form our identities. Furthermore, these legal ground rules are all the more effective because they are not visible as law. Rather than think of legal permission as law, we tend to think of it as individual freedom, the market, or culture.

The realist insight was epitomized by the critique of the state's powerful role in determining the background rules for social action and maintaining an unequal distribution of wealth, particularly through the use of contract and property law.[27] Realists rejected the claims of classical theorists that contracts and property rights were part of a private law system based on individual

such that both lawyer and client can be considered more or less powerful, even at the same time." Sarat & Felstiner, *supra* note 56, at 19.

[26] Dworkin continues: "It is sword, shield, and menace: we insist on our wage, or refuse to pay our rent, or are forced to forfeit penalties, or are closed up in jail, all in the name of what our abstract and ethereal sovereign, the law, has decreed.... We are subjects of law's empire." Ronald Dworkin, *Law's Empire*, at vii (1986).

[27] While this story has been told many times by many different scholars, I rely here primarily on Gary Peller, *The Metaphysics of American Law*, 73 Cal. L. Rev. 1151 (1985); Joseph William Singer, *Legal Realism Now*, 76 Cal. L. Rev. 465 (1988).

autonomy rather than legal coercion.[28] Realists argued that contracts are public, rather than private, because individuals ask the state to enforce them by using law to aid one party against the other.[29] Likewise, they claimed that property is not a natural right protected by the state only in the rare event of a threat of dispossession, but a right created by the state to exclude others generally. Thus, the "law of property helps me directly only to exclude others from using the things which it assigns to me."[30] The law, then, does not merely protect owners in their possessions, but also creates both owners and possessions, by creating and enforcing a right called property.

Property and contract rights together have powerful state-sanctioned distributional effects.[31] Property rights affect the relative bargaining power of the parties and hence the contract terms that can be bargained for; the terms of the contract in turn affect the ability of the parties to increase their power and possessions.[32] "The distribution of market power is thus only partly a function of private decisions of market actors; to a substantial extent, it is determined by the legal definition and allocation of property rights."[33] Thus the realists showed that conditions and relationships which were popularly thought to be nonlegal, like class or employment, were largely determined by law.[34]

[28] *Lochner v. New York*, 198 U.S. 45 (1905), is the now infamous expression of the classical approach to contract. The *Lochner* Court understood the power of the state to legislate and the power of the individual to contract as two separate and competing powers, and concluded that the statute at issue was "an illegal interference with the rights of individuals, both employers and employes [sic], to make contracts regarding labor upon such terms as they may think best.... Statutes of the nature of that under review, limiting the hours in which grown and intelligent men may labor to earn their living, are mere meddlesome interferences with the rights of the individual." 198 U.S. at 61.

[29] *See, e.g.*, Morris Cohen, *The Basis of Contract*, 46 Harv. L. Rev. 553, 562 (1933); *cf* Jay M. Feinman & Peter Gabel, *Contract Law as Ideology*, in *The Politics of Law: A Progressive Critique* 373 (David Kairys ed., 1990) (tracing the history of contract law through its ideological imagery).

[30] Morris Cohen, *Property and Sovereignty*, 13 *Cornell L.Q.* 8, 12 (1927).

[31] *See id.* at 13 ("The extent of the power over the life of others which the legal order confers on those called owners is not fully appreciated by those who think of the law as merely protecting men in their possession."); Robert L. Hale, *Coercion and Distribution in a Supposedly Non-Coercive State*, 38 Pol. Sci. Q. 470,478 (1923) ("The distribution of income, to repeat, depends on the relative power of coercion which the different members of the community can exert against one another.... The resulting distribution is very far from being equal, and the inequalities are very far from corresponding to needs or to sacrifice.").

[32] Singer, *supra* note 61, at 489. Put bluntly, "Property law, when combined with contract law, delegates to property owners the power to coerce nonowners to contract on terms imposed by the stronger party." *Id.* at 490. The only pressure operating to counteract the power of coercion is the relatively weak power of the nonowner to withhold her labor. *Id.*

[33] *Id.* at 488.

[34] Peller, *supra* note 61, at 1237 (explaining that the realist contention "was that the distinctions between the terms public and private, free will and coercion, were constructed in the very opinions which purported to proceed from them").

The realist reconceptualization of law is captured in their view of the employer-employee relationship, a relationship they saw not as defined by two autonomous agents, whose actions were dictated by culture, but as a relationship determined by legal coercion. Law, by creating owners, also transforms nonowners into laborers, who need certain possessions to survive. As Robert Hale puts it:

> Unless, then, the non-owner can produce his own food, the law compels him to starve if he has no wages, and compels him to go without wages unless he obeys the behests of some employer. It is the law that coerces him into wage-work under penalty of starvation- unless he can produce food.... [B]ut in every settled country there is a law which forbids him to cultivate any particular piece of ground unless he happens to be an owner.[35]

Where we still tend to think of law as guiding employment relationships only at the margins, putting a floor on wages, a ceiling on hours, or governing the rules of a strike, the realists saw law as creating both employers and employees, and structuring that relationship in its most mundane and intimate aspects.

As the realists revealed, law reaches into our lives in its absence as much as in its presence. Affirmative laws create the rights of property owners. But the absence of law also creates rights of a sort. In the employment context, the absence of a federal law prohibiting employers from discriminating against people on the basis of sexual orientation means that where no local or state law dictates otherwise, law affirmatively gives employers permission to discriminate openly against gay, lesbian, or transgendered employees, by refusing to grant such employees a remedy for discrimination.[36]

Duncan Kennedy, who, as a critical legal scholar, can be seen as taking up where the realist project left off, contends that the pervasive distributional

---

[35] Hale, *supra* note 65, at 473; *see generally* Barbara H. Fried, The Progressive Assault on Laissez Faire: Robert Hale and the First Law and Economics Movement (1998). Hale's position can be distinguished from the standard Marxist critique of capital by the emphasis he puts on the ability of both workers and consumers to exert some counter-coercion on labor. Hale, *supra* note 65, at 474.

[36] Title VII of the Civil Rights Act of 1964 prohibited discrimination on the basis of race, color, religion, sex, or national origin. 42 U.S.C. § 2000e-2(a) (1964). With passage of the Age Discrimination in Employment Act, 29 U.S.C. § 621 (1967), and the Americans with Disabilities Act, 42 U.S.C. § 12,102(2) (1991), age and disability have been added as protected categories. Federal legislation to prohibit discrimination on the basis of sexual orientation has been introduced in Congress but has not passed. Employment Non-Discrimination Act, S. 2056, 104th Cong. (1996); S. 1276, 106th Cong. (1999). The Employment Non-Discrimination Act has been reintroduced in the 107th Congress as Title V to the Protecting Civil Rights for All Americans Act, S. 19, 107th Cong. (2001).

effects of law are not just felt in economic relations, but in all relations of power.[37] The relative power of men and women or blacks and whites is primarily constituted not through culture, but through law. For example, according to Kennedy, the historical legality of marital rape and battery as well as their current under-enforcement are part of the legal background rules that define the possibilities of male behavior, and hence structure the relations between men and women, even in the context of nonviolent relationships.[38]

> Since we can imagine a legal program that would radically reduce the incidence of rape, the impact of rape on the relative bargaining power of nonviolent men and women is a function of the legal system.

> This is only the beginning of the story. The relative bargaining power of men and women when they confront one another from gendered positions is affected by hundreds of discrete legal rules. For example, the following legal choices structure women's bargaining power within marriage: the legalization of contraception and abortion, limited protection against domestic abuse, no-fault divorce, a presumption of custody in the mother, some enforcement of child support rules, and alimony without a finding of fault in the husband.[39]

One version of the critique offered by the realists and further developed by critical legal theorists is that virtually all human action, from going to bed to going to work, is either implicitly or explicitly defined and structured by law, which operates all the more effectively for appearing not to be law.[40]

B. The Power of Culture

Second, law as culture might mean emphasizing the pervasive power of culture, a power that might be conceived as either excluding the possibility of a legal realm that could be articulated without recourse to culture, or establishing the possibility of cultural regulation that functioned independently of law.[41] Either way, law is a colony in culture's empire, and sometimes a rather powerless one.

---

[37] Duncan Kennedy, *The Stakes of Law, or Hale and Foucault!, in* Sexy Dressing Etc.: Essays on the Power and Politics of Cultural Identity 83 (1993).

[38] *Id.* at 103–04; *see also* Duncan Kennedy, *Sexual Abuse, Sexy Dressing, and the Eroticization of Domination, in* Sexy Dressing Etc., *supra* note 71, at 126. In other respects Kennedy's book is a great example of a synthetic approach to law and culture.

[39] *See* Kennedy, 1993, at 104.

[40] Mark Tushnet suggested to me a wonderful example of the invisibility of ground rules: There are implicit rules that most people recognize governing whether it is okay to let someone cut into a line, and whether it is better to let them in ahead of you or behind you, but the more powerful and less visible ground rule is evinced by the fact of the line itself.

[41] I associate this second version of the power of culture with some social norms scholarship. *See, e.g.,* Robert Ellickson, Order Without Law: How Neighbors Settle Disputes (1991).

For example, on most roads there is a legal speed limit; there are formal laws, usually enacted by state legislatures, that set the posted maximum speed.[42] Despite the existence of formal law, it is culture that actually determines the "legal" speed limit. The speed limit that is enforced, by the police and in traffic court, and hence operates as the de facto "legal" speed limit, is the limit set by the conventions of drivers – conventions which vary depending on the stretch of road, the time of day, the prevailing conditions, or the habits of a particular city or geographic region.[43]

Moreover, changes in the formal speed limit often have little or no lasting impact on the speed at which motorists drive.[44] Montana, which has seen the most fluctuation in its legal speed limit, provides the most vivid example. For almost twenty years prior to the federally-imposed, fifty-five mile-per-hour speed limit in 1975, Montana had no set speed limit and operated under what it called its "Basic Rule," which simply required a daytime speed that was reasonable and prudent under the prevailing conditions.[45] In 1995, after almost twenty years under the federal speed limit, Montana returned to using its Basic Rule.[46] Robert King and Cass Sunstein have concluded, in reviewing the history of the Montana speed limit, that the changes in the law had little impact on the behavior of drivers.[47] Montana motorists

---

[42] In 1974, in response to the Arab oil embargo, Congress passed a federally- imposed fifty-five mile-per-hour speed limit in an effort to save fuel. Law of Jan. 4, 1975, Pub. L. No. 93–643, § 102(b), 88 Stat. 2281 (1975), *repealed by* National Highway System Act of 1995, 23 U.S.C. § 101 (1995). With full federal highway funds as an incentive, every state eventually complied. *See* Tyee Palmaffy, *Don't Brake for Big Government*, J. Am. Citizenship Pol. Rev., Sept-Oct. 1996, at II. In 1995 the newly Republican Congress, with the reluctant support of President Clinton, repealed the federal speed limit and returned authority to the states. National Highway System Act of 1995, 23 U.S.C. § 101 (1995). All states except Hawaii have since raised their highway speed limits to between sixty-five and seventy-five miles-per-hour for cars. *Maximum Speed Limits in Each State, at* http://web.missouri.edu/~c669885/ncaslllimits.html (last updated Feb. 13, 2000).

[43] *See* Ronald J. Krotoszynski, *Building Bridges and Overcoming Barricades: Exploring the Limits of Law as an Agent of Transformational Social Change*, 47 Case W. Res. L. Rev. 423, 424 n.3 (1997) ("[N]on-compliance was greatest in the western United States, whose long expanses of sparsely populated land created a culture among Westerners that demanded higher speed limits.").

[44] *See id.* (suggesting that lower speed limits imposed in response to the oil crisis in the 1970s did not change most people's driving habits); Quentin Hardy, *Transportation: Westerners Rev Up To Speed Legally Again*, Wall St. J., Nov. 13, 1995, at B1 (citing both federal and local statistics to show that changes in the speed limit "don't seem to affect driving behavior much").

[45] Mont. Code Ann. § 61–8–303 (1973).

[46] Tom Kentworthy, *New Life in the Fast Lane: Wide-Open Throttles in Wide Open Spaces*, Wash. Post, Dec. 9, 1995, at A3. Montana subsequently imposed a numerical speed limit in 1999. Mont. Code Ann. § 61–8–303 (1999).

[47] Robert E. King & Cass R. Sunstein, *Doing Without Speed Limits*, 79 B.U. L. Rev. 155, 162–68 (1999).

effectively ignored the federal fifty-five mile-per-hour speed limit when it was imposed and did not drive significantly faster once it was rescinded.[48] Indeed, current speed limits suggest that, if anything, the impact appears to have moved in the opposite direction, with states setting the formal legal speed limit to correspond roughly with the general practice of motorists in that state.

Culture can also be said to dictate a "legal" speed limit that differs from either the formal speed limit or the one determined by driving conventions. The color of one's car, or more important still, the color of one's skin, will change the legally enforced speed limit and traffic laws generally. In this case, the shared yet contested meaning of race, combined with a subculture of policing, means that African-American drivers are far more likely to be stopped by police than white drivers, even when they are a smaller percentage of the total drivers in a particular area. This practice is so common that it is now popularly known as "DWB," Driving While Black.[49] David Cole, in his widely lauded book on race and class in the criminal justice system, has collected evidence suggesting that there is a consistent and gross disparity between the rate at which blacks and whites are subject to pretextual stops.[50] For example, a review conducted in the early 1990s of more than one thousand traffic stops on one stretch of interstate highway in Florida "found that while about 5 percent of drivers on that highway were dark-skinned, nearly 70 percent of those

---

[48] *Id.* at 160, 163. Their ability to flout the federal speed limit was undoubtedly aided by the law in Montana that required a mere five-dollar fine for speeding, payable in cash on the spot. Kentworthy, *supra* note 80, at A3. King and Sunstein report that during the first few months of Montana's return to the Basic Rule, total average speeds increased only negligibly, from seventy-two to seventy-four miles-per-hour. King & Sunstein, *supra* note 81, at 163. The one exception to the constancy of driver behavior were tourists. According to King and Sunstein, the "repeal of the national speed limit turned Montana into a national speed magnet." *Id.* at 164 (recounting the exploits of "speed tourists" and test drivers).

[49] *See, e.g.,* David A. Harris, *"Driving While Black" and All Other Traffic Offenses: The Supreme Court and Pretextual Traffic Stops,* 87 J. Crim. L. & Criminology 544 (1997) [hereinafter Harris, *"Driving While Black"*]; David A. Harris, *The Stories, the Statistics, and the Law: Why "Driving While Black" Matters,* 84 Minn. L. Rev. 265 (1999) [hereinafter Harris, *Stories*]; Katheryn K. Russell, *"Driving While Black": Corollary Phenomena and Collateral Consequences,* 40 B.C. L. Rev. 717 (1999); David A. Harris, *Driving While Black: Racial Profiling on Our Nation's Highways,* ACLU Special Report (June 1999); John Lamberth, *Driving While Black; A Statistician Proves That Prejudice Still Rules the Road,* Wash. Post, Aug. 16, 1998, at C1.

[50] David Cole, No Equal Justice: Race and Class in the American Criminal Justice System 25, 34–41 (1999) (discussing studies done in California, Maryland, Florida, Colorado, and New Jersey). While the studies vary in the size of the area under investigation and in design, Cole's conclusion that "traffic stops are routinely used as a 'pretext' to stop minority drivers" is compelling and widely regarded as sound. *Id.* at 38; *see also* Harris, *Stories, supra* note 83, at 275–88 (detailing the studies done in New Jersey, Maryland, and Ohio).

stopped were black or Hispanic."[51] On Interstate 95 in Maryland, between
1995 and 1997, 29% of the drivers stopped and 70% of those searched were
black, although African-American drivers made up only 17.5% of the traffic on
that road.[52] The statistical disparity is striking and consistent with studies done
in other states.[53]

A cultural practice of targeting minority drivers persists in spite of the posted
speed limit or other formal traffic laws and, more seriously, in spite of the
Equal Protection Clause's guarantee that the Fourth Amendment's promise of
freedom from unreasonable searches and seizures applies equally regardless of
race. In an interesting and ironic twist, the law has made it nearly impossible
to use a constitutional challenge to halt this cultural practice – another, more
sinister version of law acquiescing to culture. In 1996, in *Wren v. United States*,[54]
the Supreme Court held that as long as there is an observed traffic violation,
no matter how minor, a stop is reasonable under the Fourth Amendment,
even if the traffic violation is pretextual and not ultimately enforced.[55] Because
driving is so minutely regulated and technical traffic violations so common,
Wren essentially allows officers to make stops for any motive.[56] Moreover, the
Court explicitly rejected the argument "that the constitutional reasonable-
ness of traffic stops depends on the actual motivations of the individual officers involved."[57] As Cole points out, *Wren* "allows officers who have no more
basis for suspicion than the color of a driver's skin to make a constitutional
stop."[58] Harris takes the point further, contending that *Wren* not only approves
such stops but implicitly approves the actual practice of using such stops

---

[51] Cole, *supra* note 84, at 37. This study also suggests that the practice is more accurately called
      "Driving While Brown."
[52] Lamberth, *supra* note 83, at CI. The results of this study are even more astounding once we
      consider that it was conducted *after* the Maryland State Police had settled a lawsuit against
      them alleging racial profiling practices. As part of the settlement, the police agreed to issue a
      policy barring the practice, to train police in the new policy, and to submit to monitoring of all
      stops that resulted in a search. Cole, *supra* note 84, at 36.
[53] The rolling study Lamberth conducted in Maryland used the same technique as a study he
      had done of a stretch of the New Jersey Turnpike. In the New Jersey study, African Americans
      made up 13.5% of the total number of drivers, 15% of the speeders, and 35% of those pulled
      over. Lamberth, *supra* note 83, at CI. As Lamberth points out, "blacks were 4.85 times as likely
      to be stopped as were others." *Id.* While Lamberth did not study the rate of searches, he notes
      that police data showed that over 73% of those arrested along the turnpike were black. *Id.*
[54] 517 U.S. 806 (1996).
[55] *Id.* at 819. The case arose out of a stop of two black men in a new car. The plainclothes vice-
      squad officers contended that the car was stopped for too long at a stop sign, made a turn
      without signaling, and proceeded at an unreasonable speed. *Id.* at 808.
[56] *Id.* at 810.
[57] *Id.* at 813. While intentionality does not matter for Fourth Amendment purposes, it may form
      the basis of an Equal Protection Clause challenge. *Id.*
[58] Cole, *supra* note 84, at 39.

disproportionately against African Americans and Hispanics.[59] Hence the law here aids in the triumph of culture by providing some protection for a cultural practice that is otherwise potentially illegal.[60]

C. Law as Culture as Law

Third, law as culture might mean emphasizing the mutuality and endless recycling between formal legal meaning-making and the signifying practices of culture, demonstrating that, despite their denials and antagonisms, these processes are always interdependent. The Supreme Court's famous decision in *Miranda v. Arizona*[61] and its recent reconsideration of that case in *Dickerson v. United States*[62] exemplify the constitutive nature of law and culture: The legal rule laid down in *Miranda* so effectively infiltrated cultural practice that forty years later the cultural embeddedness of Miranda warnings provided the justification for recognizing the constitutional status of the rule.

In *Miranda*, the Court was confronted with the problem of confessions resulting from custodial interrogation practices by police that effectively infringed the privilege against self-incrimination afforded by the Fifth Amendment.[63] The Court consciously sought a rule that would change culture in the narrow sense, by altering law-enforcement practices that ranged from the psychologically menacing to the physically brutal.[64] By requiring that custodial interrogations begin with a warning to the suspect that "he has the right to remain silent, that anything he says can be used against him in a court of law, that he has the right to the presence of an attorney, and that if he cannot afford an attorney one will be appointed for him,"[65] the Court not only changed

---

[59] Harris, "*Driving While Black,*" *supra* note 83, at 560.

[60] It is also possible to characterize this practice as the power of law over culture in that it takes law to protect the cultural practice; however, given the conflicting and unresolved impulses in the law (between protecting police discretion and protecting people equally from police abuses of discretion), it makes more sense to think of this problem as the power of culture over law. One might also argue that it could be thought of as the third option of synthesis – law as always culturally informed and culture as always legally informed to the extent that it is nearly impossible to distinguish them. Here a cultural practice conflicts with the law, but with law's approval. Likewise, the meaning of race and racial discrimination is both culturally and legally informed.

[61] 384 U.S. 436 (1966).

[62] 120 S. Ct. 2326 (2000).

[63] 384 U.S. at 439.

[64] *Id.* at 445–55. The Court dedicated considerable time to documenting historical and contemporary interrogation practices that it gleaned from studies and police manuals. It concluded that "such an interrogation environment is created for no purpose other than to subjugate the individual to the will of his examiner," and such coercion is incompatible with the principle "that the individual may not be compelled to incriminate himself." *Id.* at 457–58.

[65] *Id.* at 479.

police practices, but also altered culture in the broadest sense – it created new meanings which circulated globally. The legal rule found its way not only into police stations, but into television stations, movies, children's games, as well as the popular imagination of Americans and foreigners alike. The Miranda warnings became part of culture.

While one might say that *Miranda* had a more profound impact on popular culture than it did on the specific practices of law enforcement,[66] its impact in both contexts is complex and intertwined. In one sense, the effects of *Miranda* fit within the first paradigm of law as culture in which most cultural acts, symbols, and practices are traceable to the presence or absence of legal rules. Certainly, the broad cultural salience of the Miranda warnings depended upon their widespread adoption within specific legal contexts. This reading, however, misses the interdependence of legal and cultural meanings. Although the legal rule had dramatic cultural influence, the influence was not unidirectional: It is plausible that, as the warnings gained cultural significance, their very familiarity made them both more mandatory and less meaningful in the context of actual interrogations.[67] One might also argue that it was culture in the narrow sense that created the need for the warnings in the first instance; they were a legal safeguard against police interrogation practices that were themselves a kind of cultural struggle over law's reach and authority.

The Supreme Court's reconsideration last term of its famous *Miranda* decision evinces the third paradigm, the near-total entanglement of law and culture. At issue in *Dickerson* was whether the warnings spelled out in *Miranda* were required by the Fifth Amendment of the Constitution or were merely a prophylactic evidentiary rule meant to safeguard constitutional rights, but not required by the Constitution itself. Two years after *Miranda*, Congress had enacted a statute that sought to undermine the Miranda warnings by making the admissibility of a confession depend only on a finding of voluntariness.[68] If the *Dickerson* Court had concluded that the Miranda warnings were not constitutionally required, then Congress would have had the authority to legislate evidentiary rules governing confessions, and the statute might have overruled *Miranda* more than thirty years ago. Despite some tough cases to the contrary,[69]

---

[66] Mike Seidman has argued that *Miranda* did not change the methods by which police obtained confessions, but instead provided a relatively easy way to sanitize confessions against claims of coercion. Louis Michael Seidman, Brown *and* Miranda, 80 Cal. L. Rev. 673, 744–45 (1992).

[67] For a discussion of the cultural feedback loop between *Miranda* and television, see Susan Bandes & Jack Beerman, *Lawyering Up*, 2 Green Bag 5, II, 13–14 (1998).

[68] 18 U.S.C. § 3501 (1994).

[69] In his dissent in *Dickerson*, Justice Scalia made effective use of *Michigan v. Tucker*, 417 U.S. 433 (1974); *Oregon v. Hass*, 420 U.S. 714 (1975); *New York v. Quarles*, 467 U.S. 649 (1984); and *Oregon v. Elstad*, 470 U.S. 298 (1985) on this score. *See* 120 S. Ct. at 2340–42 (Scalia, J., dissenting).

the Court in *Dickerson* confirmed that *Miranda* was a constitutional decision entitled to stare decisis protection and thus upheld it.[70]

What is most interesting about *Dickerson* is that the majority seemed to uphold the constitutional status of *Miranda* without a majority of the Court actually believing that Miranda warnings were ever constitutionally required. As Justice Scalia pointed out in dissent, Justices Kennedy, O'Connor, and Rehnquist, who each joined the *Dickerson* majority, had previously participated in undercutting the constitutional rationale of *Miranda*.[71] Moreover, the *Miranda* court itself had anticipated and encouraged legislative experimentation with warnings, admitting that "we cannot say that the Constitution necessarily requires adherence to any particular solution for the inherent compulsions of the interrogation process as it is presently conducted."[72] Although the *Dickerson* majority appeared united by a commitment to stare decisis, it was an odd sort of stare decisis, in that the Court was faithful less to legal precedent, and more to what that precedent had come to signify in popular culture. After *Miranda*, law had transformed culture; in *Dickerson*, culture transformed law. The *Dickerson* Court quickly and confidently declined to overrule *Miranda* because the decision "has become embedded in routine police practice to the point where the warnings have become part of our national culture."[73] Precisely because of its cultural ubiquity, a decision that the Court, had been retreating from for some time was explicitly upheld, and upheld as a constitutional rule. The twist, however, is that the Court found that the warnings were constitutionally required not because the Constitution demanded them but because they had been popularized to the point that they were culturally understood as being constitutionally required.

In *Dickerson*, the synthesis of law and culture is complete: Law became so thoroughly embedded in culture that culture became the rationale for law. While it is possible to read *Miranda* as a triumph of law over culture and *Dickerson* as a triumph of culture over law, I think such readings overlook the way in which both opinions participate in a broader narrative, in which law and culture are mutually constituted, and legal and cultural meanings are

---

[70] Interestingly, the *Dickerson* Court did not quite conclude that the *Miranda* warnings *were* constitutionally required. Rather, it held more obliquely that "*Miranda* announced a *constitutional rule* that Congress may not supersede legislatively." 120 S. Ct. at 2336 (emphasis added). Needless to say, this rhetorical avoidance sent Scalia, writing in dissent, into mouth-foaming fits. *See id.* at 2337–38 (Scalia, J., dissenting).

[71] *Id.* at 2337 (citing Davis v. United States, 515 U.S. 452 (1994); Duckworth v. Eagan, 492 U.S. 195 (1989); *Elstad*, 470 U.S. at 298; *Quarles*, 467 U.S. at 649).

[72] Miranda v. Arizona, 384 U.S. 436, 467 (1966).

[73] 120 S. Ct. at 2336.

produced precisely at the intersection of the two domains, which are themselves only fictionally distinct.

Conclusion

I have tried to explore three different versions of what law as culture has meant and might mean. I have also briefly sketched a method for trying to apply the synthetic version of law as culture. Outlining the task of a cultural interpretation of law this broadly has the advantage of leaving room for variations on the theme, improvisations of approach, and engagement with the tools of other disciplines. Whereas a positivist scholar of law and culture might consider theoretical variety to be a vice,[74] I consider it a virtue. To my mind, one of the gifts of cultural studies is the hybrid vigor of theoretical mixing. I agree with Geertz that the object of analysis should determine the theory and not the other way around;[75] to script a theoretical method tightly would risk "locking cultural analysis away from its proper object, the informal logic of actual life."[76]

This raises the problem of formulating abstract theories at all, such as the one in this Essay. I have provided a provisional framework for a cultural interpretation of law that I realize will (or will not) be persuasive only in the context of specific applications. While I cannot dispute that theoretical formulations "stated independently of their applications ... seem either commonplace or vacant,"[77] I think that such a sketch, as well as the formulations of law as culture that animate it, is valuable to the extent it enables scholars of law and culture to work toward some sort of agreement, however tentative, about what it is that we are doing. As scholars in a field that is still forming, more theoretical guidance, with plenty of room for dissent, would, I think, be helpful. A more coherent framework and a more consistent vocabulary would encourage this sort of work – work which at its best invites attention to issues of justice, power, recognition, and self-definition. To focus on culture is to locate the ways in which law influences who we are and who we aspire to be, and moves us beyond the standard critique of what the law is and what we want it to be. Kahn is right to insist that the crucial "issue is not whether law makes us better off, but rather what it is that the law makes us."[78] As Sarat

---

[74] *See, e.g.,* Ellickson, *supra* note 75, at 149 (criticizing the failure of the law-and-society school to develop a unified, monolithic theory of human nature, culture, and social control).

[75] Geertz, *supra* note 108, at 24–25 ("This is the first condition for cultural theory: it is not its own master. As it is unseverable from the immediacies thick description presents, its freedom to shape itself in terms of its internal logic is rather limited.").

[76] *Id.* at 17.

[77] *Id.* at 25.

[78] Kahn, *supra* note 2, at 6.

and Kearns so eloquently note, "we come, in uncertain and contingent ways, to see ourselves as the law sees us; we participate in the construction of law's 'meanings' and its representations of us even as we internalize them, so much so that our own purposes and understandings can no longer be extricated from those meanings."[79] Thus we all, in the most intimate sense, stand to gain from understanding law as culture.

There is, lastly, the issue of the complexity and uncertainty that attends scholarship of this kind. Some consider it a serious drawback that it is messy and makes appraisal so difficult.[80] With respect to appraisal, Guyora Binder and Robert Weisberg suggest that we judge legal representations of the social and law itself "aesthetically rather than epistemologically ... according to the society it forms, the identities it defines, the preferences it encourages, and the subjective experience it enables."[81] My hope is that the appraisal of such work could be both aesthetic and epistemological. With respect to its messiness, I suspect that the cultural study of law will never attain the status of law-and-economics within law schools, precisely because, rather than simplify law, it complicates it.[82] I count myself among those who consider the complexity of the endeavor a virtue. That is why our agreements as to method can and should be only rough. A cultural interpretation of law, like interpretive anthropology, is an enterprise "whose progress is marked less by a perfection of consensus than by a refinement of debate. What gets better is the precision with which we vex each other."[83]

---

[79] Sarat & Kearns, *supra* note 7, at 7–8.

[80] Ellickson, *supra* note 75, at 149.

[81] Binder & Weisberg, *supra* note 2, at 463.

[82] Jeffery Cole, *Economics of Law: An Interview with Judge Posner*, I Litig. 23, 26 (1995) (quoting Judge Posner as saying, "There are simplifiers and complicators, and I'm a simplifier. I don't much like it when postmodern scholars talk about nuance and thick description and complexity and the need for constant qualification.").

[83] Geertz, *supra* note 108, at 29.

Excerpts From:

Ruskola, Teemu (2002) Legal Orientalism. *Michigan Law Review* 101(1):179–234.

Reproduced with permission by the author.

LEGAL ORIENTALISM

Teemu Ruskola

The goal of this Article is not to defend Chinese law, whether past, present, or future. Ultimately, the answer to the question whether or not there is law in China is always embedded in the premises of the questioner: it necessarily depends on the observer's definition of law. Hence, my aim here is not to "prove" that there is in fact such a thing as a tradition of Chinese "law." Indeed, there already exists a considerable scholarly literature on Chinese law (however defined), and among students of Chinese law the idea of China's inherent lawlessness – at least in the crude form of the thesis – is a discredited notion.[84]

However, outside of the academic study of Chinese law, ideas of China's lawlessness continue to abound. Indeed, one of the primary obstacles to a serious discussion of Chinese law are the blank stares with which one is frequently met upon confessing an interest in the subject: "What Chinese 'law'? There is no law in China!" (Sometimes followed by a more tentative, "*Is* there law in China?") Unlike the more traditional comparativist who studies French or German law, for example, the student of Chinese law frequently needs to convince her audience that the subject matter exists in the first place.

In this Article, however, I do not address the substantive arguments in the debate on law's existence in China. I do so not because there is no merit in engaging in this debate,[85] but because for present purposes, my primary

[84] *See generally* Gerrit W. Gong, The Standard of 'Civilization' in International Society 130–63 (1984).

[85] For one thing, many studies have already debunked the thesis that the Chinese legal tradition is exclusively penal. *See, e.g.,* Civil Law in Qing and Republican China (Kathryn Bernhardt & Philip C.C. Huang eds., 1994); Philip C.C. Huang, Civil Justice in China: Representation and Practice in the Qing (1996). Thomas Metzger goes so far as to suggest that by late Qing the Chinese suffered not from an absence of law but, if anything, an excessive concern for it, or "overlegality." Thomas A. Metzger, The Internal Organization of Ch'ing Bureaucracy: Legal, Normative, and Communication Aspects 18 (1973). In addition to the discovery of Chinese "civil law," there are also many defenses of Confucian traditions of "liberalism" and "constitutionalism" as well as various Chinese conceptions of "rights." An eclectic selection of this large literature includes Stephen C. Angle, Human Rights and Chinese Thought (2002); Confucianism and Human Rights (Wm. Theodore de Bary & Tu Weiming eds., 1998); Wm. Theodore Debary, The Liberal Tradition in China (1983); Janet E. Ainsworth, *Interpreting*

interest is in analyzing how the West has constructed its cultural identity against China in terms of law. Why, despite vigorous efforts to debunk it, does the view of China's lawlessness continue to prevail, not only in the popular opinion and among policy-makers, but even among legal scholars who do not specialize in China as well as China scholars who do not specialize in law?[86] Chinese civil law, for example, has been discovered and re-discovered periodically in the West. What preconceptions make it possible for it to be discovered and forgotten again so quickly, leaving it to wait for yet another round of "discovery"?

Stated differently, this Article is an attempt to take account of the context in which the study of Chinese law necessarily unfolds, and to understand the historicity of contemporary scholarship. What can we learn from the history of comparative law and, indeed, from the history of Chinese legal history?[87] I suggest that by considering legal Orientalism as an ongoing cultural tradition we can understand better why even today claims about the status of Chinese law are so relentlessly *normative*. Why is it that the statement that China lacks "law" (again, however defined) is almost never simply a factual claim but constitutes an implicit indictment of China and its cultural traditions?

Legal Subjects of Orientalism

Structurally, Orientalism as a discourse entails the projection onto the Oriental Other of various sorts of things that "we" are not. Given law's role in the constitution of subjects and national "imagined communities," how do Americans imagine themselves as legal subjects? How does the American legal subject differ from the Chinese legal subject? A fully contextualized genealogy of legal Orientalism is hardly possible within the confines of a single article. What follows is a sketch of the broad outlines of one possible genealogy, focusing on the ways in which legal subjectivity has constituted a standard for measuring non-Western societies' – here, China's-civilizational fitness to enter into "law's republic."[88]

Sacred Texts: Preliminary Reflections on Constitutional Discourse in China, 43 Hastings L.J. 273 (1992); Wm. Theodore de Bary, *The "Constitutional Tradition" in China*, 9 J. Chinese L. 7 (1995); Ju-ao Mei, *China and the Rule of Law*, 5 Pac. Aff. 863 (1932); Richard Vuylsteke, *Tung Chung-shu: A Philosophical Case for Rights in Chinese Philosophy*, *in* Law and Society: Culture Learning Through Law 303 (1977).

[86] I have participated in the debate myself by arguing that China in fact has a tradition of "corporation law" despite historic claims to the contrary. *See* Ruskola, *Conceptualizing Corporations and Kinship*, *supra* note 15.

[87] David M. Halperin, St. Foucault: Towards a Gay Hagiography 13 (1995).

[88] *Cf* Frank Michelman, *Law's Republic*, 97 Yale L.J. 1493 (1988).

American Legal Orientalism

Hegel, Marx, and Weber are classical European Orientalists whose work ultimately affirms the superiority of Western civilization and law.[89] However, they
do not exhaust the universe of legal Orientalisms, which vary by historical and
cultural context. The anti-immigrant Orientalism of nineteenth-century United
States provides an example of a peculiarly American form of Orientalism.[90] As
one historian of Chinese immigration observes, nineteenth-century Americans
viewed almost every aspect of Chinese life as an illustration of their backwardness: "wearing white for mourning, purchasing a coffin while still alive,
dressing women in pants and men in skirts, shaking hands with oneself in
greeting a friend, writing up and down the page, eating sweets first and soup
last, etc."[91]

The usefulness of this particular Orientalist discourse lay in its role in jus-
tifying the legal exclusion of Chinese immigrants at that historical moment.
Indeed, the text of a 1878 report by the California State Senate Committee on
Chinese Immigration sounds as though it had been excerpted directly from
Hegel's *Philosophy of History*:

> The Chinese are ... able to underbid the whites in every kind of labor. They
> can be hired in masses; they can be managed and controlled like unthinking
> slaves. But our laborer has an individual life, cannot be con-trolled as a slave
> by brutal masters, and this individuality has been required by the genius of

[89] To be sure, in Marx's case even the modern Western legal civilization may ultimately be destined to wither away together with the state, but as the penultimate way station to Utopia
it certainly represents a higher stage in the development of historical materialism than the
despotic law of Oriental civilizations. As Marx states unequivocally, colonial rule in Asia had a
dual mission, "one destructive, the other regenerating – the annihilation of old Asiatic society,
and the laying of the material foundations of Western society in Asia." Karl Marx, *The Future
Results of British Rule in India, in* The Marx-Engels Reader 659, 659 (Robert C. Tuckered., 2d
ed. 1978). Again, wishing to neither accuse nor excuse the three thinkers considered here, *cf
supra* note 139, I am evaluating their work along only *one* narrow dimension: what their work
has to say about China and its relation to the West. That is, I am not seeking to shame them in
an act of "postcolonial revenge" (to borrow Leela Gandhi's stark phrase) but simply examining
them as historical artifacts. *See* Leela Gandhi, Postcolonial Theory, at x (1998). Or, as Said
might put it, I am viewing Orientalist texts as part of the worlds in which they existed, since
texts, "even when they appear to deny it ... are nevertheless part of the social world, human
life, and of course the historical moments in which they are located and interpreted." Edward
Said, The World, the Text, and the Critic 4 (1983).

[90] *See generally* Keith Aoki, *"Foreign-ness" and Asian American Identities*, 4 Ucla Asian Pac. Am.
L.J. 1, 7–44 (1996) (describing the history of "American Orientalism"); Neil Gotanda, *Exclusion
and Inclusion: Immigration and American Orientalism, in* Across the Pacific: Asian Americans
and Globalization 129 (Evelyn Hu-DeHart ed., 1999); *see also* Lisa Lowe, Immigrant Acts: On
Asian American Cultural Politics 1–36 (1996).

[91] Stuart Creighton Miller, The Unwelcome Immigrant: The American Image of the Chinese
1785–1885, at 27–28 (1969).

our institutions, and upon these elements of character the State depends for defense and growth.[92]

Such sentiments may have very much a nineteenth-century flavor, but consider also the following analysis of the Chinese immigration exclusion, made by a federal judge in the 1920s:

> The yellow or brown racial color is the hallmark of Oriental despotisms, or was at the time the original naturalization law was enacted. It was deemed that the subjects of these despotisms, with their fixed and ingrained pride in the type of their civilization, which works for its welfare by subordinating the individual to the personal authority of the sovereign, as the embodiment of the state, were not fitted and suited to make for the success of a republican form of Government. Hence they were denied citizenship.[93]

To the judge, it was thus self-evident that the Congress's exclusion of the Chinese from immigration was not based on "color" but *cultural* disqualification for citizenship.[94] That is, the Chinese were so radically "un-legal" that they were simply not capable of the kind of self-governance that was required by America's "republican form of Government."

Although the power of Orientalist tropes lies precisely in their irrefutability by empirical evidence, it bears repeating that even historically, from the very genesis of the Chinese immigration exclusion, the perception of Chinese Americans as being either unable or unwilling to resort to law for their rights has been simply inaccurate. Even though one prominent justification for the Chinese exclusion laws was the putative inability of the Chinese even to comprehend the notion of individual rights and thus qualify for America's "Republican form of Government,"[95] ironically the immediate response of the

---

[92] State of California, Senate Special Committee on Chinese Immigration, *quoted in* Tomas Almaguer, Racial Fault Lines: The Historical Origins of White Supremacy in California 174 (1994). These conclusions were foreshadowed by a joint special committee of the U.S. Congress: "To admit these vast numbers of aliens to citizen- ship and the ballot would practically destroy republican institutions on the Pacific coast, for the Chinese have no comprehension of any form of government but despotism, and have not the words in their own language to describe intelligibly the principles of our representative system." Report of Joint Special Committee to Investigate Chinese Immigration, s. Rep. No. 689, 44th Cong., 2nd Sess. (1877), *quoted in* Leti Volpp, *"Obnoxious to Their Very Nature": Asian Americans and Constitutional Citizenship*, 5 Citizenship Stud. 57, 63 (2001).

[93] Terrace v. Thompson, 274 F. 841, 849 (W.D. Wash. 1921), *affd*, 263 U.S. 197 (1923).

[94] *Id.* ("It is obvious that the objection on the part of Congress is not due to color, *as color*, but only to color as an evidence of a type of civilization which it characterizes.") (emphasis added).

[95] *Cf supra* text accompanying note 156.

Chinese to their exclusion was the paradigmatically "American" one: to insist on their legal rights in federal court.[96]

Toward an Ethics of Orientalism

Although the focus of this Article is on sketching the broad contours of certain historically dominant representations of Chinese law in the West, one may still fairly ask what, if anything, all of this has to do with understanding China and Chinese law today. How *should* we use "law" to understand China, or "China" to understand law?

The moral of this Article is not to issue a categorical imperative that comparative lawyers must cease Orientalizing China, that it must never constitute a mere means in our own projects of legal self-definition. While such moralizing is perhaps rhetorically satisfying, a categorically anti-Orientalist morality is simply not possible. Prejudices, in the neutral Gadamerian sense, can only be managed, not eliminated. As Gadamer observes, for better or worse, "the fundamental prejudice of the Enlightenment is the prejudice against prejudice itself, which denies tradition its power."[97] In the end, "belonging to a tradition is a condition of hermeneutics,"[98] and traditions inevitably prejudice us in the sense of disposing us to see the world in light of our preconceptions – whether those preconceptions be positive or negative.

Thus, there is no innocent knowledge to be had, and we have little choice *but* to Orientalize – to always anticipate China and its legal traditions in terms of our own biases. Moreover, not only are we inevitably always engaged in Othering and essentializing China and Chinese law as we seek to understand them, but the Chinese, likewise, essentialize us, the West. Moreover, both we and the Chinese essentialize our own traditions as well: the Chinese "self-Orientalize" and Americans "self-Americanize," as it were.

As examples of Chinese self-essentialization, consider again the fact that for centuries it was the official, state-sponsored Confucian view that law played only a minimal role in governance of the Chinese empire which was ideally ruled by morality – yet in fact the state developed a sophisticated legal system to carry out its policies. But insofar as Confucianism privileged law over morality and the state identified Chinese-ness with Confucianism, it was ideo-

---

[96] *See* Christian G. Fritz, *A Nineteenth Century "Habeas Corpus Mill": The Chinese Before the Federal Courts in California*, 32 Am. J. Legal Hist. 347 (1988).

[97] Gadamer, *supra* note 24, at 270.

[98] *Id.* at 291; *see also id.* at 277 ("[I]t is necessary to fundamentally rehabilitate the concept of prejudice.").

logically imperative to insist that China was a government of men (of superior virtue), not of (mere instrumental) laws.[99]

Consider again also the notion of a stable, enduring China. This myth is not just a Western fantasy but a Confucian one as well. Confucius himself insisted, rather disingenuously, that his project of reforming Chinese state and society was simply a return to a past Golden Age – a mere reaffirmation of an ancient tradition rather than a fundamental reorganization of a world that he found corrupt and lacking in morality.[100] Indeed, ever since Confucius (and even before him), nearly all Chinese projects of fundamental social transformation have sought to retroject their Utopias onto a distant past, so as to honor a strong cultural prejudice against radical change.

To be sure, since the Communists' rise to power in 1949, at least the Chinese state has rejected the past unequivocally as a source of legitimacy. However, even that rejection is premised on a selfOrientalization of that past. That is, although the Sinicized version of Marxism may well represent a significant transformation, even the Maoist variety is ultimately driven by a need to see the Chinese past as irredeemably "feudal," stagnantly waiting for Communism to rescue it from its ahistorical trap. Hence, many Chinese historians have internalized some of Marx's Orientalist understandings of the world as part of their self-understanding.[101] The accomplished legal historian Jing Junjian,

---

[99] *Cf supra* text accompanying notes 72–73.

[100] *Cf* Confucius, The Analects, Bk. VII, Ch. 1 (D.C. Lau trans., 1979) ("The Master said, 'I transmit but do not innovate; I am truthful in what I say and devoted to antiquity...' ").

[101] On Marxist historiography in China, see generally Arif Dirlik, Revolution and History: Origins of Marxist Historiography in China, 1919–1937 (1978). *Cf* Partha Chatterjee, Nationalist Thought and the Colonial World: A Derivative Discourse? (1986) (analyzing the adoption of the European ideology of "nationalism" by the Indian state). To the extent that "Chineseness" is premised on *not* being "Western," Wang Ning calls the phenomenon "Occidentalism" – ultimately another mode of self-Orientalism in that it still defines itself primarily in relation to "the West." *See* Wang Ning, *Orientalism versus Occidentalism?*, 28 New Literary Hist. 57 (1997). As an example, consider the satirical observation made by Lu Xun, China's leading literary modernist, in 1934: "[B]ecause we have been suffering from [foreign] aggression for years, we make enemies to this 'foreign air.' We even go one step further and deliberately run counter to this 'foreign air': as they like to act, we would sit still; as they talk science, we would depend on divination; as they dress in short shirts, we would put on long robes; as they emphasize hygiene, we would eat flies; as they are strong and healthy, we would rather stay sick." Lu Xun, *Reflections Starting from My Son's Photographs*, quoted in Zhang Longxi, *Western Theory and Chinese Reality, supra* note 68, at 105–06; *see also* Chen Xiaomei, Occidentalism: A Theory of Counter-Discourse in Post-Mao China 5 (1995) (observing that Chinese "Occidentalism," or self-definition against the Western Other, is "primarily a discourse that has been evoked by various and competing groups within Chinese society for a variety of different ends, largely, though not exclusively, within domestic Chinese politics"). For an alternative definition of "Occidentalism" (referring to the West's self- essentialization), see *infra* note 195.

for example, paints a rich, even dynamic view of the legal regulation of the economy during the Qing – yet, almost contradicting his own evidence, in the end he nevertheless concludes that "Chinese law was permeated by the same basic principles from beginning to end."[102]

And just as the Chinese tend to self-Orientalize their own past as lawless and unchanging, I have suggested above that Americans tend to "self-Americanize" themselves as inherently legal. Intriguingly, although Americans often do "place a high cultural valuation on change,"[103] which also serves to condemn China's legal tradition as "stagnant," in the domestic context Americans are capable of valuing *lack* of change as well. Just as Confucianism sought political stability in respecting the forms of governance established by the founder of each dynasty, so many Americans too take pride in the fact that their Constitution has remained unaltered since its adoption in the wake of the

---

[102] Jing Junjian, *Legislation Related to the Civil Economy in the Qing Dynasty*, in *Civil Law In Qing And Republican China*, *supra* note 21, at 42, 82; *see also* Chen Duanhong, *Opposition – The Future of Chinese Constitutionalism from the Perspective of Administrative Litigation*, 4 Zhongwai Faxue [*Peking U. L.J.*]1 (1995) (painting a Hegelian image of traditional Chinese law as paternalistic rule where subjects were reduced to the position of children); Liang Zhiping, *Explicating "Law": A Comparative Perspective of Chinese and Western Legal Culture*, 3 J. Chinese L. 55, 91 (1989) ("Obviously, China's traditional legal concepts are incapable of accommodating the rich essence of modern legal concepts .... We must expose and criticize past history and consciously recognize the traditions that we inherited unintentionally."). And just as the indigenous Chinese legal tradition tends to be reduced to an Orientalist stereotype, idealized notions of Western law have come to constitute the paradigmatic form of "law." *See, e.g.,* Gao Hongjun, *Two Modes of the Rule of Law*, in *Yifa Zhiguo*, Jianshe Shehui Zhuyi Fazhi Guojia [Ruling the Country According to Law, Constructing a Socialist Rule of Law State] 262, 266–67 (Liu Hainian et al. eds., 1996) (relying on Roberto Unger's Eurocentric account of legal development). *Cf* Alford, *The Inscrutable Occidental*, *supra* note 59. Ironically, the "cutting edge" of much contemporary Chinese legal theory thus consists of retellings of European Enlightenment narratives. *See, e.g.,* Yan Cunsheng, *Rationalization Is the Core of Legal Modernization*, 1 Faxue [Law Science Monthly]8 (1997); Du Wanhua, *The Dualistic Social Structure and Jurisprudential Reflections Thereon*, 1 Xiandai Faxue [Modern Legal Studies] 5 (1996) (drawing on Hobbes, Kant, Locke and Rousseau, among others); Bei Yue, *Human Rational Agreement and the Origin of Legal Rules*, 1 Xiandai Faxue [Modern Legal Studies] 8 (1997) (social contract narrative). To be sure, there is nothing "wrong" about legal self-Orientalism. As Gayatri Spivak observes, "Programs of cultural self-representation are never correct or incorrect. They are the substance of cultural inscriptions." Spivak, A Critique Of Postcolonial Reason, *supra* note 64, at 341. Yet insofar as legal self- Orientalism is based on an incomplete reading of the Chinese past, it can at least be criticized for seeking to ground itself in untenable history and for unnecessarily restricting the ability of contemporary Chinese law reformers to draw on the resources of China's legal past. In this context, it is perhaps noteworthy, as Xiaobing Tang observes, that Said's critique of Orientalism "has never really entered into the general cultural-intellectual discourse [of contemporary China] with a palpable impact." Xiaobing Tang, *Orientalism and the Question of Universality: The Language of Contemporary Chinese Literary Theory*, 1 Positions 389, 389 (1993).

[103] Cohen, Discovering History, *supra* note 39, at 6.

Founding.[104] Yet while a real or perceived lack of change in China's political culture is usually classified negatively as "stagnation," a similar lack of change in the American case represents the positive quality of "stability": not slavery to tradition but an admirable fidelity to who We the People "really" are. Indeed, consider the tremendous amounts of scholarly energy that constitutional Originalists, for example, devote to explaining why contemporary Americans ought to be ruled by an agreement hammered out by a group of property-owning white men in Philadelphia in 1789. The expectation that these men should be able to rule us from their graves is surely as much a form of ancestor worship as any advocated by Confucius, yet here it is one that confirms Americans' identity as essentially, solidly American.[105]

But if this is indeed the melancholic conclusion – we cannot help essentializing others, and even ourselves – what is a comparative lawyer to do? If we accept the premise that prejudices ultimately constitute the very "conditions of understanding,"[106] we need not find an Archimedean point of observation in order to understand at all: perfection is not required, even if we may wish to strive for it. Instead of a simplistic morality of anti-Orientalism – "Thou shalt not Orientalize" – which would effectively end comparative law, we are allowed to proceed with our enterprise. Indeed, comparison is ultimately the *only* way for us to encounter and enter into relationships with others.[107]

Yet while morality may have no place in comparative law, ethics must. By "morality," I mean normative systems that posit a pre-given moral subject and then elaborate guidelines for proper actions by that subject.[108] By "ethics," in contrast, I refer to normative systems that are concerned, not with what a pre-given subject may or may not do, but rather with the construction of that subject. Instead of assuming an ethical subject and then regulating it, ethics regulates the *conditions* under which subjects emerge. What comparative law

---

[104] To be sure, the Constitution has been amended several times, but at least in the popular view – if not that of constitutional theorists – Americans continue to live under the "same" Constitution. *Cf.* Bruce Ackerman, We The People: Foundations (1991).

[105] As another example of Confucian-like self-projection into tradition, consider Western appeals to an idealized "classical antiquity" (to be strictly distinguished from Eastern-influenced Hellenism, for example) and the need to "preserve[] it within Western culture as the heritage of the past." Gadamer, *supra* note 24, at 287. Reminding us that Orientalist discourses are constitutive not only of the Oriental as an object but also of the Western subject, James Carrier uses the term "Occidentalism" in a similar fashion to describe the ways in which anthropological studies of "the Orient" have contributed to the idealization of "the West." James G. Carrier, *Occidentalism: The World Turned Upside-Down*, 19 Am. Ethnologist 195 (1992).

[106] Gadamer, *supra* note 24, at 277–307.

[107] *Cf.* Charles Taylor, *Comparison, History, Truth, in* Philosophical Arguments 147, 150 (1995) ("[O]ther-understanding is always in a sense comparative.").

[108] Christianity and Kantian ethics are paradigmatic examples of morality in this sense.

needs, then, is an ethics of Orientalism, rather than an impossible morality of anti-Orientalism.

That is, even as we continue to compare and necessarily Orientalize as well, we must consider the effects that our comparisons have on others.[109] To the extent that the categories we employ always impose limits on what we can discover in the world, it is a fundamental effect of our acts of comparison that they in part *produce* the objects that are being compared – for example, the American "legal subject" and the Chinese "nonlegal non-subject." We must therefore consider the ways in which our comparisons subject others, in both senses of the term: recognize them as free subjects and also limit their freedom as subjects.[110]

Today, many American policy-makers still view the Chinese as essentially lawless and unindividuated subjects of Oriental Despotism, the latest despot being the Communist Party, rather than the imperial state. In its current incarnation this view underwrites the political and economic project of making China open its markets for Western investment and trade: those favoring China's entry into the World Trade Organization and other international commercial and trade law regimes claim that China's participation will eventually transform its population into viable subjects of the rule of law. This particular Orientalist view risks rendering the mission of American law in China from (relatively harmless) legal tourism to the imposition of neo-liberalism under the alibi of law reform.[111]

There is also a deep irony to this view, given that in the American domestic context it is precisely the all *too* successful economic integration of Chinese Americans that renders them suspect as legal subjects: even as citizens, they are believed to exercise their agency primarily through economic rather than legal and political means, at least according to their media portrayals.[112]

Yet whatever the differences among the above Orientalisms, they support an overly idealized self-image of the American legal subject and an unduly negative view of the Chinese (non)legal (non)subject: Chinese are ruled by

---

[109] The ethical conception of Orientalism can be also thought of as a kind of "strategic essentialism," as elaborated by Spivak, *Subaltern Studies, supra* note 64, *i.e.,* a practice of essentializing the other for only certain purposes and with an awareness of its consequences.

[110] *Cf supra* note 112.

[111] This is not to suggest that there is no indigenous Chinese demand for law reform. Quite clearly, many Chinese *do* favor law reform, as well as China's participation in the W.T.O. There is nothing inherently objectionable about the pursuit of these goals in themselves. What *is* questionable is these projects' implicit assumption (made equally commonly by both American law-exporters and Chinese law-importers) about the self-evident Western-ness of all possible forms of legal modernity, and the expectation that the expansion of markets will naturally "civilize" Chinese subjects of despotism into (liberal) legal subjects.

[112] *Cf supra* text accompanying notes 182–183.

morality, Americans by law; Chinese are lemmings, Americans individuals; Chinese are despotic, Americans democratic; China is changeless, America dynamic. Together, these notions form an analytically indissoluble complex of meanings so that often to invoke one is to invoke them all. The problem is not that these Orientalisms make assumptions about Chinese legal subjectivity – that is unavoidable – but that these assumptions essentially foreclose the possibility of any real communication between the American legal subject and its Chinese would-be counterpart. To the extent that they view the American legal subject as the paradigmatic and authentic case, they implicitly authorize it to teach the Chinese *how to become* (real) legal subjects. And until that lesson has been imparted, there is little that Chinese law can offer to American law, which is hardly a promising recipe for cross-cultural understanding. Indeed, insofar as this conception of the legal subject holds the potential for delegitimizing all other legal traditions, legal Orientalism is built into the very definition of "law," which, along with the kind of individual subjectivity it implies, becomes one of the West's key contributions to the modern world.[113]

Yet whether we articulate our criticisms in terms of human rights or some other discourse, we must not proceed to condemn China without a fair hearing. Often, Chinese legal practices are judged by irrelevant character evidence, based on assumptions about the "despotic" and "irrational" nature of the Chinese, for example. Equally frequently, the Chinese legal system is presumed guilty before evidence has been even offered – or when it is offered, too often it is Orientalist hearsay with a history of several centuries. And all too often the entire process seems to center around us, and the project of proving the innocence of *our* norms and practices, derivatively by challenging those of China. Finally, there is the ultimate structural question of all Orientalist epistemologies: why is China always cast as the defendant and the West as the judge – and the jury?[114]

---

[113] As Peter Fitzpatrick observes, manufacturing myths about other societies' law is an inevitable part of legitimating one's own. *See* Peter Fitzpatrick, The Mythology of Modern Law (1992).

[114] *Cf* Leti Volpp, *Feminism vs. Multiculturalism*, 101 Colum. L. Rev. 1181 (2001) (analyzing ways in which discourses of Western legal feminism posit non-Western cultural practices as patriarchal and thus find multiculturalism oppositional to feminism).

Excerpts From:

Mutua, Makau W. (2001) Savages, Victims, and Saviors: The Metaphor of Human Rights. *Harvard International Law Journal* 42(1):201–245. Reproduced with permission.

SAVAGES, VICTIMS, AND SAVIORS: THE METAPHOR OF HUMAN RIGHTS

Makau W. Mutua[115]

I. Introduction

The human rights movement[116] is marked by a damning metaphor. The grand narrative of human rights contains a subtext that depicts an epochal contest pitting savages, on the one hand, against victims and saviors, on the other.[117]

---

[115] Professor of Law and Director, Human Rights Center, State University of New York at Buffalo School of Law. S.J.D., Harvard Law School, 1987; LL.M., Harvard Law School, 1985; LL.M., University of Dar-es-salaam, 1984; I.L.B., University of Dar-es-salaam, 1983; Co-Chair, 2000 Annual Meeting of the American Society of International law. In March 1999, an early draft of this article was presented at the Faculty Workshop Series at Harvard Law School. In November 1999, a later version was presented at Yale Law School under the auspices of the Orville Schell Center for International Human Rights. I am greatly indebted to the participants at both for their valuable comments. I am also grateful to the following colleagues who enriched this article with their insightful conversations: William Alford, Guyora Binder, Christine Desan, Gerald Frug, Maty Ann Glendon, Paul Kahn, Duncan Kennedy, Randall Kennedy, Martha Minow, Spencer Ovenon, Richard Parker, Peter Rosenblum, James Silk, Joel Singer, Anne-Mane Slaughter, Lucie White, and David Wilkins. I wish especially to thank Leila Hilal, David Kennedy, Frank Michelman, and Henry Steiner for closely reading a draft of this article and making critically significance and vital comments and suggestions.

[116] For the purposes of this Article, the "human rights movement" refers co that collection of norms, processes, and institutions that traces its immediate ancestry to the Universal Declaration of Human Rights (UDHR),adopted by the United Nations in 1948. Universal Declaration of Human Rights, G.A. Res. 217(III), U.N. GAOR, 3d Sess., l83d meg. at 71, U.N. Doc. A/810 (1948) [hereinafter UDHR]. The UDHR, the first human rights document adopted by the United Nations, is the textual foundation of the human rights movement and has been referred to as the "primal parent" of most other human rights documents. Henry J. Steiner, *Political Participation as a Human Right*,1 Harv. Hum. Rts. Y.B. 77, 79 (1988). Elsewhere, Steiner and Philip Alston call the UDHR "the parent document, the initial burst of Idealism and enthusiasm, terser, more general and grander than the treaties, in some sense the constitution of the entire movement ... the single most invoked human rights instrument." Henry J. Steiner & Philip Alston, International Human Rights in Context: Law, Politics, Morals 120 (1996).

[117] This oppositional duality is central to the logic of Western philosophy and modernity. As described by David Slater, this binary logic constructs historical imperatives of the superior and the inferior, the barbarian and the civilized, and the traditional and the modern. Within chis logic, history is a linear, unidirectional progression with the superior and scientific Western civilization leading and paving the way for others to follow. *See generally* David Slater, *Contesting Occidental Visions of the Global: The Geopolitics of Theory and North-South Relations*, Beyond Law, Dec. 1994, ac 97, 100–01.

The savages-victims-saviors (SVS)[118] construction is a three-dimensional compound metaphor in which each dimension is a metaphor in itself.[119] The main authors of the human rights discourse,[120] including the United Nations, Western states, international non-governmental organizations (IN–Gos),[121] and senior Western academics, constructed this three-dimensional prism. This rendering of the human rights corpus and its discourse is unidirectional and predictable, a black-and-white construction that pits good against evil.

This Article attempts to elicit from the proponents of the human rights movement several admissions, some of them deeply unsettling. It asks that human rights advocates be more self-critical and come to terms with the troubling rhetoric and history that shape, in part, the human rights movement. At the same time, the Article does not only address the biased and arrogant rhetoric and history of the human rights enterprise, but also grapples with the contradictions in the basic nobility and majesty that drive the human rights project – the drive from the unflinching belief that human beings and the political societies they construct can be governed by a higher morality. This first section briefly introduces the three dimensions of the SVS metaphor and how the metaphor exposes the theoretical flaws of the current human rights corpus.

The first dimension of the prism depicts a savage and evokes images of barbarism. The abominations of the savage are presented as so cruel and unimaginable as to represent their state as a negation of humanity. The human rights story presents the state as the classic savage, an ogre forever bent on

---

[118] This Article hereinafter refers to the "savages-victims-saviors" metaphor as "SVS." The author uses the term "metaphor" to suggest a historical figurative analogy within human rights and its rhetoric and discourse.

[119] Each of the three elements of the SVS compound metaphor can operate as independent, stand-alone metaphors as well. Each of these three separate metaphors is combined within the grand narrative of human rights to compose the compound metaphor.

[120] I have elsewhere grouped the major authors of human rights as belonging to four dominant schools: conventional doctrinalists, who are mostly, though not exclusively, human rights activists; conceptualizers, mostly senior Western academics who systematize human rights discourse; multiculturalists or pluralists, who are mainly non-Western; and instrumentalists or political strategists, who are Western states and Western dominated intergovernmental organizations such as the United Nations and the World Bank. *See generally* Nfakau wa Murua, *The Ideology of Human Rights*, 36 Va. J. Int'l L. 589, 594–601(1996).

[121] Human rights international non-governmental organizations (INGOs) are typically "First World" non-governmental organizations (NGOs) that concentrate on human rights monitoring of, reporting on, and advocacy in Third World" states. These INGOs share a fundamental commitment to the proselytization of Western liberal values, particularly expressive and political participation rights. *See* Henry J. Steiner, Diverse Partners: Non-Governmental Organizations in the Human Rights Movement 19 (1991). For a further explanation of the term "Third World," see *infra* note 23.

the consumption of humans.[122] Although savagery in human rights discourse connotes much more than the state, the state is depicted as the operational instrument of savagery. States become savage when they choke off and oust civil society.[123] The "good" state controls its demonic proclivities by cleansing itself with, and internalizing, human rights. The "evil" state, on the other hand, expresses itself through an illiberal, anti-democratic, or other authoritarian culture. The redemption or salvation of the state is solely dependent on its submission to human rights norms. The state is the guarantor of human rights; it is also the target and *raison d'etre* of human rights law.[124]

But the reality is far more complex. While the metaphor may suggest otherwise, it is not the state per se that is barbaric but the cultural foundation of the state. The state only becomes a vampire when "bad" culture overcomes or disallows the development of "good" culture. The real savage, though, is not the state but a cultural deviation from human rights. That savagery inheres in the theory and practice of the one-party state, military junta, controlled or closed state, theocracy, or even cultural practices such as the one popularly known in the West as female genital mutilation (FGM),[125] not in the state per se. The state itself is a neutral, passive instrumentality – a receptacle or an empty vessel – that conveys savagery by implementing the project of the savage culture.

The second dimension of the prism depicts the face and the fact of a victim as well as the essence and the idea of victimhood. A human being whose "dignity and worth" have been violated by the savage is the victim. The victim

[122] The human rights corpus is ostensibly meant to contain the state, for the state is apparently the *raison d'etre* for the corpus. *See* Henry J. Steiner, *The Youth of Rights*, 104 Harv. L. Rev. 917, 928–33 (1991) (reviewing Louis Henkin, The Age Of Rights (1990)). Thus the state is depicted as the "antithesis of human rights; the one exists to combat the other in a struggle for supremacy over society." Makau wa Mutua, *Hope and Despair for a New South Africa: The Limits of Rights Discourse*, 10 Arv. Hum. Rts. J. 63, 67 (1997).

[123] In Western thought and philosophy, the state becomes savage if it suffocates or defies civil society. *See generally* John Keane, *Despotism and Democracy, in* Civil Society and the State 35 (John Keane ed., 1988).

[124] Mutua, *Hope and Despair for a New South Africa: The Limits of Rights Discourse, supra* note 7, at 67.

[125] There has been considerable debate among scholars, activists, and others in Africa and in the West about the proper term for this practice entailing the surgical modification or the removal of some portions of the female genitalia. For a survey of the debate, see Hope Lewis, *Between Irua and "Female Genital Mutilation": Feminist Human Rights Discourse and the Cultural Divide*, 8 Harv. Hum. Rts. J. 1, 4–8 (1995); Hope Lewis & Isabelle R. Gunning, *Cleaning Our Own House: "Exotic" and Familial Human Rights Violations*, 4 Buff. Hum. Rts. L. Rev. 123, 123–24 n.2 (1998). *See also* Isabelle R. Gunning, *Arrogant Perception, World Traveling and Multicultural Feminism: The Case of Female Genital Surgeries*, 23 Colum. Hum. Rts. L. Rev. 189, 193 n.5 (1991–92).

figure is a powerless, helpless innocent whose naturalist attributes have been negated by the primitive and offensive actions of the state or the cultural foundation of the state. The entire human rights structure is both anti-catastrophic and reconstructive. It is anti-catastrophic because it is designed to prevent more calamities through the creation of more victims. It is reconstructive because it seeks to re-engineer the state and the society to reduce the number of victims, as it defines them,[126] and prevent conditions that give rise to victims. The classic human rights document – the human rights report – embodies these two mutually reinforcing strategies. An INGO human rights report is usually a catalogue of horrible catastrophes visited on individuals. As a rule, each report also carries a diagnostic epilogue and recommended therapies and remedies.[127]

The third dimension of the prism is the savior or the redeemer, the good angel who protects, vindicates, civilizes, restrains, and safeguards. The savior is the victim's bulwark against tyranny. The simple, yet complex promise of the savior is freedom: freedom from the tyrannies of the state, tradition, and culture. But it is also the freedom to create a better society based on particular values. In the human rights story, the savior is the human rights corpus itself, with the United Nations, Western governments, INGOs, and Western charities as the actual rescuers, redeemers of a benighted world.[128] In reality,

---

[126] The human rights movement recognizes only a particular type of victim. The term "victim" is not deployed popularly or globally but refers rather to individuals who have suffered specific abuses arising from the state's transgression of *internationally recognized human rights*. For example, the human rights movement regards an individual subjected to torture by a state as a victim whereas a person who dies of starvation due to famine or suffers malnutrition for lack of a balanced diet *is* not regarded as a human rights victim. The narrow definition of the victim in these instances relates in part to the secondary status of economic and social rights in the jurisprudence of human rights. *See generally* U.N.Escor, 7th Sess., Supp 2, at 82, U.N. Doc. E/1993/22 (1992) (criticizing the emphasis placed upon civil and political rights over economic, social, and cultural rights).

[127] The arc and science of human rights reporting was pioneered and perfected by Amnesty International (AI), the International Commission of Jurists (ICJ), and Human Rights Watch (HRW), the three oldest and most influential INGOs. Other INGOs as well as domestic human rights groups have mimicked this reporting. On the character, work, and mandate of NGOs and INGOs, see generally Nigel Redley, *The Work of Non-Governmental Organization in the World-Wide Promotion and Protection of Human Rights*, 9011 U.N. Bull Hum Rts. 84, 85 (1991), *excerpted in* Steiner & Allston, *supra* note 1, at 476–79; Peter R. Baehr, *Amnesty International and Its Self-Imposed Limited Mandate*, 12 Neth. Q. Hum. Rts. 5 (1994); Jerome Shestack, *Sisyphm Endures: The International Haman Rights NGO*, 24 N.Y.L. Sch. L. Rev. 89 (1978–79); Theo van Boven, *The Role of Non-Governmental Organization in International Human Rights Standard-Setting: A Prerequisite of Democracy*, 20 C\1. W. Lnt'l L.J. 207 (1989–90).

[128] Kenneth Roth, the Executive Director of HRW, underscored the savior metaphor when he powerfully defended the human rights movement against attacks that it had failed to move

however, these institutions are merely fronts. The savior is ultimately a set of culturally based norms and practices that inhere in liberal thought and philosophy.

The human rights corpus, though well-meaning, is fundamentally Eurocentric,[129] and suffers from several basic and interdependent flaws captured in the SVS metaphor. First, the corpus falls within the historical continuum of the Eurocentric colonial project, in which actors are cast into superior and subordinate positions. Precisely because of this cultural and historical context, the human rights movement's basic claim of universality is undermined. Instead, a historical understanding of the struggle for human dignity should locate the impetus of a universal conception of human rights in those societies *subjected* to European tyranny and imperialism. Unfortunately, this is not part of the official human rights narrative. Some of the most important events preceding the post-1945, United Nations-led human rights movement include the anti-slavery campaigns in both Africa and the United States, the anti-colonial struggles in Africa, Asia, and Latin America, and the struggles for women's suffrage and equal rights throughout the world.[130]

But the pioneering work of many non-Western activists[131] and other human rights heroes are not acknowledged by the contemporary human rights movement. These historically important struggles, together with the norms anchored in non-Western cultures and societies, have either been

---

the international community to stop the 1994 mass killings in Rwanda. He dismissed those attacks as misguided, arguing that they amounted to a call to close "the fire brigade because a building burned down, even if it was a big building." Kenneth Roth, Letter to the Editor, *Human-rights Abuses in Rwanda, Times Literary Supp.*, Mar. 14, 1997, at 15. Turning to various countries in Africa as examples, he pointed to the gratitude of Africans, who with the help of the human rights movement, threw off dictatorial regimes and inaugurated political freedom. *Id.* He argued, further, that in some countries, "like Nigeria, Kenya, Liberia, Zambia, and Zaire [now Democratic Republic of the Congo], the human-rights movement has helped numerous Africans avoid arbitrary detention, violent abuse and other violations." *Id.*

[129] This Article contends that the participation of non-European states and societies in the enforcement of human rights cannot in itself universalize those rights. It is important to note that the terms "European" or "Eurocentric" are used descriptively and do not necessarily connote evil or undesirability. They do, however, point to notions of cultural specificity and historical exclusivity. The simple point is that Eurocentric norms and cultures, such as human rights, have either been imposed on, or assimilated by, non-European societies. Thus the current human rights discourse is an important currency of cross- cultural exchange, domination, and valuation.

[130] Margaret E. Keck & Kathryn Sikkink, Activists Beyond Borders: Advocacy Net- works in International Politics 39–58 (1998).

[131] *See, e.g.*, Josiah Mwangi Karluki, "Mau Mau" Detainee: The Account by a Kenyan African of His Experiences in Detention Camps, 1953–1960 (1963); Kwame Nkrumah, Autobiography of Kwame Nkrumah (1973); Mohandas K. Ghandi, An Autobiography: The Story of My Experiments with Truth (1957).

overlooked or rejected in the construction of the current understanding of human rights.

Second, the SVS metaphor and narrative rejects the cross-contamination[132] of cultures and instead promotes a Eurocentric ideal. The metaphor is premised on the transformation by Western cultures of non-Western cultures into a Eurocentric prototype and not the fashioning of a multicultural mosaic.[133] The SVS metaphor results in an "othering" process that imagines the creation of inferior clones, in effect dumb copies of the original. For example, Western political democracy is in effect an organic element of human rights.[134] "Savage" cultures and peoples are seen as lying outside the human rights orbit, and by implication, outside the regime of political democracy. It is this distance from human rights that allows certain cultures to create victims. Political democracy is then viewed as a panacea. Other textual examples anchored in the treatment of cultural phenomena, such as "traditional" practices that appear to negate the equal protection for women, also illustrate the gulf between human rights and non-liberal, non-European cultures.

Third, the language and rhetoric of the human rights corpus present significant theoretical problems. The arrogant and biased rhetoric of the human rights movement prevents the movement from gaining cross-cultural legitimacy.[135] This curse of the SVS rhetoric has no bearing on the substance of the normative judgment being rendered. A particular leader, for example, could be labeled a war criminal, but such a label may carry no validity locally because of the curse of the SVS rhetoric.[136] In other words, the SVS rhetoric

[132] The author uses the term "cross-contamination" facetiously here to refer to the idea of "cross-fertilization." Many Western human rights actors see the process of multiculturalization in human rights as contaminating as opposed to cross-fertilizing in an enriching way. For example, Louis Henkin has accused those who advocate cultural pluralism or diversity of seeking to make human rights vague and ambiguous. Louis Henkin, The Age of Rights, at x (1990). In other words, he casts cross-fertilization as a negative process, one that is contaminating and harmful to the clarity of human rights.

[133] Slater argues that the "Western will to expand was rooted in the desire to colonize, civilize and possess the non-Western society; to convert what was different and enframed as inferior and backward into a subordinated same." Slater, *supra* note 2, at 101.

[134] For a discussion on the relationship among human rights, political democracy, and constitutionalism, see Steiner & Alston, *supra* note 1, at 710–25.

[135] Since the rhetoric is flawed, those who create and promote it wonder whether it will resonate "out there" in the Third World. The use of the SVS rhetoric is in itself insulting and unjust because it draws from supremacist First World & Third World hierarchies and the attendant domination and subordination which are essential for those constructions.

[136] For example, Serbs sympathized with former Yugoslav President Slobodan Milosevic possibly because they felt he had been stigmatized by the West. Milosevic played to locals' fears of the West and used the arrogance of the discourse to blunt the fact that he is an indicted war criminal. *See e.g.*, Niles Lathem, *Defiant Milosevic: Hell, No, I won't go!*, N.Y. Post, Aug. 7, 1999, at 10.

may undermine the universalist warrant that it claims and thus engender resistance to the apprehension and punishment of real violators.

The subtext of human rights is a grand narrative hidden in the seemingly neutral and universal language of the corpus. For example, the U.N. Charter describes its mandate to "reaffirm faith in fundamental human rights, in the dignity and worth of the human person, in the equal rights of men and women and of nations large and small."[137] This is certainly a noble ideal. But what exactly does that terminology mean here? This phraseology conceals more than it reveals. What, for example, are fundamental human rights, and how are they determined? Do such rights have cultural, religious, ethical, moral, political, or other biases? What exactly is meant by the "dignity and worth" of the human person? Is there an essentialized human being that the corpus imagines? Is the individual found in the streets of Nairobi, the slums of Boston, the deserts of Iraq, or the rainforests of Brazil? In addition to the Herculean task of defining the prototypical human being, the U.N. Charter puts forward another pretense – that all nations "large and small" enjoy some equality. Even as it ratified power imbalances between the Third World[138] and the dominant American and European powers, the United Nations gave the latter the primary power to define and determine "world peace" and "stability."[139] These fictions of neutrality and universality, like so much else in a lopsided world, undergird the human rights corpus and belie its true identity and purposes. This international rhetoric of goodwill reveals, just beneath the surface, intentions and reality that stand in great tension and contradiction with it.

This Article is not merely about the language of human rights or the manner in which the human rights movement describes its goals, subjects, and intended outcomes. It is not a plea for the human rights movement to be more sensitive to non-Western cultures. Nor is it a wholesale rejection of the idea of human rights.[140] Instead, the Article is fundamentally an attempt at

---

[137] U.N. Charter Pmbl.

[138] The term "Third World" here refers to a geographic, political, historical, [and] developmental paradigm. It is a term that is commonly used to refer to non-European, largely non-industrial, capital-importing countries, most of which were colonial possessions of European powers. As a political force, the Third World traces its origins to the Bandung Conference of 1955 in which the first independent African and Asian states sought to launch a political movement to counter Western hegemony over global affairs. *See* Robert-Mortimer, The Third World Coalition in Global Affairs (1984), *See also* Makau Mutua, *What is TWAIL?*, in Proc. 94th Ann. Meeting-Am. Soc'y Int'l L. (forthcoming 2001).

[139] Dianne Otto, *Subalternity and International Law: The Problems of Global Community and the Incommensurabilty of Difference*, 5 Soc. & Legal Stud. 337, 339–40 (1996).

[140] I have argued elsewhere that all human cultures have norms and practices that both violate and protect human rights. Fundamental to this idea is the notion that all cultures construct their view of human dignity. What is needed is not the imposition of a single culture's

locating – philosophically, culturally, and historically – the normative edifice of the human rights corpus. If the human rights movement is driven by a totalitarian or totalizing impulse, that is, the mission to require that all human societies transform themselves to fit a particular blueprint, then there is an acute shortage of deep reflection and a troubling abundance of zealotry in the human rights community. This vision of the "good society" must be vigorously questioned and contested.

Fourth, the issue of power is largely ignored in the human rights corpus. There is an urgent need for a human rights movement that is multicultural, inclusive, and deeply political. Thus, while it is essential that a new human rights movement overcome Eurocentrism, it is equally important that it also address deeply lopsided power relations among and within cultures, national economies, states, genders, religions, races and ethnic groups, and other societal cleavages. Such a movement cannot treat Eurocentrism as the starting point and other cultures as peripheral. The point of departure for the movement must be a basic assumption about the moral equivalency of all cultures. Francis Deng has correctly pointed out that to "arrogate the concept [of human rights] to only certain groups, cultures, or civilizations is to aggravate divisiveness on the issue, to encourage defensiveness or unwarranted self-justification on the part of the excluded, and to impede progress toward a universal consensus on human rights."[141]

The fifth flaw concerns the role of race in the development of the human rights narrative. The SVS metaphor of human rights carries racial connotations in which the international hierarchy of race and color is reintrenched and revitalized. The metaphor is in fact necessary for the continuation of the global racial hierarchy. In the human rights narrative, savages and victims are generally non-white and non-Western, while the saviors are white. This old truism has found new life in the metaphor of human rights. But there is also a sense in which human rights can be seen as a project for the redemption of the redeemers, in which whites who are privileged globally as a people – who have historically visited untold suffering and savage atrocities against non-whites – redeem themselves by "defending" and "civilizing" "lower," "unfortunate," and "inferior" peoples. The metaphor is thus laced with the pathology of self-redemption.

---

template of human dignity but rather the mining of all cultures to craft a truly universal human rights corpus. *See generally* Makau wa Mutua, *The Banjul Charter and the African Cultural Fingerprint: An Evaluation of the Language of Duties*, 35 Va. Int'l L. 339 (1995)).

[141] Francis M. Deng, *A Cultural Approach to Human Rights Among the Dinka, in* Human Rights in Africa: Cross-Cultural Perspectives 261, (Abdullahi A. An-Na'im & Francis M. Deng eds., 1990).

As currently constituted and deployed, the human rights movement will ultimately fail because it is perceived as an alien ideology in non-Western societies. The movement does not deeply resonate in the cultural fabrics of non-Western states, except among hypocritical elites steeped in Western ideas. In order ultimately to prevail, the human rights movement must be moored in the cultures of all peoples.[142]

The project of reconsidering rights, with claims to their supremacy, is not new. The culture of rights in the present milieu stretches back at least to the rise of the modern state in Europe. It is that state's monopoly of violence and the instruments of coercion that gave rise to the culture of rights to counterbalance the abusive state.[143] Robert Cover refers to this construction as the myth of the jurisprudence of rights that allows society to both legitimize and control the state.[144] Human rights, however, renew the meaning and scope of rights in a radical way. Human rights bestow naturalness, transhistoricity, and universality to rights. But this Article lodges a counterclaim against such a leap. This Article is certainly informed by the works of critical legal scholars,[145] feminist critics of rights discourse,[146] and critical race

---

[142] But genuine reconstructionists must not be mistaken with cynical cultural manipulators who will stop at nothing to justify repressive rule and inhuman practices in the name of culture. Yash Ghai powerfully exposed the distortions by several states of Asian conceptions of community, religion, and culture to justify the use of coercive state apparatuses to crush dissent, protect particular models of economic development, and retain political power within the hands of a narrow, largely unaccountable political and bureaucratic elite. Yash Ghai, *Human Rights and Governance: The Asia Debate*, 15 Austl. Y.B. Int'l L. 1 (1994). Such cultural demagoguery is clearly as unacceptable as is the insistence *by* some Western academics and leaders of the human rights movement that the non-West has nothing to contribute to the human rights corpus and should accept the human rights corpus as a gift of civilization from the West. *See* Aryeh Neier, *Asia's Unacceptable Standard*, 92 Foreign Policy 42 (1993). Henkin has written that the United States viewed human rights "as designed to improve the condition of human rights in countries other than the United States (and a very few like-minded liberal states)." Henkin, *supra* note 17, at 74. Elsewhere, Henkin has charged advocates of multiculturalism and ideological diversity in the reconstruction of human rights with desiring a vague, broad, ambiguous, and general text of human rights, one that would be easily manipulated by regimes and culture bent on violating human rights. *Id.* at x.

[143] *See* Robert M. Cover, *Obligation: A Jewish Jurisprudence of the Social Order*, 5 J.L. & Religion 65 (1987).

[144] *Id.* at 69. *See also* John Locke, Two Treatises of Government (Peter Laslett ed., Cambridge Univ. Press 1988) (1690).

[145] For examples of critical legal scholarship, see generally Karl E. Klare, *The Public/Private Distinction in Labor Law*, 130 U. Pa.L. Rev. 1358 (1982); Mark Tushnet, *An Essay on Rights*, 62 Thx. L. Rnv. 1363 (1984).

[146] For examples of feminist critiques of the law, see generally Frances Olsen, *Statutory Rape: A Feminist Critique of Rights Analysis*, 63 Tex.L. Rev. 387 (1984); Elizabeth M. Schneider, *The Dialectic of Rights and Politics: Perspectives From the Women's Movement*, 61 N.Y.U.L. Rev. 589 (1986).

theorists.[147] Still, the approach of this Article differs from all three because it seeks to address an international phenomenon and not a municipal, distinctly American question. The critique of human rights should be based not just on American or European legal traditions but also on other cultural milieus. The indigenous, non-European traditions of Asia, Africa, the Pacific, and the Americas must be central to this critique. The idea of human rights – the quest to craft a universal bundle of attributes with which all societies must endow all human beings – is a noble one. The problem with the current bundle of attributes lies in their inadequacy, incompleteness, and wrong-headedness. There is little doubt that there is much to celebrate in the present human rights corpus just as there is much to quarrel with. In this exercise, a sober evaluation of the current human rights corpus and its language is not an option – it is required.[148]

Conclusion

The promise that human rights holds out to the Third World is that problems of cruel conditions of life, state instability, and other social crises can be contained, if not substantially eliminated, through the rule of law, grants of individual rights, and a state based on constitutionalism. Through the metaphor of human rights and its grand narrative, the Third World is asked to follow a particular script of history. That script places hope for the future of the international community in liberal nationalism and democratic internal self-determination. The impression given is that a unitary international community is possible within this template if only the Third World followed suit by climbing up the civilizational ladder. However, I argue that this historical model, as now diffused through the human rights movement, cannot respond to the needs of the Third World absent some radical re-thinking and restructuring of the international order.

The human rights movement must abandon the SVS metaphor if there is going to be real hope in a genuine international discourse on rights. The

---

[147] For examples of critical race theory scholarship, see generally Critical Race Theory: The Key Writings That Formed the Movement (Kimberle Crenshaw et al. eds., 1995); Kimberle Williams Crenshaw, *Race, Reform, and Retrenchment: Transformation and Legitimation in Antidiscrimination Law*, 101 Harv. L. Rev. 1331 (1988). For examples of critical race feminism, an offshoot of critical race theory, see generally Critical Race Feminism: A Reader (Adrien Katherine Winged., 1997); Leila Hilal, *What Is Critical Race Feminism?*, 4 Buff. Hum. Rts. L. Rev. 367 (1997) (reviewing Critical Race Feminism: A Reader (Adrien Katherine Wing ed., 1997)).

[148] For other probing critiques of the human rights movement, see Raimundo Panikkar, *Is the Notion of Human Rights a Western Concept?*, 120 Diogenes 75 (1982); Bilahari Kausikan, *Asia's Different Standard*, 92 Foreign Policy 24 (1993); Josiah A.M. Cobbah, *African Values and the Human Rights Debate: An African Perspective*, 9 Hum. Rts. Q. 309 (1987).

relentless efforts to universalize an essentially European corpus of human rights through Western crusades cannot succeed. Nor will demonizing those who resist these efforts achieve a truly international approach. The critiques of the corpus from Africans, Asians, Muslims, Hindus, and a host of critical thinkers from around the world are the one avenue through which human rights can be redeemed and truly universalized. This multiculturalization of the corpus could be attempted in a number of areas: balancing between individual and group rights, giving more substance to social and economic rights, relating rights to duties, and addressing the relationship between the corpus and economic systems. This Article does not develop those substantive critiques, but it is important that these issues be raised. Further work must done on these questions to chart out how such a vision affects or distorts non-European societies.

Ultimately, a new theory of internationalism and human rights, one that responds to diverse cultures, must confront the inequities of the international order. In this respect, human rights must break from the historical continuum – expressed in the metaphor and the grand narrative of human rights – that keeps intact the hierarchical relationships between European and non-European populations. Nathaniel Berman is right in his prognosis of what has to be done.

> The contradictions between commitments to sovereign equality, stunning political and economic imbalances, and paternalistic humanitarianism cannot be definitively resolved logically, doctrinally, or institutionally; rather, they must be confronted in ongoing struggle in all legal, political, economic, and cultural arenas. Projections of a unitary international community, even in the guise of the inclusive U.N., or a unified civilizational consensus, even in the guise of human rights discourse, may be provisionally useful and important but cannot indefinitely defer the need to confront these contradictions.[149]

This Article has viewed the human rights text and its discourse as requiring the typology of state based on constitutionalism and political democracy.[150] The logic of the human rights text is that political democracy is the only political system that can guarantee or realize the fundamental rights it encodes.[151]

---

[149] Berman, *supra* note 133, at 478.
[150] *See generally,* Henry J. Steiner, *Do Human Rights Require a Particular Form of Democracy?,* *in* Democracy, The Rule of Law and Islam 193 (Eugene Cotran & Abdel Omar Sherif eds., 1999).
[151] Steiner, for example, does not dispute that the human rights text requires a political democracy. He argues that it in fact does impose just such a model. But he correctly points out that the model envisaged is not "detailed and complete." *Id.* at 200. The "essential elements" of a

As Henry Steiner points out, the basic human rights texts, such as the ICCPR, "should be understood not as imposing a universal blueprint of the myriad details of democratic government but rather as creating a minimum framework for popular participation, individual security, and nonviolent change."[152] However, the point then is that if this were a game or sport, its essence would have been decided, leaving those who adopt it only the option of tweaking or revising the rules governing it without transforming its purpose. It is in this construction that the SVS metaphor comes to life.

Using political democracy as one medium through which the human rights culture is conveyed, one is able to capture the imperial project at work. First, the choice of a political ideology that is necessary for human rights is an exclusionary act. Thus, cultures that fall outside that ideological box immediately wear the label of the savage. To be redeemed from their culture and history, which may be thousands of years old, a people must then deny themselves or continue to churn out victims. The savior in this case becomes the norms of democratic governments, however those are transmitted or imposed on the offending cultures. Institutions and other media – both those that purport to have a universalist warrant and those that are the obvious instruments of a particular nation's foreign policy and its interests – are critical to the realization of the grand script and metaphor of human rights explored in this Article. However, the imposition of the current dogma of human rights on non-European societies contradicts conceptions of human dignity and rejects the contributions of other cultures in efforts to create a universal corpus of human rights. Proponents of human rights should first accept the limitations of working within the metaphor. Then they must reject it and seek a truly universal platform.

Stepping back from the SVS rhetoric creates a new basis for calculating human dignity and identifies ways and societal structures through which such dignity could be protected or enhanced. Such an approach would not assume, *ab initio,* that a particular cultural practice was offensive to human rights. It would respect cultural pluralism as a basis for finding common universality on some issues. With regard to FGM, for instance, such an approach would first excavate the social meaning and purposes of the practice, as well as its effects, and then investigate the conflicting positions over the practice in that society. Rather than demonizing and finger-pointing, under the tutelage of outsiders and their local supporters, the contending positions would be carefully

democratic government that the human rights instruments impose do not constitute a complete blueprint but rather "leave a great deal open for invention, for political variation, for progressive development of the very notion of democracy." *Id.*

[152] *Id.* at 200 – 01.

examined and compared to find ways of either modifying or discarding the practice without making its practitioners feel shameful of their culture and of themselves. The zealotry of the SVS approach leaves no room for a deliberative intra-cultural dialogue and introspection.

The purpose of this Article is not to raise or validate the idea of an original, pure, or a superior Third World society or culture. Nor is it to provide a normative blueprint for another human rights corpus, although such a project must be pursued with urgency. Rather, the Article is a plea for a genuine cross-contamination of cultures to create a new multicultural human rights corpus. The human rights movement should rethink and re-orient its hierarchical, binary view of the world in which the West leads the way and the rest of the globe follows. Human rights can play a role in changing the un-just international order and particularly the imbalances between the West and the Third World. Still, it will not do so unless it stops working within the SVS metaphor. Ultimately, the quest must be for the construction of a human rights movement that wins for all.

3   Producing Legal Knowledge

This chapter is concerned with the production of legal knowledge, and the cultural logics and epistemological foundations within any society on which legal knowledge is based. The sociology of knowledge literature tells us that social organizations and structures, and the knowledge systems they engender, are constitutively linked, in turn shaping the way people think, socialize, and relate to each other (Swidler and Arditi 1994; McCarthy 1996). Exploring how we know what we know, and the ways that some knowledge becomes more authoritative than others, is the starting point for nurturing dialogue across different cultures with different knowledge systems and understandings about a person's place in the world. In the current age of globalization, it is vital to appreciate the complex plurality of epistemologies within, between, and across nations, localities, and regions that inform a diversity of legal conceptions, consciousness, and meaning (see for example Valverde 2012). Without such an appreciation, there can never be real legal collaboration between a global North and global South sufficient to deal with the world's pressing issues such as global poverty, global health, and global environmental deterioration.

Historically, European nations downplayed the existence of epistemological plurality, particularly in the contexts of colonialism and imperialism when Western cultural understandings and legal knowledge were most aggressively imposed upon others:

> The epistemological privilege granted to modern science from the seventeenth century onwards, which made possible the technical revolutions that consolidated Western supremacy, was also instrumental in suppressing other, non-scientific forms of knowledges and, at the same time, the subaltern social groups whose social practices were informed by such knowledges.... There is, thus, an epistemological foundation to the capitalist and imperial order that the global North has been imposing on the global South (Santos et al. 2007:xix).

Laurelyn Whitt, in her remarkable book *Science, Colonialism, and Indigenous Peoples*, which analyzes a colonial history of competing epistemologies, adds:

> the ideology of western science, wedded as it is to the thesis of value-neutrality, insists that issues of power do not enter into knowledge making or shape the dynamics of knowledge systems. The relations of domination and assimilation which characterize imperialism (whether in its historical or contemporary variants) ... are thus neither acknowledged or acknowledgeable (Whitt 2009:219; see also Woo 2011).

Today, there is an imperative to acknowledge this colonial legacy and to attempt to come to terms with the historical privileging of Western epistemology and Euro-American legal knowledge on the global stage. Without such an acknowledgment it will remain very difficult to nurture true exchange across the world's enduring epistemological divides.[1] Unfortunately, while "there has been a growing recognition of the cultural diversity of the world ... the same cannot be said of the recognition of the epistemological diversity in the world, that is, in the diversity of knowledge systems underlying the practices of different social groups" (Santos et al. 2007:xix). This lack of recognition of different epistemological systems creates enormous hurdles in the context of global governance and any sincere efforts toward global cooperation.[2] Hence, for scholars adopting a global sociolegal perspective three central questions that should always be asked are (1) whose legal knowledge is in play; (2) what cultural biases does such knowledge embody and convey; (3) and what alternative or additional forms of legal knowledge and consciousness may be present that up to now, given the historical dominance of a Euro-American formal understanding of law, have been silenced, ignored, or deemed irrelevant.

THE SCIENCE OF LAW

Euro-American law schools are in the business of training the next generation of legal practitioners and have vested interests in promoting an instrumental view of the law (see Introduction). One of the goals in the law school curriculum is to neutralize any moral considerations in legal determinations (Williams 1991; Mertz 2001). Law deliberately cuts away the messy lived experiences of people by simplifying facts down to a principle that can be applied

---

[1]   Of course, a diversity of epistemologies raises all sorts of methodological and practical issues revolving around communication, translation, and vernacularizing of world views that go beyond the scope of this brief discussion (see Merry 2006; Santos 2007).

[2]   On the challenge of indigenous knowledge systems, see Oguamanam 2006; Anderson 2009; Minkkinen 2009; Whitt 2009; Black 2010; Goldberg-Hiller and Silva 2011.

to multiple situations (Darian-Smith 2008). In addition, legal pedagogy reinforces a linear, chronological sense of time and a particular understanding of causality.[3] However, perhaps the most important goal of any law school training is to present legal knowledge as rational, logical, and reasoned. Max Weber recognized more than 100 years ago that law, as part of the modern bureaucratic state, was essential in formalizing and legitimizing state processes of domination (Deflem 2008; see also Kennedy 2004). "Whether law is characterized as a system of social organization, dispute resolution, or a means of particularized justice, its contemporary claim to justification rests largely upon its appeal to being founded upon and driven by reason drawing on firmly established principles" (Butler 2003:209).

Undergirding law's rational objectivity is the assumption that legal knowledge, like scientific knowledge, is capable of being classified, categorized, predicted, and replicated across different jurisdictions, cases, and legal actors. This assumption supports the claim that law can be universally applied to all situations and all subject-citizens and allows the adoption of legal fictions such as the standardized image of the "reasonable man" or "reasonable person." As the legal anthropologist Beth Mertz has argued in her analysis of law school training, the "distinctive epistemology that underlies legal language, as it is taught in doctrinal classrooms, fits very well with the overall goals and features of the legal system as it is taught in the United States" (Mertz 2001:93). As a result, stripped from most law school curriculums are complex contextualizing facts and historically structured inequities of power that frame and inform any given case and any set of actors.

Thinking of law as a science was a concept first introduced in the United States by the dean of Harvard Law School, Christopher C. Langdell, upon his appointment in 1870. Langdell was keen to standardize the emerging legal profession, and one of his innovations was to introduce the case method as taught in legal textbooks. Not coincidentally, this urge to professionalism also granted elite law schools the ability to monitor incoming law students to ensure that they were of a particular socioeconomic class, ethnicity, and gender (Darian-Smith 2010a).[4] Perhaps more importantly, the urge to present

---

3   According to the sociologist Andrew Abbott, in most Western systems of meaning the occurrence of events or actions are assumed to adopt a particular causal sequence and represent a particular way of social ordering (Abbott 2001). Yet time is not experienced by everyone in the same way, as noted in particular by anthropologists, a point that will be explored more fully in Chapter 4 (see Wilkinson 1987; Greenhouse 1996; Engel 1987; French 2001; Richland 2008).

4   "The first African American known to graduate from Harvard Law School was George Lewis Ruffin, who attended the Law School in 1867 and graduated in 1869. He was followed by a number of African Americans, each of whom became prominent members of the legal

law as an objective science distinct from politics and cultural values served well the interests of nineteenth-century corporate capitalists who were keen to present their successes based on personal merit rather than birth right and class elitism. At the same time it ensured the prominence and power of professional lawyers (Hall and Karsten 2009). As Shiela Jasonoff and other scholars have shown, there is a long-standing co-production between law and science in Western societies, with science providing law with objective authority and technical expertise, and law in turn becoming "deeply intertwined with the production of science, technology, and medicine" (Jasanoff 1987, 1992; Lynch 2004:162; see also Silbey 2008a, 2008b). The result of this mutual collaboration was the creation of what is called "legal positivism." Legal positivism, based in statistics, forensics, and experimentation, defines the modern science and authority of law (Samuel 2009; Bederman 2010).

Today there remains a need – perhaps more than ever before given the crisis of legitimacy in Western law – for lawyers and policy makers alike to maintain the myth that law is scientifically based, objective, and floats about the mêlée of social forces and political interests (see Banakar 2011). In recent years, scholars have exerted considerable efforts to create a standardized legal language and system of legal meaning. With the use of software technologies, new legal ontologies or classificatory systems are being created that are more adaptive to shifting political and legal contexts.[5] What these software projects claim is that the meaning of legal terms, and relationships between those terms, are available for mapping across national borders, cultural knowledges, and diverse legal systems.

Up to a point it is possible to create a more uniform system of rules between particular legal cultures and jurisdictions. However, the scope and applicability of these new legal programs are severely limited. They are bound to the (1) legal meanings found in legal texts, reports, and documents, (2) formal legal arenas such as courtrooms, governmental assemblies, and places of legal adjudication, (3) the vocabularies of European-based languages, primarily

---

community and well-known jurists serving in the state courts. In 1957, Harvard Law School produced its first female graduate, Millicent Fenwick" (Ogletree 2009:6).

5   Through Web-based tools such as OWL (Web Ontology Language http://www.w3.org/TR/ owl-features/) and the ESTRELLA Project (European Project for Standardized Transparent Representations in Order to Extend Legal Accessibility http://www.estrellaproject.org/), Web-based platforms are being created for knowledge production. According to the Web site of the Leibniz Center for Law where ESTRELLA is based: "We have longstanding experience in the development of legal ontologies, automatic legal reasoning and legal knowledge-based systems, (standard) languages for representing legal knowledge and information, user-friendly disclosure of legal data, and the application of information technology in education and legal practice" (http://www.leibnizcenter.org/).

English, and (4) common law and civil law legal systems. There is virtually no accommodation made for the production of legal meaning outside conventional Euro-American legal spaces, places, forums, vocabularies, cultural logics, and textual modes of communication.

If we accept that law is a cultural artifact, as discussed in Chapter 2, how do new software projects seeking to standardize legal knowledge account for cultural and social pluralities? In exploring structures of legal knowledge, how is it possible to accommodate customs, ideologies, and visual, aural, and symbolic modes of communication that do not easily translate into Euro-American-based legal concepts or legal interpretations? Can there really be a universal science of law as most Western legal practitioners and policy makers would have us believe?

AESTHETICS, NETWORKS, AFFECTS

Against the scientific claims and universal aspirations of mainstream Euro-American law, a few sociolegal scholars are developing theoretical models that challenge the authority of legal positivism and its built-in assumptions of objectivity and rationality. These scholars are often associated with critical legal schools of thought that have emerged over the past thirty years – cultural legal studies, feminist legal theory, critical race theory, actor-network theory, affect theory, and so on. Together these critical perspectives use a variety of theoretical frames and methodological approaches from the humanities and social sciences, often analyzing a diverse range of materials in addition to more obvious forms of legal texts. These materials include literatures, narratives, rhetoric, consciousness, ideology, symbolism, metaphor, images, music, custom, space, time, history, imagination, and sensory experiences. The critical perspectives and the materials analyzed are not mutually exclusive fields of inquiry and often overlap and inform each other. So for instance, it is possible to be a feminist international law scholar who examines the semiotic dimensions of human rights violations in times of war through exploring readings of nineteenth-century novels (see Tiefenbrun 2010). Together these critical legal perspectives, informed by rich mixed-method analyses, can be grouped as a rubric of inquiry called sociolegal aesthetics (which I will shortly explain more fully).

In this commentary, I very briefly discuss actor-network theory and affect theory as two of the more recent theoretical positions seeking to challenge legal positivism. I cannot begin to do justice to these two forms of critique or to the ever-widening range of sociolegal subfields that engage with aesthetics, as each is the subject of considerable bodies of scholarship in its own right. The more obvious of these subfields are law and literature,[6] law and memory,[7] law and senses,[8] law and rhetoric,[9] and law and semiotics.[10] Together these modes of inquiry share a concern with breaking through the assumptions of law as a positivist scientific enterprise. Moreover, they share a concern to move away from thinking about the rights-bearing individual as a standardized abstraction without a personal history and devoid of such things as ethnicity, race, sex, age, class, ideology, or religion (Geary 2001; see also Passavant 2001). Against the pressures of law school pedagogy, professional lawyers and conventions of legal practice, sociolegal scholars are deliberately folding back into legal inquiry the social, cultural, political, and economic contexts of legal engagement.

However, as Jon Goldberg-Hiller has elegantly argued, not all law and society scholars willingly embrace sociolegal aesthetics and its implications (Goldberg-Hiller 2008). A primary reason for this reluctance – at least in the United States – is that sociolegal aesthetics moves analysis away from progressive instrumentalism that informed early law and society scholarship emerging out of the legal realism movement and civil rights era as discussed in the Introduction. According to David Trubek, a leading figure in the law and society movement, "While the Law and Society movement succeeded in creating a new object of study and a new domain of knowledge, it did so within a 'legally-constructed' domain. Thus, Law and Society knowledge, while different from the traditional knowledges produced in the legal academy, necessarily reflects the needs and interests of legal elites" (quoted in Tomlins 2000:959).

In contrast to this normative impulse to reform the law from within,[11] an aesthetic approach is primarily concerned with exploring new imaginings of legal possibility and meaning in spaces, times, and practices typically not seen as "legal" (see Kahn 1999:40; Goldberg-Hiller 2011). This requires, in turn, exploring new forms of politics that previously have gone unrecognized or acknowledged within a law school or social science paradigm. Moreover,

---

[6] *See*, for example, West 1985; Aristodemou 2000; Binder and Weisberg 2000; Dolin 2007; Reichman 2009; Raffield 2010.

[7] *See*, for example, Markovits 2001; Savelsberg and King 2007; Gurnham 2009.

[8] *See*, for example, Hibbits 1994; Bently and Flynn 1996; Douzinas and Nead 1999; Geary 2004; Valverde 2006; Rhode 2010; Cooper 2011 and the special issue on law and love in the *Law Review*, Quinnipiac University School of Law 2010 28(3).

[9] *See*, for example, White 1985; Butler 2006, 2010; Constable 2007.

[10] *See*, for example, Wagner et al. 2005; Tiefenbrun 2010.

[11] This impulse was clearly demonstrated in scholarship by scholars associated with the Critical Legal Studies movement (Tomlins 2000) and more recently in the work by scholars associated with the ELS and NLR movements as discussed in the Introduction.

a politics of aesthetics engages with chaotic, messy, disruptive, and often counterintuitive realities (see Latour 2010; Rancière 2010). How people read and experience signs, symbols, smells, images, and stories and how these comprehensions influence human behaviors and social relations across various times and spaces are becoming increasingly central concerns for a critical – and dare I say it – younger generation of sociolegal scholars.

What do we mean by legal aesthetics? The study of aesthetics has a long historical and philosophical intellectual history in Western thought (Eagleton 1990; also Barron 2000). For our purposes here, aesthetics is not understood in conventional terms of artistic beauty or good taste, but (as suggested by Pierre Schlag) in terms of its more general post-Kantian application as sensation, perception, and norms that inform how one knows what one knows in the world, and how this experiential knowledge connects to political power (Schlag 2002; Goldberg-Hiller 2008). As early as the 1950s, the anthropologist Edmund Leach argued that "[l]ogically, aesthetics and ethics are identical. If we are to understand the ethical rules of a society, it is aesthetics that we must study" (Leach 1954:12). More recently, Peter Goodrich has noted, "A reading of the legal text which ignores the power of its imagery or the aesthetics of its reception is a reading which is in many senses beside the point in that it ignores precisely that dimension of the text and its contents which performs the labor of signification and so gives text its effect" (Goodrich 1991:236–238). And more recently still, Pierre Schlag in his discussion on the aesthetics of American law has stated, "the aesthetic pertains to the forms, images, tropes, perceptions and sensibilities that help shape the creation, apprehension, and even identity of human endeavors, including, most topically, law" (Schlag 2002:1050; see also Manderson 2000; Geary 2001, 2004; Kenyon and Rush 2004).

Drawing on these insights, Brian Butler argues that the legitimacy of law itself is in fact bound up with its particular aesthetic form of reason and authority. According to Butler:

> Law deals with various aesthetic concerns explicitly and implicitly, but is at its core a more aesthetic shaped enterprise than we generally think. It is quite odd that a domain of social practice so thoroughly overdetermined symbolically, can be viewed as if it were immune to and independent of aesthetics ... Aesthetics need not (indeed cannot) take us beyond the limits of rational inquiry and argument ... We can always attempt to argue rationally between aesthetic accounts and premises of the law (Butler 2003:215).

If, as suggested by Butler, formalized legal reasoning is itself an aesthetic form, then a new set of analytical possibilities emerges. It should be possible to move beyond the simplistic dichotomies positing law's superiority based on reason, objectivity, and abstraction as against the unreasoned, subjective passion of individuals. Law, in other words, should not be thought of as devoid of emotion, imagination, or subjectivity, just as aesthetics is not devoid of rationality or logic. Argues Bent Flyvbjerg, focusing only on rationality distorts understanding because:

> the rule-based, rational mode of thinking generally constitutes an obstacle to good results, not because rules and rationality are problematic in themselves, but because the rational perspective has been elevated from being necessary to being sufficient, even exclusive. This has caused people and entire scholarly disciplines to become blind to context, experience, and intuition, even though these phenomena and ways of being are at least as important and necessary for good results as are analysis, rationality, and rules (Flyvbjerg 2001:24; see also Flyvbjerg et al. 2012).

The problem in acknowledging that law is, in part, aesthetically constituted challenges the dominant Western perception of law as a scientific and reasoned enterprise that operates above the mêlée of common human actions, emotions, and desires. In short, by acknowledging an aesthetic dimension within law, what becomes unsettled is the foundational myth of Western law's rational core. Moreover, if sociolegal scholars are to take legal aesthetics seriously it follows that we must also "respect the particular, the diverse, the local" (Manderson 2000:200–201). For acknowledging law contains aesthetic dimensions begs the question: whose emotions, imaginaries, or subjectivities are prioritized, silenced, marginalized, or emergent within law itself? These are intrinsically political and potentially transgressive forms of inquiry in that they expose the centrality of power and social exclusion in Western law. As Chris Cunneen has remarked with respect to cultural criminology, focusing on the aesthetic dimensions of knowledge production "provides a powerful voice for those who may not be able to utilize the language of law or academia ... and by doing this, it provides the opportunity to hear the voices of those outside the traditional corridors of power" (Cunneen 2010:135). It is no surprise, then, that lawyers, politicians, and policy makers (and the scholars who serve them) are anxious to claim law as an empirical science and concurrently discredit explorations of the aesthetic dimensions of law.

Actor-network theory is a relatively new theoretical orientation emerging alongside the array of critical legal perspectives mentioned earlier. However, actor-network theory is more radical in that it rejects the role causal logic plays in creating meaningful legal interaction. Instead, it presents a model that posits contradiction, ambiguity, juxtaposition, contingency, alliance, and connectivity as referential conceptual relations to explain processes of legal understanding and practices of legal meaning. Actor-network theory seeks to move beyond the conventional dichotomies of structure/agency, material/ social, and human/non-human to explore how people, ideas, and objects circulate to construct systems of experience and meaning. In actor-network theory there is a co-production and interdependence between natural, social, technological, and material realms that conventional Western understandings of agency, time, and space cannot adequately accommodate. According to this theory, actions and impacts work across networks of interconnection, but do not always work in the same way or travel along in the same sequential direction (see Latour 1993, 2004).

Bruno Latour first articulated and applied actor-network theory to try to understand the production of scientific knowledge in the laboratories of the Salk Institute (Latour 1986). More recently, he has applied the concept of network to try to understand the constitution of legal knowledge. Focusing on French administrative law, and specifically the offices located in the Palais-Royal of the Conseil d'Etat, Latour conducted an ethnographic study of legal files as they wound their way across various clerical desks, were stacked in various piles, and stored in appropriate pigeonholes (Latour 2004, 2010; Levi and Valverde 2008). Throughout this lengthy meandering process, Latour observed the building of the legal case and argument through the addition of paper clips, slips of paper, and a complex layering of legal commentary (Latour 2010). Notes Latour: "The collective manipulation of the file is essential for this complex alchemy through which elements of facts are incessantly kneaded, leafed through, summarized, forgotten, rediscovered and finally glued together, hooked up and juxtaposed to elements of text" (Latour 2010:91–92). Like a good detective, Latour illuminates through exacting detail the myriad of ways empirical evidence is woven together and put into acceptable legal format, in turn producing legal documents that in the end are upheld as legitimate and authoritative. Latour's central concern is to show the unforeseen and unremarked upon ways – the actor-networks – in which "the central institutions of our culture produce truth" (Latour 2010:ix)

Actor-network theory has been criticized for its privileging certain sets of interactions, actors, and epistemological perspectives over others (see Star 1991; Strathern 1996; Jasanoff 2004; Wilson 2007; Gershon 2010). Moreover, actor-network theory has been taken to task for its assumption that the category of law exists as a pre-given entity (Pottage 2012), and similarly constructions of class, race, and gender exist a priori to networks and do not, in fact, emerge out of network interactions (Haraway 1997). Comments Shiela Jasanoff, "when actor-network theory confronts the nature of power, as if often does, it side-steps the very questions about people, institutions and preferences that are of greatest political concern. Who loses and who wins through the constitution of networks? How are benefits and burdens (re)distributed by or across them?" (Jasanoff 2004:23).

Despite these limitations, actor-network theory should be congratulated for its focus on intertextuality, the value of the non-human and material, and its attempts to move beyond conventional Western understandings of legal knowledge production. For these reasons it has been taken up by a few socio-legal scholars from various disciplinary fields (Law and Hassard 1999; Riles 1999, 2006, 2011; Valverde 2005, 2008; Bhandar 2009a; Guggenheim 2010; also see special issue *Journal of Law and Society* March 2012). These scholars provocatively seek to expose the limitations of our conventional epistemological understandings and demonstrate that we should not take "the substance or constitution of any particular objects for granted" (Bhandar 2009a:328). By deliberately emphasizing the agency in people as well as in objects such as "machines, animals, texts, money, architectures," this approach offers a corrective to the dominant causal logic of positivist law that marginalizes material objects (Law 1992:2). As John Law has remarked, "Actor-network theory is analytically radical in part because it treads on a set of ethical, epistemological and ontological toes. In particular, it does not celebrate the idea that there is a difference in kind between people on the one hand, and objects on the other" (Law 1992:3). On this point, Brenna Bhandar has persuasively argued:

> In thinking through the role that technologies and non-human things (for instance, machines, or scientific artefacts such as statistics, or legal artefacts such as court documents) play in particular networks of production, we gain new insights in how meaning and knowledge themselves are transformed over the course of time. In other words, the concept of a network of relations between things (humans and non-human actors) can yield different insights about the making of spaces, things, people, relations and significantly, knowledge forms (Bhandar 2009a:3260).

Affective social theory, sometimes called the "the affective turn," is another innovative theoretical response to the dominance of positivist legal knowledge (Clough 2007). This theoretical perspective, like actor-network theory, underscores the interconnections between the social and the material and seeks to move away from a purely "cognitive register" (Buchanan and Johnson 2009:35). However, unlike actor-network theory, affect theory underscores the significance of emotion, imagination, and the unconscious, as well as the performativity of the body through new technologies and sites of scientific exploration (such as the brain). These interconnections are seen as crucial in understanding the mutual construction of subjectivity and political action (Clough 2000, 2007; Massumi 2002a; Malabou 2008).

Affective social theory requires us to rethink our assumed epistemological frames and open ourselves up to emergent possibilities. According to Patricia Clough, affect theory forces us to "rethink empiricism, realism, physicality, causality, quantum ontology, and probabilistic epistemology" (Clough 2010:224). "What is at stake," adds Nigel Thrift, "is a different model of what thinking is, one that extends reflexivity to all manner of actors, that recognizes reflexivity as not just a property of cognition and which realizes the essentially patchy and material nature of what counts as thought" (Thrift 2004:59).

To date, affective social theory has not had much impact in Euro-American sociolegal scholarship and appears most often in the context of human geography. That being said, it has been picked up by scholars seeking to change how law is taught in law schools (Maharg and Maughan 2011) and is evident across a scattering of sociolegal scholarship exploring processes of legal consciousness and imagination (see Buchanan and Johnson 2009; also Sarat 2000; Reichman 2009). While few sociolegal scholars explicitly identify with affect social theory, the insights of theorists such as Henri Bergson, Gilles Deleuze, and Félix Guattari who inform affect theory have had a more general impact on law and society scholarship in their bringing into question the conventional relationship between institutions of power and people by highlighting issues of receptivity and experience (see for example, Hyde 1997; Rhode 2010). Together these theoretical perspectives have nurtured new understandings about how law is constituted and legal knowledge produced. Rejecting a conventional top-down perspective, which assumes law acts upon the abstract "reasonable man/person," this critical body of scholarship takes into account multiple subjective interpretations of legal meaning and how law, in turn, is affected by and constituted through the people, narratives, emotions, things, places, and events that it seeks to regulate.

DECOLONIZING LEGAL KNOWLEDGE

A general concern with legal aesthetics – including more recent actor–network theory and theories about affect – highlights an intellectual trend amongst critical law and society scholars. This trend seeks a bottom-up approach to legal knowledge, focusing on subjective and cultural interpretations of law and at the same time moving away from a state-centrist paradigm by challenging the prevalent assumption that legal engagement is framed by and through national jurisdictions. These innovative theoretical perspectives attempt, above all, to decolonize the dominant and homogenous forms of Western legal knowledge and present alternative and complimentary systems of knowing existing within and beyond the global North. Whether one embraces these innovative theoretical perspectives or not, the attempt to destabilize dominant legal paradigms and legal assumptions should be welcomed by anyone who takes seriously the need to adopt a global sociolegal perspective.

Overcoming the dominance of a Euro-American based "monoculture of knowledge" is essential to fully engage with and participate in the diverse epistemologies that inform our contemporary world (see Pieterse and Parekh 1995; Dhanda and Parashar 2009). This does not mean that scientific knowledge and the legal knowledge it engenders must always be resisted or denigrated, but it does mean that it is necessary to appreciate that this kind of world view is both limited and one of many (Wallerstein 2001). Moreover, such an appreciation must understand that these alternative knowledge systems are not fixed and mutually exclusive any more than are Western scientific and legal systems of knowledge. Epistemological world views are internally contested as they develop over time and in relationship to each other – they are in fact relational epistemologies. As Santos and his colleagues remind us:

> The epistemic diversity of the world is open, since all knowledges are situated. There are neither pure nor complete knowledges; there are constellations of knowledges. The claim of the universal character of modern science is increasingly displayed as just one form of particularism, whose specificity consists of having the power to define all the knowledges that are its rivals as particularistic, local, contextual, and situational (Santos et al. 2007:xl-xli).

The hope for a more equitable and inclusive global future lies in the possibilities of co-alliance and co-production of knowledge between different social groups and cultural traditions. However, this first requires acknowledging the reality of epistemological diversity, and then making sincere attempts to decolonize the dominant Euro-American legal system (see Mutua and Swadener 2011; Miller 2012; Smith 2012). Only then may it be possible to work through the enduring legacies of colonialism and legal power that continue to inform the North/South asymmetrical power relations and its disproportionate impact on the poor, the rural, and the indigenous peoples of the world. Yet, as Santos and his colleagues further remind us, any hope in the co-production of new shared knowledge may come at a considerable price. "The recognition of epistemological diversity is a highly contested terrain because in it converge not only contradictory epistemological and cultural conceptions but also contradictory political and economic interests" (Santos et al. 2007:xli). With this caution in mind, we need to move beyond Western political and economic interests sustained by a dominant Euro-American legal epistemology and push toward finding common ground within the overlapping human interests of the masses of people living in a global South and global North (see Hosseini 2010). This will require critiquing Western legal knowledge and its inherent Eurocentric biases. Specifically, it will require sociolegal scholars to challenge law's scientific claims and open up the legal field to a range of images, symbols, cosmologies, ideologies, senses, emotions, and non-textual networks of communication that inform alternative legal epistemologies, legal histories, and legal consciousness.

LIST OF SUGGESTED READINGS

1. Bhandar, Brenna (2009) Constituting Practices and Things: The Concept of the Network and Studies in Law, Gender and Sexuality. *Feminist Legal Studies* 17:325–332.
2. Black, C.F. (2010) *The Land is the Source of the Law: A Dialogic Encounter with Indigenous Jurisprudence.* New York: Routledge-Cavendish.
3. Buchanan, Ruth and Rebecca Johnson (2009) Strange Encounters: Exploring Law and Film in the Affective Register. *Studies in Law, Politics, and Society* 46:33–60.
4. Constable, Marianne (2007) *Just Silences: The Limits and Possibilities of Modern Law.* Princeton, NJ: Princeton University Press.
5. Cooper, Davina (2011) Reading the State as a Multi-Identity Formation: The Touch and Feel of Equality Governance. *Feminist Legal Studies* 19:3–25.
6. Douzinas, Costas and Lynda Nead (eds.) (1999) *Law and the Image: The Authority of Art and the Aesthetics of Law.* Chicago: University of Chicago Press.
7. Geary, Adam (2001) *Law and Aesthetics.* Oxford: Hart Publishing.
8. Hibbits, Bernard J. (1994) Making Sense of Metaphors: Visuality, Aurality, and the Reconfiguration of American Legal Discourse. *Cardozo Law Review* 16:229–356.
9. Kenyon, Andrew and Peter Rush (eds.) (2004) An Aesthetics of Law and Culture: Texts, Images, Screens. Special Issue. *Studies In Law, Politics and Society* 34.
10. Latour, Bruno (2010) *The Making of Law: An Ethnography of the Conseil d'État.* Cambridge: Polity Press.
11. Macaulay, Stewart (1987) Images of Law in Everyday Life: The Lessons of School, Entertainment, and Spectator Sports. *Law & Society Review* 21:185–218.

12. Riles, Annalise (1999) *The Network Inside Out*. Ann Arbor: University of Michigan Press.

13. Santos, Boaventura de Sousa (ed.) (2007) *Another Knowledge is Possible: Beyond Northern Epistemologies*. London and New York: Verso.

14. Savelsberg, Joachim J. and Ryan D. King (2007) Law and Collective Memory. *The Annual Review of Law and Social Science* 3:189–211.

15. Valverde, Mariana (2005) Authorizing the Production of an Urban Moral Order: Appellate Courts and Their Knowledge Games. *Law & Society Review* 39(2):419–456.

16. Wagner, Anne, Tracey Summerfield and Farid Samir Benavides Vanegas (eds.) (2005) *Contemporary Issues of the Semiotics of Law: Cultural and Symbolic Analyzes of Law in a Global Context*. Oxford and Portland: Hart Publishing.

17. West, Robin (1985) Jurisprudence as Narrative: An Aesthetic Analysis of Modern Legal Theory. *New York University Law Review* 60:145–211.

18. White, James Boyd (1985) *Essays on Rhetoric and Poetics of the Law*. Madison: University of Wisconsin Press.

Excerpts From:

Berman, Paul Schiff (2010) Toward a Jurisprudence of Hybridity. *Utah Law Review* 1:11–29.

Reproduced with permission from the author.

TOWARD A JURISPRUDENCE OF HYBRIDITY

Paul Schiff Berman[12]

Introduction

Debates about non-state normative communities often devolve into clashes between two polarized positions. On the one hand, we see the desire to eradicate difference through forced obeisance to a single overarching state norm. On the other, we see claims of complete autonomy for non-state lawmaking, as if such non-state communities could plausibly exist in isolation from the communities that both surround and intersect them.

Neither of these positions takes seriously the importance of engagement and dialogue across difference. Navigating difference doesn't require either assimilation or separation; it requires negotiation. Legal pluralists have long charted this process of negotiation,[13] noting, for example, that colonial legal

---

[12] © 2010 Paul Schiff Berman, Dean and Foundation Professor of Law, Sandra Day O'Connor College of Law, Arizona State University. This essay is based on a presentation delivered at the Non-State Governance Symposium, held at the University of Utah in February 2009. I am grateful to participants in that symposium for useful comments and suggestions. Portions of this essay have appeared in Paul Schiff Berman, The New Legal Pluralism, 5 *Annual Rev. of L. & Soc. Science* 225 (2009); Paul Schiff Berman, Federalism and International Law Through the Lens of Legal Pluralism, 73 *Mo. L. Rev.* 1151 (2008); Paul S. Berman, Global Legal Pluralism, 80 *S. Cal. L. Rev.* 1155 (2007); and Paul Schiff Berman, The Globalization of Jurisdiction, 151 *U. Penn. L. Rev.* 311 (2002). For a video of the author's remarks at the Non-State Governance Symposium, visit http://www.ulaw.tv/watch/631/non-state-governance-symposium -paul-berman.

[13] *See, e.g.*, Sally Falk Moore, *Legal Systems of the World: An Introductory Guide to Classifications, Typological Interpretations, and Bibliographical Resources, in* Law and the Social Sciences 11, 15 (Leon Lipson & Stanton Wheeler eds., 1986) ("[N]ot all the phenomena related to law and not all that are lawlike have their source in government."). For further discussions of legal pluralism, see generally Boaventura De Sousa Santos, Toward a New Legal Common Sense: Law, Globalization, and Emancipation 85–98 (2d ed. 2002); Carol Weisbrod, Emblems of Pluralism: Cultural Differences and the State (2002); Franz von Benda-Beckmann, *Who's Afraid of Legal Pluralism?*, 47 J. Legal Pluralism & Unofficial L. 37 (2002); Keebet von Benda-Beckmann, *Transnational Dimensions of Legal Pluralism, in* Begegnung Und Konflikt Eine Kulturanthropologische Bestandsaufnahme 33 (2001); David M. Engel, *Legal Pluralism in an American Community: Perspectives on a Civil Trial Court*, 1980 Am. B. Found. Res. J. 425; Marc Galanter, *Justice in Many Rooms: Courts, Private Ordering, and Indigenous Law*, 19 J. Legal Pluralism 1, 27–34 (1981); John Griffiths, *What Is Legal Pluralism?*, 24 J. Legal Pluralism & Unofficial L. 1 (1986); Law and Globalization from Below: Towards a Cosmopolitan Legality (Boaventura de Sousa Santos & César A. Rodríguez-Garavito eds., 2005); Sally Engle Merry,

systems did not eradicate indigenous systems (even when they tried to).[14] Instead, there was a layering and intermingling of systems. And, just as important, actors strategically used the variety of fora to gain leverage and make their voices heard.

But legal pluralists have usually stopped at the descriptive. Thus, while they have catalogued the myriad ways in which state and non-state lawmaking interact, they have not taken the next step and attempted to articulate the normative jurisprudence that might flow from these observations. After all, it is one thing to say that as a descriptive matter interactions among legal and quasi-legal systems operating in the same social field inevitably occur; it is quite another to argue (as I will attempt to do here) that such messy interactivity is actually a potentially *desirable* feature to build into legal and political systems.

I call this messy interactivity a jurisprudence of hybridity, and I argue that such a jurisprudence may actually be preferable to either a hierarchical jurisprudence whereby the hegemonic state imposes a universal norm, or a separatist jurisprudence whereby non-state communities attempt to maintain complete autonomy.[15] Why do I prefer a jurisprudence of hybridity? First, such a jurisprudence acknowledges the reality that people hold multiple community affiliations, rather than dissolving that multiplicity into either universality or separatism. Second, developing procedural mechanisms, institutions, or discursive practices that acknowledge hybridity helps to ensure that multiple communities are at least taken seriously and given a voice. Third, providing space for multiple communities may result in better substantive decisions because there is more space for variations and experimentation.[16]

International Law and Sociolegal Scholarship: Toward a Spatial Global Legal Pluralism, 41 Stud. In L., Pol. & Soc'y (Special Issue) 149 (2008); Sally Engle Merry, *Legal Pluralism*, 22 L. & Soc'y Rev. 869, 870 (1988); Sally Falk Moore, *Law and Social Change: The Semi-Autonomous Social Field as an Appropriate Subject of Study*, 7 Law & Soc'y Rev. 719 (1973); Balakrishnan Rajagopal, *The Role of Law in Counter-Hegemonic Globalization and Global Legal Pluralism: Lessons from the Narmada Valley Struggle in India*, 18 Leiden J. Int'l L. 345 (2005); Brian Z. Tamanaha, *A Non-Essentialist Version of Legal Pluralism*, 27 J.L. & Soc'y 296 (2000); Gunther Teubner, *Global Bukowina: Legal Pluralism in the World Society*, in Global Law Without A State 3 (Gunther Teubner ed., 1997).

[14] *See, e.g.*, Leopold Pospisil, *Modern and Traditional Administration of Justice in New Guinea*, 19 J. Legal Pluralism 93 (1981) (examining the change from a traditional to a modern legal system in New Guinea).

[15] This is a position I advance at greater length in Paul S. Berman, *Global Legal Pluralism*, 80 S. Cal. L. Rev. 1155 (2007).

[16] In focusing on the pluralist opportunities inherent in jurisdictional redundancy, I echo the insights of Robert Cover. *See* Robert M. Cover, *The Uses of Jurisdictional Redundancy: Interest, Ideology, and Innovation*, 22 Wm. & Mary L. Rev. 639 (1981). Although his essay was focused particularly on the variety of official law pronouncers in the U.S. federal system, Cover

Of course, acknowledging non-state community affiliations does not necessarily mean that they are the *same* as state communities. Most important, states usually (though not always) possess greater access to coercive power such as armies, police officers, and the like. Thus, it will often be agents of the state who determine the parameters of accommodation to non-state norms, so one should not naively assume that there is no hierarchy here.

Moreover, building mechanisms for acknowledging and accommodating multiple community affiliations does not mean states should always *defer* to those communities. For example, some community norms are sufficiently repressive, violent, and/or profoundly illiberal that they might not be followed. I argue here only that such norms should be *considered*, not that they should always win. But if they are considered, then when a decision maker refuses to defer, that decision maker will at least be required to justify why deference is impossible. As we will see, requiring such justifications acknowledges and respects community norms even when they don't win and forces the decision maker to offer a compelling justification on the other side of the ledger to explain why deference is impossible. It seems to me that this process of acknowledgment and justification is a good thing.

In this Essay, I start by referencing work of sociologists and political theorists analyzing interpersonal and societal communication, and I contrast a vision whereby difference is overcome by assuming commonality with one in which "otherness" is seen as an inevitable part of human interaction. I argue that it is unwise to attempt to "overcome" difference by trying to forge sameness. Yet, it is equally unwise, in a globally integrated world, to expect that walls of separation (either literal or conceptual) will be effective. Thus, we should aspire to a state of unassimilated otherness in an integrated community. In such a state, we seek communication across difference rather than annihilation of difference.

Then, I turn to law and survey three different procedural mechanisms that are or could be examples of a jurisprudence of hybridity with regard to non-state communities. First, I examine the idea of building margins of appreciation into

celebrated the benefits that accrue from having multiple overlapping jurisdictional assertions. Such benefits included greater possibility for error correction, a more robust field for norm articulation, and a larger space for creative innovation. And though Cover acknowledged that it might seem perverse "to seek out a messy and indeterminate end to conflicts which may be tied neatly together by a single authoritative verdict," he nevertheless argued that we should "embrace" a "system that permits tensions and conflicts of the social order" to be played out in the jurisdictional structure of the system. *Id.* at 682. Thus, Cover's pluralism, though here focused on U.S. federalism, can be said to include the creative possibilities inherent in multiple overlapping jurisdictions asserted by both state and non-state entities in whatever context they arise.

constitutional jurisprudence to allow some scope for local and non-state community variation. Second, I explore the possibility that limited autonomy or participation regimes can help ensure some scope for non-state norms. And third, I suggest that thinking of non-state norms through the prism of conflict of laws doctrines – jurisdiction, choice of law, and recognition of judgments – might be preferable to the more mechanistic ways in which clashes between state and non-state norms are often judged.

The excruciatingly difficult case-by-case questions concerning how much to defer and how much to impose are probably impossible to answer definitively and are, at any rate, beyond the scope of this Essay. The crucial antecedent point, however, is that although people may never reach agreement on *norms*, they may at least acquiesce in *procedures, institutions, or practices* that take hybridity seriously, rather than ignoring it through assertions of either universalist state imperatives or inflexible conceptions of non-state autonomy. A jurisprudence of hybridity, in contrast, seeks to preserve the spaces of opportunity for contestation and local variation that legal pluralists have long documented, and therefore a focus on hybridity may at times be both normatively preferable and more practical precisely because agreement on substantive norms is so difficult. And again, the claim is only that the independent values of pluralism should always be factored into the analysis, not that they should never be trumped by other considerations.

Of course, one thing that a jurisprudence of hybridity will *not* do is provide an authoritative metric for determining which norms should prevail in this messy hybrid world. Nor does it answer the question of who gets to decide. Indeed, pluralism fundamentally challenges both the positivist and natural rights-based assumption that there can ever be a single answer to such questions. For example, as noted previously, the state's efforts to squelch a non-state community are likely only to be partial, so the state's assertion of its own trumping authority is not the end of the debate, but only one gambit in an ongoing normative discourse that has no final resolution.[17] Likewise, there is no external position from which one could make a definitive statement as to who is authorized to make decisions in any given case. Rather, a statement of authority is itself inevitably open to contest. Power disparities matter, of course, and those who wield coercive force may be able to silence competing

---

[17] Lauren Benton, *Making Order out of Trouble: Jurisdictional Politics in the Spanish Colonial Borderlands*, 26 L. & Soc. Inquiry 373, 375–76 (2001) (describing jurisdictional politics in seventeenth-century New Mexico and observing that, while "the crown made aggressive claims that royal authority and state law superseded other legal authorities," in reality, "[j]urisdictional disputes became not just commonplace but a defining feature of the legal order").

voices for a time. But even that sort of temporary silencing is rarely the end of the story, either. Thus, instead of the unitary answers assumed by universalism and separatism, a jurisprudence of hybridity is a "jurisgenerative" model[18] focusing on the creative interventions offered by various normative communities, drawing on a variety of normative sources in ongoing political, rhetorical, and legal iterations.[19]

At the same time, mechanisms, institutions, and practices of the sort discussed in this Essay require actors to at least be willing to take part in a common set of discursive forms. This is not as idealistic as it may at first appear. Indeed, as Jeremy Waldron has argued, "[t]he difficulties of inter-cultural or religious-secular dialogue are often exaggerated when we talk about the incommensurability of cultural frameworks and the impossibility of conversation without a common conceptual scheme. In fact, conversation between members of different cultural and religious communities is seldom a dialogue of the deaf . . . ."[20] Nevertheless, it is certainly true that some normative systems deny even this limited goal of mutual dialogue. Such systems would (correctly) recognize the liberal bias within the hybrid vision I explore here, and they may reject the vision on that basis. For example, although abortion rights and antiabortion activists could, despite their differences, be said to share a willingness to engage in a common practice of constitutional adjudication, those bombing abortion clinics are not similarly willing; accordingly, there may not be any way to accommodate such actors even within a more pluralist, hybrid framework. Likewise, communities that refuse to allow even the participation of particular subgroups, such as women or minorities, may be difficult to include within the pluralist vision I have in mind. Of course, these groups are undeniably important forces to recognize and take account of as a descriptive matter. But from a normative perspective, an embrace of a jurisprudence of hybridity need not commit one to a worldview free from judgment, where all positions are equivalently embraced. Thus, I argue not necessarily for undifferentiated inclusion, but for a set of procedural mechanisms, institutions,

---

[18] *See* Robert M. Cover, *The Supreme Court, 1982 Term—Foreword: Nomos and Narrative,* 97 Harv. L. Rev. 4, 11–15 (1983).

[19] *Cf.* Seyla Benhabib, Another Cosmopolitanism 49 (2006) ("Whereas natural right philosophies assume that the principles that undergird democratic politics are impervious to transformative acts of popular collective will, and whereas legal positivism identifies democratic legitimacy with the correctly generated legal norms of a sovereign legislature, jurisgenerative politics is a model that permits us to think of creative interventions that mediate between universal norms and the will of democratic majorities.").

[20] Jeremy Waldron, *Public Reason and "Justification" in the Courtroom,* 1 J.L., Phil. & Culture 107, 112 (2007).

and practices that are more likely to expand the range of voices heard or considered, thereby creating more opportunities to forge a common social space than either statism or separatism.[21]

II. A Jurisprudence of Hybridity

Now we turn to explore three possible mechanisms that might form components of a jurisprudence of hybridity. Each of these mechanisms is premised on the idea of multiple community affiliation. Therefore, instead of insisting that one affiliation necessarily trumps the others, we seek ways of fostering dialogue and mutual accommodation if possible. And if accommodation is not possible, a jurisprudence of hybridity at least requires an explanation of why it is impossible to defer.

A. Margins of Appreciation

One mechanism of accommodation can be drawn from the jurisprudence of the European Court of Human Rights (ECHR): the oft-discussed "margin of appreciation" doctrine.[22] The idea here is to strike a balance between deference to national courts and legislators on the one hand, and maintaining "European supervision" that "empower[s the ECHR] to give the final ruling" on whether a challenged practice is compatible with the Convention, on the other.[23] Thus, the margin of appreciation allows domestic polities some room to maneuver in implementing ECHR decisions to accommodate local variation. How big that margin is depends on a number of factors including, for example, the degree of consensus among the member states. Thus, in a case involving parental rights of transsexuals, the ECHR noted that because there was as yet no common European standard and "generally speaking, the law appears to be in a transitional stage, the respondent State must be afforded a wide margin of appreciation."[24]

Affording this sort of variable margin of appreciation usefully accommodates a limited range of pluralism. It does not permit domestic courts to fully ignore the supranational pronouncement (though domestic courts have

---

[21] This focus on jurisgenerative structures, rather than on the necessary inclusion of, or deference to, all points of view, may differentiate a jurisprudence of hybridity from multiculturalism.

[22] A particular useful, succinct summary can be found in Laurence R. Helfer & Anne-Marie Slaughter, *Toward a Theory of Effective Supranational Adjudication*, 107 Yale L.J. 273, 316–17 (1997). My discussion here largely tracks theirs.

[23] Sunday Times v. United Kingdom, 30 Eur. Ct. H.R. (ser. A) at 276 (1979).

[24] X v. United Kingdom, 24 Eur. Ct. H.R. 143, 169 (1997); *see also* Otto-Preminger Inst. v. Austria, 19 Eur. Ct. H.R. 34 (ser. A) at 58 (1995) (finding that the lack of a uniform European conception of rights to freedom of expression "directed against the religious feelings of others" dictates a wider margin of appreciation).

sometimes asserted greater independence[25]). Nevertheless, it does allow space for local variation, particularly when the law is in transition or when no consensus exists among member states on a given issue. Moreover, by framing the inquiry as one of local consensus, the margin of appreciation doctrine disciplines the ECHR and forces it to move incrementally, pushing towards consensus without running too far ahead of it. Finally, the margin of appreciation functions as a signaling mechanism through which "the ECHR is able to identify potentially problematic practices for the contracting states before they actually become violations, thereby permitting the states to anticipate that their laws may one day be called into question."[26] And, of course, there is reverse signaling as well, because domestic states, by their societal evolution away from consensus, effectively maintain space for local variation. As Laurence Helfer and Anne-Marie Slaughter have observed, "The conjunction of the margin of appreciation doctrine and the consensus inquiry thus permits the ECHR to link its decisions to the pace of change of domestic law, acknowledging the political sovereignty of respondent states while legitimizing its own decisions against them."[27] A similar sort of interaction could be established by a constitutional court adopting some form of the classic concept/conception distinction[28] with regard to the adoption of norms by other actors. Thus, an entity such as the ECHR could, for example, articulate a particular concept of rights while recognizing that the way this right is implemented is subject to various alternative conceptions. Thus, legal regimes could usefully adopt margins of appreciation with regard to non-state community norms. Such a flexible approach might allow communities more leeway in trying to make statements of rights work within a particularized community context.

[25] *See, e.g.*, Nico Krisch, *The Open Architecture of European Human Rights Law*, 71 Mod. L. Rev. 183, 196–97 (2008) (discussing the interaction between the ECHR and state constitutional courts).

[26] Helfer & Slaughter, *supra* note 33, at 317 (citing Laurence R. Helfer, *Consensus, Coherence and the European Convention on Human Rights*, 26 Cornell Int'l L.J. 133, 141 (1993)) (noting that the Convention "puts other less progressive states on notice that the laws may no longer be compatible with the Convention if their nationals were to challenge them."). For an example of this type of signaling, see J.G. Merrills, The Development of International Law by the European Court of Human Rights 81 (2d ed. 1993) (1986) (interpreting the ECHR's statement in *Rees v. United Kingdom*, 106 Eur. Ct. H.R. (ser. A) at 19 (1986), that "[t]he need for appropriate legal measures [to protect transsexuals] should therefore be kept under review having regard particularly to scientific and societal developments" as a "strong hint that while British practice currently satisfied [the Convention], the Court's duty to interpret the Convention as a living instrument may lead it to a different conclusion in the future.").

[27] Helfer & Slaughter, *supra* note 33, at 317.

[28] *See, e.g.*, Ronald Dworkin, Law's Empire 71 (1986) (discussing the difference between "concept" and "conception" as "a contrast between levels of abstraction at which the interpretation of the practice can be studied").

B. Limited Autonomy Regimes

As noted above, interactions between state and non-state law pose a particular kind of margin of appreciation issue. Here, as with the supranational/national dialectic, we have two different normative orders that can neither ignore nor eliminate the other. Thus, the question becomes what mechanisms of pluralism can be created to mediate the conflicts? This problem classically arises in the context of religion or ethnicity, though it is in no way limited to such communities. Nevertheless, an overview of mechanisms for managing religious and ethnic (or linguistic-group) hybridity may shed light on the possibility of building institutions to address non-state normative communities in a variety of settings.

In a useful summary, Henry Steiner has delineated three distinct types of autonomy regime.[29] The first allows a territorially concentrated ethnic, religious, or linguistic minority group limited autonomy within the nation-state.[30] The precise contours of this autonomy can vary considerably from situation to situation. However, such schemes can include the creation of regional elective governments, command of local police, control over natural resources, management of regional schools, and so on.[31] With regard to language, communities may be empowered to create language rights within their regions.[32]

Of course, non-state normative communities are often dispersed throughout a state, making it[33] difficult to create specific local zones of autonomy. In such cases, other potential autonomy regimes may be more effective.[34] A second

---

[29] Henry J. Steiner, *Ideals and Counter-Ideals in the Struggle over Autonomy Regimes for Minorities*, 66 Notre Dame L. Rev. 1539, 1541–42 (1991) (identifying three different types of autonomy regimes for ethnic minorities including a power-sharing regime, a territorial regime, and an autonomy regime).

[30] *See, e.g.*, Will Kymlicka, Politics in the Vernacular: Nationalism, Multiculturalism, and Citizenship 156–59 (2001) (arguing that the creation of linguistically homogeneous, separate institutions for minority subgroups within a larger federal structure will foster the participation of minority groups in democracy by giving them the autonomy to control cultural policy).

[31] *See* Steiner, *supra* note 40, at 1542 (listing examples).

[32] *See, e.g.*, Wouter Pas, *A Dynamic Federalism Built on Static Principles: The Case of Belgium*, in *Federalism, Subnational Constitutions, And Minority Rights* 157, 158–59 (G. Alan Tarr, Robert F. Williams & Josef Marko eds., 2004) ("[I]n 1970, the Belgian State was divided into four territorial linguistic regions: The Dutch-speaking region, the French-speaking region, the bilingual region of Brussels-Capital, and the German-speaking region.... The authorities in each region may, in principle, only use the official language of that region in their dealings with citizens. In some municipalities, where a significant number of the inhabitants speak another language, special provisions were enacted to give individuals the right to continue to use their own language in their relations with the local authorities.") (citation omitted).

[33] *See, e.g.*, Cristina M. Rodriguez, *Language and Participation*, 94 Cal. L. Rev. 687, 744 (2006) ("Devolution to minority-run institutions will not help secure rights for disparate ethnic groups spread out over a nation's territory ....").

[34] See id.

possibility, therefore, involves direct power-sharing arrangements.[35] "Such regimes carve up a state's population in ethnic terms to assure one or several ethnic groups of a particular form of participation in governance or economic opportunities."[36] Thus, we may see provisions that set aside a fixed number of legislative seats, executive branch positions, or judicial appointments to a particular religious or ethnic minority group.[37] In addition, legislators who are members of a particular minority group may be granted the ability to veto proposed measures adversely affecting that group.[38] Alternatively, states may enact rules requiring formal consultation before decisions are taken on issues that particularly impact minority communities.[39]

Finally, a third autonomy regime contemplates the reality that members of an ethnic community may invoke the idea of a personal law that is carried with the individual, regardless of territorial location. This personal law is often religious in character, and it reflects a primary identification with one's religious or ethnic group, rather than the territorially delimited community of the nation-state.[40]

Accordingly, state law may seek to create what are essentially margins of appreciation to recognize forms of autonomy for these identities.[41] "Like power sharing, a personal law can provide an important degree of autonomy and cohesion even for minorities that are territorially dispersed."[42]

The question of accommodation to personal law is not a new one, nor is it limited to religious groups. In ancient Egypt, foreign merchants in commercial disputes were sometimes permitted to choose judges of their own nationality so foreigners could settle their dispute "in accordance with their own foreign laws and customs."[43] Greek city-states adopted similar rules.[44] Later, legal systems

---

[35] *See, e.g.,* Ivo D. Duchacek, *Federalist Responses to Ethnic Demands: An Overview, in Federalism and Political Integration* 59, 67, 71 (Daniel J. Elazar ed., 1979) (arguing that fostering democratic pluralism and an open political system is one way to meet ethnic demands); Arend Lijphart, *The Power-Sharing Approach, in* Conflict and Peacemaking in Multiethnic Societies 491 (J. Montville ed. 1990).

[36] Steiner, *supra* note 40, at 1541.

[37] *Id.* at 1541–42.

[38] Id.

[39] *Id.* at 1542.

[40] *See, e.g.,* Chibli Mallat, *On the Specificity of Middle Eastern Constitutionalism*, 38 Case W. Res. J. Int'l L. 13, 47 (2006) (contrasting the "personal model" with the "territorial model").

[41] Chibli Mallat calls this scheme "'communitarian' (or personal) federalism." *Id.* At 51.

[42] Steiner, *supra* note 40, at 1542.

[43] Coleman Phillipson, The International Law and Custom of Ancient Greece and Rome 193 (1911).

[44] *See* Douglas M. Macdowell, The Law In Classical Athens 220, 222–24 (H. H. Scullard ed., 1978) (noting that the Athenian legal system provided "xenodikai" or "judges of aliens" to handle an influx of cases involving foreign citizens in the first half of the fifth century).

in England and continental Europe applied personal law to foreign litigants, judging many criminal and civil matters based not on the territorial location of the actors, but on their citizenship.[45] In the ninth century, for example, King Edgar allowed Danes to be judged by the laws of their homeland.[46] Likewise, William the Conqueror granted eleventh-century French immigrants the right to be judged by rules based on their national identity.[47] Foreign merchants trading under King John, in the twelfth and thirteenth centuries, were similarly governed by the law of their home communities.[48]

As noted previously, the relationship between state and personal law frequently arose in colonial settings where western legal systems were layered on top of the personal laws and customs of indigenous communities. Indeed, in the colonial context, margins of appreciation and other forms of accommodation were often invoked as governing legal principles. For example, English courts were empowered to exercise the jurisdiction of the English courts of law and chancery only "as far as circumstances [would] admit."[49] Likewise, with respect to personal laws, the Straits Settlements Charter of 1855 allowed the courts of judicature to exercise jurisdiction as an ecclesiastical court "so far as the religions, manners and customs of the inhabitants admit."[50] "By the end of the colonial era, indigenous law was recognized as law proper by all the colonial powers."[51]

Today, particularly in countries with a large minority Muslim population, many states maintain space for personal law within a nominally Westphalian

---

[45] *See* Marianne Constable, The Law of the Other: The Mixed Jury and Changing Conceptions of Citizenship, Law, and Knowledge 7 (1994).

[46] *Id.* at 8.

[47] *Id.* at 10.

[48] *Id.* at 12–13.

[49] Siak v. Drashid, [1946] 1 Malayan L.J. 147, 152 (App. Ct. Sept. 13, 1941).

[50] Roland St. John Braddell, The Law of the Straits Settlements: A Commentary 17 (3d ed. 1982). Interestingly, in the era prior to the Age of Empire, English courts would only defer to indigenous laws of Christian communities. For example, in *Calvin's Case*, 7 Co. Rep. 1 a, [18a] (1608), *reprinted in* 77 Eng. Rep. 377, 398 (1932), Lord Coke stated that if a King conquers a Christian kingdom, "he may, at his pleasure, alter the laws of the kingdom, but until he [does] so the ancient laws ... remain. But if a Christian king should conquer the kingdom of an infidel, and bring them under his subjugation, [then] ipso facto, the laws of the infidels are abrogated, for that they are not only against Christianity but against the law of God and of nature, contained in the decalogue ...." However, by at least 1774, that distinction appears to have fallen into disrepute. *See, e.g.*, Campbell v. Hall, (1774) 98 Eng. Rep. 848 (K.B.) at 882 ("Don't quote the distinction [between Christians and non-Christians] for the honour of my Lord Coke.").

[51] David Pearl, Interpersonal Conflict of Laws in India, Pakistan, and Bangladesh 26 (1981). Pearl excludes Germany and notes that the recognition of indigenous law created an internal conflicts of law regime, which seems implicitly to recognize some sort of autonomous legitimacy for indigenous practices.

legal structure. These nation-states – ranging from Canada to the United Kingdom to Egypt to India to Singapore – recognize parallel civil and religious legal systems, often with their own separate courts.[52] And civil legal authorities are frequently called on to determine the margin of appreciation to be given to such personal law. For example, the Indian Supreme Court has famously attempted to bridge secular and Islamic law in two decisions involving Muslim women's right to maintenance after divorce.[53] At the same time, issues arise concerning the extent to which members of a particular religious or ethnic community can opt *out* of their personal law and adopt the law of the nation-state. For example, in 1988 a Sri Lankan court decided that a Muslim couple could adopt a child according to state regulation but could not confer inheritance rights on their adopted child because Islamic Law did not recognize adoption.[54] Even outside of the context of Islamic law, the United States Supreme Court has at times deferred to the independent parallel courts maintained by Indian populations located within U.S. territorial borders.[55] And beyond judicial bodies, we will increasingly see other governmental entities, such as banking regulators, forced to oversee forms of financing that conform to religious principles.[56] These sorts of negotiations, like all the limited autonomy regimes surveyed in this section, reflect official recognition of essential hybridity that the state cannot wish away.

C. Conflicts of Laws

Because non-state lawmaking is not usually conceived of as law, we do not usually think of clashes between state and non-state law through the prism of conflicts of law jurisprudence. But we could. Indeed, the three classic legal doctrines often grouped together under the rubric of conflict of laws – jurisdiction, choice of law, and judgment recognition – are specifically meant to manage hybrid legal spaces. However, although these doctrines are where one would most expect to see creative innovations springing forth to address

[52] *See* Bharathi Anandhi Venkatraman, *Islamic States and the United Nations Convention on the Elimination of All Forms of Discrimination Against Women: Are the Shari'a and the Convention Compatible?*, 44 Am. U. L. Rev. 1949, 1984 (1995); DeNeen L. Brown, *Canadians Allow Islamic Courts to Decide Disputes: Sharia Gains Foothold in Ontario*, Wash. Post, Apr. 28, 2004, at A14 (discussing an Islamic Court of Civil Justice in Ontario, staffed by arbitrators trained in both Sharia and Canadian civil law).

[53] *See* Latifi v. Union of India, A.I.R. 2001 S.C. 3958, 3973; Mohammed Ahmed Khan v. Shah Bano Begum, (1985) 3 S.C.R. 844 (India).

[54] *See, e.g.* Ghouse v. Ghouse, (1988) 1 Sri L.R. 25, 28.

[55] *See* Santa Clara Pueblo v. Martinez, 436 U.S. 49, 71–72 (1978).

[56] *See, e.g.*, Tavia Grant, *Sharia-Compliant Finance Is Increasingly Popular, Globe & Mail* (Toronto), May 7, 2007, https://secure.globeadvisor.com/servlet/ArticleNews/story/RTGAM/20070507/wrislam07.

hybridity, they have only infrequently been used in this way. Thus, it may be helpful to consider how communities could use choice-of-law and judgment recognition doctrines to manage the reality of multiple community affiliation.

To illustrate, I explore two well-known cases in which the U.S. Supreme Court was forced to determine how state-based lawmaking would interact with the norms of a religious community. First, in *Bob Jones University v. United States*, the Court addressed an IRS decision to deny tax-exempt status to a religious school that interpreted Christian scriptures to forbid "interracial dating and marriage."[57] Second, in *Employment Division, Department of Human Resources of Oregon v. Smith*, the question was whether a general state statute forbidding certain narcotics should be applied to an Indian tribe's religious practice that included the use of peyote.[58] To my mind, viewing these conflicts as choice-of-law questions makes the analytical framework more coherent (though, it should be noted, no less difficult).

Turning to *Bob Jones*, the Internal Revenue Service had interpreted Section 501(c)(3) of the Internal Revenue Code, which gives tax-exempt status to qualifying charitable institutions, to apply to schools only if such schools have a "racially nondiscriminatory policy as to students."[59] Accordingly, the Service denied tax exemption to Bob Jones University, which had not admitted blacks at all until 1971, and had admitted them thereafter but had forbidden interracial dating, interracial marriage, the espousal of violation of these prohibitions, and membership in groups that advocated interracial marriage.[60] Crucial to the case was the fact that the university grounded its rule not on racial attitudes, but on Biblical scripture. The school therefore considered the exclusion of interracial dating to be a principal tenet of its religious community.[61] Nevertheless, although the text of section 501(c)(3) did not speak to racial discrimination at all, the Supreme Court upheld the IRS determination, finding the service's interpretation of the code provision to be permissible.[62]

Robert Cover, in his article *Nomos and Narrative*, has famously criticized the reasoning of the *Bob Jones* decision, even while agreeing with the Court's result. According to Cover, the Court assumed "a position that places nothing at risk and from which the Court makes no interpretive gesture at all, save the quintessential gesture to the jurisdictional canons: the statement that an

[57] 461 U.S. 574, 580–82 (1983).
[58] 494 U.S. 872, 874 (1990).
[59] *Bob Jones*, 461 U.S. at 579.
[60] *Id.* at 580–81.
[61] *Id.* at 580.
[62] *Id.* at 595.

exercise of political authority was not unconstitutional."[63] In particular, Cover argued that, by grounding its decision on an interpretation of the Internal Revenue Code, the Court had sidestepped the crucial constitutional question of whether Congress could grant tax exemptions to schools that discriminated on the basis of race.[64] This was a problem for Cover because he believed that if a state legal authority were going to "kill off" the competing normative commitment of an alternative community, it should do so based on a profound normative commitment of its own.[65] By avoiding the constitutional question, Cover complained, the Court had disserved both the religious community – whose normative commitments would be placed at the mercy of mere public policy judgments – and disserved racial minorities – who "deserved a constitutional commitment to avoiding public subsidization of racism."[66]

In contrast, had the clash between the university's religious rule and the IRS code, or between the religious rule and the United States Constitution, been viewed as a choice-of-law decision, two aspects of the case would have been clarified. First, the Court would have analyzed and defined the relevant community affiliations at stake. Second, the Court would have been forced to grapple with the strength of its commitment to the principle of nondiscrimination, just as Cover urged. As a result, instead of simply asserting federal law, a conflicts analysis encourages negotiation among the different norms advanced by different communities.

A more cosmopolitan and pluralist vision of conflict of laws recognizes that people and groups hold multiple community affiliations and takes those affiliations seriously. Thus, when a non-state legal practice is largely internal and primarily reflects individuals' affiliation with the non-state community, the practice should be given more leeway than when the state itself is part of the relevant affiliation. In this case, the issue at stake was a tax exemption, a quintessentially state matter. Indeed, Bob Jones University was asking for a particular benefit for charitable organizations that was contained in the United States tax code. Therefore, for these purposes the place of the university within the nation-state was the most salient tie, making application of the federal law more justifiable. In contrast, as we shall see, other non-state normative commitments do not implicate the nation-state so directly.

Moreover, even if the relevant community tie were largely with the religious community itself, certain norms might be held so strongly by the nation-state community that such norms would be applied *regardless* of the community

---

[63] Cover, *supra* note 6, at 66.
[64] *Id.*
[65] *See id.* at 53–60.
[66] *Id.* at 67.

affiliation. In choice-of-law analysis, this is usually called the public policy exception, and it allows courts to refuse to apply foreign law that would otherwise apply, if those legal norms are sufficiently repugnant. However, as noted previously, application of the public policy exception is rare, both as a normative and descriptive matter. Thus, if a court asserts such an exception, it must justify the use of public policy grounds by reference to precisely the sorts of deeply held commitments that Cover envisioned. In the *Bob Jones* case, for example, it might be that the nation-state's deep commitment to eradicating racial discrimination would independently justify overriding the religious norms, regardless of the community affiliation analysis.

Accordingly, a conflicts approach would not simply throw the claim of protected religious insularity to the mercy of political or bureaucratic judgments. Taking the ban on interracial dating seriously as law and performing a choice-of-law analysis would create the obligation to engage in crucial line drawing. And although the community affiliation and public policy exception analyses *in this case* might justify application of state law, that will not always be the case.

Consider, by way of contrast, *Employment Division, Department of Human Resources of Oregon v. Smith*, in which the Supreme Court refused to extend First Amendment protection to the religious use of peyote.[67] There, unlike the tax exemption at issue in *Bob Jones*, the Indian tribe was not negotiating its relationship with the state; rather the use of peyote was part of a purely internal religious practice open primarily (or exclusively) to members of that community. Thus, a choice-of-law analysis based on community affiliation might well result in deference to the non-state norm. Moreover, the normative commitment to drug enforcement is perhaps better characterized as a governance choice than as an inexorable normative command. As such, the public policy exception is arguably less appropriate in this context than when addressing racial discrimination. Applying these principles, a choice-of-law analysis might well have permitted the religious practice in *Smith*.

In the end, however, I am less concerned with the particular outcome than with the analytical framework. Conceiving of these clashes between religious and state-based norms in conflicts terms reorients the inquiry in a way that takes more seriously the non-state community assertion. As a result, courts must wrestle both with the nature of the multiple community affiliations potentially at issue and with the need to articulate truly strong normative justifications for not deferring to the non-state norm. Both consequences make the choice-of-law decision a constructive terrain of engagement among multiple

[67] 494 U.S. 872 (1990).

normative systems, rather than an arm of state government imposing its normative vision on all within its coercive power.

Of course, this vision is not unproblematic. Two related objections immediately present themselves. First, a choice-of-law rule that tends to defer to non-state norms when they implicate only internal community affiliation might be seen to rest on the often-criticized distinction between public and private action. Indeed, the idea of deference in this context might come to look like the classic state deference to family privacy or autonomy.[68] And just as family privacy was often invoked to shield domestic violence and gender hierarchy, so too may deference to "internal" community norms become deference to fundamentally illiberal norms.

Second, as in the family context, we may make a mistake by assuming that the non-state community at issue is monolithic. Indeed, it may be that some members of the relevant community would prefer to have the *state* norm applied to their situation. As Judith Resnik has noted, Cover's vision of multiple norm-generating communities did not address the problem of conflict "*within* [such] communities about their own practices and authoritative interpretations."[69] Yet, such "contestation from within"[70] (which is likely to occur along the fault lines of power hierarchies within the community) is an almost inevitable part of community norm creation. Thus, the choice-of-law question becomes, in part, a question of whose voices within a community are heard by which speakers of nation-state power.

As to the concern that too much deference to "private" norms within a community will overly empower illiberal communities, it is important to remember that, because of the public policy exception, these norms, if sufficiently abhorrent, need not be applied by the state authority. After all, a lynch mob may also be a statement of community norms, but it need not for that reason necessarily be embraced. The object of a choice-of-law analysis is not to blindly follow non-state community norms, but to ensure that if a state asserts its own norms it does so self-consciously. Indeed, simply identifying the state's jurispathic power does not necessarily mean that we must reject all exercises of that power.[71] Even Cover recognized the utility of a state court's speaking in "imperial mode."[72] He noted that, when judges kill off competing law by

[68] *See, e.g.,* Frances E. Olsen, *The Myth of State Intervention in the Family,* 18 U. Mich. J. L. Reform 835, 836–37 (1985).

[69] Judith Resnik, *Living Their Legal Commitments: Paideic Communities, Courts, and Robert Cover,* 17 Yale J.L. & Human. 17, 27 (2005).

[70] *Id.*

[71] *See id.* at 25.

[72] *See* Cover, *supra* note 6, at 13–14.

asserting that *"this one* is law," they may do violence to the competing visions, but they also enable peace both because too much law is too chaotic to sustain and because some laws are simply too noxious to be applied.[73] The point then is simply to make sure that the imposition of imperial, jurispathic law is not done blindly or arrogantly, but with intentionality and a respect for the other sources of lawmaking that are being displaced.[74] A conflicts analysis at least opens space for such self-consciousness and care.

More difficult is the problem of how to respond to Resnik's arguments about inevitable conflicts within a non-state community concerning the content of that community's norms. Certainly the existence of significant disagreement within the community might be factored into the decision of whether to apply the state norm. Thus, if some substantial portion of the non-state community were clamoring for the application of *state* law, such clamoring might blunt somewhat the need to defer to the non-state norm.

More important, in thinking about how to address disputes within a non-state community, we must distinguish between two types of challenges. One concerns the proper understanding of what the content of the community's law *actually is*, and the other concerns what that law *ought to be*. For example, in *Santa Clara Pueblo v. Martinez*, a woman who was a member of an Indian tribe challenged her tribe's refusal to consider her children to be tribal members.[75] She did so, however, not based on an argument that the tribe had improperly interpreted its own community law (which based tribal membership on the father's tribal membership, not the mother's). Instead, she argued that the tribe's law was inconsistent with a federal equal protection statute.[76] Thus, the case did not present a contestation about the content of the community's norms; it merely raised a choice-of-law issue about whether the tribal law or the federal statute should govern. And however difficult the resolution of that choice-of-law question might be, it does not raise the conundrum of how to determine the appropriate content of the non-state norms in the first place.

Finally, in those relatively infrequent situations when the actual content of the non-state norm *is* at issue, courts can seek evidence to determine that community's governing norm. Historical documentation, anthropological

---

[73] *See id.* at 53.
[74] *See* Resnik, *supra* note 80, at 25 ("[Cover] wanted the state's actors ... to be uncomfortable in their knowledge of their own power, respectful of the legitimacy of competing legal systems, and aware of the possibility that multiple meanings and divergent practices ought sometimes to be tolerated, even if painfully so.").
[75] 436 U.S. 49, 49 (1978).
[76] *Id.* at 51.

testimony, and evidence of ongoing practice might all be relevant. And again, to the extent that there are concerns that the non-state norm is the product of hierarchy, those concerns can be factored into the choice-of-law inquiry itself; they do not render it impossible to determine the content of the norm.

Conclusion

A jurisprudence of hybridity does not, of course, make it any easier to reach actual decisions in individual cases. Indeed, determining when to defer to a non-state norm and when not, when to allow a margin of appreciation and when to insist on a state norm, when to carve out zones of autonomy and when to encroach on them – these are all issues that are probably impossible ever to resolve satisfactorily. And I do not suggest that merely adopting a more inclusive set of jurisprudential or institutional mechanisms will eliminate clashes between state and non-state normative communities. Such clashes are both inevitable and unlikely ever to be dissolved.

But the relevant question, it seems to me, is not whether law can eliminate conflict, but whether it has a chance of mediating disputes among multiple communities. And this question becomes increasingly important as normative communities increasingly overlap and intersect. Accordingly, instead of bemoaning the messiness of jurisdictional overlaps, we should accept them as a necessary consequence of the fact that communities cannot be hermetically sealed off from each other. Moreover, we can go further and consider the possibility that this jurisdictional messiness might, in the end, provide important systemic benefits by fostering dialogue among multiple constituencies, authorities, levels of government, and non-state communities. In addition, jurisdictional redundancy allows alternative ports of entry for strategic actors who might otherwise be silenced.

Most fundamentally, all of this interaction is elided or ignored if we continue to think and speak as if legal and quasi-legal spheres can be formally differentiated from each other. Instead, we need to accept and perhaps even celebrate, the potentially jurisgenerative and creative role law might play in a plural world. Indeed, it is only if we take multiple affiliation seriously, if we seek dialogue across difference, if we accept unassimilated otherness, that we will have some hope of navigating the hybrid legal spaces that are all around us.

Excerpts From:

Butler, Brian E. (2003) Aesthetics and American Law. *Legal Studies Forum*
27(1):203–220.

AESTHETICS AND AMERICAN LAW

Brian E. Butler (2003)

I. Introduction

Pierre Schlag in "The Aesthetics of American Law"[77] argues for an investigation of the aesthetic attributes of law. Aesthetics, Schlag contends, is broader
than an understanding of beauty, and is better seen as a discipline that
"pertains to the forms, images, tropes, perceptions, and sensibilities that help
shape the creation, apprehension, and even identity of human endeavors,
including, most topically, law."[78] Schlag identifies and deploys four "recurring
forms," the: (1) grid aesthetic; (2) energy aesthetic; (3) perspective aesthetic;
and (4) the dissociative aesthetic, to explain various aspects of legal theory and
practice.[79] The main point of Schlag's "The Aesthetics of American Law" is
that not only do aesthetic issues influence the decisions and internal workings
of law, but aesthetics "bring what we call law into being."[80]

Some issues in American law have a direct connection to aesthetics, but the
aesthetic issues are resolved by ordinary legal procedures (although both philosophical and jurisprudential issues may be raised, even if unaddressed by these
legal procedures). Obscenity laws which separate legitimate art from pornogra-
phy are a clear example. Courts deal with municipal aesthetic regulations[81] and
decide what is permissible architecturally and what is legally prohibited. And still
more obviously, free speech issues intersect constantly with artistic creativity.[82]

---

[77] Pierre Schlag, *The Aesthetics of American Law*, 115 Harv. L. Rev. 1047 (2002).

[78] *Id.* at 1050.

[79] *Id.* at 1051–1052.

[80] *Id.* at 1053. I agree with Schlag's claim that aesthetics permeates the internal workings of law
and conspires to bring law into being. But there is more to the aesthetic analysis of law than
Schlag explores in his "The Aesthetics of American Law." In this essay I highlight some issues
which Schlag either gives short shrift or ignores altogether. Further, I will argue that Schlag's
characterization of aesthetics is, in a fundamental way, misleading.

[81] *See* Randall Cude, *Beauty and the Well-Drawn Ordinance: Avoiding Vagueness and
Overbreadth Challenges to Municipal Aesthetic Regulations*, 6 J. Law & Pol'y 853 (1998).

[82] An interesting example of this is the controversy surrounding Serra's *Tilted Arc*. *See* Richard
Serra, *Art and the Law: Suppression and Liberty – The Titled Arc Controversy*, 19 Cardozo Arts
& Ent. L. J. 39 (2001).

We also find aesthetic issues decided by courts in the area of copyright law[83] and environmental law.[84] In all of these areas, aesthetic issues are determined through legal mechanisms.

Beyond the substantive legal issues raised by aesthetics and addressed directly by the law, Schlag is concerned about still broader issues of textual interpretation (of interest to both courts and jurisprudential scholars) and philosophical issues common to both law and aesthetics, and it is those broader, global philosophical issues which I address here.[85]

I begin by exploring the claim that artistic expressions influence the way law is practiced. The effects can be found detrimental or edifying. For instance, some scholars find the influence of modern media detrimental to the neutrality and fairness promised by way of legal process. Other scholars, particularly those associated with the field of "law and literature," argue that literature may be helpful in sensitizing legal professionals to the broader context and intricacies within which law is enacted and practiced.

Law itself may be considered as a form of artistic production. And even it is not an art in itself, we may find in the study of legal practice aesthetic qualities associated with authority and reason, the primary virtues associated with law. Since both reason and authority are contested concepts, and law attempts to objectify these ideas with concrete symbols, we may find that a study of aesthetics allows us to expose presuppositions about authority, reason and the relationship between them as they relate to the rule of law. Finally, I return to Schlag's analysis and argue that he has offered a flawed conception of what labeling something "aesthetic" means in the study of law and jurisprudence.

II. Influences of Art on Law

The products of cultural art influence legal practice in various ways and with varying results. The argument over results is taken up by Richard Sherwin in *When Law Goes Pop*[86] where he claims that an ever-present contemporary media has a detrimental effect upon the legal profession, that the law has been so infected by television and film representations of law and lawyers that

---

[83] *See e.g.,* Alfred Yen, *Copyright Opinions and Aesthetic Theory*, 71 So. Calif. L. Rev. 247 (1998).

[84] For environmental laws *see* John Costonis, Icons And Aliens (Urbana: University of Illinois Press, 1989).

[85] In recent years, scholars have begin to address these philosophical issues of aesthetics and law. *See* Costas Douzinas & Lynda Neal, Law and the Image (Chicago: University of Chicago Press, 1999); Adam Gearey, Law and Aesthetics (Oxford: Hart Publishing, 2001); Roberta Kevelson (ed.), Law and Aesthetics (New York: Peter Lang, 1992); Desmond Manderson, Songs Without Music: Aesthetic Dimensions of Law and Justice (Berkeley: University of California Press, 2000).

[86] Richard Sherwin, When Law Goes Pop: The Vanishing Line Between Law and Popular Culture (Chicago: University of Chicago Press, 2000).

legal practice has been irretrievably altered.[87] Sherwin argues that this media infection of the law has so detrimentally "thinned" legal meanings that law has become spectacle. The "customary balance within the legal system among disparate forms of knowledge, discourse, and power" are "flattened out as they yield to the compelling visual logic of film and TV images and the market forces that fuel their production."[88] Law, according to Sherwin, had traditionally refused to privilege a single source of knowledge.[89] But with the influence of the media, legal storytelling is now beginning to adapt to the expectations of TV storytelling. The courtroom is now awash in the images and metaphors drawn from mass media. While "law cases enact a battle for reality," the fight must now take place within the (reductionist) options offered by the media.[90] Sherwin finds that this "estheticization of the real"[91] conflates law with the media images of law and in doing so delegitimates legal practice by calling into question the "autonomy" of law and the justice of individual case results. Law, infected by popular culture, also loses its ability to act as a check upon popular passions. What is offered by the media is stereotypes and intensified passions, not the reasoned articulations about particulars that might lead to justice.

Sherwin goes on to seek out sources of narrative meaning that will help combat the leveling aspects of pop culture. In doing so, he repeats, if in altered form, the conventional belief that images, as opposed to argument, short-circuit our reasoning abilities and aim at baser (less rational) faculties such as those related to physical consumption and pleasure. In other words, image-based persuasion is a shallow and pernicious form of "illicit persuasion."[92] Sherwin is concerned that an "image-based" justice can be so seductive that it sweeps away the "actual facts and applicable case law."[93]

The conclusion offered by Sherwin in *When Law Goes Pop* is that pop culture subverts the legitimate aspects of legal practice – the specific institutional competencies of the legal system – and substitutes simplifying images for the more rational processes and competing literary narratives traditionally deployed in law courts.[94] Whether Sherwin's descriptions of traditional law or

---

[87] *Id.* at ix.
[88] *Id.* at 4.
[89] *Id.* at 216.
[90] *Id.* at 24.
[91] *Id.* at 26.
[92] *Id.* at 243.
[93] *Id.* at 193.
[94] One aspect of Sherwin's argument that seems clearly problematic is his emphasis upon in-court proceedings. Most aspects of legal practice are more literary and office-bound. If this is accepted, then it becomes difficult to see how media images can be as influential as argued in the book.

the effect of modern media on contemporary legal practice are to be accepted is less important than his larger philosophical argument that aesthetic products of modern culture have deep and influential effects upon the practice of law.

In contrast to Sherwin's claims, other scholars who accept the premise that law is influenced by culture and art do not find the same negative effects and results as does Sherwin. For example, we find that some cultural products, most significantly the literary novel, have an edifying effect on law and legal actors. Martha Nussbaum, in *Poetic Justice*, argues that legal argumentation and judicial decision-making would be greatly improved if lawyers and judges adopted a diet of novel reading.[95] In contrast to the technical, legalistic style of today's legal opinions, "the novel constructs a paradigm of a style of ethical reasoning that is context-specific without being relativistic, in which we get potentially universalizable concrete prescriptions by bringing a general idea of human flourishing to bear on concrete situation, which we are invited to enter through the imagination."[96] Nussbaum argues that legal reasoning (of the best kind) requires sympathy for the human condition, and for particularities, that other formal modes of legal reasoning and reasoning based on law and economics cannot provide. Nussbaum finds the novel effective in stimulating the ability to imagine oneself in the place of another, and therefore prompts a more nuanced version of justice than results from impersonal, institutional driven approaches to law (qualities of law which some find to be its most distinct virtues). If this argument is correct, legal education would need to make place for the reading of novels as well as judicial opinions (a practice some law teachers have already adopted). Following Nussbaum, we may find that "images" (construed broadly) made available by culture deepen meanings and expand the arguments we find in law rather than flatten them.

With both Sherwin and Nussbaum we find thoughtful explorations of how artistic products influence practices within the realm of law. But there is another more intimate way to explore the connection of law with aesthetic issues. As Schlag hints, law can be investigated as an aesthetic product in its own right.

III. Law as Literature

The most common and accessible characterization of law as an aesthetic enterprise can be found by legal scholars associated with the "law and literature" movement, which is part of what may now be called "narrative

---

[95] Martha Nussbaum, Poetic Justice (Boston: Beacon Press, 1995).

[96] *Id.* at 8. Nussbaum's analysis of *Bowers v. Harwick* provides a convincing example of how legal argumentation uses the strategy of distancing and generality to reach insensitive and unjustified conclusions.

jurisprudence."[97] As Robin West argues, even jurisprudential and legal theorists (writing in what they assume are abstractions), "persistently employ narrative plots at strategic points in their arguments."[98] Consequently, a schema like Northrop Frye's aesthetic theories can be adapted by West to analyze the aesthetic modes of modern jurisprudence.

The rhetorical and narrative strategies of law reviews – the traditional source of commentary on legal doctrine – is called into question by Patricia Williams's critique of legal reasoning and legalistic attitudes of law students in *The Alchemy of Race and Rights*.[99] Williams recounts how she provided a law review with a manuscript which centered on a racially charged experience at Benetton's. Williams describes how her law review article changed as it went through multiple edits authored by the student editors of the law review. As she tells it, in the first edit all the painful emotions of the experience were eliminated in favor of the "passive impersonal."[100] In the second edit all references to Benetton's were eliminated for "legal" reasons. Finally, another edit eliminated all references to her race. Arguing against the changes, she was told by the student editor she was being too emotional. "What was most interesting to me in this experience," says Williams, "was how the blind application of principles of neutrality, through the device of omission, acted either to make me look crazy or to make the reader participate in old habits of cultural bias."[101] She concludes that the "impersonal" writing demanded by the law review was a form of "denial of self." We may indeed want to deny the self, but we should, argues Williams, "be clearer about that as the bottom line of the enterprise. We should also acknowledge the extent to which denial of one's authority in authorship is not the same as elimination of oneself; it is a ruse, not reality."[102] Williams sees this formulaic and impersonal writing style as entailing a legal education that enforces an "aesthetic of uniformity."[103] It is this aesthetics of law review style – a stylized neutrality – which eliminates significant human experiences from the realm of the "legally cognizable."

---

[97] Richard Posner has argued that the claims of the "law and literature" scholars are overstated. *See* Richard Posner, Law and Literature: A Misunderstood Relation 79 (Cambridge: Harvard University Press, 1988). Posner does, however, concede that the study of literature may properly sensitize lawyers to the "great issues that law intersects." *Id.* at 175.

[98] Robin West, *Jurisprudence as Narrative: An Aesthetic Analysis of Modern Legal Theory*, 60 N.Y.U. L. Rev. 145–146 (1985).

[99] Patricia Williams, The Alchemy of Race and Rights (Cambridge: Harvard University Press, 1991).

[100] *Id.* at 47.

[101] *Id.* at 48.

[102] *Id.* at 92.

[103] *Id.* at 117.

Beyond analysis of the literary elements of jurisprudential theory and law review article aesthetics is an analysis of legal practice as a literary enterprise. Desmond Manderson claims that "the discourse of law is fundamentally governed by rhetoric, metaphor, form, images, and symbols."[104] Thomas Beebee argues that "judicial procedure constructs not just law itself, but also reality," therefore law is a type of "poesis."[105] A proper understanding of legal practice would highlight its constructive poesis. Law as poesis is a place where narrative possibilities compete for the right to be held as "the" true description of the world. Law, in this sense is creative every bit as much as it is reactive in nature, a fact that both traditional theories of law and an aesthetics of law must explain. A theory that ignores the creative aspect of law can be seen as descriptively false.

Further, admission of the poesis of law and the creative side of legal practice, forces acceptance of a new self-image for legal practitioners, with new obligations. For example, Adam Gearey in *Law and Aesthetics* observes that awareness of the proactive, constructive side of law, should push us towards a "Nietzschean aesthetic responsibility" where law is based upon a duty to create.[106] Reading the law as a creative literary practice has been the foundation of James Boyd White's scholarly writing over the past thirty years. White sees the literary and rhetorical aspect of law as placing legal activity in the realm of the humanities rather than as a social science.[107] The main question, in this view of the law, is "what worlds, what communities, our expressions and writings create. In our hands, what kind of theater can the law be, or become."[108] With this view of law, our view of lawyers, our sense of legal argumentation, and the role of judges changes (as do so many other aspects and "images" of the law).

Even if the hope for Nietzschean creativity is discounted (as I think it should be), and lawyers are not expected to be artists, it seems hard to argue against some of the "law as literature" claims. The greater part of law is a language-based product. Lawyers and judges make up a profession of writers. Case law, statutes, and constitutions are all written documents. Acknowledging the craft and influence of writing shows a close connection between law and aesthetic issues. And yet, the consciousness of the law's (and lawyers) literary qualities have remained marginal in both legal education and the practice of law.

---

[104] Desmond Manderson, Songs Without Music: Aesthetic Dimensions of Law and Justice ix (Berkeley: University of California Press, 2000).

[105] Thomas Beebee, The Legal Theaters of Bertolt Brecht in Law and Aesthetics 37–67, at 43 (Roberta Kevelson ed., New York: Peter Lang, 1992).

[106] Adam Gearey, Law and Aesthetics 56–58 (Oxford: Hart Publishing, 2001).

[107] James Boyd White, Heracles' Bow: Essays on the Rhetoric and Poetics of the Law xii (Madison: University of Wisconsin Press, 1985).

[108] *Id.* at 26.

IV. The Aesthetics of Authority and the Aesthetics of Reason

Why are the literary aspects of law so often ignored, the aesthetic aspects of law so conspicuously discounted? Law and legal practice purport to be a "discipline" and an academic subject of study that need not claim allegiance to either the social sciences or the humanities. Yet, if the law stands apart as a discipline, it must still justify itself. The most important type of justification law offers – in over abundance – is that it produces results that are derived from legitimate authority. Yet, law signals its authority via aesthetic means. As Peter Goodrich explains, law "is in many aspects to be taken as a plastic art, of architecture, statuary, dress, heraldry, painting and insignia – gold rings, rods, coifs, seals and rolls – which provide popular consciousness with a Justice which can be seen and remembered."[109] We are presented the law by way of the judge's robe, the ritualistic invocation of oaths and seals – all clearly aim at reinforcing the appearance of authority.[110] Apparent even to lay observers, the activities of the law, especially trials, take place within temple-like structures. In comparison to other public institutions, law seems more aesthetically charged with symbolic meanings than any other branch of the government. Even the most visible institution in the private side of law, the law firm, is aesthetically packaged so as to attach its power to the authority of tradition, culture and knowledge.

The aesthetics of authority offered by law is, in many ways, similar to the aesthetics of authority found in religious practices. Robes, rituals and grandiose buildings are common to both, as are the esoteric texts and specialized methods of interpretation. Also common to both religion and law are ritualistic appeals to the traditions and legitimacy of institutional hierarchies. Law, like religion, is tethered to its metaphysical transcendental sources of authority. Yet, in modern society law is largely viewed as a domain detached from religious sources of justification; law purports to replace religion with a metaphysics of democratic procedure and "reason."

Whether law is characterized as a system of social organization, dispute resolution, or a means of particularized justice, its contemporary claim to justification rests largely upon its appeal to being founded upon and driven by reason drawing on firmly established principles. It is reason and principle that we assume to be the basis for justness of court decisions. (A bad judicial decision

---

[109] Peter Goodrich, "The Iconography of Nothing: Blank Spaces and the Representation of Law in *Edward VI and the Pope*," In *Costas Douzinas & Lynda Neal (eds.), Law and the Image: The Authority of Law and the Aesthetics of Law* 89–114, at 206 (Chicago: University of Chicago Press, 1999).

[110] *See* Peter Winn "Legal Ritual," in Roberta Kevelson (ed.), Law and Aesthetics 401–442 (New York: Peter Lang, 1992) (discussion of the relation of law and ritual).

is, thus, attributed to bad reasoning.) Law's claim to legitimate authority rests, in large part, upon its characterization as a system ruled by reason, reason which must be presented in its symbols, symbols used operationally by legal practitioners so routinely that they become a form of popular consciousness.

Beginning with Blackstone's *Commentaries*, according to Daniel Boorstin, we find an "aesthetics of reason" used to justify English common law.[111] According to Boorstin, Blackstone's aesthetics of reason in law was assumed to have been discovered in nature.[112] It was an aesthetics of simplicity, symmetry, and balance, but also an aesthetics which contemplated disorder, complexity, and obscurity. It was, from beginning to end, a "rationalist aesthetic."[113] For Blackstone, the aesthetics of the common law naturally mirrored nature, a nature made beautiful because it was a manifestation of universal laws of reason.

Janice Toran identifies a similar attitudinal aesthetic in contemporary legal reformers.[114] According to Toran, aesthetic considerations such as simplicity, elegance, and coherence are factors which directly influence legal decisions.[115] Adam Geary describes this as "a belief in the inherent worth of form."[116] This aspect of law often carries with it a sense of harmony; everything in its own proper place. The questionable move here is to assume that we are talking about reason (in the rhetoric of neutrality and objectivity) and not aesthetics.

Law may be guided by reason, but the law provides no means by which to test its system of guidance other than to appeal to its own internal formalistic criteria. As Adam Geary puts it, "law is a kind of confidence trick, as way of making society appear. If one is not aware that legal concepts are reified and abstracted, they appear to have some kind of foundational substance, a kind of autonomy or independent being. This loses sight of the notion that the system manufactures its own conditions of legitimacy and then attempts to legislate them as *a priori* universals that have a legitimizing effect through their appeal to reason."[117]

The best example of this type of circular and insular internal justification grounded in an aesthetics of reason is Ronald Dworkin's theory of "law as

---

[111] Daniel Boorstin, The Mysterious Science of the Law (Gloucester: Peter Smith, 1973). It is important to note that Blackstone's *Commentaries* is generally acknowledged to be one of the most important influences in the practice of early American law.

[112] *Id.* at 90.

[113] *Id.* at 104.

[114] Janice Toran, *'Tis a Gift to be Simple: Aesthetics and Procedural Reform*, 89 Mich. L. Rev. 352 (1990).

[115] *Id.* at 355.

[116] Adam Geary, Law and Aesthetics 4 (Oxford: Hart Publishing, 2001).

[117] *Id.* at 32.

integrity."[118] Dworkin's theory rests upon a strong attachment to the concept of "principle" and his view of "rights as trumps."[119] A principled system of law is largely characterized as one that rejects "checkerboard" laws and results. The checkerboard effect results in similar legal events distinguished in an "arbitrary" manner on grounds which vary case to case. But just what exactly is a similar case and when is treatment arbitrary? And why do checkerboard laws fail at offering anything more than arbitrary distinctions? These are, of course, key issues in most legal philosophy. Dworkin's explanation is telling. First, he admits that checkerboard laws may hypothetically succeed in providing fair solutions[120] (and he further admits that some non-checkerboard laws are unjust[121]). So the dilemma: "we have no reason of justice for rejecting the checkerboard strategy in advance, and strong reasons of fairness for endorsing it. Yet our instincts condemn it."[122] The solution: we oppose checkerboard laws because "we say that a state that adopts these internal compromises is acting in an unprincipled way."[123] They don't live up to the vision of law as integrity that Dworkin offers. So how does Dworkin help us understand his "legal integrity" argument? The law is to be imagined as "chain novel." And it is with the "chain novel" metaphor and image that Dworkin's grounds his jurisprudence in aesthetics.

According to Dworkin judges should interpret laws as if they were authors of a chain novel where a "group of writers writes a novel *seriatim*; each novelist in the chain interprets the chapters he has been given in order to write a new chapter." The interpretive rule that governs the enterprise is that each author "has the job of writing his chapter so as to make the novel being constructed the best it can be."[124] First, note the Latin flourish – a legal profession favorite. Second, note that "best" here rests largely upon an assumption that unity is better than fragmentation.[125] This seems to be an aesthetic preference that Dworkin finds no reason to justify but can assume as a given.

The two tests that the law and the chain novel must pass are "fit" and the result must reflect the "best all things considered,"[126] both of which even Dworkin admits are largely aesthetic considerations.[127] The circularity of this

---

[118] Ronald Dworkin, Law's Empire (Cambridge: Harvard University Press, 1986).
[119] "Rights as trumps" is one of many powerful images found in Dworkin's jurisprudence. The seductive nature of Dworkin's arguments rests largely upon his masterful use of vivid imagery.
[120] *Id.*
[121] *Id.* at 180.
[122] *Id.* at 182.
[123] *Id.* at 183.
[124] *Id.* at 229.
[125] *Id.*
[126] *Id.* at 230–231.
[127] *Id.* at 231.

theory should be apparent as well as is Dworkin's belief in the inherent worth of form, in the equation of reason with simplicity and coherence. It is meant to look like rigorous and principled reasoning, although most of the more important questions go unanswered. While both Geary and White would have the lawyer, judge, and scholar ask which narrative possibility creates the "best" world, Dworkin's integrity thesis places us squarely in the realm of law as a separate domain. Dworkin's judge makes law the best it could be – not the world.

Returning to Schlag's exploration of law and aesthetics, we find Schlag arguing that "Dworkin achieved his elegant solution only by climbing to an exceedingly rarefied level of abstraction," offering a jurisprudence "never touching the ground, always spinning in on itself."[128] Aesthetics teaches that law most surely cannot be separate and apart from the world in which we must both produce and judge the law's results. But this isn't to condemn Dworkin because his jurisprudence is determined by aesthetic principles, but rather due to the fact that his adopted aesthetic is not the most desirable one.

V. Pierre Schlag's View of Aesthetics

There are aesthetic aspects to law that Schlag either ignores or glosses too quickly. More importantly, there is an aspect of Schlag's analysis I think seriously misleading, primarily his conception of what attaching the label "aesthetic" means to a discipline or dispute.

The attachment of the label "aesthetic" to a discipline is important because, as Schlag claims, aesthetic issues "shape the ways in which we think law, do law, and imagine law's future directions. They shape its very identity."[129] This shaping is a substantial part of legal education where students are inculcated "sub rosa [with] a certain aesthetic of social and economic relations."[130] Finally, this aesthetic shaping (and the inculcation of an aesthetics) is of practical importance because our aesthetic conceptions of law become so convincing that they make our conclusions seem required and inevitable when they are neither necessary nor particularly appealing.[131]

The labeling of an aesthetic enterprise is first broached by Schlag when he states his own aims in writing the article. Describing the article itself as an aesthetic project, Schlag views his work as "an attempt to awaken in the reader a sensitivity for and a recognition of the different aesthetics of law." Yet, he "cannot "define" these aesthetics or "prove" their existence" but can only show

---

[128] *Id.*
[129] *Id.* at 1102.
[130] *Id.* at 1104.
[131] *Id.* at 1114.

"how it feels to enact or inhabit a particular aesthetic."[132] For Schlag, once a project is labeled aesthetics in nature, reasoning and argument are at an end. What is now demanded of the reader is no longer the capacity to reason but "a certain imaginative empathy."[133]

> Once a dispute becomes explicitly a contest of aesthetics, there is not a whole lot more to say other than, "Well, that's just the way I see things." The obvious reply, "Well, you should see things my way," is perhaps worth a try, but it is just as likely to meet with the answer, "I tried, but I just don't see it that way.[134]

This is a view of aesthetics as the limit of the rational, a view consistent with Sherwin's claim that images (drawn from popular culture) short-circuit the law's reasoning processes. For Schlag, once this characterization of aesthetics and reason is accepted, "a great number of jurisprudential problems become at once clear, rationally insoluble, and no longer terribly interesting."[135] That is, the issues become largely a matter of "I just do or don't see it that way."

This, I think, is a serious misunderstanding of what labeling something aesthetic entails. First, the argument falls prey to something very analogous to that of thinking that aesthetics only deals with issues of beauty. As any person familiar with modern art knows, even a narrow picture of aesthetic issues must include with beauty, issues of the ugly, the sublime, and the meaningful (and how we are to talk about and represent these notions). We have, with these issues, a combining of the sensory and the cognitive in ways that make them inseparable. But this does not mean that the cognitive, and our "rational" capacities become irrelevant and may not still be dispositive of many issues. Indeed, the agreement in scholarly circles on distinctions about the nature and quality of various works of art can be properly attributed to rational argumentation. That mistakes will be made and adjustments necessary is not a counter-example but simply suggests that rationality should not be associated with certainty in any field. The view of the aesthetic as the limit of the rational is a symptom of a conception of reason too attached to architectonic distinctions and purified realms of objectivity. The reductionist conclusion that aesthetics is the limit of the rational is analogous to the mistaken idea that moral beliefs are best characterized as simply emotive preferences and cannot be explored or resolved by rational argument.

[132] *Id.* at 1054.
[133] *Id.*
[134] *Id.* at 1105–1106.
[135] *Id.* at 1102.

This leads to a second worrisome aspect of Schlag's characterization of aesthetics as offering four "meta-aesthetics" (or "meta-analogies") that determine choices. The main problem here is that we are given a top-down (deductive) view of the influence of aesthetics on legal practice and theory. The aesthetic is, I contend, in a far more intimate relationship with the rational than Schlag suggests and is admittedly less "univocal." In contrast to Schlag, I find multiple, overlapping, intersecting types of reasoning in law, and that these forms of reasoning rely upon aesthetic images and aesthetic argument. In my view, we need a less hierarchical picture of legal argumentation, one which does not seek to make it immune from influences from the most humble of the "lower" sources.

In law (and aesthetics), the questions often come down to analogies and our ways of seeing the world. Some are more useful, more accurate, and more seductive, more beautiful, than others. We choose an analogy for its usefulness, its aesthetics, and through traditional means of argumentation and reason. Aesthetic stances are not self-enclosed and homogeneous domains, therefore we can reason from one to the other; we can reason within them, between them, and around them. Even if one aesthetic is dominant, we may by way of argument, find that we can be convinced that another analogy (or aesthetic) is more justified. This calls into question the impression Schlag gives that one can reason within an aesthetic but not between them.[136]

Adopting a more cognitive-oriented, nuanced conception of aesthetic, allows us to see that the distinction between argument form and aesthetic form is not one of type but of degree. From this juncture we can see that the claim that law is inherently an aesthetic enterprise is not nearly so radical as it sounds. It is a matter of seeing how people argue for their aesthetic beliefs (and the conclusions that follow from them) instead of stopping with a platitude: "There is no accounting for taste." If we find Dworkin's jurisprudential theory misleading as well as aesthetically determined, we don't have to say, "I just see things differently" but things like, "Dworkin's theories always seem to have the feel of a foregone conclusions," or, "While I often agree with Dworkin's ultimate conclusions the reasons he offers often seem insubstantial." With statements of this kind, the reasoning process remains intact and can now begin in earnest. We have not used aesthetics to end the conversation with the claim and the impasse: "We just choose to differ." While a person who desires clarity over descriptive accuracy might want to see aesthetics as non-cognitive and reason, at its best, purified of aesthetic bias (what Schlag describes as aesthetic

---

[136] *See e.g., id.* 1109–1110.

"skewing"[137]), this position does not lend itself to our best understanding of the workings of law, lawyers, and judges.

VI. Conclusion

In this survey of the ways that aesthetics is implicated in our understanding and practice of law, one thing becomes clear – aesthetic issues are unavoidable. Law deals with various aesthetic concerns explicitly and directly, but is at its core a more aesthetic-shaped enterprise than we generally think. It is quite odd that a domain of social practice so thoroughly overdetermined symbolically, can be viewed as if it were immune to and independent of aesthetics. Or worse, aesthetics is viewed as the basis for bias, emotion, and pernicious passions. But we might note, that an impoverished sensitivity to the aesthetic nature of a discipline is not the same thing as lacking an aesthetic. Law's aesthetic gains legitimacy as it denies its aesthetic and holds itself forth as a highly formalized aesthetics of reason and authority, a fetish of form. But this is a highly questionable source of legitimacy.

While Pierre Schlag is right to see aesthetic issues as being constitutive of legal practices the conclusion he draws from this premise is misleading. We need not conclude that a dispute, legal problem, or legal practice, viewed as a contest of aesthetics means that we end the conversation with, "Well, that's just the way I see things." Aesthetics need not (indeed cannot) take us beyond the limits of rational inquiry and argument. The aesthetic is always in an intimate relationship with the rational. We can always attempt to argue rationally between aesthetic accounts and premises of the law just as we have learned to do in dealing with any art.

BIBLIOGRAPHY

Beebee, Thomas O. 1992. "The Legal Theaters of Bertolt Brecht." Pp. 37–67 in *Law and Aesthetics*, edited by Roberta Kevelson. New York: Peter Lang.

Binder, Guyora. 2001. "The Poetics of the Pragmatic: What Literary Criticisms of Law Offers Posner." *Stanford Law Review* **53**: 1509–1540.

Boorstin, Daniel J. 1973. *The Mysterious Science of the Law: An Essay on Blackstone's* Commentaries, *Showing How Blackstone's Eighteen Century Ideas of Science, Religion, History, Aesthetics, and Philosophy, Made of the Law at Once a Conservative and a Mysterious Science* Gloucester: Peter Smith.

---

[137] *Id.* at 1109.

Braun, Christopher K. 1992. "Pro Bono Habits: Signs, Confession and Play." Pp. 69–94 in *Law and Aesthetics*, edited by Roberta Kevelson. New York: Peter Lang.

Caudill, David S. 1992. "Psyche as Legal Text: Lacan's Return to Freud the Semiotician." Pp. 117–150 in *Law and Aesthetics*, edited by Roberta Kevelson. New York: Peter Lang.

Costonis, John J. 1989. *Icons and Aliens: Law, Aesthetics, and Environmental Change.* Urbana: University of Illinois Press.

Cude, Randall J. 1998. "Beauty and the Well-Drawn Ordinance: Avoiding Vagueness and Overbreadth Charges to Municipal Aesthetic Regulations." *Journal of Law and Policy* 6: 853–913.

Douzinas, Costas. 1992. "The Alta(e)rs of Law: The Judgment of Legal Aesthetics." *Theory Culture, and Society* 94: 93–117.

Douzinas, Costas & Lynda Neal. 1999. *Law and the Image: The Authority of Art and the Aesthetics of Law.* Chicago: University of Chicago Press.

——— 1999. "Prosophon and Antiprosophon: Prolegomena for a Legal Iconology." Pp. 36–67 in *Law and the Image: The Authority of Art and the Aesthetics of Law*, edited by Costas Douzinas, and Lynda Nead. Chicago: University of Chicago Press.

Douzinas, Costas & Ronnie Warrington. 1992. "Signifying Alta(e)rs: The Aesthetics of Legal Judgment." Pp. 151–175 in *Law and Aesthetics*, edited by Roberta Kevelson. New York: Peter Lang.

Dworkin, Ronald. 1986. *Law's Empire.* Cambridge: Harvard University Press.

Eisele, Thomas D. 1992. "The Activity of Being a Lawyer: The Imaginative Pursuit of Implications and Possibilities." Pp. 177–204 in *Law and Aesthetics*, edited by Roberta Kevelson. New York: Peter Lang.

Foster, Hal. 1999. "Obscene, Abject, Traumatic." Pp. 240–256 in *Law and the Image: The Authority of Art and the Aesthetics of Law*, edited by Costas Douzinas, and Lynda Nead. Chicago: University of Chicago Press.

Frank, Jerome. 1947. "Words and Music: Some Remarks on Statutory Interpretation." *Columbia Law Review* 47: 1259–1278.

Gabel, Peter. 1984. "Symposium: A Critique of Rights: The Phenomenology of Rights-Consciousness and the Pact of the Withdrawn Selves." *Texas Law Review* 62: 1563–1598.

Gearey, Adam. 2001. *Law and Aesthetics.* Oxford: Hart Publishing.

Goodrich, Peter. 1999. "The Iconography of Nothing: Blank Spaces and the Representation of Law in *Edward VI and the Pope*." Pp. 89–114 in *Law and the Image: The Authority of Art and the Aesthetics of Law*, edited by Costas Douzinas, and Lynda Nead. Chicago: University of Chicago Press.

—— 1992. "Specula Laws: Image, Aesthetic and Common Law." Pp. 205–225 in *Law and Aesthetics*, edited by Roberta Kevelson. New York: Peter Lang.

Haldar, Piyel. 1999 "The Function of the Ornament in Quintilian, Alberti, and Court Architecture." Pp. 117–136 in *Law and the Image: The Authority of Art and the Aesthetics of Law*, edited by Costas Douzinas and Lynda Nead. Chicago: University of Chicago Press.

Hibbitts, Bernard J. 1994. "Making Sense of Metaphors: Visuality, Aurality, and the Reconfiguration of American Legal Discourse." *Cardozo Law Review* 16: 229–356.

Jay, Martin. 1999. "Must Justice Be Blind? The Challenge of Images to the Law." Pp. 19–35 in *Law and the Image: The Authority of Art and the Aesthetics of Law*, edited by Costas Douzinas and Lynda Nead. Chicago: University of Chicago Press.

Kang, John M. 1997. "Deconstructing the Ideology of White Aesthetics." *Michigan Journal of Race and Law* 2: 283–359.

Kevelson, Roberta. 1992. *Law and Aesthetics*. New York: Peter Lang.

—— 1992. "Introduction: Dialectic, Conflicts in Cultural Norms, Laws and Legal Aesthetic." Pp. 1–19 in *Law and Aesthetics*, edited by Roberta Kevelson. New York: Peter Lang.

—— 1992. "Semiotics and the 'Art of Discovery' in Law." Pp. 245–279 in *Law and Aesthetics*, edited by Roberta Kevelson. New York: Peter Lang.

Kurzon, Dennis. 1992. "Poetic Language and Court Opinions." Pp. 281–302 in *Law and Aesthetics*, edited by Roberta Kevelson. New York: Peter Lang.

Levinson, Sanford. 1982. "Law as Literature." *Texas Law Review* 60: 373–403.

Llewellyn, Karl. 1941–42. "On the Good, the True, the Beautiful in Law." *University of Chicago Law Review* 9: 224–265.

Malkan, Jeffrey. 1998. "Literary Formalism, Legal Formalism." *Cardozo Law Review* 19: 1393–1439.

Manderson, Desmond. 1994. "Health and the Aesthetics of Health-An Historical Case Study." *Journal of Contemporary Health Law and Policy* 11: 85–109.

—— 2000. *Songs Without Music: Aesthetic Dimensions of Law and Justice*. Berkeley: University of California Press.

Manderson, Desmond & David Caudill. 1999. "Symposium: Modes of Law: Music and Legal Theory-An Interdisciplinary Workshop Introduction." *Cardozo Law Review* 20: 1325–1329.

Moran, Leslie J. 1992. "'Skeleton Arguments': The Art of Corporate Criminal Capacity." Pp. 303–324 in *Law and Aesthetics*, edited by Roberta Kevelson. New York: Peter Lang.

Nead, Lynda. 1999. "Bodies of Judgment: Art, Obscenity, and the Connoisseur." Pp. 203–225 in *Law and the Image: The Authority of Art and the Aesthetics of Law*, edited by C. Douzinas, and L. Nead. Chicago: University of Chicago Press.

Nussbaum, Martha C. 1995. *Poetic Justice*. Boston: Beacon Press.

Packer, Mark. 1996. "The Aesthetic Dimension of Ethics and Law: Some Reflections on Harmless Offense." *American Philosophical Quarterly* 33(1): 57–74.

Posner, Richard A. 1988. *Law and Literature: A Misunderstood Relation*. Cambridge: Harvard University Press.

Rosenberg, Gerald N. 1991. *The Hollow Hope: Can Courts Bring About Social Change?* Chicago: University of Chicago Press.

Sarat, Austin & Thomas R. Kearns. 1996. *Legal Rights: Historical and Philosophical Perspectives*. Ann Arbor: University of Michigan Press.

—— 1996. "Narrative Strategy and Death Penalty Advocacy." *Harvard Civil Rights-Civil Liberties Law Review* 31: 353–381.

Schlag, Pierre. 2002. "The Aesthetics of American Law." *Harvard Law Review* 115: 1047–1118.

Schrader, Scott. 1991. "Politics, Law, and Society: Icons and Aliens: Law, Aesthetics, and Environmental Change." *Michigan Law Review* 89: 1789–1799.

Schwartz, Louis B. 1987. "Justice, Expediency, and Beauty." *University of Pennsylvania Law Review* 136: 141–182.

Scott, William T. 1992. "Aspects of 'Value' in Aesthetic Communication." Pp. 355–375 in *Law and Aesthetics*, edited by Roberta Kevelson. New York: Peter Lang.

Serra, Richard. 2001. "Art and the Law: Suppression and Liberty the Tilted Arc Controversy." *Cardozo Arts and Entertainment Law Journal* 19: 39–49.

Skeel, David A. 1992. "Notes Toward an Aesthetics of Legal Pragmatism." *Cornell Law Review* 78: 84–105.

Sherwin, Richard K. 2000. *When Law Goes Pop: The Vanishing Line Between Law and Popular Culture*. Chicago: University of Chicago Press.

Stevens, Wilf. 1993. "Imagining Justice: Aesthetics and Public Executions in Late Eighteenth-Century England." *Yale Journal of Law and the Humanities* 5: 51–78

Sunstein, Cass. 1996. *Legal Reasoning and Political Conflict*. Oxford: Oxford University Press.

Toran, Janice. 1990. "'Tis a Gift to be Simple: Aesthetics and Procedural Reform." *Michigan Law Review* 89: 352–397.

West, Robin. 1985. "Jurisprudence as Narrative: An Aesthetic Analysis of Modern Legal Theory." *New York University Law Review* 60: 145–211.

White, James Boyd. 1985. *Heracles' Bow: Essays on the Rhetoric and Poetics of the Law.* Madison: University of Wisconsin Press.

Williams, Patricia J. 1991. *The Alchemy of Race and Rights.* Cambridge: Harvard University Press.

Winn, Peter A. 1992. "Legal Ritual." Pp. 401–440 in *Law and Aesthetics*, edited by R. Kevelson. New York: Peter Lang.

Winter, Steven L. 1989. "Transcendental Nonsense, Metaphoric Reasoning, and the Cognitive Stakes for Law." *University of Pennsylvania Law Review* 137: 1105–1237.

Yen, Alfred C. 1998. "Copyright Opinions and Aesthetic Theory." *Southern California Law Review* 71: 247–297.

Young, Alison. 1992. "'Nothing Out of the Ordinary': The Criminality of the Feminine Body." Pp. 443–462 in *Law and Aesthetics*, edited by Roberta Kevelson. New York: Peter Lang.

Excerpts From:

Anker, Kristen (2005) The Truth in Painting: Cultural Artifacts as Proof of Native Title. *Law Text Culture* 9: 91–124.

Reproduced with permission of the author and *Law Text Culture*.

THE TRUTH IN PAINTING: CULTURAL ARTIFACTS AS PROOF OF NATIVE TITLE

Kristen Anker (2005)

Introduction – "Walking All Over Their Painting"

On the front cover of the Oxford *Companion to Aboriginal Art and Culture* an Aboriginal man in a red loin cloth appears dancing on a brightly coloured canvas. He is dwarfed by the size of the painting, and is doubly lost amid the 'riotous colour', the lines, circles and swirls of his platform, the Ngurrara Canvas II. This is Nyilpirr Spider Snell, an artist from the Kimberley/Great Sandy Desert region of North Western Australia, performing the *Kurtal* – or snake dreaming dance – in Canberra to 'remind those sitting on the High Court of the depth of [his peoples'] claim' (*Native Title Newsletter* 2002: 4).

The painting is a collaboration of around 50 artists, produced when the Walmajarri, Wangkajunga, Mangala and Juwaliny peoples were asked to prepare a map of their traditional area for a Native title claim (see Figure 3). They decided to do it this way, each person painting a section which represents their own areas of responsibility on the land and in lore. The result, although not employing cartographic conventions, is described as a map and shows the freshwater holes (*Uila*) and other sites in the desert in spiritual and physical relation to each other, as well as representing the relationships between the painters themselves (Chance 2001: 28–40). In giving evidence about the connection of the claimants to the land during a plenary session[138] before the National Native Title Tribunal in 1997, each witness stood on their respective portion of the canvas and recounted the stories associated with it.

But what exactly does a painting prove? One painter described the importance of the Ngurrara Canvas:

> I believe that [native title] is about blackfella law. The painting is only for proof. When I go to court to tell my story, I must listen very carefully before I open my mouth. Maybe the *kartiya*[139] will say, "We don't believe you." That's why we made this painting, for evidence. We have painted our story for native title people, as proof. We want them to understand, so that they

---

[138] Claimants have to pass an initial registration test with the Tribunal, demonstrating that there is sufficient factual basis for their claim: *Native Title Act* 1993 (Cth) s190B(5). As of 1 July 2005 the claim is still in mediation: National Native Title Tribunal File No WC96/32.

[139] White people.

Figure 3. Ngurrara, an 8 x 5 metre canvas was acquired by the National Museum of Australia and unveiled in Canberra on September 2, 2009. Reproduced with permission. AAP Image/Mark Graham.

> know about our painting, our country, our *ngurrara*. They are all the same thing (Ngarralja Tommy May, in Chance 2001: 38).

In one respect, the painting is seen as a way to communicate knowledge to non-Aboriginal people and to the courts. Proof of knowledge about country and traditional law is the measure of entitlement under the *Native Title Act* 1993 (Cth). But the knowledge of which Ngarralja Tommy May speaks is not something which the painting 'points to'. This would be the conventional understanding that evidence is something that testifies to the external real world of facts. The painting *is* the country, we are told. 'They are all the same thing.' This statement suggests that evidence about traditional knowledge is itself evidence of a different way of knowing. The painting is powerful because in proving a different kind of title to that familiar to the common law, it engages in the very question of what entitlement is. The painting is not just a fact about law, it is law.

Second, the painting is seen to address the need for credibility in making a claim, the need to appear truthful. The relation of truth to evidence in Western law is complicated. While the function of evidence is to elicit the facts, where facts are taken to correspond directly to an external reality, the court usually has before it only some form of statement that the facts claimed are true. Evidence is then what allows the court to increase or decrease the weight of probability in assessing that a claim is true. This might include evidence about the character of a witness in order to infer the likelihood that they are making truthful statements. Assessments of credibility are also likely to be influenced by more subtle cultural indicators such as dress and manner (Timony 2000). So what is it about a painting that could show the credibility of a witness? Do paintings have their own truth?

Third, the painting is described as representing a map of the claimants' country.[140] Maps of the more conventional variety have been central to native title claims, as they have been central to the development of Anglo-Australian land law and to the project of colonisation in general. Boaventura de Sousa Santos has written that both maps and law make claims to authoritatively represent reality (1987). The use of such a painting in evidence may undermine the exclusivity of both western cartography and western law because it suggests that in order to recognise a different kind of title, the common law might also have to consider a different way of conceiving of entitlement and representing the land. The painting may well act as a kind of map in the claimants' case, but it does more than just indicate the geographic parameters of the claim. It makes a normative claim about the basis for entitlement and the manner in which it can be proved that resists reduction to a set of rights and interests over a bounded territory.

Thus I will disassemble the painting's function along three axes, all of which see it targeting a particular orthodoxy in the common law and pushing towards a realisation of the transformative and plural character of evidentiary practices in native title. Part 2 takes up the claim that the Ngurrara Canvas is law. Although subordinated to the category of 'fact', the painting must be taken on its own terms in order for it to be meaningful as proof, including a very different person-place relation as the basis for entitlement and the point that, for the claimants, the painting embodies the law. The most obvious challenge here is to the idea of the state as the sole source of law, but other assumed attributes of law – that it consists of public, verifiable and positive statements of principle, for example – are also resisted. In Part 3, I will argue that the painting makes a claim to credibility that confronts conventional legal understandings of truth because it operates aesthetically, rhetorically and therefore a-rationally. Lastly, to read the painting as a map entails a challenge to the European valuation of land, the way it is thought and depicted. Where maps have historically colluded with property law in order to communicate a particular mode of entitlement, the canvas insists on disrupting the universality of this vision. In

---

[140] Aboriginal painting from other regions have also been described as geographic maps: for example Pintupi Western Desert acrylic dot paintings (Myers 2002: 34) and Yolngu bark painting in Arnhem Land (Morphy 1998: 24)

all three instances, there is a strong normative aspect to the canvas which is missed in a conventional reading of it as something purely factual, purely aesthetic or purely cartographic. I will show that it is this much larger challenge which must be met if Australia is, as was claimed for the recognition of native title in *Mabo* (1992), to have rejected *terra nullius*.

The Ngurrara Canvas operates in a number of frames.[141] It contains designs that originate in body and ground painting associated with traditional ceremonies and law, but it is transposed onto the western format of a flat canvas and in acrylic paint of a much wider palate than was earlier available. It is not a map of the claim area in the conventional sense anticipated by the National Native Title Tribunal personnel, and yet it is comprehensible as such in the context of a growing public awareness of the way Indigenous art can represent traditional relationships to 'country'. It articulates a claim in a language alien to the rational legal discourse of the court, and yet it can still have rhetorical power – 'It was, one tribunal member said, the most eloquent and overwhelming evidence that had ever been produced [in the tribunal]. The Aborigines could proceed to court' (Brooks 2003).

Ngurrara as truth

Like Ngarralja Tommy May, other painters are confident of the ability of the Ngurrara Canvas to convince others of the truth of their claim (see also ABC Radio National 1997). For the court or the tribunal, the truth of the claim will come down to the authenticity of what is presented as traditional laws and customs connecting the claimants to the land. How is it possible for the canvas to do this work?

A *The normal course of evidence in the common law*

In the conventional positivist view of law, evidence is the process by which the facts of the case are brought before the judge or jury so that they may establish what happened. Once facts are characterised, the relevant legal principle will then be applied so as to produce the decision of the case. The assumptions of what William Twining calls the 'Rationalist Tradition' of evidence scholarship, implicit in most contemporary work on evidence, are that events and facts have an existence independent of human observation, that true statements correspond with facts, and that present knowledge about past events is theoretically possible, if typically incomplete (Twining 1985: 12–4). Although

---

[141] My intellectual debt here is to Howard Morphy's image of the frame in relation to Yolngu art (1991: 21–32), and Richard Mohr's analysis of change and continuity in law with frames as a semiotic device (2002).

in practice we can never perfectly establish the truth of a statement of fact, we can filter the process – through the rules of admissibility – so that only evidence that tends to increase or decrease the *probability* that a statement of fact is true is allowed to be introduced. This includes details suggestive of whether the witness is being truthful or otherwise, that is, their credibility.

The 'normal course of evidence' is taken as a reasoned process of revealing the world through the senses of the witness or the court itself, via eyewitness or expert testimony, documentation or exhibited objects. These either constitute the 'fact' in question itself (the witness saw the accused stab the victim) or by inference attest to the occurrence of the fact in question (the witness saw the accused running away from the victim with a bloodied knife in hand). A brief survey of contemporary texts indicates that there are few challenges to this paradigm (Cross & Tapper 1985: 16–37, Ligertwood 1993: 4, Howard 2000: 2). Murphy, for instance, admits that 'facts' in court are a matter of what the court can be persuaded to believe rather than what is true, but proceeds as if this process of persuasion is uncontentious or uninteresting (1995: 1–16). And yet, as evidence is a matter of persuasion, it is never a purely 'rational' exercise. Whether facts are true or relevant to the question on trial, or can be inferred from other facts, depends on the experience or intuition of the trier of fact. Persuasion takes place by rhetorical and emotional means as well as by 'logic', as practitioners are well aware. But the challenge that these points pose for the Rationalist Tradition is more than just an admission of some extra factors added to a core of facts, or a suspicion that the work of most litigators is in manipulating the trier of fact into arriving at the judgment that will suit their client. None of this challenges the proposition that the truth is 'out there'. The relevance of outlook and experience, however, goes also to the heart of the concepts of logic, rationality and knowledge itself, as feminist and critical race scholars have argued: our background, values and experience affect not only what we know, but how we know (Alcoff & Potter 1993, Delgado 1995, Harmon 1999, Nicholson 2000).

Critical legal scholars have likewise argued that the process of judgment is neither rational nor determinate, and that both facts and law are highly constructed, dependent on language, reasoning and discourse for their representation (Hutchinson & Monahan 1984). Consequently, 'the legal representation of fact is normative from the start' and is telling of a particular way of imagining the world (Geertz 1983: 174). The fallacy of the correspondence theory of facts (where statements are considered to correspond directly to aspects of or events in the real world that exist apart from human discourse) is hinted at by the vernacular of practitioners who often speak of the 'coherence' of evidence as a narrative as a test for the plausibility of that evidence (Twining 1985: 183,

Jackson 1988). How we assess the truthfulness of a story depends on how well it 'hangs together', and this relies in turn on cultural experience with styles of narrative. Playing on standard stories also has the effect of pre-empting judgment – if a woman can be cast successfully as a damsel in distress, or a wicked stepmother, we can guess whether the decision will be in her favour or not (see Sarmas 1994).

Other scholars point to the integral role that our senses play in the way we respond to law to the fact, that it is sometimes the aesthetics of legal drama and discourse that makes certain decisions possible. For example, Desmond Manderson argues that it was the visual impact of the scarred body of the plaintiff in *Natanson v Kline*, her heart beating visibly through ribs damaged by radiation in a mastectomy procedure, that lead to a new legal principle of informed consent, when those before her had failed in similar claims (2000: 41). The aesthetics of a body, or a painting, or a judicial decision, imply a moral standard. Likewise, they demand a moral judgment.

Perceiving evidence as rhetorical, narrative, aesthetic and normative puts paid to the premises of the Rationalist Tradition. Instead, the hearing of evidence produces a sort of translation of what is taken to be the 'real world' – other places and other times – into the terms of law; it renders a world in which law's principles make sense. In the process it establishes both the separation of law from society and its mastery over society (Mohr 1999). The translation and the constitution of the law/world hierarchy is a play which is dramatised in various ways – the architecture and dress of the court, the presentation of witnesses, exhibits, experts, documents.

Conventionally, however, for all the symbolic significance of wigs and gowns in evoking the majesty of the law, and the historical origins of the forms of order, these aspects of law are mostly considered to be little more than window dressing, peripheral to the substance of either law or fact (Haldar 1994: 188). But the window's frame, like the frame on a painting, plays a role that is not merely extraneous. It constitutes the object, says what is inside and out, is at once a part of the scene while seeming external to it. It tells us, in both legal and aesthetic terms, what is available for judgment (Derrida 1987: 57).

The frame here is more that just the interpretive context of a 'frame of reference'; it has the sense of selection, delimitation, constitution. The frame as an analytic device is bound up in the philosophical question of 'the limit'. In distinguishing between a thing and what it is not – a painting from the wall, an object of beauty as opposed to its ornamentation, fact from law, law from everything else – there is a question of what happens at the border (the limit) between the thing and the not-thing. A frame (*parergon*) does the job of maintaining this limit, it 'delimits' the subject (work, *ergon*) captured within it.

But the status of the parergon as neither inside nor outside, and yet maintaining the inside from the outside, makes it a paradox. In order to imagine how the parergon operates, Derrida, in *The Truth in Painting*, denotes the frame structurally with the figure of a laced boot (from Van Gogh's painting): it laces the edges together by passing through them in a repeated and reversible movement, from outside to inside, from under to over. A frame thus 'cuts out but also sews back together. By an invisible lace which pierces the canvas – passes into it then out of it in order to sew it back onto its milieu, its internal and external worlds' (1987: 304).

Consequently, when the courtroom, the gavel, the leatherbound law report say 'what passes by me is the law' they are neither superfluous, nor quarantining the law off from the world, but are rather performing this lacing role. It is by virtue of the law's frame that the outside becomes represented in the *ergon*, that scraps of the world, 'footprints, fingerprints, chance memories captured by a witness' come to correspond to 'the "whole truth and nothing but the truth" of an event' once brought within the walls of the court (Haldar 1994: 192). In native title cases, some of these frames help constitute the world for the court: a microphone in a bush hearing gives a witness voice, a piece of canvas makes *ngurrara* into a map, a loincloth signifies Aboriginality. The means by which things become what they are. The two senses of frame – *ergon* and frame of reference – are related, for something does not become a 'thing' to be interpreted until it has been framed 'off' from everything else. Each framing then also implies a frame of reference, a weaving between the thing and its context.

B The painting as supplementary evidence

The positivist paradigm for evidence would allow that paintings, dances, songs, and pitching the court in a desert river bed to visit country, are merely novel ways to introduce facts about Indigenous rights and interests in land into evidence. But how are these 'facts' communicated? Without further explanation, a man dancing on a canvas does not immediately say much to a court. An explanation can indicate the significance of the dance, the song, the iconography to the facts at issue – how the claimants are connected to the land and what their rights are over it. But then, as far as the court is concerned, what does the painting add to the explanation?[142] The presentation of cultural evidence communicates in ways supplementary to the facts proper: by appeal

---

[142] I am questioning the position of Western evidence here, not the position of the Ngurrara claimants, who have clearly expressed the view that this was their preferred method of giving testimony, and the way they feel best able to express themselves.

to the senses through colour and rhythm, a sense of space and a smell of dust; and by referents in intercultural knowledge between Indigenous and colonial cultures. Does it *look* like an authentic demonstration of Aboriginal law and culture? Does this man seem to know how to move about the canvas in an Aboriginal way? (Does it tell the story that the court needs to hear?)

For the court, evidence will be judged credible if it gels with expectations of authentic culture (the 'feel' and the 'look') and if the witnesses display 'genuine' knowledge in their testimony. For this, any observer will rely on a repertoire of cultural precedents, among them a likely awareness of paintings as a particularly high-profile site for debates about authenticity and Indigenous culture in recent decades.

The use of acrylic colours to paint Dreaming designs on boards for sale emerged in Pupunya (in the Central Desert) in the 1970s. With support from the government under the new policy of self-determination, and interest from painters for whom commercial values complimented their own views of the paintings as culturally 'dear', a modest market developed in 'Aboriginal acrylic paintings'. While Indigenous artefacts had earlier held only ethnographic interest for Western audiences (Short 1991: 218, Morphy 1991: 22), they now represent a category of 'fine art' in galleries the world over (Myers 2002: 64).

The appeal of these paintings to a Western public has been multi-faceted. In Australia, a new 'national consciousness' lead people to formulate Aboriginal culture as distinctive of a uniquely Australian identity which was, significantly, linked to its land. Internationally, responses to Aboriginal art were themed around an interest in 'the Other' and a nostalgia for place and spirituality, a 'conceptual return to our lost ("primitive") selves' (Myers 2002: 201, 283–6). While acrylic paintings represented an idea of Aboriginal authenticity, however, debates raged around the negative effects of commercialisation and industry on the 'traditional' nature, and therefore the value, of such art. On the other hand, it seems that despite the use of new materials and the influence of advisors in tailoring work for a market with particular visual expectations (Myers 2002: 284, 289), the paintings continue to hold the layered significance of designs that were previously painted on bodies, objects and in the sand, to enact stories from the Dreaming and the geographical places belonging to the painter.

This is what interests the court – that something traditional 'is there' in the painting. But like most work in galleries, acrylic paintings are intercultural objects, produced in a complex world of government policy, the consumer market, art criticism and land claims as well as distinctly Indigenous purposes. Non-Indigenous ideas of 'pure tradition' are in themselves hybrid events, products of the colonial encounter and textually mediated efforts to explain the inexplicable.[143] The Ngurrara Canvas has a specifically contemporary purpose, but is also continuous with an inherited mandate to look after country; it is not a 'title deed' and represents something quite different to 'property', and yet, if reiterated over time, it can come to be understood in those terms because property and title deed will *themselves* undergo a semiotic shift (Mohr 2002).

So the world of facts in native title does not exist 'out there'; it is created for the court by the supplementary evidence in the physical and aesthetic being of the painting or other evidence. In the *Lardil Peoples* example, a principle of exclusive possession comes into being when, through the event of oral questioning, someone articulates what they do when asking permission. The manifestation of Ngurrara/country in the canvas brings the claimants' law into the terms of the law of the court at the same time as it marks a distinction between the two. More than pointing out that the painting convinces of the truth of its object because it matches stereotypes of cultural authenticity, I am arguing that the excluded supplement of the common law 'proper', whether a-rationality and aesthetics in the question of proof, or Indigenous law in the question of sovereignty, always makes a return and so effects a transformation on what *is* proper to the law. The general point here is that the recognition of native title is not the application of a label (property) to an external phenomenon (Indigenous law) by an unassailable common law. What is there in evidence is mixed up in the exigencies of proof – all law becomes articulated and made present in certain ways in response to a challenge or a need to explain and justify and so is intrinsically hybrid.

In stating that the 'facts' of Indigenous culture and law do not exist in any objective way for the court, I do not mean that giving evidence is a chimera. It is a practice itself, meaningful, for example, in terms of obligations to care for country or to represent Dreaming relations in pictorial form. It is also a practice for *kartiya*, one that constitutes spaces and relationships in particular ways and one that is required to transform law 'into a living reality, a concrete experience' (Tait 1999). If, in the usual environment of the court room, symbols and practices work to consolidate the power and authority of western law, then being a visitor on, for example, Walmajarri homeland potentially destabilises that frame of reference by immersing the court in another world. If evidence is the law's way of framing the world to make it available for judgment, then the intercultural frames of a native title hearing push towards the possibility of other views on the world and other sorts of judgments. A closer reading of the Ngurrara Canvas as a map of country will provide one example.

---

[143] A sobering analysis of one of the earliest ethnographic studies by Spencer and Gillen is given by Elizabeth Povinelli (2002: 71–109).

Ngurrara as Map

Through the approximations I ascribed to Indigenous visual culture above –
iconography, representation of topography, lexicon – the common reference
to paintings as maps is understandable; they both encode the land. Within the
native title frame, paintings can thus be accepted in the role of marking out
an area of claim, in the way that a cartographic map would. And yet, unlike
a topographical map, it would be useless to an uninitiated person trying to
find their way, for the map and the canvas are premised on incongruent ways
of reading the land. The question I wish to address here is what this habit of
reading has to do with entitlement to property.

A *Cartography and the common law*

In addition to the principles of proof discussed above, property has its own
requirements. In the Torrens system of land titles now operating in Australia,
proof of title depends on establishing that the person claiming title is the
person who is registered as the proprietor of an interest on the register of the
state or territory-wide Land Titles Office (or equivalent).[144] This system is the
apotheosis of a long process of the 'dephysicalisation' (Vandevelde 1980: 329)
of real property in the common law, where title to land was gradually, and
now almost completely, removed from material events on the land.[145]

In spite of this development, the common law presupposes a resource of
memory. In medieval and preliterate times, where the performance of rituals
such as turning turf or exchanging objects marked the conveyance of land
to a new owner, the objects worked as a guarantee of title 'only because they
were fixed as reference points within a medieval art of recollection, which
recorded cultural events by associating them metaphorically or metonymi-
cally with things and their images' (Pottage 1994: 361). So the functional locus
of title was in the local knowledge about boundaries and transfers; the ritual of
transfer merely underlined the accumulated practice of neighbours and past
owners as to who held what rights and where.

The advent of cartography eventually facilitated the removal of property from local knowledge onto a more abstract domain, first of the paper
title, and more recently, of the register. In a more rapidly changing social,
political and economic context, individual memories could no longer give
certainty. Increased communication led to a perception of local spaces

---

[144] As long as no exceptions to the indefeasibility of title apply, for example,*Real Property Act* 1900
   (NSW) s42.
[145] Some rare exceptions include the doctrine of adverse possession, and the provision of ease-
   ments by prescription.

as parts of a whole, matched by the increased availability of maps which placed land onto a homogenising, linear grid. Industrialisation led to a growth in urban areas and rapid changes in topography that confused and outstripped local memory, at the same time as creating the need for, and perception of, land as a commodity. Proof of title in the common law context is thus dominated by a logic of exchange and abstraction. Every time we use the title system, we bring that logic into being as a (naturalised) way of perceiving land.

Native title evidence is introduced into this frame of reference. Memory and practice as a resource in proving title is at once deeply familiar and pointedly forgotten in modern property. It is easy to accept that a painting stands in for memory in the same way as a title deed (or the register) does for common law property, while overlooking the performative, constitutive role that earlier rituals actually played and that the technology of title continues to play, and so missing the subtleties of what native title is performing and bringing into being.

The critical context for this performance, in Australia, is the way the same disciplines of cartography and property that in England facilitated industrialisation worked in concert to offer up a vision of a land available for acquisition. Since its inception in the European imagination,[146] *Terra Australis* was represented cartographically as a blank space within the initially vague outlines of its coast (Ryan 1996: 115–7). The impression of collusion between this and the legal doctrine of *terra nullius* – a legal blank space – is hard to avoid. Once physical colonisation of Australia began, representations of its landscape in the sketches and journals of early explorers followed a similar trope. The monotonous, undifferentiated mass of land in the interior resisted being read, for example for signs of water, in the way that 'normal' landscape could be read.[147] Landscape also *became* monotonous because of the imperative to move through space in exploration – the apparent absence of geographical 'milestones' frustrated an explorer's desire to sense progress and direction (Carter 1988: 247).

New maps inscribed colonial qualities over Indigenous (unreadable) ones: the blankness was marked by features of European creation – fences, houses, roads. Locations are specified through coordinates of latitude and longitude that take Greenwich, London – the heart of the British Empire – as their

---

[146] Pythagoras devised a concept of a southern landmass counterbalancing the northern one in the 5th century BC, and a *Terra Australis* appeared on the medieval *mappae mundi* (Eisler 1995: 8–11).

[147] A similar experience was had by European settlers of the Canadian prairies, who were at a loss to know how to paint in the 'absence' of scenery (Rees 1982).

point of reference (Reilly 2003: 3). Indigenous placenames were laid over with names bestowed by explorers who created a landscape in the act of naming. Names reference the imperial act of possession or the experience of exploration itself – Victoria, Queensland, Cape Tribulation, Lake Disappointment.

In an attempt to manage the vastness and unfamiliarity of the land, both written accounts and early landscape painting made use of the comforting European ideals of the 'picturesque,' an aesthetic in which the land appears as a scene arranged for the viewer – vivid green foliage, ornamental avenues of trees and the like – and, moreover, as naturally awaiting the arrival of sheep and cattle (Appleton 1975: 25–39, Sturt & Mitchell in Ryan 1996: 74–6). It is a short step from rightfully enjoying the view to rightfully enjoying ownership. Kooris,[148] when present, were corralled by the 'picturesque' as part of the scenery – they belonged to the known rather than existing as knowers (or owners) themselves and so did not disturb the fantasy of *terra nullius*.

Although native title is a form of land ownership that in some sense operates outside the grid of registration, it is in other ways incorporated into the same non-Indigenous view of land through the processes of representation used in native title claims. Maps, as Alexander Reilly explains, are everywhere in native title, and '[t]he ability to represent relationships to land and waters cartographically is central to the process' (2003: 3). Maps are used to specify the external boundaries of the claim area and the extent of other land tenures,[149] and to indicate the various aspects of the claimants' connection to the country through symbols that represent Dreaming tracks, and other sites of significance to them, alongside the symbols of European settlement – roads, fences and homesteads. Such maps embody both the possibility of co-existence, and the limitations of the recognition of Indigenous relationships to country because in being reduced to a singular, unambiguous discourse, Indigenous spaces are subjected to a deeper process of colonisation (Reilly 2003).

The significance of maps as representations to questions of proof is that they belong to an aesthetic that semiotically communicates entitlement. The act of representing space positions people with respect to the world. Perspectivalism 'helps constitute an apparent divide between the "sovereign eye" of the observer and the space of the "external world"' (Blomley 1998: 575) that makes domination and surveillance possible and natural (Cosgrove 1984: 25). In cartography, even the implicit sense of observation is erased. The flatness of projection is a view from no-where and the naturalness of this particular vision is perfected. The cartographic aesthetic thus achieves the necessary conditions for

---

[148] As early landscape painting was mainly from areas in the South East, the people depicted were Kooris.

[149] Required by *Native Title Act* 1993 s62.

ownership: a subject 'eye/I' that can only relate to the objectified land through possession, and a grid of infinitely exchangeable portions. It also excludes other perspectives by creating the illusion that these qualities inhere in the land rather than existing as properties of vision (Bender 1999: 32).

The Ngurrara Canvas, on the other hand, has a spatial organisation in which there are no portions, only places known and named. If dot paintings can sometimes resemble aerial photographs, they are far more significant for positioning people in, in relation to, and because of, the landscape. Such land could never be a possession; it is more like family. The relationship is one of care and stewardship.

The Ngurrara Canvas is coined as a map because that is the term to which the claimants responded. The analogy also permits the uninitiated to understand the painting as a representation of the relative position of places in the land. But the painting embodies an alternative aesthetic that contests all three aspects of the legality of entitlement: objectification, commodification and exclusion. As a map, the painting is not simply assimilated to the Cartesian worldview, but participates in shifting the terms in which maps are understood. It introduces a multiplicity to the monopoly over vision, a perspective in which people are in not absent from the map, and a relationship with land that forms an alternative mode of entitlement.

To the court, the Ngurrara Canvas both represents and demonstrates, through performance, the existence of property rights via matters of entitlement under traditional law. But what the painting represents and performs is something larger than what is forensically captured as the frame of traditional law: western titles are also performative, and in this intercultural arena, the evidentiary process hosts a shifting conversation about what land (and with it identity and entitlement) can possibly mean, and performs the fact of that plurality. Although not superseding the technical requirement in section 62(2)(b) of the *Native Title Act* that a cadastral map of the claim area be provided – and so never 'officially' a map – Ngurrara as map nonetheless puts into relief the fact that land titles are a complex of habits of vision, practices with respect to the world and the methods of representation that link the two.

B Physical Country

If *Ngurrara* is a map, this map *is* also the country, filled with significant places, connected by stories. Giving evidence on the painting is the next best thing to standing on the land (Chance 2001: 40). Where physical country is understood to be fully integrated both into an Indigenous notion of law and one of identity, it makes sense that, as Kathryn Trees has explained in relation to the hearings for the Miriuwung-Gajerrong claim, witnesses do not merely feel more comfortable giving evidence on their home country than in the foreign territory of a courtroom (although that is one way of expressing it); their ability and authority to speak about certain places may literally depend on their being physical present (2002).

The practice of permitting hearings 'on country' would seem to go further than merely increasing 'access to the facts' because it contemplates the normative impact of being on country to the witnesses. Chief Justice Black of the Federal Court writes that:

> The new practice is a recognition that, for many claimants, their relationship to country is not able to be explained in the abstract, and that it is necessary to be on country to gain a true appreciation and understanding of that relationship and the claimants' evidence about it. It is also an acknowledgment that, under traditional law, some evidence can only be given on country, and that there will be many cases in which it would be quite wrong to expect claimants to talk about their relationship to country by reference to maps prepared by non-indigenous people (Black 2002: 18).

Under the *Native Title Act*, taking account of the cultural concerns of claimants and witnesses is part of the balancing process of procedural fairness (*Native Title Act* section 82). But is there more at stake? If giving evidence on country is a source of authority for Aboriginal people, is there a conversely unsettling process going on here for the court? How does it affect the processes of law 'for judges to sit in the desert under trees or in tents for 4–6 weeks at a time to hear evidence, with limited facilities and very few formalities' (Black 2002: 18)?

The physical site of the court and its surroundings are conventionally seen as extraneous to the operation of law. As we saw, however, this window dressing communicates a great deal about the law, and even makes judgment itself possible. Even in a desert setting the idiom of order familiar in courtroom architecture (Haldar 1994) is apparent: during the Miriuwung-Gajerrong hearing, a picnic table was transformed into a judges' bench with a red cloth; maps and stacks of legal papers reinforced the value of the written word; the judge and the lawyers sat on raised chairs and heard from witnesses while they, too were sitting in chairs rather than on the ground; microphones designated who the court would listen to; the whole arrangement enhanced the position of the judge – the performance was for him, who sat in objective distance from it all (Reilly 1996: 203–5). Sometimes such degrees of formality are even requested – as when the Karajarri community invited the court to robe – to reflect the significance of the proceedings for the claimants (Anderson 2003: 135).

There are clues as to how an experience of physical country might affect judgment. Reilly writes that the court looked uncomfortable in its new setting on the riverbed of Miriuwung-Gajerrong country (1996: 205). In *De Rose v State of South Australia* (hereinafter *De Rose Hill*), O'Loughlin J mentions six of the 13 sites visited during the hearing. Unusually for a native title judgment, he gives some brief descriptions of physical aspects of the sites. For instance, the site at Intalka was said to be 'a rocky gorge of spectacular beauty, spoilt by the presence of three large rusted water tanks' (*De Rose Hill*: [384]). Some of the significance of the places to the claimants was described – where the ancestor Beings had traveled through, places of danger and death – and the association of ancestor Beings with physical features of the land was a recurring part of the hearing (*De Rose Hill*: [387]).

We can only speculate as to the effect on the trial judge of travelling round to these various sites with elderly Yankunytjatjara and Pitjantjatjara people, at times obviously impressed by the landscape and the stories associated with it (for example *De Rose Hill*: [410]). Perhaps there are some clues to his surprising findings that the claimants had lost their spiritual connection to the place (*De Rose Hill*: [910–915]), however, from the fact that the claim area comprised a cattle station. Alongside emu eggs transposed into boulders and *TUukurpa*[150] tracks there were fences, water bores and cattle. This is contested land, and the presence of European artefacts in the landscape represents a *fait accompli* in the competition between two groups of people.

Just as the legal doctrine of *terra nullius* was accompanied by cartographic and artistic representations that all spoke to a particular way of seeing the land and the Kooris, Murris, Wiradjuris and others who lived there, a reversal of the doctrine relies on an ability to see the land as peopled, as belonging to someone, as known to someone. It is possible to consider that hearings 'on country' merely enable a more comprehensive presentation of the facts required to prove native title. This is a perspective that poses few challenges to the positivist conception of law and evidence. However, I would argue that a hearing on country enables the change of view required to fully reverse terra nullius in all its constituent parts by physically locating the court in what was previously a blank space, and populating it – with ancestors, stories, law and people themselves. In contrast to the positivist conception, this argument proposes a law which, like the specific instance of *terra nullius*, is part of a larger complex of seeing, representing and being in the world.

---

[150] Dreaming, or ancestral Beings.

Conclusion

When the High Court spoke of native title as an 'intersection between two normative systems' (*Yorta Yorta*: 550) it was as a device to explain the recognition by the common law of rights arising in traditional Indigenous law: the intersection happened once, at the time sovereignty was claimed. Because there can only be one law and one sovereign, recognition relates to property rights alone. But the reference in the definition of native title to the internal perspective of claimant groups – what does Walmajarri law say – means that in the process of proof, what Walmajarri law says about property rights soon unravels into larger and more fundamental questions. Partly because of the inherent requirements of proving customary entitlement as a fact in court, and partly because the Federal Court has been directed to take Aboriginal and Torres Strait Islander cultural concerns into account, some kind of 'profound shift' is visible in the necessity to take seriously the daily realities of the claimants' lives and the way they think: there are unfamiliar rules about who can speak about what and where they can speak; some people aren't supposed to look at other people; this rock is an emu egg; strangers have to be 'watered' before they enter this place; this painting is the country.

The need for elements of Indigenous law to be taken as principles of interpretation in proof means that the intersection of the 'two normative systems' is not a dead letter, but a live quotidian interaction. The dynamics of this can be understood in part by considering how forms of evidence particular to native title, and especially paintings such as the Ngurrara Canvas, communicate their significance by operating within different cultural frameworks. A painting that draws on traditional designs from the Kimberleys works on levels pertinent to the painters in terms of embodying Dreaming stories and their connections to places and ancestral Beings. It is one way of fulfilling a traditional obligation to 'care for country' and it in fact performs that relationship to country. For the court, this manner of proof is inevitably read against common law notions of proof, title and the modes of imagination and representation, such as cartography, that support them. Reiteration over time of Indigenous modes of expressing connection to country through Dreaming stories and designs can begin to stand in for these western phenomena – maps, title deeds – within both contexts. In response, the phenomena themselves begin to undergo shifts.

But the intersection is more than simply the traditional law and custom frame caught within the common law frame. Such a painting is not a 'purely' Indigenous object, produced for internal purposes. Already there is a recent and high-profile history of Aboriginal painting for a Western market that involves desires for cultural pride and economic independence on behalf of the painters, as well as changing Western aesthetic criteria, ideas of landscape and, for non-Indigenous Australians in particular, a search for a distinctive national identity. The Ngurrara Canvas was painted for an additional specific purpose, the native title claim, but its power as a communicative tool relies on this history of Aboriginal mainstream art and the ability of a non-Indigenous audience to perceive the painting as meaningful. Through its address to the senses, the Ngurrara Canvas may also compel others – without further rational explanation – to recognise in the common law what is a compulsion under law for the claimants.

Lastly, the use of the painting as a physical platform for delivering evidence on country introduces a final frame that draws all the others together. To stand on a painting that represents parts of the country in order to talk about those places and its laws embodies the connection in Walmajarri and Wangkajunga ontology between land, people, stories and designs and so brings home a radically different knowledge about land to that of the court. But its spatiality allows it to invoke the concept of maps, while challenging the way of seeing and understanding land that western cartography represents. Standing on a painting that is a map of country from another way of seeing thus confronts the physical and the representational aspects of *terra nullius* – we are here on this country and this is the way it looks to us.

This intersection through the processes of giving evidence is not, despite my emphasis on dialogue, a fluid semiotic free-for-all. Meaning (or knowledge) and power are bound together, and in native title, it is the *kartiya* who have the power to disseminate some interpretations, to quash others, and to back those interpretations with the force of the state. After all, the Ngurrara Canvas does not fulfill the requirements of s62 for a map of the claim area. Others before me have despaired that what is proper to Indigenous peoples, whether in art or in native title, is inevitably erased by the colonial leviathan which at best holds an inventive monologue with itself. Such a view would mean that even when, like the Ngurrara claimants, agency is asserted through cultural means, the terms on which they are received are not of their making – if not property, title, or proof, then dance, painting and 'Aboriginal or Torres Straight Islander' trap them in a diorama from which there is no escape. While it may return land to their control or engender pride in aspects of culture, the native title process is stressful, often requires the breach of secrecy laws, and always demands that claimants represent themselves through foreign languages, ideas and technologies.

I do not claim that in using the Ngurrara Canvas as evidence some kind of 'true' recognition of the painting's meaning has taken place, but rather that the processes of interpretation and meaning making are more complex, plural and shifting than the conventional model of proof would allow. In a 'clash' of laws, judges may wield the force of law, but the source of law as legal meaning remains a deeply social, and inescapably plural, process (see Cover 1983). For law more generally the implications are that some of its neat divisions have to be rethought, in particular, the singular location of law in the state, the separation of fact and law, the rationality of proof, and the idea of property as distinct from a broad ontology of place.

As Fred Myers argues in relation to Aboriginal art, by the very fact that it provokes exposure to a paradox, Aboriginal art has influenced the parameters of art criticism and discourse. The same prospect exists in native title: the involvement of Indigenous claimants in native title processes is not only supplying answers to the questions posed by the common law, but changing the nature – the how and the what – of the questions, themselves.

REFERENCES

ABC Radio National 1997 'Art Work as Evidence in Native Title Claim' *Law Report* July 15 available at

Alcoff L and Potter E 1993 *Feminist Epistemologies* Routledge New York.

Anderson L 2003 'The Law and the Desert: Alternative Methods of Delivering Justice' *Journal of Law and Society* 30/1: 120–36

Appleton J 1975 *The Experience of Landscape* John Wiley & Sons London

Attwood B 2003 *Rights for Aborigines* Allen & Unwin Crows Nest

Bender B 1999 'Subverting the Western Gaze: Mapping Alternative Worlds' in Ucko and Layton 1999: 31–45

Bennet L and Feldman M 1981 *Reconstructing Reality in the Courtroom* Rutgers University Press New Brunswick

Black M 2002 'Developments in Practice and Procedure in Native Title Cases' *Public Law Review* 13/March: 16–25

Blomley N 1998 'Landscapes of Property' *Law and Society Review* **32**/3: 567–612

Carter P 1988 *The Road to Botany Bay: An Exploration of Landscape and History* Knopf New York

Brooks G 2003 'The Painted Desert' *New Yorker* July **28**: 60–7

Chance I ed 2001 *Kaltja Now* Wakefield Press Adelaide

Childs M and Ellison L eds 2000 *Feminist Perspectives on Evidence* Cavendish Publishing London

Cosgrove D 1984 *Social Formation and Symbolic Landscape* Croom Helm London

Cover R 1983 'The Supreme Court, 1982 Term: Forward: Nomos and Narrative' *Harvard Law Review* **97**: 4–68

Cross R and Tapper C 1985 *Cross on Evidence* Butterworths London (6th edn)

Delgado R ed 1995 *Critical Race Theory: The Cutting Edge* Temple University Press Philadelphia

Derrida J 1987 *The Truth in Painting* Trans G Bennington and McLeod I University of Chicago Press Chicago

Eades D 1988 'They Don't Speak an Aboriginal Language, or Do They?' *in* Keen **1988**: 87–115

Edmonds M 1994 *Claims to Knowledge, Claims to Country: Native Title, Native Title Claims and the Role of the Anthropologist* Aboriginal Studies Press Canberra

Edwards W H 1998 *Traditional Aboriginal Society* Macmillan Education Australia South Yarra (2nd edn)

Eisler W 1995 *The Furthest Shore: Images of Terra Australis from the Middle Ages to Captain Cook* Cambridge University Press Cambridge

Geertz C. 1983 *Local Knowledge: Further Essays in Interpretive Anthropology* Basic Books New York

Haldar P 1994 'In and Out of Court: On Topographies of Law and the Architecture of Court Buildings (A Study of the Supreme Court of the State of Israel)' *International Journal for the Semiotics of Law* **7**/20: 185–200

Harley B. 1992 'Rereading the Maps of the Columbian Encounter' *Annals of the Association of American Geographers* **82**/3: 522–42

Harmon L. 1999 'Etchings on Glass: Reflections on the Science of Proof' *South Texas Law Review* **40**/2: 483–508

Howard M. 2000 *Phipson on Evidence* Sweet & Maxwell London (15th edn) Hutchinson A and Monahan P 1984 'Law, Politics and Critical Legal Scholars: The Unfolding Drama of American Legal Thought' *Stanford Law Review* **36**: 199–245

Jackson B 1988 *Law, Fact and Narrative Coherence* Deborah Charles Publications Merseyside

Keen I ed 1988 *Being Black: Aboriginal Cultures in 'Settled' Australia* Aboriginal Studies Press Canberra

Kerruish V and Perrin C 1999 'Awash in Colonialism: A Critical Analysis of the Federal Court Decision in the matter of *The Members of the Yorta Yorta Aboriginal Community v Victoria*' *Alternative Law Journal* **24**/1: 3

Kleinart S and Neale M eds 2000 *Oxford Companion to Aboriginal Art and Culture* Oxford University Press London and Canberra

Ligertwood L 1993 *Australian Evidence* Butterworths Sydney

Manderson D 2000 *Songs Without Music: Aesthetic Dimensions of Law and Justice* University of California Press Berkeley

Mohr R 1999 'In Between Power and Procedure: Where the Court Meets the Public Sphere' *Journal of Social Change and Critical Inquiry* 1: <http://www.uow.edu.au/arts/joscci/joscci1/index.html>

—— 2002 'Shifting Ground: Context and Change in Two Australian Legal Systems' *International Journal for the Semiotics of Law* 15/1: 1–24

Morphy H 1983 '"Now You Understand": An Analysis of the Way Yolngu Have Used Sacred Knowledge to Retain Their Autonomy' in Peterson et al 1983: 110–45

—— 1991 *Ancestral Connections: Art and an Aboriginal System of Knowledge* University of Chicago Press Chicago

—— 1998 'The Art of Northern Australia' in Edwards 1998: 6–29

Munn N 1973 *Walpiri Iconography: Graphic Representation and Cultural Symbolism in a Central Australian Society* University Press Ithaca Cornell

Murphy P 1995 *Murphy on Evidence* Blackstone Press Ltd London (5th edn) Myers F 2002 *Painting Culture: The Making of an Aboriginal High Art* Duke University Press Durham

Native Title News Letter 2002 No. 3 May-June.

Neate G 2003 'Land, Law and Language: Some Issues in the Resolution of Aboriginal Land Claims in Australia' International Association of Forensic Linguists 11 July 2003 Sydney: available at http://www.nntt.gov.au/ metac-ard/files/iafl/eates_IAFL_speech_July_2003.pdf

Nicholson D 2000 'Gender, Epistemology and Ethics: Feminist Perspectives on Evidence Theory' in Childs and Ellison 2000: 13–37

Pannel S 1994 'Mabo and Museums: "The Indigenous (Re)Appropriation of Indigenous Things"' *Oceania* 65/ 1: 18–39

Peterson N and Langton M eds 1983 *Aborigines, Land and Land Rights* Australian Institute of Aboriginal Studies Canberra

Pottage A 1994 'The Measure of Land' *Modern Law Review* 57/3: 361–84

Povinelli E 2002 *The Cunning of Recognition: Indigenous Alterities and the Making of Australian Multiculturalism* Duke University Press Durham

Rees R 1982 'Painting, Place and Identity: A Prairie View' in Sadler and Carson 1982: 117–41

Reilly A 1996 'Entering a Dream: Two Days of a Native Title Trial in the North-East Kimberley' *Law/Text/Culture* 4: 196–211

—— 2000 'The Ghost of Trugannini: Use of Historical Evidence as Proof of Native Title' *Federal Law Review* 28/3: 453–75

—— 2003 'Cartography and Native Title' *Journal of Australian Studies* 79: 3–14

Rose D B 1994 'Whose Confidentiality? Whose Intellectual Property?' in Edmonds 1994: 1–11

Roskill M and Carrier D 1983 *Truth and Falsehood in Visual Images* University of Massachusetts Press Amherst

Ryan S 1996 *The Cartographic Eye: How Explorers Saw Australia* Cambridge University Press Cambridge

Sadler B and Carson A eds 1982 *Environmental Aesthetics: Essays in Interpretation* University of Victoria Victoria

Santos B 1987 'Law: A Map of Misreadings – Toward a Postmodern Conception of Law' *Journal of Law and Society* 14/3: 279–302

Sarmas L 1994 'Story Telling and the Law: A Case Study of *Louth v Diprose*' *Melbourne University Law Review* 19/3: 701–28

Schreiner A 2001 'Landmarks for Aboriginal Law in Australia' Law Society Association Conference 4–7 July 2001 Budapest

Short J 1991 *Imagined Country: Environment, Culture and Society* Routledge London

Smith B 2001 *Australian Painting 1788–2000* Oxford University Press South Melbourne

Smith T 2001 'From the Desert: Aboriginal Painting 1970–90' in Smith B 2001: 496–517

Stanner W E H 'The Dreaming' in Edwards 1998: 227–51

Tait D 1999 'Boundaries and Barriers: The Social Production of Space in Magistrates' Courts and Guardianship Tribunals' *Journal of Social Change and Critical Inquiry* 1: available at http://www.uow.edu.au/arts/joscci/joscci1/index.html

Timony J 2000 'Demeanor Credibility' *Catholic University Law Review* 49/4: 903–44

Trees K 2002 'Respecting Difference: For Indigenous People Law and Cultural Memory is in the Land not Legislation' Mediating Law: Theory, Production, Culture 11th International Conference of the Law and Literature Association of Australia 29 November–1 December 2002 Melbourne

Twining W 1985 *Theories of Evidence: Bentham and Wigmore* Weidenfelt & Nicolson London

Ucko P and Layton R eds 1999 *The Archaeology and Anthropology of Landscape* Routledge London

Vandevelde K 1980 'The New Property of the Nineteenth Century: The Development of the Modern Concept of Property' *Buffalo Law Review* 29/2: 325–67

Walton W 2002 *Legal Argumentation and Evidence* Pennsylvania State University Press University Park

Cases
Commonwealth v Yarmirr (2001) 208 CLR 1
De Rose v State of South Australia (unreported O'Loughlin J 1 November 2002)
Fejo v Northern Territory (1988) 156 ALR 721
Mabo v Queensland (No 2) (1992) 175 CLR 1
Members of the Yorta Yorta Aboriginal Community v Victoria (2002) 194 ALR 538
Milirrpum v Nabalco (1971) 17 FLR 141
Neowarra v State of Western Australia (unreported Sundberg J 8 December 2003)
The Lardil Peoples v State of Queensland (unreported Cooper J 23 March 2004)
Western Australia v Ward [2002] HCA 28

Statutes
Land Rights Act 1976 (NT)
Native Title Act 1993 (Cth)
Real Property Act 1900 (NSW)

4   Reimagining Legal Geographies

This chapter examines analyses of law and space and the relations between them. These analyses have gained some prominence in critical legal studies in recent decades and underscore another arena of inquiry by sociolegal scholars engaging in a global sociolegal perspective. The interdisciplinary exploration of law's spatial dimensions reflects wider intellectual concerns with new configurations of power, agency, and knowledge and, as such, is not disconnected from the exploration of aesthetics in sociolegal scholarship as outlined in the previous chapter. Similar to a concern with legal aesthetics, an interest in the interrelations between law and space challenges a positivist perspective that posits law as an abstract set of principles to be applied across cultural contexts and fixed spaces. Against this top-down abstractionism, scholars working on law and space typically adopt a bottom-up approach that foregrounds the local conditions of people's experience and how law is imagined and what law means to individuals and communities in their everyday exchanges (Holder and Harrison 2003). Drawing on the work of human geographers, and specifically Marxist human geographers such as David Harvey and Doreen Massey, sociolegal scholars are increasingly embracing the "spatial turn" and, in so doing, bringing attention to the construction of particular places, shaping of subjective imaginaries, and positioning of legal and political possibilities within the relational spaces and places of human experience (see Blomley et al. 2001; Holder and Harrison 2003; Taylor 2006; Butler 2009).

In this chapter I do not attempt to summarize the theoretical debates seeking to define "space" and "place" and how these concepts relate to time.[1] That

[1]   For a wonderful summary of some of these debates see Harvey 2006:117–148. Other major works include Tuan 1974; Buttimer and Seamon 1980; Massey 1994, 2005; Harvey 1996; Lefebvre 1991; Soja 1990; for summaries of these debates see Neely and Samura 2011:3–8 and Cresswell 2004. To varying degrees, all of these theorists discuss space in relationship to time. However, for sociolegal scholarship specifically on time, see Engel 1987; Wilkinson 1987; Greenhouse 1996; French 2001; Richland 2008.

being said, it is important to recognize that all places are "narrated by both location in space – where we are – and location in time – where we were before and where we may be in the future" (Milner and Goldberg-Hiller 2008:236). In this way, all places intrinsically embody political trajectories in the way they become sites of imagination, experience, identity, discrimination, inclusion, and exclusion (Pile and Keith 1993; Harvey 1996; Razack 2002; Neely and Samura 2011). Doreen Massey reiterates the political nature of inquiries in to the construction of space/place/time. She argues that space matters precisely because it inflects how we think about the possibilities of future political action. Proposes Massey:

> *First*, we recognize space as the product of interrelations; as constituted through interactions, from the immensity of the global to the intimately tiny ... *Second*, that we understand space as the sphere of possibility of the existence of multiplicity in the sense of contemporaneous plurality ... If space is indeed the product of interrelations, then it must be predicated upon the existence of plurality. Multiplicity and space as co-constitutive. *Third*, that we recognize space as always under construction. Precisely because space on this reading is the product of relations-between, relations which are necessarily embedded in material practices which have to be carried out, it is always in the process of being made (Massey 2005:9).

According to Massey, space can be characterized as temporally fluid, highly contested, intrinsically politicized, historically informed, and relationally interactive. The central message is that space and its relationship to place and time are never to be assumed as given sites of fixed materiality. It is not as if one can plot spaces on a map and expect that map to remain static or represent the complex of interactions that make up that site. All maps are stylized visual representations of space that may have little to do with geopolitical realities. As such, cartographic images are always inadequate in conveying the contestations of power, shifting symbolisms, and wider political, social, and economic contexts of their making (Lewis and Wigen 1997; with respect to legal maps, see Twining 2000; Bavinck and Woodman 2009).

SPACES, TIMES, INTERLEGALITIES

Why are the concepts of space and time important to a global sociolegal perspective? The primary reason is that nineteenth- and twentieth-century modernist assumptions about space, place, and time are no longer tenable in the context of new local, national, regional, and global interconnections, tensions, and movement of legal meaning across and within borders that constitute the contemporary era. Modernist assumptions correlated state territories, legal jurisdictions, cultural identity, national history, and sovereign authority. In recent decades these linking assumptions have been delinked or unraveled. Against a backdrop of escalating global forces throughout the 1990s, a few sociolegal scholars recognized that law was being profoundly challenged by new forms of spatially constituted legal engagement. One of the most important of these scholars was Boaventura de Sousa Santos who wrote a groundbreaking essay titled "Law: A Map of Misreading. Toward a Postmodern Conception of Law" (Santos 1987). This essay raised new theoretical and empirical concerns about the ways law distorts reality and specifically about the artificial assumption presumed in conventional cartography of legal jurisdictions neatly mapping onto nation-state boundaries. Introducing the concept of "interlegalities," Santos argued that non-state law and informal legal processes are as important as official state law in any understanding of legal interaction (see Santos 1987, 1995:473; on legalities also see Ewick and Silbey 1998). The idea of decentering the importance of the nation-state (or misreading conventional maps of state and interstate power) cannot be underestimated. Even though it sounds rather obvious today, at the time this concept was enormously provocative, innovative, and prescient.

Santos' work foreshadowed what has since become a wave of scholarship grappling with the concept of law in a world of increasingly explicit globalization. Throughout the 1990s a growing appreciation of law's global geopolitical dimensions emerged alongside increasing attention being given to the scales and sites and forms of transnational and global legal processes. This was a period of new technologies and media that accelerated communication and data exchange that transcended both the boundaries and regulatory capacities of any one nation. In addition, transnational movements of money, people, and materials, and the growth of regional political and economic entities such as the European Union and the Asian Tigers (Hong Kong, Taiwan, South Korea, and Singapore), highlighted both the conceptual and regulatory inadequacies of national legal jurisdictions. More recently, cyberspace, outerspace exploration, and the increasing recognition of global climate change and world environmental devastation have pushed the conceptual frames of space and law in new directions. Together these global processes profoundly undermine the assumption of the nation-state as the jurisdictional "container" of all legal interaction (see Darian-Smith 1999; Sparke 2005; Lastowka 2010). Today, we are witnessing lawyers and scholars scrambling to come to terms with what a global legal world may look like, and what agencies and frameworks may be required for legal relations across and between states, regions, and dimensions.

Over the past two decades, sociolegal scholars such as Nicholas Blomley and David Delaney (both trained geographers) established a new wave of inquiry in law and society scholarship. Seeking to bring together the insights of human geography with those of critical legal scholars, these scholars formed an innovative field of sociolegal inquiry that is sometimes referred to as "critical legal geography" or more simply scholarship concerned with space and law. This rather loosely coalesced field is involved with various issues ranging from local zoning laws and practices of urban government, to racial formations across diasporas and economic regions, to movements of labor and human trafficking, to transnational regulatory agencies such as the IMF and the World Bank. Whether working on local, national, regional, or global legal processes or the interactions between them, scholars identifying with the field of law and geography understand that law is intrinsically spatialized. This means that whatever site or scale of legal engagement explored, there is an appreciation that law first requires designation of legitimate legal subjects to which law applies and against which it can be enforced (Fitzpatrick 1992, 2001; Engel 1993:180). In other words, law is constituted as law once it has marked off the boundaries and so legitimized the authority of its application. Argues Paul Kahn, "law's space is always bordered space … Law's space is not a thing in the world about which we can be right or wrong. It is a set of meanings displayed and maintained in an historically specific discourse that is deployed to defend particular claims to property and jurisdiction" (see Cooper 1998; Kahn 1999:56, 65; Ford 1999; Holder and Harrison 2003:Part II).

This does not mean, of course, that law's space is in some way naturalized or a pre-given. In fact, much of the sociolegal work being done on issues of law and space seeks to explore the processes by which jurisdictional boundaries are established, defended, and/or challenged (see Sarat and Umphrey 2010). Moreover, as Anne Orford, a leading international law theorist reminds us, jurisdiction and territory are not necessarily closely connected despite "the triumph of the territorial State as the dominant political form globally" (Orford 2009:982). According to Orford, the United Nation's responsibility to intervene when a state is incapable of providing security to its own citizens depends upon a "non-territorial form of jurisdiction that applies to the world as a whole" (Orford 2009:1010). This claim to a universal jurisdiction is not based in the UN's authority to control the world, but in its role in policing peoples' obligations and duties to each other.[2]

---

[2] Orford argues that the concept of universal jurisdiction, which is grounded in the United Nations and the wider international community, is analogous to the earlier Holy Roman Empire (Orford 2009:1010; on universal jurisdiction, see Reydams 2004). Orford rightly cautions that this kind of global responsibility to police needs careful checks and balances given that it could be used oppressively to justify forms of global domination.

As suggested by the concept of universal jurisdiction, law's relationship to space involves much more than demarcating boundaries of rule making and authorizing legal subjectivities (be this via national citizenship or other forms of group affiliation). Spaces of legal interaction can be ambiguous and contradictory, producing metaphors of self and collective identity as well as symbols of responsibility, belonging, and alienation (see Blandy and Silbey 2010). Spaces of legal interaction, in other words, can operate in nonmaterial and nonlinear ways to create new imaginings of subjectivity that far transcend any actual place or locality (Sarat et al. 2006; William Taylor 2006). According to David Delaney:

> As Henri Lefebvre has written, "*That* space signifies is incontestable. But *what* it signifies is *dos* and *don'ts*, that brings us back to power" (Lefebvre 1991:142, emphasis added). And *that* brings us back to law. The worlds of human experience are composed of an uncountable number and innumerable variety of social spaces. Some are global in extent, some smaller than your hand; some are fixed to particular landscapes, some are in motion. The ways in which these spaces are created and altered, assembled, disassembled, and reassembled, strongly condition what the world is like and what it is like to be in the world – that is, what this or that life is like. These spaces are meaningful. They signify, represent, and refer (Delaney 2010:4).

In thinking about how spaces "signify, represent, and refer" it is helpful to turn to specific examples. For instance, what role did city streets and urban spaces play in pro-democracy protest movements that erupted in Tunis, Cairo, and other major urban and capital cities throughout North Africa and the Middle East during 2011 and 2012? In analyzing the role of urban streets and spaces, Saskia Sessen cautions us to distinguish these spaces from the concept of public space in the European tradition (Sassen 2011). In the context of medieval Europe, city space was contested and partitioned on the basis of new alignments of property ownership and demands of citizenship among a growing merchant class. In contrast, "Today's political practices ... have to do with the production of 'presence' by those without power and with a politics that claims rights to the city and to the country rather than protection of property" (Sassen 2011:574). Building upon this current analysis of urban public space, Mohamed Nanabhay and Roxane Farmanfarmaian argue that in the context of Cairo's Tahrir Square, three intersecting spaces were essential in the pro-democracy protest movements that eventually ousted Egyptian President Hosni Mubarak in February 2011. These three spaces were the physical protests themselves, social media and the Internet, and satellite television and mainstream media (Nanabhay and Farmanfarmaian 2011). Together these intersecting spaces created the "spectacle" of Tahrir Square as a focal point for mobilizing demonstrators and communicating to international media the "spectacular" events at the local level. Under these conditions, Tahrir Square became a symbolic site of interaction and political possibility and provided a public platform and theatrical space through which tense negotiations unfolded over the course of weeks. Since the revolution, Tahrir Square has continued to be a site of ongoing public protest and mobilization in Egypt, and references to its symbolic "people power" are constantly evoked across the Middle East and other pro-democracy movements.

Another public space, and one that stands in stark contrast to Tahrir Square, is Beijing's Tiananmen Square. After the failed Chinese democratic movement and violent killing of student protestors in 1989, the public square became a site of tight military oversight, and any reference to the protests or killings have been virtually eviscerated from Chinese media archives and public memory.[3] Today, it is only when Chinese people travel outside China can they learn about the history surrounding their own Tiananmen Square. For those of us living outside China, Tiananmen Square and the protests that happened there have assumed symbolic and political resonance that far transcend its immediate spatial context in the city of Beijing or the country of China. Referring back to Delaney's point that spaces "signify, represent, and refer," Tiananmen Square harshly reminds us that processes of signification always involve elements of power, including the power to silence certain narratives and spatial experiences and to re-signify others (see also Layard 2010).

Law, as an expression and vehicle of power, is intimately and necessarily interrelated with space. Notes Nick Blomley, law and space are in fact "aspects of each other" (Blomley 2004b:29). According to Blomley:

> A prisoner without a prison, even a virtual one, is, of course, not a prisoner. A legal category such as "citizen" is meaningless without the spatial category of "territory". In turn land without an owner is an impossibility (at least within the West). When we think about it, it becomes hard to isolate the "legal" from the "spatial". Is a prison a spatial or legal category? Both are integral; both are entangled. The challenge is to find a conceptual language that allows us to think beyond binary categories such as "space" and "law" (Blomley 2004b:29–30).

---

3 Chinese director Lou Ye produced *Summer Palace* (2006), which is a movie containing re-enacted scenes of street protests and demonstrations in Tiananmen Square. The Chinese government banned the public viewing of the movie.

However, the mutual dependence between law and space Blomley points to should not be interpreted as a causal relationship such that law always acts upon space in an instrumental sense. Legal rules can shape spaces and territories. At the same time, spaces "have characteristics that affect the conditions in which power can be exercised, conflicts pursued and social control attempted" (Hirst 2005:3). Spaces and territories also shape and inform the capacity to imagine new – and revise old – legal logics and mechanisms of social ordering (Cooper 1998; Valverde 2011).

This complex intermingling between space and law can be seen, for instance, in the establishment of refugee camps. International humanitarian laws and conventions set up rules defining who is a refugee, what rights and welfare policies pertain to refugees, and what happens when a person becomes stateless. Do refugee camps force the creation of new international laws to deal with what is going on within camp boundaries, or do existing laws create the authority and legitimacy for particular locales to become new camps in the first place? The answer is not clear, nor generalizable to diverse refugee camp settings around the world. Moreover, how do memory, longing, nostalgia, and despair feature in the legally liminal spaces of refugee camps in which nationalist identities and citizenship rights are marginalized and in many cases deemed irrelevant (Ray 2002; Peteet 2005; Turner 2005; Sanyal 2009). Do these unique social places, which are technically temporary and transitional, create new forms of legality formally not available or conceivable? (See Figure 4.)

In a similar way, do zoning laws within cities create and legitimate racial discriminatory practices against certain minorities, or do existing racial prejudices sustain the creation of new zoning laws based on exclusion and inequity? A 2011 example is the French government's banning of street prayer by Muslims who often lack spaces to worship in Paris. Critics interpret the ban as racially biased and pandering to Marine Le Pen's right-wing nationalist party, which has described street prayer as an "invasion" (*New York Times* Sept. 17, 2011:6). Will the ban shore up French racism toward Muslims and generate new forms of criminality based on racialized difference? Or will the ban on public prayer – and here I admit to being rather fanciful – produce unforeseen results, such as the French government's endorsement of the building of mosques to accommodate worshippers and create new opportunities for Parisian and Muslim communities to learn to live together (see Bowen 2007, 2009). My point is that whatever the eventual outcome of this ban on public prayer, the relationship between law and space is dynamic, not necessarily connected in a linear causal sense, and often contingent upon emergent opportunities we may not be able to predict or even imagine.

Figure 4. Democratic Republic of Congo. The Congo River was the link between Kisangani and Kinshasa. Before the war (which began in 1998 and officially ended in 2003), huge barges plied the river carrying agricultural produce down river and industrial goods up. The war brought this to an end. Today, the banks of the river are littered with the rusting hulks of a transport system that has collapsed along with the economic and legal mechanisms that supported it. Abandoned boats create floating refugee camps, with people living on makeshift tents between stacks of goods on the decks. Photograph taken by Julien Harneis. February 14, 2008.

RELATIONAL PROPERTIES AND SOVEREIGNTIES

For decades, sociolegal scholars have explored the racial, gender, and class dimensions of property ownership. This is hardly surprising given that property rights, and the capacity to own property to the exclusion of others, are central pillars of modern Euro-American law and lie at the heart of social contract theory governing people's relationships to each other and the state. Property rights shape people's intimate social relationships through such things as marriage and dowry, as well as their public economic and political status with respect to the general society. In short, owning property is an essential component of, and claim to, various levels and kinds of social membership. People who do not own property in Western societies are in many ways socially invisible, politically powerless, and economically irrelevant. This is as true today as it has been for the past five centuries.

In seventeenth-century England, John Locke (1632–1704) discussed in his *Two Treatises of Government* the mechanism whereby a social contact was made between individuals and a representative form of government. He argued that people create private property rights over land by applying their own labor and making it productive, typically through farming.[4] Once having established private property rights, people want to defend those rights. Hence, Locke argued, people turn to creating a social contract whereby individuals abandon the "state of nature" and accept a ruling government and the obligations of civil society in return for the protection of their property rights, including property vested in their own bodies.

Jean-Jacques Rousseau (1712–1778), writing approximately half a century after Locke, was similarly fascinated in the role private property played in governing social and political relations. For Rousseau, the invention of private property was a pivotal moment in the evolution from what he regarded as an idyllic and peaceful pre-modern state of nature to one of modern social inequality and class conflict. In his famous work *The Social Contract* (1762), Rousseau outlined the failings of modern society, which he saw as fundamentally flawed by people's self-interested greed and inequalities of property ownership. According to Rousseau, this terrible state of affairs could be overcome and peace returned if all people would come together and submit to a general will to live together as a collective community of free and equal persons. Noted Rousseau, a central element in an individual's submission to the general will was obeying law in return for the state's protection of private property rights. Abiding by state law was the foundational platform on which could be constructed a social contract.

Today, social contract theories have been heavily critiqued by feminist and critical race theorists (see Pateman 1988; Mills 1997; Pateman and Mills 2007). These theorists argue that earlier conceptualizations of the social contract idealized the notion of who could in fact enter the contract in the first place and assumed that contracting parties consisted of white males. For instance, Carole Pateman has argued that preexisting contracts exist between men and women, whereby men maintain control over women's sexuality and reproductive rights. Hence, any notion that a social contract creates equality and a collective good must first of all account for preexisting contracts (such as marriage contracts) that deny women full emancipation (Pateman 1988). Charles Mills has made similar arguments with respect to race, arguing that racial

---

[4] This rationale also justified European colonizers taking lands from native peoples. In the new British colonies in North America, Indians who did not till and plant the land were seen as lazy and having abandoned their possessory rights (Darian-Smith 2010a:71–72).

and ethnic minorities occupy positions analogous to women in that they have been historically denied equal access to political participation. Notes Mills, the idea of a social contract has in fact served to mask socioeconomic inequalities and systematically exclude non-whites in processes of political representation (Mills 1997). Together Pateman and Mills maintain that Locke and Rousseau failed to fully consider the capacity of women and other minorities to contract in their own right, free of white male domination. The consequence of this argument is that the evolution of Euro-American property rights is predicated on exclusionary practices toward certain sectors of society.

Sociolegal scholars working on property rights have drawn heavily from the theoretical insights of feminist studies and critical race scholarship. As Margaret Davies notes in her book *Property: Meanings, Histories, Theories*, "the concept and manifestations of property in Western liberal context go far beyond legal doctrine, extending to ideologies of the self, social interactions with others, concepts of law, and social concepts of gender roles and race relations" (Davies 2007:2; see also Rose 1994). This raises questions such as, who owns property, in what ways do they own it, and what does legal possession mean materially, historically, symbolically, and metaphorically? Moreover, how does property acquisition, dispossession, and displacement relate to the shifting contours of social membership through citizenship and other markers of group identity? (Neves 2007). In what ways does the constitution of property delegate public and private spaces, in turn affirming or subverting categories of race, class, gender, age, religion, and ethnicity, as well as concepts such as privacy and labor? (i.e., Delaney 1998; Mitchell 2003; Layard 2010; Blomley 2011).

Increasingly, these kinds of questions are preoccupying critical sociolegal scholars whose studies range across time and space, including, for instance, examining the possession of overseas colonial lands in the building of European empires (Robertson 2007), the problems in granting hereditary land title to black slaves in the United States (Jones 2009), the forced relocation of Bedouins from rural to urban Israeli communities (Shamir 1996), the criminalization and "banishment" of homeless and poor from city centers (Beckett and Herbert 2010), the administration of therapeutic care to drug users through drug treatment courts and the creation of "unhealthy" city neighborhoods (Moore et al. 2011), and the removal of ethnic communities from their traditional homelands in the name of economic development in South Africa (O'Mahony and Sweeney 2010). As these examples suggest, scholars of space and law are acutely aware of the relational dimensions of property (and territoriality more generally) and the need to contextualize space within wider cultural and socioeconomic explorations. Property is not treated as an absolute or naturalized pre-given but a realm constituted through the people negotiating its assumed and contested meanings.

In a similar way to reconceptualizing property, the concept of sovereignty is also being reanalyzed in terms of its relationship to territory and non-state political activities.[5] Historically, sovereignty correlated to territory and designated the power of a state to control its bordered lands. Notes Rafael Domingo, "Sovereignty is thus a property inherent to any state, which gives it supreme power in territory, control of its legal system, and the right to recognize external bodies or entities that establish contact with it" (Domingo 2010:65). Of course, states never have been totally sovereign or independent, and impoverished nations of the world are considerably less sovereign than rich nations (Ferguson 2006). As Domingo goes on to point out, in today's world the concept of territorial sovereignty is being more severely challenged than ever before. "Nowadays, its usefulness is in doubt in an era of globalization, in which communications, commerce, and daily life have been globalized, creating a dense web of human interaction and an interdependence of relations incompatible with its theoretical assumptions" (Domingo 2010:65–66). Wendy Brown, a leading feminist scholar and political theorist, also describes how territorial sovereignty is waning in today's contemporary world. However, she is quick to note that this does not mean that states matter less or that sovereignty is being somehow eliminated and that we now live in a post-sovereign world (Brown 2010b). Rather, Brown argues, states are being pulled apart from their territories with the rise of the global political economy and religiously sanctioned political violence. As a result, this destabilization of territoriality is creating – somewhat ironically – a surge in efforts by states to build walls around their borders and to reassert autonomy and containment (Brown 2010b).

Helen Stacy, a scholar of international law, builds on these theoretical discussions about the changing nature of sovereignty in the twenty-first century and argues for the need to reconceptualize sovereignty in terms of "relational sovereignty" (Stacy 2003, 2009). She suggests that the concept of sovereignty is being "defined by a different nature of the social contract, a contract that must account for the increasingly complex range of transnational interactions

---

[5] In recent years the concept of sovereignty has attracted significant attention in the theoretical works of scholars such as Georges Bataille, Carl Schmitt, Jean-Luc Nancy, Michele Foucault, Judith Butler, and Georgia Agamben. The concept of sovereignty and the implications of exceptionalism have been at the core of much recent sociolegal scholarship (i.e., Anghie 2005, 2009; Sarat and Clarke 2008; Barbour and Pavlich 2010). Further complicating these debates has been the work of scholars examining minority groups within states, sometimes referred to as "stateless nations" such as the Catalonians in the Basque region, and scholars focusing on "quasi-sovereign" states such as Palestinian-controlled territory in Gaza and the West Bank.

under the conditions of globalization, and also the enlarging role of international human rights norms as benchmarks of good governance and good sovereignty" (Stacy 2003:2004). Stacy argues that sovereignty must attach "itself to the people of the state, not merely the state itself, in a multi-directional social contract." In this way, "relational sovereignty places a higher obligation on the sovereign state to care for and regulate the behavior of its citizens both inside and outside state borders ... The sovereign's duty to protect and deter should follow the citizen, rather than stopping at the border" (Stacy 2003:2050–2051, 2049). In other words, Stacy argues, sovereignty has to delink itself from the state as the spatial container of its obligations. In contrast to conventional notions of sovereignty, relational sovereignty "takes its contours from the relationships between citizens, their governments, and the international community" (Stacy 2003:2044).

In burgeoning theories and public conversations[6] about the social contract and how this may relate to a state's sovereign responsibilities it becomes clear that conventional notions of law and space are no longer viable in the twenty-first century. There is an emerging disjuncture between law and space as historically conceived in a Westphalian world view of autonomous states interacting with each other, regulated by positivist national legal systems. This disjuncture is widening and deepening, despite the United States claiming an exceptional status and denying its interdependence with the rest of the world and its consequent international and global obligations (see Agamben 2005; Butler 2006). As scholars note, "Absolute sovereignty continues to be invoked by politicians and states intent on insulating themselves from international criticism and accountability" (Clarke and Whitt 2007:18). Against state resistance to shifting geopolitical realities, concepts such as relational sovereignty can be seen as efforts to move the focus away from state-to-state relations based on relative power and competition for resources and markets toward activities affecting people on various fronts and that can no longer be regulated and contained within national state borders (i.e., labor, environment, immigration, health).

That being said, the preceding discussions about rethinking property and sovereignty in relational terms tend to get bogged down by the enduring

---

[6] Interestingly, not only are academics concerned about the changing context of the social contract. What the social contract means and what obligations state governments owe their citizens has entered public political debate in the United States in the lead up to the 2012 presidential elections. See "Video: The Elizabeth Warren Quote Every American Needs To Hear," MoveOn.org, Sept. 21, 2011. Online at: http://www.moveon.org/r?r=264488&id=31551–17916434-quBVm5x&t=4 (retrieved on April 20, 2012).

dominance of nation-states and national law. Hence, as Doreen Massey points out, "On the one hand space and places are increasingly the product of global flows; on the other hand we work with a politics both official and unofficial that is framed by a territorial imagination and formal structure" (Massey 2007:14). So although some sociolegal scholars are increasingly acknowledging different ways of relating to property and territory, such as homeless peoples' relationship to public space (Blomley 2011), transnational adoption and reconfigurations of "motherhood" and "home" (Yngvesson 2010), or genetic materials such as cells and genes being reterritorialized as objects of property (Whatmore 2003), these alternative spatial-legal interrelations are typically seen as marginal or powerless against the dominant authority of national geographies. Nation-states are interpreted as continuing to function as relatively fixed political and territorial entities against which non-state actors (and things) and their relationships to places, properties, homelands, and sovereignties (however defined) are posited. In other words, pluralized ways of knowing and experiencing law and space are not seen as dislodging or destabilizing state systems in any significant sense. National laws and their correlative jurisdictional territories continue to provide the dominant spatial context and frame of mainstream legal scholarship.

LAW IN THE WORLD

Andreas Philippopoulos-Mihalopoulos laments the continuing dominance of the nation-state in analyses of law and space and suggests such literature represents a kind of "parochialism" (Philippopoulos-Mihalopoulos 2010:190). This parochialism constructs "space in a narrow, legalistic way as jurisdiction" and considers the space of law as the nation as opposed to the world. The result is that the space of law is not in any way disturbed or questioned, and the status quo is ultimately maintained. Hence, while "Law's spatial turn promises to bring forth a space within the law both welcoming and terrifying in its capacity to disorientate and destabilize," for Philippopoulos-Mihalopoulos this opening up of subversive possibility is squandered by scholars who cling to analyzing the limits of space as contained by national jurisdictions (Philippopoulos-Mihalopoulos 2010:202; see also Delaney 2003; Blomley 2004b).

In a similar vein, David Delaney describes the work in critical legal geography as at an impasse (Delaney 2010:12). Argues Delaney:

> Scholars tend to focus on particular spatial issues or contexts at the "law-space nexus", such as public space, Indian reservations, refugee camps,

voting districts, borders, colonies, or cities. This reinforces the archipelagic effect in the field as a whole. Each of these contexts is surrounded by an invisible boundary that cuts it off from other contexts or other dimensions of spatio-legality. Wider connections or more pervasive processes are thereby made invisible, filtered out, or excluded by the boundaries of inquiry. This fragmentation is compounded by a like parcelization from the legal side of social spatialization, through, say, property law, immigration law, municipal law, voting rights, civil rights, constitutional law, or international law that has a dispersal effect that deflects attention away from social phenomena and experiential realities that are not so easily cabined. Also lost is any larger sense of more extensive constellations or configurations that are not discernable through these refracting lenses (Delaney 2010:12–13).[7]

However, a few sociolegal scholars are not shying away from exposing some of the ways spaces may be subverting and radicalizing the constitution and production of law. Such work explores how law's cultural logics may be spatially and temporally challenged from various sources and directions, be these at local, regional, national, international, transnational, or global levels. This research typically adopts a bottom-up ethnographic approach that allows for close analysis of people's relations with various, often overlapping, legal systems (see Chapter 2). Appreciating that law is pluralized across time and space, scholars are keen to examine whether such plurality may in fact create hybrid epistemologies and various ways of knowing, experiencing, and performing law (see Blomley 2004a; Benton 2005; Mawani 2009; Valverde 2009, 2011; Guggenheim, 2010; Keenan 2010). As Franz von Benda-Beckmann, Keebet von Benda-Beckman, and Anne Griffiths argue, to date most of the work in the geography of law focuses on state law in industrialized countries in Europe and the United States. "However, many people live under plural legal constellations. For example, they negotiate one set of rules relating to personal law, such as customary law, with another such as religious or international human rights law (reflecting a more transnational dimension), along with state law that also reflects a degree of heterogeneity" (Benda-Beckman

---

7   Moreover, Delaney suggests that conventional understandings of space as the external or material world, and law as primarily composed of words, rhetoric, ideology, discourse, and meaning, intrinsically limits the critical edge of sociolegal scholarship. "In this framing law is to space as mind is to body. Law signifies a realm of meaning (making), legal meanings are 'inscribed' onto segmented materialities, social spaces 'contain' meanings and so on. This deeper metaphysics of legal geography has effects that are rarely noticed. Among these is the perpetuation of a cognitive centrifugal force that impedes investigation of the richness of the mutual constitutivity of the legal and the spatial, and so short-circuits analysis of how their practical intertwinings are accomplished and transformed. This has the further effect of impeding a greater appreciation of why (and how) they matter" (Delaney 2010:13).

et al. 2009b:4; see also Drummond 2006; Benda-Beckmann 2009; Griffiths 2009). These legal anthropologists argue for the need to recalibrate the relationship that exists between law and social space "under plural legal conditions." Accordingly:

> Under plural legal conditions, often a result of colonial rule, diverse and often contradictory notions of spaces and boundaries and their legal relevances come to coexist. The ways in which physical spaces, boundaries or borderlands are conceived and made legally relevant varies considerably within and across legal orders. Relations between space and social organization, the temporality of constructions of space and place, the scale on which they operate, and the political loading and moral connotations pertaining to specific spaces may all differ (Benda-Beckman et al. 2009b:4).

In today's globalizing world, indigenous perspectives are becoming increasingly relevant in thinking through a range of interlegalities and spatial connections of "law in the world." An exciting body of literature is emerging within postcolonial and indigenous studies that explores how plural legal conditions may be challenging the epistemological foundations and positivist assumptions of modern Western law (Black 2010; Goldberg-Hiller and Silva 2011).[8] In the context of critical legal geography, both native and nonnative scholars are examining concepts such as property, identity, territoriality, and sovereignty within non-Western conceptual, spatial, and temporal frames (Deloria 1996, 1998; Biolsi 2005; Cattelino 2006, 2007; Muldoon 2008; Richland 2010, 2011; Cheyfitz 2011). According to Alan Clarke and Laurelyn Whitt, legal scholars are paying more attention to indigenous perspectives because they suggest new ways to conceptualize a system of global governance that simultaneously allows for greater control by communities at local levels (Clarke and Whitt 2007; see also Skibine 2009). As Clarke and Whitt go on to say, rethinking sovereignty as interdependent and relational helps ensure the future protection of human rights by preventing abusive states from hiding behind claims that they exist autonomously and have absolute control over their citizens. In the twenty-first century, who has control over who has become one of the major issues confronting aspirations by international communities to establish institutions of global governance and legal accountability. How human rights rhetoric and related institutions and agencies may be mobilized to adequately

---

[8] As discussed in Chapter 3, this body of scholarship takes seriously the plural legal underpinnings of contemporary conflicts across and between indigenous and non-indigenous communities (Ivison 2002; Barker 2005; Wiessner 2008). Significantly, these scholars do not assume the dominance of Euro-American law, and so they do not marginalize or see as irrelevant competing legal epistemologies above and below the level of the state (Santos 2007; Skibine 2009; Chapman 2009).

historicize and remember – as well as challenge and change – the legal, spatial, and temporal conditions of domination and inequality is the subject of the next chapter.

LIST OF SUGGESTED READINGS

1. Butler, Chris (2009) Critical Legal Studies and the Politics of Space. *Social & Legal Studies* 18(3):313–332.
2. Santos, Boaventura de Sousa (1987) Law: A Map of Misreading. Toward a Postmodern Conception of Law. *Journal of Law and Society* 14(3):279–302.
3. Holder, Jane and Carolyn Harrison (eds.) (2003) *Law and Geography*. Current Legal Issues. 2002 Vol. 5. Oxford: Oxford University Press.
4. Ford, Richard (1999) Law's Territory (a History of Jurisdiction). *Michigan Law Review* 97(4):843–930.
5. Benda-Beckmann, Franz von, Keebet von Benda-Beckmann and Anne Griffiths (eds.) (2009) *Spatializing Law: an Anthropological Geography of Law in Society*. Farnham, Surrey: Ashgate.
6. Blandy, Sarah and David Silbey (2010) Law, Boundaries and the Production of Space. *Social & Legal Studies* 19(3):275–284.
7. Blomley, Nicholas, David Delaney and Richard Ford (eds.) (2001) *The Legal Geographies Reader: Law, Power and Space*. Oxford: Blackwell.
8. Delaney, David (2010) *The Spatial, the Legal and the Pragmatics of World-Making. Nomospheric Investigations*. Milton Park, Oxon: Routledge-Cavendish.
9. Griffiths, Anne (2009) Law, Space, and Place: Reframing Comparative Law and Legal Anthropology. *Law & Social Inquiry* 34(2):495–507.
10. Lastowka, Greg (2010) *Virtual Justice: The New Worlds of Online Worlds*. New Haven: Yale University Press.
11. Lynch, Mona (2001) From the Punitive City to the Gated Community: Security and Segregation Across the Social and Penal Landscape. *Miami Law Review* 56:89–112.
12. Manderson, Desmond (ed.) (2005) Legal Spaces. Special Issue. *Law Text Culture* 9(1).
13. Merry, Sally Engle (2008) International Law and Sociolegal Scholarship: Toward a Spatial Global Legal Pluralism. Special Issue: Law and Society Reconsidered. *Studies in Law, Politics, and Society* 41:149–168.
14. Philippopoulos-Mihalopoulos, Andreas (2010) Law's Spatial Turn: Geography, Justice and a Certain Fear of Space. *Law, Culture and the Humanities* 7(2):187–202.

15. Sparke, Matthew (2005) *In the Space of Theory: Postfoundational Geographies of the Nation-State.* Minneapolis: University of Minnesota Press.
16. Taylor, William (ed.) (2006) *The Geography of Law: Landscape, Identity and Regulation.* Oxford: Hart Publishing.

Excerpts From:

Coutin, Susan Bibler (2010) Confined Within: National Territories as Zones of Confinement. *Political Geography* 29:200–208. Reproduced with permission.

CONFINED WITHIN: NATIONAL TERRITORIES AS ZONES OF CONFINEMENT

Susan Bibler Coutin[9]

Abstract

Keywords: Immigration Deportation Detention Territory, El Salvador, United States

The securitization of immigration has led to increased reliance on border enforcement, detention, and deportation to control unauthorized movements. Based on a case study of the ways that Salvadoran immigrants to the United States have experienced these tactics, this paper analyzes the spatial implications of current enforcement strategies. As movement across borders becomes more difficult for the unauthorized, national territories become zones of confinement. This carceral quality is a dimension of national territory in that undocumented and temporarily authorized migrants cannot exit their countries of residence without losing territorially-conferred rights, while if they are deported, their countries of origin become extensions of the detention centers they occupied before exit. This transformation of national spaces is accompanied by internal differentiation, as interior enforcement confines migrants to subnational spaces where they must remain to avoid detection or harassment. Securitization thus entails both extraterritoriality, that is the extension of U.S. legal regimes into foreign territories, and intraterritoriality, or the operation of different legal regimes within national territories. The paper also highlights the ways that securitization contributes to multidimensionality, such that spatial locations are rendered ambiguous, both inside and outside at the same time. Finally, the paper considers how these spatial transformations redefine citizenship and belonging.

Over the past two decades, immigration receiving states have resorted to extraordinary spatial tactics to prevent irregular migrants from accessing the legal rights conferred by territorial presence. These tactics include excising territory for immigration purposes, locating customs inspections abroad such that travelers "enter" national space before leaving their destinations, policing

[9] Dept. of Criminology, Law and Society, University of California, Irvine, Irvine, CA 92697–7080, USA; Dept. of Anthropology, University of California, Irvine, Irvine, CA 92697–7080, USA.

migrants and would-be migrants in countries of transit and exit, and defining the international spaces of airports as outside of national territory (Coutin, 2007; Hyndman & Mountz, 2008; Mountz, 2010; Raustiala, 2009). These spatial tactics have coincided with an intensification of immigration enforcement more generally. In the United States, stiffened enforcement has included mandatory detention, militarization of the U.S. Mexico border, workplace raids, state and local initiatives that target undocumented immigrants, police enforcement of immigration laws, restricting access to driver's licenses and identity documents, reducing means of legalization, targeting aliens with criminal convictions, increased deportations, bars on legal reentry following deportation, and prosecuting immigration offenses (Andreas, 2000; Cole & Dempsey, 2002; Coleman, 2007; Coutin, 2005; Eagly, 2008; Hing, 2006; Inda, 2006; Kanstroom, 2000, 2007; Nevins, 2002; Scalia & Litras, 2002; Walters, 2002). Like territorial excision, these law enforcement practices have significant spatial implications. I argue that the increased securitization of immigration makes national spaces akin, in certain respects, to detention centers. This carceral quality is a dimension of national territory in that undocumented and temporarily authorized migrants cannot exit their countries of residence without losing territorially-conferred rights, while if they are deported, their countries of origin become extensions of the detention centers they occupied before exit. This transformation of national spaces is accompanied by internal differentiation, as interior enforcement confines migrants to subnational spaces where they must remain to avoid detection or harassment. As, in the United States, "persons" are increasingly treated as "immigrants" (Varsanyi, 2008), alienage is embodied within noncitizen subjects as a dimension of personhood. The proliferation of law enforcement practices also has a spillover effect, such that citizens too must pass through inspection points, obtain passports to travel, demonstrate proof of legal residency and so forth. Treating residents, legal or otherwise, as potentially undocumented thus transforms the nature of citizenship itself.

Detention centers are key to this reconstitution of both persons and territories. As Nicholas De Genova (2002) has noted, immigration law enforcement is designed less to produce deportations than deportability; that is, a relatively small number of actual deportations give undocumented migrants a sense of vulnerability and thus constitute them as illegal and disposable workers. Likewise, increased emphasis on detention and deportation exacerbates migrants' alienage and illegality. Even migrants who are not apprehended experience exclusionary tactics such as being denied access to employment, housing, higher education, social services, healthcare, and public benefits. Such exclusionary practices situate migrants ambiguously as outside of national territory even when, physically, they are within. Through such spatial ambiguity, undocumented migrants' illegal status maps onto their physical location, making the space that they occupy a special case of what Raustiala (2009: 5) refers to as intra-territoriality, that is, "when different areas within a sovereign state have distinct legal regimes." Detention centers also have transnational effects in that it is the prospect of being detained and incarcerated following reentry that makes deportees' countries of origin places of confinement for deportees. As foreign territories become extensions of detention centers, a territorial transference, of sorts, occurs. Deportation and immigration enforcement thus also exemplify extraterritoriality, which occurs "when domestic law extends beyond sovereign borders" (Raustiala, 2009: 5). The fact that national territories in some ways resemble detention centers – both of these confine, both restrict movement – challenges liberal notions of nations as entities through which individuals can realize their capacities (Collier, Maurer, & Suárez-Navaz, 1995). At the same time, differences between national territories and detention centers – after all, the undocumented do cross-borders and are not formally confined – suggest the limits of securitization. Thus, increases in the size of the undocumented population have given rise to renewed calls for a path to legalization.

A number of factors are responsible for the new enforcement practices that have produced these territorial reconfigurations. First, the globalization of labor markets has led to a renewed emphasis on the forms of social control that produce deportability, such that migrant laborers are present and exploitable (De Genova, 2002; De Genova & Peutz, 2010; Wishnie, 2003, 2007–2008). Second, reliance on such labor has made undocumented immigration part of the "shadow economy" of neoliberalism and global restructuring (Coutin, Maurer, & Yngvesson, 2002; see also Heyman & Smart, 1999). Migrants travel illicitly, but produce remittances, which are then incorporated into national and international financial accounts, even as the dispersal of workers through deportation has made labor available for such transnational enterprises as call centers (Hernandez & Coutin, 2006). Third, neoliberalism has exacerbated social conflict, giving rise to intensified wars on crime and on terror. Criminal problems, such as gang violence, are increasingly viewed as cross-border phenomena that require transnational policing efforts, while the war on terror ignores national boundaries and treats its targets as aliens or even as inhuman (Cole & Dempsey, 2002; Raustiala, 2009). Fourth, investments in security apparatuses, such as detention centers, weaponry, and personnel, create a need for targets, contributing further to the production of illegality (Welch, 2002). Finally, current enforcement policies respond as well to fantastic constructions of "illegal aliens" as "other" (Chavez, 2001, 2008; Inda,

2006). It appears entirely counterproductive to disrupt family and community relationships by irrevocably exiling a legal permanent resident for a minor offense, yet such disruptions occur regularly. Such social and psychological costs suggest that there is also an irrational component to current deportation policies.

The spatial reconfigurations wrought by current immigration enforcement tactics demonstrate that the interplay between law and territoriality is complex. In the Westphalian system of governance, law and space are supposed to map onto each other neatly (Raustiala, 2009). Law defines the state and its subjects and is supposed to pervade national territory. In contrast to earlier, feudal forms of spatiality, in which being closer to the center was important, within the Westphalian system, national territory is supposed to be equivalent throughout. Being next to the border or within the interior of a country is supposed to be legally equivalent (Chavez, 1992; Ngai, 2004). Legal responses to unauthorized migration disrupt such spatial configurations. Law complexly acknowledges yet prohibits the presence of the undocumented. Unauthorized migrants become territorial persons with specified legal rights even as a host of enforcement practices situate them outside of the polity, allegedly "in the shadows" or "underground" (Bosniak, 2006; Motomura, 2006; Varsanyi, 2008). Physically present but legally ambiguous, undocumented immigrants interrupt the legal continuity of national space. Furthermore, as the literature on trans-migration demonstrates, migrants participate in multiple national economies and social networks, and therefore can be said to occupy multiple national spaces at the same time (Hondagneu-Sotelo & Avila, 1997). As they exist in multiple places simultaneously, migrants create opportunities for territorial interpenetration – through "alien" presences, "foreign" nations also enter. The ambiguity of presence and absence, rights and illegality, makes national territories multidimensional. On the one hand, the exclusion of undocumented immigrants permits national territories to remain whole, while on the other hand, the physical presence of excluded individuals creates "holes" within legal jurisdictions.

My analysis of the ways that current immigration enforcement tactics reconfigure spaces and persons derives from my own recent research regarding a group of migrants who are ambiguously situated; namely Salvadorans who were born in El Salvador but raised in the United States, the so-called "1.5 generation." Because of El Salvador's historical relationship to the United States, these migrants' legal statuses and spatial locations are particularly complex. During the 1980s, El Salvador was hailed as the "backyard" of the United States by the Reagan administration, which invested heavily in combating guerilla movements during the Salvadoran civil war. As a result, Salvadoran migrants were largely denied asylum during the 1980s but more recently have been regarded as having a "special" relation to the United States. As President Clinton stated during a May 1997 meeting with the Central American presidents, "These Central American countries are in a rather special category. After all, the United States Government was heavily involved with a lot of these countries during the time of all this upheaval" (Clinton, 1997: 571). This "special" relationship has been acknowledged legally, in that Salvadoran migrants were granted Temporary Protected Status (TPS), first due to the 1980–1992 Salvadoran civil war, then due to massive earthquakes that occurred in 2001. TPS confers work authorization but not the right to leave and reenter the United States or to become a legal permanent resident. Long-time Salvadoran migrants have also been permitted to apply for legal permanent residency under the Nicaraguan Adjustment and Central American Relief Act (NACARA). At the same time, Salvadoran migrants, especially youth, have been targets of anti-gang and immigration enforcement policies, contributing to rising deportation rates. The United States and El Salvador continue to collaborate around security issues, particularly, combating transnational gangs. Although the experiences of migrants from different nations differ, this case study illustrates the kinds of territorial forms that current immigration enforcement practices may produce.

In this paper, I draw primarily on interviews that I conducted in Southern California and El Salvador between 2006 and 2008 focusing on the experiences of 1.5 generation Salvadoran migrants. 104 individuals were interviewed altogether, and are identified here only through pseudonyms. Interviewees included 1.5 generation migrants, as well as some individuals who were born in the United States, who immigrated to the United States as adolescents, or who work with immigrant youth. Most interviewees originally entered the United States without authorization, and most acquired U.S. citizenship, legal permanent residency, or Temporary Protected Status, while a few remained undocumented. Just under half did not obtain U.S. citizenship and were eventually deported. My interpretation of the interview material is informed by my prior fieldwork within community organizations that sought legal status for Salvadoran immigrants, as well as my previous interviews with migrants, community activists, legal service providers, and U.S. and Salvadoran officials involved in formulating policies regarding Salvadorans living in the United States (Coutin, 1993, 2000, 2007). My analysis is organized around three forms of confinement potentially experienced by the undocumented: de facto confinement to national territory, formal confinement in a detention center, and de facto confinement within one's country of origin following deportation.

Unauthorized Presence

Unauthorized immigrants experience a de facto confinement to U.S. territory both through increased border enforcement and through the acquisition of what Motomura (2006: 10) calls "territorial personhood," that is, the way that "simply being present in the United States bestows certain minimum rights on lawful immigrants and other noncitizens." When they enter or remain in the United States without authorization, migrants acquire an illegal persona. They become "illegal" in that their very presence is an infringement of U.S. territory, an interruption of space that is otherwise jurisdictionally whole. Unauthorized migrants can be denied housing (in certain cities), employment, welfare benefits, medical care, in-state tuition, access to public universities, and other key services (Rodriguez, 2008). At the same time, due to their presence within U.S. borders, these migrants acquire rights that are denied to individuals who are outside of the United States. Unauthorized migrants are able to attend public schools, receive emergency room care, and obtain an attorney at public expense if accused of a criminal offense.

Although it confers rights, territorial personhood also traps within U.S. borders those who are unauthorized or only temporarily authorized. The very conflation of legality and territoriality (Raustiala, 2009) that is supposed to keep the unauthorized out also makes those who acquire rights by virtue of being present reluctant to lose them by leaving. The legality of migrants who have temporary authorization, such as TPS or a pending application for asylum, is ambiguous. Such individuals may possess work permits, driver's licenses, and social security cards, and therefore appear to be documented. At the same time, such migrants are not eligible for legal permanent residency and, as individuals who entered without authorization or overstayed visas, are in many ways like the undocumented. If they leave the United States without first securing advanced parole from immigration authorities, TPS recipients and asylum applicants lose their status, and become ineligible to reenter. Advanced parole is granted for only a limited time (a few weeks or months) on the grounds of an emergency such as a serious illness or a death in the family. Even if they secure advanced parole, temporarily authorized migrants must be careful not to accumulate more than six months of absences because doing so would define their stay in the United States as discontinuous and would make them ineligible for remedies such as cancellation of removal (which requires ten years of continuous presence in the United States). Unauthorized migrants do not have a legal status to lose, yet territorial personhood still traps them. Unauthorized migrants cannot apply for advanced parole, and therefore do not have a legal means of reentry if they leave the United States. Continuous presence was an eligibility requirement for legalization under IRCA, and therefore could be required in any future legalization program that might be created. Furthermore, unauthorized immigrants develop considerable social ties such as jobs, family, home ownership, community involvement that would be jeopardized by leaving the country without a legal means of reentry. And, as Monica Varsanyi (2007, 2008: 879) notes, in the United States, there has long been a tension between "intensive border militarization" and "lax internal immigration enforcement," permitting undocumented immigrants to feel that they have become part of U.S. communities, even as their presence is officially prohibited. Earlier patterns of cyclical but unauthorized migration have been made difficult by stiffened border enforcement, further confining the undocumented to U.S. territory (Bean et al., 1990; Gutierrez, 1995).

Interviews with undocumented or temporarily authorized Salvadorans convey their sense of confinement. Monica Ramirez, a 20-year-old college student and TPS recipient, was frustrated that she could not travel to El Salvador to study and to visit her father, from whom she had been separated since the age of eight. She stated, "When I was in high school, I always wanted to go visit El Salvador because I would, like, hear [of] people going. That was my thing, like, 'Oh I want to go visit my family.' And my dad even..., just you know go back to, like, my childhood place." Marisol Sanabria, a 19-year-old undocumented college student who immigrated to the United States at the age of five, described even greater deprivation. Raised in Los Angeles in Boyle Heights, Marisol complained that when people asked her about life in El Salvador, she had to admit, "'I really don't know' because my mom all her life she worked, you know, and she never had the chance to like teach me how to cook like pupusas [a popular Salvadoran dish] and stuff like that. I feel like left out some part of my life – there's like a culture, like there's something missing from me." Marisol believed that, if she were to obtain legal status, she could fill this hole by traveling to El Salvador.

Monica and Marisol's experiences were echoed by Manuel Cañas, a 29-year-old airport worker and TPS recipient, who, when asked whether he would like to one day become a U.S. citizen, responded immediately:

> I would love to be a US citizen. Because to be honest, I want to visit my country. I haven't been there since I left. I know that everything has changed, you know? My uncle was telling me that El Salvador isn't the way that it used to be. All those forests that used to be there are all cut down and there are houses. The ranch that we used to go to, my aunt's ranch, it's gone. It's all houses now. All that has totally changed. What I love about my country is the way it used to be. Even though the war was going on, but it was a beautiful place.

Like Monica and Marisol, Manuel chafed at his inability to relive childhood memories, update his knowledge of El Salvador, and visit friends and relatives. Significantly, no legal barrier prevents these migrants from leaving the United States or from entering El Salvador. Rather, they are confined by their inability to reenter this country legally, in short, by their dependence on the (albeit limited) territorial personhood that their presence in the United States affords them. Of course, poverty, language barriers, and racial and ethnic differences, all of which are linked to immigration status in complex ways, can also exacerbate confinement.

Both undocumented and temporarily authorized migrants are confined to U.S. territory as a whole, but the undocumented also experience confinement to more local settings. For them, highway checkpoints, I.D. checks at airports, and the possibility of border patrol agents boarding trains and buses create internal boundaries. The existence of such internal boundaries is also linked to what Monica Varsanyi (2008) refers to as the "rescaling" of citizenship, that is the increased ability of states and local governments to set and enforce immigration policies, whether these be prohibiting police from questioning individuals regarding their immigration status, or at the opposite extreme, establishing penalties for landlords who rent to undocumented immigrants (see also Bosniak, 2006; Rodriguez, 2008; Spiro, 1997; Wishnie, 2003, 2004). For the undocumented, U.S. territory is legally differentiated internally, though such intra-territoriality (Raustiala, 2009) may not be apparent to legal residents. Marisol Sanabria, for example, discovered what it meant to lack papers when her mother told her that she could not participate in a class trip:

> In middle school I remember there was a field trip. I don't know where, I think it was out of the country. And I was asking my mom, "I really want to go, I really want to go." But I never knew that, to be honest, I never knew what was the difference to have papers and not have papers. Until that moment that she told me, "well you can't get out of the country, you know, can't go out of the state." And I'm like, "I [will] use my school I.D., I'd do anything. I'm a student you know."

Similarly, Beatriz Gonzales, a Mexican immigrant and youth organizer, described how she learned that she was undocumented:

> At the age of 15, 16, 17, like your peers, like you start talking about getting a license. So I remember enrolling in the drivers ed. class, thinking, "Okay, by next year I'm going to have my papers. So I can enroll in the class, get the permit now, and I know I'll have a year to get my license." And so that kind of made you feel normal. Because "Well, I'm in the class and I'm doing the same thing that other youth are doing at the same age." Well – when everyone started getting their license, they were like, "Beatriz, why haven't you?

Why haven't you?" And I'm like, "Oh, well, um, I'm not going to have a car, so I'm not going to get my license."

The inability to drive legally, described by Beatriz, further confines undocumented migrants geographically, thus contributing to the internal differentiation and multidimensionality of national territory.

As unauthorized migrants are confined to particular spaces, their illegal status also becomes confined to minimalized yet potentially powerful segments of their lives and beings. In the passages that are quoted above, both Beatriz and Marisol thought that they were "normal," that they were like their friends or like other students. Marisol's comment, "I [will] use my school I.D. – I'm a student you know" draws attention to the way that, at young ages, unauthorized migrants' status as students (a benefit of territorial personhood) seems to trump and thus erase their illegality (Gonzales, 2008). Nonetheless, illegality remains lurking, to emerge in particular contexts, such as when seeking a driver's license, applying for college, or considering an opportunity to travel within or outside of the United States. The discrepancy between the "normalcy" of their everyday lives and the "abnormality" of being undocumented is both mind-boggling and experientially wrenching for undocumented youth. Beatriz, for example, described having to live in multiple yet incompatible realities: "I think that one of the biggest challenges for undocumented youth is that they function in both worlds. The world where being undocumented doesn't matter. And then the other world is where being undocumented IS the point that matters and affects everything." In this movement between worlds, unauthorized migrants' abilities to confine (and thus largely ignore) their own illegality shift. Illegality is a relationship between legal space and unauthorized presences that interrupt space. Because space is not always defined primarily in legal terms, the salience of migrants' illegality can also vary. Being undocumented can "not matter" or "affect everything," depending on these migrants' social location. Thus, migrants embody illegality in ways that mirror territorial confinement. Just as U.S. territory becomes internally differentiated for unauthorized migrants (through being restricted to local spaces) so too does illegality become a component of undocumented migrants' physical being.

Detention

Intensified immigration enforcement has led to renewed emphasis on detention, giving detention centers a territorial significance that is not unlike excised territory or the international space of the airport. As "portals," detention centers are spatially ambiguous, located within and outside of the nation at the same time. Unlike prisons, where convicts serve out their sentences, detention

centers house individuals while they are in removal proceedings or are awaiting deportation. A rise in apprehension rates coupled with the elimination of
bail for most detainees has meant that more noncitizens are spending more
time in detention. Detention is an administrative form of custody rather than
a punishment. While a U.S. citizen and an undocumented immigrant who
are charged with a crime share the same due process rights throughout their
involvement with the criminal justice system, this formal equality appears to
evaporate as soon as prisoners are transferred into immigration custody, where
their lack of U.S. citizenship becomes particularly salient. This evaporation
of formal equality is also a product of a shift between the mandate that states
and local governments treat immigrants as "persons" under the U.S. constitution, and plenary power which allows the federal government to treat migrants
as "aliens" or "nonpersons" and therefore as subject to "rules that would be
unacceptable if applied to citizens" (Mathews v. Diaz, 1976: 1891, quoted in
Varsanyi, 2008: 879). Such differences in legal rights may be a key factor in the
increasing tendency for U.S. authorities to charge noncitizens with immigration violations instead of with crimes (Cole & Dempsey, 2002; Eagly, 2008).

In detention centers, the spatial ambiguity of unauthorized presence is inten-
sified. For example, detainees' accounts of being taken into immigration cus-
tody convey their sense of being "removed" before they are actually deported.
Pablo Ramirez was at home, getting ready for work, when Immigration and
Customs Enforcement (ICE) agents arrived to detain him and his brother,
Jorge. Pablo recounted,

> We had papers. We had our green cards. And we thought with the green
> card, we were citizens, basically. I remember that when ICE came to pick us
> up at the house, they said, "Where's your green card?" And usually, I used to
> carry it in my wallet. I took it out and said, "So what're you going to do now?"
> And he's like, "Well, you ain't an American citizen. So you're going back
> to your country no matter what." And right then and there, he just, boom!
> Flipped it over and broke it in half.

The destruction of a detainee's green card at the moment of apprehension appears to be something of a ritual, as I heard similar stories from other
interviewees. This act symbolically removes the legal protection that permitted migrants to remain in the country. Furthermore, once they are in immigration custody, migrants often discover that they can never again return to
their homes and communities. One interviewee who had this experience was
Marcus Lopez, who was taken into immigration custody while on probation
for statutory rape (a crime that, during our interview, he denied committing).
One day, when he presented himself to his probation officer, "there were two

guys sitting on the desk. They just told me, 'You got a warrant to get you deported. This is INS.' Locked me [up]. I lost everything. My car just got thrown in the streets. The house [was lost]." Although he had simply been performing a routine activity, Marcus found himself seemingly irrevocably pulled into another space, the detention center, where he was removed from the people, places, and relationships that made up his life, and where his only means of exit was deportation.

A further indication of the territorial ambiguity of the detention center is the fact that there, the territorial personhood that unauthorized immigrants had enjoyed previously is considerably eroded. Detainees are not charged with crimes, are not serving a specified sentence, have no predetermined release date, do not have public defenders, often lack the right to be released on bail, and frequently become convinced that it is useless to fight deportation because they cannot win. They are serving what one interviewee referred to as "dead time" – "time that you're not guilty of. You're just locked up." Their family, community, and employment relationships are disrupted, and they are subjected to frequent and unannounced transfers to other detention centers. Of course, detainees technically have not yet exited the United States. They may have a right to an immigration hearing, they can still receive visits from relatives, they have the privilege of hiring an attorney at their own expense, and there is always a chance that a few could prevail in court and win release. Detention center conditions nonetheless seem designed to convince migrants that they are on their way out.

Marcus Lopez described the many frustrations that he experienced after being detained during the visit to his probation officer. Marcus had immigrated to the United States at the age of 12 to live with his father. He completed high school and married his U.S. citizen girlfriend, with whom he had a child, and had qualified for a work permit through a pending application for residency under the Nicaraguan Adjustment and Central American Relief Act. Before he could become a resident, however, he was convicted of petty theft and committing a sexual offense with a minor (a charge that he said was fabricated). He was attempting to turn his life around when he was taken into immigration custody. He recounted:

> And they wouldn't even let me see the judge. I requested it so many times.
> Even though when the detective, officer, from INS took me to the headquar-
> ters of INS in Baltimore, I told him, "I'm married to a US-born citizen." He
> said, "We don't care. That's not the way we work." And we got there, finger-
> printed me. He said, "Would you like to see a judge?" I say, "Yes." He said, "If
> my supervisor approves it, you're able to see it." He did not. They denied it. I
> would send letters from the detention center requesting a judge or a trial or

something to fight the case. They would never respond. They would just be a pain to us. They would force you to sign your own deportation, saying that you are agreeing to get deported." So that's what they'd say. "Okay, if you don't want to sign, just stay here. You're going to be here 12 years, if you want to." And the treatment when you get deported is like you're a dog. To them, it is like we are clowns. Almost like we are from another planet. That's how they treat you.

Practices such as frequent transfers, denying detainees a hearing before an immigration judge, lengthy procedural delays, and continual pressure to sign deportation papers appeared designed to convince detainees that it was hopeless to attempt to return to their previous lives. Like Marcus, many interviewees were told repeatedly by guards, immigration officials, and fellow detainees that fighting their cases would lead only to endless detention. Mandatory detention policies significantly undercut exercise of the appeal process. Amilcar Mejia was unique among interviewees in that he won his immigration case, only to have the judge's decision over-turned on appeal. Because he did not want to remain in detention, Amilcar chose to sign deportation papers rather than continuing to appeal.

As their territorial personhood is eroded, detainees experience themselves as foreign (see also Yngvesson & Coutin, 2006). Many interviewees were legal permanent residents or at least work permit holders prior to being detained. Their criminal convictions made them ineligible to retain their residency, thus stripping them of their U.S. legal personae and leaving only an alienage that was not even temporarily authorized. This stripping away was akin to banishment. According to Beccaria, banishment

> nullifies all ties between society and the delinquent citizen. The citizen dies and the man remains. With respect to the body politic, [civil death] should produce the same effect as natural death. (Beccaria, 1963: 53, brackets in original; quoted in Walters, 2002: 269)

The "man" who remains after ties to society have been nullified is nothing but a body, an extralegal being, an alien. Interviewees, who in many cases thought of themselves as quasi-citizens, discovered that, through detention, they became this alien. Francisco Ramirez, brother to Pablo and Jorge, whose experiences were described above, used an analogy to explain how, through detention and deportation, a single facet of an individual's experience or being comes to dominate and thus erase all else. Picking up a mug that happened to be sitting on the table during our interview, Francisco commented, "See this cup? You don't see the white [background], but what stands out more is the black spot, that logo there. That's what they see. They don't see what's around it, they only see that one little dot, that one little stain."

Removed from their communities, with diminished territorial personhood, detainees are to a large degree already "elsewhere," therefore deportation is the seemingly inevitable realization of the illegality experienced in detention. Deportation situates deportees within another national territory, namely, their country of origin. There, their inability to legally reenter the United States makes this new territorial location to some degree an extension of the detention center.

Deportation

Deportation is territorially complex. On the one hand, it "sorts" citizens and territories, such that individuals are returned to their country of citizenship. On the other hand, the enforcement practices associated with deportation disrupt territorial demarcations by enforcing one country's laws in another country's territory. The deportations that I analyze here are thus instances of extraterritoriality (Raustiala, 2009) in at least two senses: first, they enable U.S. immigration officials to act within the territory of El Salvador, and second, migrants' countries of origin are places of confinement for deportees. Although a few deportees may return willingly, most experience deportation as an act of force, an expulsion that releases them from ICE custody but subjects them to surveillance and policing in their country of origin. Though deportees enjoy the right to exit their countries, this right is not particularly meaningful if there is nowhere to go. For deportees who spent a significant portion of their lives in the United States, therefore, presence within their country of origin is simultaneously absence from the United States, and is therefore akin to exile. Furthermore, deportees' prior history – the normalcy that they established in the United States and that was erased through detention and deportation – continues to differentiate them from other Salvadorans, placing them apart, and, once again, creating internal spatial boundaries. Such differentiation can be life-threatening, as deportees are subjected to harassment from police, security guards, or gang members. The risk of harassment (or worse) hampered deportees' abilities to move within their own national territories, and thus further extends the confinement that these migrants experienced in the United States.

The sense that national territories are zones of confinement is conveyed by some deportees' description of their lives in El Salvador as a "sentence." For example, when asked to describe his future plans, Amilcar Mejia responded, "I guess I have no plans. This [living in El Salvador] is just part of my sentence. I'm just going it day by day. Just a little bit more freedom. I guess I haven't settled in yet, it hasn't kicked in. That I'm destined to be here for the rest of my life. I guess it hasn't set in that this is a life sentence. I just don't want to accept it." The temporal suspension of the detention center – "dead" time, seemingly endless detention while fighting deportation – continues through such uncertainty, even as judges' specifications of the penalties that deportees will incur upon reentering without authorization appear to limit the time that deportees must spend outside of the United States. For instance, Javier Ayala, who had lived in the United States from the age of eight to the age of twenty-five, commented, "I went before the judge, I signed the deportation, and the judge said, 'We're going to give you five years [during which time] you cannot enter the United States. If you do, we're going to give you up to 25 years, and a fine of $25,000.'" Interviewees were unclear what would occur at the end of the specified period – could they then reenter the United States legally, if they were eligible for a family visa petition? Or would the convictions that, in many cases, had resulted in their deportations also make them ineligible for legal reentry? In essence, the exile that they were experiencing appeared to be indefinite, and in fact, aggravated felons and those who reenter the country without authorization following deportation are subject to a permanent bar on lawful reentry (Chacon, 2007).

Of course, deportees were not actually confined and therefore enjoyed much greater liberty than they had when they were in detention, a fact that many interviewees appreciated. Remarking on what appeared to him to be the greater permissiveness of Salvadoran law, Wilbur Quezada, a deportee who had been convicted on drug-related charges in the United States, commented, "Because one is in one's own country, one has more freedom to do what seems appropriate to one... Here, one has more liberty." In El Salvador, deportees potentially could work, form families, and enjoy leisure activities.

Deportees nonetheless experienced severe restrictions on their movement and activities, and thus experienced a form of intra-territoriality (Raustiala, 2009) that parallels that experienced by unauthorized migrants living in the United States. To cope with the risk of harassment by police, security guards, and gang members, those interviewees who had the economic means to do so removed themselves from the general population. Such interviewees avoided areas that were known to be gang territory, rented homes in middle class (and therefore relatively secure) neighborhoods, and purchased cars so that they would not have to travel by bus. Some interviewees prominently displayed their work badges when they were out in public so that they would not be mistaken for gang members. Cesar, who had put his English skills to good use by getting a job at a call center, told me, "Every time I walk, I walk with my badge. 'I work, man!' I wear it on my days off."

In short, although interviewees were not formally confined, their lives in El Salvador were defined in relation to the (im)-possibility of returning legally to the United States (see also Shachar, 2007). Some interviewees had attempted to return, only to be deported again by Mexican or U.S. authorities. Interviewees found themselves weighing the possibility of being reunited with family members and securing more lucrative jobs in the United States against the risks of traveling without authorization, the high fees charged by smugglers, the possibility of prison time for unlawful reentry, and, even if they successfully evaded detection, the pressure of having to live as a fugitive. Victor commented, "It's feo (literally, "ugly") to live under this fear. Trapped. You want to do what is right, but no, 'the things of the street,' 'hide yourself, they'll pick you up.' No, hombre!" Similarly, Lorenzo, who had been a legal permanent resident before being deported due to drug convictions and who had already served a four year prison sentence for unlawful reentry, explained his thinking about making another reentry attempt: "I'm scared. Because if I get busted crossing, I'm going back to the BoP [Federal Bureau of Prisons]. For reentry again. This time, I'm gonna get double time. 8 years. So I really don't know what to do. I'm so confused. I need time. I miss my family so much! I'm really hurt!!" One interviewee had seriously considered paying doctors to alter his fingerprints so that he could return to the United States with a new identity, however, he feared that his fingers would melt or that he would be left with no feeling. The severe deprivation that makes such extreme actions conceivable demonstrates the way that deportation traps detainees.

Conclusion

In his recent book about the history of territoriality, Kal Raustiala notes that paradoxically, "the legal differences inherent in the Westphalian system of territorial sovereignty create strong incentives for extraterritoriality" (2009: 230). This paradox is borne out in the case analyzed in this paper. The contradictions that unauthorized migrants, detainees, and deportees experience within and between their legal identities and territorial locations are a function of complex relationships between bodies, law and space. In a jurisdictionally ideal world, bodies are lawfully present within particular nationally bounded spaces. Law is thus mapped onto bodies through legal status, whether temporary or permanent. In the case of unauthorized immigrants, an unlawfully present body interrupts this mapping, creating holes, of sorts, within national territories. Through legal measures designed to exclude (and thus reduce the draw for) unauthorized migrants, bodies are located "outside," in the "underground" that the undocumented allegedly occupy. At the same time, unauthorized immigrants acquire limited legal rights due to their territorial presence. The unauthorized therefore live with a continual ambiguity: their lives may be "normal" and completely "abnormal" (illegal) at the same time.

Detention centers are designed to remove those whose presence may be unauthorized, and therefore reinforce the Westphalian system of sovereignty. Yet, as portals, detention facilities, which have become more central to immigration enforcement, also partake of spatialized enforcement tactics that externalize spaces in an effort to prevent access to U.S. territory. Detention centers thus also disrupt national territories. Such disruptions of space are furthered by deportation, a border control mechanism that is considered a hallmark of sovereignty. At the same time, in that deportation extends confinement, migrants' countries of origin become extensions of US detention centers, producing further territorial displacements.

The securitization of immigration therefore has complex spatial implications. Enforcement practices that produce deportability (De Genova, 2002), detention, and actual deportation fracture territories, such that the United States is comprised of both an "underground" and an "above ground," detention centers become borders of nations, and foreign territories become the "outside" occupied by migrants whose presence is prohibited "within." The presence of unauthorized migrants makes national territories multidimensional, both in the sense that enforcement practices confine migrants to particular subnational spaces, and in that space takes on different meanings in the presence of the unauthorized. Intra-territoriality, that is, the operation of different legal regimes within the same national territory, comes about not only through jurisdictional designations, such as demarcating a reservation as a different sort of sovereign territory (Raustiala, 2009), but also through the presence of people subject to proceedings in which certain constitutional rights (such as the right to an attorney at public expense) do not apply. Multidimensionality and the "holes" created by the presence of alien persons also permit a sort of territorial transference through which migrants occupy multiple national spaces at the same time, and territories, in a sense, interpenetrate. Likewise, enforcing U.S. immigration laws defines other nations, such as El Salvador, as the "outside" of the United States, making them territorially ambiguous. As the place to which deportees are, in their view, "sentenced," foreign territories become part of the U.S. immigration enforcement regime.

The securitization of immigration and the spatial implications of enforcement tactics contribute to the reformulation of citizenship and membership more broadly. There are clear connections between the territorial splintering that is entailed in confinement and what Mae Ngai (2004: 5) refers to as the "impossibility" of the illegal alien as "a person who cannot be and a problem that cannot be solved" (see also Bosniak, 2006). These migrants embody contradictory legal identities – unauthorized yet territorially present, prohibited yet retaining traces of a prior legal existence, foreign yet national.

Deportation would seem to resolve ambiguity by sorting out the legally authorized and unauthorized. Nevertheless, within their countries of origin, deportees can once again experience themselves as foreign. This foreignness is not only a matter of acculturation to U.S. society but also of the imposition of a legal identity – "Salvadoranness" – defined in relation to what deportees are *not* –not U.S. citizens, not legal permanent residents, not present within U.S. territory, not permitted to reenter the United States. This redefinition is made clear in the following exchange between two deportees who were interviewed in El Salvador:

> Amilcar: Our mentality [living in the United States], our thought was, we thought, "Wait a minute, I'm a green card holder, that should automatically make me a citizen. My mom's a citizen, my dad's a citizen, my sister's a citizen. Everybody over there's a citizen!" So it's like. Why am I not a citizen?
> Jorge: Because you're Salvadorean, man.
> Amilcar: Now, I'm Salvadorean.

In this excerpt, Amilcar says, "Now, I'm Salvadorean," suggesting that he became Salvadoran, in contrast to his earlier legal identity as a green card holder and quasi-U.S. citizen, through the process of detention and deportation. His identity as Salvadoran results from a stripping away of the legal personae he had occupied in the United States, but Salvadoranness is not simply what is "left" when his U.S. legal identity (in his case, as a legal permanent resident) is removed, rather it is, in some sense newly reconstituted. Even though Amilcar probably also considered himself Salvadoran at earlier points in his life, through deportation, he became legally Salvadoran in a way that he had not been previously. Their legal identity as Salvadoran citizens resituates deportees within El Salvador even as the fact that this legal status was established definitively in the United States, prior to their deportation, sets them apart. Such redefinitions of citizenship, as seemingly arbitrarily allocated, potentially alienable, and constituted through security procedures, surely have ramifications for even native born citizens who nonetheless must travel through checkpoints, prove their legal status in order to obtain a driver's license, and defend themselves against suspicions of being aliens. Enforcement tactics that treat all residents as potentially suspect (though, given racial profiling, not to the same degree) have important implications that are worthy of further study.

Acknowledgments

I am grateful to CARECEN Los Angeles, CARECEN Internacional, and Homies Unidos, El Salvador for their assistance with this project. In particular,

I thank Dan Sharp, Henry Aguilar, Luis Perdomo, Jesus Aguilar, Tony Azucar, and Samuel Uribe, and all of the individuals who participated in interviews or otherwise helped with the project. Katie Dingeman, Tim Goddard and Sylvia Valenzuela served as research assistants. This research was supported through funds from the National Science Foundation's Law and Social Sciences Program, Award #SES-0518011. Earlier versions of this paper were presented at the American Anthropological Association, the Association of American Law Schools, and Princeton University. I thank Chowra Makaremi and Carolina Kobelinsky, Josiah Heyman, Leti Volpp, Dirk Hartog, and Carol Greenhouse as well as audiences for discussions of the paper. Alison Mountz posed the question that inspired this paper. Anonymous reviewers' comments were very helpful!

REFERENCES

Andreas, P. (2000). *Border games: Policing the US-Mexico divide.* Ithaca: Cornell.

Bean, F. D., Edmonston, B., & Passel, J. S. (1990). Undocumented migration to the United States: IRCA and the experience of the 1980s. Santa Monica: Rand Corporation.

Beccaria, C. (1963). On crimes and punishments. Indianapolis: Bobbs-Merrill. p. 53.

Bosniak, L. (2006). *The citizen and the alien: Dilemmas of contemporary membership.* Princeton: Princeton University Press.

Chacon, J. M. (July 2007). Unsecured borders: immigration restrictions, crime control, and national security. *Connecticut Law Review,* **39**, 1827–1891.

Chavez, L. (1992). *Shadowed lives: Undocumented immigrants in American society.* Fort Worth, TX: Harcourt, Brace, Jovanovich.

—— (2001). *Covering immigration: Popular images and the politics of the nation.* Berkeley: University of California Press.

—— (2008). *The Latino threat: Constructing immigrants, citizens, and the nation.* Stanford: Stanford University Press.

Clinton, W. J. (1997). Public papers of the presidents of the United States: William J.

Clinton. 1997 (in two books). Book II – July 1 to December 31, 1997. Washington, DC: U.S. Government Printing Office, Office of the Federal Register, National Archives and Records Administration. p. 571.

Cole, D., & Dempsey, J. X. (2002). *Terrorism and the constitution: Sacrificing civil liberties in the name of national security.* New York: The New Press.

Coleman, M. (2007). A geopolitics of engagement: neoliberalism, the war on terrorism, and the reconfiguration of US immigration enforcement. *Geopolitics,* **12**(4), 607–634.

Collier, J. F., Maurer, B., & Suárez-Navaz, L. (1995). Sanctioned identities: legal constructions of modern personhood. *Identities*, 2(1–2), 1–27.

Coutin, S. B. (1993). *The culture of protest: Religious activism and the U.S. sanctuary movement*. Boulder, CO: Westview Press.

—— (2000). *Legalizing moves: Salvadoran immigrants' struggle for U.S. Residency*. Ann Arbor: University of Michigan Press.

—— (2005). Contesting criminality: illegal immigration and the spatialization of illegality. *Theoretical Criminology*, 9(1), 5–33.

—— (2007). *Nations of emigrants: Shifting boundaries of citizenship in El Salvador and the United States*. Ithaca: Cornell University Press.

Coutin, S. B., Maurer, B., & Yngvesson, B. (2002). In the mirror: the legitimation work of globalization. *Law and Social Inquiry*, 27(4), 801–843.

De Genova, N. P. (2002). Migrant 'illegality' and deportability in everyday life. *Annual Review of Anthropology*, 31, 419–447.

De Genova, N., & Peutz, N. (Eds.). (2010). *The deportation regime: Sovereignty, space, and the freedom of movement*. Durham, NC: Duke University Press.

Eagly, I. (12 September 2008). The impact of immigration raids and community response. Paper presented at the conference, "Immigrants' Rights: From Global to Local," Inaugural Symposium, Loyola Public Interest Law Foundation and The Los Angeles Public Interest Law Journal, Loyola Law School, Los Angeles.

Gonzales, R. G. (2008). Born in the shadows: The uncertain futures of the children of unauthorized Mexican migrants. Unpublished dissertation. Irvine: Department of Sociology, University of California.

Gutierrez, D. (1995). *Walls and mirrors: Mexican Americans, Mexican immigrants and the politics of ethnicity*. Berkeley: University of California Press.

Hernandez, E., & Coutin, S. B. (2006). Remitting subjects: migrants, money, and states. *Economy and Society*, 35(2), 185–208.

Heyman, J. McC., & Smart, A. (1999). States and illegal practices: an overview. In J. McC. Heyman (Ed.), *States and illegal practices* (pp. 1–24). New York: Berg.

Hing, B. O. (2006). *Deporting our souls: Values, morality and immigration policy*. Cambridge: Cambridge University Press.

Hondagneu-Sotelo, P., & Avila, E. (1997). "I'm here, but I'm there": the meanings of Latina transnational motherhood. *Gender & Society*, 11(5), 548–571.

Hyndman, J., & Mountz, A. (2008). Another brick in the wall? Neo-refoulement and the externalization of asylum by Australia and Europe. *Government and Opposition*, 43(2), 249–269.

Inda, J. (2006). *Targeting immigrants: Government, technology, and ethics*. Malden, MA: Blackwell Publishing.

Kanstroom, D. (2000). Deportation, social control, and punishment: some thoughts about why hard laws make bad cases. *Harvard Law Review*, 113(8), 1890–1935.

—— (2007). *Deportation nation: Outsiders in American history.* Cambridge: Harvard University Press.

Legomsky, S. H. (2006). The USA and the Caribbean interdiction program. *International Journal of Refugee Law*, 18(3–4), 677–695.

Motomura, H. (2006). Americans in waiting: The lost story of immigration and citizenship in the United States. New York: Oxford University Press. p. 10.

Mountz, A. (2010). *Seeking asylum: Human smuggling and bureaucracy at the border.* Minneapolis: University of Minnesota Press.

Nevins, J. (2002). *Operation gatekeeper: The rise of the 'illegal alien' and the making of the U.S. Mexico boundary.* New York: Routledge.

Ngai, M. (2004). *Impossible subjects: Illegal aliens and the making of modern America.* Princeton: Princeton University Press. p. 5.

Raustiala, K. (2009). *Does the constitution follow the flag? The evolution of territoriality in American law.* New York: Oxford University Press. pp. 5, 230.

Rodriguez, C. M. (2008). *The significance of the local in immigration regulation. Michigan Law Review*, 106, 567–642.

Scalia, J., & Litras, M. F. X. (2002). Immigration offenders in the federal criminal justice system, 2000. Bureau of Justice Statistics Special Report. Washington, DC: Office of Justice Programs, U.S. Department of Justice.

Seattle School of Law. (2008). Voices from detention: A report on human rights violations at the Northwest detention center in Tacoma, Washington. Seattle: Seattle University School of Law International Human Rights Clinic in Collaboration with OneAmerica.

Shachar, A. (2007). The shifting border of immigration regulation. *Stanford Journal of Civil Rights & Civil Liberties*, 3, 175–193.

Spiro, P. J. (1997). Learning to live with immigration federalism. *Connecticut Law Review*, 29, 1627–1646.

—— (2006). Perfecting political diaspora. *NYU Law Review*, 81, 207–233.

USCIS (United States Citizenship and Immigration Services). (2008). Credible fear screenings. Available at http://www.uscis.gov/portal/site/uscis/menuitem.5af9bb95919f35e66f614176543f6d1a/?vgnextoid¼44d28d86c76oac 110VgnVCM1000004718190aRCRD&vgnextchannel¼3a82ef4c766fd010V gnVCM1000000ecd190a RCRD Accessed 17.10.08.

Varsanyi, M. W. (2007). Documenting undocumented migrants: the matrículas consulares as neoliberal local membership. *Geopolitics*, 12, 299–319.

——— (2008). Rescaling the 'alien,' rescaling personhood: neoliberalism, immigration, and the state. *Annals of American Geographers*, 98(4), 877–896.

Walters, W. (2002). Deportation, expulsion, and the international police of aliens. *Citizenship Studies*, 6(3), 265–292.

Welch, M. (2002). *Detained: Immigration laws and the expanding I.N.S. jail complex*. Philadelphia: Temple University Press.

Weiss, M., & Collins, J. (October 10, 2008). Una comunidad desgarrada por la migra.

La Opinión. Available at www.laopinion.com Accessed 11.10.08.

Wishnie, M. J. (2003). Emerging issues for undocumented workers. *University of Pennsylvania Journal of Labor and Employment Law*, 6, 497.

——— (2004). State and local police enforcement of immigration laws. *University of Pennsylvania Journal of Constitutional Law*, 6, 1084.

——— (2007–2008). Labor law after legalization. *Minnesota Law Review*, 92, 1446.

Yngvesson, B., & Coutin, S. B. (2006). Backed by papers: undoing persons, histories, and return. *American Ethnologist*, 33(2), 177–190.

Excerpts from:

Ferguson, James and Gupta, Akhil (2002) Spatializing States: Toward an Ethnography of Neoliberal Governmentality. *American Ethnologist*, 29(4):981–1002.

Reproduced by permission of the American Anthropological Association. Not for Sale or further production.

SPATIALIZING STATES: TOWARD AN ETHNOGRAPHY OF NEOLIBERAL GOVERNMENTALITY

James Ferguson and Akhil Gupta (2002)

Recent years have seen a new level of anthropological concern with the modern state. In part, the new interest in the state arises from a recognition of the central role that states play in shaping "local communities" that have historically constituted the objects of anthropological inquiry; in part, it reflects a new determination to bring an ethnographic gaze to bear on the cultural practices of states themselves. An important theme running through the new literature has been that states are not simply functional bureaucratic apparatuses, but powerful sites of symbolic and cultural production that are themselves always culturally represented and understood in particular ways. It is here that it becomes possible to speak of states, and not only nations (Anderson 1991), as "imagined" – that is, as constructed entities that are conceptualized and made socially effective through particular imaginative and symbolic devices that require study (Bayart 1993; Bernal1997; Cohn 1996; Comaroff 1998; Coronil 1997; Corrigan and Sayer 1985; cf. Fallers 1971; Geertz 1980; Joseph and Nugent 1994; Nugent 1997; Scott 1998; Taussig 1996).

In this article, our contribution to this literature is twofold. First, we argue that discussions of the imagination of the state have not attended adequately to the ways in which states are spatialized.[10] How is it that people come to

[10] There is a long and rich tradition of studies by geographers and social theorists on the social construction of space under conditions of modernity and postmodernity. Building on an old, if often undervalued, tradition of spatial thinking within Marxism (esp. the seminal work of Henri Lefebvre [1991]), social geographers like David Harvey (1985a, 1985b, 1990) and Doreen Massey (1984, 1994) have shown how changing forms of capitalist production have structured urban spaces and the social experiences that unfold within them. Meanwhile, theorists of globalization, such as Saskia Sassen, have shown how state practices of regulation (from immigration control to financial regulations) intersect with transnational flows of capital to generate highly differentiated national and subnational economic zones within an increasingly global economic space (1991, 1996, 1998). But although such contributions help to show how states say act to construct social and economic space and to shape the way that places are built, experienced, and inhabited, they do not deal with the related but distinct question that concerns us here: How are states themselves spatialized?We have also benefited greatly from a recent body

experience the state as an entity with certain spatial characteristics and properties? Through what images, metaphors, and representational practices does the state come to be understood as a concrete, overarching, spatially encompassing reality? Through specific sets of metaphors and practices, states represent themselves as reified entities with particular *spatial* properties (specifically, what we will describe as properties of "vertical encompassment").[11] By doing so, they help to secure their legitimacy, to naturalize their authority, and to represent themselves as superior to, and encompassing of, other institutions and centers of power. We refer to the operation of these metaphors and practices as "the spatialization of the state." In the first part of this article, we identify some key methods through which states achieve this spatialization and seek to show, via an ethnographic example, that mundane bureaucratic state practices are integral to such achievements.

In the second part of the article, we build on this discussion by showing its relevance to the question of globalization. We argue that an increasingly transnational political economy today poses new challenges to familiar forms of state spatialization. After developing a concept of transnational governmentality, we discuss the relation between weak African states and an emerging network of international organizations and transnational nongovernmental organizations (NGOs), and show how these developments confound conventional understandings of state spatiality. We suggest that attention to the changing forms of state spatialization might enrich the anthropology of the state and clarify certain aspects of the contemporary politics of globalization.

Part One: The Spatialized State

Conceptual Issues

Two images come together in popular and academic discourses on the state: those of *verticality* and *encompassment*. *Verticality* refers to the central and pervasive idea of the state as an institution somehow "above" civil society, community, and family. Thus, state planning is inherently "top down" and state actions are efforts to manipulate and plan "from above," while "the grassroots" contrasts with the state precisely in that it is "below," closer to the ground, more authentic, and more "rooted." The second image is that of *encompassment:* Here the state (conceptually fused with the nation) is located within an ever widening series of circles that begins with family and local community

of work in anthropology that seeks to understand ethnographically the spatial consequences of state policies (see, e.g., Bernal 1997; Darian-Smith 1999; Grant 1995; Herzfeld 1991; Merry 2001; and Verdery 1996). It is this literature that has enabled us to pursue our own, slightly different, question of how the state itself is spatialized.

[11] Ann Anagnost presents a wonderful example of this phenomenon in her discussion of splendid China (1997:161–175).

and ends with the system of nation-states.[12] This is a profoundly consequential understanding of scale, one in which the locality is encompassed by the region, the region by the nation-state, and the nation-state by the international community.[13] These two metaphors work together to produce a taken-for-granted spatial and scalar image of a state that both sits above and contains its localities, regions, and communities.

Such images of state vertical encompassment are evident, for instance, in scholarly discussions of so-called state-society relations, a topic that has dominated recent discussions of the state in political science and political theory. The idea of "civil society" has been embraced both by neoliberal advocates of structural adjustment in Africa and India and, for different reasons, by many of their strongest critics (cf. Ferguson in press). But whatever else might be said about the opposition between state and civil society, it is evident that it normally brings with it a quite specific, if often unacknowledged, image of vertical encompassment, one in which the state sits somehow "above" an "on the ground" entity called "society."[14] The state, of course, has long been conceived in the West, through an unacknowledged "transcoding" of the body politic with the organismic human body (Stallybrass and White 1986), as possessing such "higher" functions as reason, control, and regulation, as against the irrationality, passions, and uncontrollable appetites of the lower regions of society.[15]

It is therefore unsurprising that where Western political theory has opposed civil society to the state, it has often been as a kind of buffer between the low and the high, an imagined middle zone of contact or mediation between the citizen, the family, or the community, on the one hand, and the state, on the other.[16] For Hegel (to take one foundational instance), the state was literally

[12] A different kind of critique of this position has been advanced by Marilyn Strathern (1995), who argues that just because anthropology appears to route its knowledge through persons, it does not follow that the person constitutes an elementary scale of social organization. Maurer (1998) offers an example of how spatial and statist projects converge when encompassment is realized through incorporation.

[13] That spatial encompassment is often imagined in terms of such neatly nested circles does not imply that regions, localities, or communities really do fit so neatly within the "higher" levels that supposedly encompass them – indeed, a range of phenomena from borderlands to transnational communities in practice confound this image. Part two develops the implications of this observation.

[14] The concept of "civil society" clearly grows out of a specific, European history; like Chatterjee (1990), we emphasize the historical and cultural particularity of the concept, even as we are concerned with its operational universalization as part of the standard package of institutional and ideological forms that have come to be as widely distributed as the modern state itself. But it is not simply the category, "civil society," that requires to be seen in its cultural particularity, but a larger imaginary topography through which the state and society are visualized in relation with each other.

[15] Verdery makes a very interesting connection between the nation and the body (1996:63).

[16] Not all theorists have made such an opposition; indeed, the earliest writers on civil society (e.g., Locke) saw "civil society" as synonymous with "political society" (see Taylor 1990:105).

"mind objectified" (1942:156), and civil society precisely the intermediary between the foundational natural particularity of the family and the ideal universality of the state. The state was therefore "higher" than civil society (ethically as well as politically) and also encompassed it.[17]

Few scholars today, of course, would endorse Hegel's conception of the state bureaucracy as the embodiment of society's highest collective ideals, and feminist criticism has long since laid bare the maneuvers through which the separation of a public, political "society" from a private, personal "family" naturalized patriarchal domination (e.g., Ferguson 1984; Pateman 1988; Rosaldo 1980; Yanagisako and Collier 1987). But the old topographic metaphor that allowed civil society to appear as a zone of mediation between an "up there" state and an "on the ground" community continues to be omnipresent and surprisingly resistant to critical scrutiny. Participants in recent debates on the public sphere (e.g., Calhoun 1992) and civil society (Chatterjee 1990; Cohen and Arato 1992; Harbeson et al. 1994; Taylor 1990) advance diverse political and theoretical positions; but they largely share a commonsense topography within which the object of their theorizing lies in some sense "between" the state and the communities, interest groups, and life worlds that states must govern.

An imagined topography of stacked, vertical levels also structures many taken-for-granted images of political struggle, which are readily imagined as coming "from below," as "grounded" in rooted and authentic lives, experiences, and communities. The state itself, meanwhile, can be imagined as reaching down into communities, intervening, in a "top down" manner, to manipulate or plan society. Civil society, in this vertical topography, appears as the middle latitude, the zone of contact between the "up there" state and the "on the ground" people, snug in their communities. Whether this contact zone is conceived as the domain of pressure groups and pluralist politics (as in liberal political theory) or of class struggle in a war of position (as in Gramscian Marxism), the vertical topography of power has been an enormously consequential one.

Picturing the state's relation to society through the image of vertical encompassment fuses in a single, powerful image a number of analytically distinct propositions. Is the state's encompassing height a matter of superior rank in a political hierarchy? Of spatial scale? Abstraction? Generality of knowledge and interest? Distance from nature? The confusion engendered by bundling these distinct propositions together is in fact productive, in the Foucauldian

---

[17] On the history of the concept of civil society, see Burchell 1991; Chatterjee 1990; Comaroff and Comaroff 1999; and Seligman 1992.

sense, in that it constructs a commonsense state that simply *is* "up there" somewhere, operating at a "higher level." The point is not that this picture of the "up there" state is false (still less that there is no such thing as political hierarchy, generality of interest, etc.), but that it is constructed; the task is not to denounce a false ideology, but to draw attention to the social and imaginative processes through which state verticality is made effective and authoritative.

Images of state vertical encompassment are influential not only because of their impact on how scholars, journalists, officials, activists, and citizens imagine and in-habit states, but because they come to be embedded in the routinized practices of state bureaucracies. The metaphors through which states are imagined are important, and scholarship in this area has recently made great strides.[18] But the understanding of the social practices through which these images are made effective and are experienced is less developed. This relative inattention to state practices seems peculiar, because states in fact invest a good deal of effort in developing procedures and practices to ensure that they are imagined in some ways rather than others (Scott 1998). They seem to recognize that a host of mundane rituals and procedures are required to animate and naturalize metaphors if states are to succeed in being imagined as both higher than, and encompassing of, society.

The importance of the mundane rituals and routines of state spatialization is easily recognized where the regulation and surveillance of the borders of nation-states is concerned. But the policing of the border is intimately tied to the policing of Main Street in that they are acts that represent the repressive power of the state as both extensive with the territorial boundaries of the nation and intensively permeating every square inch of that territory, respectively.[19] There is more to state spatialization, though, than policing or repression. State benevolence, no less than coercion, must also make its spatial rounds, as is

---

[18] See especially such contributions as Bayart's (1993) discussion of "eating" as a metaphor of state power in Africa and Mbembe's (1992) analysis of how the imagery of the vulgar and the grotesque in the popular culture of Cameroon comes to invest the symbols of state power. The ways that the spatial metaphors of vertical encompassment that we discuss here may coexist with other metaphors for picturing states are a rich ground for future investigation. Other important contributions to a lively recent discussion on the state in postcolonial Africa include Bayart et al. 1999; Chabal and Daloz 1999; Mamdani 1996; and Werbner and Ranger 1996.

[19] One particularly clear example of such policing is provided by the treatment received by Mexican laborers in the United States at the hands of the INS and the police, which demonstrates quite clearly that the border is not just a line that one crosses into a zone of safety but a zone of exclusion that permeates the interior of the territory of the nation-state (see, for instance, Chavez 1998). Heyman (1998) goes even further in making an explicit connection between control of the U.S.-Mexico border and foreign wars such as Vietnam through the trope of illegality.

clear, for instance, in the ritual tours of U.S. presidents who drop from the sky in helicopters to dispense aid in the wake of natural disasters.

Although such spectacular examples make convenient illustrations, it may be more important to look at the less dramatic, multiple, mundane domains of bureaucratic practice by which states reproduce spatial orders and scalar hierarchies.[20] Any attempt to understand state spatialization, therefore, must simultaneously attend to theoretical understandings and bureaucratic embodiment. The force of metaphors of verticality and encompassment results both from the fact that they are embedded in the everyday practices of state institutions and from the fact that the routine operation of state institutions *produces* spatial and scalar hierarchies.

Part Two: Transnational Governmentality – Contemporary Challenges to State Spatialization

Governmentality and the Global

In the previous section, we showed some of the means through which a state may be able to create, through mundane and unmarked practices, a powerful impression of vertical encompassment of the "local." But such efforts by states to establish their superior spatial claims to authority do not go uncontested. This is especially true at a time when new forms of transnational connection are increasingly enabling "local" actors to challenge the state's well-established claims to encompassment and vertical superiority in unexpected ways, as a host of worldly and well-connected "grassroots" organizations today demonstrate. If state officials can always be counted on to invoke the national interest in ways that seek to encompass (and thereby de-value) the local, canny "grassroots" operators may trump the national ace with appeals to "world opinion" and e-mail links to the international headquarters of such formidably encompassing agents of surveillance as Amnesty International, Africa Watch, or World Vision International. The extent to which states are successful in establishing their claims to encompass the local is therefore not preordained, but is a contingent outcome of specific sociopolitical processes. And, as the precarious situation of many states in Africa today makes especially clear, the state has no automatic right to success in claiming the vertical heights of sovereignty.

In thinking about the relation between states and a range of contemporary supranational and transnational organizations that significantly overlap their traditional functions, we have found it useful to develop an idea of

---

[20] The term *order* is here used both in its directive intent as well as in its organizing con notations.

transnational governmentality, borrowing and extending the idea of "governmentality" first introduced by Michel Foucault (1991). Foucault draws attention to all the processes by which the conduct of a population is governed: by institutions and agencies, including the state; by discourses, norms, and identities; and by self-regulation, techniques for the disciplining and care of the self. Political economy as knowledge and apparatuses of security as technical means have operated on the population as a target to constitute governmentality as the dominant mode of power since the 18th century (Foucault 1991:102). Governmentality is concerned most of all with "the conduct of conduct" (Dean 1999:10), that is, with the myriad ways in which human conduct is directed by calculated means. Foucault was interested in mechanisms of government that are found within state institutions and outside them, mechanisms that in fact cut across domains that we would regard as separate: the state, civil society, the family, down to the intimate details of what we regard as personal life. Governmentality does not name a negative relationship of power, one characterized entirely by discipline and regulation; rather, the emphasis is on its productive dimension.

More recently, scholars working in this tradition have sought to refine the analysis of governmentality to deal with the shift from the Keynesian welfare state toward so-called free-market policies in Western democracies. Although this move to neoliberalism has often been understood (and variously celebrated or lamented, depending on one's politics) as a "retreat" or "rolling back" of the state, Barry et al. stress that it has, rather, entailed a transfer of the operations of government (in Foucault's extended sense) to non-state entities, via "the fabrication of techniques that can produce a degree of 'autonomization' of entities of government from the state" (1996:11–12). The logic of the market has been extended to the operation of state functions, so that even the traditionally core institutions of government, such as post offices, schools, and police are-if not actually privatized-at least run according to an "enterprise model" (Burchell 1996). Meanwhile, the social and regulatory operations of the state are increasingly "de-statized," and taken over by a proliferation of "quasi-autonomous nongovernmental organizations" (Rose 1996:56).[21] But this is not a matter of less government, as the usual ideological formulations would have it. Rather, it indicates a new modality of government, which works by creating mechanisms that work "all by themselves" to bring about governmental results through the devolution of risk onto the "enterprise" or

[21] A good example is provided by the privatization of prisons: Increasingly, private companies have taken over the job of constructing and operating prisons for the state. Once an "enterprise model" becomes dominant, there is little reason for many state functions to be performed by state institutions.

the individual (now construed as the entrepreneur of his or her own "firm") and the "responsibilization" of subjects who are increasingly "empowered" to discipline themselves (see Barry et al. 1996; Burchell 1996; D. Burchell et al. 1991; O'Malley 1998; Rose 1996; Rose and Miller 1992).

Such extensions of the Foucauldian concept of governmentality to neoliberalism are undoubtedly illuminating and suggestive. But they remain strikingly Eurocentric, and closely tied to the idea of the territorially sovereign nation-state as the domain for the operation of government.[22] We propose to extend the discussion of governmentality to modes of government that are being set up on a global scale. These include not only new strategies of discipline and regulation, exemplified by the WTO and the structural adjustment programs implemented by the IMF, but also transnational alliances forged by activists and grassroots organizations and the proliferation of voluntary organizations supported by complex networks of international and transnational funding and personnel. The outsourcing of the functions of the state to NGOs and other ostensibly non-state agencies, we argue, is a key feature, not only of the operation of national states, but of an emerging system of transnational governmentality.

The increasing salience of such processes ought to bring into question the taken-for-granted spatial and scalar frames of sovereign states. But instead of spurring a wholesale rethinking of spatial and scalar images, what we find is that received notions of verticality and encompassment have been stretched – often improbably – to adapt to the new realities. Thus, institutions of global governance such as the IMF and the WTO are commonly seen as being simply "above" national states, much as states were discussed vis-a-vis the grassroots. Similarly, the "global" is often spoken of as if it were simply a superordinate scalar level that encompasses nation-states just as nation-states were conceptualized to encompass regions, towns, and villages.

Struggles between agencies that are attempting to foster global government and their critics have made headlines first in Seattle in November and December 1999, then in Washington, D.C., in April 2000, and, more recently (September 2000), in Prague. One of the most interesting aspects of these protests, as well as of the documentary coverage and commentary about them,

---

[22] It is striking, for instance, that Rose (1996:53) characterizes "advanced liberalism" as a set of strategies that "can be observed in national contexts from Finland to Australia" without any discussion of the vast range of national contexts (most of the world, it would seem) to which his account does not apply. Nor is there any consideration of the relations between the breakdown of notions of welfare at the national level and those of development at the international, or of the ways that the proliferation of "quasi-autonomous NGOs" might be linked to changes in the role and function of the nation-state within a global system.

is the difficulty experienced by participants and observers alike in articulating the role of the national state vis-a-vis "global" agreements and "grassroots" protests. Are the institutions that promote globalization, such as the World Bank, the IMF, and the WTO, making policy decisions that affect the lives of people all over the world without the normal mechanisms of democratic accountability, as the protestors charge? Or are these international bodies merely facilitating efforts at "good governance" proposed and enforced by national governments, as they counter? Observers and commentators struggle to make sense of this situation. Journalists note that the protestors consist of seemingly unrelated groups that are protesting for very different causes and reasons; moreover, many of the "grassroots groups" opposing globalization are themselves arguably leading examples of it: well-organized transnational organizations with offices or affiliations spread out across the world, coordinating their demonstrations over the internet, and even in real-time (during the events) by cellular phones and walkie-talkies.

The confusion evident in the understandings both of important agencies of globalization and of the activist groups that oppose them (as well as those who report on them and study them) is at least in part about how states are spatialized and what relations exist between space and government. Processes of globalization have disturbed the familiar metaphors and practices of vertical encompassment (still taken for granted by the participants in debates on globalization, including journalists and academics), and the new landscape that is emerging can be understood only through a rethinking of questions of space and scale. To accomplish such a rethinking, it will be necessary to question both commonsense assumptions about the verticality of states as well as many received ideas of "community," "grassroots" and the "local," laden as they are with nostalgia and the aura of authenticity.[23]

The State

If, as some neoliberal theorists of state and society suggest, domination is rooted in state power, then rolling back the power of the state naturally leads to greater freedom, and ultimately to "democratization." But the argument is revealed to be fallacious if one observes that, in Africa and elsewhere, domination has long been exercised by entities other than the state. Zambia, to take an example, was originally colonized (just a little over a hundred years ago) not by any government, but by the British South Africa Company, a private

---

[23] Recently, a great many anthropologists have been concerned to problematize the traditional anthropological notion of the "local" (although usually without relating this notion to the question of state spatialization). For reasons of space, we will not review this literature here, but only refer the reader to our extensive discussion of this issue in Gupta and Ferguson 1997.

multinational corporation directed by Cecil Rhodes. Equipped with its own army, and acting under the terms of a British "concession," it was this private corporation that conquered and "pacified" the territory, setting up the system of private ownership and race privilege that became the colonial system. Today, Zambia (like most other African nations) continues to be ruled, in significant part, by transnational organizations that are not in themselves governments, but work together with powerful First World states within a global system of nation-states that Frederick Cooper has characterized as "internationalized imperialism."[24]

Perhaps most familiarly, international agencies such as the IMF and World Bank, together with allied banks and First World governments today often directly impose policies on African states. The name for this process in recent years has been "structural adjustment," and it has been made possible by both the general fiscal weakness of African states and the more specific squeeze created by the debt crisis. The new assertiveness of the IMF has been, with some justification, likened to a process of "re-colonization," implying serious erosion of the sovereignty of African states (e.g., Saul 1993). It should be noted that direct impositions of policy by banks and international agencies have involved not only such broad, macroeconomic interventions as setting currency exchange rates, but also fairly detailed requirements for curtailing social spending, restructuring state bureaucracies, and so on. Rather significant and specific aspects of state policy, in other words, are, for many African countries, being directly formulated in places like New York, London, Brussels, and Washington.

As critics have pointed out, such "governance" of African economies from afar represents a kind of transfer of economic sovereignty away from African states and into the hands of the IMF. Yet, because it is African governments that remain nominally in charge, it is easy to see that they are the first to receive the blame when structural adjustment policies begin to bite. At that point, democratic elections (another "adjustment" being pressed by international donors) provide a means whereby one government can be replaced by another; but because the successor government will be locked in the same financial vice-grip as its predecessor, actual policies are unlikely to change. (Indeed, the IMF and its associated capital cartel can swiftly bring any government that tries to assert itself to its knees, as the Zambian case illustrates vividly.) In this way, policies that are in fact made and imposed by wholly

---

[24] We borrow this evocative term from remarks made by Cooper (1993). It should be noted, however, that we are here connecting the term to larger claims about transnational governmentality that Cooper may not have intended in his own use of the term.

unelected and unaccountable international bankers may be presented as democratically chosen by popular assent. In this way, "democratization" ironically serves to simulate popular legitimacy for policies that are in fact made in a way that is less democratic than ever (cf. Ferguson 1995).

"The Grassroots"

Civil society often appears in African Studies nowadays as a bustle of grassroots, democratic local organizations. As Jane Guyer has put it, what this ignores is "the obvious: That civil society is made up of international organizations" (1994:223). For, indeed, the local voluntary organizations in Africa, so beloved of civil society theorists, very often, on inspection, turn out to be integrally linked with national and transnational-level entities. One might think, for instance, of the myriad South African community groups that are bankrolled by USAID or European church groups (Mayekiso 1996; Mindry 1998); or of the profusion of local Christian development NGOs in Zimbabwe, which may be conceived equally well as the most local, grassroots expressions of civil society, or as parts of the vast international bureaucratic organizations that organize and sustain them (Bornstein 2001). When such organizations begin to take over the most basic functions and powers of the state, as they very significantly did, for instance, in Mozambique (Hanlon 1991), it becomes only too clear that NGOs are not as "NG" as they might wish us to believe. Indeed, the World Bank baldly refers to what they call BONGOs (bank-organized NGOs) and even GONGOs (government-organized NGOs).

That these voluntary organizations come as much from "above" (international organizations) as from "below" (local communities) is an extremely significant fact about so-called civil society in contemporary Africa. For at the same time that international organizations (through structural adjustment) are eroding the power of African states (and usurping their economic sovereignty), they are busy making end runs around these states and directly sponsoring their own programs and interventions via NGOs in a wide range of areas. The role played by NGOs in helping Western development agencies to get around uncooperative national governments sheds a good deal of light on the current disdain for the state and celebration of civil society that one finds in both the academic and the development literature right now.

But challengers to African states today are not only to be found in international organizations and NGOs. In the wake of what is widely agreed to be a certain collapse or retreat of the nation-state all across the continent, we find forms of power and authority springing up everywhere that have not been well described or analyzed to date. These are usually described as "subnational," and usually conceived either as essentially ethnic (the old primordialist view), or alternatively (and more hopefully) as manifestations of a newly resurgent civil society, long suppressed by a heavy-handed state. Yet, can we really assume that the new political forms that challenge the hegemony of African nation-states are necessarily well conceived as "local," "grassroots," "civil," or even "subnational"?

Guerrilla insurrections, for instance, not famous for their civility, are often not strictly local or subnational, either – armed and funded, as they often are, from abroad. Consider Savimbi's Uniao Nacional para a Independencia Total de Angola (UNITA) movement in Angola: long aided by the CIA, originally trained by the Chinese government, with years of military and logistic support from apartheid South Africa, and funding from sources that range from the international diamond trade to donations from U.S. church groups. Is this a subnational organization? A phenomenon of an emerging civil society? Or consider the highly organized transnational forms of criminality that so often exist in such a symbiotic partnership with the state that we may even come to speak, as Bayart et al. have recently suggested (1999), of "the criminalization of the state" in many parts of Africa. Can such developments be grasped within the state-society or local-global polarities? What about transnational Christian organizations like World Vision International, which play an enormous role in many parts of contemporary Africa, organizing local affairs and building and operating schools and clinics where states have failed to do so (Bornstein 2001)? Are such giant, transnational organizations to be conceptualized as "local"? What of humanitarian organizations such as Oxfam, Cooperative for Assistance and Relief Everywhere (CARE), or Doctors Without Borders, which perform statelike functions all across Africa?

Such organizations are not states, but are unquestionably statelike in some respects. Yet they are not well described as subnational, national, or even supranational. They ignore the nation-building logic of the old developmentalist state, which sought to link its citizens into a universalistic national grid (D. Scott 1998) and instead build on the rapid, deterritorialized point-to-point forms of connection (and disconnection) that are central to both the new communications technologies and the new, neoliberal practices of capital mobility (Ferguson 1999, 2001). Local and global at the same time, such entities are transnational-even, in some ways, anational; they cannot be located within the familiar vertical division of analytic levels presented above. Not coincidentally, these organizations and movements that fall outside of the received scheme of analytic levels are also conspicuously understudied – indeed, they have until recently been largely invisible in theoretical scholarship on African politics, tending to be relegated instead to "applied," problem-oriented studies.

In all of these cases, we are dealing with political entities that may be better conceptualized not as "below" the state, but as integral parts of a transnational apparatus of governmentality. This apparatus does not replace the older system of nation-states (which is, let us be clear, not about to disappear), but overlays and coexists with it. In this optic, it might make sense to think of the new organizations that have sprung up in recent years not as challengers pressing up against the state from below but as horizontal contemporaries of the organs of the state – sometimes rivals; sometimes servants; sometimes watchdogs; sometimes parasites; but in every case operating on the same level, and in the same global space.

The implication is not simply that it is important to study NGOs and other transnational non-state organizations, or even to trace their interrelations and zones of contact with the state. Rather, the implication is that it is necessary to treat state and non-state governmentality within a common frame, without making unwarranted assumptions about their spatial reach, vertical height, or relation to the local. Taking the verticality and encompassment of states not as a taken-for-granted fact, but as a precarious achievement, it becomes possible to pose the question of the spatiality of contemporary practices of government as an ethnographic problem.

Conclusion: Toward an Ethnography of Neoliberal Governmentality

Studying the relationship between states, space, and scale opens up an enormous empirical and ethnographic project, one that has not been systematically pursued in anthropological analysis. In this article, we have drawn attention to two central features of state spatialization, *verticality* and *encompassment*. These images of space and scale are not "mere" metaphors. What gives verticality and encompassment their efficacy as commonsensical features of states is their embeddedness in a host of mundane bureaucratic practices, as the examples from the ICDS program in India demonstrate. Instead of understanding space as a preexisting container and scale as a natural feature of the world in which states operate, we have argued that states themselves *produce* spatial and scalar hierarchies. In fact, the production of these hierarchies is not incidental but central to the functioning of states; they are the raison d'etre of states (and perhaps their raison d'etat). It might be worth rereading the ethnographic record to reinterpret the data concerning how state claims to verticality and encompassment have been legitimized and substantiated in everyday life in a multiplicity of empirical situations around the world (although the data might well be too thin in many cases to carry out such a project).

Although the spatial and scalar *ideologies* of states have always been open to critique, the new practices associated with neoliberal globalization have opened up opportunities for a deeper questioning. In a global order where the organization of capitalism coexisted more easily with the hegemony of nation-states, statist projects of verticality and encompassment seemed "natural" and were usually easily incorporated into the everyday routines of social life. However, the conflicts engendered by neoliberal globalization have brought the disjuncture between spatial and scalar orders into the open, revealing the profoundly transnational character of both the "state" and the "local," and drawing attention to crucial mechanisms of governmentality that take place outside of, and alongside, the nation-state. Claims of verticality that have historically been monopolized by the state (claims of superior spatial scope, supremacy in a hierarchy of power, and greater generality of interest and moral purpose) are being challenged and undermined by a transnation-alized "local" that fuses the grassroots and the global in ways that make a hash of the vertical topography of power on which the legitimation of nation-states has so long depended. For increasingly, state claims of encompassment are met and countered by globally networked and globally imaged organiza-tions and movements – manifestations of "the local" that may claim (in their capacity as ecological "guardians of the planet," indigenous protectors of "the lungs of the earth," or participants in a universal struggle for human rights) a wider rather than narrower spatial and moral purview than that of the merely national state.

We do not mean to suggest that such transnationalized local actors always win their fights, or that national states have become incapable of exercising their authority over localities. Neither do we intend to imply that states' new difficulties in spatializing their authority are likely to usher in a new era of enlightenment and greater public good. (On the contrary, the diminishment of state authority is as likely to undermine the position of subaltern groups as it is to enhance it, as the recent political history of much of Africa in particular shows). That state claims to vertical encompassment are today increasingly precarious does not mean that they no longer exist; as we have shown, vertical encompassment continues to be powerfully institutionalized and instantiated in daily practices. If the nature of these institutions and the sites of this instan-tiation are being transformed, it is precisely to these transformations that we must attend in our empirical investigations.

What is necessary, then, is not simply more or better study of "state-society interactions" – to put matters in this way would be to assume the very oppo-sition that calls for interrogation. Rather, the need is for an ethnography of encompassment, an approach that would take as its central problem the understanding of processes through which governmentality (by state and non-state actors) is both legitimated and undermined by reference to claims of superior spatial reach and vertical height. Indeed, focusing on governmentality calls into question the very distinction insisted on by the term *nongovernmental organization,* emphasizing instead the similarities of technologies of government across domains.

An ethnography of the spatiality of governmentality has to confront several problems. First, as originally formulated by Foucault (1991), "governmentality" as a form of power exercised over populations assumes the frame of the nation-state. Extending this concept to account for neoliberal globalization forces us to reformulate the spatial and scalar assumptions of governmentality.[25] For example, we cannot just think of transnational governmentality as a form of global government, a suprastate that is superimposed on various nation-states much as the European Union is on its member governments. Institutions of global governance are not simply replicating on a bigger scale the functions and tasks of the nation-state, as both proponents and opponents of transnational governmentality often assume. Verticality and encompassment continue to be produced, but not in the same way by the same institutions or groups. Globalized "grassroots" groups and nongovernmental organizations are good examples of how scales have collapsed into each other. Neil Smith has attempted to understand this phenomenon of the "active social and political connectedness of apparently different scales" (1992:66) by referring to such activities in terms of "jumping scales." John Ruggie (1993) has attempted to understand the reconfiguration of territorial sovereignty in the world system as forming an "unbundled space" where nation and state are not homologous in their control and regulation of territory. Other forms of spatial and scalar production are clearly imposing themselves on state spatiality and territoriality (Brenner 1997; Storper 1997; Swyngedouw 1997). At the same time, different institutions and organizations, including nation-states and metastates like the European Union, are attempting to reinstate verticality and encompassment in territories that are not necessarily contiguous, or united in cultural, political, and economic spheres. The ethnographic challenge facing us today with neoliberal globalization is to understand the spatiality of all forms of government, some of which may be embedded in the daily practices of nation-states while others may crosscut or superimpose themselves on the territorial jurisdiction of nation-states.

Such an approach might open up a much richer set of questions about the meaning of transnationalism than have been asked up to now. It is not a

---

[25] Sally Merry (2001) has developed the idea of "spatial governmentality" to draw attention to forms of governmentality that seek to regulate people indirectly through the control and regulation of space.

question of whether a globalizing political economy is rendering nation-states weak and irrelevant, as some have suggested, or whether states remain the crucial building blocks of the global system, as others have countered. For the central effect of the new forms of transnational governmentality is not so much to make states weak (or strong), as to re-configure states' abilities to spatialize their authority and to stake their claims to superior generality and universality. Recognizing this process might open up a new line of inquiry into the study of governmentality in the contemporary world.

REFERENCES CITED

Anagnost, Ann 1997 *National Past Times: Narrative, Representation, and Power in Modern China*. Durham, NC: Duke University Press.

Anderson, Benedict R. 1991 *Imagined Communities: Reflections on the Origin and Spread of Nationalism*. 2nd edition. New York: Verso.

Bayart, Jean-Francais 1993[1989] The State in Africa: The Politics of the Belly. New York: Longman. Bayart, Jean-Francais, Stephen Ellis, and Beatrice Hibou, eds.

―― 1999 The Criminalization of the State in Africa. Bloomington: Indiana University Press. Barry, Andrew, Thomas Osborne, and Nikolas Rose, eds. 1996 *Foucault and Political Reason: Liberalism, Neo-Liberalism and Rationalities of Government*. Chicago: University of Chicago Press.

Bernal, Victoria 1997 Colonial Moral Economy and the Discipline of Development: The Gezira Scheme. *Cultural Anthropology* **12**(4):447–479.

Bornstein, Erica 2001 The Good Life: Religious NGOs and the Moral Politics of Economic Development in Zimbabwe. Ph.D. dissertation, Program in Social Relations, University of California at Irvine.

Brenner, Neil 1997 Global, Fragmented, Hierarchical: Henri Lefebvre's Geographies of Globalization. *Public Culture* **10**(1):135–167.

Burchell, Graham 1991 Peculiar Interests: Civil Society and Governing "The System of Natural Liberty." In The Foucault Effect: Studies in Governmentality. Graham Burchell, Colin Gordon, and Peter Miller, eds. Pp. 119–150. Chicago: University of Chicago Press.

―― 1996 Liberal Government and Techniques of the Self. In Foucault and Political Reason: Liberalism, Neo-liberalism and Rationalities of Government. Andrew Barry, Thomas Osborne, and Nikolas Rose, eds. Pp. 19–36. Chicago: University of Chicago Press.

Burchell, Graham, Colin Gordon, and Peter Miller, eds. 1991 *The Foucault Effect: Studies in Governmentality*. Chicago: University of Chicago Press.

Calhoun, Craig, ed. 1992 *Habermas and the Public Sphere*. Cambridge, MA: MIT Press.

Chabal, Patrick, and Jean-Pascal Daloz 1999 Africa Works: Disorder as Political Instrument. Bloomington: Indiana University Press.

Chatterjee, Partha 1990 A Response to Taylor's "Modes of Civil Society." *Public Culture* 3(1):119–132.

Chavez, Leo R. 1998 Shadowed Lives: Undocumented Immigrants in American Society. Fort Worth: Harcourt Brace College Publishers.

Cohen, Jean L., and Andrew Arato 1992 *Civil Society and Political Theory.* Cambridge, MA: MIT Press.

Cohn, Bernard S. 1996 *Colonialism and Its Forms of Knowledge.* Princeton: Princeton University Press.

Comaroff, John L. 1998 Reflections on the Colonial State, in South Africa and Elsewhere: Factions, Fragments, Facts and Fictions. *Social Identities* 4(3):321–361.

Comaroff John L., and Jean Comaroff, eds. 1999 *Civil Society and the Political Imagination in Africa.* Chicago: University of Chicago Press.

Cooper, Frederick 1993 Historicizing Development. Workshop. Emory University, Atlanta, December.

Coronil, Fernando 1997 *The Magical State: Nature, Money, and Modernity in Venezuela.* Chicago: University of Chicago Press.

Corrigan, Philip, and Derek Sayer 1985 *The Great Arch: English State Formation as Cultural Revolution.* New York: Basil Blackwell.

Darian-Smith, Eve 1999 *Bridging Divides: The Channel and English Legal Identity in the New Europe.* Berkeley: California University Press.

Dean, Mitchell 1999 *Governmentality: Power and Rule in Modern Society.* Thousand Oaks, CA: Sage Publications.

Fallers, Lloyd A. 1971 *The Social Anthropology of the Nation-State.* Chicago: Aldine.

Ferguson, Kathy E. 1984 *The Feminist Case Against Bureaucracy.* Philadelphia: University of Pennsylvania Press.

Ferguson, James 1995 From African Socialism to Scientific Capitalism: Reflections on the Legitimation Crisis in IMF-ruled Africa. In Debating Development Discourse: Popular and Institutionalist Perspectives. David Moore and Gerald Schmitz, eds. Pp. 129–148. New York: St. Martins Press.

—— 1999 *Expectations of Modernity: Myths and Meanings of Urban Life on the Zambian Copperbelt.* Berkeley: University of California Press.

—— 2001 Global Disconnect: Abjection and the Aftermath of Modernism. In The Anthropology of Globalization. Jonathan Javier Inda and Renato Rosaldo, eds. Pp. 136–153. New York: Blackwell.

—— In press Transnational Topographies of Power: Beyond "the State" and "Civil Society" in the Study of African Politics. In The Forces of

Globalization. Gabrielle Schwab, ed. New York: Columbia University Press.

Foucault, Michel 1991 Governmentality. In The Foucault Effect: Studies in Governmentality. Graham Burchell, Colin Gordon, and Peter Miller, eds. Pp. 87–104. Chicago: University of Chicago Press.

Geertz, Clifford 1980 *Negara: The Theatre State in Nineteenth-Century Bali*. Princeton: Princeton University Press.

Grant, Bruce 1995 *In the Soviet House of Culture: A Century of Perestroikas*. Princeton: Princeton University Press.

Gupta, Akhil 1995 Blurred Boundaries: The Discourse of Corruption, the Culture of Politics, and the Imagined State. *American Ethnologist* 22(2):375–402.

Gupta, Akhil, and James Ferguson, eds. 1997 *Culture, Power, Place: Explorations in Critical Anthropology*. Durham, NC: Duke University Press.

Guyer, Jane 1994 The Spatial Dimensions of Civil Society in Africa: An Anthropologist Looks at Nigeria. In Civil Society and the State in Africa. John W. Harbeson, Donald Rothchild, and Naomi Chazan, eds. Pp. 215–30. Boulder: Lynne Rienner Publishers.

Hanlon, Joseph 1991 Mozambique: Who Calls the Shots? Bloomington: Indiana University Press.

Harbeson, John W., Donald Rothchild, and Naomi Chazan, eds.1994 Civil Society and the State in Africa. Boulder: Lynne Rienner Publishers.

Harvey, David 1985a *Consciousness and The Urban Experience: Studies in the History and Theory of Capitalist Urbanization*. Baltimore: Johns Hopkins University Press.

—— 1985b *The Urbanization of Capital: Studies in the History and Theory of Capitalist Urbanization*. Baltimore: John Hopkins University Press.

—— 1990 *The Condition of Postmodernity: An Enquiry into the Origins of Cultural Change*. Cambridge, MA: Blackwell.

Hegel, Georg Wilhelm Friedrich 1942[1821] *Philosophy of Right*. Thomas Malcolm Knox, trans. Oxford: Clarendon Press

Herzfeld, Michael 1991 *A Place of History: Social and Monumental Time in a Cretan Town*. Princeton: Princeton University Press.

Heyman, Josiah McC. 1998 State Escalation of Force: A Vietnam/US-Mexico Border Analogy. In State and Illegal Practices. J. M. Heyman, ed. Pp. 285–314. Oxford: Berg.

Joseph, Gilbert M., and Daniel Nugent, eds.1994 *Everyday Forms of State Formation: Revolution and the Negotiation of Rule in Modern Mexico*. Durham, NC: Duke University Press.

Lefebvre, Henri 1991 *The Production of Space*. Cambridge, MA: Blackwell.

Mamdani, Mahmood 1996 *Citizen and Subject: Contemporary Africa and the Legacy of Late Colonialism.* Princeton: Princeton University Press.

Massey, Doreen 1984 *Spatial Divisions of Labour: Social Structures and the Geography of Production.* London: Macmillan.

Massey, Doreen 1994 *Space, Place and Gender.* Minneapolis: University of Minnesota Press.

Maurer, Bill 1998 *Recharting the Caribbean: Land, Law, and Citizenship in the British Virgin Islands.* Ann Arbor: The University of Michigan Press.

Mayekiso, Mzwanele 1996 *Township Politics: Civic Struggles for a New South Africa.* New York: Monthly Review Press.

Mbembe, Achille 1992 The Banality of Power and the Aesthetics of Vulgarity in the Postcolony. *Public Culture* 4(2):1–30.

Merry, Sally Engle 2001 Spatial Governmentality and the New Urban Social Order: Controlling Gender Violence Through Law. *American Anthropologist* 103(1):16–29.

Mindry, Deborah 1998 "Good Women": Philanthropy, Power, and the Politics of Femininity in Contemporary South Africa. Ph.D. dissertation, Program in Social Relations, University of California at Irvine.

Mitchell, Timothy 1991 The Limits of the State: Beyond Statist Approaches and Their Critics. *American Political Science Review* 85(1):77–96.

Nugent, David 1997 *Modernity at the Edge of Empire: State, Individual, and Nation in the Northern Peruvian Andes, 1885–1935.* Stanford: Stanford University Press.

O'Malley, Pat 1998 *Indigenous Governance. In Governing Australia: Studies in Contemporary Rationalities of Government.* Mitchell Dean and Barry Hindess, eds. Pp. 156–72. Cambridge: Cambridge University Press.

Pateman, Carole 1988 *The Sexual Contract.* Stanford: Stanford University Press.

Rosaldo, Michelle Z. 1980 The Use and Abuse of Anthropology: Reflections on Feminism and Cross-Cultural Understanding. Signs: *Journal of Women in Culture and Society* 5(3):389–417.

Rose, Nikolas 1996 *Governing "Advanced" Liberal Democracies. In Foucault and Political Reason: Liberalism, Neo-liberalism and Rationalities of Government.* Andrew Barry, Thomas Osborne, and Nikolas Rose, eds. Pp. 37–64. Chicago: University of Chicago Press.

Rose, Nikolas, and Peter Miller 1992 Political Power beyond the State: Problematics of Government. *British Journal of Sociology* 43(2):172–205.

Ruggie, John 1993 Territoriality and Beyond: Problematizing Modernity in International Relations. *International Organization* 47(1):139–174.

Sassen, Saskia 1991 *The Global City: New York, London, Tokyo.* Princeton: Princeton University Press.

—— 1996 *Losing Control? Sovereignty in an Age of Globalization*. New York: Columbia University Press.

—— 1998 *Globalization and Its Discontents: Essays on the New Mobility of People and Money*. New York: New Press.

Saul, John S. 1993 *Recolonization and Resistance: Southern Africa in the 1990s*. Trenton: Africa World Press.

Scott, James C. 1998 *Seeing Like a State: How Certain Schemes to Improve the Human Condition Have Failed*. New Haven, CT: Yale University Press.

Seligman, Adam B. 1992 *The Idea of Civil Society*. Princeton: Princeton University Press.

Smith, Neil 1992 Contours of a Spatialized Politics: Homeless Vehicles and the Production of Geographical Scale. *Social Text* 33:54–81.

Stallybrass, Peter, and Allan White 1986 *The Politics and Poetics of Transgression*. Ithaca: Cornell University Press.

Storper, Michael 1997 *Territories, Flows, and Hierarchies in the Global Economy. In Spaces of Globalization: Reasserting the Power of the Local.* Kevin R. Cox, ed. Pp. 19–44. New York: The Guilford Press.

Strathern, Marilyn 1995 *The Relation: Issues in Complexity and Scale.* Cambridge: Prickly Pear Press.

Swyngedouw, Erik 1997 *Neither Global Nor Local: "Glocalization" and the Politics of Scale. In Spaces of Globalization: Reasserting the Power of the Local.* Kevin R. Cox, ed. Pp. 137–166. New York: The Guilford Press.

Taussig, Michael 1996 *The Magic of the State*. New York: Routledge.

Taylor, Charles 1990 Modes of Civil Society. *Public Culture* 3(1):95–118.

Vail, Leroy, ed. 1991 *The Creation of Tribalism in Southern Africa*. Berkeley: University of California Press.

Verdery, Katherine 1996 *What Was Socialism, and What Comes Next?* Princeton: Princeton University Press.

Werbner, Richard, and Terence Ranger, eds. 1996 *Postcolonial Identities in Africa*. Atlantic Highlands, NJ: Zed Books.

Wilmsen, Edwin N., and Patrick McAllister, eds.1996 *The Politics of Difference: Ethnic Premises in a World of Power*. Chicago: University of Chicago Press.

Yanagisako, Sylvia J., and Jane F. Collier 1987 *Toward a Unified Analysis of Gender and Kinship. In Gender and Kinship: Essays Toward a Unified Analysis.* Jane F. Collier and Sylvia J. Yanagisako, eds. Pp 14–50. Stanford: Stanford University Press.

Excerpts From:

Hernández-López, Ernesto (2010) Guantanamo as a "Legal Black Hole": A Base for Expanding Space, Markets, and Culture. *University of San Francisco Law Review* 45(Summer):141–213.

Reproduced with permission of the *University of San Francisco Law Review*.

GUANTANAMO AS A "LEGAL BLACK HOLE": A BASE FOR EXPANDING SPACE, MARKETS, AND CULTURE

Ernesto Hernández-López (2010)

Introduction

Why Does the U.S. Naval Station at Guanta´namo Bay, Cuba[26] ("Guanta´namo" or "GTMO") appear as a "legal black hole"?[27] It's been labeled a "quirky outpost" with an "unusual jurisdictional status"[28] and an anomalous legal zone.[29] After eight years, nearly 800 persons have been detained on the base.[30] Cases from this year show that elemental legal questions about the base still daunt courts.[31] Uighurs, Turkic Muslims from China, are no longer in the same custody as other War on Terror base detainees but are unable to leave GTMO.[32] Five Uighurs remain at GTMO, awaiting

[26] The acronyms "GTMO" or "Gitmo" refer to the U.S. Naval Station at Guanta´namo Bay, Cuba. For the U.S. Navy's website, visit U.S. Navy CNIC: Naval Station Guantanamo Bay, http://www.cnic.navy.mil/guantanamo/index.htm (last visited July 30, 2010).

[27] Lord Johan Steyn, Judicial Member of the House of Lords, Twenty-Seventh F.A. Mann Lecture, Guantanamo Bay: The Legal Black Hole (Nov. 25, 2003), http://www.statewatch.org/news/2003/nov/guantanamo.pdf; *see also* Clive Stafford Smith, *America's Legal Black Hole*, L.A. Times, Oct. 5, 2007, http://articles.latimes.com/2007/oct/05/opinion/oe-smith5.

[28] Boumediene v. Bush, 128 S. Ct. 2229, 2279, 2293 (2008) (Roberts, C.J., dissenting).

[29] Gerald L. Neuman, *Anomalous Zones*, 48 Stan. L. Rev. 1197, 1201 (1996) [hereinafter Neuman, *Anomalous Zones*] (describing the base as an anomalous legal zone with "legal rules," fundamental to larger policies, "locally suspended" in a geographic area); *see also* Gerald L. Neuman, *Closing the Guantanamo Loophole*, 50 Loy. L. Rev. 1, 3–5, 42–44 (2004) [hereinafter Neuman, *Guantanamo Loophole*].

[30] *Names of the Detained in Guantanamo Bay, Cuba*, Wash. Post, http://projects.washingtonpost.com/guantanamo/ (last visited July 30, 2010) [hereinafter *Names of the Detained*, Wash. Post].

[31] Written mostly in the spring of 2010, this Article analyzes various evolving policy and litigation developments concerning Guanta´namo detentions. The detainee numbers used, reports referred to, and litigation developments presented are undoubtedly not uniform throughout the Article, since they all describe different time periods as changes transpire. While these issues develop on a constant basis, the Article's main argument, that Empire and the law of extraterritorial authority are mutually influential, remains constant. Even if Guanta´namo detentions end or new doctrines change the course of detainee and executive litigation strategies, this Article provides significant insights on Empire and law's extraterritorial application.

[32] *See* Robert Barnes, *Supreme Court Dismisses Case Involving Resettlement of Guantanamo Detainees*, Wash. Post, Mar. 2, 2010, http://www.washingtonpost.com/wp-dyn/content/article/2010/03/01/AR2010030101140.html. *See generally* Caprice L. Roberts, *Rights, Remedies, & Habeas Corpus – The Uighurs, Legally Free While Actually Imprisoned*, 24 Geo. Immigr. L.J. 1 (2009).

acceptable offers of resettlement.[33] District court habeas proceedings illustrate disagreement on basic le- gal issues such as the scope of detention authority, its legal source, the required nexus between detainee and terrorist groups, and how to treat statements coerced during torture.[34] This anomaly spreads to Afghanistan,[35] with the Bagram detention center also characterized as a "black hole."[36] One of the most controversial expressions of American power, GTMO floats as a jurisdictional island in a sea of legal anomaly terrorized by growing legal complexity in one of "the longest wars in American history."[37] If GTMO detentions end for the 174 remaining detainees,[38]

[33] *See* Lyle Denniston, *New Defeat for Detainees: No Fact-Gathering Allowed*, Scotus Blog (May 28, 2010, 11:20 AM), http://www.scotusblog.com/2010/05/new-defeat-for-de-tainees/#more-20880; Marcia Coyle, *Court Deals Uighurs Another Setback in Quest for Release into U.S.*, Blt: Blog Legaltimes (May 28, 2010, 13:11), http://legaltimes.typepad.com/blt/2010/05/court-deals-uighurs-another-setback-in-quest-for-release-into-us.html. At this time, the status of these detainees remains in flux. They are not "detained" with persons the Government argues are combatants or waiting relocation, military commissions, or other proceedings, but they remain on the base and cannot leave. *See* Letter from Elena Kagan, U.S. Solicitor General, to William K. Suter, Clerk of the Supreme Court of the United States (Feb. 19, 2010), http://www.scotusblog.com/wp-content/uploads/2010/02/SG-Kiyemba-letter-2-19-10.pdf (reporting five Uighur detainees will remain at the base, once two Uighurs leave GTMO for Switzerland, out of an initial 22 detainees and that the remaining Uighurs should receive resettlement offers). As of October 5, 2010, the five detainees have been at Guanta´namo for eight years; they include Yusef Abbas, Hajiakbar Abdulghupur, Saidullah Khalik, Ahmed Mohamed, and Abdul Razak. *The Guanta´namo Docket: Citizens of China*, N.Y. Times, http://projects.nytimes.com/guantanamo/country/china (last visited Oct. 12, 2010). For specific information and documents concerning their detention, see *id.*

[34] *See generally* Benjamin Wittes Et Al., The Emerging Law of Detention: The Guanta´Namo Habeas Cases as Lawmaking (2010), http://www.brookings.edu/~/media/Files/rc/papers/2010/0122_guantanamo_wittes_chesney/0122_guantanamo_wittes_chesney.pdf (examining legal issues developing in detainee habeas corpus proceedings since *Boumediene*).

[35] *See* Maqaleh v. Gates, 605 F.3d 84 (D.C. Cir. 2010) (holding the Suspension Clause does not extend to the Bagram detention facility); *see also* Kal Raustiala, *Is Bagram the New Guanta´namo? Habeas Corpus and* Maqaleh v. Gates, Asil Insight (June 17, 2009), http://www.asil.org/insights090618.cfm. This case is referred to as both "Al Maqaleh" and "Maqaleh." For the sake of consistency, this Article uses the term "Maqaleh."

[36] *See* Editorial, *Bagram: A Legal Black Hole?*, L.A. Times, May 26, 2010, http://arti- cles.latimes.com/2010/may/26/opinion/la-ed-bagram-20100526; Tom Reifer, *Secrecy, Torture & Human Rights: US War Crimes, European Complicity, and International Law*, Transnat'l Inst. May 2010, http://www.tni.org/article/secrecy-torture-human-rights-us-war-crimes-eu- ropean-complicity-and-international-law.

[37] Boumediene v. Bush, 128 S. Ct. 2229, 2262 (2008) (referring to the War on Terror since Sept. 11, 2001).

[38] The New York Times reports 174 detainees remain at the base. *The Guanta´namo Docket: Detainees Held*, N.Y. Times, http://projects.nytimes.com/guantanamo/detainees/ held (last visited Oct. 5, 2010) [hereinafter *The Guanta´ namo Docket: Detainees Held*, N.Y. Times]. While this Article highlights demographic and numerical data on the detainees, qualitative and personal narratives of the detainees and attorneys should not be ignored. For examples of these important perspectives, see Witness to Guanta´ Namo, http://www.witnesstoguantanamo.com/

an event predicted since January 2009,[39] these experiences will inform future extraterritorial authority.

Referring to the concept of Empire, this Article argues that U.S. foreign relations capitalize on the base's jurisdictional ambiguities. Anomaly on the base is not an aberration but instead manifests Empire's intended legal objectives.[40] These objectives articulate American assumptions regarding expanding authority, overseas market access, and cultural superiority. These three factors – space, markets, and culture – are essential for empires throughout world history.[41] Paraphrasing Alejandro Colás's foci on Empire's material, cultural, and political attributes, this Article defines Empire as metropolitan rule that subordinates overseas populations. Empire can only exist when the following are found: an expanding territory under political rule that lacks any identified limit, a protection of economic markets to sustain consumption and expansion, and an ideology of superiority to legitimize expansion.[42] When examining detainee rights, Guantánamo's anomaly appears as a legal black hole, but in reality, Empire purposefully crafts such ambiguities as part of larger objectives.

As described below, Guantánamo operates as a base for imperial objectives concerning space, markets, and culture. Base occupation since 1898 and detentions since 2002 suggest this.[43] Reflecting "Empire as space," GTMO relies on legal interpretations of extraterritoriality, which facilitate expansion with no defined spatial limit or border. Functional approaches to constitutional protections on GTMO, as seen in *Boumediene v. Bush*,[44] exemplify this flexible expansion.[45] Market protection in the Caribbean and Central America were integral to the base's purpose after 1898. Currently, "Empire as markets" refers to GTMO detentions that allow for intelligence gathering

---

index.html (last visited July 30, 2010) (providing a systemic compilation of videotaped interviews of detainees and witnesses) and The Guantá Namo Lawyers: Inside a Prison Outside the Law (Mark P. Denbeaux et al. eds., 2009) (offering narratives from detainee attorneys).

[39] *See* Exec. Order No. 13,492, 74 Fed. Reg. 4897 (Jan. 27, 2009), *available at* http://edocket.access. gpo.gov/2009/pdf/E9–1893.pdf (ordering the disposition of all detainees at Guantánamo and prompt closure of base detention facilities as "soon as practicable" but no later than January 22, 2010).

[40] For an excellent, concise description of the base's legal anomaly and its role in informal Empire, the Cold War, refugee detention, and the War on Terror, see Amy Kaplan, *Where is Guantánamo?, in* Legal Borderlands: Law and the Construction of American Borders 239–66 (Mary L. Dudziak & Leti Volpp eds., 2006).

[41] Throughout this Article, the idea of Empire as space, markets, and culture refers to Alejandro Colás's theory on Empire. *See* Alejandro Colá S, Empire 5 (2007). Dr. Colás's book, *Empire*, examines the social and political organization of empires throughout world history. *Id.*

[42] *Id.* at 5–7.

[43] *See* discussion *infra* Part II.

[44] Boumediene v. Bush, 128 S. Ct. 2229 (2008).

[45] *See* discussion *infra* Part II.A.

and support the geopolitics of energy security in the Persian Gulf and Central Asia.[46] "Empire as culture" concerns how base detentions discriminate by targeting Middle Eastern, Arab, and Central Asian nationalities.[47]

Evident with detentions, base jurisdiction has been excluded from checks in the Constitution and international law by capitalizing on anomalous sovereignty demarcations between Cuba and the United States.[48] As the first U.S. base overseas, GTMO has "legally" been under American control since a lease agreement in 1903.[49] Agreements with Cuba provide the United States

---

[46] *See* discussion *infra* Part II.B.

[47] *See* discussion *infra* Part II.C.

[48] *See* Neuman, *Anomalous Zones, supra* note 4, at 1228–33; Neuman, *Guantanamo Loophole, supra* note 4, at 1, 3–5, 42–44 (describing how the base was used to detain asylum- seekers and avoid constitutional and international law protections). *See also* Sale v. Haitian Ctrs. Council, Inc., 509 U.S. 155, 158–59 (1993) (rejecting challenges to U.S. detention authority by Haitians detained at Guanta´namo after attempting to illegally enter the United States); Cuban Am. Bar Ass'n, Inc. v. Christopher, 43 F.3d 1412, 1430 (11th Cir. 1995) (finding aliens on the base are "without legal rights that are cognizable" in U.S. courts); Haitian Ctrs. Council, Inc. v. McNary, 969 F.2d 1326, 1347 n.19 (2d Cir. 1992) (finding constitutional claims for asylum detainees likely succeeding in court); Haitian Refugee Ctr., Inc. v. Baker, 953 F.2d 1498, 1506 (11th Cir. 1992) (finding constitutional rights do not apply to asylum detainees). For a description of the international law implicated in base detentions, see Diane Marie Amann, *Guanta´ namo*, 42 Colum. J. Transnat'l L. 263 (2004).

[49] Agreement Between the United States and Cuba for the Lease of Lands for Coaling and Naval Stations, U.S.-Cuba, Feb. 23, 1903, T.S. No. 418, [hereinafter U.S.-Cuba Feb. 1903 Lease], *available at* http://avalon.law.yale.edu/20th_century/dip_cuba002.asp; *see also* Lease to the United States by the Government of Cuba of Certain Areas of Land and Water for Naval or Coaling Stations in Guantanamo and Bahia Honda, U.S.-Cuba, July 2, 1903, T.S. No. 426, [hereinafter U.S.-Cuba July 1903 Lease], *available at* http://avalon.law.yale.edu/20th_century/ dip_cuba003.asp (specifying tariff, maritime, and remuneration for U.S. occupation). Cuba contests the legality of these agreements and refuses to cash the checks that the United States provides each year in the amount of $4,085 for the lease. Kaplan, *supra* note 15, at 244; *see* Kathleen T. Rhem, *Guantanamo Bay Base Has Storied Past*, U.S. Department Def. (Aug. 24, 2004), http://www.defense.gov/news/newsar- ticle.aspx?id=25469; Michael J. Strauss, *Guanta´ namo Bay and the Evolution of International Leases and Servitudes*, 10 N.Y. City L. Rev. 479, 505–06 (2007). For descriptions of Cuba's legal arguments against base occupation, see Kal Raustiala, *The Geography of Justice*, 73 Ford- Ham L. Rev. 2501, 2539–40 (2005) [hereinafter Raustiala, *The Geography of Justice*]; Robert L. Montague, III, *A Brief Study of Some of the International Legal and Political Aspects of the Guantanamo Bay Problem*, 50 Ky. L.J. 459, 471–75 (1962); Joseph Lazar, *International Legal Status of Guantanamo Bay*, 62 Am. J. Int'l L. 730 (1968); Gary L. Maris, *Guantanamo: No Rights of Occupancy*, 63 Am. J. Int'l L. 114, 115–16 (1969). *See generally* Felipe Pe´rez Roque, Minister of Foreign Affairs of the Republic of Cuba, Statement at the High-Level Segment of the Human Rights Council (June 20, 2006), http:// www.cubaminrex.cu/english/Speeches/FPR/2006/FPR_200606i.htm (referring to the base as a "concentration camp"); Felipe Pe´rez Roque, Minister of Foreign Affairs of the Republic of Cuba, Statement to the Local and Foreign Media, at the Ministry of Foreign Affairs, Cuba Off. Site Embassy (Dec. 10, 2007), http://embacu.cubaminrex.cu/Default.aspx?tabid=5604 (demanding that the U.S. government close the "torture center" at Guanta´namo because it is "cruel, inhumane and degrading" and occupied illegally).

with "complete jurisdiction and control" for an indefinite period, while affirming Cuba's "ultimate sovereignty" over the base.[50] GTMO reflects the imperial qualities of space, markets, and culture, through U.S. authority over base territory in Cuba. It has served American foreign relations objectives in a Sphere of Influence (1898–1940), Cold War (1946–1991), and War on Terror (2002–).[51] Even though President Obama called for a closure of the GTMO detention center by February 2010, detentions still continue. The Pentagon has spent nearly $2 billion since 2001 to improve the base,[52] while Congress and the American public actively resist any relocation of detainees to the United States.[53]

Initial interests in the base were expressed in the Platt Amendment, agreements between the United States and Cuba in 1903 and 1934, and Caribbean and Central American geopolitics. Explicit War on Terror interests include detentions for intelligence, situated within American authority but securely distanced from terrorist violence.[54] The U.S. government presumed that this location avoided potential legal checks such as detainee access to courts, interference from foreign governments, and protections in constitutional, international, and foreign law.[55] Detentions close to terrorist groups in the

[50] U.S.-Cuba Feb. 1903 Lease, *supra* note 24, at art. III; *see also* Treaty Between the United States of America and Cuba Defining Their Relations, U.S.-Cuba, May 29, 1934, 48 STAT. 1682 [hereinafter U.S.-Cuba 1934 Treaty] (rescinding the Platt Amendment but confirming U.S. occupation of Guanta´namo until the United States unilaterally leaves or Cuba and the United States mutually agree to end occupation). *See generally* Lester H. Woolsey, *The New Cuban Treaty*, 28 Am. J. Int'l L. 530 (1934).

[51] *See generally* Ernesto Herna´ndez-Lo´ pez, Boumediene v. Bush *and Guanta´ namo, Cuba: Does the "Empire Strike Back"?*, 62 Smu L. Rev. 117, 153–167 (2009) [hereinafter Herna´ndez-Lo´ pez, Boumediene v. Bush *and Guanta´ namo, uba*] (describing sovereignty's role in supporting the base's strategic objectives).

[52] Scott Higham & Peter Finn, *At least $500 Million Has Been Spent Since 9/11 on Renovating Guantanamo Bay*, Wash. Post, June 7, 2010, http://www.washingtonpost.com/wp- dyn/content/article/2010/06/06/AR2010060604093.html.

[53] *See* Ken Gude, Ctr. for Am. Progress, Getting Back on Track to Close Guantanamo: How to Get to Zero 4–5 (2009), http://www.americanprogress.org/issues/2009/11/pdf/closing_guantanamo.pdf (describing Congressional budgetary and policy resistance to relocating detainees within the United States).

[54] *See* discussion *infra* Part II.B.

[55] *See, e.g.*, Boumediene v. Bush, 476 F.3d 981, 990–93 (D.C. Cir. 2007), *rev'd*, Boumediene v. Bush, 128 S. Ct. 2229 (2008); Memorandum from Patrick F. Philbin and John C. Yoo to William J. Haynes, II, Possible Habeas Jurisdiction over Aliens Held in Guantanamo Bay, Cuba (Dec. 28, 2001), *in* The Torture Papers: The Road to Abu Ghraib 29–37 (Karen J. Greenberg & Joshua L. Dratel eds., 2005) [hereinafter Philbin & Yoo Memo]; John Yoo, War by Other Means: An Insider's Account of the War On Terror 142–43 (2006) (explaining how court decisions on rights for refugees detained on the base suggested habeas corpus jurisdiction would not extend to Guanta´namo).

Persian Gulf and Central Asia[56] would derail intelligence and war efforts.[57] In this context, GTMO plays a vital role in Empire's expanding authority.

Framed by Alejandro Cola´s's conception of Empire as space, markets, and culture,[58] this Article suggests that GTMO is a legal anomaly that serves foreign relations objectives of protecting expanding American influence,[59] economic interests overseas,[60] and perceived cultural superiority.[61] This Article provides legal, historical, and social science analysis to begin exploring how anomaly feeds imperial objectives in extraterritorial jurisdiction. These arguments are presented as preliminary hypotheses, as the Supreme Court,[62] Court of Appeals for the District of Columbia Circuit,[63] the District Court for the District of Columbia,[64] the Obama administration,[65] and Congress[66] address

---

[56] This Article utilizes geographic indicators to highlight where the War on Terror is being fought, its regional influence, and where terrorists attack civilians, threaten U.S. energy security, or maintain bases of operations. It uses "Persian Gulf" to refer to the region comprised of Saudi Arabia, Bahrain, the United Arab Emirates, Iraq, Iran, Oman, Yemen, Qatar, and Kuwait, which all influence regional foreign relations and thus global access to energy resources. Other terms used include the "Middle East," "Near East," and "Arabian Peninsula." The Article does not use these latter terms as much, in an effort to isolate the specific geographic areas with geopolitical influence. It uses the term "Central Asia" to refer mostly to Afghanistan and Pakistan but also to Turkmenistan, Azerbaijan, Georgia, Armenia, Uzbekistan, Kazakhstan, and Kyrgyzstan. Other classifications could include "South Asia," "Middle East," "Near East," or "Asia" but seem imprecise and do not highlight their proximity to War on Terror fighting and/or energy resources. Ultimately, this Article could use many potential indicators; surely all suffer from imprecision or perhaps over inclusion. Moreover, this Article uses "Persian Gulf" and "Central Asia" for sake of simplicity and internal consistency.

[57] *See* discussion *infra* Part II.B.1.

[58] Cola´ S, *supra* note 16.

[59] *See* discussion *infra* Part II.

[60] *See* discussion *infra* Part II.B.2.

[61] *See* discussion *infra* Part II.C.1.

[62] *See* discussion *supra* note 7.

[63] A court of appeals decided its first appeal of a Guanta´namo habeas corpus proceeding in *Al-Bihani v. Obama*, 590 F.3d 866 (D.C. Cir. 2010). It also recently ruled on a habeas corpus appeal from a detainee held at Bagram in Afghanistan. Maqaleh v. Gates, 605 F.3d 84 (D.C. Cir. 2010).

[64] Del Quentin Wilber, *U.S. Appeals Court Wary of Habeas Corpus Challenge by Detainees in Afghanistan*, Wash. Post, Jan. 8, 2010, http://www.washingtonpost.com/wp-dyn/con- tent/ article/2010/01/07/AR2010010703205.html.

[65] *See generally* Robert M. Chesney & Benjamin Wittes, *The Courts' Shifting Rules on Guanta´ namo Detainees*, Wash. Post, Feb. 5, 2010, http://www.washingtonpost.com/wpdyn/content/ article/2010/02/04/AR2010020403910.html (explaining how the courts have had to fill gaps in the substantive law of detention because the Supreme Court has been silent and because Congress and the President provide minimal guidance); Gude, *supra* note 28 (describing the challenges, created by all three branches, in ending detentions and administering habeas proceedings, criminal trials, and military commissions).

[66] *See* Gude, *supra* note 28

complex legal issues about the base.[67] The doctrine, theory, and context presented spark larger questions on how War on Terror lawmaking relates to spatial, economic, and cultural assumptions. Imperial objectives created the need for policies to detain nearly 800 persons over an eight-year period (even now as 174 men remain detained).[68] The base's long legal history, coupled with a significant detention program, offers substantial material to start identifying how this legal anomaly – and legal anomalies in general – suits Empire.[69]

While this Article's claims are neither conclusive nor based on extensive empirical analysis, they attempt to spur scholarly inquiry. More research is needed into the theory, doctrine, and context behind Empire, legal anomaly, extraterritorial authority, detention, and foreign relations in the War on Terror. This Article's greatest promise may not be in providing complete answers now. Instead, its value comes from posing larger questions on law and extraterritorial jurisdiction. This Article's conclusions – in Part I and the Conclusion – begin to pose these questions.

This Article makes three initial arguments. First, Guanta´namo's anomaly facilitates flexible control of overseas territory by limiting public obligations to protect individual rights. This reflects Empire as space.[70] Inside the base and evident in detainee challenges, there is a degree of uncertainty or even permitted denial of constitutional and international law obligations.

[67] Since *Boumediene*, the judiciary finds itself in the position of having to define the substantive norms and procedures to be used in GTMO habeas corpus proceedings. After the 2008 Supreme Court decision, the Executive and Congress have not clarified various legal issues concerning detention authority and the procedures for habeas corpus proceedings. Although the Obama administration began a review of detention practices and announced it would end base detention by the end of January 2010, detentions still continue. The administration explored relocating detainees to a former prison in Illinois, but these plans faced political resistance in Congress and popular discourse. For excellent descriptions of how the law of overseas detention must respond to policy and jurisprudential developments, see Gude, *supra* note 28 and Wittes Et Al., *supra* note 9.

[68] See *The Guanta´namo Docket: Detainees Held*, N.Y. Times, *supra* note 13; *see also Names of the Detained*, Wash. Post, *supra* note 5.

[69] Empire is intimate to the base's history. *Cf.* Helmut Rumpf, *Military Bases on Foreign Territory, in* 3 Encyclopedia of Public International Law 381, 382–83 (Peter MacAlister-Smith ed., 1992) (describing Guanta´namo's foundation during U.S. imperialism and explaining that such bases were the start of colonial expansion); Raustiala, *The Geography of Justice, supra* note 24, at 2545–46 (describing base creation and the present lease as "remnants of the age of empire").

[70] See Cola´ S, *supra* note 16, at 31. This Article uses Yi-Fu Tuan's definition of "space" Space is more abstract than "place." Space represents "openness, freedom, and threat [of the unfamiliar]," while "place" concerns what "we get to know" and endow with value. Yi-Fu Tuan, Space and Place: The Perspective of Experience 6 (1977). As such, "Empire as space" refers to the potential abstract locations where American authority may rule and that require flexible and adaptable borders.

This uncertainty and denial creates a legal black hole.[71] In *Boumediene v. Bush*, the Court even comments on turning the Constitution on or off at the base.[72] This aids expanding U.S. jurisdiction and control, while flexibly evading public limitations. Jurisprudence on extraterritorial authority, such as the *Insular Cases*[73] (1910–1920) and the Guantánamo cases (2004–2010), points to how overseas control benefits from these limits.[74] For both periods, American law has perceived extraterritorial authority as avoiding the checks that would apply domestically. In *Boumediene*, the Supreme Court affirmed that the Constitution's Suspension Clause, including habeas corpus rights, "has full effect" on the base.[75] Jurisprudence since *Boumediene* solidifies a functional and flexible approach for determining if constitutional protections check authority overseas.[76] This Article describes anomaly's role in *Kiyemba v. Obama*, concerning Uighur detainees unable to leave the base,[77] district court habeas proceedings since 2008, with ambiguity clouding issues such as detention authority and evidentiary matters,[78] and *Maqaleh v. Gates*, concerning

---

[71] *See* Steyn, *supra* note 2. Smith, *supra* note 2. Hari M. Osofsky offers an elaborate discussion of "justice wormholes," like black holes, as "governmentally-constructed links between legal spaces devoid of … procedural or substantive protection." Hari M. Osofsky, *The Geography of Justice Wormholes: Dilemmas from Property and Criminal Law*, 53 Vill. L. Rev. 117, 117 (2008). For descriptions of black holes and the philosophy behind states of exception to the rule of law, see Noa Ben-Asher, *Legal Holes*, 5 Unbound: Harv. J. Legal Left 1 (2009), http:// www.legalleft.org/?p=188. For an examination of how human rights treaties apply in extra-territorial settings, see Ralph Wilde, *Legal "Black Hole"? Extraterritorial State Action and International Treaty Law on Civil and Political Rights*, 26 Mich. J. Int'l L. 739 (2005). For an analysis of how eliminating black holes or "grey holes" is impracticable, see Adrian Vermeule, *Our Schmittian Administrative Law*, 122 Harv. L. Rev. 1095 *passim* (2009). *But see* Stephen I. Vladeck, *The Long War, the Federal Courts, and the Necessity/Legality Paradox*, 43 U. Rich. L. Rev. 893 (2009) (presenting the danger in reasoning that "necessity" and national security emergencies require judicial deference, by relating War on Terror jurisprudence and poli-cies with jurisprudence and policies during the Japanese-American internment during World War II).

[72] Boumediene v. Bush, 128 S. Ct. 2229, 2236, 2259 (2008).

[73] *See generally* Ernesto Hernández-López, *Guantánamo Outside and Inside the U.S.: Why is an American Base a Legal Anomaly?*, 18 Am. U. J. Gender Soc. Pol'y & L. 471 (2010) (describ-ing the *Insular Cases* as "empire as space"); Hernández-López, Boumediene v. Bush *and Guantánamo, Cuba*, *supra* note 26, at 181–86 (examining how foreign sovereignty is similarly checked in the *Insular Cases* and War on Terror cases).

[74] *See* discussion *infra* Part II.A.

[75] *Boumediene*, 128 S. Ct. at 2262 (referring to U.S. Const. art. I, § 9, cl. 2). *See generally* Gerald L. Neuman, *The Habeas Corpus Suspension Clause After Boumediene v. Bush*, 110 Colum. L. Rev. 537 (2010) [hereinafter Neuman, *The Habeas Corpus Suspension Clause After Boumediene v. Bush*] (arguing *Boumediene* affirms that the Suspension Clause guarantees some judicial review, for citizens and noncitizens, against unlawful detention).

[76] *See* discussion *infra* Part II.A.1.

[77] *See* discussion *infra* Part II.A.2.

[78] *See* discussion *infra* Part II.A.3.

similar proceedings for detainees in Afghanistan.[79] This evolving doctrine expands anomalies within extraterritorial authority. It functions as Empire as space.

Second, the base protects economic markets abroad. Historically, it bolstered "sphere of influence" objectives regarding Cuba, the Caribbean, and the Panama Canal.[80] This Article offers preliminary in- sight into GTMO's effective role in current overseas market protections.[81] The base supports intelligence gathering needed for War on Terror efforts in the Persian Gulf and Central Asia. These regions are also of vital economic and strategic importance to the United States because of their energy resources or geographic proximity to such resources. Terrorists[82] threaten these markets directly by attacking the energy industry and indirectly by destabilizing regional states and global markets. Accordingly, terrorists threaten vital resource supplies for global energy demand. GTMO detentions are justified because they obtain intelligence to combat these threats. These threats are of explicit concern to national security, but they also disrupt the geopolitics of energy markets in the region. Government and public discourse contend that terrorism threatens national security and that this threat justifies an American military response and increased executive authority.[83] This Article does not deny that terrorism

---

[79] *See* discussion *infra* Part II.A.4.

[80] *See generally* Bartholomew H. Sparrow, *The Insular Cases and the Emergence of American Empire* (2006) (describing the Insular Cases as providing a legal framework to support informal Empire, of which overseas military bases were a central component); Robert Freeman Smith, *Latin America, the United States and the European Powers, 1830–1930, in* The Cambridge History of Latin America: Volume IV C. 1870 to 1930, at 83–119 (Leslie Bethell ed., 1986) [hereinafter Freeman Smith] (describing the international rivalries and subsequent increase in involvement of the United States in Central America and the Caribbean, especially in planning for and protecting the Canal). Legal anomaly also characterized the U.S. Panama Canal Zone and the lease agreement with Panama. *See* Neuman, *Guantanamo Loophole, supra* note 4, at 15–23.

[81] *See* discussion *infra* Part II.B.

[82] President George W. Bush defined "terrorism" as "premeditated, politically motivated violence perpetuated against innocents." The National Security Strategy Of The United States Of America 5 (2002), *available at* http://georgewbush-whitehouse.archives. gov/nsc/nss/2002/index.html [hereinafter The National Security Strategy].

[83] This Article argues that the Bush and Obama administrations share much in common in terms of how the executive branch interprets what limits, if any, check its detention authority and extraterritorial authority. Concerning Afghanistan detentions, see Christopher Weaver, *Obama Administration On Detention Policy: What He Said,* Propublica, (Feb. 23, 2009, 5:31 PM), http://www.propublica.org/article/obama-administration-on-detention- policy-what-he-said. For an analysis of how Obama and Bush have very similar War on Terror policies and legal arguments, see Jack Goldsmith, *The Cheney Fallacy: Why Barack Obama is Waging a More Effective War on Terror than George W. Bush,* New Republic, (May 18, 2009, 12:00 AM), http://www.tnr.com/article/politics/the-cheney-fallacy?id=1e733cac-c273-48 e5-9140-80443ed1f5e2.

kills innocent civilians and threatens national security (both domestically and overseas), but it suggests material interests have enormous influences on U.S. foreign policy in the Persian Gulf and Central Asia.[84] It may be negligent for scholars to ignore regional geopolitics and resource challenges. The base's legal anomaly effectively subsidizes intelligence gathering – perhaps even out-sources torture in its support – aiding economic objectives in the Persian Gulf and Central Asia. With an eye on geopolitics in these regions, GTMO's role in intelligence reflects the idea of Empire as markets.

Third, culturally the base promotes an ideology of American superiority with manipulations of sovereignty and consequential racial-based exclusions. American jurisdiction on the base is defined in reference to sovereignty, with Cuba denied full sovereignty.[85] Historically, international law explicitly used cultural reasoning to exclude certain populations from sovereignty. This is evident in the Treaty of Paris of 1898, ceding Cuba to the United States from Spain, and the Platt Amendment, requiring a U.S.-protector role and base in Cuba.[86] Cubans as a Hispanic, black, and mixed-race population could not be fully sovereign or self-govern. With provisions specifically limiting Cuban sovereignty, the Platt Amendment and base agreements articulate these assumptions. Today, racial implications take the form of the denial of rights protections for detainees, because they are simultaneously outside U.S. and Cuban sovereignty. Some have argued constitutional rights only apply in U.S. sovereign territory and not in GTMO.[87] Detention is primarily reserved for Central Asian, Middle- Eastern, or Arab identities.[88] Guanta´namo reflects

---

[84] *See generally* Leo Panitch & Sam Gindin, *The Unique American Empire, in* The War On Terrorism And The American 'Empire' After The Cold War 24 (Alejandro Cola´s & Richard Saull eds., 2006) (presenting American Empire's objectives to protect global capitalism and to serve as global police for neoliberal policies, increasing the importance of overseas military bases and intelligence).

[85] The Platt Amendment required Cuba to provide a base; GTMO became that base. An Act Making Appropriation for the Support of the Army for the Fiscal Year Ending June Thirtieth, Nineteen Hundred and Two, 31 Stat. 895, 897 (1901) [hereinafter Platt Amendment – U.S. Appropriations]. *See generally* Herna´ndez-Lo´ pez, Boumediene v. Bush *and Guanta´ namo, Cuba, supra* note 26, at 153–67 (describing how the Platt Amendment began as a letter from Secretary of War Elihu Root, was included in congressional appropriations, an international treaty, and Cuban law, and checked Cuban sovereignty as a U.S. protectorate).

[86] *See* discussion *infra* Part I.B; *see also* Herna´ndez-Lo´ pez, Boumediene v. Bush *and Guanta´ namo, Cuba, supra* note 26, at 129–49.

[87] *See* Brief for the Respondents at 14–24, Boumediene v. Bush, 128 S. Ct. 2229 (2008) (Nos. 06–1195 & 06–1196). *Cf. The Legal Basis for Detaining Al Qaida and Taliban Combatants,* U.S. Department Def. (Nov. 14, 2005), www.defenselink.mil/news/Jul2007/Legal%20basis%20 Guantanamo%20Detainees%20OGC%20FINAL.pdf. (reporting that there is "no question that under the law of war" the United States may detain persons "who have engaged in unlaw-ful belligerence for the duration of hostilities, without charges or trial").

[88] *See* discussion *infra* Part II.C.

law's cultural assumptions that Cuba could not be sovereign, with American superiority justifying a base for over a century. Cultural exclusions produced an overseas base. They now sustain detention inside it, reflecting GTMO's contribution to Empire as culture.

Concentrated Trends in Detainee Nationalities

GTMO's role in Empire as culture is consistent with preliminary analysis of detainee demographics. This analysis suggests that detention is reserved mostly for specific nationalities; the majority of detainees are nationals from Afghanistan, Saudi Arabia, Yemen, or Pakistan. The War on Terror articulates American values of cultural superiority and duty. Base detainee nationality patterns are consistent with these cultural assumptions. Here, the early argument is that base detentions overwhelmingly focus on specific nationalities. While detentions may not have explicit racist or national origin motives, their result is de facto discriminatory. GTMO detention appears to be more likely for certain nationalities. The total detainee population has included over forty-seven nationalities, including European, Canadian, and Australian nationals.[89] But when these numbers are sorted by nationality, the most represented groups point to detention-nationality patterns. As such, a detention program at a specific location lasting at least eight years with detainees distanced from American and foreign law inspires asking: Who is or has been detained there?

We can draw only preliminary inferences, because since 2002 detainee population information has been incomplete, imperfect, controlled for security reasons, and has changed with transfers, releases, and litigation. This Article works with three databases accessible online from the Brookings Institution, Washington Post, and New York Times, developed since Pentagon disclosures in the spring of 2006. The Brooking Institution notes that the Pentagon has "consistently refused to comprehensively identify" the detainees, and despite information releases, it "always maintained ambiguity" and declines to give a precise number of those actually held.[90] Despite these compilations, information is "strangely obscure" with changes to the population's makeup remaining "fuzzy."[91]

---

[89] *Names of the Detained*, WASH. POST, *supra* note 5.
[90] Benjamin Wittes, Zaahira Wyne, Erin Miller, Julia Pilcer, & Georgina Druce, Brookings Inst., The Current Detainee Population of Guanta´ Namo: An Empirical Study 1, 3 (2008), http://www.brookings.edu/reports/2008/1216_detainees_wittes.aspx?rssid=wittesb (follow "Full Report" hyperlink) [hereinafter Wittes & Wyne].
[91] *Id.* at 3.

The Brookings Institution reported that as of October 21, 2009, 221 detainees remained,[92] while recent reports say 174 remain.[93]

Countries with 70 or more detainees include Afghanistan, Saudi Arabia, Yemen, and Pakistan.[94] Two hundred nineteen detainees are of Afghan nationality, 140 detainees are of Saudi Arabian nationality, 109 detainees are of Yemeni nationality, and 70 detainees are of Pakistani nationality.[95] Countries with the next largest number of detainees include Algeria and China, having 25 and 22 nationals detained respectively.[96] The third largest set consists of countries that have had between 10 and 20 nationals detained: Morocco, Kuwait, Sudan, Tajikistan, and Tunisia.[97] Iraq, Syria, and Russia each have 9 detainees.[98] Countries with less than 10 detainees include: Jordan, the United Kingdom, France, Bahrain, Egypt, Uzbekistan, Turkey, Somalia, Iran, Kazakhstan, Mauritania, West Bank, Australia, Belgium, Canada, Malaysia, United Arab Emirates, Palestine, Bangladesh, Denmark, Azerbaijan, Sweden, Spain, Chad, Qatar, Turkmenistan, Uganda, Maldives, Ethiopia, Tanzania, Indonesia, and Kenya.[99] The New York Times *Guanta´namo Docket* reports similar trends regarding the citizenship of detainees.[100]

Drawing inferences from the law's cultural assumptions and its consequential racial exclusions for this population is difficult.[101] Detainee nationalities suggest they are from the Persian Gulf or Central Asia, regions vital to American security in terms of the War on Terror and energy supplies. One place to start is by ordering the population by geographic origin based on nationality. Broken up, using U.S. Department of State geographic

---

[92] Benjamin Wittes, Zaahira Wyne, Erin Miller, Julia Pilcer, & Georgina Druce, Brookings Inst., The Current Detainee Population of Guanta´Namo: An Empirical Study 1 (2008), http://www. brookings.edu/reports/2008/1216_detainees_wittes.aspx?rssid=wittesb (follow "View Updates as of October 21, 2009" hyperlink).

[93] *The Guanta´namo Docket: Detainees Held*, N.Y. Times, *supra* note 13.

[94] *Names of the Detained: Results*, Wash. Post, *supra* note 356

[95] *Id.*

[96] *Id.*

[97] *Id.*

[98] *Id.*

[99] *Id.*

[100] *The Guanta´namo Docket: Countries of Citizenship*, N.Y. Times, http://projects.nytimes. com/guantanamo/detainees/by-country/page/1 (last visited July 23, 2010).

[101] The numeric data presented in this subsection is imperfect, for a variety of methodological and sourcing reasons. This Article does not pretend to offer a thorough statistical analysis. This early and rudimentary demographic analysis is offered only to spur more thorough examinations and to motivate questions about detention trends and their influence on extraterritorial jurisdiction and Empire. The data provided is quite limited and far from conclusive. Any examination of detainee demographics is hindered by concerns about the ramifications of disclosure, the developing nature of numbers due to relocations and litigation, and databases that use different reporting criteria.

categories,[102] detainees represent 18 Near Eastern states, 8 South and Central Asian states, 7 African states, 4 East Asian and Pacific states, and 10 European and Eurasia states.[103] This provides for 377 detainees from the Near East and 319 from South and Central Asia. These two regions' combined result equals 696 of the 779 detainees, constituting 89.4% from the Near East and South or Central Asia. Put simply, detainees seem to overwhelmingly be from these regions.

Critical Race Questions Raised by Nationalities

Localizing racial categories for detainees under U.S. law is quite complex. For this, the Article emphasizes critical race approaches.[104] Base detainees' shared nationalities and geographic origin point to Empire as culture, with detention being de facto discriminatory. Because American law reserves detentions primarily for Arabs and South and Central Asians, detention practices are discriminatory. They bolster goals of American superiority by excluding certain populations from protections. Critical race legal theory offers various analytical tools explaining how racially neutral or color-blind legal policies, such as base detentions for enemy combatants and intelligence gathering, discriminate against populations of color.[105] Here, the idea is that race is socially constructed and not necessarily something biological or static.[106] Social thoughts, political contests, and assumptions create racial categories.[107] By designating

[102] The U.S. State Department groups countries into the following regions: Africa (Sub-Sahara), East Asia and the Pacific, Europe and Eurasia, the Near East (North Africa and the Middle East), South and Central Asia, and the Western Hemisphere. *Countries & Regions*, U.S. Department St., http://www.state.gov/countries/ (last visited July 20, 2010).

[103] These figures use the Washington Post database. *Names of the Detained*, Wash. Post, *supra* note 5.

[104] It can be argued that many of the detainee identities are white for domestic U.S. law purposes, yet the law perpetually discriminates against detainees by classifying them as enemy aliens, disloyal, or passionately violent. *See generally* John Tehranian, Whitewashed: America's Invisible Middle Eastern Minority (2009).

[105] Liberal theory's assumptions regarding "formal equality" and meritocracy overlook where de facto discrimination exists. *See Introduction, in* Critical Race Theory: The Key Writings that Formed the Movement, at xiv–xvii (Kimberlé eds., 1995). With GTMO, liberal assumptions operate on two general planes. First, an American base was obtained by the consent of two sovereign states. In reality, the negotiation was grossly unequal and was an exercise of imperial power. This created an anomalous space in American and international law at Guantánamo. Second, the objectives of the detention program have no racial intent or impact. Detention is for security and intelligence-gathering purposes. Detainee nationalities and the neo-savagery tropes implicit in the "unlawful enemy combatant" classification suggest that detention racializes Arab and South and Central Asians. See generally Mégret, supra note 333.

[106] *See* Michael Omi & Howard Winant, Racial Formation in the United States: From the 1960s to the 1980s, at 68 (1st ed. 1986).

[107] *See, e.g.*, Race And Races: Cases and Resources for a Diverse America (Juan F. Perea et al. eds., 2000) (illustrating the historical process of how various groups are treated as "different" by American history and the law).

categories, excluding rights protections, or affirming certain privileges, the law may racialize certain populations. Base detentions and classifications as "unlawful enemy combatants" create proxies in American law to exclude persons from rights protections.[108] Referring to American law's racialization of foreigners and the War on Terror, critical race legal scholarship inspires similar inquiries on base detentions, race, and notions of American superiority. Natsu Taylor Saito explains how, historically with Chinese Americans, Japanese Americans, Asian Americans, and Native Americans, U.S. law has categorized "foreigners," "others," or noncitizens to then exclude them from rights protections in domestic and international law.[109] These exclusions are interdependent on legal normativity in U.S. foreign relations and domestic civil rights.[110] Highlighting how the notion of sovereignty contains exclusionary assumptions on territory and collective identity, Tayyab Mahmud explains how this process naturally characterizes migrants as permanent outsiders and threats.[111] Accordingly, these examples inspire asking how American superiority and notions of Arabs and Central Asians as outsiders frame jurisprudence to exclude detainees from rights protections. Guantánamo's legal anomaly, effectively excluding rights protections, provides the instruments to affirm imperial power.

Critical race theory similarly elucidates how immigration and alienage law stems from, and never fully breaks with, social mechanisms to exclude certain races from American rights protections. Importantly, the *Boumediene* Court found that alien detainees did have habeas corpus rights on the base.[112] This holding has not been without controversy, since it was argued aliens did not have these constitutional rights on non-sovereign territory, and aliens generally enjoy less constitutional rights than citizens.[113]

Kevin Johnson describes how alienage serves as a proxy for race in U.S. law. He ties in history, social, legal, foreign, and domestic analyses. Immigration

---

[108] When incorporated by the Court in *Hamdi*, the "unlawful enemy combatant" classification did not enjoy firm doctrinal support. *Cf.* Martinez, *supra* note 203, at 785–87 (explaining that no statute had defined or used the term and that the laws of war and international humanitarian law do not frequently use the term).

[109] Natsu Taylor Saito, *Alien and Non-Alien Alike: Citizenship, "Foreignness," and Racial Hierarchy in American Law*, 76 Or. L. Rev. 261, 263–66, 289–92 (1997); Natsu Taylor Saito, *Crossing the Border: The Interdependence of Foreign Policy and Racial Justice in the United States*, 1 Yale Hum. Rts. & Dev. L.J. 53, 56 (1998).

[110] Natsu Taylor Saito, From Chinese Exclusion to Guantá Namo Bay: Plenary Power and the Prerogative State 6 (2007).

[111] Tayyab Mahmud, *Migration, Identity, & the Colonial Encounter*, 76 Or. L. Rev. 633, 634 (1997).

[112] Boumediene v. Bush, 128 S. Ct. 2229, 2259–60 (2008).

[113] *Id.* at 2293–307 (Scalia, J., dissenting).

law, with explicit intent or ignored effect, discriminates against citizens and noncitizens of color. From the late nineteenth century to the present, this includes Chinese exclusion, Japanese internment, national origin quotas, war on illegal aliens (i.e., Mexican immigrants), and Haitian interdiction.[114] Johnson explains not only how social biases feed lawmaking but how racism provided the initial reasoning for sovereignty-based immigration doctrine.[115] This doctrine, known as the plenary power doctrine, justifies why Congress and the Executive have plenary powers in foreign relations, overseas territories, and immigration matters.[116] This frames how American law approaches base detention, by focusing jurisprudence on national security, base location, and detainee alienage. Following these insights, this Article starts posing larger questions on how Empire (as space, markets, and culture) creates the need for these doctrines.

Lastly, critical race theory illuminates how domestic War on Terror policies inherently discriminate against Arabs, Muslims, and those who appear as such.[117] As a result, base detainees share much in common culturally and racially with the domestic victims of the War. Susan Akram and Kevin Johnson show how immigration law, building on notions of "otherness" in race, national origin, religion, culture, and political ideology, plays a key role in government attacks on Arabs and Muslims.[118] September 11, 2001 permitted American law to add to exclusionary assumptions of foreigners as disloyal, engrained in social attitudes, policy, and legal precedent.[119] The social effect of the law's discrimination has been to foster public targeting of those who appear Middle Eastern, Arab, or Muslim,[120] tolerate

---

[114] See Kevin R. Johnson, *Race, the Immigration Laws, and Domestic Race Relations: a "Magic Mirror" into the Heart of Darkness*, 73 Ind. L.J. 1111, 1119–44 (1998).

[115] See Kevin R. Johnson, *Race and Immigration Law and Enforcement: A Response To Is There a Plenary Power Doctrine?*, 14 Geo. Immigr. L.J. 289, 291 (2000).

[116] See, e.g., Sarah H. Cleveland, *Powers Inherent in Sovereignty: Indians, Aliens, Territories, and the Nineteenth Century Origins of Plenary Power Over Foreign Affairs*, 81 Tex. L. Rev. 1, 10–13 (2002); Saito, *supra* note 383, at 6.

[117] David Cole explains the process of sacrificing noncitizen rights for national security is not limited to this War and provides numerous examples of such occurrences in American history; he explains that the elimination of noncitizens' rights is the first step to eliminating citizens' rights. David Cole, *Enemy Aliens*, 54 Stan. L. Rev. 953, 955, 959 (2002).

[118] Susan M. Akram & Kevin R. Johnson, *Race, Civil Rights, and Immigration Law after September 11, 2001: The Targeting of Arabs and Muslims*, 58 N.Y.U. Ann. Surv. Am. L. 295, 299 (2002).

[119] See Thomas W. Joo, *Presumed Disloyal: Executive Power, Judicial Deference, and the Construction of Race Before and After September 11*, 34 Colum. Hum. Rts. L. Rev. 1, 2 (2002).

[120] Leti Volpp, *The Citizen and the Terrorist*, 49 Ucla L. Rev. 1575, 1577 (2002); See also Leti Volpp, *The Culture of Citizenship*, 8 Theoretical Inquiries L. 571, 581–82 (2007).

"[r]acial [v]iolence as [c]rimes of [p]assion,"[121] or mix religion and race into "terror-profiling."[122]

In summation, this subsection illustrates how cultural assumptions of American superiority and Cuban inferiority produced an American base within Cuban territory. These cultural assumptions helped craft base occupation of effectively indefinite duration with a jurisdiction anomalously between Cuban and American sovereignty. Ironically, current detainees argue their detention is indefinite, and they suffer from anomalous jurisdiction between branches of U.S. government and between sovereign states. Legal approaches in several treaties, the Platt Amendment, and contemporary foreign relations confirm how cultural assumptions shaped extraterritorial authority. For the United States, this power represented an Anglo and civilized population in a hemisphere of inferior communities with de jure sovereignty and an inability to self-govern. The base and the corresponding legal anomaly were the product of Empire as culture.

Since the detention location is the product of cultural assumptions and detentions tend to concentrate on certain nationalities, this subsection poses one question: Does detention authority rely on cultural assumptions regarding detainees who are primarily Arab, Middle Eastern, or Central Asian?

Conclusion

This Article has offered preliminary suggestions as to why Empire purposefully creates Guantánamo's jurisdictional anomalies. For the past eight years, legal contests and public discourse worldwide have debated whether the plight of nearly 800[123] really makes the base a legal black hole. Despite four Supreme Court decisions, endless diplomatic efforts, congressional debates, executive policy, and multiple litigation efforts, a substantial number of men remain detained on the base, effectively for an indefinite period. Two years after the Supreme Court in *Boumediene* held that detainees may contest the legality of their detention in district court habeas proceedings, anomaly still clouds this litigation in myriad ways.[124]

This anomaly is the product of Empire. It is crafted for the benefit of American foreign relations, since base occupation started in 1903 but most apparent with ongoing detention. Detainee rights, or lack thereof, are just one

---

[121] Muneer I. Ahmad, *A Rage Shared by Law: Post-September 11 Racial Violence as Crimes of Passion*, 92 Calif. L. Rev. 1259, 1302 (2004).

[122] Margaret Chon & Donna E. Arzt, *Walking While Muslim*, 68 Law & Contemp. Probs. 215, 218 (2005).

[123] *See Names of the Detained*, Wash. Post, *supra* note 5.

[124] Boumediene v. Bush, 128 S. Ct. 2229, 2240 (2008).

aspect of the base's anomaly. To open the general question of how Empire profits from jurisdictional anomalies, this Article explores the base's role in serving an American Empire. Since its creation a century ago, legal anomaly on the base furthers foreign relations objectives regarding expanding authority, overseas market access, and cultural superiority. This Article provides a contextual picture of how Guantánamo influences and is influenced by Empire. With this, the Article's ultimate objective is to pose questions about Guantánamo's law and Empire's space, markets, and culture.

As Alejandro Colás describes, three factors – space, markets, and culture – are essential and required for empires throughout world history. Analyzing a series of examples in world history, he demonstrates that empires need expanding territory under political rule, lacking any identified limit, protection of overseas resource markets, and ideologies of superiority.[125] These factors refer to Empire as space, markets, and culture, respectively. This Article uses this framework to examine how American foreign relations profit from the base's legal anomaly and how the law contributes to this.

Suggesting Empire as space, functional approaches to constitutional protections on GTMO result in a flexible expansion of American power, possibly without limits. Detention jurisprudence since 2008 elucidates these doctrinal developments. These include: a functional test for constitutional protections overseas fashioned by the Supreme Court in *Boumediene*;[126] an anomalous judicial power to order a detainee's release, suggested in *Kiyemba*;[127] district court habeas proceedings illustrating abundant legal confusion concerning the scope and source of detention authority and what evidence is permitted;[128] and similar approaches in Afghanistan, as suggested in *Maqaleh*.[129] This developing doctrine inspires asking: Is it Empire as space, with flexible borders or no boundaries, when extraterritorial jurisprudence poses no spatial or geographic limits to American authority?

Current Empire as markets refers to detention's implicit role in supporting American geopolitics of energy security in the Persian Gulf and Central Asia. With bases and operations in these regions, terrorists – mostly Al Qaeda and Taliban – attack civilian populations worldwide, including the U.S. homeland but especially in the Persian Gulf and Central Asia. Simultaneously, the United States views these regions as strategically important to its energy security. Intelligence gained through Guantánamo detentions and by other

---

[125] COLÁS, *supra* note 16, at 18.
[126] *See* discussion *supra* Part II.A.1.
[127] *See* discussion *supra* Part II.A.2.
[128] *See* discussion *supra* Part II.A.3.
[129] *See* discussion *supra* Part II.A.4.

methods helps counter terrorist operations abroad. Targeting these regions, terrorists directly attack the energy industry and indirectly destabilize access to these markets. Recent violence in Saudi Arabia, Iraq, and Yemen suggests this. Afghanistan's location, adjacent to Caspian Sea energy sources, Iran, China, Russia, India, and Pakistan, points to its unique geopolitical significance. American economic and geopolitical interest in these regions goes far beyond the War on Terror. Detentions for intelligence help protect these energy markets and bolster American geopolitical power in these regions. With these early hypotheses, this Article asks: Are overseas markets effectively protected with Guanta´namo detentions and corresponding intelligence, suggesting the base supports Empire as markets?

The base's role in Empire as culture concerns how detentions discriminate by focusing on certain nationalities (e.g., Middle Eastern, Arab, or Central Asian). Detention occurs on base territory acquired with justifications of American superiority and Cuban inferiority, after the War of 1898 and with the Platt Amendment. The executive branch and courts determine American jurisdiction on the base in reference to sovereignty, with Cuba denied full sovereignty. Current racial implications concern the denial of rights protections for detainees, because they are simultaneously outside U.S. and Cuban sovereignty. It was argued that constitutional rights require presence in U.S. sovereign territory (i.e., not in GTMO). Guanta´namo reflects the law's cultural assumptions that Cuba could not be sovereign and the United States was superior. These cultural exclusions produced an overseas base. They now sustain detention inside it. Cultural assumptions embedded in the base's legal history plus current detention patterns suggest asking: Does detention authority rely on cultural assumptions regarding detainees who are primarily of Arab, Middle Eastern, or Central Asian nationalities?

In conclusion, the preceding paragraphs described how American Empire produced legal anomaly on the base and how this anomaly contributes to Empire. Recent detentions suggest the base appears like a legal black hole. Global assumptions – broader than individual rights or executive authority to detain – motivate this anomaly. If the War on Terror ever ends or base detentions cease, Guanta´namo detention cases will inform future approaches to American extraterritorial authority. This law shapes current and future approaches to individual rights, foreign relations, war, national security, interrogations/torture/intelligence, and military deference. Scholars, lawyers, and policymakers should explore the motivations and effects of these legal instruments. Accordingly, this Article briefly examines relevant doctrine, sheds light on foreign relations history, and applies theory on Empire to ask: What is Guanta´namo's role in Empire as space, markets, and culture?

5   Securing Peoples

Within the field of law and society, no arena of inquiry has grown as fast as that analyzing the abuse of human rights and the application and implementation of human rights discourses and remedies. In the past, sociolegal scholars typically focused on the civil and political rights of individuals within the context of nation-states. More recently, sociolegal scholars have moved beyond analysis of peoples' domestic rights vis-à-vis the state to look to the application and implementation of human rights discourses in international and global contexts. This more expansive body of scholarship is concerned with the degree to which international legal norms, and specifically the United Nation's 1945 Charter and 1948 Universal Declaration of Human Rights, have become mobilized, institutionalized, and enforced and, in turn, shaped mechanisms and strategies of political accountability.

In this chapter, I am not attempting to chart the enormous body of sociolegal literature on human rights. However, what I do is lay out a very brief history of the emergence of human rights because this background continues to inform assumptions that human rights intrinsically represent an ethics of progress. As I will discuss, in the context of twenty-first century globalization, assumptions about the universal application of human rights and its embodiment of progress and democracy are now being seriously questioned and challenged (see Brysk 2002; Sarat 2011). In particular, the transitional justice literature highlights just how limited and inadequate a conventional human rights approach has become in contexts of deliberate state and non-state violence, mass movements of people fleeing conflict, and the millions of people who are without citizenship or any form of political representation. The transitional justice literature suggests an urgent need to shift gears and rethink the future of international human rights and humanitarian law as they are applied in contexts not framed or informed by state institutions or state-enforced legalities.

My underlying objective in this chapter is to emphasize that sociolegal scholarship on human rights will have to increasingly confront these new geopolitical realities of non-state violence in the absence of state protections that are
an intrinsic – but often unrecognized – by-product of economic globalization
and the increasingly aggressive global quest for profitable resources (Ferguson
2006). One strategy discussed is to move away from thinking in terms of individual people with state-protected rights and to reflect more creatively about
individuals living in specific locales where collective rights and community
responsibilities feature prominently. In this configuration of new legal spaces,
how may alternative constructions of self and subjectivity refashion the concept of human rights as it has been historically conceived? Another possible
strategy discussed is to engage with the idea of human security and explore
how a human security framework may be more effectively enforced than
conventional human rights. Both of these discussions highlight the prevailing assumptions built into an international human rights discourse, premised
as it is on understandings of autonomous individuals and sovereign states. A
global sociolegal perspective underscores the limits of these assumptions and
asks how a human rights discourse may remain applicable and relevant in
the coming decades to various political, religious, and cultural communities
around the world (see, for example, Onuma 2010; Simmons 2011).

HUMAN RIGHTS AS AN ETHICS OF PROGRESS

In Europe and the United States, against the turbulent background of the
American War of Independence (1776) and the French Revolution (1789), a
notion of human rights emerged based on a person's inalienable rights to life,
freedom, and liberty (Hunt 2008). Encapsulated in the French Declaration
of the Rights of Man and the American Bill of Rights was the idea that all
individuals have, by virtue of their humanity, certain inalienable rights that
the state is obligated to defend. In practical terms, this meant that a person's
human rights were limited to the extent that the state would defend them. A
person's status as citizen was seen as key in determining the degree to which a
liberal democratic state would involve itself, or not, in defending any notion
of rights and freedoms.

Historically, the concept of rights can be broken down into various categories, such as civil and political rights, as well as cultural, social, and economic
rights. These different kinds of rights include, to varying degrees, the belief
that all people are created equal in nature. Some of these rights, such as the
right to vote and the right to be politically represented, are based on a person's
status as a citizen of a state. In contrast, cultural, social, and economic human

rights, at least in theory, are not necessarily linked to a person's status with respect to state institutions but are supposedly determined on the basis of all peoples' intrinsic human dignity.

Despite the lofty principles of human dignity embodied in human rights language, the history of human rights is actually one of violence, oppression, and exploitation. Imperial expansion and colonialism saw the conquest and occupation by European nations of large areas of Africa, the Americas, and the Asia-Pacific from the sixteenth to the twentieth centuries. During these centuries of colonial control, classificatory schemas were established whereby people were determined to be Christian or non-Christian, citizens or noncitizens, civilized or savage.

These schemas of mankind were based on hierarchical understandings of race which presumed that different human characteristics, such as intelligence, correlated to a person's ethnic identity and racial characteristics. Hierarchies of race ranked white European males as superior and darker skinned peoples as inferior. In the nineteenth and early twentieth centuries, pseudoscientific schema based on eugenics lent legitimacy to popular theories about racialized hierarchies of people. Eugenics sought to classify mankind on the basis of genes and improve humanity through selective breeding, sterilization, and other horrifying social policies (Darian-Smith 2010a).

On the basis of how a person was classified, certain political, civil, cultural, social, and economic rights were granted. Those people considered racially inferior, and less than human, were denied rights and privileges linked to citizenship. As a result, "While the colonizing West brought the constitutive aspects of the human rights tradition – sovereignty, constitutionalism, and ideas of freedom and equality – their beliefs about anthropology effectively excluded non-European peoples from human rights benefits" (Stacy 2009:12). However, the exclusion of non-European peoples from the benefits of an international human rights discourse began to change with the decolonialization movement after WWII in the mid-to-late twentieth century (see Burke 2010). The decolonization era saw the withdrawal of many European powers from their former colonies, and a growth in world attention focused on how best to implement human rights in new self-governing state systems emerging in Africa, Asia, and the Pacific. In this context delegates from formerly colonized countries joined the international forum of the United Nations and helped to draft the Universal Declaration of Human Rights. The discussions between representatives from former colonized and colonizing countries were often bitter and tense (Anderson 2003; Eckel 2010). After years of heated debate, the end result in the Universal Declaration was to de-link human rights from citizenship by stating that people, as bearers of human rights, were self-determining sovereign actors whether or not a given state recognized them as such. In other words, the Universal Declaration attempted to move human rights discourse away from its former dependence on nation-states as the grantor and enforcer of a person's rights. The Geneva Conventions and Helsinki Agreement of 1975 furthered this agenda, as did the growing international attention to the proliferation of human rights abuses in Latin America and Eastern Europe throughout the 1980s and 1990s. Recent advances have been made on this front through the establishment of the International Criminal Court (ICC) in 2002, which can prosecute any individual for crimes against humanity and is not limited to individuals who have operated in their capacity as state officials (see Hajjar 2004). Despite these advances, however, protecting the principle of an individual's right to self-determination has not yet been fully realized in international law (Stacy 2009).

Implementing a human rights framework has brought empowerment and in some cases actual relief to impoverished peoples and oppressed minorities. International human rights discourse, in conjunction with the rise of local civil society organizations and NGOs such as Human Rights Watch, have been enormously successful in diminishing abuses against women, indigenous peoples, and ethnic and religious minorities in recent decades (see Charlesworth and Chinkin 2006; Merry 2006; Goodale and Merry 2007; An-Na'im 2008). At the same time, however, human rights rhetoric can be used in negative ways, create unforeseen results, and may be in fact part of the problem in the seeking of global equality (Kennedy 2002). As sociolegal scholar Bob Nelson reminds us, "The dialectic character of law means that it sometimes is an instrument of social justice, and sometimes is an institution that produces and legitimates hierarchies of race, gender, and class" (Nelson 2001:36).

Complicating the effectiveness of an international human rights regime is the premise that it is universal in its application (Pahuja 2011). This premise disavows that human rights rhetoric and the human rights movement in general is, at its core, a European project that expresses the "ideology, ethics, aesthetic sensibility and political practice of a particular western eighteenth through twentieth-century liberalism" (Kennedy 2002:114). The human rights premise of universal neutrality is questioned by indigenous and postcolonial scholars who, among others, are deeply skeptical that modern Western law as promulgated in the Universal Declaration can operate as a rational and objective enterprise devoid of European cultural assumptions, values, and biases (An-Na'im and Deng 1990; Preis 1996; Anghie et al. 2003; Baxi 2006a; Chimni 2006; Maduagwu 2009). Critical sociolegal scholars point to the liberal ideologies and values embedded in human rights discourse that tend to compromise, and in some instances marginalize, non-Western perspectives. Specifically, these scholars are concerned that Euro-American liberal values simplistically envisage individuals as autonomous actors, present states as defenders of an individual's rights, and imply that the concept of justice is fixed and universally recognized.

Indigenous and postcolonial scholars have a sound historical basis for their skepticism about Western law and the human rights regime and movement that it engenders. For the past 400 years, the Enlightenment's triumphant narratives of reason and objectivity were employed by European leaders to argue that Western law was universal and therefore applicable to all colonized communities. Euro-American law has been a most effective weapon in institutionalizing colonial oppression and the imperial exploitation of non-European peoples (see Darian-Smith 2010a). Western liberal values – in claiming universal applicability – intrinsically deny historical legacies of colonialism and imperialism that continue to inform and frame discussions of human rights and humanitarian interventions. Accordingly, asks the sociolegal scholar Onuma Yasuaki:

> how should we reconcile human rights with diverse cultures, religions, political and/or economic systems, social practices, as well as criticisms, negative memories and grudges of people in the non-Western world? In other words, what will be, what should be, the relationship between human rights and diverse civilizations and cultures that may have regarded, and still regard, human rights as alien to them? (Onuma 2010:374).

Balakrishnan Rajagopal adds that this failure to acknowledge legacies of cultural diversity presents long-term consequences. "By ignoring the history of imperialism, by endorsing wars while opposing their consequences, and by failing to link itself with social movements of resistance the main protagonists of the Western human rights discourse are undermining the future of human rights itself" (Rajagopal 2006:775).

Against the normative Western assumptions embedded in human rights discourse, some critical scholars point out that individuals live in communities and that a person's rights may include relations of collective responsibility and accountability (see Nedlesky 2011). These scholars also point out that a focus on an individual's relationship to a state is limited given that in many cases state governments are in fact the primary perpetrators of human rights abuses (Godoy 2002). Moreover, the concept of justice is not a fixed absolute but must be understood in terms of a person's comparative and relational social contexts (Sen 2009). Above all, scholars critical of an international human rights regime object to the assumption that such rights embody a modernist ethics of progress that metaphorically positions the global South as the "victim" and the global North as the "savior" (Mutua 2001:205; Douzinas 2007; Skouteris 2010). In other words, there is a built-in inference in the recognizing and enforcing of human rights that it will automatically bring democratic reform to those people who are "less enlightened." This is an extremely powerful assumption and one that is often difficult to refute.

The Western liberal bias built into human rights discourse becomes particularly problematic when naïve presumption of progress and reform are coupled with a focus on oppressed victims. Such a focus precludes full engagement with the structural socioeconomic inequalities and asymmetries of power within any one society that have historically positioned certain peoples in positions of oppression and "victimhood" in the first place (see Darian-Smith 2000). In human rights discourse, a focus on the relationship of victim and savior creates a lens through which some histories are prioritized and others are marginalized or even denigrated. This liberal interpretation and representation of particular histories may create – even for the most well-intentioned scholars, activists, policy makers and bureaucrats – unforeseen political, cultural, and economic complications. As noted by the international law scholar David Kennedy, "the remove between human rights professionals and the people they purport to represent can reinforce a global divide of wealth, mobility, information and access to audience. Human rights professionals consequently struggle, ultimately in vain, against a tide of bad faith, orientalism, and self-serving sentimentalism" (Kennedy 2002:121).

For example, in 1991 Colombia introduced a new constitution that recognized minority rights and was viewed by many as a huge breakthrough in institutionalizing democratic reforms. However, as Diana Bocarejo has argued, the new constitution and its open embrace of liberal values also set up a dynamic in which different rights discourses were forced to compete for recognition and resources. Today, there is much bitterness between indigenous and peasant communities precisely because the state gives priority to indigenous peoples' rights to undeveloped land over peasant's rights to agrarian land (Bocarejo 2009). In this case the native peoples' history of colonial victimization trumped the peasants' history of exploitation irrespective of the fact that both minority groups are largely powerless and oppressed.

In a similar vein, Kristen Drybread compellingly narrates the rising prominence of a universal human rights discourse in Brazil after the fall of the military dictatorship in the 1980s. In an effort to institutionalize reform, the state introduced the Children and Adolescents Act of 1990 which conceded that children were rights-bearing citizens and as a consequence deserving of state support. However, Drybread points out, despite the progressive liberal nature of the legislation, it in effect backfired when applied to Brazilian street children. This was because the state refused to deal with and regulate the structural inequalities and lack of opportunities for poor children that made living on the streets, at least for some, more attractive than being reformed in state-run institutions. The Brazilian government's unwillingness to develop the bureaucratic apparatus and support structures necessary to vindicate children's rights inadvertently contributed to subverting them (Drybread 2009; on children's rights in another context, see Lazarus-Black 1994).

As the preceding examples from Colombia and Brazil suggest, it cannot always be assumed that state recognition of human rights will automatically bring about reform and progress and rescue those perceived to be victims. Even when states are consciously trying to improve the conditions of their citizens, human rights legislation and the politics of its implementation may not have the desired impact or consequences. The difficulties of implementation are further compounded if racial, ethnic, or religious minorities are involved because these are communities typically long oppressed by state systems and are justifiably wary and reluctant to embrace so-called policies and strategies of reform. In short, although huge advances have been made over the past half decade in the quest for global justice and equality, it is not enough to rely upon the human rights movement that in a variety of ways may be exacerbating social inequalities and reinforcing structural inequities (see Dickinson et al. 2012).

GLOBALIZATION, VIOLENCE, AND TRANSITIONAL JUSTICE

As discussed, even when states are consciously trying to improve the plight of their citizens, policies recognizing human rights may not have the desired impact or consequences. But within an international human rights frame, what is the appropriate response when states are not attempting to introduce reform but rather are themselves the perpetrators of gross atrocities and violence on civilians? In certain regions of the world, namely Africa, Central America, and Eastern Europe, this scenario has dominated the political landscape in recent decades. These postcolonial and post-communist regions fundamentally disrupt the liberal Western assumptions built into human rights discourses that position the state as the defender of humanity. In these regions of the world, state systems are unstable and volatile. Many countries are now designated "failed states" or weak states, which typically means the state is losing control over its territory and can no longer effectively and legitimately provide for its citizens (Chomsky 2007). As a result, new patterns of organized violence have erupted that involve intra-state civil wars and populist uprisings, many of which spill out beyond national borders and involve mass movements of people across geopolitical regions fleeing discrimination, ethnic cleansing, and genocide. As the Fund for Peace notes, the world is now experiencing a new class of global conflict. "Approximately 2 billion people live in countries that run a significant risk of collapse. These insecure and unstable states are breeding grounds for terrorism, organized crime, weapons proliferation, humanitarian emergencies, environmental degradation, and political extremism – threats that will affect everyone."[1]

Mary Kaldor, Herfried Münkler, and other scholars have characterized the era of violence that has emerged since the end of the Cold War as a period of "new wars" (Münkler 2004; Kaldor 2006). What these scholars argue is that contemporary violence is no longer dominated by "old" wars between states as determined from above by state leaders. Today's new wars involve a range of decentralized state and non-state actors "such as paramilitary units, local warlords, criminal gangs, police forces, mercenary groups and also regular armies, including breakaway units from regular armies" (Kaldor 2006:9). These warring groups exert force from below at local and regional levels, and they base their politics not on ideological party divides but on a politics of identity that nurtures ethnic and religious hatred (Kaldor 2006). In these new wars, violence is the primary mode of political mobilization, and the primary objective by warlords and other disparate leaders is to maintain control through fear. As a result, the leaders of these new wars, unlike the leaders of old wars prior to the mid-twentieth century, do not seek peaceful solutions but rather seek to exacerbate the conditions for chaos and anarchy.

Notably, Kaldor sees these new wars as a result of economic and political globalization. She argues that with increasing global interconnectedness and interdependency, state autonomy has been challenged by regional and international forms of oversight and accountability. One consequence of globalization is that large numbers of state governments are aligning themselves with corporate interests and in the process compromising their

[1] According to the Fund for Peace, "A state that is failing has several attributes. One of the most common is the loss of physical control of its territory or a monopoly on the legitimate use of force. Other attributes of state failure include the erosion of legitimate authority to make collective decisions, an inability to provide reasonable public services, and the inability to interact with other states as a full member of the international community. The 12 indicators cover a wide range of state failure risk elements such as extensive corruption and criminal behavior, inability to collect taxes or otherwise draw on citizen support, large-scale involuntary dislocation of the population, sharp economic decline, group-based inequality, institutionalized persecution or discrimination, severe demographic pressures, brain drain, and environmental decay. States can fail at varying rates through explosion, implosion, erosion, or invasion over different time periods." Accessed 28 October 2011. Online at: http://www.fundforpeace.org/global/?q=fsi-faq.

historical responsibilities for the welfare of their citizens (Kaldor 2006). This creates volatile political and economic environments that strain state institutions, structures, and unilateral powers, undermine a sense of social contract between people and governments, and grant opportunities for new forms of violence to erupt. Kaldor goes on to say that the "impact of globalization is visible in many of the new wars" that are not contained within state borders, do not employ centralized state institutions, and create new local/global divides between

> those members of a global class who can speak English, have access to faxes, the Internet and satellite television, who use dollars or euros or credit cards, and who can travel freely, and those who are excluded from global processes, who live off what they can sell or barter or what they receive in humanitarian aid, whose movement is restricted by roadblocks, visas and the cost of travel, and who are prey to sieges, forced famines, landmines etc (Kaldor 2006:5).

James Ferguson further complicates the relationship between new forms of organized violence and the neoliberal forces of economic globalization in his book *Global Shadows: Africa in the Neoliberal World Order* (2006). Ferguson's examination of the role of Africa in the contemporary global political economy raises many interesting insights that I cannot do justice to here. What I want to focus on is his analysis of the mineral extraction industry in Africa, and specifically the extraction of oil from offshore platforms. Ferguson argues against conventional wisdom that failed states are unattractive sites for foreign investment because they are torn apart by ethnic violence, lawlessness, and corruption. To the contrary, Ferguson notes that countries such as Angola now have booming economies based on oil and mineral extraction despite being ravaged by civil war between 1975 and 2002. In fact the new wars of intra-state violence in Angola and other African countries provide the opportunity for transnational corporations to come in, set up highly securitized production sites and enclaves peopled by corporate and local governmental elites, and extract oil reserves with little regulatory oversight and minimal engagement with or responsibility to local communities. According to Ferguson, "The apparently chaotic and undoubtedly violent surroundings may well discourage traditional investors and 'reputable' firms. But for more 'flexible' actors, innovations in both mining and private security increasingly allow operations to proceed without the added expense of securing and regulating an entire national space" (Ferguson 2006:206).

While Ferguson does not suggest any causal connection between transnational corporatism and local civilian violence, the predatory connection hovers throughout his analysis. Moreover, in his discussion of Africa he sees parallels emerging in other places around the world. With respect to the war in Iraq, Ferguson writes:

> Like wartime Angola, Iraq currently boasts of a continuing oil production in the midst of apparent chaos and war. One can imagine that, under conditions of prolonged civil strife, the private forces guarding the oil installations may well be a more durable contribution to the Iraqi landscape than either the American occupation or its rhetorical commitment to "democracy" and "nation-building" (Ferguson 2006:210).

In many ways Ferguson's book prefigures the arguments made in Naomi Klein's book *The Shock Doctrine: The Rise of Disaster Capitalism* (2007). In this book Klein describes how "disaster capitalism" takes advantage of situations where effective national order is dismantled. In other words, she argues that contemporary capitalism is well equipped to exploit national chaos and disaster situations. It does not matter if chaos is brought about by intentional policies implemented through the World Bank or the IMF, by unforeseen natural disasters, or by the calculated declaration of war by a powerful state against a weaker one (Klein 2007). Klein's argument globalizes Ferguson's insights about African states in profoundly alarming ways.

Whether all contemporary warfare can be classified as a "new war" is debatable. Mary Kaldor makes this argument and includes in her discussion the war in Iraq (Kaldor 2007). However, this argument is not without critics (Nickels 2009). However, what is certain is that all contemporary conflict, even that ostensibly between states, utilizes mercenary units known as PMCs or private military companies as part of their defense strategies (Kinsey 2006). The United States, Australia, Canada, Britain, and other Western nations are increasingly dependent upon private companies such as Blackwater and Erinys to fight for them in military contexts as well as protect their oil and mineral "extraction production" overseas (see Singer 2003; Pelton 2007; Fainaru 2009). These private military firms are also needed to maintain these states' domestic and offshore internment camps for so-called enemy combatants, illegal immigrants and those deemed to be political refugees. This outsourcing and privatizing of security creates all sorts of problems in terms of maintaining control, oversight, and accountability of state-authorized violence (Eckert 2009). Diana Sidakis takes this problem one step further, arguing "In the case of private military companies, the role of the state has been to shield the industry from meaningful human rights obligations" (Sidakis 2009:80).

Outsourcing the means of war underscores that, along with new kinds of warfare, there are emerging different forms, levels, and degrees of state engagement in warring activities and that these interrelated features are becoming the norm in all global conflict. In this context it is important to heed the words of Mary Kaldor. Drawing on her characterization of new wars, Kaldor warns that analysts of contemporary warfare must appreciate the underlying vested economic and political interests in the continuation of violence (Kaldor 2006:95). Historically, of course, in all wars some people have made money at the expense of other people's misfortunes. The difference today is that this exploitative dimension of warfare is explicitly encouraged and supported by state/corporate coalitions and alignments. It is somewhat disquieting to think about the United States' war on drugs[2] and war on terror,[3] which are open-ended, racially charged, without viable long-term solutions, and making some of the parties involved extremely rich. On these fronts, these so-called wars are not dissimilar from the open-ended civil wars that have raged for decades in parts of Africa. Kaldor's point is that if we do not heed the economic logic that creates and perpetuates modern warfare, the well-intentioned efforts of international efforts to deal with past and present conflict and the human rights abuses that accompany such violence may in fact be counterproductive (Kaldor 2006).

In recent decades, UN-sponsored humanitarian intervention and transitional justice mechanisms have escalated to meet the demands presented by a proliferation of new wars and related human rights abuses. Transitional justice mechanisms seek to help countries transitioning from authoritarian to democratic systems and from civil war to peace. Through UN-sponsored trials, tribunals and commissions in post-conflict societies, transitional justice processes help (1) prosecute perpetrators of human rights abuse, (2) foster justice and reconciliation among traumatized communities, (3) encourage a collective national memory of the past, and (4) above all, nurture state building through the institutionalizing of the rule of law and liberal political values (Minow 1998; Kent 2012;). The primary presumption behind a transitional justice paradigm was – and is – that if a country can become politically stable and embrace democratic reform, it will then be better positioned to

---

[2] It is not commonly known that the U.S. Drug Enforcement Administration (DEA) extends its reach way beyond its national borders in its goals to wipe out drug cartels in Central and South America. To further its mission, and reminiscent of former counter-insurgency operations by the United States in Latin America, the DEA deploys five commando-style squads of trained special agents, planes, and helicopters in countries such as Honduras, Guatemala, Belize, and the Dominican Republic. "Because they are considered law enforcement agents, and not soldiers, their presence on another country's soil may raise fewer sensitivities about sovereignty" (*New York Times* May 17, 2012 p. 4; see also Baum 1997; Provine 2007, 2011).

[3] Dick Cheney, it should be remembered, at the time of his being appointed vice president by George W. Bush in 2000, was CEO of Halliburton, which was one of the largest oil and construction companies in the world with connections to militaries in several countries.

participate in a global political economy and embrace development strategies (Paris 2004). Despite postcolonial critics pointing to the fetishizing of law in these contexts of law and disorder (Comaroff and Comaroff 2006; Rajagopal 2008), over the past three decades the transitional justice paradigm has gone from strength to strength. During this period, over thirty-five international truth commissions and forty international courts have been set up around the world (Stanley 2009:56; on the history of truth commissions, see Hayner 2011). This UN mission of bringing "justice" to war-torn countries and enabling a "transition" from conflict to peace has been furthered by the establishing of the International Criminal Court in 2002[4] and the UN-endorsed principle of the "responsibility to protect" or RtoP, which was established in 2005 (http:// www.responsibilitytoprotect.org/).

Some sociolegal scholars argue that the transitional justice paradigm in the form of trials, tribunals, and truth commissions has its intellectual roots in the post–WWII Nuremberg and Tokyo trials (Teitel 2003; Goldstone and Smith 2009; see also Elster 2004). Other scholars, however, argue that transitional justice really only became an established way to deal with war criminals and war victims in the late 1980s and early 1990s (Arthur 2009; Bell 2009). This was the result of the revelation of ethnic cleansing and genocide in the former Yugoslavia, Rwanda, and East Timor. Because of the scale of these violent episodes, and the past failures of national governments to establish peace in other war-torn contexts,[5] it was deemed appropriate that an international body should intervene to help national efforts of peace building.

Today, many international humanitarian and human rights lawyers, policy makers, politicians, and NGOs firmly uphold the appropriateness and neces-sity of a transitional justice paradigm (Sikkink 2011; see also Amar 2012). That being said, transitional justice processes are not always successful in terms of effectively prosecuting perpetrators of crime, satisfying the quest for justice and reconciliation, or establishing long-term peace (Nettlefield 2010; see also Sikkink and Walling 2007; Braithwaite 2011; White and Perelman 2011). As a result, among legal practitioners and commentators there is considerable debate as to how to improve transitional justice mechanisms (Roht-Arriaza and Mariezcurrena 2006; Van der Merwe et al. 2009; Olsen et al. 2010).

---

[4] The ICC's mandate, however, prevents it from acting with respect to crimes committed before 2002 (see Schiff 2008; Struett 2008; Hayner 2011).

[5] By this time it had become clear that national efforts to establish criminal accountability and regime change in Latin American countries such as Chile and El Salvador had failed. This failure was in part because of the widespread offer of amnesty to perpetrators of crimes by national criminal prosecutors as a transitional justice policy. (Collins 2010; see also Popkin 2000; Hayner 2011).

These commentators weigh up the relative merits of trials versus commissions (Campbell and Bell 2004), the complementariness of these two forms of investigation (Leebaw 2008; Lambourne 2009;), and the desirability of "hybrid" tribunals consisting of both international and national court judges and personnel (Kaye 2011).

However, among critical sociolegal scholars the response to unsuccessful transitional justice processes has taken a different direction. Some scholars now question the core liberal assumptions and embedded Western understandings of transition, justice, truth and state that underpin transitional justice discourses (Dembour and Kelly 2007; McEvoy 2008; Nagy 2008; Rajagopal 2008; Bowden et al. 2009; Kelsell 2009). With respect to the concept of transition, the transitional justice paradigm suggests that a break with the past is possible. As scholars point out, however, this often simplifies and obscures complex histories of violence (and colonialism) that continue to inform the present and future (Mamdani 2001; Nagy 2008). Scholars also argue that focusing on transition as a break with the past promotes a linear sense of time and causal logic, falsely implying that if certain actions are taken, ready solutions exist for recovery. Moreover, scholars point out that the concept of transition evokes a narrative of progress: from violence to peace, illiberal to liberal, despair to hope, savage to civilized (Moon 2008). This language validates and reinforces the ethics of progress built into international human rights discourses discussed earlier.

With respect to the concept of justice, problems arise because there is not a universal definition of justice (Sarat and Kearns 1996; Sen 2009). A large body of critical sociolegal scholarship on transitional justice highlights that justice is a relative term and can be experienced and understood in many different ways (Kent 2012; see also Clark 2009, 2010; Bell et al. 2004). In the words of Nicola Henry, who writes on the invisibility of wartime rape in formal transitional mechanisms:

> Justice is elusive, subjective, and even impossible. Justice is much broader than the prosecution of a few offenders; it involves not simply legal justice, but social and political justice, including both practical and symbolic forms of security, safety, and stability. The limitations of justice are also the limitations of collective memory. The collective memory of international criminal courts is thus a potent reminder of both the promise and the impossibility of justice in the aftermath of mass atrocities (Henry 2011:125).

Despite the recognition that justice is a highly contested and contingent concept, transitional justice mechanisms promote universalized legal notions of justice (Pavlich 2007). These notions feature retributive and restorative justice that foreground the individual violator and the individual rights-bearing victim. In other words, the transitional justice paradigm is conceptualized in terms of Enlightenment liberal values that focus upon individual rights and individual responsibilities. What are removed from consideration are the relational and temporal dimensions of people's experience of what constitutes justice as distinct from truth. Perhaps even more significantly, dropped from consideration are the deeply embedded structural injustices that create and maintain poverty, socioeconomic inequality, and racism and diminish capacities to recognize and exercise individual or group rights in the first place (Nagy 2008; Stanley 2009). As argued by Angelina Snodgrass Godoy in her powerful analysis of postwar violence in Guatemala, acts of collective vigilantism in the newly formed democratic state present new forms of terror that do not fit a conventional human rights paradigm of "abuses and abusers" (Godoy 2002:659). Such violence undermines the Enlightenment assumption that democracy ensures social justice and demands a rethinking of the "shifting nature of human rights today" (Godoy 2002:660).

Further compounding the conceptual limitations with respect to transition and justice is the prevailing framework of the state within which the transitional justice paradigm is situated. As a UN-sponsored initiative, transitional justice is locked into dealing with state governments and people as citizens of specific nations. As a result, it has few mechanisms for dealing with people whose primary geopolitical identity is with cities or regions rather than states (Sassen 2003, 2004), or people whose ethnic and religious identities dominate and make their formal relationship to the state largely irrelevant (Arthur 2010), or people who have been disempowered, dislocated, enslaved or made into refugees and may have limited, if any, access to state institutions (Bales 2004). Furthermore, because the transitional justice rhetoric is at its core about peacemaking and state building, alternative non-state jurisdictional, institutional, or conceptual mechanisms are often silenced or marginalized within transitional justice discourses. This raises all sorts of questions such as the following: How to deal with violence in cross-border, regional, or aspirant states such as Palestine, Northern Cyprus, and Taiwan (Geldenhuys 2009)? How to cope with the proliferation of new wars over the past thirty years that are driven by neoliberal economic forces and involve a wide variety of non-state sites, affiliations, and actors? And how to nurture bottom-up community peace processes outside formal political processes? On this last point, John Braithwaite and his colleagues note that in Bougainville it was in fact the total collapse of the state and dismantling of state institutions that created space for traditional reconciliation processes involving both women and men to be revived and shine "without police, courts and prisons" (Braithwaite et al.

2010:122). In war-ravaged Bougainville, in effect it was the lack of law – at least Western forms of law – that granted the space for recognizing suffering and reestablishing human value and dignity in terms meaningful for local communities.

How an international human rights discourse and humanitarian intervention framework will deal with these relatively recent geopolitical realities in which liberal legal assumptions may not be appropriate or applicable remains a central challenge for the future (see Ticktin 2006). Peter Hough effectively summarizes the inadequacies of conventional human rights discourse when he states:

> Human rights policies have developed significantly in recent decades but this has not yet come close to making *all* human secure. Governments tend to prioritize the rights and lesser interests of their own citizens over the fundamental rights of others, and human rights are still routinely treated as secondary to "national security" issues where the two are perceived to clash. The recent tightening up of migration laws and the increased surveillance of foreign citizens in the current "war against terrorism" in the USA and Western Europe present cases in point. The lives of far more people in today's world, however, are imperiled by human rights abuses than by terrorist or conventional military attacks. Throughout the total war era of the twentieth century a case could be made that the security of individuals was inextricably tied up with that of their states but that era has now passed into history. Today the issues that threaten people's lives bear such little relation to those issues which dominate the international political agenda ... [S]tate centrism is impeding both the study and practice of that most fundamental of political concerns: securing people (Hough 2008:19).

HUMAN SECURITY IN THE TWENTY-FIRST CENTURY

One strategy in rethinking the application of human rights discourse is to move beyond the limitations of a transitional justice paradigm (which is primarily concerned with the rebuilding of states in post-conflict environments) and to think more broadly in terms of human security (Battersby and Siracusa 2009). The idea of human security is not linked only to conflict zones and state-directed violence, and so it is more expansive in its vision, scope, and potential application. This more expansive perspective is vital given the changing nature of war as a cause and consequence of economic globalization (as discussed earlier), coupled with the enormous insecurities and risks created by mass movements of people fleeing political, economic, and religious persecution, as well as the escalating impacts of natural disasters, food and water shortages, and global climate change.

Today's global problems suggest that sociolegal scholars need to turn their sights more pointedly toward the potentials of a human security framework. This is because it is now clear that in the twenty-first century, issues of security can no longer be narrowly defined as pertaining to the military actions of nation-states. Both the types of security issues and the actors involved in the politicization and implementation of these issues have proliferated in recent decades. Some political science communities continue to debate about what constitutes a security issue and whether it should be expanded to include non-military actions. However, for many foreign policy makers, politicians, and scholars these debates appear parochial, anachronistic, and locked in a Cold War mentality. Today, a majority of analysts perceive security threats to include natural disasters such as tsunami and earthquakes, as well as economic, environmental, health, cultural, religious, educational, and criminal risks existing inside and outside national borders. Furthermore, in tandem with acknowledging the increasing number of security threats beyond the arena of military conflict, there is also the acknowledgment of increasing numbers of actors involved in security issues. These include states as well as a wide range of non-state actors such as intergovernmental organizations (i.e., United Nations and the European Union), nongovernmental organizations, banks and corporations, private security companies, militias, grassroots activists, and communities of ordinary people (see Figure 5).

Scholars and analysts examining a human security framework necessarily adopt a global perspective. In this regard, they follow an intellectual trajectory established by the Brandt Report written in 1980 by Willy Brandt and other European statesmen. In prescient language, the Brandt Report stated that "Our survival depends not only on military balance, but on global cooperation to ensure a sustainable biological environment based on equitably shared resources" (International Commission on International Development Issues [ICIDI] 1980:124). This concern for a more globalized response to inequality and insecurity was endorsed and further widened in the 1994 United Nations Human Development Report, which argued for the need to insure against both "freedom from want" and "freedom from fear."[6] The Report stated that:

> In the final analysis, human security is a child who did not die, a disease that did not spread, a job that was not cut, an ethnic tension that did not explode

---

[6] Significantly, the Report noted that while human rights and the norms and principles of international humanitarian law are essential components for the construction of human security, the concept of human security itself should not be limited to situations only of armed conflict. Expanding the application of a human security framework beyond warfare and violence to focus more generally on risk and vulnerability, the Report outlined seven areas of primary

in violence, a dissident who was not silenced. Human security is not a concern with weapons – it is a concern with human life and dignity. The idea of human security, though simple, is likely to revolutionize society in the 21st century (Human Development Report 1994:22).

More recently Peter Hough has argued, "A security issue, surely, is an issue which threatens (or appears to threaten) one's security ... If people, be they government ministers or private individuals, perceive an issue to threaten their lives in some way and respond politically to this, then the issue should be deemed to be a *security* issue" (Hough 2008:10). This prioritizing of people rather than states references a new awareness of contemporary geopolitical complexities that are destabilizing the centrality of states' economic, political, and legal power (see discussion in Chapter 4). This decentering in turn suggests a need to move beyond state military defense and interstate conflict and rethink what constitutes security threats to people living within and between and across specific countries and regions (Tadjbakhsh and Chenoy 2007).

Since the 1994 Human Development Report the concept of global human security has gained ground in intergovernmental organizations such as the United Nations and has evolved to mesh with a range of organizational interests and political agendas (see Tadjbakhsh 2007). Japan, and to a lesser degree Canada, has strongly supported the development of a human

---

concern, which included economic security, food security, health security, environment security, personal security, community security, and political security. The Report noted that together these areas require immediate attention because they transcend state borders and affect everybody irrespective of people's citizenship or territory in which they live. According to the Report, there are four essential characteristics of human security:

- Human security is a *universal* concern. It is relevant to people everywhere, in rich nations and poor. There are many threats that are common to all people, such as unemployment, drugs, crime, pollution and human rights violations. Their intensity may differ from one part of the world to another, but all these threats to human security are real and growing.
- The components of human security are *interdependent*. When the security of people is endangered anywhere in the world, all nations are likely to get involved. Famine, disease, pollution, drug trafficking, terrorism, ethnic disputes, and social disintegration are no longer isolated events, confined within national borders. Their consequences travel the globe.
- Human security is *easier to ensure through early prevention* than later intervention. It is less costly to meet these threats upstream than downstream. For example, the direct and indirect cost of HIV/AIDS (human immunodeficiency virus/acquired immune deficiency syndrome) was roughly $240 billion during the 1980s. Even a few billion dollars invested in primary health care and family planning education could have helped contain the spread of this deadly disease.
- Human security is *people-centered*. It is concerned with how people live and breathe in a society, how freely they exercise their many choices, how much access they have to market and social opportunities, and whether they live in conflict or in peace (HDR 1994:22–23). United Nations Development Programme (1994) Human Development Report. Online at: http://hdr.undp.org/en/reports/global/hdr1994/ (retrieved October 10, 2011).

Figure 5. Members of the South Central Farm attending the immigrant rights march for amnesty in downtown Los Angeles California on May Day, 2006. The banner, in Spanish, reads "No human being is illegal." Photograph taken by Jonathan McIntosh. May 1, 2006.

security framework within the context of the United Nations. For instance, Japan was the founder and main donor of the UN Trust Fund for Human Security (established 1999), and the promoter of the Commission on Human Security (established 2002) and the Friends of Human Security (established 2006).[7] However, against these promising and optimistic moves to embrace global security issues from a people-centered perspective, major setbacks have emerged over the first decade of the twenty-first century. These setbacks are a result in large part to the United States' response to 9/11 and the subsequent declaring of the so-called Wars on Terror. The wars in Afghanistan and Iraq quickly squandered any opportunity the United States' may have had to nurture the then emergent sense of a global community working together to

---

[7]   Ministry of Foreign Affairs of Japan: Human Security. Online at: http://www.mofa.go.jp/policy/human_secu/

protect all humanity. The U.S. claim of exceptionalism and national privilege, and its flagrant disregard of the norms of international law such as prohibitions against the use of torture, reintroduced a state-based geopolitical agenda. In short, in the first decade of the new century the United States selfishly pursued its own national interests over that of Afghan and Iraqi civilians as well as its own citizens (Held 2004).

In addition to the United States reaffirming the centrality of its territorial state interests over that of people, other global forces are undermining the emerging concept of human security as initially articulated in the 1994 Human Development Report. Most obviously, the logics of global capitalism to pursue profits at all costs works against a people-centered perspective that seeks to secure peoples' rights, equality, and social justice. It is important to remember that global capitalism was in full swing decades before the events of 9/11. Under the logics of global capitalism and neoliberal foreign policies, the role of governments is no longer primarily to protect citizens but rather to protect the interests of corporations. In other words, within states the role of government has been "rearticulated so that it can serve efficiently as an instrument of globalization-from-above" (Falk 1999:17). As experienced in the United States and elsewhere, for the past forty years governments have increasingly rolled back the political and civil rights of their citizens and aggressively attacked resistance emanating from labor, environmental, consumer, gay, same-sex marriage, educational, or non-Christian religious groups. Even the U.S. Patriot Act, ostensibly put into place to protect people from external terrorist threats, has been used primarily to create a sense of fear under which it is easier to quash domestic unrest and attack immigration. Given this backdrop, it may not come as a surprise that within the United States paramilitary hate groups have escalated at a stunning rate since the beginning of Barack Obama's presidency in 2008. According to a report issued by the Southern Poverty Law Center, the number of U.S.-based patriot and militia groups that have shown indications of violence rose from 824 in 2010 to 1,274 in 2011.[8]

The second front on which state governments have aided corporate elites has occurred beyond national borders and involves facilitating the exploitation of cities, islands, or regions (typically situated in the global South) for cheap labor and unregulated manufacturing production (Harvey 2005). As a result, state security functions are directed less at opposing other states as they are at serving the interests of capitalists and intergovernmental organizations

---

[8] Online at: http://www.splcenter.org/get-informed/news/southern-poverty-law-center-report-as-election-season-heats-up-extremist-groups-at (accessed 8 March 2012).

such as the WTO (Thomas 2001). The enabling of capitalist enterprise by wealthy governments in the global North has created great social, political, and economic inequalities between it and the global South. Four decades of expansionist global capitalism, coupled with the United States' aggressive defense of its national interests under the guise of fighting communism and terrorism, has created an extremely volatile global context for defending peoples' human rights and ensuring human security. Establishing a human security framework seeks to oppose, or at least moderate, corporate/state interests. It seeks to force corporations to acknowledge their direct and indirect involvement in harming innocent people caught up in the forces of a global political economy and policies of neoliberalism.

Some analysts (although remarkably few sociolegal scholars) are now beginning to appreciate that human security issues are not problems faced only by the developing nations of the world. Problems confronting Western countries such as urban violence, unemployment, epidemics, and the militarization and criminalization of segments of societies are the result of global forces as much as they are the result of national domestic policies. As discussed in the Introduction, these issues are interconnected even if not recognized as such. It is now evident that the exploitative logics of global capitalism applied by Western nations overseas in poor countries are also being applied to their own citizens (Darian-Smith 2010a:Ch 8). The Occupy Wall Street protest in New York and related demonstrations in approximately 900 cities around the world throughout 2011 suggest the emerging public realization of the "undemocratic alliance between financial interests and government" at the expense of the political, civil, social, cultural, and economic rights of ordinary people (*New York Times* November 7, 2011).

In the light of increasing public protest within Western countries as people struggle to come to terms with a crisis of legitimacy in law and government, an international human rights discourse will have to reevaluate who is the savior and who is the victim. The long-standing premise that Europeans and Americans "save" others is being questioned as it becomes apparent that these societies too need help. As Shahrbanou Tadjbakhash and Anuradha Chenoy argue, "The challenge of studying the scope of human security issues in Western societies is, perhaps, more than before and more than in other areas of the world, an imperative" (Tadjbakhsh and Chenoy 2007:243). But as Caroline Thomas notes, this kind of research faces enormous challenges precisely because it brings into question the limits of all governments to protect their internal populations (Thomas 2007:128). A human security framework, in short, challenges the continuing viability and appropriateness of any state's exclusive claim to power and authority over its citizens. A human security framework challenges the conventional state-centrist norms of international law and human rights discourse that are still based within sovereign states and interstate negotiations (Von Tigerstrom 2007; see also Sunga 2009).

Looking at these challenges more positively, a human security framework allows us to rethink debates about human rights and humanitarian intervention. According to Barbara Von Tigerstrom, the real value of privileging human security is not to provide solutions but rather "to provide or encourage an alternative way of framing and prioritizing the questions to be asked" (Von Tigerstrom 2007:112). A human security framework suggests the need to think more creatively about top-down and bottom-up forms of integrated multi-level governance that decreases harm to people and reestablishes human dignity and justice within pluralistic societies (den Boer and de Wilde 2008). This may mean embracing global institutions such as the ICC to help impose accountability from above the level of the state, city and community networks to help create security from below, as well as a range of non-state actors and NGOs who can mediate across organizations and geopolitical regions. However, as discussed in this chapter, these various actors and legal processes are difficult to implement in practice, particularly in war-torn and impoverished regions of the world that increasingly include cities within the United States and other countries of the global North. Even more problematic, perhaps, moving toward a multi-level governance system profoundly destabilizes the mutually reinforcing liberal assumptions that every person is an autonomous rights-bearing individual with ties of citizenship to a sovereign state. These assumptions are deeply embedded within the UN system and international law and – rightly or wrongly – sustain the political and economic platform upon which the legitimacy of any new multi-level governance strategies still depends.

LIST OF SUGGESTED READINGS

1. Arthur, Paige (ed.) (2010) *Identities in Transition: Challenges for Transitional Justice in Divided Societies.* Cambridge: Cambridge University Press.
2. Clarke, Karmari Maxine (2009) *Fictions of Justice: The International Criminal Court and the Challenge of Legal Pluralism in Sub-Saharan Africa.* Cambridge: Cambridge University Press.
3. Collins, Cath (2010) *Post-Transitional Justice: Human Rights Trials in Chile and El Salvador.* University Park: Pennsylvania State University Press.
4. Dickinson, Rob, Elena Katselli, Colin Murray and Ole W. Pedersen (eds.) (2012) *Examining Critical Perspectives on Human Rights.* Cambridge: Cambridge University Press.
5. Drybread, Kristen (2009) Rights-Bearing Street Kids: Icons of Hope and Despair in Brazil's Burgeoning Neoliberal State. *Law & Policy* 31(3):330–350.

6. Ferguson, James (2006) *Global Shadows: Africa in the Neoliberal World Order.* Durham and London: Duke University Press.
7. Godoy, Angelina Snodgrass (2002) Lynchings and the Democratization of Terror in Postwar Guatemala: Implications for Human Rights. *Human Rights Quarterly* **24**(3):640–661.
8. Goodale, Mark and Sally Engle Merry (eds.) (2007) *The Practice of Human Rights: Tracking Law Between the Global and the Local* (Cambridge Studies in Law and Society). Cambridge: Cambridge University Press.
9. Kaldor, Mary (2007) *Human Security: Reflections on Globalization and Intervention.* Cambridge: Polity.
10. Kent, Lia Michelle (2012) *The Dynamics of Transitional Justice: International Models and Local Realities in East Timor.* London and New York: Routledge.
11. Merry, Sally Engle (2006) *Human Rights and Gender Violence: Translating International Law into Local Justice.* Chicago: University of Chicago Press.
12. Nagy, R. (2008) Transitional Justice as Global Project: Critical Reflections. *Third World Quarterly* **29**(2):275–289.
13. Simmons, William Paul (2011) *Human Rights Law and the Marginalized Other.* Cambridge: Cambridge University Press.

Excerpts From:

Kennedy, David (2002) The International Human Rights Movement: Part of the Problem? *Harvard Human Rights Journal* 15:101–125.

THE INTERNATIONAL HUMAN RIGHTS MOVEMENT: PART OF THE PROBLEM?

David Kennedy (2002)

Reproduced with permission.

There is no question that the international human rights movement has done a great deal of good, freeing individuals from great harm, providing an emancipatory vocabulary and institutional machinery for people across the globe, raising the standards by which governments judge one another, and by which they are judged, both by their own people, and by the elites we refer to collectively as the "international community." A career in the human rights movement has provided thousands of professionals, many of them lawyers, with a sense of dignity and confidence that one sometimes can do well while doing good. The literature praising these, and other, accomplishments is vast. Among well-meaning legal professionals in the United States and Europe – humanist, internationalist, liberal, compassionate in all the best senses of these terms – the human rights movement has become a central object of devotion.

But there are other ways of thinking about human rights. As a well-meaning internationalist and, I hope, compassionate legal professional myself, I thought it might be useful to pull together in a shore list some of the questions that have been raised about international human rights by people, including myself, who worry that the human rights movement might, on balance, and acknowledging its enormous achievement, be more part of the problem in today's world than part of the solution. This Essay offers an incomplete and idiosyncratic list of such questions that might be of interest to the human rights practitioner.

I should say at the outset that the arguments I have listed are hypotheses. I have stated them as succinctly as I can, at the risk of their seeming conclusive or overly polemical. In fact, although some of them seem more plausible to me than others, to my knowledge none of them has been proven – they are in the air as assertions, worries, polemical charges. They circulate in the background of conversations about the human rights movement. And even if these potential costs *were* demonstrated, it would still be necessary to weigh them against the very real accomplishments of the human rights movement.

I. Thinking Pragmatically About Human Rights

My purpose in pulling these concerns together is to encourage other well-meaning legal professionals to adopt a more pragmatic attitude toward human rights. My hope is that we will develop a stronger practice of weighing the costs and benefits of their articulation, institutionalization and enforcement. Of course, the best human rights practitioners are already intensely strategic and practical in thinking about their work. But it is often tempting (for those within and without the movement) to set pragmatic concerns aside, to treat human rights as an object of devotion rather than calculation. And even the most intense practical evaluations of human rights initiatives too often stop short of considering the full range of potential down sides or negative knock on consequences in their enthusiasm to move forward with efforts whose upside potential seems so apparent.

A. *"Pragmatic" Always and Forever or Here and Now?*

Pragmatic evaluation means specifying the benefits and harms that might attend human rights initiatives in particular cases, under specific conditions, in particular time periods, and so forth. Those cases, conditions, times may be extremely specific (pursuing this petition will make this magistrate less likely to grant this other petition) or very general (articulating social welfare needs as individual "rights" makes people everywhere more passive and isolated) but they need to be articulated, and ultimately demonstrated, in concrete terms. At the same time, concrete does not mean sure or inevitable. The factors that influence policy making are not, by any means, all *proven* empirically. To count as a cost (or benefit), effects must be articulated in terms plausible enough to persuade people seeking to pursue human rights initiatives to take them into account.

Weighing the costs and benefits of "human rights" is difficult because the costs are often articulated in far more general terms than the benefits. The dangers on my list are often expressed as indictments of the entire human rights "idea" and "movement" in all times and places. The benefits are more often cast in immediate and local terms – these people out of this prison, those people provided with housing, this country's political process opened to elections, monitored in this way, these individuals spared the death penalty. It *is* certainly plausible that thinking about problems in the language of human rights could entail some costs (or benefits) always and everywhere, which would need to be added to each more particularized calculation. More likely, these general costs will be more or less intense in specific places and times. It may turn out that the entire human rights vocabulary or movement suffers from a blindness or works an effect that we should count as a cost. But it is far more likely that the vocabulary is used in different ways by different people, and that the movement is itself split in ways that make blindnesses more acute in some places and times than others. In weighing all this up, it is terribly hard to isolate the effects of "human rights." People in the movement also speak other languages, perhaps using the movement vocabulary of human rights to get in the door and then speaking instrumentally or ethically. People in the movement will evaluate risks, costs and benefits in quite different ways. The vocabulary and movement are themselves in flux – many of the open terms are subject to ongoing revision precisely to correct for the sorts of difficulties I have listed here. As a pragmatist, all one can do is take these possibilities into account as best one can, estimating their likelihood and augmenting or discounting risks accordingly. As a movement, one can facilitate open engagement about differing pragmatic assessments.

Imagine, for example, an effort to use the vocabulary and political capital of the international human rights movement to end capital punishment in the Caribbean. It might well turn out that leading corporate lawyers acting pro bono in London define the problem and solution differently than lawyers working with nongovernmental groups in London, and differently again from lawyers and organizers in the Caribbean. For some the anti-death penalty campaign might seem a distraction from more pressing issues, might occupy the field, might, if the campaign is successful, even legitimate other governmental (in)action or other social conditions that kill more people in the Caribbean. There might be a struggle within the movement about the usefulness of the vocabulary, or within the vocabulary about the conditions and costs of its deployment in particular places. Some people might use the death penalty, and the human rights vocabulary, to leverage interest in other issues or other vocabularies – others might use it to close off broader inquiries. Wherever you are located, if you are thinking pragmatically about devoting scarce institutional resources to furthering or limiting the effort to bring human rights to bear on the instance of Caribbean death penalty, it will be necessary to come to some conclusion, however tentative and general, about how these conflicts and divergent effects will net out. I hope that this list of critical observations about human rights might provide something of a checklist for discussions of this sort.

Finally, it only makes sense to think pragmatically about human rights in *comparative* terms. How do the costs and benefits of pursuing an emancipatory objective in the vocabulary of human rights compare with other available discourses? How do efforts to work more intently within the human rights vocabulary compare with efforts to develop alternative vocabularies? How do human rights initiatives affect these efforts? Human rights might well discourage focus on collective responsibility, might leach the spiritual from emancipatory projects, but how does this stack up against alternative vocabularies and institutions – of family, kinship, nationhood, religious conviction – or with other political or legal emancipatory rhetorics? Whose hand is strengthened or weakened by each? How do we assess the medium or long term effort to develop new vocabularies and institutions for emancipation? Again, my hope is that this list will help spark this sort of comparative analysis.

B. *Specifying the Costs and Benefits*

To weigh costs and benefits, we will need to be as articulate and concrete about the benefits as about the costs. I have not dwelt on the benefit side here, but it should be clear that people will evaluate the benefits very differently. There will be a struggle, both inside and outside the movement, about what benefits to seek and how to rank gains. Here, I have used the term "emancipation" to capture the broad range of (often conflicting) benefits people of good heart might hope to make of human rights – humanitarian, progressive, internationalist, social welfare enhancing. There might be other benefits – human rights might have aesthetic uses, might stimulate the heart or the imagination, just as they might be psychologically or ethically useful. And, of course, human rights might not be useful only for us, but for all sorts of people pursuing various projects, not all of them good-hearted. I leave the list of benefits to others.

In weighing initiatives pragmatically, it is often more useful to focus on "distributional consequences among individuals or groups" than "costs and benefits." The costs/benefits vocabulary suggests (incorrectly) that one could know at an abstract and general level what to count as a cost or a benefit of the initiative. In fact, of course, the "costs" and the "benefits" will look different and be evaluated differently by different people. For those who feel the death penalty deters, its abolition is a cost, which effects a distribution from victims to criminals. Although I speak here of costs and benefits (or the "problem" and the "solution") as if we shared very vague and general aspirations for a more humanitarian, progressive and egalitarian global society, it would probably be more accurate to think of these "benefits" as distributions of power, status and means toward those who share these objectives and away from those who don't. But let us take this general articulation as a first step. Thereafter we would need to assess, from a more particular point of view, who would win and who would lose from a human rights initiative. In that effort, we would need to recast the criticisms I list here as distributions of power that one might oppose.

II. A Short List of Pragmatic Worries and Polemical Charges

This is not a list of things unknown. All of these criticisms have been around for a long time, and the human rights movement has responded to them in a wide variety of ways. Attention is routinely given to previously under-represented rights, regions, modes of enforcement, styles of work. The human rights movement is, in many ways, now moving beyond rights, broadening its engagements and terms of reference. In many ways the movement has developed precisely by absorbing waves of criticism, often from those passionate about its possibilities and importance who cast their doubts in one or another of these terms. It would be interesting to list the reactions and reforms that these and other doubts have generated.

A. *Human Rights Occupies the Field of Emancipatory Possibility*

Hegemony as resource allocation. The claim here is that this institutional and political hegemony makes other valuable, often more valuable, emancipatory strategies less available. This argument is stronger, of course, when one can say something about what those alternatives are – or might be. But there may be something to the claim that human rights has so dominated the imaginative space of emancipation that alternatives can now only be thought, perhaps unhelpfully, as negations of what human rights asserts – passion to its reason, local to its global, etc. As a dominant and fashionable vocabulary for thinking about emancipation, human rights crowds out other ways of understanding harm and recompense. This is easiest to see when human rights attracts institutional energy and resources that would otherwise flow elsewhere. But this is not only a matter of scarce resources.

Hegemony as criticism. Human rights also occupies the field *by* implicit or explicit delegitimation of other emancipatory strategies. As an increasingly dominant emancipatory vocabulary, human rights is also a mode of criticism, among people of good will and against people of good will, when pursuing projects that, by comparison, can seem "too" ideological and political, insufficiently universal, objective, and so on. Where this is so, pursuing a human rights initiative or promoting the use of human rights vocabulary may have fully untended negative consequences for other existing emancipatory projects. Of course this takes us directly to a comparative analysis- how do we compare the gains and losses of human rights to the (potential) gains and losses of these other vocabularies and projects?

Hegemony as distortion. To the extent emancipatory projects must be expressed in the vocabulary of "rights" to be heard, good policies that are not framed that way go unattended. This also distorts the way projects are imagined and framed for international consideration. For example, it is often asserted that the international human rights movement makes an end run around local institutions and strategies that would often be better-ethically, politically, philosophically, aesthetically. Resources and legitimacy are drawn to the center from the periphery. A "universal" idea of what counts as a problem and a solution snuffs out all sorts of promising local political and social initiatives to contest local conditions in other terms. But there are other lost vocabularies that are equally global – vocabularies of duty, of responsibility, of collective commitment. Encouraging people concerned about environmental harm to rethink their concerns as a human rights violation will have bad consequences *if* it would have turned out to be more animating, for example, to say there is a duty to work for the environment, rather than a right to a clean environment.

B. *Human Rights Views the Problem and the Solution Too Narrowly*

Narrow in many ways. People have made many different claims about the narrowness of human rights. Here are some: the human rights movement foregrounds harms done explicitly by *governments* to individuals or groups – leaving largely unaddressed and more legitimate by contrast harms brought about by governments indirectly or by private parties. Even when addressing private harms, human rights focuses attention on *public* remedies – explicit rights formalized and implemented by the state. One criticizes the *state* and seeks *public* law remedies, but leaves unattended or enhanced the powers and felt entitlements of private actors. Human rights implicitly legitimates ills and delegitimates remedies in the domain of private law and non-state action.

Insulating the economy. Putting these narrowings together often means defining problems and solutions in ways not likely to change the economy. Human rights foregrounds problems of *participation* and *procedure*, at the expense of distribution, implicitly legitimating the existing distributions of wealth, status and power in societies once rights have been legislated, formal participation in government achieved, and institutional remedies for violations provided. However useful saying "that's my right" is in extracting things from the state, it is not good for extracting things from the economy, unless you are a property holder. Indeed, a practice of rights claims against the state may actively weaken the capacity of people to challenge economic arrangements.

Whether progressive efforts to challenge economic arrangements are weakened by the overwhelming strength of the "right to property" in the human rights vocabulary, or by the channeling of emancipatory energy and imagination into the modes of institutional and rhetorical interaction that are described as "public," the imbalance between civil/political and social/economic rights is neither an accident of politics nor a matter that could be remedied by more intensive commitment. It is structural, to the philosophy of human rights, to the conditions of political possibility that make human rights an emancipatory strategy in the first place, to the institutional character of the movement, or to the ideology of its participants and supporters.

Even very broad social movements of emancipation – for women, for minorities of various sorts, for the poor – have their vision blinkered by the promise of recognition in the vocabulary and institutional apparatus of human rights. They will be led away from the economy and toward the state, away from political/social conditions and toward the forms of legal recognition. It has been claimed, for example, that promoting a neutral right to religious expression in Africa without acknowledging the unequal background cultural, economic and political authority of traditional religions and imported evangelical sects will dramatically affect the distribution of religious practice. Even if we limit our thinking to the *laws* that influence the distribution of wealth, status, and power between men and women, the number of those laws that *explicitly* address "women's issues," still less "women's rights," would form an extremely small and relatively unimportant percentage. However much the human rights movement reaches out to address other background considerations affecting the incidence of human rights abuse, such "background" norms remain, well, background.

C. Human Rights Generalizes Too Much

Universal goods and evils. The vocabulary and institutional practice of human rights promotion propagates an unduly abstract idea about people, politics and society. A one-size-fits-all emancipatory practice underrecognizes and reduces the instance and possibility for particularity and variation. This claim is not that human rights are too "individualistic." Rather, the claim is that the "person," as well as the "group," imagined and brought to life by human rights agitation is both abstract and general in ways that have bad consequences.

Sometimes this claim is framed as a loss of the pre-existing diversity of experience – as a vocabulary for expressing or representing experience, human rights limits human potential. In this view, limits on pre-existing potentials and experiences are themselves bad consequences. For others who make this argument, the loss of a prior, more authentic, humane, diverse *real* experience is not the issue. Even if it turns out that behind modes of expression there is no authentic experience, much less an edenic one, *this particular vocabulary* is less useful in encouraging possibility or hope or emancipation than others that generalize less or differently.

Becoming free only as an instance of the general. To come into understanding of oneself as an instance of a pre-existing general – "I am a 'person with rights'" – exacts a cost, a loss of awareness of the unprecedented and plastic nature of experience, or a loss of a capacity to imagine and desire alternative futures. We could term this "alienation." The human rights movement proposes itself as a vocabulary of the general good – as knowledge about the shape of emancipation and human possibility chat can be "applied" and "enforced." As an emancipatory vocabulary, it offers answers rather than questions, answers that are not only outside political, ideological and cultural differences, bur also beyond the human experience of specificity and against the human capacity to hope for more, in denial of the tawdry and uncertain quality of our available dreams about and experience with justice and injustice. Rather than enabling a discussion of what it means to be human, of who is human, of how humans might relate to one another, it crushes this discussion under the weight of moral condemnation, legal adjudication, textual certainty and political power.

D. *Human Rights Particularizes Too Much*

Emancipating the "right holders." The specific way human rights generalizes is to consolidate people into "identities" on the basis of which rights can be claimed. There are two issues here: a focus on *individuals* and a focus, whether for individuals or groups, on *right-holding identity.* The focus on individuals and people who come to think of themselves as individuals blunts articulation of a shared life. The focus on discrete and insular right-holding identities blunts awareness of diversity, of the continuity of human experience, of overlapping identities. Together these tendencies inhibit expression of the experience of being part of a community.

Strengthening the state. Although the human rights vocabulary expresses relentless suspicion of the state, by structuring emancipation as a relationship between an individual right holder and the state, human rights places the state at the center of the emancipatory promise. However much one may insist on the priority or pre-existence of rights, in the end rights are enforced, granted, recognized, implemented, their violations remedied, by the state. By consolidating human experience into the exercise of legal entitlements, human rights strengthens the national governmental structure and equates the structure of the state with the structure of freedom. To be free is to have an appropriately organized state. We might say that the right-holder imagines and experiences freedom only as a *citizen.* This encourages autochthonous political tendencies and alienates the "citizen" from both his or her own experience as a person and from the possibility of alternative communal forms.

Encouraging conflict and discouraging politics among right-holders. Encouraging each person and group wishing to be free to tally the rights he/she/it holds in preparation for their assertion against the state reduces inter-group and inter-individual sensitivity. In emancipating itself, the right holder is, in effect, queue jumping. Recognizing, implementing, enforcing rights is distributional work. Encouraging people to imagine themselves as right

holders, and rights as absolute, makes the negotiation of distributive arrangements among individuals and groups less likely and less tenable. There is no
one to triage among rights and right holders – except the state. The absolutist
legal vocabulary of rights makes it hard to assess distribution among favored
and less favored right holders and forecloses development of a political process for tradeoffs among them, leaving only the vague suspicion that the more
privileged got theirs at the expense of the less privileged.

*E. Human Rights Expresses the Ideology, Ethics, Aesthetic Sensibility and
Political Practice of a Particular Western Eighteenth- through Twentieth-
Century Liberalism*

Tainted origins. Although there are lots of interesting analogies to human rights
ideas in various cultural traditions, the particular form these ideas are given in
the human rights movement *is* the product of a particular moment and place.
Post-enlightenment, rationalist, secular, Western, modern, capitalist. From a
pragmatist point of view, of course, tainted origins are irrelevant. That human
rights *claims* to be universal but *is really* the product of a specific cultural and
historical origin says nothing – unless that specificity exacts costs or renders
human rights less useful than something else. The human rights tradition
might itself be undermined by its origin – be treated less well by some people,
be less effective in some places – just as its origin might, for other audiences,
accredit projects undertaken in its name. This is the sort of thing we might
strategize about – perhaps we should downplay the universal claims, or look
for parallel developments in other cultural traditions, etc.

The movement's Western liberal origins become part of the problem (rather
than a limit on the solution) when particular difficulties general to the liberal
tradition are carried over to the human rights movement. When, for example,
the global expression of emancipatory objectives in human rights terms nar-
rows humanity's appreciation of these objectives to the forms they have taken
in the nineteenth- and twentieth-century Western political tradition. One cost
would be the loss of more diverse and local experiences and conceptions of
emancipation. Even within the liberal West, other useful emancipatory vocabularies (including the solidarities of socialism, Christianity, the labor movement, and so forth) are diminished by the consolidation of human rights as the
international expression of *the* Western liberal tradition. Other costs would be
incurred to the extent the human rights tradition could be seen to carry with
it particular down sides of the liberal West.

Human rights encourages people to seek emancipation in the vocabularies
of reason rather than faith, in public rather than private life, in law rather than
politics, in policies rather than economics. In each case, the human rights

vocabulary overemphasizes the difference between what it takes as the (natural) base and as the (artificial) domain of emancipation, and underestimates the plasticity of what it treats as the base. Moreover, human rights is too quick to conclude that emancipation *meant* progress forward from the natural passions of policies into the civilized reason of law. The urgent need to develop a more vigorous human politics is sidelined by the effort to throw thin but plausible nets of legal articulation across the globe. Work to develop law comes to be seen as an emancipatory end in itself, leaving the human rights movement too ready to articulate problems in political terms and solutions in legal terms. Precisely the reverse would be more useful. The posture of human rights as an emancipatory political project that extends and operates within a domain above or outside politics – a political project repackaged as a form of knowledge – delegitimates other political voices and makes less visible the local, cultural, and political dimensions of the human rights movement itself.

The West and the rest. The Western liberal character of human rights exacts particular costs when it intersects with the highly structured and unequal relations between the modern West and everyone else. Whatever the limits of modernization in the West, the form of modernization promoted by the human rights movement in third world societies is too often based only on a fantasy about the modern/liberal/capitalist west. The insistence on more formal and absolute conceptions of property rights in transitional societies than are known in the developed West is a classic example of this problem – using the authority of the human rights movement to narrow the range of socioeconomic choices available in developing societies in the name of "rights" that do not exist in this unregulated or compromised form in any developed western democracy.

At the same time, the human rights movement contributes to the framing of political choices in the third world as oppositions between "local/traditional" and "international/modern" forms of government and modes of life. This effect is strengthened by the presentation of human rights as part of belonging to the modern world, but coming from some place outside political choice, from the universal, the rational, the civilized. By strengthening the articulation of third world politics as a choice between tradition and modernity, the human rights movement impoverishes local political discourse, often strengthening the hand of self-styled "traditionalists" who are offered a common-sense and powerful alternative to modernisation for whatever politics they may espouse.

F. Human Rights Promises More than It Can Deliver

Knowledge. Human rights promises a way of knowing – knowing just and unjust, universal and local, victim and violator, harm and remedy – which it cannot deliver. Justice is something that must be made, experienced, articulated, performed each time anew. Human rights may well offer an index of ways in which past experiences of justice-achieved have retrospectively been described, but the usefulness of this catalog as a stimulus to emancipatory creativity is swamped by the encouragement such lists give to the idea that justice need not be made, that it can be found or simply imported. One result is a loss of the habit of grappling with ambivalence, conflict and the unknown. Taken together, belief in these various false promises demobilizes actors from taking other emancipatory steps and encourages a global misconception of both the nature of evil and the possibilities for good.

Justice. Human rights promises a legal vocabulary for achieving justice outside the clash of political interest. Such a vocabulary is not available: rights conflict with one another, rights are vague, rights have exceptions, many situations fall between rights. The human rights movement promises that "law" – the machinery, the texts, the profession, the institution – can resolve conflicts and ambiguities in society by resolving those within its own materials, and that this can be done on the basis of a process of "interpretation" that is different from, more legitimate than, politics. And different in a particularly stultifying way-as a looser or stricter deduction from a past knowledge rather than as a collective engagement with the future. In particular, the human rights movement fetishizes the judge as someone who functions as an instrument of the law rather than as a political actor, when this is simply not possible – not a plausible description of judicial behavior – given the porous legal vocabulary with which judges muse work and the likely political context within which judges are asked to ace.

Many general criticisms of law's own tendencies to overpromise are applicable in spades to human rights. The absoluteness of rules makes compromise and peaceful adjustment of outcomes more difficult. The vagueness of standards makes for self-serving interpretation. The gap between law in the books and law in action, between legal institutions and the rest of life, hollows promises of emancipation through law. The human rights movement suggests that "rights" can be responsible for emancipation, rather than people making political decisions. This demobilizes other actors and other vocabularies, and encourages emancipation through reliance on enlightened, professional elites with "knowledge" of rights and wrongs, alienating people from themselves and from the vocabulary of their own governance. These difficulties are more acute in the international arena where law is ubiquitous and unaccompanied by political dialog.

Emancipator as emancipation. Human rights offers itself as the measure of emancipation. This is its most striking, and misleading, promise. Human rights narrates itself as a universal/eternal/human truth and as a pragmatic response to injustice – there was the holocaust and then there was the genocide convention, women everywhere were subject to discrimination and then there was CEDAW. This posture makes the human rights movement *itself* seem redemptive – as if doing something *for human rights* was, in and of itself, doing something *against* evil. It is not surprising that human rights professionals consequently confuse work on the movement for emancipatory work in society. But there are bad consequences when people of good will mistake work on the discipline for work on the problem.

Potential emancipators can be derailed – satisfied that building the human rights movement is its own reward. People inside the movement can mistake reform of their world for reform of the world. What seem like improvements in the field's ability to respond to things outside itself may only be improvements in the field's ability to respond to its own internal divisions and contradictions. Yet we routinely underestimate the extent to which the human rights movement develops in response to political conflict and discursive fashion among international elites, thereby overestimating the field's pragmatic potential and obscuring the field's internal dynamics and will to power.

Think of the right to development, born less in response to global poverty than in response to an internal political conflict within the elite about the legitimate balance of concerns on the institutional agenda and to an effort by some more marginal members of that elite to express their political interest in the only available language. The move from a world of "rights" to "remedies" and then to "basic needs" and on to "transnational enforcement" reflected less a changing set of problems in the world than a changing set of attitudes among international legal elites about the value of legal formalism. The result of such initiatives to reframe emancipatory objectives in human rights terms is more often growth for the field – more conferences, documents, legal analysis, opposition and response – than decrease in violence against women, poverty, mass slaughter and so forth. This has bad effects when it discourages political engagement or encourages reliance on human rights for results it cannot achieve.

G. The Legal Regime of "Human Rights," Taken as a Whole, Does More To Produce and Excuse Violations than To Prevent and Remedy Them

Treating symptoms. Human rights remedies, even when successful, treat the symptoms rather than the illness, and this allows the illness not only to fester, but to seem like health itself. This is most likely where signing up for a norm – against discrimination – comes to substitute for ending the practice.

But even where victims are recompensed or violations avoided, the distributions of power and wealth that produced the violation may well come to seem more legitimate as they seek other avenues of expression.

Humanitarian norms excuse too much. We are familiar with the idea that rules of warfare may do more to legitimate violence than to restrain it as a result of vague standards, broad justifications, law enforcement, or prohibitions that are clear but beside the point. The same can often be said about human rights. The vague and conflicting norms, their uncertain status, the broad justifications and excuses, the lack of enforcement, the attention to problems that are peripheral to a broadly conceived program of social justice – all this may, in some contexts, place the human rights movement in the uncomfortable position of legitimating more injustice than it eliminates. This is particularly likely where human rights discourse has been absorbed into the foreign policy processes of the great powers, indeed, of all powers.

Humanitarian norms justify too much. The human rights movement consistently underestimates the usefulness of the human rights vocabulary and machinery for people whose hearts are hard and whose political projects are repressive. The United States, The United Kingdom, Russia – but also Serbia and the Kosovar Albanians – have taken military action, intervened politically, and justified their governmental policies on the grounds of protecting human rights. Far from being a defense of the individual against the state, human rights has become a standard part of the justification for the external use of force by the state against other states and individuals. The porousness of the human rights vocabulary means that the interventions and exercises of state authority it legitimates are more likely to crack political interests than its own emancipatory agenda.

Background norms do the real damage. At the same time, the human rights regime, like the law concerning war, is composed of more than those legal rules and institutions that explicitly concern human rights. The human rights movement acts as if the human rights legal regime were composed only of rights catalogs and institutions for their implementation. In fact, the law concerning torture, say, includes all the legal rules, principles, and institutions that bear on the incidence of torture. The vast majority of these rules – rules of sovereignty, institutional competence, agency, property and contract – facilitate or excuse the use of torture by police and governments.

H. The Human Rights Bureaucracy Is Itself Part of the Problem

Professionalizes the humanitarian impulse. The human rights movement attracts and demobilizes thousands of good-hearted people around the globe every year. It offers many thousands more the confidence that these matters are being professionally dealt with by those whom the movement has enlisted. Something similar has occurred within academic life – a human rights discipline has emerged between fields of public law and international law, promising students and teachers that work in the public interest has an institutional life, a professional routine and status. Professionalization has a number of possible costs. Absolute costs in lost personnel for other humanitarian possibilities. As the human rights profession raises its standards and status to compete with disciplines of private law, it raises the bar for other pro-bono activities that have not been as successful in establishing themselves as disciplines, whose practices, knowledge and projects are less systematic, less analogous to practice in the private interest. Professionalization strengthens lawyers at the expense of priests, engineers, politicians, soothsayers and citizens who might otherwise play a more central role in emancipatory efforts. At the same time, professionalization separates human rights advocates from those they represent and those with whom they share a common emancipatory struggle. The division of labor among emancipatory specialists is not merely about efficient specialization. We need only think of the bureaucratization of human rights in places like East Timor that have come within the orbit of international governance suddenly an elaborate presence pulling local elites away from their base, or consigning them to the status of local informants, attention turning like sunflowers to Geneva, New York, to the Center, to the Commission. To the work of resolutions and reports.

Perils of "representation." The professionalization of human rights creates a mechanism for people to think they are working "on behalf of" less fortunate others, while externalizing the possible costs of their decisions and actions. The representational dimension of human rights work – speaking "for" others – puts the "victims" both on screen and off. The production of authentic victims, or victim authenticity, is an inherently voyeuristic or pornographic practice that, no matter how carefully or sensitively it is done, transforms the position of the "victim" in his or her society and produces a language of victimization for him or her to speak on the international stage. The injured-one-who-is-not-yet-a-victim, the "subaltern" if you like, can neither speak nor be spoken for, but recedes instead before the interpretive and representational practices of the movement. The remove between human rights professionals and the people they purport to represent can reinforce a global divide of wealth, mobility, information and access to audience. Human rights professionals consequently struggle, ultimately in vain, against a ride of bad faith, orientalism and self-serving sentimentalism.

I. The Human Rights Movement Strengthens Bad International Governance

Weakest link. Even within international law, the modes of possible governance are far broader than the patterns worn by human rights professionals. The human rights movement is the product of a particular moment *in* international legal history, which foregrounded rules rather than standards and institutional rather than cultural enforcement. If we compare modes of governance in other fields we find a variety of more successful models-a standards/culture based environmental regime, an economic law regime embedded in private law, and so forth. The attachment to rights as a measure of the authenticity, universality, and above all as the knowledge we have of social justice binds our professional feet, and places social justice issues under the governance of the least effective institutional forms available.

Clean hands. More generally, international governance errs when it imagines itself capable of governing, "intervening" if you will, without taking responsibility for the messy business of allocating stakes in society when it intervenes only economically and not politically, only in public and not in private life, only "consensually" without acknowledging the politics of influence, only to freeze the situation and not to improve it, "neutrally" as between the parties, politically/economically but not culturally, and so forth. The human rights movement offers the well-intentioned intervener the illusion of affecting conditions both at home and abroad without being politically implicated in the distribution of stakes that results, by promising an available set of universal, extra-political legal rules and institutions with which to define, conduct and legitimate the intervention.

Governing the exception. Human rights shares with the rest of international law a tendency to treat only the tips of icebergs. Deference to the legal forms upon which human rights is built – the forms of sovereignty, territorial jurisdictional divisions, subsidiarity, consensual norms – makes it seem natural to isolate aspects of a problem that "cross borders" or "shock the conscience of mankind" for special handling at the international level, often entrenching the rest of the iceberg more firmly in the national political background. The movement's routine polemical denunciations of sovereignty work more as attestations to its continuity than agents of its erosion, limiting the aspirations of good hearted people with international and global political commitments. The notion that law sits atop culture as well as politics demobilizes people who understand their political projects as "intervention" in a "foreign" "culture." The human rights vocabulary, with its emphasis on the development of law itself, strengthens the tendency of international lawyers more broadly to concern themselves with constitutional questions about the structure of the legal regime itself rather than with questions of distribution in the broader society.

J. Human Rights Promotion Can Be Bad Politics in Particular Locations

It may be that this is all one can say – promoting human rights can sometimes have bad consequences. All of the first nine types of criticism suggested that human rights suffered from one or another design defect as if these defects would emerge, these costs would be incurred, regardless of context. Perhaps this is so. But so long as none of these criticisms have been proven in such a general way (and it is hard to see just how they could be), it may be that all we have is a list of possible down sides, open risks, bad results that have sometimes occurred, that might well occur. In some context, for example, it might turn out that pursuing emancipation as entitlement could reduce the capacity and propensity for collective action. Something like this seems to have happened in the United States in the last twenty years – the transformation of political questions into legal questions, and then into questions of legal "rights," has made other forms of collective emancipatory politics less available. But it is hard to see that this is always and everywhere the destiny of human rights initiatives. We are familiar, even in the United States, with moments of collective emancipatory mobilisation achieved, in part, through the vocabulary of rights. If we come to the recent British Human Rights Act, it seems an open question whether it will liberate emancipatory political energies frozen by the current legislative process and party structure, or will harness those political possibilities to the human rights claims of de-politicized individuals and judges. The point of an ongoing pragmatic evaluation of the human rights effort is precisely to develop a habit of making such assessments. But that human rights promotion can and has had bad consequences in some contexts does seem clear.

Condemnation as legitimation. Finally, in many contexts, transforming a harm *into* a "human rights violation" may be a way of condoning or denying rather than naming and condemning it. A terrible set of events occurs in Bosnia. We could think of it as a sin and send the religious, as illness and send physicians, as politics and send the politicians, as war and send the military. Or we could think of it as a human rights violation and send the lawyers. Doing so can be a way of doing nothing, avoiding responsibility, simultaneously individualizing the harm and denying its specificity. Thinking of atrocity as a human rights violations captures neither the unthinkable or the banal in evil. Instead we find a strange combination of clinically antiseptic analysis, throwing the illusion of cognitive control over the unthinkable, and hysterical condemnation, asserting the advocate's distance from the quotidian possibility of evil. Renaming Auschwitz "genocide" to recognize its unspeakability, enshrining its status as "shocking the conscience of mankind" can also be a way of unthinking its everyday reality. In this sense, human rights, by criminalizing harm and condensing its origin to particular violators, can serve as denial, apology, legitimation, normalization, and routinization of the very harms it seeks to condemn.

III. Conclusion

So that is the list. As I said at the outset, some of these worries seem more plausible to me than others. I would worry about some of these costs more than others. The generation that built the human rights movement focused its attention on the ways in which evil people in evil societies could be identified and restrained. More acute now is how good people, well-intentioned people in good societies, can go wrong, can entrench, support, the very things they have learned to denounce. Answering this question requires a pragmatic reassessment of our most sacred humanitarian commitments, tactics and tools.

Whatever has been the history of human rights, we do not know its future. Perhaps these difficulties will be overcome, avoided. But we will not avoid them by avoiding their articulation, discussion, assessment – by treating the human rights movement as a frail child, in need of protection from critical assessment or pragmatic calculation. At this point these remain suspicions, intuitions, hunches, by people who have seen the human rights movement from one or another point of view. Each person involved in international human rights protection will have his or her own view about which, if any, of these doubts are plausible and worth pursuing. As a profession, it would be good to have a more open conversation about worries of this sort, and to think further about how they should affect our understanding of the human rights project as a whole.

Excerpts From:

Rajagopal, Balakrishnan (2008) Invoking the Rule of Law in Post-Conflict Rebuilding: A Critical Examination. *William and Mary Law Review* 49:1347–1376. Reprinted with permission.

INVOKING THE RULE OF LAW IN POST-CONFLICT REBUILDING: A CRITICAL EXAMINATION

Balakrishnan Rajagopal[9]

Introduction

Establishing the rule of law is increasingly seen as the panacea for all the problems that afflict many non-Western countries, particularly in post-conflict settings.[10] Development experts prescribe it as the surest shortcut to market-

---

[9]   Ford International Associate Professor of Law and Development and Director, Program on Human Rights and Justice, MIT; former Human Rights Officer, United Nations High Commissioner for *Human Rights*, Cambodia. I thank Lan Cao, Robert Post, Vicki Jackson, and Jane Stromseth for a great set of intellectual exchanges during and after a symposium panel at the William & Mary School of Law, where this Article was presented. I also wish to thank the editors of the *William and Mary Law Review* for their assistance. A slightly shorter version of this Article is forthcoming in Civil War and the Rule of Law: Security, Development, Human Rights (Agnes Hurwitz, with Reyko Huang, eds., 2008).

[10]   This belief is evidenced in a plethora of official reports, articles and books in recent years. *See, e.g.,* The Secretary-General, *Report of the Secretary-General: In Larger Freedom: Towards Development, Security and Human Rights for All*, 133–39, delivered to the General Assembly, U.N. Doc. N59/2005 (Mar. 21, 2005) [hereinafter *In Larger Freedom*]; High-level Panel on Threats, Challenges & Change, Dec. 2, 2004, *A More Secure World: Our Shared Responsibility*, 145–48, U.N. Doc. N59/565 [hereinafter *A More Secure World*]; The Secretary-General, *Report of the Secretary-General: Road Map Towards the Implementation of the United Nations Millennium Declaration*, 4–32, delivered to the General Assembly, U.N. Doc. N56/326 (Sept. 6, 2001); The Secretary-General, *Report of the Secretary-General: The Rule of Law and Transitional Justice in Conflict and Post-Conflict Societies*, 2–4, delivered to the Security Council, U.N. Doc. S/2004/616 (Aug. 23, 2004) [hereinafter *Transitional Justice*]; Thomas Carothers, Promoting the Rule of Law Abroad: In Search of Knowledge (2006) [hereinafter Promoting the Rule of Law]; Jane Stromseth et al., Can Might Make Rights? Building the Rule of Law After Military Interventions (2006); Brian Z. Tamanaha, Law as a Means to an End: Threat to the Rule Of Law (2006) [hereinafter Means to an End]; Brian Z. Tamanaha, On the Rule of Law: History, Politics, Theory (2004) [hereinafter On the Rule of Law]; Agnes Hurwitz & Kaysie Studdard, Int'l Peace Acad., Rule of Law Programs in Peace Operations 3 (2005), *available at* http://www. ipacademy.org/pdfs/IPA_e_REPORT_RULE_OF_LAW.pdf.; Kirsti Samuels, *Rule of Law Reform in Post-Conflict Countries: Operational Initiatives and Lessons Learnt* (Soc. Dev. Dep't of the World Bank, Social Development Paper No. 37, 2006). For a general overview of rule of law in post-conflict settings, see David Tolbert with Andrew Solomon, *United Nations Reform and Supporting the Rule of Law in Post-Conflict Societies*, 19 Harv. Hum. Rts. J. 29 (2006). "Transitional justice" is an allied strand of literature that covers a substantial amount of the ground covered by rule of law literature. *See, e.g.,* Ruti G. Teitel, Transitional Justice (2000); Transitional Justice: How Emerging Democracies Reckon with Former Regimes (Neil J. Kritz ed., 1995).

led growth; human rights groups advocate the rule of law as the best defense against human rights abuses; and, in the area of peace and security, the rule of law is considered the surest guarantee against the reemergence of conflicts and the basis for rebuilding post-conflict societies. Indeed, the rule of law has occupied this central position at least since the early 1990s, as Thomas Carothers recognized in a well-known article on the revival of the rule of law some years ago.[11] Therefore, in a very direct sense, the rule of law has come to be considered the common element that development experts, security analysts, and human rights activists agree upon, and as the mechanism that links these disparate areas. Constitution making is also seen as a cornerstone of rule of law activities in postconflict settings,[12] but this Article focuses more on the diverse policy background against which legal reform is sought to be carried out and justified in "everyday" politics, and much less on constitution making, as such.

This Article argues that this newfound fascination with the rule of law is misplaced. Underlying this "linkage" idea is a desire to escape from politics by imagining the rule of law as technical, legal, and apolitical. In other words, there is a tendency to think that failures of development, threats to security, and human rights violations could all be avoided or managed by a resort to law. This Article traces the characteristics of this idea and the different strands of policy and disciplinary discourses that have led to this conclusion, and argues that there is, in fact, a need to retain politics at the center of the discussions of development, human rights, and security. In addition, it argues that the invocation of the rule of law hides many contradictions among the different policy agendas themselves, such as between development and human rights

---

[11] Thomas Carothers, *The Rule of Law Revival*, 77 Foreign Aff. 95, 95–106 (1998) (discussing why the rule of law is receiving a lot of recent attention, and that it is not a new idea); *see also* Thomas Carothers, Aiding Democracy Abroad: The Learning Curve 157-206 (1999).

[12] See, for example, the contributions of Vicki Jackson and Jane Stromseth in this volume. Vicki Jackson, *What's in a Name? Reflections on Timing, Naming, and ConstitutionMaking*, 49 Wm. & Mary L. Rev. 1249 (2008); Jane Stromseth, *Post-Conflict Rule of Law Building: The Need for a Multi-Layered, Synergistic Approach*, 49 Wm. & Mary L. Rev. 1443 (2008). The most extensive and thoughtful literature on constitution making and its impact on rule of law has emerged from the experience of East and Central Europe after the fall of the Berlin Wall and the break-up of the former Soviet Union, which, in turn, led to the formation of many new countries with their own constitutions and courts. *See generally* Antal Orkeny & Kim Lane Scheppele, *Rules of Law: The Complexity of Legality in Hungary, in* The Rule of Law After Communism: Problems and Prospects in East-Central Europe 55 (Martin Krygier & Adam Czarnota eds., 1999); *see also generally* The Rule of Law in Central Europe: The Reconstruction of Legality, Constitutionalism and Civil Society in the Post-Communist Countries (Jiri Priban & James Young eds., 1999); Herman Schwartz, The Struggle for Constitutional Justice in Post-Communist Europe (2000); Kim Lane Scheppele, *Guardians of the Constitution: Constitutional Court Presidents and the Struggle for the Rule of Law in Post-Soviet Europe*, 154 U. Pa. L. Rev. 1757 (2006).

or between security and human rights, that cannot be fully resolved by invoking the rule of law as a mantra. It is far more important to inquire into the real consequences of these agendas on ordinary people. Focusing attention on the rule of law as a broad, if not lofty, concept diverts attention from the coherence, effectiveness, and legitimacy of specific policies that are pursued to ensure security, promote development, or protect human rights. The rule of law agenda threatens to obfuscate the real tradeoffs that need to be made in order to achieve these worthy goals. These tradeoffs are real, partly due to the contradictions of socioeconomic development and political necessities in post-conflict settings and partly due to the contradictions between powerful third-party external actors with their own agendas and expert discourses who seek to intervene during "constitutional moments"[13] of post-conflict reconstruction in the Third World.

The post-Cold War "consensus" on the rule of law must be seen against the background of two well-known, macro-level developments. First, an increasing number of intra-state conflicts around the world have led to concerns of state failure, prompting new generations of peace operations sanctioned by the United Nations (UN) Security Council,[14] as well as situations of classic military occupations, such as the ongoing situation in Iraq. Second, the structurally violent and divisive nature of neoliberal development interventions has resulted in human rights violations and other social costs through such devices as the privatization of key national industries that increase unemployment, speculative bubbles in international finance transactions that have massive impacts on real estate and housing markets, mass population displacement and urban migration, the elimination of subsidies for food and services, and the introduction of user fees for infrastructure.[15] Against this background, the relationship between the disparate agendas of development, security, and human rights cannot be underestimated, and the invocation of the rule of law will not substitute for an honest evaluation of the costs and benefits of different policies, norms, and institutions.

Security, Development, and Human Rights: Origins and Nature of Their Relationship

The discourses of security, development, and human rights have diverse origins, but multiple, often unrecognized, intersections. Briefly put, the discourse

---

13 *See generally* Jackson, *supra* note 3.
14 *See Transitional Justice, supra* note 1, 11–12.
15 *See* Ctr. For Good Governance, A Comprehensive Guide For Social Impact Assessment (2006), *available at* http://unpan1.un.org/intradoc/groups/public/documents/CGGfUNPAN026197. pdf.

of security emerged from the realist critiques of international relations.[16] Influenced by scholars such as Hans Morgenthau, it was primarily conceived in statist terms and was focused on managing the conflicts that arose between nation-states.[17] This notion of security was predominant during the Cold War, when threats to the interstate system were perceived to be severe.[18] The security studies scholarship of this period was correspondingly dominated by political scientists who began by acknowledging the centrality of the doctrine of national security.[19]

The discourse of development, which has been much contested since its emergence in the 1940s, had its origin in colonial rule, development economics, and political development theory; it focused on the economic growth of "new" nation-states after decolonization.[20] Largely utilitarian in its calculus, the discipline of development tended to focus on measurement of aggregate indices of welfare, drawing on national income estimates from the 1940s.[21]

As can be readily seen, the discourses on security and development were natural allies. Both discourses relied heavily on the notion of the territorial nation-state and drew their force from their ability to supply content to aspects of nationalism, both territorial and developmental. The welfare of individuals, or of sub-state entities, did not figure prominently in the study of either security or development.[22] In addition, the two discourses were also linked from the beginning for different reasons. Development interventions tended to be seen by Western leaders as one of the best tools available to fight the communist menace, offering incentives for restive rural peasant populations not to rebel, while cementing the patron-client relationships between friendly regimes in power and their key domestic constituencies.[23] As U.S. Secretary

---

[16] *See* Hans J. Morgenthau & Kenneth W. Thompson, Politics Among Nations: The Struggle for Power and Peace 3–17 (6th ed. 1985).

[17] *See id.* at 451–57.

[18] *See* John Lewis Gaddis, The Cold War: A New History 92 (2005); Robert Jervis, *Was the Cold War a Security Dilemma?*, 3 J. Cold War Stud. 36, 59 (2001).

[19] *See, e.g.*, Richard A. Matthew & Leah Fraser, Global Envtl. Change & Human Sec. Program Office, Univ. of Cal. Irvine, Global Environmental Change and Human Security: Conceptual and Theoretical Issues 5 (2002), *available at* http://www.gechs.uci.edu/gechsprdraffinal.pdf.

[20] *See* Arturo Escobar, Encountering Development: The Making and Unmaking of the Third World 22 (1994); Wolfgang Sachs, The Development Dictionary: A Guide to Knowledge as Power (1992). *See generally* Ha-Joonchang, Kicking Away the Ladder: Development Strategy in Historical Perspective (2002).

[21] *See* Escobar, *supra* note 11, at 23–24; Balakrishnan Rajagopal, International Law from Below: Development, Social Movements and Third World Resistance 108 (2003).

[22] *See generally* Louis B. Sohn, *The New International Law: Protection of the Rights of Individuals Rather Than States*, 32 Am. U. L. Rev. 1 (1982) (discussing the evolution of protecting individual rights under international human rights law).

[23] *See* Gaddis, *supra* note 9, at 95–98.

of State John Foster Dulles stated in 1956, 'We are in a contest in the field of economic development of underdeveloped countries .... Defeat ... could be as disastrous as defeat in the armaments race.'[24] When radical communist movements swept to power in several Third World states during the 1950s, the response by the West was swift; the iron fist of repression and foreign intervention was brought down heavily on these countries, while the velvet glove of development was applied to pacify the restive rural masses.[25] For example, these events forced the demotion of Latin America by the United States to an "underdeveloped area," from its pre-war status as a region with a range of "developing" economies, in order to justify its foreign assistance and, therefore, security rationale.[26] Indeed, the different paradigm shifts in development discourse – for example, from growth with redistribution to poverty alleviation and basic needs in the 1970s – were explicable by the proxy wars in the Third World between the Cold War blocs.[27] The "war on poverty" announced by Robert McNamara at the World Bank in 1973 had a distinct security rationale to it.[28] Political development theorists provided theoretical support for this by justifying the importance of political stability and repression for economic growth to prevent the countries concerned from falling to the communists.[29] This focus on the linkage between security and development continues to this day, as demonstrated by the emphasis on development in the most recently published U.S. National Security Strategy, released in 2002, though with a focus on "failing" states and "the embittered few" rather than the communists.[30] Thus, the language has changed, but not the rationale.

The emergence of the human rights discourse did not fundamentally threaten this symbiotic relationship, at least not at first. Conceived as a set of state obligations towards citizens, the human rights system fit easily into the nation-state focused world of security and development.[31] The system of human rights did not pose any radical challenges to the state-centric world order, such as by pushing for extra-national obligations of states or obligations

[24] *Transcript of Dulles News Conference on Economic Contest with Soviet Union*, N.Y. Times, Jan. 12, 1956, at 10.

[25] *See* Odd Arne Westad, The Global Cold War: Third World Interventions and the Making of Our Times 111–12, 119 (2005).

[26] Devesh Kapur, John P. Lewis & Richard Webb, The World Bank: Its First Half Century 143 (1997).

[27] For a discussion, see *id.* at 215–68.

[28] *See id.* at 219–23.

[29] See Samuel P. Huntington, Political Order in Changing Societies 374–78(1968).

[30] The White House, The National Security Strategy of the United States of America 1(2002) [Hereinafter National Security Strategy], *available at* http://www.white house.gov/nsc/nss. pdf.

[31] *See* Sohn, *supra* note 13, at 9.

of non-state actors, and reaffirmed the same goals that development and security regimes set for themselves.[32] To the extent that there appeared to be any contradictions, human rights law provided for exemptions within the terms of the treaties themselves. For example, the law itself allowed violations, where needed, to preserve political stability through the concept of public emergency laid down under Article 4 of the International Covenant on Civil and Political Rights (ICCPR).[33] Economic and social rights were conceived of in promotional terms under the International Covenant on Economic, Social and Cultural Rights (ICESCR), which did not seriously threaten the dominant role of the state in the economy by imposing legal limits on the state's ability to guide economic development.[34] Many states in the West, especially European nations and the newly independent Third World countries, widely subscribed to this position during the 1960s.[35] Given the largely voluntarist premises of international human rights law,[36] states could choose to undertake limited obligations that they were comfortable with. Despite this compatibility, the human rights discourse remained largely isolated from the discourses of security and development until the 1970s and was largely dominated by lawyers.[37]

Significant changes since the 1970s began blurring the lines among the discourses of development, security, and human rights. The story of the relationship between development and human rights is well-chronicled elsewhere,[38] but the following key developments in that relationship should be noted:

- The expansion of the notion of development to include human development measures at the level of the family and the household, chiefly evidenced through UNDP reports;[39]
- The emergence of the language of social progress and development from the Declaration of Tehran (1967) and culminating in the U.N. General

---

[32] *See id.*

[33] International Covenant on Civil and Political Rights, art. 4, Mar. 23, 1976, 999 U.N.T.S. 171 [hereinafter ICCPR].

[34] *See* International Covenant on Economic, Social and Cultural Rights art. 6, Jan. 3, 1976, 993 U.N.T.S. 3 [hereinafter ICESCR].

[35] Farroukh Jhabvala, *On Human Rights and the Socio-Economic Context, in* Third World Attitudes Toward International Law 296 (Frederick Snyder & Surakiart Sathirathai eds., 1987).

[36] *See, e.g.,* The Third Comm., *Report of the Third Committee on Human Rights Questions: Human Rights Questions, Including Alternative Approaches for Improving the Effective Enjoyment of Human Rights and Fundamental Freedom*, 4–15, U.N. Doc. A/56/583/Add.2 (Dec. 11, 2001) *(prepared by* Juraj Priputen).

[37] Rajagopal, *supra* note 12, at 216–18.

[38] *See, e.g., id.* at 171–232.

[39] *See id.* at 222–24.

Assembly Resolution on Right to Development in 1986. This move followed two decades of attempts by Third World countries to elevate development as an international legal norm that would impose legal obligations on rich countries, both to abstain from intervening in Third World developmental strategies, such as the pursuit of an industrial policy, and to provide more development assistance;[40]

- The emergence of the governance agenda in development policy since the late 1980s, focusing attention on governmental failures as the reason behind developmental failures. Arising from the experience of Sub-Saharan Africa, this move saw the failure of development as the result of the absence of adequate institutions, both political and economic. At issue was the lack of transparency and accountability of government. This contrasted with the early explanations for the failure of development, which had focused on the absence of the right capital and prices and the absence of an appropriate policy framework for economic growth. This new focus on governance – or good governance in the literature of the World Bank-neatly coincided with the rise of the institutionalist turn in development economics, which came to see the legal frameworks of property and contracts as the source of economic growth. This newfound interest in institutions and legal norms had the effect of bringing human rights, which also focused primarily on legal reform, closer to development;[41]

- The emergence of rights-based approaches to development since the 1990s in multilateral and bilateral development agencies, combined with a new interest in economic, social, and cultural rights. The move towards a rights-based approach was driven by a paradigm shift within development that began to see development itself as freedom, while retaining a belief that such a new paradigm could lead to changes at the project level, where development is "delivered" to its beneficiaries. The new interest in economic and social rights was driven in large part by the constitutionalization and judicialization of these rights, as part of a wave of democratic transitions and constitution making across the world;[42]

- High-profile global campaigns involving civil society actors in various countries around the issues of displacement and damage to the environment in countries like Brazil and India, which led, in turn, to the adoption of better standards by the World Bank on internal displacement and respect for indigenous peoples' rights during the 1980s and to the establishment of the World Bank Inspection Panel in the early 1990s. These mobilizations, which were

---

[40] *See id.* at 216–22.
[41] *See id.* at 218, 224-25; Kapur Et Al., *supra* note 17, at 532–33.
[42] *See* Rajagopal, *supra* note 12, at 217–32.

simultaneously global and local, provided the political background to the move to bring human rights and development closer.[43]

The discourse of security, too, began to change. First, it was expanded to include understandings of environmental security, focusing attention on environmental damage as the cause and consequence of violent conflicts, including conflicts relating to natural resources.[44] The traditional notion of security was also increasingly challenged by new notions of human security, which emphasized the security of human beings over states.[45] Second, the notion of international security was expanded to include intra-state conflicts, which were proliferating rapidly after the end of the Cold War.[46] As the Report of the International Commission on Intervention and State Sovereignty noted, the changing nature of armed conflict in the world was reflected by the fact that 90 percent of people killed in armed conflicts in the late twentieth century were civilians, whereas it had been only one out of ten at the beginning of the twentieth century.[47] Third, the source of threats to world order had also been seen to change from classic state-based threats to non-state threats, including terrorism, drug trafficking, and transnational organized crime.[48] This expanded understanding of security shared many common elements with the most evolved thinking in development, which together indicated that the older consensus on the development-security linkage had broken down and been replaced with a new one, which had human rights at its core.

This was problematic, however. The language of human rights had since then been appropriated as part of numerous peoples' struggles around the world, and it could not so readily be deployed as a tool of governance in the

---

[43] *See id.* at 245–63.

[44] There is a very rich and complex literature on environmental security. A good source is the Environmental Change and Security Program at the Woodrow Wilson Center for International Scholars, http://www.wilsoncenter.org/index.cfm?fuseaction=topics.home&topic_id=1413 (last visited Feb. 18, 2008). For two recent samples of the literature, see Environmental Peacemaking (Ken Conca & Geoffrey D. Dabelko eds., 2002) and Violent Environments (Nancy Lee Peluso & Michael Watts eds., 2001).

[45] *See, e.g.,* osita Agbu, West Africa's Trouble Spots And The Imperative For Peace-Building 3–5 (2006).

[46] Andrea Strimling, *The Federal Mediation and Conciliation Service: A Partner in International Conflict Prevention*, 2 Pepp. Disp. Resol. L.J. 417, 419 (2002).

[47] Int'l Comm'n On Intervention & State Sovereignty: The Responsibility To Protect 13 (2001).

[48] *See generally* Raphael Perl, Cong. Research Serv., Terrorism And National Security: Issues And Trends (Dec. 21, 2004), *available at* http://www.fas.org/irp/crs/IB10119.pdf (examining international terrorism and the U.S. policy response); John R. Wagley, Cong. Research Serv., Transnational Organized Crime: Principal Threats And U.S. Responses (Mar. 20, 2006), *available at* http://www.fas.org/sgp/crslnatsed RL33335.pdf (examining the growing threat of transnational organized crime to national and global security).

fields of development or security.[49] In other words, development and security experts were working with relatively conflict-free notions of human rights that could be used to program activities in their respective fields, and this proved to be a problem. For every attempt to engage in "rights talk" by a development agency, a local actor such as a nongovernmental organization (NGO) or a social movement would offer an oppositional reading of rights.[50] Rights discourse is, in fact, constantly appropriated for oppositional struggles,[51] which makes it a particularly difficult device for governance strategies. For example, the World Commission on Dams attempted to build a new set of prescriptions for better dam building based on a human rights-influenced "rights and risks" approach.[52] For large dam-building states like India and China, this attempt to use human rights as a basis of governance proved to be too discomforting and they ended up rejecting the report of the Commission.[53] However, for the NGOs and social movements of the people displaced by dams, the "rights and risks" approach provided a minimal political safeguard that their interests would be taken into account.[54] This counter-hegemonic function of rights, as it has been called elsewhere,[55] proved sufficiently problematic for the fields of development and security. Thus, the links with the human rights discourse may, as a result, be in the process of being replaced with another, more malleable, discourse on the rule of law, as will be elaborated below. The relationship between development, security, and human rights had become confusingly self-referential and circular, each discourse pointing to the other as either the precondition for its own success or the reason for its failure. Notions such as human development and human security also muddied the waters by often equating their meaning to the full achievement of human rights, without being clear about how each is distinct.[56]

---

[49] *See* Dustin N. Sharp, *Prosecutions, Development, and Justice: The Trial of Hissein Habre*, 16 Harv. Hum. Rts. J. 147, 161–65 (2003) (discussing the differences between human rights and development discourses).

[50] *See* Henry J. Steiner, *The University's Critical Role in the Human Rights Movement*, 15 Harv. Hum. Rts. J. 317, 319 (2002); Joel P. Trachtman, *Welcome to Cosmopolis, World of Boundless Opportunity*, 39 Cornell Int'l L.J. 779, 787 (2006).

[51] *See, e.g.*, Steiner, *supra* note 41, at 319.

[52] World Comm'n on Dams, Dams and Development: A New Framework for Decision-Making 197–211 (2000), *available at* http://www.dams.org/docslreportlwcdch7.pdf [hereinafter Dams and Development].

[53] *See* Rajagopal, *supra* note 12, at 219.

[54] Dams and Development, *supra* note 43, at 207.

[55] *See* Rajagopal, *supra* note 12 at 245–58; *see also* Balakrishnan Rajagopal, *Counter-Hegemonic International Law: Rethinking Human Rights and Development as a Third World Strategy*, 27 Third World Q., 767, 767 (2006).

[56] *See, e.g.*, Comm'n on Human Sec., Human Security Now 11–12 (2003) [hereinafter Human Security Now); U.N. Dev. Programme, Human Development Report 2000, at 127 (2000).

For now, it should be noted that the new post-Cold War consensus on development, security, and human rights could be said to have the following characteristics. First, there has been a move away from the nation-state as the focus of development towards the individuals and various subgroups (women, children, small farmers, etc.) living within it. Second, state failure is regarded as responsible for common and grave challenges in the fields of security, development, and human rights and, therefore, saving "failed states" is seen as a priority for the international community. Third, there has been a corresponding redefinition of sovereignty from that of a right of a state to exclusive domestic control, to a responsibility of a state to protect its citizens. Finally, there is now a focus on the rule of law as the tool that will help achieve the goals of development, security, and human rights.

Rule of Law and Security: Problems of Legitimacy

As was explained earlier, the concept of international security has fundamentally changed in recent years: the former state-based, territorial notion of security has now been supplanted by a more comprehensive notion of security.[57] The 2004 report of the High Level Panel on Threats, Challenges and Change, created by the U.N. Secretary-General, describes this as follows: "Any event or process that leads to large-scale death or lessening of life chances and undermines States as the basic unit of the international system is a threat to international security."[58] It then goes on to include six clusters of threats within this definition: environmental and social threats including poverty, infectious disease, and environmental degradation; interstate conflict; internal conflict, including civil war, genocide, and other large-scale atrocities; nuclear, radiological, chemical, and biological weapons; terrorism; and transnational organized crime.[59] With this holistic approach, the report joins a chorus of calls to expand the narrow definition of state security to include environmental security and human security.[60] Indeed, the National Security Strategy of the United States makes this linkage between poverty and security quite clear and asserts that poverty can make weak states vulnerable to terrorist networks and drug cartels within its borders.[61] With this move, poverty itself becomes a security threat, so that the means of responding to it become more militarized. Poverty alleviation-through the Millennium Development Goals, for example – becomes a means of addressing a security threat, as opposed to a

---

[57] *See supra* Part I.
[58] *A More Secure World, supra* note 1, at 25.
[59] *Id.*
[60] Human Security Now, *supra* note 47, at 4.
[61] *See* National Security Strategy, *supra* note 21.

set of tools that are required either because of moral duties towards the poor or because of a broad-based economic development strategy.[62] *Ergo*, a logical conclusion from this new approach would be that military interventions to secure development goals or to deal with environmental catastrophes would be legitimate and perhaps even lawful. This is not a fanciful line of thinking: one could recall the important, perhaps unwitting, role that the UNDP's Arab Human Development Report played in supporting the neoconservative argument for the Iraq war, by pointing to the role of gender inequality and poverty in Arab "backwardness."[63] The timing of that report did not hurt the broad U.S. agenda of modernizing the Middle East by force. Rather, it helped generate a hegemonic consensus that forcible intervention was for the good of the Arab people. Of course, human rights-based arguments have been used many times by hegemonic states to justify their interventions, in the form of the doctrine of humanitarian intervention.[64] Human rights groups such as Human Rights Watch were similarly inadvertent allies of the Iraq war effort by refusing to evaluate the legality of the war effort itself, while highlighting the terrible human rights record of the Iraqi regime,[65] thereby bolstering the argument of the war hawks that the use of force was justified against the Baghdad dictator. Similarly, the aftermath of the Asian tsunami in early 2005 saw a tremendous level of military intervention and jockeying between states that were eager to show how capable their respective military forces were in responding to natural disasters.[66] This "securitization of everything" is in this sense not new, though it is the first time that a U.N.-appointed panel is endorsing such a broad definition. What does one make of this move, and how is this related to the rule of law?

One could begin by noting that the term "rule of law" is not used in the High Level Panel report itself. The sections which seem most pertinent to

---

[62] Indeed, this could be said to be one of the weaknesses of the U.N. report on the Millennium Development Goals, to the extent that the report advocates what could be termed as a "Washington Consensus Plus" approach to poverty alleviation rather than encouraging plural paths of economic development. *See* Millennium Project, Report to the U.N. Secretary-General, Investing in Development: Practical Plans to Achieve the Millennium Development Goals 8–10 (2005).

[63] U.N. Dev. Programme, Arab Human Development Report (2002). For a commentary, see Thomas L. Friedman, Op-Ed., *The Arabs at the Crossroads*, N.Y. Times, July 3, 2002, at A23.

[64] *See, e.g.*, Fernandoteson, Humanitarian Intervention: An Inquiry into Law and Morality 175–79 (1997).

[65] *See, e.g.*, Justice For Iraq: A Human Rights Watch Policy Paper (Human Rights Watch, 2002), *available at* http://www.hrw.org/backgrounder/mena/iraq1217bg.htm.

[66] One writer referred to this as "competitive compassion" between aid-giving nations. *See* P.S. Suryanarayana, *International Solidarity*, Frontline, Jan. 15, 2005, *available at* http://www.hinduonnet.com/tline/fl2202/stories/20050128006312400.htm.

the issue in the report concern Parts 3 and 4, which deal, inter alia, with the role of the Security Council.[67] Here, the report firmly supports the view that the Security Council must be the sole authority to authorize the use of force, in cases which fall outside the purview of Article 51 of the U.N. Charter.[68] This commitment to multilateralism is coupled with an acknowledgement that the Council needs to be reformed, and with two proposed models for change in the membership of the Council.[69] While this commitment to seek structural change in the way the current international order is managed is to be welcomed, the report is silent on the question of the Council's compliance with international law, and only refers to the Council's lack of accountability through the rather weak call for "civil society engagement."[70] Similarly, though the report recognizes that the "war on terrorism" within many countries has itself emerged as a major threat to human rights and the rule of law,[71] it offers no concrete recommendations for making the war on terrorism conform to human rights or the rule of law. The Secretary-General's own report, which builds on the High Level Panel report, continues in the same vein, by failing to address the Security Council's own history of noncompliance with human rights standards, or about the problematic aspects of the "war on terror."[72] The Security Council's record since the end of the Cold War has raised problematic questions about its commitment to human rights, ranging from policy failures – such as the failure to take action in specific human rights crises[73] – to active collaborations in human rights violations by imposing economic sanctions that lead to large numbers of deaths, providing the cover of legitimacy to wars of aggression. The key problem here arises from the fact that the Secretary-General uses the term "rule of law" to mean many things, including multilateralism, a commitment to the U.N. Charter, and human rights principles. While this maximalist approach to the meaning of rule of law may be, and indeed is, laudable, the Security Council will find it almost impossible to comply with such an expanded notion of the rule of law in its own actions, at least as judged by its past record. In addition, the implications of a broad approach to defining security are not readily apparent, especially relating to the role of the Security Council. Would the Council be expected to act under Chapter VII of the U.N. Charter to end massive human

---

[67] *See A More Secure World, supra* note 1, at 59–92.
[68] *See* U.N. Charter art. 51, para. 1 (describing the meaning of and process for the exercise of the right of self-defense for nation-states).
[69] *See A More Secure World, supra* note 1, at 79–81.
[70] *See id.* at 83.
[71] *Id.* at 48.
[72] *See In Larger Freedom, supra* note 1.
[73] *See infra* note 128 and accompanying text.

insecurity of any kind, including those caused by poverty or natural disasters? That seems unlikely and even unwise, as it would multiply the grounds – and pre-texts – for use of force in international relations at a time of hegemonic relations between states.

These two related failures – the failure to critically focus on the Security Council and the failure to critically evaluate the "war against terrorism" – are in fact very much interrelated. They undermine the whole attempt to articulate a broad notion of security as it raises concerns that an unaccountable Security Council, even if it is expanded numerically, may turn out to flout human rights and the rule of law in the name of responding to myriad non-traditional threats. It also raises important questions of legitimacy of Security Council actions under Chapters VI and/or VII of the U.N. Charter to pursue rule of law programs in peace operations, when the Council itself overlooks the rule of law in its own functioning. The U.N. Secretary-General in fact sees this connection quite clearly. In his speech at the opening of the 59th session of the General Assembly in 2004, Kofi Annan stated: "Those who seek to bestow legitimacy must themselves embody it; and those who invoke international law must themselves submit to it."[74] He further added that "[e]very nation that proclaims the rule of law at home must respect it abroad; and every nation that insists on it abroad must enforce it at home."[75] These Delphic pronouncements point to an important truth: that the absence of the rule of law – however one may define it – in domestic contexts has to be linked with the absence of the rule of law at the international level. This absence of the rule of law is not merely evidenced by the more obvious example of the U.S. decision to side-step the Security Council in its war against Iraq. More problematically, it relates to the actions of the Security Council itself as it authorizes what many consider to be arbitrary, if not unlawful actions through its counter-terrorism committee, created under Security Council Resolution 1373.[76] Many of its actions arguably flout basic protections extended under human rights treaties and available under customary international law, such as the presumption of innocence, the right to confront one's accusers, and

---

[74] Press Release, The Secretary-General, Rule of Law at Risk Around the World, Says Secretary-General in Address to General Assembly, U.N. Doc. SG/SM/9491(Sept. 21, 2004).

[75] *Id.*

[76] *See, e.g.,* Human Rights Watch, Hear No Evil, See No Evil: The U.N. Security Council's Approach to Human Rights Violations in the Global Counter-Terrorism Effort 4–7 (2004). For a review of some of the problems of legitimacy and the level of contention at the Security Council, see generally Jose E. Alvarez, *The Security Council's War on Terrorism: Problems and Policy Options, in* Judicial Review of the Security Council by Member States (Erika de Wet & Andre Nollkaemper eds., 2003); Edward Luck, *Tackling Terrorism, in* The UN Security Council: From the Cold War to the 21st Century 85, 93–98 (David M. Malone ed., 2004).

even the right to a remedy, which are not automatically available under the Council's procedures. The perceived absence of the rule of law – especially in its expanded meaning that includes human rights – in the actions of the Security Council makes it more difficult to advance those notions within domestic contexts, especially through peace operations authorized by the Council itself. This "legitimacy deficit" is compounded by a gathering sense that for all the talk about "comprehensive security" in the High Level Panel report, it remains overwhelmingly focused on the idea that the proper response to terrorism consists of rebuilding and strengthening so-called weak or failed states.[77] In this new world of strong states, softer goals such as development, environmental protection, and human rights are likely to take a backseat, while nation-building strategies are likely to focus on the imposition of order from the outside,[78] evoking concerns about the return of formal colonialism. Such an externally driven approach is unlikely to elicit much concern for the rule of law, however narrowly or broadly it is defined. These concerns, which matter for the legitimacy of the rule of law in the domain of security, need to be addressed much more robustly.

Conclusion

The discourses of security, development, and human rights have gradually merged. The key challenges to security are now seen to come not from invading armadas of strong states but from wellorganized groups of transnationally linked terrorists who operate in "failed" or weak states that are unable or unwilling to stop them. Security is also now more broadly conceived to mean human and state security. Development challenges are currently thought to arise from the absence of viable state institutions including a judiciary and formal laws that protect property and contracts. Human rights challenges are also increasingly seen as particularly acute in situations where states have failed or are too weak to stop massive abuses. There is, in other words, a consensus that state failure or failure of governance is the root of all the problems in these

[77] This is not surprising since the discourse of failed or weak states had already emerged as part of the mainstream policy and legal discourse in the 1990s and the link between weak states and U.S. national security had been well recognized. For a critical review of the failed states idea, see generally Ruth Gordon, *Saving Failed States: Sometimes a Neocolonialist Notion*, 12 Am. U. J. Int'l L. & Pol 'Y 903 (1997). On weak states and U.S. national security, see generally Jeremy Weinstein et al., Ctr. for Global Dev., on the Brink: Weak States and US National Security (June 8, 2004), *available at* http://www.cgdev.org/doc/books/weakstates/Full_Report. pdf.

[78] *See* Necla Tschirgi, Int'l Peace Acad., Post-Conflict Peacebuilding Revisited: Achievements, Limitations, Challenges 16–18 (Oct. 7, 2004), *available at* http://www.ipacademy.org/pdfs/ POST_CONFLICT_PEACEBUILDING.pdf.

disparate areas of security, development, and human rights. This consensus has in turn led to a focus on the rule of law as a way of rebuilding or strengthening the state. But using the rule of law as a way to build up states will not resolve the tensions between the disparate agendas of development, security, and human rights themselves. It is not argued here that the rule of law is a pernicious idea or a Trojan horse. Effective governance of any society cannot rest on any basis other than law. But the term "rule of law" is currently capable of just too many disparate meanings depending on the international policy agenda in which it is invoked.

The invocation of the rule of law will be of limited relevance if there are conflicts between the agendas themselves – that is, between human rights and development or between human rights and security – and will not resolve fundamental contradictions between these various agendas. The current discourse, reflected in the High Level Panel report and the Secretary-General's reports, is remarkably conflict-free and assumes a harmonious and mutually reinforcing relationship between development, human rights, and security. This assumption is unwarranted, and even perhaps ideological. Promoting the rule of law as part of disparate policy agendas also creates uncertainty in terms of the outcomes of programmatic approaches – in other words, it is not clear who will be the losers and who will be the beneficiaries as a result of the implementation of these various policy agendas. A commitment to the formalization of informal property may mean, for example, that foreign investors are able to buy more land in an urban area and local entrepreneurs are bought out. This may indeed be the outcome that a particular society and government desires to achieve. But it does not help to camouflage that outcome in the language of the rule of law as though the outcome is justified by the very rationality and objectivity of the law itself.

Neither does a commitment to the rule of law as a way to rebuild or strengthen the state answer the question of how large or small the state needs to be. Nor does it resolve the question of whether the state needs to be strong in some areas while weak in others. The answers to these questions are likely to vary dramatically depending on the local/national contexts and the particular policy components of the agendas themselves. Finally, the commitment to establish the rule of law within failed states will be fundamentally undermined if the international rule of law is not given greater consideration, especially where rule of law programs are pursued through peace operations authorized by the Security Council. It is most unfortunate that the recent flood of U.N. reports does not deal with this issue with the seriousness it requires.

Excerpts From:

Erbeznik, Katherine (2011) Money Can't Buy You Law: The Effects of Foreign Aid on the Rule of Law in Developing Countries. *Indiana Journal of Global Legal Studies* 18(2):873–900.

MONEY CAN'T BUY YOU LAW: THE EFFECTS OF FOREIGN AID ON THE RULE OF LAW IN DEVELOPING COUNTRIES

Katherine Erbeznik (2011)

Introduction

The rule of law is often touted as a panacea for problems facing the developing world.[79] It is thought to obviate violent conflicts and allay post-conflict turmoil.[80] It also is attributed with the power to accelerate economic development and protect human rights.[81] With all of the wonders the rule of law is credited with providing, it may be a surprise to learn that despite decades of reform efforts, very few of these wonders have been realized.[82] Blame for the disappointing result of international efforts to build the rule of law in developing countries may not lie with the rule of law itself; it might just be the panacea everyone hopes. The problem is that despite decades of experience, there is still no blueprint for how to build the rule of law where it is lacking.[83] Efforts to build the rule of law without such a blueprint have often been disastrous for the presumed beneficiaries.

This Note does not attempt the herculean task of drawing the needed blueprint, supposing one could even be drawn. Instead, this Note addresses a further potential roadblock to rule of law reform: foreign aid.[84] While the target

---

[79] E.g., Thomas Carothers, The Rule-of-Law Revival, in Promoting the Rule of Law Abroad: In Search of Knowledge 3 (Thomas Carothers ed., 2006) [collection hereinafter Promoting the Rule of Law Abroad].

[80] See, e.g., Chandra Lekha Sriram, Prevention and the Rule of Law: Rhetoric and Reality, in Civil War and the Rule of Law: Security, Development, Human Rights 71 (Agnès Hurwitz & Reyko Huang eds., 2008) [collection hereinafter Civil War And The Rule Of Law] (examining the rule of law as a tool for conflict prevention); see also William G. O'Neill, UN Peacekeeping Operations and Rule of Law Programs, in supra, at 91 (arguing that "the rule of law is an essential prerequisite for building a modicum of trust in war-torn societies").

[81] For the relationship between the rule of law and economic development, see generally Kenneth W. Dam, The Law-Growth Nexus: The Rule of Law and Economic Development (2006).

[82] See, e.g., Stephen Golub, A House Without a Foundation, in Promoting the Rule of Law Abroad, supra note 1, at 105, 112–15.

[83] See Thomas Carothers, The Problem of Knowledge, in Promoting the Rule of Law Abroad, supra note 1, at 15.

[84] Foreign aid can be used to describe various sorts of international assistance, from technocratic expertise to monetary transfers. For the purpose of this Note, foreign aid is used to describe

of monetary transfers of foreign aid is often economic development or poverty reduction and only indirectly the improvement or development of the rule of law,[85] targeting economic development through foreign aid often has deleterious consequences on the rule of law. There is a growing economic literature that highlights the negative consequences foreign aid can have on economic development. This Note draws on that literature to explore the ways in which foreign aid may negatively impact rule of law reform efforts. It concludes that not only can money not buy the rule of law, but it can hinder rule of law reform as well.

I. The Rule of Law

The rule of law is seen as a fundamental element of developed countries; an element that developing countries must foster in order to escape the trenches of poverty. This part explores what the rule of law means and why efforts to foster it in developing countries have been unsuccessful.

A. Defining the Rule of Law

The rule of law is an expansive concept, subject to multiple meanings.[86] It can refer to a set of rules that binds governments and individuals,[87] the presence and quality of specific legal or political institutions,[88] or the adequate protection of equality or human rights.[89] Formal theories define the concept as a system of rules that are transparent, public, and enforced regularly, predictably, and equally against all persons, both citizens and political elites.[90] In particular, government accountability to the rule of law is held as the sine qua non of the rule of law,[91] and it comprises a core tenet of formal theories of the rule of law. The institutional approach defines the rule of law as a set of specific formal institutions, such as written legal codes, independent judiciaries,

---

monetary transfers. The main point is that such monetary transfers undermine technocratic assistance and rule of law reform.

[85] See Golub, supra note 4, at 107, 109.

[86] See generally Rachel Kleinfeld, Competing Definitions of the Rule of Law, in Promoting the Rule of Law Abroad, supra note 1, at 31. For a taxonomy of various rule of law concepts, see Richard H. Fallon, Jr., "The Rule of Law" as a Concept in Constitutional Discourse, 97 Colum. L. Rev. 1 (1997); William C. Whitford, The Rule of Law, 2000 Wis. L. Rev. 723.

[87] See Kleinfeld, supra note 8, at 36–44.

[88] See id. at 47–48.

[89] See id. at 44–46. See generally Brian Z. Tamanaha, On the Rule of Law: History, Politics, Theory 91–113 (2004) (providing an in-depth look at formal and substantive theories of the rule of law, and the differences between the two).

[90] Kleinfeld cites Friedrich Hayek as a principal proponent of predictability as a by-product of the rule of law. Kleinfeld, supra note 8, at 42–44 (referring to Hayek's work in The Road To Serfdom (1994)). Fallon cites both Hayek and John Rawls as holding this "formalist" view of the rule of law. Fallon, supra note 8, at 16.

[91] Kleinfeld, supra note 8, at 37.

effective law enforcement bodies,[92] and democratic government.[93] According to the substantive approach, the rule of law requires the realization of certain normative values, such as substantive equality or the protection of human rights.[94] These concepts are not mutually exclusive; in fact, substantive theories encompass certain formal rule of law elements,[95] and both substantive and formal theories include institutional elements.

In theory, it does not matter whether the rule of law has one meaning or many. The trouble lies in evaluating the efficacy of rule of law reform efforts without defining what would count as successful reform,[96] for the "know it when you see it" approach is untenable.[97] Furthermore, promoting one conception of the rule of law may often conflict with the promotion of another.[98] It is, therefore, important to postulate what meaning of the rule of law is being used here to evaluate whether foreign aid undermines that concept.

This Note focuses on the formal rule of law theory,[99] because, at a minimum, the rule of law encompasses the idea of a well-ordered society; one in which there is a "government of laws, and not of men."[100] The formal rule of law is as much a political and cultural concept as it is a legal one.[101] In this sense, the rule of law is both a set of formal rules, which are public and transparent, and to which both the government and its citizens are held accountable, and a set of social norms, which reflect a cultural commitment to submit to the formal

---

[92] Id. at 47–48.

[93] See Tamanaha, supra note 11, at 91, 99–101. Tamanaha sees democracy as an extension of the "formal" rule of law concept. Democratic accountability and rule making may be part of a "thicker" formal rule of concept – that is, with more requirements, but democracy itself is best understood as an institution.

[94] See Kleinfeld, supra note 8, at 44–46.

[95] Jane Stromseth et al., Can Might Make Rights? 70–71 (2006).

[96] See Thom Ringer, Note, Development, Reform, and the Rule of Law: Some Prescriptions for a Common Understanding of the "Rule of Law" and Its Place in Development Theory and Practice, 10 Yale Hum. Rts. & Dev. L.J. 178, 182 (2007) (explaining that if rule of law reforms are to be effective, they "must establish clear institutional benchmarks," yet "conceptual anarchy about the meaning of the rule of law is likely to produce competing and conflicting benchmarks in different states and systems").

[97] Stromseth et al., supra note 17, at 56–58.

[98] E.g., Kleinfeld, supra note 8, at 59–61.

[99] For a more detailed description of a formal rule of law concept, see Robert S. Summers, A Formal Theory of the Rule of Law, 6 Ratio Juris 127 (1993).

[100] Mass. Const. Art. XXX (drafted by John Adams). The rule of law concept has a long pedigree, tracing its roots to Plato and, more recently, Adams. See DAM, supra note 3, at 13. By adopting this concept of the rule of law, it does not follow that *expressio unius est exclusio alteruis*. That is to say, by adopting the formal rule of law concept, I am not making an evaluative judgment about the superiority of formal concepts over substantive ones. The formal rule of law is a necessary, though perhaps not sufficient, condition for having a rule of law society.

[101] Kleinfeld, supra note 8, at 51; see also Rosa Ehrenreich Brooks, The New Imperialism: Violence, Norms, and the "Rule of Law," 101 Mich. L. Rev. 2275, 2285–86 (2003).

law as a means of dispute resolution or democratic decision-making process.[102] Indeed, it is the failure to recognize this cultural and political content in the formal rule of law that has undermined efforts to build the rule of law in developing countries.[103]

B. Building the Rule of Law in Developing Countries

The last century saw the emergence of new nations, as many countries in Africa and Asia broke free of their colonial masters.[104] It also saw the collapse of the Soviet Union,[105] after which countries comprising the Eastern Bloc regained their independence. These transformations provided a unique opportunity for countries to unshackle themselves from historical traditions and build new economic and political institutions.[106] Inspired by this opportunity, a development industry has emerged, drawing economists, political scientists, lawyers, and technocrats into its fold. Development efforts have focused on economic, legal, and political institutions, including democratic transition to economic development to rule of law reform. Yet, despite the plethora of experts and outpouring of development aid, results have often been disappointing.[107] One explanation of why this is the case is offered in the following sections.

The next two sections discuss rule of law reform efforts and the challenges that those efforts face. These sections conclude that rule of law reform will continue to produce lukewarm results unless political elites adopt the will to enact reforms. In other words, there must be sincere demand for rule of law reform before the development industry can assist in the supply, and currently, that demand is lacking.[108]

1. Rule of Law Reform

The problem with past rule of law reform efforts is that reformers tried to promote the formal rule of law by focusing solely on its institutions, such as legal codes, judiciaries, and police forces. This furthers the myth that

---

[102] Brooks, supra note 23, at n. 50. Friedrich Hayek is thought to espouse the rule of law theory adopted here by Brooks. See Tamanaha, supra note 11, at 58 (citing Friedrich A. Hayek, The Constitution of Liberty 206 (1960)).

[103] Brooks, supra note 23, at 2289.

[104] Carothers, supra note 5, at 16.

[105] Brooks, supra note 23, at 2278.

[106] See, e.g., Francis Fukuyama, State-Building: Governance and World Order in the 21st Century 2 (2004).

[107] Brooks, supra note 23, at 2280.

[108] Fukuyama, for example, expresses reservations about external actors' ability to create demand for institutions. Fukuyama, supra note 28, at 32–42. Carothers also recognizes that one of the primary obstacles to rule of law reform is a lack of the will to reform. Carothers, supra note 1, at 4.

technocratic expertise must rewrite legal codes to mirror the legal codes of Western societies,[109] train judiciaries to think and act like Western judiciaries, and modernize legal institutions to make them as efficient as legal institutions in Western societies.[110] Rule of law reform efforts that embody this myth assume a "build it and they will come"[111] approach, meaning if the "right" formal institutions are in place, the rule of law will simply emerge. However, good laws are meaningless if they are not followed or enforced, training the judiciary or police force is pointless if the incentives for corruption are not mitigated, and efficient legal institutions are just for show if no one trusts or uses them.[112] While the rule of law does encompass the idea of transparent and public laws, equal and predictable enforcement, and accountability, it is more than a set of formal institutions. The fallacy of this approach is that it ignores the political or cultural element of the rule of law.[113]

The cultural or political element of the rule of law is the relationship that citizens and political elites have with their legal institutions and each other; it is a cultural commitment to the law as a guide to behavior and "the project of law itself."[114] It is not enough to have a written legal code; there must also be a social commitment to abide by those laws, especially on the part of the political elite.[115] Likewise, it is not enough that the judiciary is trained to be impartial. Individual judges must have an incentive to be impartial, which would require, for example, reducing the substantial political and financial rewards, such as promotions and bribes, for partial conduct. Lastly, it is not enough for the judicial process to run efficiently; ordinary citizens must have access to legal institutions and trust that outcomes will be fair.[116] This trust is only possible if the government and political elite abide by the laws, especially when it is not in their individual interest to do so. Without any effort to address the cultural or political elements of the rule of law, reform efforts will stall.

Addressing this cultural or political element of the rule of law requires, at a minimum, fostering the will to reform on the part of the government and

---

[109] While there is room for debate as to whether Western societies, like the United States or Great Britain, exhibit the rule of law as it is defined in this Note, they are generally thought to be the closest to the norm.

[110] See generally Kleinfeld, supra note 8, at 47–54 (discussing the conventional thinking of practitioners engaged in institution modeling).

[111] Golub, supra note 4, at 106; see also Stromseth et al., supra note 17, at 73.

[112] Stromseth et al., supra note 17, at 76, 178–80.

[113] See id. at 75–77; Brooks, supra note 23, at 2284–86.

[114] Stromseth et al., supra note 17, at 75.

[115] See Carothers, supra note 1, at 7–8 (explaining that the crucial step in rule of law reform lies with government officials refraining from placing themselves above the law).

[116] See Carothers, supra note 5, at 20–21.

political elite.[117] While empowering citizens is also a crucial element of fostering a rule of law culture,[118] recalcitrant government officials and political elites can undermine such empowerment. The will to reform is more than simply a desire for reform; it requires political restraint to see such reform through.

2. Challenges to Rule of Law Reform

"[P]eople respond to incentives."[119] It takes great willpower to resist the rewards or punishments that incentives deliver.[120] Promoting the will to reform on the part of political elites, therefore, requires the difficult task of changing the incentive structures such individuals face. Some recommendations, for example, have focused on curbing corruption by increasing salaries in the police and judicial sectors, while also increasing oversight by state reformers.[121] While these recommendations are helpful, in practice the implementation of them has not solved the problem of corruption, in part because "it is extremely difficult to politely dislodge an ingrained culture of corruption at the highest levels."[122] This is true when the payoff of corruption to the individual is greater than the potential costs to that individual.[123] If the payoff of political restraint for each individual is minimal, then that individual will have little incentive to exercise restraint, especially when no one else exercises such restraint.[124] The will to reform, therefore, suffers from a collective action problem and is further hampered by the commitment problem, which is characterized by the resistance to change of those who currently benefit from the status quo.[125] The collective action and commitment problems help to explain why the will to reform often does not emerge despite the likelihood that, in the

---

[117] Id. at 22.

[118] Stromseth et al., supra note 17, at 340–46.

[119] William Easterly, The Elusive Quest for Growth: Economists' Adventures and Misadventures in the Tropics 143 (2002) (arguing that incentives matter for economic growth).

[120] See id. (equating changing incentives to "cutting away brambles" that block one's path).

[121] See, e.g., Stromseth et al., supra note 17, at 213, 240–43.

[122] Madalene O'Donnell, Corruption: A Rule of Law Agenda?, in Civil War and the Rule of Law, supra note 2, at 240.

[123] See id. at 227 ("The single greatest challenge [reformers] face is intense opposition from political and economic elites who benefit tremendously from corruption.").

[124] For a game-theoretic discussion of corruption and collective action, see Jakob Svensson, Foreign Aid and Rent-Seeking, 51 J. Int'l Econ. 437 (2000).

[125] See Karla Hoff & Joseph E. Stiglitz, Exiting a Lawless State, 118 Econ. J. 1474, 1474–77 (2008) (discussing one type of coordination and commitment problem inherent in moving to the rule of law from the lawless state). For the idea that collective action can only succeed when all participants perceive that they are better off under the new institution than under the status quo – that is, when the new institutions are self-reinforcing, see Barry R. Weingast, The Political Foundations of Democracy and the Rule of Law, 91 Amer. Pol. Sci. Rev. 245 (1997) (discussing the emergence and sustainability of political pacts).

aggregate, society will be better off if systemic corruption is curbed or government accountability is strengthened.

Formal and informal institutions determine the payoffs and, thus, the incentives that individuals face.[126] Institutions, in this context, refer to rules and norms, including political and cultural norms, that act as constraints on human interaction. Both formal institutions, like written legal codes and judiciaries, and informal institutions, like the rewards and punishments of corruption, inform individual action by structuring incentives.[127] "Institutions consist of formal rules, informal constraints (norms of behavior, conventions, and self imposed codes of conduct) and the enforcement characteristics of both."[128] True institutional change, and not window-dressing change, is difficult. "But even more fundamentally, this institutional evolution *takes time*."[129] "[T]he single most important point about institutional change, which must be grasped if we are to begin to get a handle on the subject, is that institutional change is overwhelmingly incremental."[130] Changes, particularly to informal constraints, tend to occur gradually because reformers or other entrepreneurial individuals take advantage of opportunities to introduce changes at the margin.[131] One reason that true change tends to be at the margin is that the "larger the number of rule changes, ceterus [sic] paribus[,] the greater the number of losers and hence opposition."[132] Attempts to impose new formal institutions by fiat, such as by rewriting laws or holding formal elections for democratic government, impose new costs and benefits by changing the formal rules. Those who benefit from the old institutions face new costs and lose old benefits. Thus, those who would lose from the new system are likely to mount a strong opposition to such changes.[133] Furthermore, even those who desire such reform may lack the commitment to it because of the personal rewards inherent in the old system. This argument helps to explain why there are so many nominal, rather than

---

[126] Douglass C. North, Institutional Change: A Framework of Analysis 1 (unpublished manuscript), available at http://129.3.20.41/eps/eh/papers/9412/9412001.pdf.

[127] See Douglass C. North, Institutions, Institutional Change and Economic Performance 3–6 (1990).

[128] North, supra note 48, at 2.

[129] Deborah Brautigam, Governance, Economy, and Foreign Aid, Stud. Comp. Int'l Dev., Fall 1992, at 3, 7.

[130] North, supra note 49, at 89.

[131] Id.

[132] North, supra note 48, at 6.

[133] Kurt Weyland, Toward a New Theory of Institutional Change, 60 World Pol. 281, 288 (2008) ("Since, according to cognitive psychology, losses weigh far more heavily than gains, [powerful actors] undertake disproportional efforts to defend the status quo."); see also Hoff & Stiglitz, supra note 47, at 1474 ("It is now well understood that [dysfunctional institutions] persist if there are politically powerful losers from reform and no way to promise them compensation credibly.").

true, democracies and why countries with similar legal codes seem to function so differently.[134] As Douglass North pointedly notes, "Formal rules may change over night, but informal constraints do not."[135]

Due to the difficulty of changing the institutions and thus the incentive structures that political elites face, the will to reform is likely to occur gradually, if at all, as a result of individuals seeking opportunities to benefit from change. Until more positive change can be observed at a societal level, such changes are likely to occur at the margin, although they can subtly change the costs and benefits all others face. The change itself may appear to be sudden or drastic, such as when a dictator unexpectedly agrees to subject himself to a democratic election, but it can usually be explained by marginal changes that alter the incentives of the dictator, rendering a seemingly drastic change less risky than maintaining the status quo.[136] If this analysis of informal institutional change is true, it explains why rule of law reform efforts have not been successful. Rule of law reform efforts have focused on one-size-fits-all solutions that are not sensitive to these entrepreneurial opportunities for real change and ignore the difficulty of changing informal institutions, cultural and political norms, and the incentives such institutions naturally create.

The will to reform is difficult to achieve in the best of circumstances, and very little is known about how to foster it. Working against reform efforts are elements that support the status quo and undermine the incentives for change. The next part explores how foreign aid can be one hindrance to reform.

II. The Unintended Consequences of Foreign Aid

Foreign aid, whether in the form of Official Development Assistance (ODA) or conditional loans, presents a further challenge to rule of law reform because

---

[134] See North, supra note 49, at 101; Weingast, supra note 47, at 254–55 (providing an explanation for the differences between democracy in the United States and democracy in Latin America).

[135] North, supra note 48, at 8. For the idea that formal rules are more susceptible to change than informal, cultural rules, see Gérard Roland, Understanding Institutional Change: Fast-Moving and Slow-Moving Institutions (unpublished manuscript), available at http://www.econ.berkeley.edu/~groland/pubs/gr3.pdf; Stromseth et al., supra note 17, at 313 (noting that post-intervention societies may be more susceptible to institutional change due to the breakdown of the "old" institutions).

[136] See Avner Greif & David D. Laitin, A Theory of Endogenous Institutional Change, 98 Am. Pol. Sci. Rev. 633, 639 (2004) ("[I]nstitutional change should have a quality of punctuated equilibria, where change is in actuality evolutionary but apparently abrupt, typically associated with a "crisis" revealing that the previous behavior is no longer an equilibrium.") (citing Steven Krasner, Approaches to the State: Alternative Conceptions and Historical Dynamics, 16 Comp. Pol. 223, 223–46 (1984)); Weyland, supra note 55, at 288 ("When a crisis looms, the aggregate benefits arising from a transformation can finally outweigh the disproportionate concern about losses held by the defenders of the existing system.").

of its potential to perpetuate the negative incentive structures of government officials and political elites. Naturally, these consequences are unintended. The stated intent behind foreign aid efforts is to accelerate economic development and institutional reform, including rule of law reform.[137] Foreign aid is based in part on the premise that it is difficult for developing countries to make needed reforms without the help of the developed world, particularly without their financial assistance. William Easterly has called this the "white man's burden," and it is the idea that even though much of the developed world has advanced without outside assistance, the developing world cannot do the same.[138] With the white man's burden deeply ingrained in the minds of Western aid agencies, people have only recently begun to question this assumption and consider whether they are doing more harm than good.[139]

A survey of recent economic literature, primarily focused on the effects of foreign aid on economic development, reveals that foreign aid can undermine rule of law reform by reducing the costs of maintaining the status quo. In other words, foreign aid may hinder the emergence of a cultural or political commitment to the rule of law, particularly on the part of the political elite. If the cultural or political elements of the rule of law require political accountability to the rule of law and a commitment to maintaining a well-ordered society, then foreign aid can undermine that by thwarting the emergence of democracy and democratic accountability,[140] decreasing the quality of governance,[141]

---

[137] See, e.g., Margareta Sollenberg, Aid Dependence and Armed Conflict: A Re- Examination of the Evidence 2 (June 11, 2009) (unpublished manuscript), available at http://www.prio.no/upload/cscw/wg3/GROW%20net%20Workshop/Sollenberg%20Aid&Conflict%20090604%20 (Oslo).pdf ("Although aid is meant to be solely beneficial for the recipient country, the aid community as well as the research community has long been aware of the possibility that aid may sometimes do harm, despite the donors' good intentions.").

[138] William Easterly, The White Man's Burden: Why the West's Efforts to Aid the Rest Have Done So Much Ill and So Little Good 23–26 (2006). "The White Man's Burden emerged from the West's self-pleasing fantasy that 'we' were the chosen ones to save the Rest. The White Man offered himself the starring role in an ancien régime version of Harry Potter." Id. at 23.

[139] The white man's burden is obviously a caricature to some extent, though it is an apt description of some of the imperialist elements found in the development literature. Of course, it may also be the case that the developed world simply believes they can accelerate the development of the developing world through development assistance. Still, even this premise is challenged by the failure of development in many countries that have been the primary focus of development assistance.

[140] See, e.g., Stephen Knack, Does Foreign Aid Promote Democracy?, 48 Int'l Stud. Q. 251–66 (2004) (arguing there is no evidence to suggest foreign aid, in the aggregate, successfully promotes democracy).

[141] E.g., Simeon Djankov et al., The Curse of Aid, 13 J. Econ. Growth 169 (2008); Brautigam, supra note 51, at 21 (arguing that "participatory dialogue between governments and their private sector, rather than between governments and donors" is more likely to yield effective property rights and accountability); Stephen Knack, Aid Dependence and the Quality of Governance:

and encouraging violent conflict or civil war.[142] Each of these effects is a road-block to the will to reform. The following sections discuss the impact of for-eign aid on rule of law reform, focusing, in particular, on impediments like corruption, poor governance, and the lack of democratic accountability that foreign aid can create.

A. Incentives for Rent Seeking and Corruption

The role of governance in reform efforts cannot be overemphasized. "Good governance – in the form of institutions that establish a predictable, impartial, and consistently enforced set of rules ... – is crucial for sustained and rapid growth in per capita incomes of poor countries."[143] Not only is good gover-nance, as defined above, good for economic growth, but it is also synonymous with certain aspects of the formal rule of law theory.[144] While ODA, in theory, could promote good governance and the rule of law by increasing salaries and reducing corruption or by training the police and the judiciary, the unintended consequences of aid may overshadow any positive returns in these areas.[145]

Instead of promoting good governance, foreign aid can skew the incentives of governments and political elites.[146] As one economic study reveals: "Analyses

Cross-Country Empirical Tests, 68 S. Econ. J. 310, 310 (2001) (discussing evidence that "higher aid levels erode the quality of governance, as measured by indices of bureaucratic quality, corruption, and the rule of law"); Raghuram Rajan & Arvind Subramanian, Does Aid Affect Governance?, 97 Am. Econ. Rev. 322, 322 (2007) (arguing that "countries that get more aid are likely to be the ones where [the quality of governance] is most adversely affected"); Svensson, supra note 46, at 437 (finding "no evidence that ... donors systematically allocate aid to coun-tries with less corruption"). But see José Tavares, Does Foreign Aid Corrupt?, 79 Econ. Letters 99 (2003) (producing a study that shows that aid decreases corruption).

[142] See, e.g., Manuel Oechslin, Foreign Aid, Political Instability, and Economic Growth 1 (U. Zurich Inst. for Empirical Research Econ., Working Paper No. 310, 2006), available at https://editorialexpress.com/cgi-bin/conference/download.cgi?db_name=res2007&paper_id=489 (arguing that "more money in the hands of the regime fuels conflict over the distribu-tion of funds"); Sollenberg, supra note 59, at 3 (finding that "aid dependence does increase the probability of armed conflict"). But see Paul Collier & Anke Hoeffler, Aid, Policy and Peace: Reducing the Risks of Civil Conflict, 13 Def.& Peace Econ. 435, 435 (2002) (finding "that aid and policy do not have direct effects upon conflict risk"); Joppe de Ree & Eleonora Nillesen, Aiding Violence or Peace? The Impact of Foreign Aid on the Risk of Civil Conflict in Sub-Saharan Africa, 88 J. Dev. Econ. 301, 301 (2009) (finding that "increasing aid flows tends to decrease civil conflict duration"). The methodology of the Collier and Hoeffler article should be questioned, however, since it measured the effect of economic policy and foreign aid on the risk of conflict. It is unclear then what effect aid alone has on such risk. Still, because the relationship between aid and conflict is ambiguous, it is omitted from discussion here.

[143] Knack, supra note 63, at 311.

[144] See supra notes 12–13, 21–25 and accompanying text.

[145] For a similar argument about foreign aid and democratization, see Knack, supra note 62, at 251.

[146] For an argument linking foreign aid to the incentives of government officials, and in particu-lar arguing that foreign aid, in the form of unconditional monetary transfers, decreases the

of cross-country data provide evidence that higher aid levels erode the quality of governance, as measured by indices of bureaucratic quality, corruption, and the rule of law."[147] One reason for this is that foreign aid can be seen as a large prize to be won.[148] Whoever controls the government also controls the money. Thus, a moral hazard problem results in that the people who end up in power tend not to be the same people who have sincere reform efforts in mind.[149] As another study points out, "[h]igh levels of aid in countries where the political leadership does not have reform on the agenda are likely to reduce the incentive to cooperate in the sacrifices necessary for reform to occur."[150] Rule of law reform, which seeks to build a society in which government officials and political elites abide by laws, runs counter to the power-as-prize mentality because reform requires collective sacrifice on the part of political elites, who must eschew personal gain for the public good.[151] The collective sacrifice requirement suffers from a quintessential prisoner's dilemma problem in that it is always in the individual's self-interest to promote personal gain and thus not make sacrifices, regardless of whether anyone else does.[152] The result is the equilibrium position in which few political elites or government officials are prepared to make the sacrifices necessary for reform.[153]

Foreign aid also represents a potential source of rents, which is a way for the political elite to maintain power.[154] It is often easier to remain in power

incentives to institute "good policies," see Alberto Dalmazzo & Guido de Blasio, Resources and Incentives to Reform, 50 Imf Staff Papers 250 (2003).

[147] Knack, supra note 63, at 310.

[148] See Alberto Alesina & Beatrice Weder, Do Corrupt Governments Receive Less Foreign Aid? 3 (Nat'l Bureau of Econ. Research, Working Paper No. 7108, 1999) (citing Philip Lane & Aaron Tornell, The Voracity Effect, 89 Am. Econ. Rev. 22 (1999)).

[149] For example, Stephen Knack notes that "[a]id may also encourage coup attempts and political instability, by making control of the government and aid receipts a more valuable prize, reducing the prospects for democratic governance. It is widely acknowledged that violent competition for control over large-scale food aid contributed to the breakdown of government in Somalia." Knack, supra note 62, at 253 (finding overall that aid has no positive or negative effect on democracy in recipient governments).

[150] Deborah A. Brautigam & Stephen Knack, Foreign Aid, Institutions, and Governance in Sub-Saharan Africa, 52 Econ. Dev.& Cultural Change 255, 263 (2004).

[151] Id. at 256.

[152] For an overview of the prisoner's dilemma problem, see Steven Kuhn, Prisoner's Dilemma, in The Stanford Encyclopedia of Philosophy (Edward N. Zalta ed., 2009), available at http://plato.stanford.edu/archives/spr2009/entries/prisoner-dilemma/.

[153] One study by George Economides, Sarantis Kalyvitis, and Apostolis Philippopoulos finds that "the deleterious effect of aid upon incentives ... is significant only in recipient countries with relatively large public sectors. This confirms the popular belief that rent seeking and corruption take place mainly through government activities ...." Does Foreign Aid Distort Incentives and Hurt Growth? Theory and Evidence from 75 Aid-Recipient Countries, 134 Pub. Choice 463, 464 (2008). In those countries with large public sectors, "foreign aid makes ... a cooperative solution [i.e., one without rent seeking] more difficult to sustain." Id. at 484.

[154] Knack, supra note 63, at 313.

by patronage rather than by reform. "Political elites have little incentive to change a situation in which large amounts of aid provide exceptional resources for patronage and many fringe benefits (vehicles, study tours, salary increments, etc.) that would not otherwise be available to officials in low-income countries."[155] Reform is often painful and unpopular with those who benefit from the status quo. The incentive for reform is lessened when power can be retained by force or patronage without having to make unpopular reforms. Even for reform-minded elites, the incentive to forestall reform is great; "it is in the interests of all actors today to continue the benefits they get from ... receiving aid, even though this aid will create problems for future governments."[156] Given that most government officials and political elites have short time horizons,[157] it is easier to leave real reform for the next government and to take advantage of the present, personal gains from aid as they come.[158]

Lastly, foreign aid increases the opportunity for corruption, meaning "the illegal use of public office for private gain."[159] Corruption may be blatant, like the diversion of foreign aid to private Swiss bank accounts,[160] but corruption also occurs when aid money is used to provide government positions for cronies or political allies or fund projects supported by the political elites.[161] Despite arguments that aid can reduce corruption by raising the salaries of government officials, an empirical study reveals that countries that receive more aid tend to have higher corruption.[162] While it may be difficult to make a conclusive causal argument that aid causes corruption, a potential endogeneity problem is minimized because there is little risk that increased corruption causes increased aid flows.[163]

Again, there is a collective action problem involved with reducing corruption. Considering the incentives of political elites to eschew corruption through a prisoner's dilemma choice set, each individual maximizes his self-interest by engaging in corrupt behavior in both scenarios: (1) if everyone else

[155] Brautigam & Knack, supra note 72, at 263.

[156] Id. at 265.

[157] Knack, supra note 63, at 311. For an argument that foreign aid may decrease the time horizon of governments by increasing potential for conflict over the distribution of funds, see Oechslin, supra note 64.

[158] For the proposition that aid reduces the cost of "doing nothing – that is, avoiding reform," see Dani Rodrik, Understanding Economic Policy Reform, 34 J. Econ. Lit. 9, 30–31 (1996).

[159] Brautigam, supra note 51, at 13 (citing Robin Theobald, Corruption, Development and Underdevelopment (1990)).

[160] See Todd Moss & Arvind Subramanian, After the Big Push? Fiscal and Institutional Implications of Large Aid Increases 7 (Ctr. for Global Dev., Working Paper No. 71, 2005).

[161] Knack, supra note 63, at 313.

[162] Alesina & Weder, supra note 70, at 20.

[163] Id. at 6–7.

resists corrupt behavior, or (2) if everyone else engages in corrupt behavior. The decision set is identical for each actor. Thus, the equilibrium behavior is corruption, rather than restraint.[164]

Given the incentives governments face, the ineffectiveness of aid to improve governance should not be surprising. One of the problems with foreign aid or rule of law aid is that once the laws are rewritten and the judiciary is trained, reformers in aid agencies do not promote sustainable reform efforts.[165] If the aid continues despite the lack of real reform, recipient governments will do just enough to guarantee a continued flow of revenue. Real reform, however, can only go so far with a carrot-and-stick enforcement policy. Real reform also requires a commitment to reform even when no one is watching. It has been noted that "[t]he single greatest challenge [reformers] face is intense opposition from political and economic elites who benefit tremendously from corruption."[166] Rule of law reformers still do not know how to build the normative commitment to rule of law reform. Perhaps, there is no easy way to do so. In the meantime, the commitment is undermined by the subsidization of the status quo provided by foreign aid.

B. Thwarting the Emergence of Democratic Governance

Perhaps the most notable and widely discussed consequence of foreign aid stems from its effect on democracy and democratic accountability. Rentier state theory, originally modeled to explain why oil-rich Middle Eastern states tend to be authoritarian, argues that countries that rely predominantly on

---

[164] In the traditional prisoner's dilemma scenario, there are two suspects who each face the choice of testifying against the other or remaining silent. If both suspects remain silent, there is not enough evidence to charge them with the serious offense and they will each get six months in prison. However, if one testifies and the other remains silent, the one that testifies will go free, while the other will be sentenced to ten years in prison. If both suspects testify against the other, they will both get five years. Because each suspect risks going to prison for ten years if he stays silent, each suspect will testify against the other. As a result, each will get a five-year sentence. Both would be better off if they can agree to keep silent, but they cannot coordinate their actions. The collective action problem for corruption is similar in that without a disincentive to engage in corruption, each political elite would maximize his self-interest by defecting, and taking bribes, than from agreeing to eschew corruption, even if all of the other political elites agree to eschew corruption. Because each political elite gains from defecting on any agreement, the equilibrium is corruption. For an example of this type of game-theoretic response to foreign aid, see Svensson, supra note 46. Svensson concludes that this result is more prominent in societies that are politically or culturally divided. Id. at 455.

[165] The stories of aid projects rendered useless without continued monitoring on the part of the aid agencies are countless. See, e.g., Michael Maren, The Road to Hell: The Ravaging Effects of Foreign Aid and International Charity (1997). Aid agencies need to monitor these projects because none of the agencies' efforts reach the human element or the will to reform. With the will to reform, no oversight would be required.

[166] O'Donnell, supra note 44, at 227.

external rents, like oil profits or foreign aid, are less accountable to civil society than are governments that must rely on tax revenue.[167] The argument against foreign aid is that by producing external rents, the state can function without the need to tax its citizens.[168] As the flip side of the Revolutionary War slogan, "no taxation without representation," the idea of "no representation without taxation" might be equally compelling. While most recipient governments do tax their citizens to some extent, tax collection efforts are often grossly inefficient. Foreign aid reduces the pressure to introduce tax reform. Indeed, "[s]eventy-one percent of the African countries receiving more than 10% of GDP in aid in 1995 were also in the group of countries judged in an IMF study to have lower than expected tax effort."[169]

Historians and political scientists have argued that the demand for representation in government arose in response to the sovereign's attempts to raise taxes.[170] Essentially, the sovereign's need for revenue forced it into the bargaining process with citizens.[171] Without the pressure of raising revenue, the bargaining position of citizens is diminished.

> The "taxation produces representation" claim is most commonly invoked today by Middle East specialists who reason that the ability of the region's autocrats to finance themselves with non-tax revenues – primarily through oil revenues – has enabled them to avoid pressures to democratize.... [T]he discovery of oil allowed the governments of Kuwait and Qatar to stop taxing their merchant classes; relieved of taxes, the merchants relinquished their historically-established right to participate in policy making. Similarly,... a drop in foreign aid and remittances in the 1980s forced the Jordanian government to depend more heavily on taxes: from 1987 to 1992, the ratio of taxes to gross domestic product (GDP) rose from 0.13 to 0.24. Rising taxes and falling subsidies led to riots in April 1989, a revision in the election laws, and following a November 1989 vote, a more open, representative and influential parliament.[172]

The idea is that, like citizens of oil-rich countries, citizens of countries in which foreign aid makes up a significant portion of revenue will also have less bargaining power vis-à-vis the state. Less bargaining power translates into

---

[167] Michael Lewin Ross, Does Oil Hinder Democracy? 53 World Pol. 325, 329–32 (2001).

[168] See Djankov et al., supra note 63, at 3.

[169] Brautigam & Knack, supra note 72, at 264.

[170] Ross, supra note 89, at 332–33. For an argument that the sources of state revenue may have a major impact on governance in developing countries, see Mick Moore, Revenues, State Formation, and the Quality of Governance in Developing Countries, 25 Int'l Pol. Sci. Rev. 297 (2004).

[171] See Michael L. Ross, Does Taxation Lead to Representation?, 34 Brit. J. Pol. Sci. 229, 230–32 (2004).

[172] Id. at 232–33.

fewer mechanisms to hold the government accountable and less democratic representation.[173]

So, the question becomes: do international lending agents keep governments accountable? In particular, do international lending agents keep governments accountable to rule of law reform?

The simple answer to this question is no, but the reasons for this are more complex than the answer. Understanding why lending agents fail to keep governments accountable to the rule of law requires understanding the multidimensional, principal-agent relationship lurking behind this interaction. In the idealized citizen-state relationship, the citizens are the principals. They are the owners of the valuable resources and revenues that are transferred to the agent, namely the state, through taxation. In the case of foreign aid, instead of the citizens, the principals are the international lenders, while the agent is the recipient state. On this one dimension, then, the recipient state is accountable to the aid agencies. The story is more complicated, however, because the aid agencies themselves are agents for yet other principals, namely the citizens in the donor countries whose tax dollars fund the agencies.[174] Moreover, the aid agencies rely on the presumption that the recipient governments are agents of their citizens, as principals. Bertin Martens refers to this multidimensional principal- agent relationship as a "broken feedback loop" because there are no smooth channels in this relationship for proper feedback.[175]

The lack of feedback between the recipient government and its citizens has already been discussed, but what about the feedback between the recipient government and aid agencies? If citizens cannot induce the government or political elites to work toward rule of law reforms, can aid agencies? The problem here is that aid agencies have an incentive to continue producing output (i.e., increase grants and loans), regardless of whether the recipient governments reform.[176] The reason is that the principals to the aid agency–donor relationship are the citizens in donor countries, and these citizens have almost no ability to monitor the effect of aid on rule of law reform, particularly on the

---

[173] See generally id. 233–34.

[174] Easterly, supra note 60, at 169.

[175] See generally Bertin Martens Et Al., The Institutional Economics of Foreign Aid, at viii-9 (2002). See also William Easterly, Was Development Assistance a Mistake? 97 Am. Econ. Rev. 328, 330 (2007) ("Unlike the provision of domestic public goods in democracies, the recipient of aid-financed public services has no ability to register dissatisfaction through voting. With little or no feedback from the poor, there is little information as to which aid programs are working.").

[176] See generally Jakob Svensson, Why Conditional Aid Does Not Work and What Can Be Done About It?, 70 J. Dev. Econ. 381, 398 (2003) ("[T]here is a strong bias towards 'always' disbursing aid to the ex ante designated recipient, irrespective of that recipient's performance ....").

will to reform.[177] As a result, the success of the aid agencies is measured by the volume of input – money given, in other words – as opposed to output or real reform.[178] To highlight this fact, instead of complaining about the trillions of dollars of aid that has been given without any remarkable change in the rule of law or economic well-being in the recipient countries, the rhetoric in donor countries is that more aid is needed. Several influential celebrities, most notably Bono,[179] as well as prominent academics, such as Columbia University professor Jeffrey Sachs,[180] believe that doubling aid to poor countries will somehow produce a different result than the first few trillion.[181] Citizens in the donor countries "love the Big Plans, the promises of easy solutions, the utopian dreams, [and] the side benefits for rich-country political or economic interests, all of which hands the aid agency impossible tasks."[182] More importantly, they are more than willing to take on the white man's burden without demanding observable results. Thus, the aid agencies lack the incentives to demand those results from recipient countries, especially since, as this Note has argued, real results are difficult to achieve.

The other problem with aid agencies' incentives is that their continued existence depends on the premise that foreign aid can produce reform. If foreign aid is anathema to reform, the aid agency has no purpose and will not continue to be funded. As a result, agencies have an incentive not to give up on the hope that aid can bring reform and growth. This hope has spurred new trends and theories on how to make aid work for developing countries, including directing aid toward countries with better institutions and using economic sanctions to threaten governments and political elites into reform. While these efforts almost certainly result in some improvements, the unintended negative effects of aid overshadow those improvements, leaving many countries worse off after fifty years of development aid than they were before.[183] This unfortunate conclusion is especially prominent on the African continent.

---

[177] Easterly, supra note 60, at 170–71.

[178] Id. at 181–83.

[179] Bono has been an influential part of the Live 8 concert series. The message of the Live 8 movement is to "make poverty history." As part of the program, 30 million people provided their names to a list presented to then–Prime Minister Tony Blair in order to influence Great Britain's foreign aid efforts in Africa. See http://www.live8live.com.

[180] See Jeffrey Sachs, The End of Poverty: Economic Possibilities for Our Time (2005) (Bono wrote the foreword for this book and has traveled extensively with Professor Sachs throughout Africa).

[181] Easterly, supra note 60, at 170.

[182] Id. at 169.

[183] Thomas W. Dichter, Despite Good Intentions: Why Development Assistance to the Third World Has Failed 2 (2003).

Conclusion

It is the presumption of the development industry that foreign aid can promote rule of law reform by providing the resources necessary to rewrite formal legal codes, train judiciaries and police forces, and introduce technology that may help legal institutions function more efficiently. This Note has highlighted both theoretical and empirical evidence as to why foreign aid has failed to lead to rule of law reform in many countries. The fundamental problem the development industry overlooks is the lack of incentives for developing countries' government officials and political elites to aid in the reformation of the rule of law. An important aspect that is also often overlooked is that true rule of law reform will not be sustainable without a social commitment to abide by the rule of law, especially on the part of government officials and the political elite. The development industry has thus far failed to develop the underlying institutions that create this social commitment.

Contrary to what the development industry intends to achieve by offering foreign aid, aid often has the unintended consequence of subsidizing present institutions, thereby postponing the need to make necessary reforms. An influx of aid money provides few incentives for political elites to commit themselves to the sacrifices required for real reform and democratic accountability, and it enables the elite to remain in power without such reform.

While this Note has presented a pessimistic view of foreign aid and its ability to accelerate rule of law reform in developing countries, its arguments are limited to the way in which foreign aid is currently delivered. The challenges, however, are great. Previous attempts to attach conditions for reform on development assistance have failed to engender true reform, precisely because the parties on both sides – government officials, political elites, and the aid agents themselves – face incentives contrary to the end goal. The aid agents face incentives to continue giving aid even when real reform is not forthcoming, and the political elites in the recipient countries are incentivized to stifle change while continuing to receive aid revenue. If aid is to provide the means for true reform, the development industry must discover some way to overcome these adverse incentives.

6   Re-racializing the World

The sociologist Howie Winant talks about a "re-racializing" of the world in which he refers to the enduring relevance of race in understanding the global forces of the twenty-first century (Winant 2004:131). Against those who claim that race is no longer a central concern, or is less salient today than it has been in the past, Winant asserts that race remains an essential feature in understanding contemporary issues that are intrinsically global by nature (Winant 2004). In other words, thinking about race in global terms, and thinking about relations between old and new forms of racism, is central to any analysis of contemporary global problems that invariably involve racialized differences in terms of people's access to resources and opportunities. The feminist scholar and political theorist Denise Ferreira da Silva takes this line of thought further, arguing that racialized difference has in fact created the global space in which unequal power across countries and regions is formalized and ethically reinforced (da Silva 2007). The idea of race, Silva continues, lies at the heart of modern liberal thought and Enlightenment values that, over the past 400 years, have been spread worldwide through forces of colonialism and imperialism. In short, the racial is the "signifier of globality," and the contemporary reshaping of the "analytics of raciality is placing large regions of the social and global space – the ones inhabited by the others of Europe – altogether outside the domain of the operation of the law" (da Silva 2007:266–267).

Thinking about the re-racializing of the world means acknowledging the politics of race that both enables and imbues our contemporary global world. It means acknowledging that racism is produced at and occurs within all social levels and spatial scales both within and beyond nation-states. Notes Winant, "The idea that racial formation occurs on a global scale is certainly not new, but it is unusual to think of global racial patterns as being shaped 'from below.' As with other accounts of the global … the tendency is to see things from the standpoint of domination, from the 'top down'" (Winant 2004:xvii–xviii).

314

Moreover, understanding how the world is becoming re-racialized means problematizing conventional ways of thinking about racism and racial identity. This involves moving away from what W.E.B. Du Bois called the "double consciousness" of racial identity formation and accommodating a "multiple consciousness" more fitting for the contemporary multicultural global age (Winant 2004:xviii). Above all, argues Winant, we have to dispel the idea that we live in a post-racial era and come to terms with the reality that we live in a "modern world racial system." This system has a long historical legacy built upon colonial oppression and imperial capitalism.[1] Today, it has been reshaped and reframed in the face of neoliberal policies of resource extraction, demands for cheap labor, and growing inabilities to produce enough food and find enough clean water to adequately supply the world's populations. We are now living in a system of "global apartheid" as evidenced by the gross inequities of resources and power between rich and poor nations (Sen 2002b). Writes Winant:

> the North depends to an ever greater extent on its ability to exploit the South: to draw from it the cheap labor and resources it needs, to export its pollution there, and to thwart any efforts to develop in a sovereign and democratic fashion, outside the discipline of the IMF, the WTO, and the other instruments of global economic power (Winant 2004:214).

Building upon Winant's insights, it is possible to argue that Du Bois's "color line" has been re-written on a global scale as evidenced in the divide between the WTO and the Group of 77.[2]

This chapter takes as its premise the re-racializing of the contemporary global world and the enduring inequities of power and resources across nations and regions and continents that such a re-racializing engenders (Thomas 2001). I will discuss how the idea of race has been examined in the context of law and society scholarship and suggest it may need to expand its horizons to fully embrace a global sociolegal perspective. I then turn to pressing global issues that are slowly gaining legal scholarly attention but are not typically associated with sociolegal analyses of race and racism. These global issues are that of religious conflict, environmental degradation and climate change, and associated risks to vulnerable communities in terms of public health that

---

[1]   W.E.B. Du Bois was one of the first scholars to note a global system of oppression that linked domestic racism with global racism and histories of colonialism in Africa, Caribbean, and Central and South America in his booklet titled *Africa – Its Place in Modern History* (1930).

[2]   The Group of 77 at the United Nations consisted of 77 members at its establishment in 1964 but now includes 132 members. The members are developing nations, and the organization is designed to promote their common economic and political interests.

include pandemics such as tuberculosis, cholera, HIV/AIDS and H1n1. In selecting these three interrelated issues I do not want to suggest that these are the only urgent concerns emerging in the twenty-first century. But I do argue that sociolegal scholars *should* be paying attention to these three areas that undoubtedly will become of mounting concern in coming years, particularly for people living in the poor regions of the world. Importantly, the very impossibility of all three issues to be contained, constrained, and managed within national jurisdictions and geopolitical borders underscores the need to adopt a global sociolegal perspective. Together these issues urge us to seriously engage with the aspirations of global governance as one strategy to help reduce their negative impact upon everyone, no matter where one lives in the world.

Global religious conflict, global environmental degradation and climate change, and the inequities of public health are presented here as provocative domains that contain overlooked and underexplored racialized facets that sociolegal scholars of race have to date largely ignored. My hope is to show that these areas, and in fact any analysis of contemporary global problems, contain elements that impinge upon sociolegal constructions of race and racial inequality. This is the case irrespective of whether analysis is conducted through the lens of political economy, cultural studies, comparative literature, criminology, or international law. My argument is that one does not have to think of oneself as a scholar of globalization to appreciate that understanding race and practices of racism, even at the micro level, are historically and contemporaneously constituted through the global. It is only by asking new kinds of questions and posing new sets of legal and political relations across time and space that these often unseen processes of racialization may become more evident. In turn, this kind of intellectual exploration will hopefully underscore that sociolegal analyses of race are even more timely and necessary to understanding the geopolitical realities of the twenty-first century.

RACE IN GLOBAL SOCIOLEGAL PERSPECTIVE

In 2009 Laura Gómez was elected president of the U.S. Law and Society Association – the first woman of color to take up this prestigious position. In her presidential address, Gómez noted that great strides had been made over the past twenty years to make the study of race more central in law and society scholarship. Sociolegal scholars have helped nurture an understanding that race is socially and politically constructed, that racial identity and classifications of race are historically informed, fluid, and dynamic, and that racialized ideologies are deeply embedded within the foundational myths and daily contemporary practices of Euro-American law (see Gómez 2004, 2012). However,

Gómez went on to argue, despite these advances, "we still have a long way to go." In a compelling and provocative address, Gómez asserted "that we need to do much more to incorporate race and racism into the core of what we think and write about as law and society scholars" (Gómez 2012: 225; see also Obasogie 2007). As suggested by Gómez, this would involve studying race as process rather than outcome; comparatively analyzing race and racism across social groups, within racialized groups, and between national legal systems; and finally operationalizing the concept of race in more nuanced ways.

I very much agree with Gómez's argument. But in adopting a global sociolegal perspective, I have two comments that suggest that Gómez's urging for greater comparative work may not go far enough. The first comment has to do with constructions of racism. It is one step to acknowledge – as Gómez does – that racism is a global phenomenon, and hence comparative understandings of racism as it occurs elsewhere may offer new insights into one's own domestic legal arena. However, I would push Gómez to take an additional step. I suggest that any study of how race and racism are constructed within any one national legal system must *always* be understood as the product of transnational and global processes that shape and frame the emergence of specific legal cultures and racial politics in the first place. The constructed nature of race as it intersects with law is aligned to the constructed nature of nation-states – all of which are global, national, and local simultaneously. In other words, nation-states, and their legally racialized underpinnings, are not discrete geopolitical islands but historically and constitutively embedded within international and transnational processes (see, for example, Dudziak 2004). Legal constructions of race, and the shifting practices of domestic racism, have always overflowed the boundaries of national jurisdictions and been constitutively shaped by external economic, cultural, and political forces.

My second comment follows from my first. Gómez's call for sociolegal scholars to do more traditional comparative work by comparing how racism operates in different national systems unnecessarily binds scholarship to a nation-state context. This nationalist comparative work is certainly important (i.e., Telles 2002). But also important, yet often overlooked, is analysis that examines constructions of racial difference as they occur outside formal legal forums bound by state law. Such analysis situates national racial politics in a global context that, as W.E.B. Du Bois noted over eighty years ago, is laced with histories of imperialism, colonialism, and exploitation (Du Bois 1930; see also James 1938). Fortunately, contemporary scholars of race such as Paul Gilroy (1993), Edward Park and John Park (2005), Renisa Mawani (2009), Sherene Razack (2002), Donaldo Macedo and Panayota Gounari (2005), Marilyn Lake and Henry Reynolds (2008), David Theo Goldberg (2008), and Denise Ferreira da

Silva (2007) highlight in different ways the historical and global geopolitical dimensions of racialization as they play out over time in formal and informal legal settings of local, national, regional, and intercontinental scale. It is from scholars such as these, as well as the more general trend toward transnational studies (Khagram and Levitt 2008) and global history (Tyrrell 2007; Crossley 2008) that sociolegal scholars seeking to do comparative research on race should perhaps take a cue.[3] Adopting global perspectives on race does not mean that domestic racial politics should in any way be marginalized or deemed unimportant. Rather, a global perspective seeks to underscore that whether living in the United States or any other country in the world, issues of race and racism within state and sub-state systems cannot be disconnected from their wider historical formation and a range of contemporary global challenges and problems. In short, it means recognizing that domestic racial politics are constitutively linked to global racial politics and vice versa.

As discussed, in the United States, sociolegal scholarship of race and critical race theory have emerged over the past twenty years to make significant contributions to analyzing how law and other state institutions are deeply implicated in producing and maintaining racial inequalities (Crenshaw et al. 1995; Delgado 1995 ; Brown 2003; Gómez 2004, 2010). Yet despite a new generation of law and society scholars of race, and a new focus on the ways in which micro social relations substantiate and reinforce racial differences in the United States (i.e., Obasogie 2010) sociolegal scholarship on race remains surprisingly parochial (i.e., Haney-Lopez 2007).

Against this blinkered resistance to situating racial politics at state, regional, and local levels in wider global contexts, there emerges a need to decenter the nation-state in an effort to reveal the racial dimensions of transnational interconnections between peoples, places, and economies. In any discussion of law and racism, it is important to foreground capitalism and its drive for material resources, cheap labor, and the constant need to open new consumer markets. Capitalism did not produce racism in any causal sense because racist practices existed long before the modern capitalist system was first institutionalized in England under a Protestant regime in the sixteenth and seventeenth centuries. That being said, modern, full-scale, capitalist enterprise has been very much involved in exploiting cheap labor and, in turn, creating labor hierarchies. And labor hierarchies have pivoted primarily on racial differences that determine an individual's capacity to garner higher or lower wages. From the early colonial

---

[3] A global approach to history "often requires us to move beyond a national framework of analysis, to explore connections between people, societies and events usually thought of as distinct and separate"(Curthoys and Lake 2005:6–10; see also Mazlish and Buultjens 1993; Reichard and Dickson 2008).

era on, labor has been a site of explicit and dynamic racialization (Ignatiev 1995; Darian-Smith 2010a). It is in this context that Howie Winant calls the Atlantic slave trade "the first truly multinational capitalist enterprise" (Winant 2004:87).

The racialization of labor continues today in the growing global gap between rich and poor. As has been remarked upon by many scholars and economists, the exploitation of the many by the few is today's economic reality (Carbado 2002; Stiglitz 2012). Over the past forty years the world has become increasingly dominated by neoliberal logics that promote and prioritize the interests of corporations over the interests of people. In economic terms, this new form of globalized exploitation is what is known as a post-Fordist process, whereby financial and political power settles in a core group of entrepreneurs and multinational corporations who outsource work and services to temporary workers in underdeveloped and developing nations. This outsourcing is most profitable when the labor pools are comprised of poor and desperate workers willing to accept terrible labor conditions, job insecurity, and minimal wages. As a result, the gap between the wealthy global North and the impoverished global South has not been closed – nor has it come even close to it – since the decolonization movements in the middle of last century. In fact, notes sociologist Bill Robinson, "Broad swaths of humanity have experienced absolute downward mobility in recent decades. Even the IMF was forced to admit in a 2000 report that 'in recent decades, nearly one-fifth of the world's population has regressed. This is arguably one of the greatest economic failures of the 20th century'" (Robinson 2011). Of significance is that much of the world's population that has regressed live in the global South, in countries racially and ethnically different from Europeans. It is thus impossible to talk about global interactions and interconnections, which have been enabled by new forms of technology, communication, international legal instruments, and economic agencies such as the World Bank and the IMF, without also speaking of the racial implications behind today's global processes (see Figure 6).

The contemporary re-racialization of the world is driven by a political economy of imperialism and racial discrimination that reinforces and perpetuates racial divides between the global North and South, but also within nations and amongst local communities (Sen 2002b). The logics of neoliberalism that the global North has applied to the global South for decades have also been insidiously working within advanced industrialized states and their domestic policies. This can be seen in the United States (and to a lesser degree in Britain, Australia, and elsewhere) in practices of city segregation (Nightingale 2012), mass incarceration (Lynch 2009; Alexander 2010), as well as in the persistent and aggressive dismantling of trade unions, workers' job security, labor conditions, social security benefits, public education, and so

Figure 6. World Bank Protester, Jakarta, Indonesia. Photograph taken by Jonathan McIntosh. 2004.

on. As a result, social contracts between governments and their citizens have been broken, and public service jobs, public health, public education, public transport, public security, public environments, and people's futures have all been compromised, perhaps even sacrificed. Unfortunately, but not surprisingly, racial, ethnic and gender minorities within Western nations have been disproportionately affected by these dismantling processes of neoliberal policy (see Pateman and Mills 2007; Tavernise 2011).

In sum, today what we are witnessing in the re-racialization of the contemporary world is a global political economy that still depends on maintaining racial hierarchies within and between the global North and South. According to the international legal theorist B.S. Chimni, "The colonial period saw the complete and open negation of the autonomy of the colonized countries. In the era of globalization, the reality of dominance is best conceptualized as a more stealthy, complex and cumulative process " (Chimni 2006:26; see also Bhattacharyya et al. 2001). Euro-American law and international legal agencies – perhaps unintentionally but nonetheless effectively – play a significant role in sustaining these enduring relations of oppression. This involvement is primarily practiced through denying adequate legal access to marginalized communities and in turn sustaining and enforcing racial biases in favor of the capitalist enterprise. However, as the Occupy Wall Street and related protests around the world in 2011 indicate, many people living in advanced industrialized nations can no longer remain indifferent and ignore that systemic poverty is being institutionalized not just in the global South but in all countries, regions, and cities, including their own (see Kaldor 2006; Pogge 2008). These activist movements punctuate the growing global outrage against the neoliberal exploitative economic reality and its social, political, and racial consequences.

Taking seriously the idea of the world's re-racialization means moving beyond the pretense that we live in a post-race and color-blind era where the idea of "race" no longer has relevance (Getches 2001; Goldberg 2008; Alexander 2010; Lentin 2011). It means fighting against what Winant calls "a new form of racial hegemony."[4] For sociolegal scholars of race, it highlights the limits of state-centered approaches to racialized issues such as incarceration, immigration, criminalization, drugs, urban violence, voting rights, labor discrimination, and the rolling back of political and civil rights (i.e., Frymer 2005; Lynch 2009; Hagan 2010; Beckett and Herbert 2011; Provine 2011). These issues are, of course, immensely important and precisely because of this import should be situated within a global sociolegal framing. In other words, one can and should study localized processes that inform constructions of racialization, whilst at the same time being attentive to how a global perspective may proffer new ways of thinking about how and why localized processes play out in the different and dynamic ways that they do. In addition, sociolegal scholarship on race should expand its horizons and explore the racial dimensions of a range of global issues (i.e., religious conflict, environmental degradation, health inequities) that to date have typically not been associated with sociolegal scholarship. These ignored arenas of engagement are, I suggest,

---

[4] "…we are witnessing the dawn of a new form of racial hegemony. In the twenty-first century, race will no longer be invoked to legitimate the crucial social structures of inequality, exploitation, and injustice. Appeals to white superiority will not serve, as they did in the bad old days. Law, political and human rights, as well as concepts of equality, fairness, and human difference will therefore increasingly be framed in 'race-neutral' terms. Yet the race-concept will continue to work at the interface of identity and inequality, social structure and cultural signification. The rearticulation of (in)equality in an ostensibly color-blind framework emphasizing individualism and meritocracy, it turns out, preserves the legacy of racial hierarchy far more effectively than its explicit defense. Similarly, the reinterpretation of racialized differences as matters of culture and nationality, rather than as fundamental human attributes somehow linked to phenol-type, turns out to justify exclusionary politics and policy far better than traditional white supremacists arguments can do" (Winant, cited in Khagram and Levitt 2008:100).

constitutively significant in the political and legal constructions of racial difference within any one state's domestic sphere.

RACIALIZING RELIGION

In recent years, scholarship on law and religion has become a vibrant new arena of sociolegal scholarship. Small in numbers but steadily growing, scholars in law and religion are reexamining the significance of faith in a variety of formal and informal legal forums (i.e., Barzilai 2004; Edge 2006; Mehdi et al 2008; Cane et al. 2008; Hosen and Mohr 2011).[5] Notably, these scholars are bringing into question the liberal assumption that modern democratic states are based on a separation of church and state institutions and so, by nature, are secular. This assumption rests upon a well-rehearsed and long-accepted historical narrative. Since the Enlightenment, so the narrative goes, European societies witnessed a steady decline in institutional religious practices, and as a result, public demonstrations of faith became less overt. This decline in public religiosity did not occur at the same rate or in the same manner in all countries and communities. However, it was sufficiently widespread across Europe and North America for Max Weber to argue in *The Protestant Ethic and the Spirit of Capitalism* that the rise of rationalization, particularly in the United States, had stripped the "pursuit of wealth" of all its religious and ethical meaning (Weber 1904:182). Weber, along with other social commentators such as Karl Marx, subscribed to the secularization thesis, which assumes the inevitable decline of religion as a political and economic force in society and in the minds of individuals. Secularization, and the understanding that women and men are personally responsible for their actions and not subject to the whim of God, underpins modern nationalism and imbues the ideas of "progress" and "improvement," which are emblematic of modern capitalist societies.

Over the past decade the secularization thesis has been hotly debated by sociologists of religion and political theorists who are divided on the issue of whether Western societies have become more, rather than less, religious since the Middle Ages (Taylor 2007; Bellah 2011; Butler et al. 2011; Calhoun et al. 2011). The central question is the degree to which the lessening power of religious institutions at the macro level correlates to a lessening of subjective religious belief at the individual level. Peter Berger, a leading sociologist in this

---

[5]   For instance, the Law and Religion Scholars Network publication listings give some idea of the range of scholarship that primarily focuses on the relationship of religions and state institutions. See http://www.law.cf.ac.uk/clr/networks/lrsn2.html. See generally the Center for Law and Religion at Cardiff Law School.

area, points out that the relationship between religion and modernity is very complicated and has not followed a linear or causal sequence. He notes that at times secularization has provoked strong anti-secular movements, and moreover, while some religious institutions may have lost power, other new institutions and faiths have gained power (Berger 1999). Berger, along with other scholars, argues that the secularization thesis is too simplistic, and modernity is not synonymous with secularization. In light of today's global religious conflicts and wars waged in the name of competing faiths, this argument seems entirely appropriate and applicable. As Mark Lilla alarmingly reminds us, "we have progressed to the point where we are again fighting the battles of the sixteenth century – over revelation and reason, dogmatic purity and toleration, inspiration and consent, divine duty and common decency" (Lilla 2007:3; see also Juergensmeyer 2003).

In the twenty-first century religious fervor seems to be alive and well, even amongst advanced industrialized societies typically characterized as secular (Juergensmeyer 2008). In turning attention to the ways religion plays out in public life, there is an emerging recognition that religious associations and apocalyptic visions continue to play a role in shaping domestic policies and international affairs (Jewett 2008; Hall 2009; Katzenstein 2011). In the United States, and to a lesser degree in Britain and other liberal democracies, the question of religion, both Christian and non-Christian, and the relative influence religion may have in social and political circles, has become a "hot" topic. In the post 9/11 world, references to God and Christian values are a constant theme in mainstream media. Moreover, there is a strident urgency in presenting Christianity as the "sane" religion in contrast to what is presented as the radical and irrational fundamentalism of "terrorists."[6] Commentators have bombarded the public with book titles such as *God Is Back: How the Global Revival of Faith is Changing the World* (Micklethwait and Wooldridge 2009) and *God's Century: Resurgent Religion and Global Politics* (Toft et al. 2011). Whatever side one takes in the complex debate about separation of churches and state, it now is apparent that the widespread assumption that the rule of

---

[6] This was dramatically expressed in the Republican nominee elections in the run up to the U.S. presidential election in late 2012. Almost all the Republican candidates running for office argued that the United States is not a secular society and laws should not follow the constitution but rather must be based on Christian morality. For instance, Rick Santorum declared that the United States should follow God's law, not secular laws. In a rather twisted argument given his open antagonism to Shari'a law, he stated: "Unlike Islam, where the higher law and the civil law are the same, in our case, we have civil laws. But our civil laws have to comport with the higher law.... As long as abortion is legal – at least according to the Supreme Court – legal in this country, we will never have rest, because that law does not comport with God's law" (November 19, 2011 Republican Forum, Des Moins, IA).

law epitomizes the secularism of modern societies does not stand up. Despite a long-accepted historical narrative in Western societies, Euro-American law cannot be simplistically characterized as a legal system premised on the removal of religion from politics.

Among a few sociolegal scholars the questioning of the long-accepted secularization thesis has prompted a reassessment of the development of modern nation-states and the role of secularization and religion in their formation (see Bowen 2010; (Hosen and Mohr 2011); Sullivan et al. 2011). This reassessment is necessary given that "The reemergence of competing and possible irreconcilable religious and legal systems in a postmodern twenty-first century unsettles much of the accumulated wisdom on the modernizing dimensions of early modern states and communities" (Roeber 2006:201; see also Bhandar 2009b; Bowen 2009, 2007). Against the backdrop of escalating domestic and global religious conflict, it is becoming increasingly clear that the current world is dealing with multiple secularisms in tandem with multiple religions, capitalisms, state systems, and democracies (Katzenstein 2011).

Sociolegal scholars are increasingly appreciating that secular and religious practices are not unconnected or mutually exclusive and that a separation of religion from state should be not be assumed as a given. Moreover, a few scholars are arguing that modern Western law historically developed within and out of Christian sensibilities (Novak 2000; Asad 2003; Fitzpatrick 2004; Schlag 2007; Umphrey et al. 2007; Mohr 2011). Still others point to the secular and sacred characteristics embodied in the concept of a legal subject and the challenges that religious pluralism creates for notions of secularized legal subjectivity (Naffine 2008; Mehdi et al. 2008). Against a background of increasing tension between secular state institutions and pluralized religious demands, Naomi Stolzenberg warns against simplistic polarizations between the secular and the religious. "Both sides," she cautions:

> demonize the other; both sides talk past each other, without realizing that they share a common root. In fact, religious fundamentalism and modern secularism derive from – and yet are cut off from – a common political and religious heritage, an intellectual tradition borne of the struggle to reconcile the idea of divinity with the practical needs and limitations of the mortal world (Stolzenberg 2007:31–32).

Scholarly insights of Stolzenberg and others show that Euro-American law – in ways analogous to Islamic or Native American legal systems – is not devoid of religious impulse either in its myths of legitimacy or in the formation of its foundational concepts. This line of argument suggests that law's ultimate validity appears to rest on some reference to a higher order of natural or divine authority. Such a need to refer to a higher order is particularly evident in moments of great upheaval, such as revolutions and coups. Notes Martha Umphrey, in the writing of the Declaration of Independence the American founders evoked "divine warrant" to legitimate the new order and the violence of revolution. Such moments of crisis highlight a more general legal condition. Continues Umphrey, "Law, thought to be one of the exemplary domains of secularism, instead emerges as a signal location in which the sacred has resided and continues to reside alongside and as a fundamental part of the secular" (Umphrey et al. 2007:20).

Significantly, religious and racial intolerances are not mutually exclusive practices; in many cases prejudices dovetail, overlap, and reinforce each other. The dovetailing of these processes may be obvious, but it is rarely discussed by sociolegal scholars of either religion or race. As a result, often glossed over in scholarly discussions about the development of Euro-American law is its deep entanglement in the racialization of religion (see, however, Cook 1997; Taylor 2006; Joshi 2009; Darian-Smith 2010a; Stolzenberg 2011).[7] This absence in the literature is somewhat surprising given that recognition of the intersections of religion and race is not new and has a long and well-documented legacy. From the time of the first crusades through to the Reformation in the sixteenth century, the religions of Muslims, Jews, Catholics, and Protestants was explicitly racialized, as were the religions of indigenous peoples throughout the colonial era. In the nineteenth century, African-American slavery, it should be remembered, was characterized by white Americans as a "divine institution" and the superiority of whites over blacks was interpreted as being ordained by God (Darian-Smith 2010a:128–130). A century later, the interconnections of religion and race were starkly revealed by W.E.B. Du Bois in his reflections on Jewish persecution after visiting Poland and the Warsaw Ghetto in 1949. Before his visits to Poland, Du Bois had thought of U.S. racial politics in terms of the color line and "physical and racial characteristics." But after his visits, Du Bois realized that persecution based on the color of one's skin was not so easily disentangled from persecution based on one's spiritual belief.[8] More recently, Henry Goldschmidt, in his discussion

---

[7] The racialization of religion occurs when "a specific religion becomes identified by a direct or indirect reference to a real or imagined ethnic/racial characteristic," and as a consequence renders that religion immoral, illegitimate, and harmful to the dominant culture (Joshi 2009:41).

[8] Reflecting on his experiences, Du Bois noted "the race problem in which I was interested cut across lines of color and physique and belief and status and was a matter of cultural patterns, perverted teaching and human hate and prejudice ... the ghetto of Warsaw helped me to emerge from a certain social provincialism into a broader conception of what the fight against race segregation, religious discrimination and the oppression by wealth had to

of the history of the Americas, adds, "If we fail to understand the relationships among these categories of collective identity [race, nation, religion], we will be unable to grasp the contours of our own histories ...We will misunderstand our increasingly diverse societies. And we are likely to misinterpret the sweeping social changes propelling us toward an increasingly global future" (Goldschmidt 2004:5).

A contemporary example of the blending of religious and racist intolerances is demonstrated by U.S. reactions to the 9/11 terrorist attacks. Former American president G.W. Bush framed his immediate response to the attacks in terms of a "crusade" to protect the "civilized world" from "barbarians," and over the course of his term he made frequent references to Islamic militants as "infidels." (Darian-Smith 2010a:263) Against this backdrop, notes Khyati Joshi, "Islam and its followers are perpetually associated with terrorists and terrorism, thus showing one facet of racialization where a racial stereotype is extended to a religious group" (Joshi 2009:37). Endorsement of legislation similar to that of the United States' Patriot Act (2001) by countries such as Australia, Britain, Germany, and France have enabled widespread racial profiling of dark-skinned people of Islamic faith. Today, over a decade since the attacks of 9/11, peoples from South Asia and the Middle East remain overly scrutinized and disproportionately suspected of subversive activities by police and other regulatory agencies (see Razack 2008; Bowen 2011b; Moore 2012).

G.W. Bush was the loudest public voice to evoke the rhetoric of "good western Christian" against "evil eastern Muslim" but he was by no means the only person to endorse the "clash of civilizations" rhetoric espoused by Samuel Huntington and others, which has enjoyed widespread and enduring popular support across the global North (Huntington 1996; see Said 2001; Sen 2002a). This in part may explain why a poll conducted by Britain's Equalities and Human Rights Commission in 2009 determined that religion, not race, is the most divisive issue dividing the British people today. The Commission's finding marks a dramatic shift in British social attitudes, which only a decade earlier regarded racial conflict as the most important social issue confronting the country. The emerging preoccupation with religion – rather than race – in the UK and other countries in Europe and North America may also account for the widespread public hysteria related to any discussion about accommodating Shari'a law or other non-Christian legal practices (see Chapter 2).

In the second decade of the twenty-first century, it may be possible to argue that religion is the new race. However, I would caution against substituting

become if civilization was going to triumph and broaden in the world" (Du Bois 1982: 174–175; Rothberg 2001; Darian-Smith 2012).

one form of cultural and social discrimination with another. As I have argued elsewhere, there is a need to recognize the interconnections within practices of religion and constructions of race in the shaping of collective attitudes and legal practices (Darian-Smith 2010a). This is vitally important given the global North's preoccupation – once again – with the racialization of Islam. However, the racialization of religion in the twenty-first century should be understood in the context of somewhat different conditions than it has been in the past. Today, more so than in any other historical era, all religious conflict, no matter how localized, cannot be disentangled from transnational and global forces that are imposing new pressures on local communities and the national borders in which they have been historically framed. These pressures are in the form of (1) new technologies of communication that are helping to create religious movements at grassroots levels that are not bound by geopolitical territories, (2) huge reductions in the global security of food, water, and energy that are in turn promoting new forms of regional warfare that are often expressed in terms of religious conflict, and (3) unprecedented movements of millions of people fleeing persecution, starvation, and environmental degradation and whom often carry with them different religious world views from the societies that they are forced to move to. How religious conflict will be manifested within cities, states, and regions under these escalating global economic, political, cultural, and environmental pressures is something no one can entirely predict. Unfortunately, what does appear relatively certain is that the racialization of religion in spaces and levels below and beyond that of the nation-state, and the challenges these present to legal and governmental systems, will increasingly and urgently demand the attention of sociolegal scholars.

ENVIRONMENTAL APARTHEID – TOXINS, FLOODS, DISEASES

Equally pressing and urgent, yet engaged with by even fewer sociolegal scholars than those who study religion, is the escalating crises of environmental degradation and climate change. Of particular concern are the increasing vulnerabilities of certain communities to the catastrophes of flooding, drought, starvation, poisoning, and disease. Surprisingly, even though scholarship on the environment over the past decade has increased dramatically across the social sciences and humanities, and environmental law is now taught in many schools across the United States and elsewhere, within law and society circles engagement with environmental concerns is virtually absent.[9]

---

[9] Few law and society scholars study environmental issues of any sort (for notable exceptions, see Park 1998; Yoder 2003; Elver 2008; Murdocca 2010; Morgan 2011; Farrall et al. 2012). As

The reason why this enormously urgent topic does not have a substantive presence in the current field of law and society research raises disturbing questions that are beyond the scope of discussion here. My purpose in this brief section is to point to this area of scholarship that will (I hope!) become important in the sociolegal field as we advance through the second decade of the twenty-first century. Moreover, my argument is that any serious engagement with the causes and consequences of environmental degradation and climate change will require – at the very least – adopting a global sociolegal perspective.

The environmental justice movement emerged in the United States in the early 1980s and was particularly concerned with the disproportionate risks and impacts (pollution, crime, industrial plants, noise, etc.) that environmental degradation had on poor and minority communities both in inner-city and rural areas. In the wake of the civil rights movement and Rachel Carson's book *Silent Spring* (1962), the environmental justice movement sought to bring attention to issues of racism and discrimination that were exacerbated by the socioeconomic vulnerabilities of poor and marginalized people who have limited political power and options. This concern with race, class, and gender oppression stood in stark contrast to the U.S. environmental movement in the first half of the twentieth century, which had predominantly involved white Americans interested in wildlife preservation and wilderness conservation (see Nash 1982; see also Cronon 1996; Checker 2002).

The environmental justice movement was further galvanized in the 1980s by a report titled *Toxic Wastes and Race in the United States* (1987), which was published by the United Church of Christ. The report brought widespread public attention to the intentional placement of hazardous waste sites in communities inhabited predominantly by Blacks, Latinos, Native Americans, farm workers, and the working poor. Not only did the report find that people of color are concentrated in communities with the greatest number of hazardous waste facilities but that they can expect different responses from the government when it comes to remediation. With growing public pressure, in 1992 the U.S. Environmental Protection Agency (EPA) established the Office of

---

evidenced in the *Annual Review of Law and Social Science*, which began in 2005, there are only three articles that speak to environmental concerns (out of over 200 articles); the first focuses on environmental law as it relates to Native American law (Darian-Smith 2010b), the second on the politics of carbon emission taxation (Harrison 2010), and the third is an article on environmental law and regulation that calls for greater engagement with social science research (Boyd et al. 2012). To date, there is no LSA Collaborative Research Network that specifically focuses on the environment. There is even less sociolegal literature on public health issues in national or global contexts, although a LSA Collaborative Research Network was launched on law, health, and medicine in 2012.

Environmental Justice under the presidency of H.W. Bush.[10] Two years later, president Bill Clinton signed an executive order that directed federal agencies to pay particular attention to the negative impact of environmental degradation on people of color. However, over the course of the following decade efforts to address environmental injustices were thwarted by a range of issues including increasingly aggressive resistance from congress and industry lobbyists. Under G.W. Bush the Office of Environmental Justice was severely financially constrained.

Despite the political and economic limitations imposed on the U.S. environmental justice movement, and the disappointing finding that environmental racism was even more robust in 2007 than it had been twenty years earlier (see report *Toxic Wastes and Race at Twenty: 1987–2007*), environmental justice remains a strong platform for political activism and critical scholarship within the United States and internationally (see Bullard et al. 2008). The environmental justice movement's primary goals[11] have informed a global environmental justice movement that today flourishes in regions and countries around the world (Dwivedi 2001; Walker 2009). Of course, environmental politics play out differently in various regions and places. Even the concept of "justice" means different things according to the interpretation of the actors involved (Schlosberg 2004, 2007). That being said, all environmental justice movements, whether located in the global North or global South, are concerned with the inordinate burden placed on socioeconomically disadvantaged groups, particularly women, and the explicit and implicit racism involved in resource depletion and degradation. Moreover, these movements are all concerned with reframing human rights discourse to include environmental injustices as perpetrated at the global level and to rethinking the centrality of state institutions so as to include local/regional communities, NGOs, and international law agencies in decision making over the creation and management of environmental policies (see Adeola 2000; Westra and Lawson 2001; Agyeman et al. 2003; Steady 2009).

[10] According to the U.S. Environmental Protection Agency, environmental justice is defined as "the fair treatment and meaningful involvement of all people regardless of race, color, national origin, or income with respect to the development, implementation, and enforcement of environmental laws, regulations, and policies. EPA has this goal for all communities and persons across this Nation. It will be achieved when everyone enjoys the same degree of protection from environmental and health hazards and equal access to the decision-making process to have a healthy environment in which to live, learn, and work." Online at: http://www.epa.gov/compliance/environmentaljustice/index.html.

[11] According to David Schlosberg, these are to promote the equitable distribution of environmental risks and benefits, to encourage participation by all in decision making, to recognize community ways of life and cultural difference, and to encourage communities and individuals to reach their full potential (Schlosberg 2007).

Scholars examining environmental injustice and racism approach the topic in a variety of ways. Scholars interested in a global political economy point to the ecological debt incurred by the global North in its disproportionate consumption, and in some cases explicit looting, of the natural assets of countries in the global South (see Rice 2009). Other scholars point to the exploitative attitude of the global North toward the global South as it manifests in poorer regions becoming dumping grounds for unwanted hazardous materials, pollutants, and in the last decade, mountains of e-waste. On this front it should not be forgotten that as early as 1991, Lawrence Summers, then president of the World Bank, wrote in a confidential memo:

> I think the economic logic behind dumping a load of toxic waste in the lowest-wage country is impeccable and we should face up to that ... I've always thought that countries in Africa are vastly unpolluted; their air quality is probably vastly inefficiently low compared to Los Angles ... Just between you and me, shouldn't the World Bank be encouraging more migration of the dirty industries to the Least Developed Countries? (cited in Nixon 2011:1).

Enabling the World Banks' neoliberal processes of exploitation (both in terms of resource extraction and toxic dumping) has been the IMF and many state governments whose economic policies take advantage of the global South's lack of power to respond. These policies are intrinsically racialized in that they disproportionately impact the vast populations of the global South, burdening them with environmental degradation and related health risks (Anderton et al. 1994; Park 1998; Clapp 2001; Randeria 2003). According to Nisha Thakker, in New Delhi alone there is an estimated 25,000 scrap workers, including children and elderly, foraging over toxic landfills to tear apart electronic components with their bare hands. She appropriately notes that the lack in U.S. domestic laws to prohibit the export of hazardous e-waste to poorer countries such as India is not a "morally or legally sound practice" in that it allows "those that have not benefited from electronic products to bear the burden of dealing with the dangers of their unregulated disposal" (Thakker 2006:61).

Still other scholars concerned with environmental justice focus on indigenous peoples and examine the gross violations of natural resources on traditional lands and reservations in the form of mining, hazardous waste landfills, toxic dumping, deforestation, ocean acidification, and river contamination (McGovern 1995; Murdocca 2010; Darian-Smith 2010b). More recently, the forces of climate change are being witnessed in rising seas, melting glaciers, ozone depletion, and shifting weather patterns that bring droughts, floods, and famines. Together these forces are disproportionately affecting the world's millions of indigenous peoples who are particularly dependent on natural

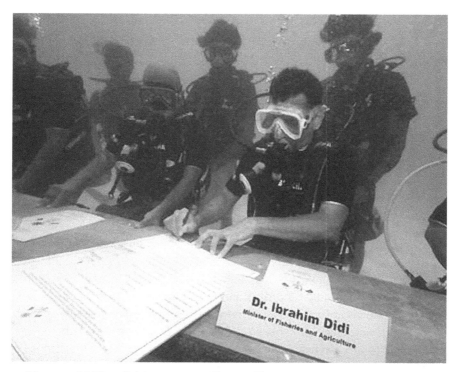

Figure 7. Maldives Cabinet signing a Climate Change Document twenty feet under the sea to protest the islands' imminent submergence. October 17, 2009. Courtesy, Wikimedia Commons.

resources for survival and, as a consequence, inordinately vulnerable (see Graham and Friederichs 2011; Hopkins 2012). One horrifying example – amongst the many currently unfolding – is that of the Maldive Islands. Here communities living on the coast are being forced to relocate to higher grounds as polar ice melts and sea levels rise, which in turn submerges their fishing villages and livelihoods. Since the islands have an average ground level of only 1.5 meters (4 ft. 11 in.) above sea level, it is anticipated that the whole archipelago will be submerged under water and the country will literally disappear within the coming decades (see Figure 7).

Rob Nixon, in his remarkable book *Slow Violence and the Environmentalism of the Poor* (2011), laments that often indigenous communities are the biggest losers in environmental degradation and climate change. This is often because minority communities have little political clout or economic recourse. Compounding this political deficit, he argues, is the fact that environmental impacts typically unfold slowly, sometimes over decades, and as a result do not attract widespread public attention and are not built into long-term strategic policies and planning to alleviate or eliminate future environmental degradation. He calls this the problem of "slow violence" whereby multinational corporations who:

> deploy depleted-uranium weaponry or dump toxic e-waste can wash their hands of the fatalities that result because what they're doing doesn't look like "real" violence. It's not immediate, spectacularly, sensationally awful ... Particularly in an age when regulatory oversight is in retreat, the agents of slow violence can build forgetfulness into their economic strategy. They know that, invariably, they won't have to pay (Dawson 2011).

In contrast to the relatively slow violence of environmental degradation and climate change, decline in levels of public health can manifest relatively rapidly, particularly among already impoverished and politically unstable communities. The most rapid, and least containable, threats to global health are pandemics, which in the past have included tuberculosis, cholera, and smallpox and more recently HIV/AIDS and H1n1 pandemics. As the anthropologist and physician Paul Farmer so movingly describes in his groundbreaking book *Pathologies of Power: Health, Human Rights, and the New War on the Poor*, the connection between poverty and disease is staggering (Farmer 2005). Moreover, the correlation between low social-economic class and poor health is further exacerbated by what he calls "the axis of race or ethnicity" in which social structures of discrimination continue to marginalize communities and individuals seen as racially or ethnically different. According to Farmer, "the dismantling of the apartheid regime [in South Africa] has not yet brought the dismantling of the structures of oppression and inequality in South Africa, and persistent social inequality is no doubt the primary reason that HIV has spread so rapidly in sub-Saharan Africa's wealthiest nation" (Farmer 2005:45; see also Heimer 2007; Klug 2012). Adds Thomas Pogge, a leading expert on global poverty, "The poor worldwide face greater environmental hazards than the rest of us: from contaminated water, filth, pollution, worms and insects" (Pogge 2008:118). People living in poverty – currently estimated to be about 1.7 billion people – are exposed to greater bodily risks in their lacking adequate means to protect themselves, access to legal protection, knowledge, and financial reserves. Moreover, "they are often obliged by dire need or debt to incur additional health risks; by selling a kidney, for instance, or by accepting hazardous work in prostitution, mining, construction, domestic service, textile and carpet production" (Pogge 2008:118).

People living in the global South face vastly different health risks than those living in the global North. Be it droughts or floods creating crises of famine, or the spread of toxins through water and air manifesting as birth defects and cancers, or the impact of drug wars and vigilante hostilities forcing people to flee and live without shelter, or more simply the steady grind of backbreaking work in mines and factories in conditions of near slavery – all of these situations place disproportionate health pressures on people living in the global South who die on average thirty years earlier than people living in the global North. Together these interrelated and cumulative global crises are insidiously and steadily re-racializing the world.

However, it should be remembered, that even within wealthy industrial nations, growing inequities with respect to access to medicine and health care are exacerbating processes of impoverishment, diminished opportunities, and racialized social and cultural differentiation. For instance, in a somewhat startling report released in 2012 by the World Health Organization and other agencies it was found that the United States ranked well below other industrialized nations in Europe in terms of its rates of premature births (Howson et al. 2012). In fact the United States ranked on par with developing nations such as Kenya, Thailand, East Timor, and Honduras. The horrifying reality is that the United States has the medical expertise to decrease rates of premature births, however, more and more women cannot afford health insurance and so are precluded from receiving prenatal health care. These women are typically from low socioeconomic backgrounds, and a disproportionate number are racial and ethnic minorities. In contrast, according to the report, Sri Lanka has state policies in place that ensure all pregnant women are visited by trained midwives, and Turkey pays for poor rural women to go to hospitals to give birth. Rates of premature births are just one indicator highlighting the intersections of poverty, health, and disease that are playing out in the global North. Relatively high rates of diabetes, obesity, cancer, tuberculosis, HIV/AIDS, and other diseases among racial and ethnic minorities in the United States and other wealthy Western nations further confirm the racialized dimensions of public health (see LaVeist 2002).

As we move toward the mid decades of the twenty-first century, sociolegal scholars will hopefully engage in the laws, politics, and policies related to the crises of environmental degradation, climate change, and related issues of declining global health both with respect to fast-moving pandemics and the slow violence caused by such things as toxins in water supplies and seeping radiation from contaminated waste. Given law and society's long-standing concern with power inequities and minority and racial oppression, crises in environment and public health – in the global North and the global South – would appear to be fields of sociolegal inquiry long overdue for sustained and deep examination. Any such engagement will necessarily require looking within and beyond the nation-state and exploring global governance mechanisms more appropriate to dealing with these massive global challenges, risks, and demands. Seeing the intersections and connections across scales, spaces, times, regions, and continents necessary to think through these urgent legal issues will require – at the very least – adopting a global sociolegal perspective.

LIST OF SUGGESTED READINGS

1. Asad, Talad (2003) *Formations of the Secular: Christianity, Islam, Modernity.* Palo Alto: Stanford University Press.

2. Bales, Kevin (2004, revised edition) *Disposable People: New Slavery in the Global Economy.* Berkeley: University of California Press.

3. Bowen, John (2009) *Can Islam Be French? Pluralism and Pragmatism in a Secularist State.* Princeton: Princeton University Press.

4. Cane, Peter, Carolyn Evans, and Zoe Robinson (eds.) (2008) *Law and Religion in Theoretical and Historical Context.* Cambridge: Cambridge University Press.

5. Da Silva, Denise Ferreira (2007) *Toward a global idea of race.* Minneapolis, University of Minnesota Press.

6. Farmer, Paul (2005) *Pathologies of Power: Health, Human Rights, and the New War on the Poor.* Berkeley: University of California Press.

7. Hosen, Nadirsyan and Richard Mohr (eds.) (2011) *Law and Religion in Public Life: The Contemporary Debate.* London and New York: Routledge.

8. Lake, Marilyn and Henry Reynolds (2008) *Drawing the Global Color Line: White Men's Countries and the International Challenge of Racial Inequality.* Cambridge: Cambridge University Press.

9. Moore, Kathleen M. (2010) *The Unfamiliar Abode: Islamic Law in the United States and Britain.* Oxford: Oxford University Press.

10. Nixon, Rob (2011) *Slow Violence and the Environmentalism of the Poor.* Cambridge, MA: Harvard University Press.

11. Sarat, Austin, Lawrence Douglas, and Martha Merrill Umphrey (eds.) (2006) *Law and the Sacred.* Palo Alto: Stanford University Press.

12. Steady, Filomina Chioma (2009) *Environmental Justice in the New Millennium: Global Perspectives on Race, Ethnicity, and Human Rights.* New York: Palgrave Macmillan.

13. Westra, Laura and Bill E. Lawson (eds.) (2001) *Faces of Environmental Racism: Confronting Issues of Global Justice.* Lanhan, MD: Rowman & Littlefield.

14. Winant, Howard (2004) *The New Politics of Race: Globalism, Difference, Justice.* Minneapolis and London: University of Minnesota Press.
15. Wright, Beverly (2003) Race, Politics and Pollution: Environmental Justice in the Mississippi River Chemical Corridor. In Julian Agyeman, Robert D. Bullard and Bob Evans (eds.) *Just Sustainabilities: Development in an Unequal World.* Cambridge, MA: MIT Press, pp. 125–145.

HOW TO JUDGE GLOBALISM

Amartya Sen

Globalization is often seen as global Westernization. On this point, there is substantial agreement among many proponents and opponents. Those who take an upbeat view of globalization see it as a marvelous contribution of Western civilization to the world. There is a nicely stylized history in which the great developments happened in Europe: First came the Renaissance, then the Enlightenment and the Industrial Revolution, and these led to a massive increase in living standards in the West. And now the great achievements of the West are spreading to the world. In this view, globalization is not only good, it is also a gift from the West to the world. The champions of this reading of history tend to feel upset not just because this great benefaction is seen as a curse but also because it is undervalued and castigated by an ungrateful world.

From the opposite perspective, Western dominance – sometimes seen as a continuation of Western imperialism – is the devil of the piece. In this view, contemporary capitalism, driven and led by greedy and grabby Western countries in Europe and North America, has established rules of trade and business relations that do not serve the interests of the poorer people in the world. The celebration of various non-Western identities – defined by religion (as in Islamic fundamentalism), region (as in the championing of Asian values), or culture (as in the glorification of Confucian ethics) – can add fuel to the fire of confrontation with the West.

Is globalization really a new Western curse? It is, in fact, neither new nor necessarily Western; and it is not a curse. Over thousands of years, globalization has contributed to the progress of the world through travel, trade, migration, spread of cultural influences, and dissemination of knowledge and understanding (including that of science and technology). These global interrelations have often been very productive in the advancement of different countries. They have not necessarily taken the form of increased Western influence. Indeed, the active agents of globalization have often been located far from the West.

To illustrate, consider the world at the beginning of the last millennium rather than at its end. Around 1000 A.D., global reach of science, technology, and mathematics was changing the nature of the old world, but the dissemination then was, to a great extent, in the opposite direction of what we see today. The high technology in the world of 1000 A.D. included paper, the printing press, the crossbow, gunpowder, the iron-chain suspension bridge, the kite, the magnetic compass, the wheelbarrow, and the rotary fan. A millennium ago, these items were used extensively in China – and were practically unknown elsewhere. Globalization spread them across the world, including Europe.

A similar movement occurred in the Eastern influence on Western mathematics. The decimal system emerged and became well developed in India between the second and sixth centuries; it was used by Arab mathematicians soon thereafter. These mathematical innovations reached Europe mainly in the last quarter of the tenth century and began having an impact in the early years of the last millennium, playing an important part in the scientific revolution that helped to transform Europe. The agents of globalization are neither European nor exclusively Western, nor are they necessarily linked to Western dominance. Indeed, Europe would have been a lot poorer – economically, culturally, and scientifically – had it resisted the globalization of mathematics, science, and technology at that time. And today, the same principle applies, though in the reverse direction (from West to East). To reject the globalization of science and technology because it represents Western influence and imperialism would not only amount to overlooking global contributions – drawn from many different parts of the world – that lie solidly behind so-called Western science and technology, but would also be quite a daft practical decision, given the extent to which the whole world can benefit from the process.

A Global Heritage

In resisting the diagnosis of globalization as a phenomenon of quintessentially Western origin, we have to be suspicious not only of the anti-Western rhetoric but also of the pro-Western chauvinism in many contemporary writings. Certainly, the Renaissance, the Enlightenment, and the Industrial Revolution were great achievements – and they occurred mainly in Europe and, later, in America. Yet many of these developments drew on the experience of the rest of the world, rather than being confined within the boundaries of a discrete Western civilization.

Our global civilization is a world heritage – not just a collection of disparate local cultures. When a modern mathematician in Boston invokes an algorithm to solve a difficult computational problem, she may not be aware that she is helping to commemorate the Arab mathematician Mohammad Ibn Musa-al-Khwarizmi, who flourished in the first half of the ninth century. (The word *algorithm* is derived from the name al-Khwarizmi.) There is a chain of intellectual relations that link Western mathematics and science to a collection of distinctly non-Western practitioners, of whom al-Khwarizmi was one. (The term *algebra* is derived from the title of his famous book *Al-Jabrwa-al-Muqabilah.*) Indeed, al-Khwarizmi is one of many non-Western contributors whose works influenced the European Renaissance and, later, the Enlightenment and the Industrial Revolution. The West must get full credit for the remarkable achievements that occurred in Europe and Europeanized America, but the idea of an immaculate Western conception is an imaginative fantasy.

Not only is the progress of global science and technology not an exclusively West-led phenomenon, but there were major global developments in which the West was not even involved. The printing of the world's first book was a marvelously globalized event. The technology of printing was, of course, entirely an achievement of the Chinese. But the content came from elsewhere. The first printed book was an Indian Sanskrit treatise, translated into Chinese by a half-Turk. The book, *Vajracchedika Prajnaparamitasutra* (sometimes referred to as "The Diamond Sutra"), is an old treatise on Buddhism; it was translated into Chinese from Sanskrit in the fifth century by Kumarajiva, a half-Indian and half-Turkish scholar who lived in a part of eastern Turkistan called Kucha but later migrated to China. It was printed four centuries later, in 868 a.d. All this involving China, Turkey, and India is globalization, all right, but the West is not even in sight.

Global Interdependences and Movements

The misdiagnosis that globalization of ideas and practices has to be resisted because it entails dreaded Westernization has played quite a regressive part in the colonial and postcolonial world. This assumption incites parochial tendencies and undermines the possibility of objectivity in science and knowledge. It is not only counterproductive in itself; given the global interactions throughout history, it can also cause non-Western societies to shoot themselves in the foot – even in their precious cultural foot.

Consider the resistance in India to the use of Western ideas and concepts in science and mathematics. In the nineteenth century, this debate fitted into a broader controversy about Western education versus indigenous Indian education. The "Westernizers," such as the redoubtable Thomas Babington Macaulay, saw no merit whatsoever in Indian tradition. "I have never found one among them [advocates of Indian tradition] who could deny that a single shelf of a good European library was worth the whole native literature of India and Arabia," he declared. Partly in retaliation, the advocates of native education resisted Western imports altogether. Both sides, however, accepted too readily the foundational dichotomy between two disparate civilizations.

European mathematics, with its use of such concepts as sine, was viewed as a purely "Western" import into India. In fact, the fifth-century Indian mathematician Aryabhata had discussed the concept of sine in his classic work on astronomy and mathematics in 499 a.d., calling it by its Sanskrit name, *jya-ardha* (literally, "half-chord"). This word, first shortened to *jya* in Sanskrit, eventually became the Arabic *jiba* and, later, *jaib*, which means "a cove or a bay." In his history of mathematics, Howard Eves explains that around 1150 a.d., Gherardo of Cremona, in his translations from the Arabic, rendered *jaib* as the Latin *sinus*, the corresponding word for a cove or a bay. And this is the source of the modern word *sine*. The concept had traveled full circle – from India, and then back.

To see globalization as merely Western imperialism of ideas and beliefs (as the rhetoric often suggests) would be a serious and costly error, in the same way that any European resistance to Eastern influence would have been at the beginning of the last millennium. Of course, there are issues related to globalization that do connect with imperialism (the history of conquests, colonialism, and alien rule remains relevant today in many ways), and a postcolonial understanding of the world has its merits. But it would be a great mistake to see globalization primarily as a feature of imperialism. It is much bigger – much greater – than that.

The issue of the distribution of economic gains and losses from globalization remains an entirely separate question, and it must be addressed as a further – and extremely relevant – issue. There is extensive evidence that the global economy has brought prosperity to many different areas of the globe. Pervasive poverty dominated the world a few centuries ago; there were only a few rare pockets of affluence. In overcoming that penury, extensive economic interrelations and modern technology have been and remain influential. What has happened in Europe, America, Japan, and East Asia has important messages for all other regions, and we cannot go very far into understanding the nature of globalization today without first acknowledging the positive fruits of global economic contacts.

Indeed, we cannot reverse the economic predicament of the poor across the world by withholding from them the great advantages of contemporary technology, the well-established efficiency of international trade and exchange, and the social as well as economic merits of living in an open society. Rather, the main issue is how to make good use of the remarkable benefits of economic intercourse and technological progress in a way that pays adequate attention to the interests of the deprived and the underdog. That is, I would argue, the constructive question that emerges from the so-called antiglobalization movements.

Are the Poor Getting Poorer?

The principal challenge relates to inequality – international as well as intranational. The troubling inequalities include disparities in affluence and also gross asymmetries in political, social, and economic opportunities and power.

A crucial question concerns the sharing of the potential gains from globalization – between rich and poor countries and among different groups within a country. It is not sufficient to understand that the poor of the world need globalization as much as the rich do; it is also important to make sure that they actually get what they need. This may require extensive institutional reform, even as globalization is defended.

There is also a need for more clarity in formulating the distributional questions. For example, it is often argued that the rich are getting richer and the poor poorer. But this is by no means uniformly so, even though there are cases in which this has happened. Much depends on the region or the group chosen and what indicators of economic prosperity are used. But the attempt to base the castigation of economic globalization on this rather thin ice produces a peculiarly fragile critique.

On the other side, the apologists of globalization point to their belief that the poor who participate in trade and exchange are mostly getting richer. Ergo – the argument runs – globalization is not unfair to the poor: they too benefit. If the central relevance of this question is accepted, then the whole debate turns on determining which side is correct in this empirical dispute. But is this the right battleground in the first place? I would argue that it is not.

Global Justice and the Bargaining Problem

Even if the poor were to get just a little richer, this would not necessarily imply that the poor were getting a fair share of the potentially vast benefits of global economic interrelations. It is not adequate to ask whether international inequality is getting marginally larger or smaller. In order to rebel against the appalling poverty and the staggering inequalities that characterize the contemporary world – or to protest against the unfair sharing of benefits of global cooperation – it is not necessary to show that the massive inequality or distributional unfairness is also getting marginally larger. This is a separate issue altogether.

When there are gains from cooperation, there can be many possible arrangements. As the game theorist and mathematician John Nash discussed more than half a century ago (in "The Bargaining Problem," published in *Econometrica* in 1950, which was cited, among other writings, by the Royal Swedish Academy of Sciences when Nash was awarded the Nobel Prize in economics), the central issue in general is not whether a particular arrangement is better for everyone than no cooperation at all would be, but whether that is a fair division of the benefits. One cannot rebut the criticism that a distributional arrangement is unfair simply by noting that all the parties are better off than they would be in the absence of cooperation; the real exercise is the choice *between* these alternatives.

An Analogy with the Family

By analogy, to argue that a particularly unequal and sexist family arrangement is unfair, one does not have to show that women would have done comparatively better had there been no families at all, but only that the sharing of the benefits is seriously unequal in that particular arrangement. Before the issue of gender justice became an explicitly recognized concern (as it has in recent decades), there were attempts to dismiss the issue of unfair arrangements within the family by suggesting that women did not need to live in families if they found the arrangements so unjust. It was also argued that since women as well as men benefit from living in families, the existing arrangements could not be unfair. But even when it is accepted that both men and women may typically gain from living in a family, the question of distributional fairness remains. Many different family arrangements – when compared with the absence of any family system – would satisfy the condition of being beneficial to both men and women. The real issue concerns how fairly benefits associated with these respective arrangements are distributed.

Likewise, one cannot rebut the charge that the global system is unfair by showing that even the poor gain something from global contacts and are not necessarily made poorer. That answer may or may not be wrong, but the question certainly is. The critical issue is not whether the poor are getting marginally poorer or richer. Nor is it whether they are better off than they would be had they excluded themselves from globalized interactions.

Again, the real issue is the distribution of globalization's benefits. Indeed, this is why many of the antiglobalization protesters, who seek a better deal for the underdogs of the world economy, are not – contrary to their own rhetoric and to the views attributed to them by others – really "antiglobalization." It is also why there is no real contradiction in the fact that the so-called anti-globalization protests have become among the most globalized events in the contemporary world.

Altering Global Arrangements

However, can those less-well-off groups get a better deal from globalized economic and social relations without dispensing with the market economy itself? They certainly can. The use of the market economy is consistent with many different ownership patterns, resource availabilities, social opportunities, and rules of operation (such as patent laws and antitrust regulations). And depending on these conditions, the market economy would generate different prices, terms of trade, income distribution, and, more generally, diverse overall outcomes. The arrangements for social security and other public interventions can make further modifications to the outcomes of the market processes, and together they can yield varying levels of inequality and poverty.

The central question is not whether to use the market economy. That shallow question is easy to answer, because it is hard to achieve economic prosperity without making extensive use of the opportunities of exchange and specialization that market relations offer. Even though the operation of a given market economy can be significantly defective, there is no way of dispensing with the institution of markets in general as a powerful engine of economic progress.

But this recognition does not end the discussion about globalized market relations. The market economy does not work by itself in global relations – indeed, it cannot operate alone even within a given country. It is not only the case that a market inclusive system can generate very distinct results depending on various enabling conditions (such as how physical resources are distributed, how human resources are developed, what rules of business relations prevail, what social-security arrangements are in place, and so on). These enabling conditions themselves depend critically on economic, social, and political institutions that operate nationally and globally.

The crucial role of the markets does not make the other institutions insignificant, even in terms of the results that the market economy can produce. As has been amply established in empirical studies, market outcomes are massively influenced by public policies in education, epidemiology, land reform, microcredit facilities, appropriate legal protections, et cetera; and in each of these fields, there is work to be done through public action that can radically alter the outcome of local and global economic relations.

Institutions and Inequality

Globalization has much to offer; but even as we defend it, we must also, without any contradiction, see the legitimacy of many questions that the anti-globalization protesters ask. There may be a misdiagnosis about where the main problems lie (they do not lie in globalization, as such), but the ethical and human concerns that yield these questions call for serious reassessments of the adequacy of the national and global institutional arrangements that characterize the contemporary world and shape globalized economic and social relations.

Global capitalism is much more concerned with expanding the domain of market relations than with, say, establishing democracy, expanding elementary education, or enhancing the social opportunities of society's underdogs. Since globalization of markets is, on its own, a very inadequate approach to world prosperity, there is a need to go beyond the priorities that find expression in the chosen focus of global capitalism. As George Soros has pointed out, international business concerns often have a strong preference for working in orderly and highly organized autocracies rather than in activist and less-regimented democracies, and this can be a regressive influence on equitable development. Further, multinational firms can exert their influence on the priorities of public expenditure in less secure third-world countries by giving preference to the safety and convenience of the managerial classes and of privileged workers over the removal of widespread illiteracy, medical deprivation, and other adversities of the poor. These possibilities do not, of course, impose any insurmountable barrier to development, but it is important to make sure that the surmountable barriers are actually surmounted.

Omissions and Commissions

The injustices that characterize the world are closely related to various omissions that need to be addressed, particularly in institutional arrangements. I have tried to identify some of the main problems in my book *Development as Freedom* (Knopf, 1999). Global policies have a role here in helping the development of national institutions (for example, through defending democracy and supporting schooling and health facilities), but there is also a need to re-examine the adequacy of global institutional arrangements themselves. The distribution of the benefits in the global economy depends, among other things, on a variety of global institutional arrangements, including those for fair trade, medical initiatives, educational exchanges, facilities for technological dissemination, ecological and environmental restraints, and fair treatment of accumulated debts that were often incurred by irresponsible military rulers of the past.

In addition to the momentous omissions that need to be rectified, there are also serious problems of commission that must be addressed for even elementary global ethics. These include not only inefficient and inequitable trade restrictions that repress exports from poor countries, but also patent laws that inhibit the use of lifesaving drugs – for diseases like AIDS – and that give inadequate incentive for medical research aimed at developing nonrepeating medicines (such as vaccines). These issues have been much discussed on their own, but we must also note how they fit into a general pattern of unhelpful arrangements that undermine what globalization could offer.

Another – somewhat less discussed – global "commission" that causes intense misery as well as lasting deprivation relates to the involvement of the world powers in globalized arms trade. This is a field in which a new global initiative is urgently required, going beyond the need – the very important need – to curb terrorism, on which the focus is so heavily concentrated right now. Local wars and military conflicts, which have very destructive consequences (not least on the economic prospects of poor countries), draw not only on regional tensions but also on global trade in arms and weapons. The world establishment is firmly entrenched in this business: the Permanent Members of the Security Council of the United Nations were together responsible for 81 percent of world arms exports from 1996 through 2000. Indeed, the world leaders who express deep frustration at the "irresponsibility" of antiglobalization protesters lead the countries that make the most money in this terrible trade. The G-8 countries sold 87 percent of the total supply of arms exported in the entire world. The U.S. share alone has just gone up to almost 50 percent of the total sales in the world. Furthermore, as much as 68 percent of the American arms exports went to developing countries.

The arms are used with bloody results – and with devastating effects on the economy, the polity, and the society. In some ways, this is a continuation of the unhelpful role of world powers in the genesis and flowering of political militarism in Africa from the 1960s to the 1980s, when the Cold War was fought over Africa. During these decades, when military overlords – Mobuto Sese Seko or Jonas Savimbi or whoever – busted social and political arrangements (and, ultimately, economic order as well) in Africa, they could rely on support either from the United States and its allies or from the Soviet Union, depending on their military alliances. The world powers bear an awesome responsibility for helping in the subversion of democracy in Africa and for all the far-reaching negative consequences of that subversion. The pursuit of arms "pushing" gives them a continuing role in the escalation of military conflicts today – in Africa and elsewhere. The U.S. refusal to agree to a joint crackdown even on illicit sales of small arms (as proposed by UN Secretary-General Kofi Annan) illustrates the difficulties involved.

Fair Sharing of Global Opportunities

To conclude, the confounding of globalization with Westernization is not only ahistorical, it also distracts attention from the many potential benefits of global integration. Globalization is a historical process that has offered an abundance of opportunities and rewards in the past and continues to do so today. The very existence of potentially large benefits makes the question of fairness in sharing the benefits of globalization so critically important.

The central issue of contention is not globalization itself, nor is it the use of the market as an institution, but the inequity in the overall balance of institutional arrangements – which produces very unequal sharing of the benefits of globalization. The question is not just whether the poor, too, gain something from globalization, but whether they get a fair share and a fair opportunity. There is an urgent need for reforming institutional arrangements – in addition to national ones – in order to overcome both the errors of omission and those of commission that tend to give the poor across the world such limited opportunities. Globalization deserves a reasoned defense, but it also needs reform.

Excerpts From:

Bowen, John R. (2004) Does French Islam Have Borders? Dilemmas of Domestication in a Global Religious Field. *American Anthropologist* 106(1):43–55.

DOES FRENCH ISLAM HAVE BORDERS? DILEMMAS OF DOMESTICATION IN A GLOBAL RELIGIOUS FIELD

John R. Bowen (2004)

Abstract

Although many accounts of transnational religious movements emphasize mobility and communication, equally important are efforts by both political actors and religious leaders to carve out distinctive national forms of religion. In this article I examine dilemmas faced by Muslims in France who seek both to remain part of the global Muslim community and to satisfy French demands for conformity to political and cultural norms. I consider the history of immigration and the importance of French notions of laïcité but emphasize the structural problem of articulating a global religious field onto a self-consciously bounded French nation-state. I then draw on recent fieldwork in Paris to analyze two recent public events in which attempts by Muslim public intellectuals to develop an "Islam of France" are frustrated by internal, structural tensions concerning religious authority and political legitimacy, and not simply by a conflict between "Muslims" and "France." [Keywords: Islam, France, transnational movements, politics, religion]

We should not depend on other countries for finding imams who speak not a word of French. – Nicolas Sarkozy, French Minister of the Interior, Paris, April 19, 2003

When government officials say "Islam de France" it means that they want to control Islam in France. – speaker at the Adda'wa mosque, Paris, May 4, 2003

In the best tradition of dialectical scholarship, anthropologists and others have been deftly plying the tensions of global and local to understand transnational phenomena. If in one moment scholars explore and celebrate new possibilities for movement and communication across political boundaries (Appadurai 1996; Castells 1996), in another they consider how new cultural boundaries may be generated by such movements, whether for "over-seas" Chinese coming "back to" the mainland (Louie 2000) or for Germans coming "back together" in a common homeland (Borneman 1992).

In this study of the interrelations of Islam and France, I analyze a third set of processes. I explore ways in which French state officials and Muslim public intellectuals attempt to control trans-state movement and communication by creating new, domesticated forms of Islam. Although scholars increasingly point out the ways in which states can subvert transstate movement by limiting access to national citizenship, social welfare benefits, and labor markets (Kumar 2002; Morris 1997; Soysal 1994), the case of France and Islam emphasizes two additional dimensions of these domestication strategies. First, the involvement of both Muslim and non-Muslim leaders indicates the reach of "governmentality" beyond the confines of the state and into "civil society" (Ferguson and Gupta 2002; Foucault 1991). Secondly, efforts to domesticate Islam create dilemmas for those Muslims who seek both to preserve their ties to a global religious field and to adapt to French political demands and social conditions.

Dilemmas of domestication do not exist exclusively for Muslims or for France. The problem of the loyalty of Protestant nonconformists was, after all, the issue that led John Locke to write his Letter *Concerning Toleration* (1689), and many modern Catholics have found themselves torn between Papal directives and national or personal norms and values (Casanova 1994; Gauchet 1998). East Asian states have developed a variety of strategies to "domesticate" Christianity (Baker 1997). In Muslim-majority countries, public intellectuals have sought to develop appropriately domesticated versions of Islam in accord with local norms and values – the vicissitudes of which I have explored elsewhere for Indonesia (2003a). Although their situation is not unique, French Muslims face particularly sharp and explicit conflicts because of the simultaneous strength of French Republican ideology and Islamic universalism. This case may therefore provide a particularly appropriate place for ethnographic exploration.

Turning on a Preposition

Most Muslims living in France probably would subscribe to the proposition that they ought to develop an "Islam of France" (Islam de France) rather than merely an "Islam in France" (Islam en France). Indeed, this opposition has become a hackneyed rhetorical device for signaling one's allegiance both to the French Republic and to Islam. Government officials and imams alike repeat it as an unquestionably good starting point for discussions regarding Islam. And, yet, agreement stops there. For some Muslims and many non-Muslims, the phrase "Islam of France" connotes an Islam of piety, without the antiquated trappings of Islamic law, and with less emphasis on the practices of prayer and sacrifice. For other Muslims it inspires an effort to rethink Islam in a European context without compromising on either its core principles or its norms and practices. For many non-Muslim French people it means cultural "assimilation" to French language and culture or social "integration" into a "mixed" society – to be demonstrated by choosing designer headscarves over the Islamic kind, eating the same food as everyone else, or interacting regularly with non-Muslims. For many in the government, however, the phrase means an Islam regulated by the state and bounded by the state's borders, with French Islamic institutions and French-trained imams.

Many Muslims living in France find themselves thereby caught between two competing sets of social norms. To the degree that they seek acceptance, recognition, or citizenship in France, many Muslims accommodate some of the demands that they assimilate. Many others, however, consider it to be a requirement of Islam that they engage in regular and often public performance of religious practices, display their cultural differences from non-Muslims through dress and choice of foods, and maintain their membership in the global *umma* (community of Muslims) beyond the borders of France. To urge that French Islam stop at Calais – or, more pertinently, at Marseille – would be to deny the intrinsically universal character of Islam and force Muslims to embody a non-Muslim version of French life.

Here I examine the range of public responses by Muslim intellectuals to these dilemmas of domestication.[12] I focus on only one of the issues facing Muslims: Is an Islam de France culturally, linguistically, and geographically limited to France? *Should* it be? What legitimate references can such an Islam make to authorities living in other, very different societies and to the normative ideas those authorities espouse? Below I present the two predominant approaches to understanding the dynamics of Islam in France, one that examines problems of integrating immigrants and another that emphasizes the importance of maintaining public religious neutrality. Each uncovers a specific dimension of the key dilemma, but both focus on the attitudes and motivations of individual Muslims. I then draw on recent fieldwork in Paris to propose a (complementary) third approach that focuses on the structural problem of articulating a global religious field onto a self-consciously bounded French nation-state – in other words, the problem posed by "*de*."[13]

This problem arises at the intersection of two broader sets of discussions about boundaries and norms. One concerns the nature of European identity that, as Talal Asad points out (2003:159–180), has required both differentiation

---

[12] I concentrate on actors and populations of North African origin or heritage and Arabic-language speakers and leave to the side the very different issues regarding West Africans (Riccio 2000) and Turks (Amiraux 2001; Frégosi 2003). In a longer work I will take up the important contrasts across European countries.

[13] Elsewhere I explore debates and differences among French Muslims concerning laïcité (2003b) and jurisprudence (2001; in press).

from non-Europe and recognition by others as "Europe." The question of Turkey's admission to the European Union, for example, raises not only concerns about human rights in Turkey but also – perhaps, more fundamentally but always more implicitly – a fear of diluting "Europe" by admitting a "non-Christian" nation. "Europe" and "France" also are challenged by new forms of citizenship (Hanagan and Tilly 1999; Kumar 2002; Soysal 1994) that draw on discourses of human rights to demand new forms of recognition beyond those offered by the nation-state.

At the same time, Muslims are debating whether a different transnational normative framework – namely, the universal way *(sharî`a)* proposed by God – ought to be further inflected by the norms of Europe, in other words, by "Europe." Are Muslims in Europe a minority and, thus, should they be given dispensations (to buy at interest, to marry and divorce in civil ceremonies) not accorded to Muslims in, say, Saudi Arabia? Or should the entire tradition of jurisprudence *(fiqh)* be rethought and, perhaps, be replaced by new forms of reasoning based on the objectives or principles of sharî`a? Each set of deliberations, on "Europe" and on "Islam," requires rethinking the relationships of space and norms; each involves simultaneous movements of closing in and opening outward.

Immigration, Assimilation, and Integration

It is not surprising that many studies of Muslims in France (and elsewhere in Europe) concern immigration: They tell a story of immigration gone awry, a problem of the insufficient assimilation, integration, insertion, or – to use the latest attempt at inoffensiveness – "mixing" *(mixité) by* individuals. The Muslims who immigrated to France after World War II were by and large unskilled male workers, recruited by government and industry from French Algeria and from the colonies or protectorates in order to facilitate the postwar economic recovery. The state acted as if their stay was temporary. Large housing projects built in suburbs or industrial enclaves maintained their isolation from the cultural mainstream, and instruction in languages of origin was intended to facilitate the families' expected "return home."[14]

Three things went wrong with this policy. First, the reception turned sour. The French economy suffered recession in the 1970s, and the immigrants

---

[14] Among English-language sources on recent immigration and citizenship, consult Feldblum 1999, Hargreaves 1995, and Noiriel 1996; an excellent "state of the art" collection in French is Dewitte 1999. Kepel 1991 remains the best overall sociological study of Muslim associations and activities in France; a recent update by the journalist for *Le Monde*, Ternissien 2002, also is useful. See Cesari 1998, 2002 for overviews, and Kastoryano 2002 for a comparative study of French and German policies and outcomes.

quickly went from being useful instruments in national growth to hostile com-
petitors for low-paying jobs. Political parties of the far right played on insecurity and racism. Secondly, immigrant workers became settled families. Many
workers sent for their families or married, and after 1974 it became legally more
difficult to immigrate unless one did so in order to "reunite a family," a change
that radically transformed the demographics of French Muslims (Belbah and
Vegliai 2003). Third, the children of North African Muslim immigrants, the
famous *beur* generation, began to demand rights of citizenship, including the
right to practice their religion unimpeded: to build mosques, to carry out public rituals, and to dress in an Islamic way (Cesari 1998). Other French residents did not always welcome these demands. The resentment over economic
competition that fueled the far right in the 1970s and early 1980s became, by
the late 1980s, resentment over cultural difference, an unalterable newness on
putatively ancient French soil. These resentments continue to simmer, aggra-
vated by fears of (sub) urban violence and international terrorism.

Although France keeps no statistics on the religious beliefs or practices of
its inhabitants, estimates of the number of Muslim residents in France today
range from four to five million people, nearly all of them immigrants and
their children, and about one-half foreign nationals. About 60 to 70 percent
of Muslim immigrants to France have come from the Maghreb: Algeria and
Morocco have contributed the largest numbers, followed by Tunisia. Turks
and West Africans form the next largest groups.[15]

Many of the French political scientists and sociologists who wrote about
Islam in the 1990s underscored the trajectory of immigration, emphasizing, in
most cases, the particular social situations facing "the youth" or "the beurs."
Studies that take into account the religious dimension of life for this second
generation (e.g., Khosrokhavar 1997; Souilamas 2001) shade into studies that
focus on local associations (Wihtol de Wenden and Leveau 2001), or problems
of violence and "incivility" in the suburbs. In the 2000s, an increasing number
of books attempt to link the two, making Islam or "Arabo-Muslim culture"
responsibility for the collapse of respect and tolerance in the public schools

---

[15] Haut Conseil (2001:36–39) follows earlier scholars in estimating the number of Muslims at
slightly over four million but insists that the number of people "of Muslim religion" would be
closer to one million, the rest being "of Muslim culture." They base their estimate of religious
Muslims on surveys concerning how often Muslims pray in mosques. Because the census is
not allowed to gather data on "faith," figures in France always have to do with immigration
history and various religious practices as determined by surveys. Deciding who is "Muslim"
for purposes of counting is, of course, contested; the government's recent decision to organize
elections for the Islamic representative body around the mosques implicitly linked mosque
attendance to the right to have a voice in this election, and, thus, to an idea of what is a
"Muslim." The decision was sharply criticized by some Muslims who do not attend mosques.

(Brenner 2002). Others (e.g., Cesari 1998) argue that, to the contrary, young Muslims are also Republicans. Despite their opposite conclusions, these studies share an analytical framework that focuses on processes of assimilation or integration as the outcome of immigration processes; processes that "worked" for the Portuguese, Italians, Poles, and so forth (see Noiriel 1996).[16]

Some French analyses of assimilation reach into the everyday lives of immigrants to measure the degree to which they lose their culturally specific behaviors and blend into a general French model. The clearest example of this approach is the study carried out by Michèle Tribalat (1996) of the National Institute for Demographic Studies (INED [Institut National d'Études Démographiques]), which postulates that assimilation implies not only the privatization of religion but also a lessened intensity of religious practices: "In sum, a laïcisation of behavior" (1996:254).

Prayer (*salât*) is one index of such a change for Tribalat, for whom reducing the number of times one prays indicates greater assimilation. Muslims and others in France often point to the regular performance of prayer as the dividing line between a "practicing" Muslim (*pratiquant*) and someone who is merely a "believing" Muslim (*croyant*), who might fast and eat only halal meat but does not pray regularly (Venel 1999:52–55). Designating someone a "pratiquant" often carries with it an implication of fanaticism, a judgment that someone is behaving or thinking in insufficiently French ways.

One incident struck me early on in my research, when a man who had converted to Islam and had been very active in Islamic education and publicity described the strategy behind a new magazine (*La Médina*) as "aiming for the nonpratiquants" among Muslims. He explained, "the pratiquants see what we write about and dismiss it, but the others will read it" (conversation with author, April 7, 2000). This man was, in fact, a regular observer of Islamic ritual duties and frequently excused himself to pray during our conversations (as he did during the very one in which he made this statement). Nevertheless, he used "nonpratiquant" to indicate someone interested in participating in French social life.[17]

---

[16] Intense debates concerning the proper terms and frameworks for studying immigration continue to take place in France. The Left at one time favored the use of the term *insertion* – often derided as "the Anglo-Saxon model" – which referred to a model in which ethnic communities exist within an overall political framework. After 1989, the year of the first election victories of the Front National and the first round of battles over headscarves on Muslim schoolgirls, the Left changed its preference to *integration*, a term preferred by the Haut Conseil à l'Intégration (2001).

[17] It is difficult to know the range of associations with the word *pratiquant*. On the one hand, one hears the use described above; it may be that the legacy of the word's use to describe a certain category of Catholics shades its meaning in these instances. On the other hand, when forced

Protesting that one does not pray regularly can be a way of assuring a nervous public that one is unlikely to be a terrorist. In early 2003, a baggage handler at Charles de Gaulle airport was falsely accused of possessing arms and sympathizing with terrorists. (It turned out that his in-laws had planted ammunition in his trunk in revenge for what they thought was his role in their sister's, his wife's, death.) Adding to the suspicions were reports that he obliged his wife to wear a head covering, but suspicion was reduced by the report by the secret police (who seem to know a great deal about each Muslim in France) that he did not perform his prayers regularly. On his release from jail, the *bagagiste complained*, "They made us out to be terrorists, whereas we are simple Muslims. We practice an Islam de France, indeed we do not always perform our prayers at the right time" (Tourancheau 2003). Not praying regularly – that is, not having the kind of "fanatical" spirit that would lead you to *insist* on praying – indicates a willingness to fit in with French society.

Exhibiting signs of insufficient assimilation can have very practical consequences for immigrants seeking acceptance as citizens. Each year the French government refuses about one-third of the applicants for admission, and some of those refusals are of candidates who meet the formal conditions for naturalization. The candidate must show "good morals" but they can also be rejected on grounds of insufficient assimilation, whether in their dress, language, their travel outside the country, or for the positions they have taken on Islam (Chattou and Belbah 2001).[18] The idea that everyday behavior could indicate one's values is perhaps unsurprising in the country where *habitus* became the basis for an excellent native social theory. The immigration approach to Muslims in France has shifted ground since the mid-1990s. Many commentators, Muslim and non-Muslims, found "assimilation" to be overly normative

to choose between labeling oneself as *pratiquant* or merely *croyant* (believing), many Muslims choose the former. The survey conducted in late September 2001 by Le Monde and others of Muslims and non-Muslims in France asked Muslims to choose a label for themselves, from "believer" (42 percent), "believer and pratiquant" (36 percent), or "of Muslim origin" (16 percent). The "believer and pratiquant" category was equal to its 1989 level but up from an intervening survey taken in 1994. We do not know how various Muslim respondents interpreted the question – which was posed in a face-to-face interview, presumably by interviewers from a range of backgrounds – nor if any of the respondents might have thought themselves to be practioners but not believers, if given the opportunity. However, *Le Monde* (October 5, 2001) interpreted the results as showing that Muslims in France are practicing their religion more and better able to do so collectively.

[18] Some highly educated Muslim candidates have been rejected on those grounds (Dhaou Meskine, personal communication, May 2003). One man, who at one time worked for the naturalization service, told me of police files emphasizing a couple's overly Islamic dress, the man's beard, and their use of Arabic as criteria for designating them as insufficiently assimilated. The public records studiously avoid mentioning such details, each of which could be challenged in court.

and proposed alternatives. Although "integration" remains in general use, it, too, has been criticized for presuming that it is up to immigrants to adapt rather than the responsibility of others to reexamine their own prejudices (Begag 2003). Most recently, "mixity" has come to denote a more general process of "social mingling," which, by focusing on the properties of territorial units (percentages of immigrants per school district, for example), avoids the problems posed in French ideological space by references to the properties of individuals (Kirszbaum 2003). But the overall analytical framework remains one of evaluating the degree to which Muslims have, or should, become culturally French.

Laïcité and the Republic

The second major analytical framework used to understand "Islam in France" draws its cultural strength from the Republic's struggle against the church, and the doctrines and laws of *laïcité* that were the outcome of that struggle. "Political laïcité," with respect to the state and its laws, requires the state to refrain from imposing a particular religion, or from allowing any religion to impose itself through the medium of the state. Article 2 of the Law of 1905 on the separation of churches and the state makes this conception clear: "The Republic does not recognize, salary, or subsidize any cult" (Baubérot 1996:29). In practice, this rule means that public employees of any kind may not display their religious affiliation.

Laïcité has a social and cultural reading as well, which goes well beyond the letter of the law and which has diffused a heritage of militant anticlericism, particularly in the milieus of teachers and professional classes.[19] "Social laïcité" demands not only a separation of state and churches but also a further privatization of religious affiliation, such that even nongovernmental actors, when they inhabit the public sphere, refrain from doing so religiously. According to this idea, French citizens become complete political individuals by being socialized in public institutions, and they retain their citizenship qualities by continuing to interact in such institutions qua citizens – and not as Muslims, Protestants, or, perish the thought, Scientologists. They recognize each other as equivalent citizens, indistinguishable on the dimension of their participation in French public life. This quality of being indistinguishable in public

---

[19] On the history and philosophy of laïcité, see Baubérot (2000) and Poulat (1997). One can trace the periods of relaxing and tightening the debates through the issues of *Le Monde de l'Éducation*. The issue of May 1999 urged the educational establishment to recognize, at last, that the fight with the Church was over, whereas the issue of May 2003, after rising tensions in the schools and Sarkozy's speech on the headscarves (see below), links headscarf-wearing to Muslims shutting themselves off from French society.

forums makes France a prime example of what Émile Durkheim thought he had isolated in premodern society, namely "mechanical solidarity."

The norm of social laïcité leads some teachers and principals of secondary schools to expel girls who come to class wearing headscarves, or some employers in private industry to demand that employees not wear "clearly Islamic" dress. When Muslim schoolgirls began to wear headscarves to school in the late 1980s, some teachers and principals resented the girls' public display of difference, and a number of prominent French intellectuals publicly cried out that the Republic was endangered (Gaspard and Khosrokhavar 1995). Within a few years the highest administrative law body, the Conseil d'État, had arrived at what would be its consistent ruling that nothing in French law prevents schoolchildren from expressing their religious beliefs by wearing garments that imply a religious affiliation, as long as such garments are not "ostentatious" and the children in question neither "proselytize" nor disturb "public order."[20] Indeed, the Conseil d'État ruled that they have the right to engage in religious self-expression in school. What the law restricts is the apparel and the conduct of teachers and other state employees; it is they who must remain neutral with respect to religion, according to the political and legal idea of laïcité.

But social laïcité indicates something quite different. Forged in the struggle against the Catholic Church for the control of schools and the minds of schoolchildren, and drummed into new teachers during their years of teacher training, the struggle of laïcité is against the intrusion of religion into the classroom. For many teachers, children should not distinguish themselves from one another on religious dimensions at school. Teachers and principals continue to expel or isolate children wearing headscarves and threaten to strike if overruled. One such incident occurred in 2002–03, when the teachers in a high school near Lyon threatened to strike if one female student was not expelled. The student had appeared in school in the most minimal of head coverings – a "bandana," as it was described – that covered neither the forehead nor the ears.[21] Two hundred of the 250 teachers signed a statement saying that: (1) the very fact the girl had refused to take it off on religious grounds made the scarf into an "ostentatious sign," (2) school policy forbids all such signs, and (3) the student should be punished (Landrin 2003). The headscarf

---

[20] The three terms in scare quotes are the three key legal terms in their French cognates; see Bowen 2001 for the jurisprudential details.

[21] Teachers seem to be more likely accept a scarf if it leaves uncovered the earlobes and the roots of the hair, and if it is colored rather than black or white. These preferences make the fact that the female student wore a bandana particularly pertinent (Landrin, 2003), an inference that was confirmed to me by Hanifa Chérifi, who exercised her function as mediator in headscarf affairs for the Department of Education in this case (personal communication, May 2003).

issue surfaced in the media again in April 2003, when Muslims attending the Union des Organisations Islamiques de France (UOIF) annual assembly (see below) booed the call by the Minister of the Interior to enforce the law requiring women to bare their heads for their identity photos. Newspaper articles in April and May 2003 replayed the arguments first heard in the 1980s, according to which the headscarf was a sign of female submission and a direct attack on the principle of laïcité (implying laïcité in its social sense). Throughout the fall of 2003, a special commission appointed by President Chirac conducted marathon hearings on the advisability of outlawing Islamic scarves in classrooms, finally advocating a ban on head scarves, large crosses, and yarmukes (Commission 2003, pt. 4.2.2.1).

Ironically, some women consider wearing the headscarf to be part of *breaking* with immigrant culture, a way of distinguishing between an Islam learned in France ("Islam *de* France") and the insufficiently Islamic traditions of the "old country" ("Islam *en* France"). As many French observers have noted, when young women choose to wear a head covering, misleadingly called *le voile* ("the veil"), it often signifies a moment of personal growth and transition – such as graduating from school, traveling to another country, beginning work, or making a break with the social norms of their family (Cesari 1998; Gaspard and Khosrokhavar 1995; Souilamas 2000; Venel 1999). Wearing a headscarf rarely is a mark of continuity in family dress but a mark of discovery and self-identification as an individual. Even the way a woman wears a headscarf may be seen either "as in the old country" – a manner of wearing the scarf that allows hair to show – or as learned in France – in which the forehead and all the hair is covered, indicating an appropriate understanding of the scarf's Islamic meaning (Venel 1999:52–55). As one woman stated, "I became a practicing Muslim, that is thanks to France, because it provides structures so that we might learn Arabic and our religion. I am glad to have come to know my religion, true Islam, because 'back there,' it is too traditional and troublesome" (Venel 1999:71). For these women, concepts of an "Islam de France" include wearing head coverings, in contrast to practices in their "country of origin."

Articulating Nation-State with Global Islam

Both of the analytical approaches discussed above focus on individuals' acceptance or refusal of certain French cultural values or practices. Disagreements among analysts rest on divergent interpretations of Muslims' attitudes and attitudes: Muslims do or do not accept the terms of the Republican social contract; the veil is or is not a sign of dissension from the common body politic, or of the submission of women to men. In these arguments, Muslims and non-Muslims, social scientists and public actors – and the separation between categories becomes markedly blurred – start from the political culture and cultural boundaries of the Republic and then measure the orientations and actions of individuals with respect to that culture. Yes, French Islam should have borders, and currently Muslims either do or do not behave accordingly.

But the remarks on headscarves quoted above suggest that, *through* their education in France, some Muslims, at least, discover the universal – and, thus, non-French, but also non-Moroccan, and so on – character of Islam, including its nonprivatized and nonlocalized dimensions (see also Eickelman 1992). At the same time, in the classical texts of Islamic jurisprudence other Muslims have found the basis for creating new forms of jurisprudence that would be specific to Europe. The universalistic and the specific intertwine in often unforeseen ways. In the remainder of this article I analyze the tensions and debates concerning the "domestication" of Islam, and the adaptation of Islamic texts, practices, and institutions to conditions within a state. These tensions arise among Muslims and among government officials as well as between the two. They are multivalent: political, linguistic, theological, and jurisprudential. They bring together debates about the fairness of French laws, the appropriateness of multilingualism, the degree to which Islamic norms should be different for different societies, and the questions of assimilation and laïcité already discussed.

The state and Muslim groups represent these issues in quite distinct ways, and on each side there are important debates and tensions. The French state has never interpreted laïcité to require that the state avoid involvement in the affairs of religious groups. If a religion achieves a presence in the public sphere, then the state considers it necessary that there be a single "privileged interlocutor," a body with which the state can negotiate practical matters involving religious practices. The precise arrangements have taken different forms for each major religion. Catholicism has its own hierarchy, with which the postrevolutionary French state has made a series of agreements, from the 1801 Concordat with Napoleon to century laws giving the state the right and duty to maintain those Church buildings that constitute part of the French heritage *(patrimoine)*. The Fédération Protestante de France, created in 1905 with the official separation of churches and state, controls the Protestant television broadcast on state television, furnishes chaplains for the army and prisons, and in general tries to "coordinate" relations with the state. Two bodies speak with the state regarding Jewish affairs: The Consistory, created by Napoleon in 1808, regulates the inspection of food (and pronounces religious discourses), while the Conseil Représentatif des Institutions Juives de France (CRIF), created as an underground network in 1943, claims to represent the many distinct associations of Jews (whether religious or secular) in politics and in public life.

The French state's relationship to Islam has been markedly different from these cases because it was shaped through colonial policy. The first mosque established in metropolitan France (the Great Mosque of Paris) was created in the period between the two world wars with the sponsorship of the Moroccan king, and then reassigned by the French Foreign Minister in 1957 to Algeria (Kepel 1991: 64–94). This sponsorship continued after Algerian independence in 1962. Despite its frequent complaints to the contrary, today the state accepts that the major mosques and Islamic associations in France are funded by foreign governments (principally Morocco, Algeria, Saudi Arabia, and Turkey) and that these governments are able and willing to exercise control over important Muslim leaders in France.

At the same time, the state has sought for years to establish a "privileged interlocutor" with the Muslim community. In December 2002, the Minister of the Interior (who is also "Minister of Cults"), Nicolas Sarkozy, gained the agreement of the major Islamic associations to participate in elections for a new representative council, the Conseil Français du Culte Musulman (CFCM). He did so by demanding that the three highest offices in the new Council be reserved for representatives of the three most influential associations: (1) the Paris mosque (controlled by Algeria), (2) the Fédération Nationale des Musulmans de France (FNMF, controlled by Morocco), and (3) the UOIF, the largest Islamic association in France with strong Moroccan leadership and ties to the Muslim Brotherhood.[22]

During this process Sarkozy boasted that he had made the rounds of the relevant foreign governments before completing his program, a statement greeted with derision by those Muslim leaders not included in the revealed triumvirate. After the April 6 and 13, 2003, elections, which gave victory to Moroccan candidates over the Algerian slates sponsored by the Paris Mosque,[23] the leader of the Paris Mosque, Dalil Boubakeur, was summoned back to Algeria to "explain himself."[24] State policy thus continues to be one of both

---

[22] Each has its own network of affiliated mosques throughout France. In response to the North African (Maghreb) domination of public Islamic activities, immigrants from Turkey formed their own association and Muslims from a broad array of places – the Comoros, the West Indies, and West Africa – formed a "non-Maghreb" interest group.

[23] Electors were named by mosques – the number of electors determined by the size of the mosque floor – and they then choose among competing slates of candidates. In most districts the UOIF, the Moroccan FNMF, and the Algerian Paris Mosque each presented slates, with some cases of joint slates and a few Turkish and independent slates as well.

[24] *Le Matin*, an Algerian paper, on April 22, 2003, titled the relevant article "Boubakeur Explains Himself." The mosque leader claimed he was tricked by the French state, which had assured him that they would not let Algeria lose strength in the Council.

direct and indirect control of French Islamic associations, through an interior discourse of citizenship and domestication and a foreign policy aimed at encouraging governments to control "their" Muslims.

Muslim associations and public actors pose the question differently, however; they situate themselves with respect to "France" (French language, French norms, and social laïcité) and with respect to the greater world of "Islam" (Arabic language, pan-Islamic religious norms, public religion). At the center of the ensuing debates are questions of how Islamic norms should be interpreted for Europe.

Language plays a role in the way Muslims position themselves on this dimension despite the fact that Arabic gradually disappears from North African-origin Muslim households. Most Muslims in France either speak Arabic or had parents who do so but only about one-half of those who heard Arabic regularly at home in turn speak it with their own children (Héran et al. 2002). Arabic continues to be the highest-status vehicle for religious knowledge, however, and many children of North African immigrants continue to hear Arabic and may turn "back" to study it. If Muslims attend a mosque or a lecture in France they usually find among their neighbors people with good French but little Arabic and people with good Arabic but little French (a distinction strongly correlated with age).[25] For this reason, many public events, include sermons, must include two languages – not only for reasons having to do with linguistic assimilation but also because of the special religious value of Arabic.[26]

"France" and "Islam" thus describe a continuum, with language and norms as key values in determining one's position along the spectrum. Among public actors, the UOIF represents itself as on the "Islam" end, with links to expertise in law or theology from Arabic-speaking countries and in particular to the renowned Egyptian scholar Sheikh Yûsuf al-Qardâwî. Qardâwî's opinions are diffused in Arabic through television (the renowned al-Jazîra station), web sites, and word of mouth.[27] On the "France" end of this spectrum lies the website www.oumma.com (formerly the review *Islam de France*). The site

[25] Of course, other Muslims in France speak languages of Turkey, West Africa, and of the many other former colonies of France. In a very few cases mosques have majority populations speaking one of these languages. I limit my remarks here to the Arabic–French opposition, in part because this opposition structures much of the public debate about Islam in France.

[26] Whether sermons should be in Arabic, in French, or in both remains a matter of variation and sometimes tension. As mentioned below, Larbi Kechat prides himself on having been the first in France to give sermons that alternate between the two languages; others reject using any language other than Arabic, the language of the revelation. The UOIF has made bilingual sermons part of their strategy to create their own version of "Islam of France."

[27] The forthcoming work of Ermete Mariani on Qardâwî, and that of Alexandre Caeiro (2003) on the European Council for Fatwa and Research will provide important understandings of the relationship between French institutions and this pan-Islamic network.

offers a secularist discourse, condemning the Union of Islamic Organizations in France (UOIF) for being "close to the Muslim Brotherhood," the phrase of disapproval used by many at this pole (and by non-Muslim French experts on Islam).[28]

These writers privately disdain the "approximate French" with which foreign-born leaders of all other movements express themselves. Many Muslims with university positions find themselves in agreement with www.oumma.com: They urge Muslims to follow a French lifestyle in France, shaping their Islam around either private prayer or an appreciation of Arabo-Muslim history and civilization (e.g., Babès 1997).[29]

Conclusion

Three major clusters of issues emerge as defining the problem of the preposition in Islam de France: the behavior of Muslims, the control by the Republic, and the adaptation of Islamic norms to France (and, more generally, to Europe).[30] All three can be understood as facets of the overall problem of boundaries and borders for a universalistic religion with socially normative pretensions. The issues of assimilation and "social laïcité" both turn on the ways in which the behaviors of Muslims are read to indicate something about their attitudes or motives. An entire ethnography of cross-cultural perceptions could be built on the ways in which some non-Muslim French people use their bodies, grimaces, and speech in describing the social orientations they impute to women wearing different styles of head coverings. Non-Muslim French friends of mine contort their faces and stiffen their posture in demonstrating the closed-off attitude they ascribe to Muslim women wearing black outfits or head coverings that descended down the back. In contrast, these same friends happily interweave their hands when recounting how other Muslim women had taken the trouble

---

[28] As of late 2002, I sensed that for some commentators – yet not the majority – the symbolic value of the Muslim Brotherhood had shifted to a relatively moderate form of Islamism when contrasted with the *salafistes* (the term now used to denote radical preachers in mosques).

[29] This avoidance of Arabic led the editors of *Islam de France* to attack the government's use of an Arabic phrase, *al-Istichara* (Consultation), to designate the on-line government journal about the process of creating the new representative Council. The editors suspected that this usage implied that Islam in France would not be totally French (Bowen 2003b).

[30] These examples are not exhaustive of public Islamic discourse presented in contemporary France. The full range includes: the secularist www.oumma.com; the sermons delivered in Arabic, French, or other languages "of origin" in France's mosques; the proselytizing activities of the Tablighi Jema'at in Paris and other large cities; the "under-the-radar" meetings with foreign religious activists; the many very public rallies aimed at building Muslim electoral muscle in the immediate suburbs of Paris and in the cities of Toulouse and Marseille; and the everyday lives of young people who adopt a wide variety of relationships to the religion and culture of their parents, or the religion presented to them as "true" Islam.

to wear flowered scarves tucked in under their blouses. When this ethnoso-ciology of Republicanism becomes the basis for police reports, employment decisions, or the expulsion from school, it becomes an enforceable demand to decide whether one is going to be part of "France" or part of "Islam."

This interpretive grid undoubtedly shapes the state's ways of regimenting Islam. Sarkozy shrewdly picked *le voile* as his prime example of the need for greater equality before the law because it showed why an active state con-trol of Islamic institutions and Muslims' behavior is required to safeguard the Republic. But that control runs deeper, including a desire to cut off French Islam from direct interference by other states and to leave such interference at the exclusive disposal of the French government. Here the state's project can at moments coincide *rhetorically* with the project of adapting Islam to French society advocated by many Muslim public intellectuals. The UOIF agreed with the Minister in advocating an Islam free of foreign intervention – one of the banners in front of the main stage even read "A Citizen's, Authentic Islam" – however, the two parties have very different, and conflicting, norma-tive horizons: the current laws of the Republic for one, the eternal rules of scripture for the other.

The entry of Islam into the public sphere in France has indeed changed the shape of the "preexisting discursive structure," as Asad (2003:185) suggests. The French state has done so by simultaneously enlarging the French national personality to include citizens of the Muslim confession *and* highlighting the importance of boundary maintenance to the preservation of the Republic. Muslims can be incorporated into "France," but only as French-speaking citizens who make an effort to leave behind their foreign attachments and to resemble other citizens in matters deemed critical to defining "France." The state thereby affirms the importance of maintaining boundaries that are both of the state and of the nation, as a counterweight to new internal pluralisms, *pace* the call by many scholars for a new pluralism of political boundaries (Connolly 1996; Soysal 1994).

This closing off of the nation-state comes just as trans-national Islamic movements continue to develop in strength and scope (Grillo 2001; Vertovec 2002; Werbner 2003), and Muslims in France seek to develop stronger relation-ships to Muslim scholars elsewhere. And yet here, too, efforts to create nation-alist inflections of a universal Islamic set of norms are increasingly challenged by Muslim scholars living outside of Europe, for whom a "European Islam" or national versions thereof smack of nationalism and of deviation from the single universal path. These scholars retain a religious legitimacy that French Muslims seek to capture. These two sets of attempts at closure, by the state and by French Muslim actors, are driven by their internal contradictions – what is

"France"? what is "Islam"? – and by their relationships to each other, clashing or coinciding over what, precisely, should be the borders of French Islam.

REFERENCES CITED

Al-Alwani, Taha Jabir 2003 *Towards a Fiqh for Minorities: Some Basic Reflections*. London: International Institute of Islamic Thought.

Amiraux, Valérie 2001 *Acteurs de l'Islam entre Allemagne et Turquie. Parcours militants et experiences religieuses*. Paris: L'Harmattan.

Appadurai, Arjun 1996 *Modernity at Large*. Minneapolis: University of Minnesota Press.

Asad, Talal 2003 *Formations of the Secular: Christianity, Islam, Modernity*. Stanford: Stanford University Press.

Babès, Leila 1997 *L'Islam Positif: La Religion des Jeunes Musulmans de France*. Paris: Les Editions de l'Atelier

Baker, Don 1997 World Religions and National States: Competing Claims in East Asia. *In* Transnational Religion & Fading States. Susanne Hoeber Rudolph and James Piscatori, eds. Pp. 144–172. Boulder: Westview Press.

Baubérot, Jean 2000 *Historie de la laïcité française*. Paris: Presses Universitaires de

France. Baubérot, Jean, ed. 1996 *La laïcité: Evolutions et enjeux*. Paris: La Documentation Française.

Belbah, Mustapha, and Patrick Vegliai 2003 Pour une histoire des Marocains en France. *Hommes et Migrations* **1242**:18–31.

Begag, Azouz 2003 *L'Intégration*. Paris: Le Cavalier Bleu Éditions.

Borneman, John 1992 *Belonging in the Two Berlins: Kin, State, Nation*. Cambridge: Cambridge University Press.

Bowen, John R. 2001 Shari`ah, State, and Social Norms in France and Indonesia. ISIM Papers No. 3. Leiden: Institute for the Study of Islam in the Modern World.

2003a *Islam, Law and Equality in Indonesia: An Anthropology of Public Reasoning*. Cambridge: Cambridge University Press.

2003b Two Approaches to Rights and Religion in Contemporary France. In *Rights in Global Perspective*. Jon Mitchell and Richard Wilson, eds. Pp. 33–53. London: Routledge.

In press Pluralism and Normativity in French Islamic Reasoning. *In* Muslim Democratization: Prospects and Policies for a Modern Islamic Politics. Robert Hefner, ed. Princeton: Princeton University Press.

Brenner, Emmanuel, ed. 2002 *Les Territoires Perdus de la République*. Paris: Mille et Une Nuits.

Caeiro, Alexandre 2002 La normativité islamique à l'épreuve de l'Occident: le cas du Conseil européen de la fatwa et de la recherche. Paris: Ecole des Hautes Etudes en Sciences sociales memoire de DEA.

Casanova, Jose 1994 *Public Religions in the Modern World.* Chicago: University of Chicago Press.

Castells, Manuel 1996 *The Rise of the Network Society.* Oxford: Blackwell.

Cesari, Jocelyne 1998 Musulmans et républicains: Les jeunes, l'islam et la France. Brussels: Éditions Complexe. 2002 Islam in France: The Shaping of a Religious Minority. *In* Muslims in the West: From Sojourners to Citizens. Yvonne Yazbeck Haddad, ed. Pp. 36–51. Oxford: Oxford University Press.

Chattou, Zoubir, and Mustapha Belbah 2001 Sujet et Citoyen: Evolutions, enjeux et significations de l'acquisition de la nationalité française par des Marocains en France. Paris: Ministère de l'Emploi et de la Solidarité.

Commission de reflexion sur l'application du principe de laïcité dans le République 2003 Rapport au Président de la République, December 11.

Connolly, W. E. 1996 Pluralism, Multiculturalism, and the Nation-State: Rethinking the Connections. Journal of Political Ideologies 1(1):53–74.

Dewitte, Philippe, ed. 1999 Immigration et integration: l'état des saviors. Paris: La Découverte.

Eickelman, Dale F. 1992 Mass Higher Education and the Religious Imagination in Contemporary Arab Societies. *American Ethnologist* 19(4):1–13.

Feldblum, Miriam 1999 Reconstructing Citizenship: The Politics of Nationality Reform and Immigration in Contemporary France. Albany: State University of New York Press.

Ferguson, James, and Akhil Gupta 2002 Spatializing States: Toward an Ethnography of Neoliberal Governmentality. *American Ethnologist* 29(4):981–1002.

Foucault, Michel 1991 Governmentality. *In* The Foucault Effect: Studies in Governmentality. Graham Burchell, Colin Gordon, and Peter Miller, eds. Pp. 87–104. Chicago: University of Chicago Press.

Frégosi, Franck 2003 Acteurs, movement et dynamiques de l'islam turc à Strasbourg. *In* De la citoyenneté locale. Rémy Leveau, Catherine Wihtol de Wenden, and Khadija Mohsen-Finan, eds. Pp. 35–56. Paris: Institut Français de Relations Internationales.

Gaspard, Françoise, and Farhad Khosrokhavar 1995 *Le foulard et la République.* Paris: La Découverte.

Gauchet, Marcel 1998 *Le Religion dans La Démocratie: Parcours de la Laïcité.* Paris: Gallimard.

Grillo, Ralph D. 2001 Transnational Migration and Multiculturalism in Europe. Oxford: Transnational Communities Working Paper WPTC-01–08.

Hanagan, Michael, and Charles Tilly, eds. 1999 *Extending Citizenship, Reconfiguring States*. Lanham, MD: Rowman and Littlefield Press.

Hargreaves, Alec G. 1995 *Immigration, "Race" and Ethnicity in Contemporary France*. London: Routledge.

Haut Conseil à l'Integration 2001 *L'Islam dans la République*. Paris: La Documentation Française.

Héran, Francois, Alexandra Filhon, and Christine Deprez 2002 La dynamique des langues en France au fil du XXe siècle. *Population and Sociétés* 376:1–4.

Kastoryano, Riva 2002 *Negotiating Identities: States and Immigrants in France and Germany*. Princeton: Princeton University Press.

Kepel, Gilles 1991 *Les banlieues de l'Islam: Naissance d'une religion en France*. Paris: Seuil.

Khosrokhavar, Farhad 1997 *L'Islam des Jeunes*. Paris: Flammarion.

Kirszbaum, Thomas 2003 *Le traitement préférentiel des quartiers pauvres*. Paris: C.E.D.O.V.

Kumar, Krishan 2002 The Nation-State, the European Union, and Transnational Identities. *In* Muslim Europe or Euro-Islam. Nezar Alsayyad and Manuel Castells, eds. Pp. 53–68. Lanham, MD: Lexington Books.

Landrin, Sophie 2003 Un bandeau porté en guise de voile sème le trouble dans un lycée lyonnais. Le Monde. fr 25.02.03.

Locke, John 1689 A *Letter Concerning Toleration*. Indianapolis: Hackett Publishing.

Masud, Muhammad Khalil 1977 *Islamic Legal Philosophy: A Study of Abu Ishaq al-Shatibi's Life and Thought*. Islamabad: Islamic Research Institute.

Morris, Lydia 1997 Globalization, Migration and the Nation-State: The Path to a Post-National Europe? *British Journal of Sociology* 48(2):192–209.

Noiriel, Gérard 1996[1988] *The French Melting Pot*. Minneapolis: University of Minnesota Press.

Poulat, Émile 1997 *La Solution laïque et ses problèmes*. Paris: Berg International.

Riccio, Bruno 2000 From "Ethnic Group" to "Transnational Community"? Senegalese Migrants' Ambivalent Experiences and Multiple Trajectories. Journal of Ethnic and Migration Studies 27(4):583–599.

Souilamas, Nacira Guénif 2000 *Des "beurettesá" aux descendantes d'immigrants nord-africains*. Paris: Grasset.

Soysal, Yasemin Nuhoglu 1994 *Limits of Citizenship: Migrants and Postnational Membership in Europe*. Chicago: University of Chicago Press.

Ternisien, Xavier 2002 *La France des mosquées*. Paris: Albin Michel.

Tourancheau, Patricia 2003 Bagagiste: le complot familial démasqué. Libération. Fr 12.01.03

Tribalat, Michèle 1996 De l'Immigration à l'Assimilation: Enquete sur les Populations d'origine Etrangère en France. Paris: La Découverte/INED.

Venel, Nancy 1999 *Musulmanes françaises: Des pratiquantes voilées à l'université.* Paris: L'Harmattan.

Vertovec, Steven 2003 *Religion and Diaspora.* Oxford: Transnational Communities Working Paper WPTC-01–01.

Werbner, Pnina S. 2002 Imagined Diasporas among Manchester Muslims. Oxford: James Currey. 2003 Pilgrims of Love: Ethnography of a Global Sufi Cult. London: Hurst and Co.

Wihtol de Wenden, Catherine, and Rémy Leveau 2001 *Le Beurgeoisie: Les trois ages de la vie associative issue de l'immigration.* Paris: CNRS Éditions.

Excerpts From:

Bullard, Robert D. (2002) Confronting Environmental Racism in the Twenty-First Century. *Global Dialogue* 4(1).

CONFRONTING ENVIRONMENTAL RACISM IN THE TWENTY-FIRST CENTURY

Robert D. Bullard (2002)

Despite significant improvements in environmental protection over the past several decades, 1.3 billion individuals worldwide live in unsafe and unhealthy physical environments. Hazardous waste generation and international movement of hazardous waste and toxic products pose some important health, environmental, legal, political and ethical dilemmas.

The systematic destruction of indigenous peoples' land and sacred sites, the poisoning of Native Americans on reservations, Africans in the Niger Delta, African Americans in Louisiana's "Cancer Alley", Mexicans in the border towns and Puerto Ricans on the island of Vieques, Puerto Rico, all have their roots in economic exploitation, racial oppression, the devaluation of human life and the natural environment, and corporate greed.

Unequal interests and unequal power arrangements have allowed poisons of the rich to be offered as short-term remedies for poverty of the poor. The last decade has seen numerous developing nations challenge the "unwritten policy" of countries belonging to the Organisation for Economic Co-operation and Development (OECD) to ship hazardous wastes into their borders. Most people-of-colour communities in the United States and poor nations around the world want jobs and economic development – but not at the expense of public health and the environment.

Why do some communities get dumped on while others escape? Why are environmental regulations vigorously enforced in some communities and not in others? Why are some workers protected from environmental and health threats while other workers (such as migrant farm workers) are allowed to be poisoned? How can environmental justice be incorporated into environmental protection? What institutional changes are needed in order to achieve a just and sustainable society? What community organising strategies and public policies are effective tools against environmental racism?

This paper analyses the causes and consequences of environmental racism and the strategies environmental justice groups, community-based organisations and government can use to improve the quality of life for their constituents.

What Is Environmental Racism?

The United States is the dominant economic and military force in the world today. The American economic engine has generated massive wealth, a high standard of living, and consumerism. This growth machine has also generated waste, pollution and ecological destruction. The United States has some of the best environmental laws in the world. However, in the real world, all communities are not created equal. Some communities are routinely poisoned while the government looks the other way.

People of colour around the world must contend with dirty air and drinking water, and the location of noxious facilities such as municipal landfills, incinerators, and hazardous waste treatment, storage and disposal facilities owned by private industry, government and even the military.[31] These environmental problems are exacerbated by racism. *Environmental racism refers to environmental policies, practices, or directives that differentially affect or disadvantage (whether intentionally or unintentionally) individuals, groups, or communities based on race or colour.* Environmental racism is reinforced by governmental, legal, economic, political and military institutions. Environmental racism combines with public policies and industry practices to provide benefits for the countries in the North while shifting costs to countries in the South.

Environmental racism is a form of institutionalised discrimination. Institutional discrimination is defined as "actions or practices carried out by members of dominant (racial or ethnic) groups that have differential and negative impact on members of subordinate (racial and ethnic) groups".[32] The United States is grounded in white racism. The nation was founded on the principles of "free land" (stolen from Native Americans and Mexicans), "free labour" (African slaves brought over in chains), and "free men" (only white men with property had the right to vote). From the outset, racism shaped the economic, political and ecological landscape of this new nation.

Environmental racism buttressed the exploitation of land, people and the natural environment. It operates as an intra-nation power arrangement – especially where ethnic or racial groups form a political and/or numerical minority. For example, blacks in the United States form both a political and numerical racial minority. On the other hand, blacks in South Africa, under apartheid, constituted a political minority and numerical majority. American and South African apartheid had devastating environmental impacts on blacks.

---

[31] See Robert D. Bullard, *Confronting Environmental Racism: Voices from the Grassroots* (Boston: South End Press, 1993). See also Luke W. Cole and Sheila R. Foster, *From the Ground Up: Environmental Racism and the Rise of the Environmental Justice Movement* (New York: New York University Press, 2000).

[32] Joe R. Feagin and Clairece B. Feagin, *Discrimination American Style: Institutional Racism and Sexism*, rev. ed. (Melbourne, Fla.: Krieger Publishing, 1986), p. 2.

Environmental racism also operates in the international arena between nations and between transnational corporations. Increased globalisation of the world's economy has placed special strains on the ecosystems of many poor communities and poor nations inhabited largely by people of colour and indigenous peoples. This is especially true of global resource extraction industries such as oil, timber and minerals. Globalisation makes it easier for transnational corporations and capital to flee to areas with the fewest environmental regulations, best tax incentives, cheapest labour and highest profits.

The struggles of African Americans in Norco, Louisiana, and of Africans in the Niger Delta are similar in that both groups are negatively affected by Shell Oil refineries and unresponsive governments. This scenario is repeated for Latinos in Wilmington (California) and indigenous people in Ecuador who must contend with pollution from Texaco oil refineries. The companies may be different, but the community complaints and concerns are very similar. Local residents have seen their air, water and land contaminated. Many nearby residents are "trapped" in their community because of inadequate roads, poorly planned emergency escape routes and faulty warning systems. They live in constant fear of plant explosions and accidents.

The Bhopal tragedy is fresh in the minds of millions of people who live next to chemical plants. The 1984 poison-gas leak at the Union Carbide plant in Bhopal, India, killed thousands of people, making it the world's deadliest industrial accident. It is not a coincidence that the only place in the United States where methyl isocyanate (MIC) was manufactured was at a Union Carbide plant in the predominately African-American town of Institute, West Virginia. In 1985, a gas leak from Institute's Union Carbide plant sent 135 residents to hospital.

Institutional racism has allowed people-of-colour communities to exist as colonies, areas that form dependent (and unequal) relationships with the dominant white society or "Mother Country" as regards their social, economic, legal and environmental administration. More than three decades ago, Stokeley Carmichael and Charles V. Hamilton offered the "internal" colonial model to explain the racial inequality, political exploitation and social isolation of African Americans:

The economic relationship of America's black communities ... reflects their colonial status. The political power exercised over those communities goes hand in glove with the economic deprivation experienced by the black citizens. Historically, colonies have existed for the sole purpose of enriching, in one form or another, the "colonizer"; the consequence is to maintain the economic dependency of the colonized".[33]

---

[33] Stokeley Carmichael and Charles V. Hamilton, *Black Power* (New York: Vintage, 1967), pp. 16–17.

Institutional racism reinforces internal colonialism. Government institutions buttress this system of domination. Institutional racism defends, protects and enhances the social advantages and privileges of rich nations. Whether by design or benign neglect, communities of colour (ranging from urban ghettos, barrios and rural "poverty pockets" to economically impoverished Native American reservations and developing nations) face some of the worst environmental problems. The most polluted communities are also the communities with crumbling infrastructure, economic disinvestment, deteriorating housing, inadequate schools, chronic unemployment, high poverty and overloaded health-care systems.

Dumping on the Poor

Hazardous waste generation and the international movement of hazardous waste still pose some important health, environmental, legal and ethical dilemmas. The "unwritten" policy of targeting Third World nations for waste trade received international media attention in 1991. Lawrence Summers, at the time chief economist of the World Bank, shocked the world and touched off an international firestorm when his confidential memorandum on waste trade was leaked. Summers wrote: " 'Dirty' Industries: Just between you and me, shouldn't the World Bank be encouraging MORE migration of the dirty industries to the LDCs [less developed countries]?"[34] Between 1989 and 1994, an estimated 2,611 metric tons of hazardous waste was exported from OECD countries to non-OECD countries.

Transboundary Waste Trade Conventions

In response to the growing exportation of hazardous wastes into their borders, the Organisation of African Unity (OAU) and the G-77 nations respectively mobilised to pass two important international agreements. On 30 January 1991, the Pan-African Conference on Environment and Sustainable Development adopted the Bamako Convention banning the import into Africa of hazardous wastes and controlling their movement within the continent.

In September 1995, the G-77 nations were instrumental in amending the Basel Convention, despite opposition from the United States, to ban the export of hazardous wastes from highly industrialised countries (specifically OECD countries and Lichtenstein) to all other countries. While Bamako and Basel may have made certain kinds of dumping formally illegal, in practice they have not prevented the transboundary movement of hazardous waste to developing countries. Loopholes still allow hazardous wastes to enter countries that

---

[34] See "Pollution and the Poor", *Economist* 322, no. 746 (15 February 1992), pp. 18–19.

do not have the resources or infrastructure to handle the wastes. For example, Joshua Karliner reports that "products such as pesticides and other chemicals banned or severely restricted by the United States, Western Europe and Japan because of their acute toxicity, environmental persistence or carcinogenic qualities are still regularly sent to the Third World".[35] Having laws or treaties on the books and enforcing them are two different things.

Whether at home or abroad, environmental racism disadvantages people of colour while providing advantages and privileges for whites.

US–Mexico Border Ecology

The conditions surrounding the more than 1,900 maquiladoras – assembly plants operated by American, Japanese and other foreign countries – located along the two thousand–mile US–Mexico border may further exacerbate the waste trade. The industrial plants use cheap Mexican labour to assemble imported components and raw material and then ship finished products back to the United States. Over half a million Mexican workers are employed in the maquiladoras.

All along the lower Rio Grande river valley, maquiladoras dump their toxic wastes into the river, from which 95 per cent of the region's residents get their drinking water. In the border cities of Brownsville (Texas) and Matamoras (Mexico), the rate of anencephaly – babies born without brains – is four times the national average. Affected families filed lawsuits against eighty-eight of the area's one hundred maquiladoras for exposing the community to xylene, a cleaning solvent that can cause brain haemorrhages and lung and kidney damage.

The Mexican environmental regulatory agency is understaffed and ill equipped to enforce its laws adequately. Many of the Mexican border towns have now become cities with skyscrapers and freeways. More important, the "brown pallor of these southwestern skies has become a major health hazard".[36]

Radioactive Colonialism and Threatened Native Lands

There is a direct correlation between exploitation of land and exploitation of people. It should not be a surprise to anyone to discover that Native Americans have to contend with some of the worst pollution in the United States. Native

[35] Joshua Karliner, *The Corporate Planet: Ecology and Politics in the Age of Globalization* (San Francisco: Sierra Club Books, 1997), p. 152.
[36] Tom Barry and Beth Sims, *The Challenge of Cross-Border Environmentalism: The US–Mexico Case* (Albuquerque, N.Mex.: Interhemispheric Resource Center, 1994), p. 37.

American nations have become prime targets for waste trading. The vast majority of these waste proposals have been defeated by grassroots groups on the
reservations. However, "radioactive colonialism" is alive and well. Radioactive
colonialism operates in energy production (mining of uranium) and the disposal of nuclear wastes on Indian lands. The legacy of institutional racism
has left many sovereign Indian nations without an economic infrastructure to
address poverty, unemployment, inadequate education and health care, and a
host of other social problems.

The threats to indigenous peoples are not confined to the United States.
Native and indigenous people all across the globe are threatened with extinc-
tion owing to the greed of mining and oil companies and "development
genocide". Sociologist Al Gedicks has traced the development of a grassroots
multiracial transnational movement that is countering this form of environmental racism.[37] Over five thousand members of the U'Wa tribe of Colombia
have organised to prevent Occidental from drilling on sacred U'Wa land.

The Threat from Military Toxins

Private industry does not have a monopoly on ecological threats to communities of colour. War and military activities are also big players. The US
Department of Defense has left its nightmarish nuclear weapons garbage on
native lands and the Pacific islands. In fact, "over the last 45 years, there have
been 1,000 atomic explosions on Western Shoshone land in Nevada, making
the Western Shoshone the most bombed nation on earth".[38] Residents of the
Marshall Islands live under a constant threat of radioactive contamination.

Corporate Polluters

The southern United States has become a "sacrifice zone" for the rest of the
nation's toxic waste. A colonial mentality exists in Dixie, where local governments and big business take advantage of people who are both politically and
economically powerless. The region is stuck with a unique legacy – the legacy
of slavery, Jim Crow and white resistance to equal justice for all. This legacy
has also affected race relations and the region's ecology.

The southern United States is characterised by "look-the-other-way environmental policies and giveaway tax breaks". It is a place where "political
bosses encourage outsiders to buy the region's human and natural resources at

---

[37] Al Gedicks, *Resource Rebels: Native Challenges to Mining and Oil Corporations* (Boston:
    South End Press, 2001).
[38] Winona LaDuke, *All Our Relations: Native Struggles for Land and Life* (Boston: South End
    Press, 1999), p. 3.

bargain prices".[39] Lax enforcement of environmental regulations has left the region's air, water and land the most industry-befouled in the United States.

Ascension Parish typifies the toxic "sacrifice zone" model. In two parish towns of Geismer and St Gabriel, eighteen petrochemical plants are crammed into a nine-and-a-half-square-mile area. In Geismar, Borden Chemicals has released chemicals into the environment which are hazardous to the health of local residents. These chemicals include ethylene dichloride, vinyl–chloride monomer, hydrogen chloride and hydrochloric acid.

Borden Chemicals has a long track record of contaminating the air, land and water in Geismar. In March 1997, the company paid a fine of $3.5 million, the single largest in Louisiana history. The company has been accused of storing hazardous waste, sludges and solid wastes illegally; of failing to install containment systems; of burning hazardous waste without a permit; of neglecting to report the release of hazardous chemicals into the air; of contaminating groundwater beneath the plant site (thereby threatening an aquifer that provides drinking water for residents of Louisiana and Texas); and of shipping toxic waste laced with mercury to South Africa without notifying the EPA, as required by law.

Louisiana could actually improve its general welfare by enacting and enforcing regulations to protect the environment. However, Louisiana citizens subsidise corporate welfare at the expense of their health and the environment. A growing body of evidence shows that environmental regulations do not kill jobs. On the contrary, the data indicate that "states with lower pollution levels and better environmental policies generally have more jobs, better socioeconomic conditions and are more attractive to new business".[40] Nevertheless, some states subsidise polluting industries in return for a few jobs. States argue that tax breaks help create jobs. However, the few jobs that are created come at a high cost to Louisiana taxpayers and the environment.

Corporations routinely pollute Louisiana's air, ground and drinking water while being subsidised by tax breaks from the state. The state is a leader in doling out corporate welfare to polluters. In the 1990s, the state wiped $3.1 billion in property taxes off the books of polluting companies. The state's five worst polluters received $111 million over the past decade.

Subsidising polluters is not only bad business, it also does not make environmental sense. For example, nearly three-quarters of Louisiana's population – more than three million people – get their drinking water from underground

---

[39] Donald Schueler, "Southern Exposure", *Sierra* 77 (November/December 1992), pp. 45–7.
[40] P. H. Templet, "The Positive Relationship between Jobs, Environment and the Economy: An Empirical Analysis and Review", *Spectrum* (spring 1995), p. 37.

aquifers. Dozens of the aquifers are threatened by contamination from polluting industries. The Lower Mississippi River Industrial Corridor has over 125 companies that manufacture a range of products, including fertilisers, gasoline, paints and plastics. This corridor has been dubbed "Cancer Alley" by environmentalists and local residents.

Economic Blackmail

Industry flight from central cities and older industrial corridors has left behind a deteriorating infrastructure, poverty and pollution. Economically depressed communities do not have a lot of choices available to them. Some workers have become so desperate that they see even a low-paying hazardous job as better than no job at all. These workers are forced to choose between unemployment and a job that may threaten their health, their family's health and the health of their community. This practice amounts to "economic blackmail". Economic conditions in many people-of-colour communities make such communities especially vulnerable to this practice.

Some polluting industries have been eager to exploit this vulnerability. Some have even used the assistance of elected officials in obtaining special tax breaks and government operating permits. State actors have done a miserable job in protecting central city residents from the ravages of industrial pollution and non-residential activities that have a negative impact on quality of life.

Racial and ethnic inequality is perpetuated and reinforced by local governments in conjunction with urban-based corporations. Race continues to be a potent variable in explaining urban land use, street and highway configuration, commercial and industrial development and industrial facility siting. Moreover, the question of "who gets what, where and why" often pits one community against another.

The promise of jobs (even low-paid and hazardous jobs) and a broadened tax base has proven to be an enticing offer in some economically impoverished communities. This scenario has been the rule in politically powerless and poor communities of colour in the United States and around the world. Toxic waste "imperialism" is a fact of life.

Workers are often forced to make personal sacrifices in terms of job security and job safety. The workplace in this case is an arena where unavoidable trade-offs are made between jobs and workplace hazards. If workers want to keep their jobs, they must work under conditions which may be hazardous to them, their families and their community. This practice amounts to "job blackmail" and is equivalent to economic bondage.

Workers of colour are especially vulnerable to job blackmail because of the threat of unemployment and their concentration in low-paying, unskilled, non-union occupations. For example, a large proportion of non-union contract workers in the oil, chemical and atomic fields are persons of colour. Over 95 per cent of migrant farm workers in the United States are Latino, African American, Afro-Caribbean and Asian. Workers of colour are over-represented in high-risk blue collar and service occupations where there is a more than adequate supply of replacement labour.

Residential Apartheid

Section 24 of the South African Constitution states that "everyone has the right: (a) to an environment that is not harmful to their health or wellbeing, and (b) to have the environment protected for the benefit of present and future generations". The Fourteenth Amendment to the US Constitution, while not speaking directly about the environment, is very much about "equal protection for all". Nevertheless, blacks in the United States and in South Africa have had to grapple with the legacy of legalised segregation or apartheid and take on the dismantling of "separate and unequal" measures.

The environmental and health crisis faced by present-day South Africa originates in the combination of poor land, forced overcrowding, poverty, the importation of hazardous waste, inadequate sewerage, the dumping of toxic chemicals into rivers, the strip-mining of coal and uranium, and outdated methods of producing synthetic fuels. Apartheid herded approximately 87 per cent of the black population into 13 per cent of the country's territory. Such a policy spelt environmental disaster.

Apartheid-type housing and development policies in the United States have resulted in limited mobility, reduced neighbourhood options, decreased environmental choices and diminished job opportunities for people of colour. Race still plays a significant part in distributing the public "benefits" and public "burdens" associated with economic growth.

The roots of discrimination are deep and have been difficult to eliminate. Home ownership is still a major part of the "American Dream". Housing discrimination contributes to the physical decay of inner-city neighbourhoods and denies a substantial segment of African Americans and other people of colour a basic form of wealth accumulation and investment through home ownership. The number of African-American homeowners would probably be higher in the absence of discrimination by lending institutions. Only about 59 per cent of the nation's middle-class African Americans own their homes, compared with 74 per cent of whites.

Eight out of every ten African Americans live in neighbourhoods where they are in the majority. Residential segregation decreases for most racial and ethnic groups with additional education, income and occupational status. However, this scenario does not hold true for African Americans. African Americans, no matter what their educational or occupational achievement or income level, are exposed to higher crime rates, less effective educational systems, high mortality risks, more dilapidated surroundings and greater environmental threats because of their race. For example, in the heavily populated South Coast air basin of the Los Angeles area, it is estimated that over 71 per cent of African Americans and 50 per cent of Latinos reside in areas with the most polluted air, while only 34 per cent of whites live in highly polluted areas.[41]

It has been difficult for millions of Americans in segregated neighbourhoods to say "not in my backyard" (Nimby) if they do not have a backyard. Nationally, 46.3 per cent of African Americans and 36.2 per cent of Latinos own their homes compared to over two-thirds of the nation as a whole. Homeowners are the strongest advocates of the Nimby positions taken against locally unwanted land uses, or Lulus, such as the construction of garbage dumps, landfills, incinerators, sewage treatment plants, recycling centres, prisons, drug treatment units and public housing projects. Generally, white communities have greater access than people-of-colour communities when it comes to influencing land use and environmental decision making.

Global Climate Justice

Finding solutions to global climate change is one of the areas that desperately need the input of those populations most likely to be negatively affected – poor people in the developing countries of the South and people of colour and the poor in the North. Global climate change looms as a major environmental justice issue of the twenty-first century. Mounting scientific evidence indicates that human activities are altering the chemical composition of the atmosphere through the build-up of greenhouse gases – primarily carbon dioxide, methane and nitrous oxide. Changing climates are expected to raise sea levels, alter precipitation and other weather conditions, threaten human health and harm fish and many types of ecosystems.

The adverse impacts fall heaviest on the poor. This deadly pattern occurs disproportionately among people of colour in the United States, who are concentrated in urban centres in the south, coastal regions and areas with substandard air quality. Climate justice links human rights and ecological sustainability. Advocates of climate justice are calling for solutions to avert global warming that do not fall hardest on low-income communities, communities of colour, or workers employed by fossil fuel industries.

---

[41] Eric Mann, *LA's Lethal Air: New Strategies for Policy, Organizing, and Action* (Los Angeles: Labor/Community Strategy Center, 1991).

Unsurprisingly, resistance to reining in climate-altering activities through the Kyoto Protocol has come largely from the fossil fuel lobby – companies that either extract, process and sell fossil fuels, generate electricity using coal, oil or gas, and car makers. Communities suffer environmental and health assaults from being fenced in with polluting industries. Giant oil companies are major contributors to both local pollution and global warming.

The impetus for climate justice will probably not come from within government. It is a sure bet that it will not come from the polluting industry. Climate justice will take root from meetings such as the 2000 Climate Justice Summit where those most affected share their common experiences and decide to take collective action. Waiting for governments to respond may be too deadly for communities of colour and the planet.

Review and Recommendations

The environmental justice movement emerged in response to environmental inequities, threats to public health, unequal protection, differential enforcement and disparate treatment received by the poor and people of colour.

Redefinition of Environmental Protection

The movement redefined environmental protection as a basic right. It also emphasised pollution prevention, waste minimisation and cleaner production techniques as strategies to achieve environmental justice for all Americans regardless of race, colour, national origin or income. Many countries have environmental and civil rights laws to protect the health and welfare of their citizens – including racial and ethnic groups. However, not all communities have received the same benefits from the application, implementation and enforcement of these laws.

A Holistic Approach to Environmental Protection

The environmental justice movement has set out clear goals of eliminating unequal enforcement of environmental, civil rights and public health laws, the differential exposure of some populations to harmful chemicals, pesticides and other toxins in the home, school, neighbourhood and workplace, faulty assumptions in calculating, assessing and managing risks, discriminatory zoning and land-use practices, and exclusionary policies and practices that prevent some individuals and groups from participating in decision making. Many of these problems could be eliminated if existing environmental, health, housing and civil rights laws were vigorously enforced in a non-discriminatory way.

Strengthen Legislation and Regulations

A legislative approach may be needed where environmental, health and worker safety laws and regulations are weak or non-existent. However, laws and regulations are only as good as their enforcement. Unequal political power arrangements, too, have allowed poisons of the rich to be offered as short-term economic remedies for poverty.

Design Strategies to Combat Economic Blackmail

Having industrial facilities in one's community does not automatically translate into jobs for nearby residents. Many industrial plants are located at the fence-line with the communities. Some are so close that local residents could walk to work. More often than not, communities of colour are stuck with the pollution and poverty, while other people commute in for the industrial jobs.

Close Corporate Welfare Loopholes

Tax breaks and corporate welfare programmes have produced few new jobs from polluting firms. However, state-sponsored pollution and lax enforcement have allowed many communities of colour and poor communities to become dumping grounds. Industries and governments (including the military) have often exploited the economic vulnerability of poor communities and states to implement their unsound and risky operations. Environmental justice leaders are demanding that no community or nation, rich or poor, urban or suburban, black or white, should be allowed to become a "sacrifice zone" or dumping ground. They are also pressing governments to live up to their mandate of protecting public health and the environment.

Forge International Co-operative Agreements

Governments will need to take responsibility and develop policies that address intra-nation and international environmental racism. The poisoning of African Americans in Louisiana's "Cancer Alley", Native Americans on reservations and Mexicans in the border towns is rooted in the same economic system, a system characterised by economic exploitation, racial oppression and devaluation of human life and the natural environment. The call for environmental and economic justice does not stop at US borders, but extends to communities and nations that are threatened by the export of hazardous wastes, toxic products and dirty industries.

Organise Globally

The environmental justice movement has begun to build a global network of grassroots groups, community-based organisations, university-based resource centres, researchers, scientists, educators and youth groups. Better communication and funding is needed in every area. Resources are especially scarce for environmental justice and anti-racist groups in developing countries. The Internet has proven to be a powerful tool for those groups that have access to the worldwide web. Erasing the "digital divide" can become a major strategy to combat environmental racism.

7   Conclusion: The Enduring Relevance of Law?

In this book I have urged scholars to adopt a global sociolegal perspective to better think about, explore, and perhaps address the escalating and urgent demands being placed on law in the early decades of the twenty-first century. This is not to suggest that sociolegal work to date has "missed the plot" or is inadequate in some way; that would be an arrogant and unproductive premise. But it is to suggest that today's urgent global challenges, risks, and demands require sociolegal scholars to open their minds and look below and beyond national jurisdictions to what may at first appear counter-intuitive or not immediately obvious. It is a call for sociolegal scholars to seek out the counter-hegemonic, to ask how A connects to G, to resist the lure of corporate funding channels, and to adopt a more expansive world view that embraces what Manfred Steger has called "the global imaginary" (Steger 2009).

As argued in this book's Introduction, "A global perspective suggests that important connections exist between events and processes even when events appear to be disconnected and separated by time, space, or even our own categories of thought" (McCarty 2012:3). A global sociolegal perspective destabilizes our modern and linear understandings of what law is, where law appears, and how law works. Moreover, a global sociolegal perspective underscores that analyzing law within nation-states cannot be disconnected from law's global historical formation – often through processes of colonialism and imperialism – as well as a range of global challenges that influence and frame every country's contemporary legal system. In short, a global sociolegal perspective means recognizing that domestic law as it plays out within states is, and always has been, constitutively linked to issues of global economic, political, and cultural power as manifested both within and beyond national jurisdictions (see Chapter 4).

I urge the adoption of a global sociolegal perspective because I want to believe in the enduring relevancy of law. Constrained by my own Western cultural baggage, I have difficulties envisaging a world without legal identities, legal restraints, legal accountabilities, and legal orderings. That being said, if law as we know it in the global North is to endure in any recognizable form, legal practitioners and legal scholars will have to reconceive its foundational premises by coming to terms with its legacies of racism, oppression, and bias. Looking forward, practitioners and scholars will also have to overcome a deeply embedded legal orientalism that posits Western law, and its nation-state structure, as superior to all other legal systems and as a result entitles it to be the dominant way of legally framing the world (Fraser 2005). This parochial position is offensive to billions of people living around the globe. The United States does not have a monopoly on justice, freedom, and democracy, despite widespread beliefs in American exceptionalism that conveniently justifies the country's lack of commitment to international law and resistance to emerging strategies of global governance. Individuals living in villages, cities, regions, and countries in the global South treasure justice and freedom as much as their counterparts living in the global North. However, they may conceptualize these values rather differently and seek them in a variety of ways that people living in Western nations may not be able to immediately recognize or understand (Sen 2009). Being sensitive to and inclusive of a plurality of legal concepts and meanings is the first step in adopting a global sociolegal perspective (see Chapter 3).

Even within Western nations claiming to be the defenders of democracy, it is becoming increasingly obvious that "equality and justice for all" is a hollow refrain. The logics of unregulated capitalism that have for the past forty years enabled the West to imperiously exploit the rest are now manifesting themselves within the neoliberal heartlands. Hence, the growing inequities and racial, religious, gender, and class discriminations within advanced industrialized nations – as articulated by the Occupy movement – parallels the vast disparities of power and wealth between the global North and global South. Whether people can see these global interconnections is another matter. As the prize-winning author Arundhati Roy has commented:

> I hope that the people in the Occupy movement are politically aware enough to know that their being excluded from the obscene amassing of wealth of US corporations is part of the same system of the exclusion and war that is being waged by these corporations in places like India, Africa and the Middle East ... So whether this movement is a movement for justice for the excluded in the United States, or whether it is a movement against an international system of global finance that is manufacturing levels of hunger and poverty on an unimaginable scale, remains to be seen (Roy 2011).

Western nations' legal superiority is not just offensive. It is also profoundly dangerous. Of course, well-intentioned international humanitarian efforts and vast numbers of NGOs championing the rhetoric of human rights and democracy have enabled significant improvements in many people's lives (see Chapter 5). However, although these international efforts bring some measure of relief to millions of people around the world, they have also brought new dangers. Imposing Euro-American structures of power and legality on non-Western local communities can inadvertently dismantle social and cultural support networks and make marginalized people even more vulnerable. No matter how much foreign aid is given by rich to poor nations to help them install democratic procedures, without humanitarian agencies paying close attention to localized and informal political norms, this aid may actually do more harm than good (see Klug 2002). In an analysis of how foreign aid can actually create disincentives for governments of developing countries to seek democratic legal reform, Katherine Erbeznik powerfully argues "money can't buy you law" (Erbeznik 2011). Other ways that the exportation of Western law may do unanticipated harm is revealed in Jothie Rajah's examination of Singapore's authoritarian state system. Here, Rajah argues, the state manipulates liberal legal rhetoric by claiming to embrace the rule of law while simultaneously denying basic rights and preventing judicial independence. Perversely, Singapore's apparent adoption of the rule of law legitimates and shores up an authoritarian regime that maintains power through surveillance, violence, and corruption (Rajah 2011; see also Archibugi and Croce 2012). These examples are sobering moments that give pause and demand reflection.

However, perhaps one of the most unpredictable consequences of exporting Western law to non-Western societies arises in the context of Thailand. As elegantly argued by David Engel and Jaruwan Engel, the legal consciousness of ordinary people in Thailand has not been profoundly impacted by the country's embracing of industrialization and modernity, including the establishing of formal tort law for personal injuries. In contrast to a dominant presumption that legal liberalism heightens people's understanding of their legal rights, the authors argue that in Thailand the opposite is occurring. Thai people do not express "an intensified commitment to the ideology of liberal legalism either as a framework for interpreting experience or a set of practices for obtaining justice" (Engel and Engel 2010:158–159). When personal injury is suffered, Thai people absorb the problem rather than actively seek legal recourse as they did previously, primarily through local customary law. In other words, ordinary people do not turn to previous local forms of redress or to the new state system of tort law. As a result, both informal and formal law matters less than it did before. Conclude the authors:

> The residents of northern Thailand may speak for others around the world when they characterize the law as increasingly remote and justice in this lifetime as more unattainable than ever before. If so, it is the decline of law that demands our attention, and its absence from everyday life may be the hallmark of our age (Engel and Engel 2010:161).

Perhaps it should not perhaps come as a surprise that ordinary Thai people see law as increasingly irrelevant in their lives, or only available to those with money and power. These same attitudes are percolating within the United States, the UK, Australia, Germany, France, and other Western nations that are similarly experiencing crises in the legitimacy and relevance of law. As discussed in the Introduction, today law is regarded by more and more people as explicitly instrumental in its serving corporate and political elites (Tamanaha 2006). Unlike moments in the past, such as in the civil rights era of the 1960s, law is not typically embraced for its emancipatory potential or seen as a strategy by which to resist or change the status quo. This current feeling of despondency about the legitimacy of law is even more pronounced within minority communities whose ethnic, racial, or religious identities are often interpreted as barriers to full and equal legal access and legal redress (see Chapter 6).

In the current crisis of legal legitimacy, it would be foolish to turn our backs on lessons learned from ordinary people living in villages and cities in places such as Thailand. Here the local customary laws and cultural ties of village life are unraveling as people are being forced to move away from their homes and families. Here local legal systems that were relatively accountable in that they were ultimately based on collective trust and the maintenance of social harmony are being undermined. Here we can see the emergent realization that law has become a commodity and that without economic resources ordinary people cannot afford legal access and justice. Here, paradoxically, the forces of modernity and capitalist enterprise are making the promise of legalized democracy increasingly disingenuous and the role of law in people's daily lives increasingly irrelevant.

It is not helpful to romanticize local legal systems of customary law in Thailand. However, it is important to think about the elements of legal engagement that are being lost in the shift toward an explicitly instrumentalist understanding of law that is now becoming globally hegemonic. What we can identify as now missing may inform possible ways to resurrect the legitimacy and relevance of law. These are the features of legal systems – both informal and formal – that are desired by people living across the global North and global South and from all cultures, races, religions, ethnicities, classes, genders, and so on. These are the shared commonalities that everyone can agree are needed for legal systems to function as integral components of social living. In other words, by looking at communities undergoing rapid processes of modernization, as well as frankly examining the limitations in Western nations' legal systems, we may be able to recover common practices and shared legal experiences that are not embedded in any one ideology or religious cosmology or cultural value system, but are basic needs and values that all people deem important. These needs would include such things as people feeling safe in their homes and having adequate food and water, health care, a sense of belonging, and a voice in their community. And these values would include people feeling that they can trust the system of justice, however articulated, and that it is in some way accountable, transparent, and fair in ways that are meaningful to those participating in it.

There are, of course, even within Western state legal systems, examples in which localized and alternative concepts of justice are granted to be of value. We can see this process operating in places such as Native American tribal courts (Richland 2011; Spruhan 2012), domestic and family courts in which non-Christian religious laws are allowed to play a part (Bowen 2011a), community restorative justice programs (Gilbert and Settles 2008), and in the increasing use of teen courts where first-time juvenile offenders are judged by peer juries of other juveniles (Forgays et al. 2004). And we can see the appreciation of local knowledge and meaning gaining prominence in international legal arenas such as the hybrid courts of transitional justice efforts. In these courts local people are involved in determining what constitutes appropriate punishments and processes of reconciliation in the rebuilding of post-conflict community equilibrium. Typically, these moments of allowed legal pluralism are occurring at the margins and peripheries of societies where the economic stakes are low and the political ramifications deemed inconsequential. However, if we take these moments together and focus on what they share in terms of making law meaningful and legitimate, then it may be possible to recover features of legality that can create an ethical framework generalizable to a range of legal forums.

The recovery of law as a legitimate and ethical framework, and one that sincerely respects the concept of legal plurality, is vital for the future stability of all state and non-state legal systems. And it is particularly vital for the building of global governance mechanisms appropriate for the regulation and management of escalating global problems. Unfortunately, the challenges, risks, and demands of the twenty-first century are complex and cumulative. In the global

South, and to a lesser degree in the global North, these challenges include a range of state and non-state corporate-sponsored militias seeking security over minerals, water, and food; mass migrations of people fleeing civil war, genocide, oppression, and starvation; millions of stateless people permanently living as temporary refugees in detention centers, refugee camps, and residential sweatshops; rising health risks, lack of health care, and vulnerabilities to disease and pandemics; and escalating religious and ethnic conflicts that often make relocation impossible and the future unbearable. And all of these issues must be contextualized against a backdrop of widespread environmental degradation and the rapidly growing negative impacts of climate change that disproportionately affect the poor, the marginalized, and the indigenous.

Against this backdrop of impending doom and chaos, global governance aspirations offer a glimmer of hope. But this hope will never begin to be realized until, as David Held reminds us, "a sustained effort [is] undertaken to generate new forms of global political legitimacy for international institutions involved in security and peace-making ... Many parts of the world will need convincing that the UN's – not to mention the Western-based coalition's – interest in security and human rights for all peoples and regions is not just a product of short-term geopolitical or geoeconomic interests" (Held 2004:145–146). Sociolegal scholars are uniquely situated to help in this process of generating new forms of political and legal legitimacy in the context of globalization. By exposing legal inequities within and beyond state systems, sociolegal scholars are positioned to explore the constitution and articulation of new forms of legal knowledge, legal authority, and legal accountability appropriate for a multicultural, multireligious, and multiracial global order. The first step in this process, as I have argued throughout this book, is to adopt a global sociolegal perspective that challenges our taken-for-granted assumptions about what law is, where law appears, and how law works and opens up space for fresh thinking about emergent legal possibilities.

Bibliography

Abbott, Andrew (2001) *Time Matters: On Theory and Method*. Chicago: University of Chicago Press.

Abel, R.L. (1973) Law Books and Books about Law. *Stanford Law Review* 14:805–829.

—— (ed.) (1995) *The Law and Society Reader*. New York: New York University Press.

—— (2010) Law and Society: Project and Practice. *Annual Review of Law and Social Science* 6:1–23.

Adeola, Fancis O. (2000) Cross-National Environmental Injustice and Human Rights Issues. *American Behavioral Scientist* 43(4):686–706.

Agamben, Giorgio (2005) *State of Exception*. Chicago: University of Chicago Press.

Agyeman, Julian, Robert Bullard, and Bob Evans (eds.) (2003) *Just Sustainabilities: Development in an Unequal World*. Cambridge, MA: MIT Press.

Ahdar, Rex and Nicholas Aroney (eds.) (2010) *Shari'a in the West*. Oxford: Oxford University Press.

Akram, Susan M. (2000) Orientalism Revisited in Asylum and Refugee Claims. *International Journal of Refugee Law* 12(1):7–40.

Alexander, Michelle (2010) *The New Jim Crow: Mass Incarceration in the Age of Colorblindness*. New York: The New Press.

Allen, Stephen and Alexandra Xanthaki (eds.) (2011) *Reflections on the UN Declaration on the Rights of Indigenous Peoples (Studies in International Law)*. Oxford: Hart Publishing.

Amar, Paul (ed.) (2012) *Global South to the Rescue: Emerging Humanitarian Superpowers and Globalizing Rescue Indsustries*. New York: Routledge.

Anders, Gerhard (2009) The New Legal Order as Local Phenomenon: The Special Court for Sierra Leone. In Benda-Beckmann, Franz von, Keebet von Benda-Beckmann, and Anne Griffiths (eds.) *Spatializing Law: An Anthropological Geography of Law in Society*. Farnham, Surrey: Ashgate, 137–156.

Anderson, Benedict (1983) *Imagined Communities: Reflections on the Origin and Spread of Nationalism*. London and New York: Verso.

Anderson, Carol (2003) *Eyes Off the Prize: The United Nations and the African American Struggle for Human Rights, 1944–1955*. Cambridge: Cambridge University Press.

Anderson, Jane (2009) *Law, Knowledge, Culture: The Production of Indigenous Knowledge in Intellectual Property.* Cheltenham, UK and Northampton, MA: Edward Elgar.

Anderton, D., A. Anderson, et al. (1994) Environmental Equity: The Demographics of Dumping. *Demography* 31(2):229–248.

Anghie, Anthony (2005) *Imperialism, Sovereignty, and the Making of International Law.* Cambridge: Cambridge University Press.

—— (2006) The Evolution of International Law: Colonial and Postcolonial Realities. *Third World Quarterly* 27(5):739–753.

—— (2009) Rethinking Sovereignty in International Law. *Annual Review of Law and Social Science* 5:291–310

Anghie, Anthony, Bhupinder Chimni, Karin Mickelson, and Obiora Okafor (eds.) (2003) *The Third World and International Order: Law, Politics and Globalization.* Leiden: Brill.

Anker, Kirsten Jane (2005) The Truth in Painting? Cultural Artifacts as Proof of Native Title *Law/ Text/ Culture* 9:91–124.

—— (2007) *The Unofficial Law of Native Title: Indigenous Rights, State Recognition and Legal Pluralism in Australia.* Doctoral thesis, Faculty of Law, University of Sydney.

An-Na'im, Abdullahi Ahmed (2008) Why Should Muslims Abandon Jihad? Human Rights and the Future of International Law. In Richard Falk, Balakrishnan Rajagopal, and Jacqueline Stevens (eds.) *International Law and the Third World: Reshaping Justice.* London and New York: Routledge-Cavendish, 81–94.

An-Na'im, Abdullahi Ahmed and Francis Mading Deng (eds.) (1990) *Human Rights in Africa: Cross-Cultural Perspectives.* Washington, DC: The Brookings Institute.

Antons, Christopher (2009) *Traditional Knowledge, Traditional Cultural Expressions and Intellectual Property in the Asia-Pacific Region.* London: Kluwer Law International.

Appelbaum, Richard, William L.F. Felstiner, and Voklmar Gessner (eds.) (2001) *Rules and Networks: The Legal Structure of Global Business Transactions.* Oxford: Hart Publishing.

Archibugi, Daniele and Mariano Croce (2012) Legality and Legitimacy of Exporting Democracy. In Richard Falk, Mark Juergensmeyer, and Vesselin Popovski (eds.) *Legality and Legitimacy in Global Affairs.* Oxford: Oxford University Press, 414–438.

Arias, S. and B. Warf (eds.) (2008) *The Spatial Turn: Interdisciplinary Perspectives.* New York: Routledge.

Aristodemou, Maria (2000) *Law and Literature: Journeys from Her to Eternity.* Oxford: Oxford University Press.

Arthur, Paige (2009) How Transitions Reshaped Human Rights: A Conceptual History of Transitional Justice. *Human Rights Quarterly* 31(2):321–367.

Arthur, Paige (ed.) (2010) *Identities in Transition: Challenges for Transitional Justice in Divided Societies.* Cambridge: Cambridge University Press.

—— (2003) *Formations of the Secular: Christianity, Islam, Modernity.* Palo Alto, CA: Stanford University Press.

Bales, Kevin (2004) *Disposable People: New Slavery in the Global Economy.* Revised edition. Berkeley: University of California Press.

Banakar, Reza (2011) Having One's Cake and Eating It: The Paradox of Contextualization in Socio-Legal Research. *International Journal of Law in Context* 7(4):487–503.

Banakar, Reza and Max Travers (eds.) (2002) *An Introduction to Law and Social Theory.* Oxford: Hart Publishing.

Barbour, Charles and George Pavlich (eds.) (2010) *After Sovereignty: On the Question of Political Beginnings.* Abingdon and New York: Routledge.

Barkan, Steven E. (2008) *Law and Society: An Introduction.* Upper Saddle River, NJ: Prentice Hall.

Barker, Joanne (2005) *Sovereignty Matters: Locations of Contestation and Possibility in Indigenous Struggles for Self-Determination.* Lincoln: University of Nebraska Press.

Barron, Anne (2000) Spectacular Jurisprudence. *Oxford Journal of Legal Studies* 20(2):301–315.

Bartholomew, Amy (2012) Defending Legality in the Age of Empire's Law. In Richard Falk, Mark Juergensmeyer, and Vesselin Popovski (eds.) *Legality and Legitimacy in Global Affairs.* Oxford: Oxford University Press, 92–126.

Barzilai, Gad (2004) Legal Categorizations and Religion: On Politics of Modernity, Practices, Faith, and Power. In Austin Sarat (ed.) *The Blackwell Companion to Law and Society.* Oxford: Blackwell, 392–409.

—— (2008) Beyond Relativism: Where Is Political Power in Legal Pluralism? *Theoretical Inquiries in Law* 9(2):395–416.

Basaran, T. (2008) Security, Law, Borders: Spaces of Exclusion. *International Political Sociology* 2(4):339–354.

Battersby, Paul and Joseph M. Siracusa (2009) *Globalization & Human Security.* New York: Rowman & Littlefield.

Baum, Dan (1997) *Smoke and Mirrors: The War on Drugs and the Politics of Failure.* Boston, MA: Back Bay Books.

Bavinck, Maarten and Gordon R. Woodman (2009) Can There Be Maps of Law? In Benda-Beckmann, Franz von, Keebet von Benda-Beckmann, and Anne Griffiths (eds.) *Spatializing Law: an Anthropological Geography of Law in Society.* Farnham, Surrey: Ashgate, 195–218.

Baxi, Upendra (2006a) *The Future of Human Rights.* Oxford: Oxford University Press.

—— (2006b) What May the "Third World" Expect from International Law? *Third World Quarterly* (Special Issue: Reshaping Justice – International Law and the Third World) 27(5):713–726.

Beckett, Katherine and Steve Herbert (2010) *Banished: The New Social Control in Urban America.* Oxford: Oxford University Press.

Bederman, David J. (2010) *Custom as a Source of Law.* Cambridge: Cambridge University Press.

Bell, Christine (2009) Transitional Justice, Interdisciplinarity and the State of the "Field" or "Non-Field". *International Journal of Transitional Justice* 3(1):5–27.

Bell, Christine, Colm Campbell, and Fionnuala Ní Aoláin (2004) Justice Discourses in Transition. *Social & Legal Studies* 13(3):305–328.

Bellah, Robert N. (2011) *Religion in Human Evolution: From the Paleolithic to the Axial Age.* Cambridge, MA: The Belknap Press of Harvard University Press.

Benda-Beckmann, Franz von (2002) Who's Afraid of Legal Pluralism? *Journal of Legal Pluralism* 47:37–82.

Benda-Beckmann, Franz von, Keebet von Benda-Beckmann, and Julia Eckert (eds.) (2009) *Rules of Law and Laws of Ruling: On the Governance of Law.* Surrey: Ashgate.

Benda-Beckmann, Franz von, Keebet von Benda-Beckmann, and Anne Griffiths (eds.) (2009a) *The Power of Law in a Transnational World: Anthropological Enquiries.* New York and Oxford: Berghahn Books.

—— (2009b) Space and Legal Pluralism: An Introduction. In Benda-Beckmann, Franz von, Keebet von Benda-Beckmann, and Anne Griffiths (eds.) *Spatializing Law: An Anthropological Geography of Law in Society.* Farnham, Surrey: Ashgate, 1–29.

Benda-Beckmann, Keebet von (2009) Anthropological Perspectives on Law and Geography. *PoLAR* **32**(2):265–278.

Bently, Lionel and Leo Flynn (eds.) (1996) *Law and the Senses: Sensational Jurisprudence.* London and Chicago: Pluto Press.

Benton, Lauren (2005) Legal Spaces of Empire: Piracy and the Origins of Ocean Regionalism. *Comparative Studies in Society and History* **47**(4):700–724.

—— (2010) *A Search for Sovereignty: Law and Geography in European Empire 1400–1900.* Cambridge: Cambridge University Press.

Berger, Peter L. (1999) The Desecularization of the World: A Global Overview. In Peter L. Berger (ed.) *The Desecularization of the World: Resurgent Religion and World Politics.* Grand Rapids: William B. Eerdmans, 1–18.

Berman, Paul Schiff (2005) From International Law to Law and Globalization. *Columbia Journal of Transnational Law* **43**:485–556.

—— (2010) Toward a Jurisprudence of Hybridity. *Utah Law Review* **1**:11–29.

Bhandar, Brenna (2009a) Constituting Practices and Things: The Concept of the Network and Studies in Law, Gender and Sexuality. *Feminist Legal Studies* **17**:325–332.

—— (2009b) The Ties that Bind: Multiculturalism and Secularism Reconsidered. *Journal of Law and Society* **36**(3):301–326.

Bhatia, Vijay K., Christopher N. Candlin, and Paola Evangelisti Allori (eds.) (2008) *Language, Culture and the Law: The Formulation of Legal Concepts across Systems and Cultures.* Bern and New York: Peter Lang.

Bhattacharyya, Gargi, John Gabriel, and Stephen Small (2001) *Race and Power: Global Racism in the Twenty-First Century.* London and New York: Routledge.

Bierman, Leonard and Michael A. Hitt (2007) The Globalization of Legal Practice in the Internet Age. *Indiana Journal of Global Legal Studies* **14**(1):29–34.

Binder, Guyora and Robert Weisberg (2000) *Literary Criticisms of Law.* Princeton, NJ: Princeton University Press.

Biolsi, Thomas (2005) Imagined Geographies: Sovereignty, Indigenous Space, and American Indian Struggle. *American Ethnologist* **32**(2):239–259.

Bjola, Corneliu and Markus Kornprobst (eds.) (2011) *Arguing Global Governance: Agency, Lifeworld, and Shared Reasoning.* London and New York: Routledge.

Black, C.F. (2010) *The Land Is the Source of the Law: A Dialogic Encounter with Indigenous Jurisprudence.* New York: Routledge-Cavendish.

Blandy, Sarah and David Silbey (2010) Law, Boundaries and the Production of Space. *Social & Legal Studies* **19**(3):275–284.

Blij, Harm de (2009) *The Power of Place: Geography, Destiny, and Globalization's Rough Landscape.* Oxford: Oxford University Press.

Blomley, Nicholas (1994) *Law, Space and the Geographies of Power.* London: Guildford Press.

—— (2004a) Flowers in the Bathtub: Boundary Crossings at the Public-Private Divide. *Geoforum* 36:281–296.

—— (2004b) From "What?" to "So What?": Law and Geography in Retrospect. In Jane Holder and Carolyn Harrison (eds.) (2003) *Law and Geography.* Oxford: Oxford University Press, 17–34.

—— (2011) *Rights of Passage: Sidewalks and the Regulation of Public Flow.* New York: Routledge/Taylor & Francis Group.

Blomley, Nicholas, David Delaney, and Richard Ford (eds.) (2001) *The Legal Geographies Reader: Law, Power and Space.* Oxford: Blackwell.

Bocarejo, Diana (2009) Deceptive Utopias: Violence, Environmentalism, and the Regulation of Multiculturalism in Colombia. *Law & Policy* 31(3):307–329.

Bohm, Robert (2007) Capital Punishment and Globalization. In Gregg Barak (ed.) *Violence, Conflict, and World Order: Critical Conversations on State-Sanctioned Violence.* New York: Rowman & Littlefield, 231–248.

Bond, Patrick (2012) *Politics of Climate Justice: Paralysis Above, Movement Below.* Durban: University of KwaZulu-Natal Press.

Bonnor, Chris (2007) *The Stupid Country: How Australia Is Dismantling Public Education.* Sydney: University of New South Wales.

Bonsignore, John J. et al. (eds.) 2005. *Before The Law: An Introduction to the Legal Process.* 8th edition. Boston: Houghton Mifflin Company.

Borgen, Christopher (2007) Imagining Sovereignty, Managing Session: The Legal Geography of Eurasia's "Frozen Conflicts". *Oregon Review of International Law* 9:477–534.

Bowden, Brett (2005) The Colonial Origins of International Law: European Expansion and the Classical Standard of Civilization. *Journal of the History of International Law* 7:1–23.

Bowden, Brett, Hilary Charlesworth, and Jeremy Farrall (eds.) (2009) *The Role of International Law in Rebuilding Societies after Conflict.* Cambridge: Cambridge University Press.

Bowen, John R. (2004) Does French Islam Have Borders? Dilemmas of Domestication in a Global Religious Field. *American Anthropologist* 106(1):43–55.

—— (2007) *Why the French Don't Like Headscarves: Islam, the State, and Public Space.* Princeton, NJ: Princeton University Press.

—— (2009) *Can Islam Be French? Pluralism and Pragmatism in a Secularist State.* Princeton, NJ: Princeton University Press.

—— (2010) Secularism: Conceptual Genealogy or Political Dilemma? *Comparative Studies in Society and History* 52(3): 680–694.

—— (2011a) How Could English Courts Recognize Shariah? *St. Thomas Law Review* 7(3):411–435.

—— (2011b) How the French State Justifies Controlling Muslim Bodies: From Harm-Based to Values-Based Reasoning. *Social Research* 78(2):1–24.

Boyd, William, Douglas Kysar, and Jeffrey J. Rachlinski (2012) Environment, the Law, and Regulation. *Annual Review of Law and Social Science* 8.

Boyle, Elizabeth H. and Sharon E. Preves (2000) National Politics as International Process: The Case of Anti-Female-Genital-Cutting Laws. *Law & Society Review* 34(3):703–737.

Boyle, Elizabeth Herger (2002) *Female Genital Cutting: Cultural Conflict in the Global Community.* Baltimore: Johns Hopkins University.

Bracey, Dorothy H. (2006) *Exploring Law and Culture.* Long Grove, IL: Waveland Press.

Braithwaite, John (2011) Partial Truth and Reconciliation in the *longue durée. Contemporary Social Science* 6(1):129–146.

Braithwaite, John, Hilary Charlesworth, and Peter Reddy (2010) *Reconciliation and Architectures of Commitment.* Canberra: ANU Press.

Braithwaite, John and Peter Drahos (2000) *Global Business Regulation.* Cambridge: Cambridge University Press.

Brody, David (2010) *Visualizing American Empire: Orientalism and Imperialism in the Philippines.* Chicago: University of Chicago Press.

Brown, D.A. (ed.) (2003) *Critical Race Theory: Cases, Materials and Problems.* St. Paul, MN: Thomson/West.

Brown, Michael F. (2004) *Who Owns Native Culture?* Cambridge, MA: Harvard University Press.

Brown, Wendy (2010a) Without Quality Public Education, There Is No Future for Democracy. *The California Journal of Politics & Policy* 2(1).

—— (2010b) *Walled States, Waning Sovereignty.* Brooklyn, NY: Zone Books.

Browne-Marshall, Gloria J. (2007) *Race, Law, and American Society. With a Foreword by Derrick Bell.* New York and London: Routledge.

Brysk, Alison (2000) *From Tribal Village to Global Village: Indian Rights and International Relations in Latin America.* Stanford, CA: Stanford University Press.

—— (ed.) (2002) *Globalization and Human Rights.* Berkeley: University of California Press.

Brysk, Alison and Gershon Shafir (eds.) (2004) *People Out of Place: Globalization, Human Rights and the Citizenship Gap.* New York: Routledge.

Buchanan, Patrick J. (2011) "A Fire Bell in the Night for Norway." Online at http://www.amconmag.com/blog/2011/07/25/a-fire-bell-in-the-night-for-norway/ (retrieved September 4, 2011).

Buchanan, Ruth and Rebecca Johnson (2009) Strange Encounters: Exploring Law and Film in the Affective Register. *Studies in Law, Politics, and Society* 46:33–60.

Bullard, Robert D. (2002) Confronting Environmental Racism in the Twenty-First Century. *Global Dialogue* 4(1).

Bullard, Robert D., Paul Mohai, Robin Saha, and Beverly Wright (2008) "Toxic Wastes and Race at Twenty: Why Race Still Matters After All of These Years." *Lewis & Clark Environmental Law Journal* 38(2):371.

Burke, Roland (2010) *Decolonization and the Evolution of International Human Rights.* Philadelphia: University of Pennsylvania Press.

Butler, Brian E. (2003) Aesthetics and American Law. *Legal Studies Forum* 27(1):203–220.

Butler, Chris (2009) Critical Legal Studies and the Politics of Space. *Social & Legal Studies* 18(3):313–332.

Butler, Judith (2006) *Precarious Life: The Powers of Mourning and Violence*. London: Verso.

—— (2010) *Frames of War: When Is Life Grievable?* London: Verso.

Butler, Judith, Jürgen Habermas, Charles Taylor, and Cornel West (2011) *The Power of Religion in the Public Sphere*. New York: Columbia University Press.

Buttimer, Anne and David Seamon (eds.) (1980) *The Human Experience of Space and Place*. New York: St Martin's Press.

Cain, Herman (2011) "I Would Not" Appoint a Muslim in My Administration. *Fox News*, March 28.

Calavita, Kitty (2010) *Invitation to Law and Society: An Introduction to the Study of Real Law* (Chicago Series in Law and Society). Chicago: University of Chicago Press.

Calhoun, Craig, Mark Juergensmeyer, and Jonathan Van Antwerpen (eds.) (2011) *Rethinking Secularism*. Oxford: Oxford University Press.

Camilleri, Joseph A. and Jim Falk (2009) *Worlds in Transition: Evolving Governance across a Stressed Planet*. Surrey: Edward Elgar.

Campbell, Colm and Vikki Bell (2004) Out of Conflict: Peace, Change and Justice. *Social & Legal Studies* 13(3):299–304.

Candelario, Ginneta E. B. (2007) *Black behind the Ears: Dominican Racial Identity from Museums to Beauty Shops*. Durham, NC: Duke University Press.

Cane, Peter, Carolyn Evans, and Zoe Robinson (eds.) (2008) *Law and Religion in Theoretical and Historical Context*. Cambridge: Cambridge University Press.

Carbado, D.W. (2002) Race to the Bottom. *UCLA Law Review* 49:1283.

Carson, Rachel (1962) *Silent Spring*. New York: Houghton Mifflin Company.

Cattelino, Jessica (2006) Florida Seminole Housing and the Social Meanings of Sovereignty. *Society for Comparative Study of Society and History* 48(3):699–726.

—— (2007) Florida Seminole Gaming and Local Sovereign Interdependency. In D. Cobb and L. Fowler (eds.) *Beyond Red Power: Rethinking Twentieth-Century American Indian Politics*. Santa Fe, NM: School of American Research Press, 262–279.

CBS (2010) Fears of Sharia Law in America Grow among Conservatives. October 13. Online at: http://www.cbsnews.com/8301–503544_162–20019405–503544 (accessed August 19, 2011).

Chakrabarty, D. (2000) *Provincializing Europe: Postcolonial Thought and Historical Difference*. Princeton, NJ: Princeton University Press.

Chambliss, Elizabeth (2008) When Do Facts Persuade – Some Thoughts on the Market for Empirical Legal Studies. *Law & Contemporary Problems* 71(2):17–40.

Chanock, Martin (2007) *The Making of South African Legal Culture 1902–1936: Fear, Favour and Prejudice*. Cambridge: Cambridge University Press.

Chapman, Chelsea (2009) The Ontological Problem with Sovereignty: Indigenous Nations, Territoriality, and the Making of Natural Resources in Alaska. http://papers.ssrn.com/sol3/papers.cfm?abstract_id=1579776 (accessed September 27, 2011).

Charlesworth, Hilary and C. Chinkin (2006) Building Women into Peace: The International Legal Framework. *Third World Quarterly* 27(5):937–957.

Charters, Claire and Rodolfo Stavenhagen (eds.) (2010) *Making the Declaration Work: The United Nations Declaration on the Rights of Indigenous Peoples*. Published by the International Group for Indigenous Affairs. Copenhagen, Demark.

Checker, M. 2002. "It's in the Air": Redefining the Environment as a New Metaphor for Old Social Justice Struggles. *Human Organization* **61**(1):94–105.

Cheyfitz, Eric (2011) What Is a Just Society? Native American Philosophies and the Limits of Capitalism's Imagination: A Brief Manifesto. *Sovereignty, Indigeneity, and the Law.* Special issue edited by Eric Cheyfitz, N. Bruce Duthu, and Shari M. Huhndorf. *South Atlantic Quarterly* **110**(2):291–308.

Chimni, B.S. (2006) Third World Approaches to International Law: A Manifesto. *International Community Law Review* **8**:2.

Chomsky, Noam (2007) *Failed States: The Abuse of Power and the Assault on Democracy.* New York: Holt Paperbacks.

Clapp, Jennifer (2001) *Toxic Exports: The Transfer of Hazardous Wastes from Rich to Poor Countries.* Ithaca, NY: Cornell University Press.

Clark, Phil (2009) Grappling in the Great Lakes: The Challenges of International Justice in Rwanda, the Democratic Republic of Congo and Uganda. In Brett Bowden, Hilary Charlesworth, and Jeremy Farrall (eds.) *The Role of International Law in Rebuilding Societies After Conflict.* Cambridge: Cambridge University Press, 244–269.

—— (2010) *The Gacaca Courts, Post-Genocide Justice and Reconciliation.* Cambridge: Cambridge University Press.

Clarke, Alan W., Laurie Anne Whitt, Eric Lamber, and Oko Elechi (2004) Does the Rest of the World Matter? Sovereignty, International Human Rights Law and the American Death Penalty. *Queen's Law Journal* **30**:260–400.

Clarke, Alan W. and Laurelyn Whitt (2007) *The Bitter Fruit of American Justice: International and Domestic Resistance to the Death Penalty.* Boston: Northeastern University Press.

Clarke, Karmari Maxine (2009) *Fictions of Justice: The International Criminal Court and the Challenge of Legal Pluralism in Sub-Saharan Africa.* Cambridge: Cambridge University Press.

Cleary, Edward L. and Timothy J. Steigenga (eds.) (2004) *Resurgent Voices in Latin America: Indigenous Peoples, Political Mobilization, and Religious Change.* New Brunswick, NJ: Rutgers University Press.

Clough, Patricia Ticineto (2000) *Autoaffection: Unconscious Thought in an Age of Teletechnology.* Minneapolis: University of Minnesota Press.

—— (2007) Introduction. In Patricia Ticineto Clough and Jean Halley (eds.) (2007). *The Affective Turn: Theorizing the Social.* Foreword by Michael Hardt. Durham, NC and London: Duke University Press, 1–33.

—— (2010) Afterword: The Future of Affect Studies. *Body & Society* **16** (1):222–230.

Clough, Patricia Ticineto and Jean Halley (eds.) (2007) *The Affective Turn: Theorizing the Social.* Foreword by Michael Hardt. Durham, NC and London: Duke University Press.

Cohn, Bernard S. (1996) *Colonialism and Its Forms of Knowledge.* Princeton, NJ: Princeton University Press.

Collier, Jane F., Bill Maurer, and Liliana Suarez-Navaz (1996) Sanctioned Identities: Legal Constructions of Modern Personhood. *Identities* **2**(1–2):1–27.

Collins, Cath (2010) *Post-Transitional Justice: Human Rights Trials in Chile and El Salvador.* University Park: Pennsylvania State University Press.

Comaroff, Jean and John Comaroff (1991) *Of Revelation and Revolution: Christianity, Colonialism, and Consciousness in South Africa.* Vol. 1. Chicago: University of Chicago Press.

—— (2006) *Law and Disorder in the Postcolony.* Chicago: University of Chicago Press.

Connolly, Anthony J. (2010) *Cultural Difference on Trial: The Nature and Limits of Judicial Understanding.* Farnham, UK and Burlington, VT: Ashgate.

Constable, Marianne (2007) *Just Silences: The Limits and Possibilities of Modern Law.* Princeton, NJ: Princeton University Press.

Cook, Anthony E. (1997) *The Least of These: Race, Law, and Religion in American Culture.* New York: Routledge.

Cooper, Davina (1998) *Governing Out of Order: Space, Law and the Politics of Belonging.* London and New York: Rivers Oram Press.

—— (2011) Reading the State as a Multi-Identity Formation: The Touch and Feel of Equality Governance. *Feminist Legal Studies* **19**:3–25.

Cosgrove, Denis (1999) Introduction: Mapping Meaning. In Denis Cosgrove (ed.) *Mappings.* London: Reaktion Books, 1–23.

Cotterrell, Roger (2003) *The Politics of Jurisprudence: A Critical Introduction to Legal Philosophy.* 2nd edition. Oxford: Oxford University Press.

—— (2004) Law in Culture. *Ratio Juris* **17**(1):1–14.

—— (2006) *Law, Culture and Society: Legal Ideas in the Mirror of Social Theory.* Aldershot: Ashgate.

—— (2009) Spectres of Transnationalism: Changing Terrains of Sociology of Law. *Journal of Law and Society* **36**(4):481–500.

Coutin, Susan Bibler (2000) *Legalizing Moves: Salvadorian Immigrants' Struggle for US Residency.* Ann Arbor: University of Michigan Press.

—— (2007) *Nations of Emigrants: Shifting Boundaries of Citizenship in El Salvador and the United States.* Ithaca, NY: Cornell University Press.

—— (2010) Confined Within: National Territories as Zones of Confinement. *Political Geography* **29**:200–208.

Coutin, Susan Bibler, Bill Maurer, and Barbara Yngvesson (2002) In the Mirror: The Legitimation Work of Globalization. *Law & Social Inquiry* **27**(4):801–843.

Crenshaw, K., N. Gotanda, G. Peller, and K. Thomas (eds.) (1995) *Critical Race Theory: The Key Writings That Formed the Movement.* New York: New Press.

Cresswell, Tim (2004) *Place: A Short Introduction.* Hoboken, NJ: Wiley-Blackwell.

Cronon, W. (1996) The Trouble with Wilderness: or, Getting Back to the Wrong Nature. In W. Cronon (ed.) *Uncommon Ground: Rethinking the Human Place in Nature.* New York: W.W. Norton and Company, 69–90.

Crossley, Pamela Kyle (2008) *What Is Global History?* Cambridge: Polity Press.

Cuban, Larry (2004) *The Blackboard and the Bottom Line: Why Schools Can't Be Businesses.* Cambridge, MA: Harvard University Press.

Cunneen, Chris (2010) Framing the Crimes of Colonialism: Critical Images of Aboriginal Art and Law. In K. Hayward and M. Presdee (eds.) *Framing Crime: Cultural Criminology and the Image.* London and New York: Routledge, 115–137.

Curthoys, Ann and Marilyn Lake (2005) *Connected Worlds: History in Transnational Perspective.* Camberra: ANU E Books.

Da Silva, Denise Ferreira (2007) *Toward a Global Idea of Race.* Minneapolis: University of Minnesota Press.

Darian-Smith, Eve (1998) Review of Boaventura de Sousa Santos *Toward a New Commonsense: Law, Science, and Politics in the Paradigmatic Transition. Law & Social Inquiry* **23**(1):81–120.

—— (1999) *Bridging Divides: The Channel Tunnel and English Legal Identity in the New Europe.* Berkeley: University of California Press.

—— (2000) Structural Inequalities in the Global Legal System. *Law and Society Review* **34**(3):809–828.

—— (2004) *New Capitalists: Law, Politics and Identity Surrounding Casino Gaming on Native American Land.* Belmont: Wadsworth.

—— (2008) Precedents of Injustice: Thinking about History in Law and Society Scholarship. (Special issue: Law and Society Reconsidered). *Studies in Law, Politics, and Society* **41**:61–81.

—— (2010a) *Religion, Race, Rights: Landmarks in the History of Modern Anglo-American Law.* Oxford: Hart.

—— (2010b) Environmental Law and Native American Law. *Annual Review of Law and Social Science* **6**:359–386.

—— (2012) Re-Reading W.E.B. Du Bois: The Global Dimensions of the US Civil Rights Struggle. *Journal of Global History* Vol.7(3):483–505.

Davies, Margaret (2007) *Property: Meanings, Histories, Theories (Critical Approaches to Law).* Abingdon and New York: Routledge-Cavendish.

—— (2011) The Future of Secularism: A Critique. In Nadirsyan Hosen and Richard Mohr (eds.) *Life and Religion in Public Life: The Contemporary Debate.* London and New York: Routledge, 52–66.

Dawson, Ashley (2011) Slow Violence and the Environmentalism of the Poor: An Interview with Rob Nixon. *Social Text* August 31.

de Toqueville, Alexis (1835) *Law and Democracy in America.*

Deflem, Mathieu (2008) *Sociology of Law: Visions of a Scholarly Tradition.* Cambridge: Cambridge University Press.

Delaney, David (1998) *Race, Place, and the Law, 1836–1948.* Austin: University of Texas Press.

—— (2003) Beyond the Word: Law as a Thing of This World. In Jane Holder and Carolyn Harrison (eds.) *Law and Geography.* Oxford: Oxford University Press, 67–84.

—— (2010) *The Spatial, the Legal and the Pragmatics of World-Making. Nomospheric Investigations.* Milton Park, Oxon: Routledge-Cavendish.

Delgado, E. (ed.) (1995) *Critical Race Theory: The Cutting Edge.* Philadelphia: Temple University Press.

Deloria, Vine Jr. (1996) Self-Determination and the Concept of Sovereignty. In John R. Wunder (ed.) *Native American Sovereignty (Native Americans and the Law).* New York: Routledge, 118–124.

—— (1998) *The Nations Within: The Past and Future of American Indian Sovereignty.* Austin: University of Texas Press.

Dembour, M.B. and T. Kelly (eds.) (2007) *Paths to International Justice: Social and Legal Perspectives.* Cambridge: Cambridge University Press.

den Boer, Monica and Jaap de Wilde (eds.) (2008) *The Viability of Human Security.* Amsterdam: Amsterdam University Press.

Dezalay, Yves and Bryant G. Garth (1998) *Dealing in Virtue: International Commercial Arbitration and the Construction of a Transnational Legal Order.* Chicago: University of Chicago Press.

—— (2002) *The Internationalization of Palace Wars: Lawyers, Economists, and the Contest to Transform Latin American States.* Chicago: University of Chicago Press.

—— (2010) *Asian Legal Revivals: Lawyers in the Shadow of Empire.* Chicago: University of Chicago Press.

—— (eds.) (2011) *Lawyers and the Rule of Law in an Era of Globalization.* London: Routledge.

Dhanda, Amita and Archana Parashar (eds.) (2009) *Decolonisation of Legal Knowledge.* New Delhi: Routledge.

Dickinson, Rob, Elena Katselli, Colin Murray, and Ole W. Pedersen (eds.) (2012) *Examining Critical Perspectives on Human Rights.* Cambridge: Cambridge University Press.

Dieter, Richard C. (2003) International Influence on the Death Penalty in the U.S. *Death Penalty Information Center, Foreign Service Journal.* Online at: http://www. deathpenaltyinfo.org/node/984 (retrieved November 28, 2011).

Dolin, Kieran (ed.) (2007) *A Critical Introduction to Law and Literature.* Cambridge: Cambridge University Press.

Domingo, Rafael (2010) *The New Global Law.* Cambridge: Cambridge University Press.

Douzinas, Costas (2007) *Human Rights and Empire.* London: Routledge-Cavendage.

Douzinas, Costas and Lynda Nead (eds.) (1999) *Law and the Image: The Authority of Art and the Aesthetics of Law.* Chicago: University of Chicago Press.

Drummond, Susan G. (2006) *Mapping Marriage Law in Spanish Gitano Communities.* Vancouver: University of British Columbia Press.

Drybread, Kristen (2009) Rights-Bearing Street Kids: Icons of Hope and Despair in Brazil's Burgeoning Neoliberal State. *Law & Policy* 31(3):330–350.

Du Bois, W.E.B. (1930) *Africa – Its Place in Modern History.* Girard, KS: Haldeman-Julius Publications.

—— (1982) "The Negro and the Warsaw Ghetto." In *Writings by Du Bois in Periodicals Edited by Others,* compiled and edited by Herbert Aptheker Volume 4 1945–1961. Millwood, New York: Kraus-Thomson, 173–176.

Dudziak, Mary (2004) Brown as a Cold War Case. *Journal of American History* 91(1):32–42.

—— (2010) Law, War and the History of Time. *California Law Review* 98:1669–1710.

Dudziak, Mary L. and Leti Volpp (eds.) (2006) *Legal Borderlands: Law and the Construction of American Borders (A Special Issue of American Quarterly).* Baltimore: Johns Hopkins University Press.

Dwivedi, R. (2001) Environmental Movements in the Global South: Issues of Livelihoods and Beyond. *International Sociology* 16(1):11–31.

Eagleton, Terry (1990) *The Ideology of the Aesthetic.* Oxford: Basil Blackwell.

Eckel, Jan (2010) Human Rights and Decolonization: New Perspectives and Open Questions. *Humanity* 2010:111–135.

Eckert, Amy (2009) Outsourcing War. In Amy Eckert and Laura Sjoberg (eds.) *Rethinking the 21st Century: 'New' Problems, 'Old' Solutions*. London and New York: Zed Books, 136–154.

Edge, Peter (2006) *Religion and Law: An Introduction*. Aldershot: Ashgate.

Elster, John (2004) *Closing the Books: Transitional Justice in Historical Perspective*. Cambridge: Cambridge University Press.

Elver, Hilal (2008) International Environmental Law, Water and the Future. In Richard Falk, Balakrishnan Rajagopal, and Jacqueline Stevens (eds.) *International Law and the Third World: Reshaping Justice*. London and New York: Routledge-Cavendish, 181–198.

—— (1987) Law, Time, and Community. *Law & Society Review* 21:605–638.

Engel, David M. (1993) "Law in the Domains of Everyday Life: The Construction of Community and Difference" In A. Sarat and T.M. Kearns (eds.) *Law in Everyday Life*. Ann Arbor: University of Michigan Press, 123–170.

—— (2005) Globalization and the Decline of Legal Consciousness: Torts, Ghosts, and Karma in Thailand. *Law & Social Inquiry* 30(3):469–514.

Engel, David M. and Jaruwan Engel (2010) *Tort, Custom and Karma: Globalization and Legal Consciousness in Thailand*. Palo Alto, CA: Stanford Law Books.

Engle, Karen (2010) *The Elusive Promise of Indigenous Development: Rights, Culture, Strategy*. Durham, NC: Duke University Press.

Erbeznik, Katherine (2011) Money Can't Buy You Law: The Effects of Foreign Aid on the Rule of Law in Developing Countries. *Indiana Journal of Global Legal Studies* 18(2):873–900.

Esquirol, Jorge (2011) Interview. *Institute for Global Law & Policy. Harvard Law School*. Online at: http://www.harvardiglp.org/new-thinking-new-writing/interview-with-iglp-contributor-prof-jorge-esquirol/ (retrieved December 1, 2011).

Ewick, Patricia (2004) Consciousness and Ideology. In Austin Sarat (ed.) *The Blackwell Companion to Law and Society*. Oxford: Blackwell, 80–95.

—— (2008) Embracing Eclecticism. Special Issue: Law and Society Reconsidered. *Studies in Law, Politics, and Society* 41:1–18.

Ewick, Patricia and Susan S. Silbey (1998) *The Common Place of Law: Stories from Everyday Life*. Chicago: University of Chicago Press.

Fainaru, Steve (2009) *Big Boy Rules: America's Mercenaries Fighting in Iraq*. Cambridge, MA: Da Capo Press.

Falk, Richard (1995) *On Humane Governance: Toward a New Global Politics*. Cambridge: Polity Press.

—— (1998) *Law in an Emerging Global Village: A Post-Westphalian Perspective*. Ardsley, NY: Transnational Publishers.

—— (1999) Pursuing the Quest for Human Security. In Majid Tehranian (ed.) *Worlds Apart: Human Security and Global Governance*. London and New York: I.B. Tauris Publishers (in Association with the Toda Institute for Global Peace and Policy Research), 1–22.

—— (2009) *Achieving Human Rights*. New York: Routledge.

—— (2012) Remembering the Best and Worst of 2011. Online at: http://richardfalk.wordpress.com (retrieved January 3, 2012).

Falk, Richard, Balakrishnan Rajagopal, and Jacqueline Stevens (eds.) (2008) Special Issue – Reshaping Justice – International Law and the Third World. *Third World Quarterly* 27(5):709–957.

Falk, Richard, Mark Juergensmeyer, and Vesselin Popovski (eds.) (2012) *Legality and Legitimacy in Global Affairs*. Oxford: Oxford University Press.

Farmer, Paul (2005) *Pathologies of Power: Health, Human Rights, and the New War on the Poor*. Berkeley: University of California Press.

Farrall, Stephen, Tawhida Ahmed, and Duncan French (eds.) (2012) *Criminological and Legal Consequences of Climate Change*. Oxford: Hart Publishing.

Feeley, Malcolm (2001) Three Voices of Socio-Legal Studies. *Israel Law Review* 35:175.

Ferguson, James (2006) *Global Shadows: Africa in the Neoliberal World Order*. Durham, NC and London: Duke University Press.

Ferguson, James and Akhil Gupta (2002) Spatializing States: Toward an Ethnography of Neoliberal Governmentality. *American Ethnologist* 29(4):981–1002.

Fitzpatrick, Peter (1984) Law and Societies. *Osgoode Hall Law Journal* 115.

—— (1992) *The Mythology of Modern Law*. London: Routledge

—— (2001) *Modernism and the Grounds of Law*. Cambridge: Cambridge University Press.

—— (2004) "We Know What It Is When You Do Not Ask Us": The Unchallengeable Nation. *Law Text Culture* 8(1):263–286.

Flood, John (2002) Globalisation and Law. In Reza Banakar and Max Travers (eds.) *An Introduction to Law and Social Theory*. Oxford: Hart Publishing, 311–328.

Flyvbjerg, Bent (2001) *Making Social Science Matter: Why Social Inquiry Fails and How It Can Succeed Again*. Cambridge: Cambridge University Press.

Flyvbjerg, Bent, Todd Landman, and Stanford Schram (eds.) (2012) *Real Social Science: Applied Phronesis*. Cambridge: Cambridge University Press.

Foblets, Marie-Claire and Alison Dundes Renteln (eds.) (2009) *Multicultural Jurisprudence: Comparative Perspectives on the Culture Defense*. Oxford: Hart Publishing.

Ford, Richard (1999) Law's Territory (a History of Jurisdiction). *Michigan Law Review* 97(4):843–930.

Forgays, Deborah Kirby, Lisa DeMilio, and Kim Schuster (2004) Teen Courts: What Jurors Can Tell Us about the Process. *Juvenile and Family Court Journal* 55(1):25–33.

Foucault, Michel (1986) Of Other Spaces. *Diacritics* 16:22–27.

Francavigilia, Richard (2011) *Go East, Young Man: Imagining the America West as the Orient*. Logan: Utah State University Press.

Franco, Ferrarotti (1990) *Time, Memory and Society* (Contributions in sociology, No. 91).

Fraser, Nancy (2005) Reframing Justice in a Global World. *New Left Review* 36:1–19.

French, Rebecca (2001) Time in the Law. *University of Colorado Law Review* 72(3):663–748.

Friedman, Lawrence M. (2002) One World: Notes on the Emerging Legal Order. In Likosky, Michael (ed.) *Transnational Legal Processes*. Dayton, OH: Butterworths LexisNexis, 23–40.

—— (2005) Coming of Age: Law and Society Enters an Exclusive Club. *Annual Review of Law and Social Science* 2005(1):1–16.

Friedman, Lawrence M., Rogelio Pérez-Perdomo, and Manuel A. Gómez (eds.) (2011) *Law in Many Societies: A Reader*. Stanford, CA: Stanford University Press.

Friedrichs, David O. (2011) *Law in Our Lives: An Introduction.* 3rd edition. Oxford: Oxford University Press.

Frymer, P. (2005) Racism Revised: Courts, Labor, Law, and the Institutional Construction of Racial Animus. *American Political Science Review* 99(3):373–387.

Garth, Bryant and Joyce Sterling (1998) From Legal Realism to Law and Society: Reshaping Law for the Last Stages of the Activist State. *Law & Society Review* 32:409–471.

Gathii, James Thuo (1998) International Law and Eurocentricity. *European Journal of International Law* 9:184–211.

Geary, Adam (2001) *Law and Aesthetics.* Oxford: Hart Publishing.

——— (2004) Love and Death in American Jurisprudence: Myth, Aesthetics, Law. *Studies in Law, Politics and Society* 33: 3–23.

Geertz, Clifford (1983) *Local Knowledge: Further Essays in Interpretive Anthropology.* New York: Basic Books.

Geldenhuys, Deon (2009) *Contested States in World Politics.* New York: Palgrave Macmillan.

Genn, H. and S. Wheeler (2006) Law in the Real World: Improving Our Understanding of How Law Works. London: Nuffield Foundation.

Gershon, Ilana (2010) Bruno Latour (1947–). In Jon Simons (ed.) *Agamben to Zizek: Contemporary Critical Theorists.* Edinburgh: Edinburgh University Press, 161–176.

Getches, David (2001) Beyond Indian Law: The Rehnquist Court's Pursuit of States' Rights, Color-Blind Justice and Mainstream Values. *Minnesota Law Review* 86:267–362.

Gibson, James L. (2004) Truth, Reconciliation, and the Creation of a Human Rights Culture in South Africa. *Law & Society Review* 38(1):5–40.

Gilbert, Michael J. and Tanya L. Settles (2008) Community-Based Justice in Northern Ireland and South Africa. *International Criminal Justice Review* 18:83–105.

Gilroy, Paul (1993) *The Black Atlantic: Modernity and Double-Consciousness.* Cambridge, MA: Harvard University Press.

Godoy, Angelina Snodgrass (2002) Lynchings and the Democratization of Terror in Postwar Guatemala: Implications for Human Rights. *Human Rights Quarterly* 24(3):640–661.

Goldberg, David Theo (2008) *The Threat of Race: Reflections on Racial Neoliberalism.* Oxford: Wiley-Blackwell.

Goldberg, David Theo, Michael Musheno, and Lisa C. Bower (eds.) (2001) *Between Law and Culture: Relocating Legal Studies.* Minneapolis and London: University of Minnesota Press.

Goldberg-Hiller, Jonathan (2008) Deconstructing Law and Society: A Sociolegal Aesthetics. *Studies in Law, Politics, and Society* 41:83–120.

——— (2011) Persistence of the Indian: Legal Recognition of Native Hawaiians and the Opportunity of the Other. *New Political Science* 33(1):23–44.

Goldberg-Hiller, Jonathan and Neal Milner (2002) Reimagining Rights: Tunnels, Nations, Spaces. *Law and Social Inquiry* 27(2):339–368.

Goldberg-Hiller, Jonathan and Noenoe K. Silva (2011) Sharks and Pigs: Animating Hawaiian Sovereignty against the Anthropological Machine. *The South Atlantic Quarterly* Spring 110(2):429–446.

Golder, Ben and Peter Fitzpatrick (2009). *Foucault's Law.* New York: Routledge.

Goldschmidt, Henry (2004) Introduction: Race, Nation, and Religion. In Henry Goldschmidt and Elizabeth McAlister (eds.) *Race, Nation, and Religion in the Americas*. Oxford: Oxford University Press, 3–31.

Goldstone, Richard J. and Adam M. Smith (2009) *International Judicial Institutions: The Architecture of International Justice at Home and Abroad*. Abingdon and New York: Routledge.

Gómez, Laura E. (2004) A Tale of Two Genres: On the Real and Ideal Links Between Law and Society and Critical Race Theory. In Austin Sarat (ed.) *The Blackwell Companion to Law and Society*. Oxford: Blackwell, 453–470.

—— (2010) Understanding Law and Race as Mutually Constitutive: An Invitation to Explore an Emerging Field. *Annual Review of Law and Social Science* 6:487–505.

—— (2012) Looking for Race in all the Wrong Places. *Law & Society Review* 46(2):221–245.

Goodale, Mark (2006) Reclaiming Modernity: Indigenous Cosmopolitanism and the Coming of the Second Revolution in Bolivia. *American Ethnologist* 33(4):634–649.

Goodale, Mark and Sally Engle Merry (eds.) (2007) *The Practice of Human Rights: Tracking Law Between the Global and the Local* (Cambridge Studies in Law and Society). Cambridge: Cambridge University Press.

Goodrich, Peter (1991) Specula Laws: Image, Aesthetic, and Common Law. *Law and Critique* 2(2):233–254.

Gover, Kirsty (2011) *Tribal Constitutionalism: States, Tribes, and the Governance of Membership*. Oxford: Oxford University Press.

Graham, Lorie M. and Nicole Friederichs (2011) Indigenous Peoples, Human Rights, and the Environment. *Yale Human Rights and the Environment Dialogues* Spring.

Greenhouse, Carol J. (1996) *A Moment's Notice: Time Politics across Cultures*. Ithaca, NY: Cornell University Press.

Gregory, John S. (2003) *The West and China Since 1500*. Basingstoke, Hampshire: Palgrave Macmillan.

Griffiths, Anne (2002) Legal Pluralism. In Reza Banakar and Max Travers (eds.) *An Introduction to Law and Social Theory*. Oxford: Hart Publishing, 289–310.

—— (2009) Law, Space, and Place: Reframing Comparative Law and Legal Anthropology. *Law & Social Inquiry* 34(2):495–507.

Guardiola-Rivera, Oscar (2010) *What If Latin America Ruled the World? How the South Will Take the North Through the 21st Century*. London: Bloomsbury.

Guggenheim, Michael (2010) The Laws of Foreign Buildings: Flat Roofs and Minarets. *Social & Legal Studies* 19(4):441–460.

Gurnham, David (2009) *Memory, Imagination, Justice: Intersections of Law and Literature*. Farnham: Ashgate.

Hagan, John (2010) *Who Are the Criminals: The Politics of Crime Policy from the Age of Roosevelt to the Age of Reagan*. Princeton, NJ: Princeton University Press.

Hajjar, Lisa (2004) Chaos as Utopia: International Criminal Prosecution as a Challenge to State Power. *Studies in Law, Politics, and Society* 31:3–23.

Haldar, Piyel (2007) *Law, Orientalism and Postcolonialism: The Jurisdiction of the Lotus Eaters*. Abingdon: Routledge-Cavendish.

Hall, John R. (2009) *Apocalypse: From Antiquity to the Empire of Modernity*. New York: Polity Press.

Hall, Kermit L. and Peter Karsten (2009) *The Magic Mirror: Law in American History.* 2nd edition. Oxford: Oxford University Press.

Halliday, Fred (1996) *Islam and the Myth of Confrontation: Religion and Politics in the Middle East.* London: I.B. Tauris.

Halliday, Terence C. (2009) Recursivity of Global Normmaking: A Sociolegal Agenda. *Annual Review of Law and Social Science* 5:263–289.

Halliday, Terence and Pavel Osinky (2006) Globalization of Law. *Annual Review of Sociology* 32: 447–470.

Halliday, Terence, Lucien Karpik, and Malcolm M. Feeley (eds.) (2007) *Fighting for Political Freedom: Comparative Studies of the Legal Complex and Political Liberalism.* Oxford: Hart Publishing.

Halliday, Terence and Bruce Carruthers (2009) *Bankrupt: Global Lawmaking and Systemic Financial Crisis.* Palo Alto, CA: Stanford University Press.

Haney-Lopez, Ian (ed.) (2007) *Race, Law and Society.* Aldershot: Ashgate.

Haraway, Donna J. (1997) *Modest_Witness@Second_Millenium.FemaleMan_Meets_OncoMouse: Feminism and Technoscience.* London: Routledge.

Harrison, Kathryn (2010) The Comparative Politics of Carbon Taxation. *Annual Review of Law and Social Science* 2010 6:507–529.

Harvey, David (1996) *Justice, Nature and the Geography of Difference.* Oxford: Blackwell.

——— (2005) *A Brief History of Neoliberalism.* Oxford: Oxford University Press.

——— (2006) *Spaces of Global Capitalism: Towards a Theory of Uneven Geographical Development.* London: Verso.

Hasan, Mehdi (2011) It's Time to Lay the Sharia Bogeyman to Rest. *New Statesman* 140(21):16.

Hayner, Priscilla B. (2011) *Unspeakable Truths: Transitional Justice and the Challenge of Truth Commissions.* 2nd edition. New York and London: Routledge.

Heimer, Carol (2007) Old Inequalities, New Disease: HIV/AIDS in Sub-Saharan Africa. *Annual Review of Sociology* 33:551–577.

Held, David (2004) *Global Covenant: The Social Democratic Alternative to the Washington Consensus.* Cambridge: Polity Press.

——— (2009) Restructuring Global Governance: Cosmopolitanism, Democracy and the Global Order. *Millennium. Journal of International Studies* 37(3):535–547.

Held, David, Anthony McGrew, David Goldblatt, and Jonathan Perraton (1999) *Global Transformations: Politics, Economics, and Culture.* Palo Alto, CA: Stanford University Press.

Held, David and M. Koenig-Archibugi (eds.) (2003) *Taming Globalization.* Cambridge: Polity Press.

Hellum, Anne, Shaheen Sardar Ali, and Anne Griffiths (eds.) (2011) *From Transnational Relations to Transnational Laws: Northern European Laws at the Crossroads.* Burlington, VT: Ashgate.

Henry, Nicola (2011) *War and Rape: Law, Memory and Justice.* New York and London: Routledge.

Hernandez-Lopez, Ernesto (2009) *Boumediene v. Bush* and Guantanamo, Cuba: "Does the Empire Strike Back"? *SMU Law Review* 62:117.

——— (2010) Guantanamo as a "Legal Black Hole": A Base for Expanding Space, Markets, and Culture. *University of San Francisco Law Review* 45:141–213.

Hibbits, Bernard J. (1994) Making Sense of Metaphors: Visuality, Aurality, and the Reconfiguration of American Legal Discourse. *Cardozo Law Review* 16:229–356.

Hirst, Paul (2005) *Space and Power: Politics, War and Architecture.* Cambridge: Polity Press.

Holder, Jane and Carolyn Harrison (eds.) (2003) *Law and Geography.* Current Legal Issues. 2002 Vol. 5. Oxford: Oxford University Press.

Hopkins, James (2012) Tribal Sovereignty and Climate Change: Moving Toward Intergovernmental Cooperation. *Arizona Legal Studies* Discussion Paper No.12–07.

Horwitz, Morton J. (1979) *The Transformation of American Law, 1780–1860.* Cambridge, MA: Harvard University Press.

Hosen, Nadirsyan and Richard Mohr (eds.) (2011) *Law and Religion in Public Life: The Contemporary Debate.* London and New York: Routledge.

Hosseini, S.A. Hamed (2010) *Alternative Globalizations: An Integrative Approach to Studying Dissident Knowledge in the Global Justice Movement.* London and New York: Routledge.

Hough, Peter (2008) *Understanding Global Security.* 2nd edition. London and New York: Routledge.

Howson, CP, MV Kinney, and JE Lawn (2012) *Born Too Soon: The Global Action Report on Preterm Birth.* Worth Health Organization. Geneva.

Human Development Report (1994) Published for the United Nations Development Programme. Oxford and New York: Oxford University Press.

Hunt, Alan (1993) *Explorations in Law and Society: Toward a Constitutive Theory of Law.* London: Routledge.

Hunt, Lynn (2008) *Inventing Human Rights.* New York: W.W. Norton.

Hunter, Rosemary (2008) Would You Like Theory With That? Bridging the Divide between Policy-Orientated Empirical Legal Research, Critical Theory and Politics. In Special Issue: Law and Society Reconsidered. *Studies in Law, Politics, and Society* 41:121–148.

Huntington, Samuel (1996) *The Clash of Civilizations and the Remaking of the World Order.* New York: Simon and Schuster.

Hyde, Alan (1997) *Bodies of Law.* Princeton, NJ: Princeton University Press.

ICIDI (1980) *North-South: The Report of the International Commission on International Development Issues.* London: Pan Books.

Ignatiev, Noel (1995) *How the Irish Became White.* New York: Routledge.

Ivison, Duncan (2002) *Postcolonial Liberalism.* Cambridge: Cambridge University Press.

Ivison, Duncan, Paul Patton, and Will Sanders (eds.) (2000) *Political Theory and the Rights of Indigenous Peoples.* Cambridge: Cambridge University Press.

Jacobson, Matthew Frye (1998) *Whiteness of a Different Color: European Immigrants and the Alchemy of Race.* Cambridge, MA: Harvard University Press.

James, C.L.R. (1938) *The Black Jacobins: Toussaint L'Ouverture and the San Domingo Revolution.* New York: Dial Press.

Jasanoff, Sheila (1987) Biology and the Bill of Rights: Can Science Reframe the Constitution. *American Journal of Law and Medicine* 13:249–289.

—— (1992) Science, Politics, and the Renegotiation of Expertise at EPA. *Osiris* 7:195–217.

—— (2004) Ordering Knowledge, Ordering Society. In Sheila Jasanoff (ed.) *States of Knowledge: The Co-Production of Science and Social Order*. London and New York: Routledge, 13–45.

Jewett, Robert (2008) *Mission and Menace: Four Centuries of American Religious Zeal*. Minneapolis: Fortress Press.

Jones, Bernie D. (2009) *Fathers of Conscience: Mixed Race Inheritance in the Antebellum South*. Athens: University of Georgia Press.

Joshi, Khyati Y. (2006) *New Roots in America's Sacred Ground: Religion, Race, and Ethnicity in Indian America*. New Brunswick, NJ: Rutgers University Press.

—— (2009) The Racialization of Religion in the United States. In Warren J. Blumenfeld, Khyati Y. Joshi, and Ellen E. Fairchild (eds.) *Investigating Christian Privilege and Religious Oppression in the United States*. Rotterdam and Taipei: Sense Publishers, 37–56.

Juergensmeyer, Mark (2003) *Terror in the Mind of God: The Global Rise of Religious Violence*, 3rd Edition (Comparative Studies in Religion and Society, Vol. 13). Berkeley: University of California Press.

—— (2008) *Global Rebellion: Religious Challenges to the Secular State, from Christian Militias to Al Qaeda*. Berkeley: University of California Press.

Kahn, Paul W. (1999) *The Cultural Study of Law: Reconstructing Legal Scholarship*. Chicago: University of Chicago Press.

Kaiser, Wolfram and Peter Starie (eds.) (2009) *Transnational European Union: Toward a Common Political Space*. Milton Park, Oxon: Routledge.

Kaldor, Mary (2006) *New & Old Wars: Organized Violence in a Globalized World*. 2nd edition. Palo Alto, CA: Stanford University Press.

—— (2007) *Human Security: Reflections on Globalization and Intervention*. Cambridge: Polity.

Katzenstein, Peter J. (2011) Civilizational States, Secularisms, and Religions. In Craig Calhoun, Mark Juergensmeyer, and Jonathan Van Antwerpen (eds.) *Rethinking Secularism*. Oxford: Oxford University Press, 145–165.

Kaye, David A. (2011) *Justice Beyond the Hague: Supporting the Prosecution of International Crimes in National Courts*. Council on Foreign Relations. Council Special Report No. 61, June.

Keenan, Sarah (2010) Subversive Property: Reshaping Malleable Spaces of Belonging. *Social & Legal Studies* 19(4):423–439.

Keith, Michael and Steve Pile (eds.) (1993) *Place and the Politics of Identity*. London and New York: Routledge.

Kelsell, T. (2009) *Culture under Cross-Examination: International Justice and the Special Court for Sierra Leone*. Cambridge: Cambridge University Press.

Kennedy, David (2002) The International Human Rights Movement: Part of the Problem? *Harvard Human Rights Journal* 15:101–125.

Kennedy, Duncan (1997) Review of the Rights of Conquest. *American Journal of International Law* 91:745–748.

—— (2004) The Disenchantment of Logically Formal Legal Rationality or Max Weber's Sociology in the Genealogy of the Contemporary Mode of Western Legal Thought. *Bepress Legal Series*. Paper 148.

Kent, Lia Michelle (2012) *The Dynamics of Transitional Justice: International Models and Local Realities in East Timor*. London and New York: Routledge.

Kenyon, Andrew and Peter Rush (eds.) (2004) An Aesthetics of Law and Culture: Texts, Images, Screens. Special Issue. Vol. 34 *Studies In Law, Politics and Society.*

Khagram, Sanjeeve and Peggy Levitt (eds.) (2008) *The Transnational Studies Reader: Intersections and Innovations.* London and New York: Routledge.

Kinsey, Christopher (2006) *Corporate Soldiers and International Security: The Rise of Private Military Companies.* London and New York: Routledge.

Klein, Naomi (2007) *The Shock Doctrine: The Rise of Disaster Capitalism.* New York: Metropolitan Books.

Klug, Heinz (2002) Hybrid(ity) Rules: Creating Local Law in a Globalized World. In Dezalay, Yves and Bryant G. Garth (eds.) *Global Prescriptions: The Production, Exportation, and Importation of a New Legal Orthodoxy.* Ann Arbor: University of Michigan Press, 276–305.

—— (2012) Access to Medicines and the Transformation of the South African State: Exploring the Interactions of Legal and Policy Changes in Health, Intellectual Property, Trade, and Competition Law in the Context of South Africa's HIV/AIDS Pandemic. *Law & Social Inquiry* 37(2):297–329.

Krugman, Paul (2012) Ignorance is Strength. *New York Times,* March 8.

LaChappelle, Nicholas Levi (2012) *Placing the American Death Penalty in Global Context: A Test of the Marshall Hypothesis.* Master's thesis, University of California, Santa Barbara.

Lake, Marilyn and Henry Reynolds (2008) *Drawing the Global Color Line: White Men's Countries and the International Challenge of Racial Inequality.* Cambridge: Cambridge University Press.

Lambourne, W. (2009) Transitional Justice and Peacebuilding after Mass Violence. *International Journal of Transitional Justice* 3(1):28–48.

Lastowka, Greg (2010) *Virtual Justice: The New Worlds of Online Worlds.* New Haven, CT: Yale University Press.

Latour, Bruno (1986) *Laboratory Life: The Construction of Scientific Facts.* With Steve Woolgar. Princeton, NJ: Princeton University Press.

—— (1993) *We Have Never Been Modern.* Translated by Catherine Porter. Cambridge, MA: Harvard University Press.

—— (2004) *Politics of Nature: How to Bring the Sciences into Democracy.* Translated by Catherine Porter. Cambridge, MA: Harvard University Press.

—— (2010) *The Making of Law: An Ethnography of the Conseil d'État.* Cambridge: Polity Press.

LaVeist, Thomas A. (ed.) (2002) *Race, Ethnicity, and Health: A Public Health Reader.* San Francisco: Jossey-Bass.

Law, John (1992) Notes on the Theory of the Actor Network: Ordering, Strategy and Heterogeneity. *Center for Science Studies, Lancaster University.* Online at: http://comp.lancs.ac.uk/sociology/soc054jl.html (accessed January 12, 2011).

Law, John and John Hassard (eds.) (1999) *Actor Network Theory and After.* London: Blackwell.

Layard, Antonia (2010) Shopping in the Public Realm: A Law of Place. *Journal of Law and Society* 37(3):412–441.

Lazarus-Black, Mindie (1994) Alternative Readings: The Status of the Status of Children Act in Antiqua and Barbuda. *Law & Society Review* 28(5):993–1008.

Lazarus-Black, Mindie and Susan Hirsch (eds.) (1994) *Contested States: Law, Hegemony and Resistance*. New York: Routledge.

Leach, Edmund (1954) *Political Systems of Highland Burma*. Cambridge, MA: Harvard University Press.

Leebaw, B. (2008) The Irreconcilable Goals of Transitional Justice. *Human Rights Quarterly* **30**(1):95–118.

Lefebvre, Alexander (2008) *The Image of the Law: Deleuze, Bergson, Spinoza*. Stanford, CA: Stanford University Press.

Lefebvre, Henri (1991) *The Production of Space*. Translated by D. Nicholson-Smith. Oxford: Blackwell.

Lentin, Alana (2011) What Happens to Anti-Racism When We Are Post Race? *Feminist Legal Studies* **19**:159–168.

Lentin, Alana and Gavan Titley (2011) *The Crises of Multiculturalism: Racism in a Neoliberal Age*. London: Zed Books.

Levi, Ron and Mariana Valverde (2008) Studying Law by Association: Bruno Latour Goes to the Conseil d'Etat. *Law & Social Inquiry* **33**(3):805–825.

Levine, Felice (1990) "His" and "Her" Story: The Life and Future of the Law and Society Movement. *Florida State University Law Review* **18**:69.

Lewis, Martin W. and Karen E. Wigen (1997) *The Myth of Continents: A Critique of Metageography*. Berkeley: University of California Press.

Likosky, Michael (ed.) (2002) *Transnational Legal Processes*. Dayton, OH: Butterworths LexisNexis.

Lilla, Mark (2007) *The Stillborn God: Religion, Politics, and the Modern West*. New York: Alfred A. Knopf.

Linde-Laursen, Anders (2010) *Bordering: Identity Processes between National and Personal*. Farnham and Burlington, VT: Ashgate.

Little, Douglas (2008) *American Orientalism: The United States and the Middle East since 1945*. Chapel Hill: University of North Carolina Press.

Locke, John (1993 [1690]) *Two Treaties of Government*. New York: Everyman Paperbacks.

Lowe, A. Vaughan (2002) Foreword. In Likosky, Michael (ed.) *Transnational Legal Processes*. Dayton, OH: Butterworths LexisNexis, v–viii.

Lynch, Michael (2004) Circumscribing Expertise: Membership Categories in Courtroom Testimony. In Sheila Jasanoff (ed.) *States of Knowledge: The Co-Production of Science and Social Order*. London and New York: Routledge, 161–180.

Lynch, Mona (2000) On-line executions: The symbolic use of the electric chair in cyberspace. *PoLAR: Political and Legal Anthropology Review* **23**:1–20.

—— (2001) From the Punitive City to the Gated Community: Security and Segregation across the Social and Penal Landscape. *Miami Law Review* **56**:89–112.

—— (2009). *Sunbelt Justice: Arizona and the Transformation of American Punishment*. Palo Alto, CA: Stanford University Press.

Macaulay, Stewart (1987) Images of Law in Everyday Life: The Lessons of School, Entertainment, and Spectator Sports. *Law & Society Review* **21**:185–218.

—— (2005) The New versus the Old Legal Realism: "Things Ain't What They Used to Be". *Wisconsin Law Review* 2005:365–403.

Macaulay, Stewart, Lawrence Friedman, and Elizabeth Mertz (eds.) (2007) *Law in Action: A Socio-Legal Reader*. New York: Foundation Press.

Macedo, Donaldo and Panayota Gounari (eds.) (2005) *The Globalization of Racism*. Boulder, CO: Paradigm Publishers.

Mackenzie, John M. (1995) *Orientalism: History, Theory, and the Arts*. Manchester: Manchester University Press.

Maduagwu, Michael (2009) Human Rights and the Challenges of Intercultural Dialogue in the Twenty-first Century: A Perspective from Sub-Saharan Africa. In Marie-Luisa Frick and Andreas Oberprantacher (eds.) *Power and Justice in International Relations: Interdisciplinary Approaches to Global Challenges*. Farnham: Ashgate, 173–192.

Maharg, Paul and Caroline Maughan (2011) *Affect and Legal Education: Emotion in Learning and Teaching the Law*. Farnham, Surrey: Ashgate.

Malabou, Catherine (2008) *What Should We Do with Our Brain? (Perspectives in Continental Philosophy)*. Translated by Sebastian Rand. New York: Fordham University Press.

Mamdani, M. (2001) *When Victims Become Killers: Colonialism, Nativism, and the Genocide in Rwanda*. Princeton, NJ: Princeton University Press.

Manderson, Desmond (2000) *Songs without Music: Aesthetic Dimensions of Law and Justice*. Berkeley: University of California Press.

—— (2005) Legal Spaces. Special Issue *Law Text Culture* 9:1–250.

Markovits, Inga (2001) Selective Memory: How the Law Affects What We Remember and Forget about the Past – The Case of East Germany. *Law & Society Review* 35(3):513–563.

Marrie, Henrietta (2010) Indigenous Sovereignty Rights: International Law and the Protection of Traditional Ecological Knowledge. In Aileen Moreton-Robinson (ed.) *Sovereign Subjects: Indigenous Sovereignty Matters*. Sydney and Melbourne: Allen & Unwin, 47–62.

Massey, Doreen (1994) *Space, Place, and Gender*. Minneapolis: University of Minnesota Press.

—— (2005) *For Space*. London: Sage Publications.

—— (2007) *World City*. Cambridge: Polity Press.

Massumi, Brian (2002a) *Parables for the Virtual: Movement, Affect, Sensation*. Durham, NC: Duke University Press.

Massumi, Brian (ed.) (2002b) *A Shock to Thought: Expression after Deleuze and Guattari*. London and New York: Routledge.

Maurer, Bill (2004) *Pious Property: Islamic Mortgages in the United States*. New York: Russell Sage Foundation.

Mawani, Renisa (2009) *Colonial Proximities: Crossracial Encounters and Juridical Truths in British Columbia, 1871–1921*. Vancouver: UBC Press.

Mazlish, Bruce and Ralph Buultjens (eds.) (1993) *Conceptualizing Global History*. Boulder, CO: Westview Press.

McCarthy, E. (1996) *Knowledge as Culture: The New Sociology of Knowledge*. London and New York: Routledge.

McCarty, Philip (ed.) (2012) *Integrated Perspectives in Global Studies*. San Diego, CA: Cognella.

McEvoy, Kieran (2008) Letting Go of Legalism: Developing a "Thicker" Version of Transitional Justice. In Kieran McEvoy and Lorna McGregor (eds.) *Transitional Justice From Below: Grassroots Activism and the Struggle for Change.* Oxford and Portland, OR: Hart Publishing, 15–46.

McGovern, Daniel (1995) *The Campo Indian Landfill War: The Fight for Gold in California's Garbage.* Lincoln: University of Oklahoma Press.

Mehdi, Rubya, Hanna Petersen, Erik Reenberg Sand, and Gordon R. Woodman (eds.) (2008) *Law and Religion in Multicultural Societies.* Copenhagen: Djof Publishing.

Menski, Werner (2006) *Comparative Law in a Global Context: The Legal Systems of Asia and Africa.* Cambridge: Cambridge University Press.

Merry, Sally Engle (2001) Rights, Religion, and Community: Approaches to Violence against Women in the Context of Globalization. *Law & Society Review* 35(1):39–88.

—— (2006) *Human Rights and Gender Violence: Translating International Law into Local Justice.* Chicago: University of Chicago Press.

—— (2007) International Law and Sociolegal Scholarship: Toward a Spatial Global Legal Pluralism. Special Issue: Law and Society Reconsidered. *Studies in Law, Politics, and Society* 41:149–168.

Mertz, Elizabeth (2001) Teaching Lawyers the Language of the Law: Legal and Anthropological Translations. *John Marshall Law Review* 34:91–117.

Mezey, Naomi (2001) Law as Culture. *Yale Journal of Law & the Humanities.* 13:35–67.

Mgbeoji, Ikechi (2005) *Global Biopiracy: Patents, Plants, and Indigenous Knowledge.* Vancouver: UBC Press.

—— (2008) The Civilized Self and the Barbaric Other: Imperial Delusions of Order and the Challenges of Human Security. In Richard Falk, Balakrishnan Rajagopal, and Jacqueline Stevens (eds.) *International Law and the Third World: Reshaping Justice.* London and New York: Routledge-Cavendish, 151–165.

Micklethwait, John and Adrian Wooldridge (2009) *God Is Back: How the Global Revival of Faith Is Changing the World.* New York: Penguin.

Miller, Bruce Granville (2012) *Oral History on Trial: Recognizing Aboriginal Narratives in the Courts.* Vancouver: University of British Columbia Press.

Mills, Charles (1997) *The Racial Contract.* Ithaca, NY: Cornell University Press.

Milner, Neal and Jon Goldberg-Hiller (2008) Feeble Echoes of the Heart: A Postcolonial Legal Struggle in Hawai'i. *Law, Culture and the Humanities* 4:224–247.

Milun, Kathryn (2010) *The Political Uncommons: The Cross-Cultural Logic of the Global Commons.* Farnham, Surrey: Ashgate.

Minkkinen, Panu (2009) *Sovereignty, Knowledge, Law.* New York: Routledge.

Minow, Martha (1998) *Between Vengeance and Forgiveness: Facing History after Genocide and Mass Violence.* Boston: Beacon Press.

Mitchell, Don (2003) *The Right to the City: Social Justice and the Fight for Public Space.* New York and London: The Guilford Press.

Mohr, Richard (2011) The Christian Origins of Secularism and the Rule of Law. In Nadirsyan Hosen and Richard Mohr (eds.) (2011) *Law and Religion in Public Life: The Contemporary Debate.* London and New York: Routledge, 34–51.

Moon, C. (2008) *Narrating Political Reconciliation.* London: Lexington Books.

Moore, Dawn, Lisa Freeman, and Marian Krawczyk (2011) Spatio-Therapeutics: Drug Treatment Courts and Urban Space. *Social & Legal Studies* 20(2):157–172.

Moore, Kathleen M. (2007) Muslims in the United States: Pluralism under Exceptional Circumstances. *The Annals of the American Academy of Political and Social Science* 612:116–132 (Special issue on Religious Pluralism and Civil Society).

—— (2010) *The Unfamiliar Abode: Islamic Law in the United States and Britain.* Oxford: Oxford University Press.

—— (forthcoming) Muslims in the American Legal System. In Omid Safi and Juliane Hammer (eds.) *Cambridge Companion to American Islam.* Cambridge: Cambridge University Press.

Moore, Sally Falk (1992). Treating Law as Knowledge: Telling Colonial Officers What to Say to Africans about Running 'Their Own' Native Courts. *Law & Society Review* 26(1):11–46.

—— (ed.) (2004) *Law and Anthropology: A Reader.* Oxford: Blackwell.

Morgan, Bronwen (2011) *Water on Tap: Rights and Regulation in the Transnational Governance of Urban Water Services.* Cambridge: Cambridge University Press.

Morgan, Edward M. (2007) *The Aesthetics of International Law.* Toronto: University of Toronto Press.

Muldoon, Paul (2008) The Sovereign Exceptions: Colonization and the Foundation of Society. *Social & Legal Studies* 17(1):59–74.

Mungello, D. E. (2009) *The Great Encounter of China and the West, 1500–1800 (Critical Issues in World and International History).* 3rd edition. New York: Rowman & Littlefield.

Münkler, Herfried (2004) *The New Wars.* London: Polity.

Murdocca, Carmela (2010) "There Is Something in That Water": Race, Nationalism, and Legal Violence. *Law & Social Inquiry* 35(2):369–402.

Musson, Anthony (2005) *Boundaries of the Law: Geography, Gender and Jurisdiction in Medieval and Early Modern Europe.* Farnham, Surrey: Ashgate.

Mutua, Kagendo and Beth Blue Swadener (eds.) (2011) *Decolonizing Research in Cross-Cultural Contexts: Critical Personal Narratives.* New York: State University of New York Press.

Mutua, Makau W. (2001) Savages, Victims, and Saviors: The Metaphor of Human Rights. *Harvard International Law Journal* 42(1):201–245.

Nader, Laura (2009) Law and the Frontiers of Illegalities. In Franz von Benda-Beckmann, Keebet von Benda-Beckmann, and Anne Griffiths (eds.) *The Power of Law in a Transnational World: Anthropological Enquiries.* New York and Oxford: Berghahn Books, 54–73.

Naffine, Ngaire (2008) Law's Sacred and Secular Subjects. In Peter Cane, Carolyn Evans, and Zoe Robinson (eds.) (2008) *Law and Religion in Theoretical and Historical Context.* Cambridge: Cambridge University Press, 268–290.

Nagy, R. (2008) Transitional Justice as Global Project: Critical Reflections. *Third World Quarterly* 29(2):275–289.

Nanabhay, Mohamed and Roxane Farmanfarmaian (2011) From Spectacle to Spectacular: How Physical Space, Social Media and Mainstream Broadcast Amplified the Public Sphere in Egypt's 'Revolution'. *The Journal of North Africa Studies* 16(4):573–603.

Nash, Roderick (1982) *Wilderness and the American Mind*. New Haven, CT: Yale University Press.

Nayyar, Deepak (ed.) (2002) *Governing Globalization: Issues and Institutions* (Wider Studies in Development Economics). Oxford: Oxford University Press.

Nederveen Pieterse, Jan (2006) Oriental Globalization. *Theory, Culture & Society* 23:411–413.

Nedlesky, Jennifer (2011) *Law's Relations: A Relational Theory of Self, Autonomy, and Law*. Oxford: Oxford University Press.

Neely, Brooke and Michelle Samura (2011) Social Geographies of Race: Connecting Race and Space. *Ethnic and Racial Studies* 34(1):1933–1952.

Nelken, David (1981) The "Gap" Problem in the Sociology of Law: A Theoretical Review. *Windsor Yearbook of Access to Justice* 1981:35–61.

—— (2002) Comparative Studies of Law. In Reza Banakar and Max Travers (eds.) *An Introduction to Law and Social Theory*. Oxford: Hart Publishing, 329–344.

Nelson, Robert (2001) Law, Democracy, and Domination: Law and Society Research as Critical Scholarship. *Law & Society Review* 35(1):33–38.

Nettlefield, Lara J. (2010) *Courting Democracy in Bosnia and Herzegovina: The Hague Tribunal's Impact in a Postwar State*. Cambridge: Cambridge University Press.

Neves, Lino Joao de Oliveira (2007) The Struggles for Land Demarcation by the Indigenous Peoples of Brazil. In Boaventura de Sousa Santos (ed.) *Another Knowledge Is Possible: Beyond Northern Epistemologies*. London and New York: Verso, 105–119.

Newfield, Christopher (2008) *Unmaking the Public University: The Forty-Year Assault on the Middle Class*. Cambridge, MA: Harvard University Press.

Nickels, Benjamin P. (2009) Review of Mary Kaldor New & Old Wars: Organized Violence in a Globalized World, 2nd edition. *Journal of Military and Strategic Studies* 12(1):1–4.

Nightingale, Carl H. (2012) *Segregation: A Global History of Divided Cities* (Historical Studies of Urban America). Chicago: University of Chicago Press.

Nixon, Rob (2011) *Slow Violence and the Environmentalism of the Poor*. Cambridge, MA: Harvard University Press.

Nourse, V, and Shaffer G. (2009) Varieties of New Legal Realism: Can a New World Order Prompt a New Legal Theory? *Cornell Law Review* 95:61–137.

Novak, David (2000) Law: Religious or Secular? *Virginia Law Review* 86(3):569.

Obasogie, Osagie K. (2007) Race in Law & Society: A Critique. In Ian Haney-Lopez (ed.) *Race, Law and Society*. Farnham, Surrey: Ashgate, 445–464.

—— (2010) Do Blind People See Race? Social, Legal and Theoretical Considerations. *Law & Society Review* 44(3/4):585–616.

Ogletree, Charles J. (2009) From Dred Scott to Barack Obama: The Ebb and Flow of Race Jurisprudence. *Harvard Blackletter Law Journal* 25:1–39.

Oguamanam, Chidi (2006) *International Law and Indigenous Knowledge: Intellectual Property, Plant Biodiversity, and Traditional Medicine*. Toronto: University of Toronto Press.

Olsen, Tricia D., Leigh A. Payne, and Andrew G. Reiter (2010) *Transitional Justice in Balance: Comparing Processes, Weighing Efficacy*. Washington, DC: United States Institute of Peace.

O'Mahony, Lorna Fox and James A. Sweeney (eds.) (2010) *The Idea of Home in Law; Displacement and Dispossession*. Farnham, Surrey: Ashgate.

Onuma, Yasuaki (2010) *A Transcivilizational Perspective on International Law* (Hague Academy of International Law). Leiden and Boston: Martinus Nijhoff Publishers.

Orford, Anne (2009) Jurisdiction without Territory: From the Holy Roman Empire to the Responsibility to Protect. *Michigan Journal of International Law* 30(3):981–1015.

Otto, Dianne (1996) Subalternity and International Law: The Problems of Global Community and the Incommensurability of Difference. In Eve Darian-Smith and Peter Fitzpatrick (eds.) Special Issue on Law and Postcolonialism. *Social & Legal Studies* 5(3):337–364.

Pahuja, Sundhya (2011) *Decolonizing International Law: Development, Economic Growth, and the Politics of Universality.* Cambridge: Cambridge University Press.

Paraskeva, J.M. (ed.) (2010) *Unaccomplished Utopia: NeoConservative Dismantling of Public Education in the European Union.* Rotterdam: Sense Publishers.

Paris, R. (2004) *At War's End: Building Peace after Civil Conflict.* Cambridge: Cambridge University Press.

Park, John S.W. (2004) *Elusive Citizenship: Immigration, Asian Americans, and the Paradox of Civil Rights.* New York: New York University Press.

Park, John S.W. and Edward J.W. Park (2005) *Probationary Americans: Contemporary Immigration Policies and the Shaping of Asian American Communities.* New York and London: Routledge.

Park, Rozelia S. (1998) An Examination of International Environmental Racism through the Lens of Transboundary Movement of Hazardous Waste. *Indiana Journal of Global Legal Studies* 5(2):659–709.

Passavant, Paul (2001) Enchantment, Aesthetics, and the Superficial Powers of Modern Law. *Law & Society Review* 35(3):709.

Pateman, Carole (1988) *The Sexual Contract.* Stanford, CA: Stanford University Press.

Pateman, Carole and Charles Mills (2007) *The Contract and Domination.* Cambridge: Polity.

Pavlich, George (2007) Is an Ethics of Restorative Justice Possible without Universal Principles. In Gerry Johnston and Dan Van Ness (eds.) *Handbook of Restorative Justice.* Portland, OR: Willan Publishing, 615–631.

—— (2011) *Law and Society Redefined.* Oxford: Oxford University Press.

Pelton, Robert Young (2007) *Licensed to Kill: Hired Guns in the War on Terror.* New York: Broadway.

Peteet, Julie (2005) *Landscape of Hope and Despair: Palestinian Refugee Camps.* Philadelphia: University of Pennsylvania Press.

Philippopoulos-Mihalopoulos, Andreas (2010) Law's Spatial Turn: Geography, Justice and a Certain Fear of Space. *Law, Culture and the Humanities* 7(2):187–202.

Pieterse, Jan Nederveen and Bhikhu Parekh (eds.) (1995) *The Decolonization of Imagination: Culture, Knowledge and Power.* London: Zed Books.

Pile, Steve and Michael Keith (eds) (1993) *Place and the Politics of Identity.* New York: Routledge.

Pogge, Thomas (2008) Medicines for the World: Boosting Innovation without Obstructing Free Access. *Sur – International Journal on Human Rights* 5(8):117–142.

Popkin, Margaret (2000) *Peace without Justice: Obstacles to Building the Rule of Law in El Salvador.* University Park: Pennsylvania State University Press.

Pottage, Alain (2012) The Materiality of What? *Journal of Law and Society* 39(1):167–183.

Preis, A. (1996) Human Rights as Cultural Practice: An Anthropological Critique. *Human Rights Quarterly* 18:286.

Provine, Doris Marie (2007) *Unequal under Law: Race and the War on Drugs.* Chicago: University of Chicago Press.

—— (2011) Race and Inequality in the War on Drugs. *Annual Review of Law and Social Science* 7:41–60.

Raffield, Paul (2010) *Shakepeare's Imaginary Constitution: Late Elizabethan Politics and the Theatre of Law.* Oxford and Portland, OR: Hart Publishing.

Rajagopal, Balakrishnan (2003a) International Law and Social Movements: Challenges of Theorizing Resistance. *Columbia Journal of Transnational Law* 41: 412–433.

—— (2003b) *International Law From Below: Development, Social Movements and Third World Resistance.* Cambridge: Cambridge University Press.

—— (2006) Counter-Hegemonic International Law: Rethinking Human Rights and Development as a Third World Strategy. *Third World Quarterly* 27(5):767–783.

—— (2008) Invoking the Rule of Law in Post-Conflict Rebuilding: A Critical Examination. *William and Mary Law Review* 49:1347–1376.

Rajah, Jothie (2011) Punishing Bodies, Securing the Nation: How Rule of Law can Legitimate the Urban Authoritarian State. *Law & Social Inquiry* 36(4):945–970.

Rancière, Jacques (2010) *Dissensus: On Politics and Aesthetics.* Translated by Steven Corcoran. London and New York: Continuum International Publishing Group.

Randeria, Shalini (2003) Glocalization of Law: Environmental Justice, World Bank, NGOs and the Cunning State in India. *Current Sociology* 51(3/4):305–328.

Ravitch, Diane (2010) *The Death and Life of the Great American School System: How Testing and Choice Are Undermining Education.* New York: Basic Books.

Ray, Manas (2002) Growing Up Refugee: On Memory and Locality. *History Workshop Journal* 53(1):149–179.

Razack, Sherene (ed.) (2002) *Race, Space, and the Law: Unmapping a White Settler Society.* Toronto: Between the Lines.

—— (2008) *Casting Out: The Eviction of Muslims from Western Law and Politics.* Toronto: University of Toronto Press.

Reichard, Gary and Ted Dickson (eds.) (2008) *America on the World Stage: A Global Approach to US History.* Urbana: University of Illinois Press.

Reichman, Ravit (2009) *The Affective Life of Law: Legal Modernism and the Literary Imagination.* Stanford, CA: Stanford University Press.

Renteln, Alison Dundes (2004) *The Cultural Defense.* New York: Oxford University Press.

Reydams, Luc (2004) *Universal Jurisdiction: International and Municipal Legal Perspectives.* Oxford: Oxford University Press.

Rhode, Deborah L. (2010) *The Beauty Bias: The Injustice of Appearance in Life and Law.* Oxford: Oxford University Press.

Rice, James (2009) North-South Relations and the Ecological Debt: Asserting a Counter-Hegemonic Discourse. *Critical Sociology* 35(2):225–252.

Richland, Justin (2008) Sovereign Time, Storied Moments: Time, Law, and Ethnography. *Political and Legal Anthropological Review* 31(1):56–75.

—— (2009) Hopi Sovereignty as Epistemological Limit. *Wicazo Sa Review* 24(1):89–112.

—— (2010) "They Did It Like a Song": Aesthetics, Ethics and Tradition in Hopi Tribal Court. In M. Lambek (ed.) *Ordinary Ethics: Anthropology, Language, and Action.* New York: Fordham University Press, 249–272.

—— (2011) Hopi Tradition as Jurisdiction. *Law & Social Inquiry* 36(1):201–234.

Ricouer, Paul (1981) Narrative Time. In W.J.T. Mitchell (ed.) *On Narrative.* Chicago and London: University of Chicago Press, 165–186.

Riles, Annalise (1999) *The Network Inside Out.* Ann Arbor: University of Michigan Press.

—— (ed.) (2006) *Documents: Artifacts of Modern Knowledge.* Ann Arbor: University of Michigan Press.

—— (2011) *Collateral Knowledge: Legal Reasoning in the Global Financial Markets.* Chicago: University of Chicago Press.

Roberts, Dorothy E. (1999) Why Culture Matters to Law: The Difference Politics Makes. In Austin Sarat and Thomas R. Kearns (eds.) (1999) *Cultural Pluralism, Identity Politics, and the Law.* Ann Arbor: University of Michigan Press, 85–110.

Robertson, Lindsay G. (2007) *Conquest by Law: How the Discovery of America Dispossessed Indigenous Peoples of Their Lands.* Oxford: Oxford University Press.

Robinson, William (2011) Global Rebellion: The Coming Chaos? Online at: http://www.aljazeera.com/indepth/opinion/2011/11/20111130121556567265.html (retrieved March 2, 2012).

Rodríguez-Piñero, Luis (2006) *Indigenous Peoples, Postcolonialism, and International Law: The ILO Regime (1919–1989).* Oxford: Oxford University Press.

Roeber, A.G. (2006) The Law, Religion, and State-Making in the Early Modern World: Protestant Revolutions in the Works of Berman, Gorski, and Witte. *Law & Social Inquiry* 31(1):199–227.

Roediger, David R. (2007) *The Wages of Whiteness: Race and the Making of the American Working Class.* 2nd edition. London and New York: Verso.

Roht-Arriaza, Naomi and Javier Mariezcurrena (eds.) (2006) *Transitional Justice in the Twenty-First Century: Beyond Truth versus Justice.* Cambridge: Cambridge University Press.

Rose, Carol (1994) *Property and Persuasion: Essays on the History, Theory, and Rhetoric of Ownership.* Boulder, CO: Westview Press.

Rosen, Lawrence (2008) *Law and Culture: An Invitation.* Princeton, NJ: Princeton University Press.

Rothberg, Michael (2001) W.E.B. Du Bois in Warsaw. Holocaust Memory and the Color Line, 1949–1952. *The Yale Journal of Criticism* 14(1):169–189.

Roussseau, Jean-Jacques (1997) *"The Social Contract" and Other Later Political Writings (Cambridge Texts in the History of Political Thought) (v. 2).* Cambridge: Cambridge University Press.

Roy, Arundhati (2011) "The People Who Created the Crisis Will Not Be the Ones That Come Up with a Solution". Interview with Arundhati Roy in *The Guardian,* November 30.

Ruggie, John (2003) Taking Embedded Liberalism Global: The Corporate Connection. In David Held and M. Koenig-Archibugi (eds.) *Taming Globalization.* Cambridge: Polity Press, 93–129.

Ruskola, Teemu (2002) Legal Orientalism. *Michigan Law Review* 101(1):179–234.

Said, Edward W. (1978) *Orientalism.* New York: Penguin.

—— (1993) *Culture and Imperialism*. New York: Alfred A. Knopf.

—— (2001) The Clash of Ignorance. *The Nation*. October 22.

Samuel, Geoffrey (2009) Interdisciplinarity and the Authority Paradigm: Should Law Be Taken Seriously by Scientists and Social Scientists? *Journal of Law and Society* 36(4):431–459.

Samuels, Suzanne (2005) *Law, Politics, and Society*. Boston: Houghton Mifflin Company.

Santos, Boaventura de Sousa (1987) Law: A Map of Misreading. Toward a Postmodern Conception of Law. *Journal of Law and Society* 14(3):279–302.

—— (1995) *Toward a New Commonsense: Law, Science, and Politics in the Paradigmatic Transition*. London: Routledge.

—— (ed.) (2007) *Another Knowledge Is Possible: Beyond Northern Epistemologies*. London and New York: Verso.

Santos, Boaventura de Sousa and Cezar Rodriguez-Gavarito (eds.) (2005) *Law and Counter-Hegemonic Globalization: Toward a Cosmopolitan Legality*. Cambridge: Cambridge University Press.

Santos, Boaventura de Sousa, João Arriscado Nunes, and Maria Paula Meneses (2007) Introduction: Opening up the Canon of Knowledge and Recognition of Difference. In Santos, Boaventura de Sousa (ed.) *Another Knowledge is Possible: Beyond Northern Epistemologies*. London and New York: Verso, xvix–lxii.

Sanyal, Romola (2009) Contesting Refugeehood: Squatting as Survival in Post-Partition Calcutta. *Social Identities* 15(1):67–84.

Sarat, Austin (2000) Imagining the Law of the Father: Loss, Dread and Mourning in *The Sweet Hereafter*. *Law & Society Review* 34(1):3–46.

—— (2004a) Vitality Amidst Fragmentation: On the Emergence of Postrealist Law and Society Scholarship. In Sarat, Austin (ed.) *The Blackwell Companion to Law and Society*. Oxford: Blackwell, 1–11.

—— (ed.) (2004b) *The Social Organization of Law: Introductory Readings*. Oxford: Oxford University Press.

—— (ed.) (2008) Special Issue: Law and Society Reconsidered. *Studies in Law, Politics, and Society* 41.

—— (ed.) (2011) Special Issue: Human Rights: New Possibilities/New Problems. *Studies in Law, Politics, and Society* 56.

Sarat, Austin and Conor Clarke (2008) Beyond Discretion: Prosecution, the Logic of Sovereignty, and the Limits of Law. *Law & Social Inquiry* 35(2):387–416.

Sarat, Austin, Lawrence Douglas, and Martha Merrill Umphrey (eds.) (2006) *Law and the Sacred*. Palo Alto, CA: Stanford University Press.

Sarat, Austin and Thomas R. Kearns (1996) Legal Justice and Injustice: Towards a Situated Perspective. In Austin Sarat and Thomas R. Kearns (eds.) *Justice and Injustice in Law and Legal Theory*. Michigan: University of Michigan Press.

—— (eds.) (1999) *Cultural Pluralism, Identity Politics, and the Law*. Ann Arbor: University of Michigan Press.

—— (eds.) (2000) *Law in the Domains of Culture*. Ann Arbor: University of Michigan Press.

Sarat, Austin and Stuart Scheingold (eds.) (2001) *Cause Lawyering and the State in a Global Era*. Oxford: Oxford University Press.

Sarat, Austin and Susan Silbey (1988) The Pull of the Policy Audience. *Law and Policy* 10:97–168.

Sarat, Austin and Jonathan Simons (eds.) (2003) *Cultural Analysis, Cultural Studies, and the Law: Moving Beyond Legal Realism*. Durham, NC and London: Duke University Press.

Sarat, Austin and Martha Merrill Umphrey (2010) The Justice of Jurisdiction: The Policing and Breaching of Boundaries in Orson Welles' *Touch of Evil*. *English Language Notes* 48(2):110–128.

Sarkin, J. (2001) The Tension Between Justice and Reconciliation in Rwanda: Politics, Human Rights, Due Process and the Role of the Gacaca Courts in Dealing with Genocide. *Journal of African Law* 45(2):143–172.

Sassen, Saskia (2002) Opening Remarks: Producing the Transnational Inside the National. In Michael Likosky (ed.) *Transnational Legal Processes*. Dayton, OH: Butterworths LexisNexis, 189–196.

—— (2003) Towards Post-National and Denationalized Citizenship. In Engin F. Isin and Bryan S. Turner (eds.) *Handbook of Citizenship Studies*. New York: Sage, 277–291.

—— (2004) Going Beyond the National State in the USA: The Politics of Minoritized Groups in Global Cities. *Diogenes* 51(3):59–65.

—— (2008) Neither Global Nor National: Novel Assemblages of Territory, Authority and Rights. *Ethics & Global Politics* 1(1–2):61–79.

—— (2011) The Global Street: Making the Political. *Globalizations* 8(5):573–579.

Savelsberg, Joachim J. and Ryan D. King (2007) Law and Collective Memory. *Annual Review of Law and Social Science* 3:189–211.

Scarry, Elaine (2010) *Rule of Law, Misrule of Men*. Cambridge, MA: MIT Press.

Scheingold, Stuart A. (2008) Home Away from Home: Collaborative Research Networks and Interdisciplinary Socio-Legal Scholarship. *Annual Review of Law and Social Science* 4:1–12.

Schiff, Benjamin N. (2008) *Building the International Criminal Court*. Cambridge: Cambridge University Press.

Schlag, Pierre (2002) The Aesthetics of American Law. *Harvard Law Review* 115:1047–1118.

—— (2007) Law as the Continuation of God by Other Means. *California Law Review* 85(2):427–440.

Schlosberg, David (2004) Reconceiving Environmental Justice: Global Movements and Political Theories. *Environmental Politics* 13(3):517–540.

—— (2007) *Defining Environmental Justice: Theories, Movements, and Nature*. Oxford: Oxford University Press.

Scholte, Jan Aart (2011) Towards Greater Legitimacy in Global Governance. Special Issue: Legitimacy and Global Governance. *Review of International Political Economy* 18(1):110–120.

Sen, Amartya (2002a) Civilizational Imprisonments: How to Misunderstand Everybody in the World. *The New Republic*, June 10, 437–453.

—— (2002b) How to Judge Globalism. *The American Prospect*, January 1, Vol. 13.

—— (2009) *The Idea of Justice*. Cambridge, MA: The Belknap Press of Harvard University Press.

Seron, Carroll and Susan S. Silbey (2004) Profession, Science, and Culture: An Emergent Canon of Law and Society Research. In *Dictionary of Law and Society*. Oxford: Blackwell, 30–60.

Shaker, Paul and Elizabeth E. Heilman (2008) *Reclaiming Education for Democracy: Thinking Beyond No Child Left Behind*. New York and London: Routledge.

Shamir, Ronen (1996) Suspended in Space: Bedouins under the Law in Israel. *Law and Society Review* 30(2):231–258.

Shapiro, Scott J. (2011) *Legality*. Cambridge, MA: Belknap Press of Harvard University Press.

Sidakis, Diana (2009) Private Military Companies and State Sovereignty: Regulating Transnational Flows of Violence and Capital. In Franz von Benda-Beckman, Keebet von Benda-Beckman, and Julia Eckert (eds.) *Rules of Law and Laws of Ruling: On the Governance of Law*. Farnham, Surrey: Ashgate, 61–82.

Sieder, Rachel (ed.) (2002) *Multiculturalism in Latin America: Indigenous Rights, Diversity and Democracy*. London: Palgrave Macmillan.

—— (2010) Legal Cultures in the (Un)Rule of Law: Indigenous Rights and Juridification in Guatemala. In Javier Couso, Alexandra Huneeus, and Rachel Sieder (eds.) *Cultures of Legality: Judicialization and Political Activism in Latin America*. Cambridge: Cambridge University Press, 161–181.

Sikkink, Kathryn (2011) *The Justice Cascade: How Human Rights Prosecutions Are Changing World Politics*. New York: W.W. Norton & Company.

Sikkink, Kathryn and Carrie Booth Walling (2007) The Impact of Human Rights Trials in Latin America. *Journal of Peace Research* 44(4):427–445.

Silbey, Susan S. (1997) Let Them Eat Cake: Globalization, Postmodern Colonialism, and the Possibilities of Justice. *Law & Society Review* 31(2): 207–236.

—— (ed.) (2008a) Introductory Essay. In *Law and Science (I) Epistemological, Evidentiary, and Relational Engagements*. Farnham, Surrey: International Library of Essays in Law and Society, Ashgate.

—— (ed.) (2008b) Introductory Essay. In *Law and Science (II) Regulation of Property, Practices and Products*. Farnham, Surrey: International Library of Essays in Law and Society, Ashgate.

Simmons, William Paul (2011) *Human Rights Law and the Marginalized Other*. Cambridge: Cambridge University Press.

Singer, Peter (2003) *Corporate Warriors: The Rise of the Privatized Military Industry*. Ithaca, NY: Cornell University Press.

Skibine, Alex Tallchief (2009) Tribal Sovereign Interests Beyond the Reservation Borders. *Lewis & Clark Law Review*, Utah University Legal Studies Research Paper Series, Research Paper No. 08–21.

Skouteris, Thomas (2010) *The Notion of Progress in International Law Discourse*. Cambridge: Cambridge University Press.

Slaughter, Anne-Marie (2002) Breaking Out: The Proliferation of Actors in the International System. In Yves Dezalay and Bryant G. Garth (eds.) *Global Prescriptions: The Production, Exportation, and Importation of the New Legal Orthodoxy*. Ann Arbor: University of Michigan Press, 12–36.

Smith, Linda Tuhiwai (2012) *Decolonizing Methodologies: Research and Indigenous Peoples*. 2nd edition. London: Zed Books.

Soja, Edward (1990) *Postmodern Geographies*. London: Verso.

Sparke, Matthew (2005) *In the Space of Theory: Postfoundational Geographies of the Nation-State*. Minneapolis: University of Minnesota Press.

Spruhan, Paul (2012) The Meaning of Due Process in the Navajo Nation. *The Indian Civil Right Act at Forty*. Los Angeles: UCLA American Indian Studies Center Publications.

Stacy, Helen (2003) Relational Sovereignty. *Stanford Law Review* **55**:2029–2059.

—— (2009) *Human Rights for the 21st Century: Sovereignty, Civil Society, Culture*. Palo Alto, CA: Stanford University Press.

Stafford, Ned (2011) Germany Heeds Call to Block Lethal Injection Drug Supply. January 27. Online at: http://www.rsc.org/chemistryworld/News/2011/January/27011102.asp (accessed May 28, 2012).

Stanley, E. (2009) *Torture, Truth and Justice: The Case of Timore-Leste*. London and New York: Routledge.

Star, Susan Leigh (1991) Power, Technology and the Phenomenology of Conventions: On Being Allergic to Onions. In John Law (ed.) *A Sociology of Monsters: Power, Technology and the Modern World*. London: Routledge, 26–56.

Steady, Filomina Chioma (2009) *Environmental Justice in the New Millennium: Global Perspectives on Race, Ethnicity, and Human Rights*. New York: Palgrave Macmillan.

Steger, Manfred (2009) *The Rise of the Global Imaginary: Political Ideologies from the French Revolution to the Global War on Terror*. Oxford: Oxford University Press.

Stiglitz, Joseph E. (2012) *The Price of Inequality: How Today's Divided Society Endangers Our Future*. New York: W.W. Norton & Company.

Stolzenberg, Nomi (2007) "The Profanity of Law." In Austin Sarat, Lawrence Douglas, and Martha Merrill Umphrey (eds.) *Law and the Sacred*. Palo Alto, CA: Stanford University Press, 29–90.

—— (2011) Righting the Relationship between Race and Religion in Law. *Oxford Journal of Legal Studies* **31**(3):583–602.

Strathern, Marilyn (1996) Cutting the Network. *Journal of the Royal Anthropological Institute* **2**:517–535.

Struett, Michael J. (2008) *The Politics of Constructing the International Criminal Court: NGOs, Discourse, and Agency*. New York: Palgrave Macmillan.

Suchman, Mark (2006) Empirical Legal Studies: Sociology of Law, or Something ELS Entirely? *Amici* **13**(2):1–4.

Suchman, Mark C. and Elizabeth Mertz (2010) Toward a New Legal Empiricism: Empirical Studies and New Legal Realism. *Annual Review of Law and Social Science* **6**:555–79.

Suggs, Jon-Christian (2000) *Whispered Consolidations: Law and Narrative in African American Life*. Ann Arbor: University of Michigan Press.

Sullivan, Winnifred Fallers, Robert A. Yelle, and Mateo Taussig-Rubbo (eds.) (2011) *After Secular Law*. Palo Alto, CA: Stanford University Press.

Sunga, Lyal S. (2009) The Concept of Human Security: Does It Add Anything to International Theory or Practice? In Marie-Luisa Frick and Andreas Oberprantacher (eds.) *Power and Justice in International Relations: Interdisciplinary Approaches to Global Challenges*. Surrey: Ashgate, 131–146.

Swidler, Ann and Jorge Arditi (1994) The New Sociology of Knowledge. *Annual Review of Sociology* **20**:305–329.

Tadjbakhsh, Shahrbanou (2007) Human Security in International Organizations: Blessing or Scourge? *The Human Security Journal* 4(Summer).

Tadjbakhsh, Shahrbanou and Anuradha M. Chenoy (2007) *Human Security: Concepts and Implications*. London: Routledge.

Tamanaha, Brian Z. (2001) *A General Jurisprudence of Law and Society*. Oxford: Oxford University Press.

—— (2006) *Law as a Means to an End: Threat to the Rule of Law*. Cambridge: Cambridge University Press.

Tavernise, Sabrina (2011) Soaring Poverty Casts Spotlight on "Lost Decade". *New York Times*, September 13.

Taylor, Charles (2007) *A Secular Age*. Cambridge, MA: The Belknap Press of Harvard University Press.

Taylor, George H. (2006) Race, Religion and Law: The Tension between Spirit and Its Institutionalization. *University of Maryland Law Journal of Race, Religion, Gender and Class* 6:51–67.

Taylor, William (ed.) (2006) *The Geography of Law: Landscape, Identity and Regulation*. Oxford: Hart Publishing.

Teitel, Ruti G. (2003) Transitional Justice Genealogy. *Harvard Human Rights Journal* 16:69–94.

Telles, Edward E. (2002) Racial Ambiguity among the Brazilian Population. *Ethnic and Racial Studies* 25:415–441.

Thakker, Nisha (2006) India's Toxic Landfills: A Dumping Ground for the World's Electronic Waste. *Sustainable Development Law & Policy* 2006:58–61.

Thomas, Caroline (2001) Global Governance, Development and Human Security: Exploring the Links. *Third World Quarterly* 22(2):159–175.

—— (2007) Globalization and Human Security. In Anthony McGrew and Nana K. Poku (eds.) *Globalization, Development and Human Security*. Cambridge: Polity Press, 107–131.

Thrift, Nigel (2004) Intensities of Feeling: Towards a Spatial Politics of Affect. *Geografiska Annaler* 86(B):57–78.

Ticktin, Miriam (2006) Where Ethics and Politics Meet: The Violence of Humanitarianism in France. *American Ethnologist* 33(1):33–49.

Tiefenbrun, Susan (2010) *Decoding International Law: Semiotics and the Humanities*. Oxford: Oxford University Press.

Toft, Monica Duffy, Daniel Philpott, and Timothy Samuel Shah (2011) *God's Century: Resurgent Religion and Global Politics*. New York: W.W. Norton & Co.

Tolmie, Julia (1997) Pacific Asian Immigrant and Refugee Women Who Kill Their Batterers: Telling Stories That Illustrate the Significance of Specificity. *Sydney Law Review* 19(4):473–513.

—— (2002) Battered Defendants and the Criminal Defences to Murder – Lessons from Overseas. *Waikato Law Review* 10:91–114.

Tomlins, Christopher (2000) Framing the Field of Law's Disciplinary Encounters: A Historical Narrative. *Law & Society Review* 34(4):911–972.

Toxic Wastes and Race at Twenty: 1987–2007 (March 2007). A report prepared by the United Church of Christ Justice & Witness Ministeries.

Toxic Wastes and Race in the United States: A National Report on the Racial and Socio-Economic Characteristics of Communities with Hazardous Waste Sites (1987). Commission for Racial Justice, United Church of Christ.

Travers, Max (2009) *Understanding Law and Society*. Abingdon, Oxon: Routledge-Cavendish.

Trubek, David (1990) Back to the Future: The Short, Happy Life of the Law and Society Movement. *Florida State University Law Review* 18:4.

Tuan, Yi-Fu (1974) *Topophilia: A Study of Environmental Perception, Attitudes, and Values*. Englewood Cliffs, NJ: Prentice Hall.

Turner, Simon (2005) Suspended Spaces: Contesting Sovereignties in a Refugee Camp. In Thomas Blom Hansen and Finn Stepputat (eds.) *Sovereign Bodies: Citizens, Migrants, and States in a Post-Colonial World*. Princeton, NJ: Princeton University Press, 312–332.

Twining, William (2000) *Globalization and Legal Theory*. Evanston, IL: Northwestern University Press.

—— (2009) *General Jurisprudence: Understanding Law from a Global Perspective*. Cambridge: Cambridge University Press.

Tyrrell, Ian R. (2007) *Transnational Nation*. New York: Palgrave Macmillan.

Umphrey, Martha Merrill, Austin Sarat, and Lawrence Douglas (2007) The Sacred in the Law: An Introduction. In Austin Sarat, Lawrence Douglas, and Martha Merrill Umphrey (eds.) *Law and the Sacred*. Palo Alto, CA: Stanford University Press, 1–28.

Vago, Steven (2011) *Law and Society*. 10th edition. New York: Prentice Hall.

Valverde, Mariana (2005) Authorizing the Production of an Urban Moral Order: Appellate Courts and Their Knowledge Games. *Law & Society Review* 39(2):419–456.

—— (2006) *Law and Order: Images, Meaning, Myths*. New Brunswick, NJ: Rutgers University Press.

—— (2008) The Ethic of Diversity: Local Laws and the Negation of Urban Norms. *Law & Social Inquiry* 33(4):895–923.

—— (2009) Jurisdiction and Scale: Legal "Technicalities" as Resources for Theory. *Social & Legal Studies* 18(2):139–157.

—— (2011) Seeing Like a City: The Dialectic of Modern and Premodern Ways of Seeing in Urban Governance. *Law & Society Review* 45(2):277–312.

—— (2012) The Crown in a Multicultural Age: The Changing Epistemology of (Post) Colonial Sovereignty. *Social & Legal Studies* 21(1):3–21.

Van der Merwe, Hugo, Victoria Baxter, and Audrey R. Chapman (eds.) (2009) *Assessing the Impact of Transitional Justice: Challenges for Empirical Research*. Washington DC: United States Institute of Peace.

Von Tigerstrom, Barbara (2007) *Human Security and International Law*. Oxford: Hart Publishing.

Wagner, Anne, Tracey Summerfield, and Farid Samir Benavides Vanegas (eds.) (2005) *Contemporary Issues of the Semiotics of Law: Cultural and Symbolic Analyzes of Law in a Global Context*. Oxford and Portland, OR: Hart Publishing.

Walby, Kevin (2007) Contributions to a Post-Sovereignist Understanding of Law: Foucault, Law as Governance, and Legal Pluralism. *Social & Legal Studies* 16(4):551–571.

Walker, Gordon (2009) Globalizing Environmental Justice: The Geography and Politics of Contextualization and Evolution. *Global Social Policy* 9(3):355–382.

Wallerstein, I.M. (2001) *Unthinking Social Science: The Limits of Nineteenth-Century Paradigms*. Philadelphia: Temple University Press.

Walsh, Anthony and Craig Hemmens (2010) *Law, Justice, and Society: A Sociolegal Introduction*. 2nd edition. Oxford: Oxford University Press.

Warren, Kay B. and Jean E. Jackson (eds.) (2002) *Indigenous Movements, Self-Representation, and the State in Latin America*. Austin: University of Texas Press.

Weber, Max (1995[1904]) *The Protestant Ethic and the Spirit of Capitalism*. London and New York: Routledge.

West, Robin (1985) Jurisprudence as Narrative: An Aesthetic Analysis of Modern Legal Theory. *New York University Law Review* 60:145–211.

—— (1993) *Narrative, Authority, and Law*. Ann Arbor: University of Michigan Press.

Westra, Laura (2011) *Globalization, Violence and World Governance*. Leiden and Boston: Brill.

Westra, Laura and Bill E. Lawson (eds.) (2001) *Faces of Environmental Racism: Confronting Issues of Global Justice*. Lanhan, MD: Rowman & Littlefield.

Whatmore, Sarah (2003) De/Re-Territorializing Possession: The Shifting Spaces of Property Rights. In Jane Holder and Carolyn Harrison (eds.) *Law and Geography*. Current Legal Issues. 2002 Vol. 5. Oxford: Oxford University Press, 211–224.

White, James Boyd (1985) *Essays on Rhetoric and Poetics of the Law*. Madison: University of Wisconsin Press.

White, Lucie E. and Jeremy Perelman (eds.) (2011) *Stones of Hope: How African Activists Reclaim Human Rights to Challenge Global Poverty*. Stanford, CA: Stanford University Press.

Whitman, Jim (2005) *The Limits of Global Governance*. London and New York: Routledge.

Whitt, Laurelyn (2009) *Science, Colonialism, and Indigenous Peoples: The Cultural Politics of Law and Knowledge*. Cambridge: Cambridge University Press.

Wiessner, Siegfried (2008) Indigenous Sovereignty: A Reassessment in Light of the UN Declaration on the Rights of Indigenous Peoples. *Vanderbilt Journal of Transnational Law* 41:1141–1176.

Wilf, Steven (2009) The Invention of Legal Primitivism. *Theoretical Inquiries in Law* 10:485–509.

Wilkinson, Charles F. (1987) *American Indians, Time and the Law*. New Haven, CT: Yale University Press.

Wilkinson, Rorden (ed.) (2005) *The Global Governance Reader*. London and New York: Routledge.

Williams, Patricia J. (1991) *The Alchemy of Race and Rights*. Cambridge, MA: Harvard University Press.

Wilson, Richard Ashby (2007) Tyrranosaurus Lex: The Anthropology of Human Rights and Transitional Law. In Mark Goodale and Sally Engle Merry (eds.) *The Practice of Human Rights: Tracking Law Between the Global and the Local*. Cambridge: Cambridge University Press, 342–369.

Winant, Howard (2004) *The New Politics of Race: Globalism, Difference, Justice*. Minneapolis and London: University of Minnesota Press.

Wolf, Ronald Charles (2004) *Trade, Aid and Arbitrate: The Globalization of Western Law*. Aldershot: Ashgate.

Woo, Grace Li Xiu (2011) *Ghost Dancing with Colonialism: Decolonization and Indigenous Rights at the Supreme Court of Canada*. Vancouver: University of British Columbia Press.

World Migration Report 2010: *The Future of Migration: Building Capacities for Change.* Geneva: International Organization for Migration.

Wright, Beverly (2003) Race, Politics and Pollution: Environmental Justice in the Mississippi River Chemical Corridor. In Julian Agyeman, Robert D. Bullard, and Bob Evans (eds.) *Just Sustainabilities: Development in an Unequal World.* Cambridge, MA: MIT Press, 125–145.

Wyn-Jones, R. (1999) *Security, Strategy and Critical Theory.* Boulder, CO: Lynne Rienner.

Xanthaki, Alexandra (2007) *Indigenous Rights and United Nations Standards: Self-Determination, Culture and Land* (Cambridge Studies in International and Comparative Law). Cambridge: Cambridge University Press.

Yngvesson, Barbara (2010) *Belonging in an Adopted World: Race, Identity, and Transnational Adoption.* Chicago: University of Chicago Press.

Yoder, Andrew J. (2003) Lessons from Stockholm: Evaluating the Global Convention on Persistent Organic Pollutants. *Indiana Journal of Global Legal Studies* 10(2):113–156.

Yunker, James A. (2011) *The Idea of World Government: From Ancient Times to the Twenty-First Century.* Abingdon: Routledge.

Index